Charles F. Goldfarb's
XML
Handbook™

Fourth Edition

⟨!CFG ---- DXS⟩ The Charles F. Goldfarb Definitive XML Series™

Megginson
- Structuring XML Documents

McGrath
- XML by Example: Building E-commerce Applications

Floyd
- Building Web Sites with XML

Morgenthal and la Forge
- Enterprise Application Integration with XML and Java

McGrath
- XML Processing with Python

Cleaveland
- Program Generators with XML and Java

Holman
- Definitive XSLT and XPath

Walmsley
- Definitive XML Schema

Garshol
- Definitive XML Application Development

Goldfarb and Prescod
- Charles F. Goldfarb's XML Handbook™ Fourth Edition

Titles in this series are produced using XML, SGML, and/or XSL. XSL-FO documents are rendered into PDF by the *XEP Rendering Engine* from RenderX: www.renderx.com

About the Series Editor
Charles F. Goldfarb is the father of XML technology. He invented SGML, the Standard Generalized Markup Language on which both XML and HTML are based. You can find him on the Web at: www.xmlbooks.com

About the Series Logo
The rebus is an ancient literary tradition, dating from 16th century Picardy, and is especially appropriate to a series involving fine distinctions between markup and text, metadata and data. The logo is a rebus incorporating the series name within a stylized XML comment declaration.

Charles F. Goldfarb's
XML
Handbook™

Fourth Edition

- Charles F. Goldfarb
- Paul Prescod

 Prentice Hall PTR, Upper Saddle River, NJ 07458
www.phptr.com

Library of Congress Cataloging-in-Publication Data

Goldfarb, Charles F.
   Charles F. Goldfarb's XML Handbook / Charles F. Goldfarb, Paul Prescod.—4th ed.
       p. cm.—(The Charles F. Goldfarb Definitive XML Series)
   ISBN 0-13-065198-2
    1. XML (Document markup language). I. Prescod, Paul. II. Series.

   QA76.76.H94 G65 2001b
   005.7'2—dc21

Editorial/Production Supervisor: *Faye Gemmellaro*
Acquisitions Editor: *Mark L. Taub*
Editorial Assistant: *Sarah Hand*
Marketing Manager: *Bryan Gambrel*
Manufacturing Manager: *Maura Zaldivar*
Cover Designer: *Anthony Gemmellaro*
Cover Design Director: *Jerry Votta*
Series Designer: *Gail Cocker-Bogusz*

© 2002 Charles F. Goldfarb
Published by Prentice Hall PTR
Prentice-Hall, Inc.
Upper Saddle River, NJ 07458

Prentice Hall books are widely used by corporations and government agencies for training, marketing, and resale.

The publisher offers discounts on this book when ordered in bulk quantities. For more information, contact: Corporate Sales Department, Phone: 800-382-3419; Fax: 201-236-7141; E-mail: corpsales@prenhall.com; or write: Prentice Hall PTR, Corp. Sales Dept., One Lake Street, Upper Saddle River, NJ 07458.

Printed in the United States of America

10 9 8 7 6 5 4 3 2 1

ISBN 0-13-065198-2

Pearson Education Ltd.
Pearson Education Australia Pty. Limited
Pearson Education Singapore, Pte.Ltd.
Pearson Education North Asia Ltd.
Pearson Education Canada, Ltd.
Pearson Educación de Mexico, S.A. de C.V.
Pearson Education—Japan
Pearson Education Malaysia, Pte. Ltd.

involve risk and uncertainties including, without limitation: risks of intellectual property litigation; risks in technology development and commercialization; risks in product development and market acceptance of and demand for the company's products; risks of downturns in economic conditions generally and in the markets for Web, Internet, and intranet software and services markets specifically; risks associated with competition and competitive pricing pressures; risks associated with foreign sales and higher customer concentration; and other risks detailed in each company's filings with the Securities and Exchange Commission.

To Linda – With love, awe, and gratitude.

Charles F. Goldfarb

For Lilia – Your support makes it possible and your love makes it worthwhile.

Paul Prescod

Overview

Table of Contents

Contents

Preface

When Paul Prescod and I wrote the first edition of this book – four years and 100,000 copies ago – XML was brand new and the subject of extraordinary hype. It promised to provide universal data interchange, revolutionize publishing on the Web, and transform distributed computing.

Those claims were amazing, not just because of the extent of the promised impact, but because of the diversity of the areas affected. More amazingly, the claims have largely been fulfilled. With the support of the entire computer industry, an XML-based infrastructure is being constructed for modern computing; indeed, for modern business itself.

In some ways, though, the construction site resembles the Tower of Babel. The professionals in the areas affected by XML tend to talk and write about it in their own way, from each area's unique perspective, and in its specialized jargon.

But not in *The XML Handbook*!

From the first edition, our aim has been to integrate and unify the teaching of XML so that any tech industry professional can learn it, regardless of background. And by "learn it" we mean not just the technical details but the way that XML is used. Specifically:

- We use a unified standards-based vocabulary consistently. We explain when particular disciplines or industries use terms in conflicting or ambiguous ways.
- We explain all technical concepts as we introduce them, even the basics, but we don't indulge in "simplification by distortion". We clarify without sacrificing accuracy.
- We describe major trends, applications, and product categories objectively, employing the unified vocabulary, so you can see clearly how they relate to one another and to XML technology.

As a result, developers with diverse backgrounds found they could get the full picture of XML from *The XML Handbook*. Moreover, they also found they could encourage management to read the book and learn why XML is so important to the enterprise.

XML in a nutshell

HTML – the HyperText Markup Language – made the Web the world's library. XML – the Extensible Markup Language – is its sibling, and it is making the Web the world's commercial and financial hub.

In the process, the Web is becoming much more than a static library. Increasingly, users are accessing the Web for "Web pages" that aren't actually on the shelves. Instead, the pages are generated dynamically from information available to the Web server. That information can come from databases on the Web server, from the site owner's enterprise databases, or even from other websites.

And that dynamic information needn't be served up raw. It can be analyzed, extracted, sorted, styled, and customized to create a personalized Web experience for the end-user. To coin a phrase, Web *pages* are evolving into Web *services*.

For this kind of power and flexibility, XML is the markup language of choice. You can see why by comparing XML and HTML. Both are based on SGML – the International Standard for structured information – but look at the difference:

In HTML:

```
<p>P200 Laptop
<br>Friendly Computer Shop
<br>$1438
```

In XML:

```
<product>
<model>P200 Laptop</model>
<dealer>Friendly Computer Shop</dealer>
<price>$1438</price>
</product>
```

Both of these may appear the same in your browser, but the XML data is *smart* data. HTML tells how the data should *look*, but XML tells you what it *means*.

With XML, your browser knows there is a product, and it knows the model, dealer, and price. From a group of these it can show you the cheapest product or closest dealer without going back to the server.

Unlike HTML, XML allows custom tags that can describe exactly what you need to know. Because of that, your client-side applications can access data sources anywhere on the Web, in any format. New "middle-tier" servers sit between the data sources and the client, translating everything into your own task-specific XML.

But XML data isn't just smart data, it's also a smart document. That means when you display the information, the model name can be in a different font from the dealer name, and the lowest price can be highlighted in green. Unlike HTML, where text is just text to be rendered in a uniform way, with XML text is smart, so it can control the rendition.

And you don't have to decide whether your information is data or documents; in XML, it is always both at once. You can do data processing or document processing or both at the same time.

With that kind of flexibility, it's no wonder that we're starting to see a new Web of smart, structured information. It's a "Semantic Web" in which computers understand the meaning of the data they share.

Your broker sends your account data to Quicken using XML. Your imaging software keeps its templates in XML. Everything from math to multimedia, chemistry to commerce, wireless to Web services, is using XML or is preparing to start.

The XML Handbook will help you get started too!

What about SGML?

This book is about XML. You won't find feature comparisons to SGML, or footnotes with nerdy observations like "the XML empty-element tag does not contradict the rule that every element has a start-tag and an end-tag because, in SGML terms, it is actually a start-tag followed immediately by a null end-tag".[1]

Nevertheless, for readers who use SGML, it is worth addressing the question of how XML and SGML relate. There has been a lot of speculation about this.

Some claim that XML will replace SGML because there will be so much free and low-cost software. Others assert that XML users, like HTML users before them, will discover that they need more of SGML and will eventually migrate to the full standard.

The truth is that XML is a simplified subset of SGML. The subsetting was optimized for the Web environment, which implies data-processing-oriented (rather than publishing-oriented), short life-span (in fact, usually dynamically-generated) information. The vast majority of XML documents will be created by computer programs and processed by other programs, then destroyed. Humans will never see them.

Eliot Kimber, who was a member of both the XML and SGML standards committees, says:

> There are certain use domains for which XML is simply not sufficient and where you need the additional features of SGML. These applications tend to be very large scale and of long term; e.g., aircraft maintenance information, government regulations, power plant documentation, etc.

> Any one of them might involve a larger volume of information than the entire use of XML on the Web. A single model of commercial aircraft, for example, requires some four million unique pages of documentation that must be revised and republished quarterly. Multiply that by the number of models produced by companies like Airbus and Boeing and you get a feel for the scale involved.

---

1. Well, yes, I did just make that nerdy observation, but it wasn't a footnote, was it?

I agree with Eliot. I invented SGML, I'm proud of it, and I'm awed that such a staggering volume of the world's mission-critical information is represented in it.

I'm gratified that SGML made the Web possible and that the Society for Technical Communication awarded joint Honorary Fellowships to the Web's inventor, Tim Berners-Lee, and myself in recognition of the synergy.

But I'm also proud of XML. I'm proud of my friend Jon Bosak who made it happen, and I'm glad that the World Wide Web is becoming XML-based.

If you are new to XML, don't worry about any of this. All you need to know is that the XML subset of SGML has been in use for a decade or more, so you can trust it.

SGML still keeps the airplanes flying, the nuclear plants operating safely, and the defense departments in a state of readiness. You should look into it if you produce documents on the scale of an Airbus or Boeing. For the rest of us, there's XML.

About our sponsors

With all the buzz surrounding a hot technology like XML, it can be tough for a newcomer to distinguish the solid projects and realistic applications from the fluff and the fantasies. It is tough for authors as well, to keep track of all that is happening in a field expanding as rapidly as this one.

In this case, the solution to both problems was to seek support and expert help from friends in the industry. I know the leading companies in the XML arena and know they have experience with both proven and leading-edge applications and products.

In the usual way of doing things, had we years to write this book, we would have interviewed each company to learn about its strategies, products and/or application experiences, written some chapters, asked the companies to review them, etc., and gone on to the next company. To save time and improve accuracy, we engaged in parallel processing. I spoke with each sponsor, agreed on subject matter for a chapter that would fit the book plan, and asked them to write the first draft.

I used their materials as though they were my own interview notes – editing, rewriting, deleting, and augmenting as necessary to achieve my objective for the chapter in the context of the book. I used consistent standards-based terminology and an objective factual style. All sponsored chapters are identified with the name of the sponsor, and usually with the names of the experts who contributed to it. I'd like to take this opportunity to thank them for being so generous with their time and knowledge.

We are grateful to our sponsors just as we are grateful to you, our readers. Both of you together make it possible for *The XML Handbook* to exist. In the interests of everyone, we make our own editorial decisions and we don't recommend or endorse any product or service offerings over any others.

Our thirty-four sponsors are:

- Adobe Systems Incorporated, `http://www.adobe.com/products/framemaker`
- Altova, Inc., `http://www.xmlspy.com`
- Auto-trol Technology, `http://www.auto-trol.com`
- Business Layers, `http://www.businesslayers.com`
- Chrystal Software, `http://www.chrystal.com`
- eidon GmbH, `http://www.eidon-products.com`
- Four J's Development Tools, `http://www.4js.com`
- Hewlett-Packard Company, `http://www.hp.bluestone.com`
- HostBridge Technology, `http://www.hostbridge.com`
- IBM Corporation, `http://www.ibm.com/xml`
- IBM Informix, `http://www.informix.com`
- ICE Authoring Group, `http://www.icestandard.org`
- Infoteria Corporation, `http://www.infoteria.com`
- Innodata Corporation, `http://www.innodata.com`
- Intel Corporation, `http://www.intel.com/eBusiness`
- Intelligent Compression Technologies, Inc., `http://www.ictcompress.com`
- Interwoven, Inc., `http://www.interwoven.com`
- Liquent, `http://www.liquent.com`
- Microsoft Corporation, `http://msdn.microsoft.com/xml`
- Mozquito Technologies AG, `http://www.mozquito.com`
- NeoCore, `http://www.neocore.com`
- Oracle Corporation, `http://www.oracle.com/xml`
- Peregrine Systems, `http://www.peregrine.com`
- Profium Ltd., `http://www.profium.com`
- Sequoia Software, `http://www.sequoiasoftware.com`
- Software AG, `http://www.softwareagusa.com`
- Sun Microsystems, `http://java.sun.com/xml`
- Synth-Bank LLC, `http://www.synthbank.com`
- TIBCO Software Inc., `http://www.extensibility.com`

- Vertical Computer Systems/Emily Solutions,
  `http://www.emilysolutions.com`
- Voxeo Corporation, `http://community.voxeo.com`
- XCare.net, `http://www.xcare.net`
- XMLCities, Inc., `http://www.XMLCities.com`
- XyEnterprise, `http://www.xyenterprise.com`

How to use this book

The XML Handbook has eighteen parts, consisting of 69 chapters, that we intend for you to read in order.

Well, if authors didn't have dreams they wouldn't be authors.

In reality, we know that our readers have diverse professional and technical backgrounds and won't all take the same route through a book this large and wide-ranging. Here are some hints for planning your trip.

To start, you can get the best feel for the subject matter by reading the Table of Contents and the introductions to each part. The introductions are less than a page long and usually epitomize the subject area of the part in addition to introducing the chapters within it.

Part One contains introductory tutorials and establishes the terminology used in the remainder of the book. Please read it first.

Parts Two through Fourteen cover different application domains. The chapters are application discussions, case studies, and tool category discussions, plus some introductory discussions and tutorials. You can read them with only the preceding parts (especially Part One) as background, although technical readers may want to complete the remaining tutorials first.[2]

Those can be found in Parts Fifteen through Seventeen. We strove to keep them friendly and understandable for readers without a background in subjects not covered in this book. Tutorials whose subject matter thwarted that goal are labeled as being a tad tougher so you will know what to expect, but not to discourage you from reading them.

---

2. The chapters in these parts are illustrated by their sponsors' experiences and products. The organization into parts only classifies the subject matter of the chapters; there is no attempt to classify the products. A tool used to illustrate the content management part, for example, might be an appropriate choice for a portal or a publishing system.

Part Eighteen contains resources: guides to the CD-ROM and to public XML vocabularies, an acronym dictionary, and a guide to the other books in this series.

Acknowledgments

The principal acknowledgment in a book of this nature has to be to the people who created the subject matter. In this case, I take special pleasure in the fact that all of them are friends and colleagues of long standing in the SGML community.

Tim Bray and C. Michael Sperberg-McQueen were the original editors of the XML specification, later joined by Jean Paoli. Dan Connolly put the project on the W3C "to-do list", got it started, and shepherded it through the approval process.

But all of them agree that, if a single person is to be thanked for XML, it is Jon Bosak. Jon not only sparked the original ideas and recruited the team, but organized and chaired the W3C XML Working Group.

As Tim put it: "Without Jon, XML wouldn't have happened. He was the prime mover."

But before there could be an XML, or even an SGML, there had to have been ML. I continue to be grateful to Ed Mosher and Ray Lorie, my co-inventors – and namesakes – of the first markup language, IBM's GML.

Acknowledgment is due also to Norm Scharpf and the Graphic Communications Association for their support and community-building efforts on behalf of XML, a continuation of their "from day one" support of SGML.

Regarding the content of the book, Paul and I would like to thank Jean Paoli, Jon Bosak, G. Ken Holman, Bob DuCharme, Eliot Kimber, Andrew Goldfarb, Lars Marius Garshol, Lilia Prescod, and Steve Newcomb for contributing great material; Bryan Bell, inventor of MIDI, education video producer, and information system architect, for his advice and support; Steve Pepper and Bob DuCharme for talent-spotting; and Priscilla Walmsley for her insights into XML Schema.

We also thank Lilia Prescod, Thea Prescod, and Linda Goldfarb for serving as our usability test laboratory. That means they read lots of chapters and complained until we made them clear enough.

Prentice Hall PTR uses Adobe FrameMaker and other Adobe graphic arts and publishing software to produce most of its books. We thank Jennifer Brieger of Adobe for providing Paul and me with copies. We also thank David Turner of Microsoft for providing copies of its drawing tools.

Paul and I designed, and Paul implemented, an SGML-based production system for the book. It uses James Clark's Jade DSSSL processor, FrameMaker+SGML, and some ingenious FrameMaker plug-ins designed and implemented by Doug Yagaloff of Caxton, Inc. We thank Doug, and also Randy Kelley, for their wizard-level FrameMaker consulting advice.

But a great production system is nothing without a great production team. Faye Gemmellaro supervised the project for the publisher; we thank her for her dedication, attention to detail, and unfailing kindness and patience. We also appreciated her excellent rapport with the cover artist, Anthony Gemmellaro, who responded to our constantly changing complex requirements with inspired designs.[3]

We also thank Peter Snell for exercising his formidable logistic and diplomatic skills to develop our two CD-ROMs from the contributions of several hundred people.

While I do appreciate the value of computerized document processing,[4] I also appreciate the skill that only human domain authorities can bring to index construction. For this book, the authorities are Audrey and Ron Turner and their team at Soph-Ware Associates, distinguished XML consultants, developers, and trainers with whom I've worked on many projects over the years.[5]

For past editions of this book Andrew Goldfarb served as art director and artist-on-demand. For this edition he assumed the role of Managing Editor, adding the sponsorship program and other editing and production tasks to his responsibilities.[6]

Mark Taub, our Editor-in-Chief at Prentice Hall PTR, first proposed that I edit a book series on markup languages in 1993, long before markup became cool. I thank him again for his continued help, encouragement, and guidance, for both the series and *The XML Handbook*.

---

3. And thanks again to Camille Trentacoste, our previous production supervisor. Although she now has other responsibilities for Prentice Hall, she still took time to give us another fishing lesson!

4. Does that surprise you?

5. In fact, they co-wrote the first book in my Prentice Hall series, *ReadMe.1st: SGML for Authors and Editors*, among many other books and articles.

6. Andrew was once a best-selling author in his own right. For a brief period his *The Ballad of a Slow Poisoner* outranked both Stephen King and The Bible on the Barnes and Noble e-book best-seller list. Check out his non-XML art at: http://www.slowpoisoners.com/flyers

I'd also like to acknowledge a major debt to four people who supported and encouraged my efforts to develop and popularize markup languages. They epitomize vision and leadership in technical management. Norm Pass and Bobby Lie were my managers at IBM during most of the 25 years that I worked on GML and SGML. Yasufumi Toyoshima and Charles Brauer, then of Fujitsu Network Communications, were my consulting clients for six years following my retirement from IBM in 1994. They saw the potential for a Web-friendly, grammatically simple SGML subset long before I did – or anyone else I know.

As the senior author, I gave myself this preface to write. I'm senior because Paul's folks were conceiving him about the same time that I was conceiving SGML. In return, Paul got to write the history chapter, because for him it really is history.

This gives me the opportunity to thank Paul publicly for the tremendous reservoir of talent, energy, and good humor that he brought to the project. The book benefited not just from his XML knowledge and fine writing skills, but from his expertise in SGML, Jade, and FrameMaker that enabled us to automate the production of the book (with the previously acknowledged help from our friends).

Thanks, Paul.

Charles F. Goldfarb
Saratoga, CA
November 14, 2001

XML everywhere!

- By Jean Paoli
  Product Unit Manager, XML Technologies
  Microsoft Corporation
  Co-editor of the W3C XML Recommendation

- *Redmond, April 24, 1998*

Foreword

When HTML came onto the scene it sparked a publishing phenomenon. Ordinary people everywhere began to publish documents on the Web. Presentation on the Web became a topic of conversation not just within the computer industry, but within coffeehouses. Overnight, it seemed as though everyone had a Web page.

I see the same phenomenon happening today with XML. Where data was once a mysterious binary blob, it has now become something ordinary people can read and author because it's text. With XML, ordinary people have the ability to craft their own data, the ability to shape and control data. The significance of this shift is difficult to overstate, for not only does it mean that more people can access data, but that there will undoubtedly be more data to access. We are on the verge of a data explosion. One ignited by XML.

By infusing the Web with data, XML makes the Web a better place for people to interact, to do business. XML allows us to do more precise searches, deliver software components, describe such things as collections of Web pages and electronic commerce transactions, and much more. XML is changing not only the way we think about data, but the way we think about the Web.

And by doing so, it's changing the way we think about the traditional desktop application. I have already witnessed the impact of XML on all types of applications from word processors and spreadsheets to database managers and email. More and more, such applications are reaching out to the Web, tapping into the power of the Web, and it is XML that is enabling them to do so. Gone are the days of the isolated, incompatible application. Here are the days of universal access and shared data.

I joined Microsoft in the summer of 1996 with great faith in the Standard Generalized Markup Language (SGML) and a dream that its potential might one day be realized. As soon as I arrived at Microsoft, Jon Bosak of Sun Microsystems and I began discussing the possibility of creating an XML standard. Jon shared my enthusiasm for a markup language such as XML, understanding what it could mean to Web communication.

My goal in designing an XML standard was to produce a very simple markup language with as few abstractions as possible. Microsoft's success is due in no small part to its ability to develop products with mass-market appeal. It is this mass-market appeal that I wanted to bring to XML. Together with Jon and other long-time friends from the SGML world, C.M. Sperberg-McQueen, James Clark, Tim Bray, Steve DeRose, Eve Maler, Eliot Kimber, Dave Hollander, Makoto Murata, and Peter Sharpe, I co-designed the XML specification at the World Wide Web Consortium (W3C). This specification, I believe, reflects my original goals.

It was truly an exciting time. For years, we had all been part of a maverick band of text markup enthusiasts, singing its praises every chance we had, and before us was an opportunity to bring XML into the mainstream, maybe even into the operating system. At last, we were getting our chance to tell the World of the thing we had been so crazy about for all this time.

By the fall of 1996, many groups inside Microsoft, including Office, the Site Server Electronic Commerce Edition, the Data Access Group, to cite a few, were searching for an open format to enable interoperability on the Web. It was then that I began working with the managers of Internet Explorer 4, with the passionate Adam Bosworth, with Andrew Layman, with Thomas Reardon, to define the Channel Definition Format (CDF). CDF, the first major application of XML on the Web, became an immediate and incredible success, and XML started catching on like wildfire across the Web.

I remember those weeks and months that followed as a time where it seemed that every day another new group within Microsoft began coding applications using XML. Developers, left and right, were turning on to XML. They frenetically began to develop applications using XML, because XML gave them what they wanted: an easy-to-parse syntax for representing data. This flurry of activity was so great that by October of 1997, almost a year after my arrival at Microsoft, Chairman Bill Gates announced XML as "a breakthrough technology." Since that time we've never looked back.

This book is an excellent starting point where you can learn and experiment with XML. As the inventor of SGML, Dr. Charles F. Goldfarb is one of the most respected authorities on structured information. Charles has had a very direct influence on XML, as XML is a true subset of SGML, and he clearly understands the impact that XML will have on the world of data-driven, Web-based applications.

Charles and I share a common vision, that the most valuable asset for the user or for a corporation, namely the data, can be openly represented in a simple, flexible, and human-readable form. That it can easily travel from server to server, from server to client, and from application to application, fostering universal communication with anyone, anywhere. This vision can now be realized through XML.

Enjoy the book!

Jean Paoli
Product Unit Manager, XML Technologies, Microsoft Corporation
Co-editor of the XML Recommendation
Redmond, April 24, 1998

XML: Looking back and looking forward

■ By Jon Bosak
XML Architect, Sun Microsystems
Chair, W3C XML Coordination Group

■ *Los Altos, August 1999*

Prolog

The World Wide Web is a medium that gained acceptance where earlier attempts had failed by providing the right combination of simplicity and fault tolerance. Now it faces the job of reinventing itself as a scalable, industrial-strength infrastructure strong enough to carry both human communication and electronic commerce into the new century. The story of XML and its companion standards is the story of that reinvention.

XML arose from the recognition that key components of the original Web – HTML tagging, simple hypertext linking, and hardcoded presentation – would not scale up to meet future needs. Those of us involved in industrial-strength SGML-based electronic publishing before the Web came into existence had learned the hard way that nothing substantially less powerful than SGML would work over the long run.

We also realized that any solution not based on SGML – the only formal International Standard that addresses this problem – would likely employ a proprietary binary format that would require special proprietary tools. XML is the creation of a small group of SGML experts who were motivated in large part by a desire to ensure that the Web of the future would not be dominated by standards controlled by a single vendor or nation. Its adoption by the world's largest computer software and hardware companies marks a significant turning point in the struggle to keep data free.

XML is a tremendous victory for open standards. It is freely extensible, imposing no limits on the ability of users to define markup in any combination of the world's major natural languages; it is character-based and human-readable, which means that XML documents can be maintained using even the most primitive text processing tools; and it is relatively easy to implement, so users can look forward to an abundance of inexpensive commercial XML processing tools and an ever-growing number of free ones.

Most importantly, XML provides a standard framework for making agreements about communication. It allows people sharing a common data exchange problem to work out an open solution to that problem – without interference from third parties, without dependence on large software vendors, without bindings to specific tools, without language restrictions, and in a way that lets anyone with a similar problem use the same solution. While the task of defining such standards within each industry and user community still lies before us, the framework for doing so is now in place.

Nevertheless, we must not lose sight of the larger goal. True interoperability requires not just interoperable syntax, but interoperable semantics. This ultimate goal cannot be achieved with anything less than the standardization of meaning itself, at least in those areas in which we wish to achieve automatic interoperability.

The coming standardization of domain-specific element types and attributes will establish the semantically meaningful labeling of content in particular industries, but it cannot address the behavioral aspect. While interoperable behavior can always be specified using a platform-neutral programming language like Java, such a powerful tool is often disproportionate to simple tasks. Just as we cannot ask our airline pilots to be aircraft engineers, we cannot require every creator of meaning to also be a programmer.

In the areas of hypermedia linking and presentation of rendered data, we can and must establish standardized techniques for behavioral specification that are declarative enough to be usable by nonprogrammers and yet powerful enough to get the job done in industrial contexts of unlimited scale. In both areas we are being held back by early superficial successes with simple mechanisms that are easy to learn but place unacceptable limits on what can be done, just as the early success of HTML held back the adoption of extensible markup.

The parallels to be drawn among the recent histories of markup, linking, and presentation are striking.

- In all three cases, early visionaries went much farther than the majority of adopters were ready to follow.
- In all three cases, breakthroughs in public consciousness were made by relative newcomers whose major contribution was to radically simplify the early, more advanced techniques in a way that made them accessible to the first wave of implementors.
- In all three cases, the original work is now being reconsidered, as those who understand the essential coherence of the original, larger view labor patiently to reconstruct mechanisms adequate for the demands of the future.
- And in all three cases, the biggest roadblock to deployment of the more advanced solutions is the success of the limited ones that got the Web off the ground.

I have no doubt that we will eventually succeed in replacing today's anemic realization of hypertext with something closer to the ideal articulated by the visionaries of the 1960s and worked out in the research projects of the 1970s and 1980s. I also have no doubt that we will eventually achieve interoperability of formatting behavior in a way that preserves the delivery of textual semantics to Web clients while simultaneously enabling the level of typographic control associated with printed newspaper and magazine publishing. My certainty is based not on a logical analysis of the future but simply on the same from-the-trenches understanding of basic needs that motivated me to begin the XML project in the first place.

What is not clear is how long it will take for Web implementors to realize the limitations of their existing conceptions of hyperlinking and style specification in the way that the more advanced among them now understand the limitations of HTML markup. But whether it takes two years or ten, the next steps are as necessary as was the first step to XML.

The XML Handbook can help us take those steps.

Jon Bosak
XML Architect, Sun Microsystems
Chair, W3C XML Coordination Group
Los Altos, August 1999

The Who, What, and Why of XML

- ■ Why XML?
- ■ Just enough XML
- ■ XML in the real world
- ■ XML and your browser
- ■ XML and e-business
- ■ The XML Jargon Demystifier

Part One

This part is the essential introduction to everything else in the book, which is why we named it Part One! Please read it from beginning to end because each chapter builds on the preceding ones.

For example, Chapter 2's *Just enough XML* tutorial relies on insights and markup fundamentals presented in their historical and business contexts in Chapter 1. That knowledge lets Chapter 3 tackle the most fundamental issue for XML: the relationship between documents and data and what that means for applications and products.

By Chapter 4 we've covered enough to understand XML's impact on human communication over the Web, and then, in Chapter 5, how it enables computer-to-computer communication for e-business.

Finally, in Chapter 6 we can apply what we have learned to an examination of the most important terms related to XML – the ones that people misuse the most! You'll learn what they really mean, and how to decipher the intended meaning when others get them wrong.

Reading this part will prepare you for the application and tool discussions in Part 2 through Part 14. High-tech readers may want to complete the tutorials in Part 15 through Part 17 first, but others can just dip into the tutorials on a need-to-know basis.

Why XML?

▌ What is XML, really?

▌ Origins in document processing

▌ Abstraction vs. rendition

▌ Documents and data

The buzz around the Extensible Markup Language is extraordinary: already it is changing the way software is written, sold and used. All of the major software companies are enthusiastic about XML. New standards based upon it are released daily.

As you may have noticed, the XML book rack has grown from *The XML Handbook*™ and a couple of others to scores of books on every imaginable technical variation and combination. Where did this language come from and why has it become so important?

The computer world's excitement can be summarized in two words: *information interchange*. XML is about making computer systems work together through the exchange of everything from simple numbers to elaborate data structures and human-readable texts.

For instance, to make Web browsers compatible with drawing tools like Corel Draw and Adobe Illustrator, the World Wide Web Consortium created an XML-based language called the Scalable Vector Graphics language (SVG).

Similarly – but in a totally different domain – a group of accounting software vendors defined an XML-based language called Open Financial Exchange (OFX).[1] There are similar languages for virtually every industry. Each allows information interchange between potentially varied hardware, software, and operating system combinations. If you need to get two computer programs to talk about anything, experts agree that XML is a fundamental building block.

Analysis   XML is a framework for any project that involves moving information from place to place, even between different software products and platforms.

Once computers can interchange information, they can work together. This in turn allows people to work together more efficiently. It does not matter whether you are buying and selling, writing a manifesto or collecting data on the fertility rates of fruit flies – XML can be used for any kind of information interchange.

Many of the most influential companies in the software industry promote XML as the next step in the Web's evolution. How can they be so confident about something so new? More important: how can *you* be sure that your time invested in learning and using XML will be profitable?

We can all safely bet on XML because its technology is in fact very old and has been proven effective over several decades and thousands of projects. The easiest way to understand the central ideas of XML is to go back to their source, the *Standard Generalized Markup Language* (SGML).

XML is, in fact, a streamlined subset of SGML, so SGML's track record is XML's as well. SGML enables information interchange within and between some of the world's largest companies. SGML was first used for document processing but as time goes by it has become increasingly clear that with the extensible markup technology of SGML and XML, data processing and document processing are the same thing! If you understand where it all comes from, you'll understand where it – and the Web – are going.

---

1. If you're going to work with XML, you'll need to get used to contrived acronyms with the letter "X" in them.

1.1 | Text formatters and SGML

XML comes from a rich history of text processing systems. *Text processing* is the sub-discipline of *computer science* dedicated to creating computer systems that can automate parts of the document creation and publishing process. Text processing software includes simple word processors, advanced news item databases, hypertext document presentation systems and other publishing tools.

The first wave of automated text processing was computer typesetting. Authors would type in a document and describe how they would like it to be formatted. The computer would print out a document with the described text and formatting.

We call the file format that contained the mix of the actual data of the document, plus the description of the desired format, a *rendition*. Some historically important rendition notations include *troff, Rich Text Format* (*RTF* – used in some Microsoft software), and *LaTeX*.

The system would convert the rendition into something physically perceivable to a human being – a *presentation*. The presentation medium was historically paper, but eventually electronic display.

Typesetting systems sped up the process of publishing documents and evolved into what we now know as desktop publishing. Newer programs like *Microsoft Word* and *Adobe PageMaker* still work with renditions, but they give authors a nicer interface to manipulate them. The user interface to the rendition (the file with formatting codes in it) is designed to look like the presentation (the finished paper product). We call this *What You See Is What You Get* (*WYSIWYG*) publishing. Since a rendition merely describes a presentation, it makes sense for the user interface to reflect the end-product.

1.1.1 *Formatting markup*

The form of typesetting notation that predates WYSIWYG (and is still in use today) is called *formatting markup*. Consider an analogy: you might submit a manuscript to a human typesetter for publication. Imagine it had no formatting, not even paragraphs or different fonts, but rather was a single continuous paragraph that was "marked up" with written instructions for how it should be formatted. You could write very precise instructions for layout: "Move this word over two inches. Bold it. Move the next word beside it. Move the next word underneath it. Bold it. Start a new line here." and so forth. It might look like Figure 1-1.

enlarged font

Fourscore and seven years ago our fathers *— Indent and bold, up to "our"* brought forth on this continent a new nation, conceived in liberty, and dedicated to the propositions that all men are created equal. *put in italics*

new paragraph *skip a line* Now we are engaged in a great civil war, testing whether that nation, or any nation *— align text to both margins*

Figure 1-1   A manuscript "marked up" by hand

Formatting markup is very much the same. We "circle" text with instructions called *tags* or *codes* (depending on the particular formatting markup language). Here is an example of markup in one popular formatting markup language called LaTeX.

Example 1-1. A document with formatting markup

This is a marked up document. It contains words that are italicized because they are in a foreign language: \it{oo la la}, bold-faced because they are \bf{important}, small because they are \small{not important} and large, just because \large{we like large text!}

In this markup language, the curly braces describe the extent of the formatting. So the italics started with the "\it" command extend until the end of the word "la". Because the markup uses only ordinary characters on typical keyboards, it can be created using existing text editors instead of special word processors (those came later).

1.1.2 *Generalized markup*

This process is adequate if your only goal is to type documents into the computer, describe a rendition and then print them. Around the late sixties, people started wanting more from their documents. In particular, IBM asked a young researcher named Charles Goldfarb (the name may sound familiar) to build a system for storing, finding, managing, and publishing legal documents.

Goldfarb found that there were many systems within IBM that could not communicate with each other. They could not interchange information! Each of them used a different command language. They could not read each other's files, just as you may have had trouble loading *WordPerfect* files into *Word* and vice versa. The problem then, as now, was that they all had a different *representation* (sometimes also called a *file format*) for the information.

In the late sixties, Goldfarb and two other IBM researchers, Ed Mosher and Ray Lorie, set out to solve this problem. The team recognized (eventually) that the language would need to support three basic features:

Common data representation: markup
    Various computer programs and systems would need to be able to read and write information in the same representation.

Markup should be extensible
    There are an infinite variety of different types of information that must be exchanged. The markup language must be extensible enough to support them all.

Document types need rules
    There must be a mechanism for formally describing the rules shared by documents of a common type.

These principles are important far beyond the exchange of traditional documentation. In fact they underlie the exchange of any form of information whatsoever.

1.1.3 *Common data representation*

The need for a common data representation is easy to understand. Tools cannot interchange information if they do not speak the same language. As an analogy, consider the popularity of Latin terms in describing chemical and legal concepts and categories. To a certain extent, chemists and lawyers have chosen Latin as a common language for their fields. It made sense in the text processing context that the common language should be some form of markup language, because markup was well understood and very compatible with existing text editors and operating systems. Markup is like a common language shared by many disciplines.

Before SGML and XML there was no standardized data representation. Every organization or project would invent its own from scratch. This meant that many programmers spent a significant portion of their life just writing the software that understands (*parses*) all of these different representations.

1.1.4 *Customized document types*

Second, the three realized that the common format should be *specific* to legal documents while at the same time being general enough to be used for things that are completely unrelated to the law. This seems like a paradox but it is not as impossible as it sounds!

This is a little more subtle to grasp, but vital to understanding XML. The team could have invented a simple language, perhaps similar to the representation of a standard word processor, but that representation would not have allowed the sophisticated processing that was required. Lawyers and scientists both use Latin, but they do not use the same terminology. Rather they use Latin words as building blocks to create domain specific vocabularies (e.g. "habeas corpus", "ferruginous"). These domain specific vocabularies are even more important when we are describing documents to computers. Markup is the lingua franca but it must be customized (extended!) for each community, consortium or problem domain.

Just as Latin can be used to describe anything under the sun, XML can be used for legal and scientific projects, for electronic business and also for poetry. XML is great for everything from long, complicated academic documents to the business transaction documents that allow commerce to flow around the planet: purchase orders, requests for quotation, bills of lading and so forth. Because XML is so expressive, the business transaction documents can be created and consumed by computers; increasingly, they can transact business with little or no human intervention.

1.1.4.1 Computers are dumb

Usually we take for granted that computers are not very good at working with text and documents. We would never, for instance, ask a computer to search our hard disk and return a document that was a "letter" document, that was to "Martha" and that was about "John Smith's will". Even though this example seems much simpler than something a lawyer or chemist would run into, the fundamental problems are the same.

Most people recognize that the computer is completely incapable of understanding the concepts of "letter", "Martha" or "a will". Instead we might tell it to search for those words, and hope that we had included them all in the document. But what would happen if the system that we wanted to search was massive? It might turn up hundreds of unrelated documents. It might return documents that contained strings like "Martha, will you please write me a letter and tell me how John is doing?"

The fundamental problem is that the computer does not in any way understand the text. The solution is to teach the computer as much about the document as possible. Of course the computer will not understand the text in any real sense, but it can pretend to, in the same way that it pretends to understand simple data or decimal numbers.[2] We can make this possible by reducing the complexity of the document to a few structural *elements* chosen from a common vocabulary.

The elements that we use are not chosen just for the computer but also because they have significance to people and our sociological systems. We

---

2. We hope we haven't disillusioned anyone here. Computers may seem to know everything about math, but it is all a ruse. As far as they are concerned, they are only manipulating zeros and ones.

can choose elements that closely mirror the components of established, real-world document types.

One important example of this is in electronic commerce vocabularies. If corporate policy or national law requires a certain form of document be produced in order to conduct a certain kind of business, then XML allows that document type to be moved directly into a digital representation. The system can move from a manual process to a digital one without breaking any laws or corporate policies.

1.1.4.2   Computers can be trained

Once we "teach" computers about structured information, we can also program them to do things they would not have been able to otherwise. Using their new "understanding" they can help us to navigate through large documents, organize them, and automatically format the documents for publication in many different media, such as hypertext, print or tape.

In other words, we can get them to process text for us! The range of things we can get them to do with the documents is much wider than what we would get with WYSIWYG word processors or formatting markup. In the world of transaction documents, the computer typically rips the documents apart and can do a variety of things with the piecces: store them in databases, perform financial computations or anything else necessary to a business process.

Let us go back to the analogy of the typesetter working with a document marked up with a pen on paper to see why this is so powerful.

Imagine if we called her back the next day and told her to "change the formatting of the second chapter". She would have a lot of trouble mentally translating the codes for presentation back into high level constructs like sections and paragraphs.

To her, a title would only look like a line of text with a circle around it and instructions to make it italicized and 18 point. Making changes would be painful because recognizing the different logical constructs would be difficult. She probably could eventually accomplish the task by applying her human intuition and by reading the actual text. But computers do not have intuition, and cannot understand the text. That means that they cannot reliably recognize logical structure based totally on formatting. For instance they cannot reliably distinguish an italicized, 18 point title from an italicized, 18 point warning paragraph.

Even if human beings were consistent in formatting different types of documents (which we are not) computers would still have trouble. Even in a single document, the same formatting can mean two different things: italics could represent any kind of emphasis, foreign words, mathematical notations, scholarly citations or other conventions.

Note that this all comes back to our theme of information interchange, but in a subtle way. The human being has information about a document that may not show up in any particular formatted print-out (rendition) of the document. The author knows which documents are letters and which are not. The author knows which words are foreign and which are emphasized for rhetorical effect. A markup language can serve as a vehicle for the human to transmit this information *to the computer*.

We'll see that in some applications we can use markup to let computers talk to computers also! In fact, we can build systems in which each participant does not know or care whether its conversation partner is mechanical or biological.

1.1.4.3 Abstractions and renditions

Computers are not as smart as we are. If we want the computer to consider a piece of text to be written in a foreign language (for instance for spell checking purposes) then we must label it explicitly `foreign-language` and not just put it in italics! We call "foreign language" the *abstraction* that we are trying to represent, and we call the italics a particular rendition of the abstraction.

Formatting information has other problems. It is specific to a particular use of the information. Search engines cannot do very interesting searching on italics because they do not know what they mean. In contrast, the search engine could do something very interesting with `citation` elements: it could return a list of what documents are cited by other documents.

Italics are a form of markup specific to a particular application: formatting or printing. In contrast, the citation element is markup that can be used by a variety of applications. That is why we call this form of structural markup *generalized markup*. Generalized markup is the alternative to either formatting markup or WYSIWYG (lampooned by XML users as What You See is *All* You Get). Generalized markup is about getting more.

Because of the ambiguity of formatting, XML users typically do not bother to capture the document's presentational features at all, though

XML would allow it. We are not interested, for instance, in fonts, page breaks and bullets. This formatting information would merely clutter up our abstract document's representation. Although typographic conventions allow the computer to print out or display the document properly, we want our markup to do more than that. As you can imagine, removing all ambiguity is especially important in commerce applications, where millions of dollars may hinge on the proper completion of a transaction.

1.1.4.4   Stylesheets

Of course, if you are using XML for publishing, you must still be able to generate high quality print and online renditions of the document. Your readers do not want to read XML text directly. Instead of directly inserting the formatting commands in the XML document, we usually tell the computer how to generate formatted renditions *from* the XML abstraction.

For example in a print presentation, we can make the content of TITLE elements bold and large, insert page breaks before the beginning of chapters, and turn emphasis, citations and foreign words into italics. These rules are specified in a file called a *stylesheet*. The stylesheet is where human designers can express their creativity and understanding of formatting conventions. The stylesheet allows the computer to automatically convert the document from the abstraction to a formatted rendition.

We could use two different stylesheets to generate online and print renditions of the document. In the online rendition, there would be no page breaks, but cross-references would be represented as clickable hypertext links. Generalized markup allows us to easily produce high-quality print and online renditions of the same document.

We can even use two different stylesheets in the same medium. For instance, the computer could format the same document into several different styles (e.g. "New York Times" style vs. "Wired Magazine") depending on the expressed preferences of a Web surfer, or even based on which Internet service provider they use.

We can also go beyond just print and online formatting and have our document be automatically rendered into braille or onto a text-to-speech machine. XML is highly endorsed by those who promote the *accessibility* of information to the visually impaired.

Generalized markup documents are also "future-proof". They will not have to be redone to take advantage of future technologies. Instead, new stylesheets can be created to render existing documents in new ways.

Future renditions of documents might include three-dimensional virtual reality worlds where books are rendered as buildings, chapters as rooms and the text as wallpaper! Once again, the most important point is that these many different renditions will be possible without revising the document. There are millions of SGML documents that predate the Web, but many of them are now published on it.

Typically, they were republished in the Web's Hypertext Markup Language (HTML) without changing a single character of the SGML source's markup or data, or editing a single character of the generated HTML. All of the reorganization and reformatting can be done by computer programs instead of through months of re-typing. The same will be true of the relationship between XML and future representations.

The key is abstraction. SGML and XML can represent abstractions, and from abstractions you can easily create any number of renditions. This is a fact well-known to the world's database programmers, who constantly generate new renditions – reports and forms – from the same abstract data. In this sense, XML brings some of the rigor of the database world to the document world, where it has typically been lacking.

In the electronic commerce world, stylesheets can be used to make an information-dense computer-to-computer message into a visual rendition fit for human consumption. Perhaps your company policy is to require purchase orders beyond some limit to be considered by an executive. A stylesheet could turn an abstract XML document full of business process data into a familiar rows-and-columns purchase order that can be printed, touched and stapled to a wall. If some executives are comfortable working online, a different stylesheet could turn it into a transient computer window with the purchase order information at the top and two buttons: "Accept" and "Reject" at the bottom. The same information can have different renditions depending on your corporate policies and systems of the day.

1.1.4.5 Transformations

Stylesheets allow different people to consume the same information in many different ways. Sometimes computer programs also need to work with different types of information. XML allows programs to standardize certain conventions. But many programs can only work with particular XML vocabularies. For instance, if two different companies invent accounting vocabularies they will not be able to talk to each other automatically. To get these two programs to work together we need some kind of translator.

Let's go back to our Latin analogy. The translator acts as the polymath that helps the chemist and the lawyer to understand each other's variants of Latin. Translating between variants of the same language (XML or Latin) is of course easier than translating between totally proprietary languages but it still needs to be done.

In the markup world, the "translator" is a document called a *transformation specification* that tells the computer the details of the desired conversion. A language in which programmers write transformations is called a *transformation language*. There are many similarities between transformations and stylesheets. In fact, the more advanced stylesheet languages can also be used as transformation languages.

In fact, the line between stylesheets and transformation specs is blurry. Consider a stylesheet that translates XML documents from an in-house XML vocabulary into an XML vocabulary appropriate for rendering information on a handheld PDA. That stylesheet has two tasks. It needs to make the document look appropriate to the user of the handheld and also make it compatible with the software running on the handheld. It must deal with issues both of how the information looks (the traditional role of the stylesheet) and how it is represented as XML elements (the usual role of a transformation).

Many pundits consider it a weakness of XML that different software vendors may choose to use different vocabularies. But in fact the ability to invent new vocabularies is one of XML's core *strengths*. XML merely reflects the fact that the world is a diverse place and we all do different jobs with different types of information. Some level of incompatibility is the price of flexibility.

Before generalized markup, dealing with incompatible vocabularies was only a small part of the problem. Programmers would sometimes struggle to integrate computer systems that could not even agree on the order of bits required to compose a single character.

XML standardizes this detail and hundreds of others once and for all. This allows the programmer to concentrate on solving the business problem rather than on making two computer systems communicate.

1.1.5 *Rule-based markup*

Charles Goldfarb and his team (remember them?) had a third realization: if computer systems were to work with these documents reliably, the documents would have to follow certain rules. In retrospect we can see that this is important for interchanging information of all sorts, whether it is traditionally considered a document or not.

For instance a courtroom transcript might be required to have the name of the judge, defendant, both attorneys and (optionally) the names of members of the jury (if there is one). Since humans are prone to make mistakes, the computer would have to enforce the rules for us.

In other words the legal markup language should be specified in some formal way that would restrict elements appropriately. If the court stenographer tried to submit a transcript to the system without these elements being properly filled in, the system would check its *validity* and complain that it was *invalid*.

Once again, this concept is very common in the database world. Database people typically have several layers of checking to guarantee that improper data cannot appear in their databases. For instance *syntactic* checks guarantee that phone numbers are composed of digits and that people's names are not. *Semantic* checks ensure that business rules are followed (such as "purchase order numbers must be unique"). The database world calls the set of constraints on the database structure a *schema*. This word has also caught on in the XML world.

Of course, court transcripts have a different structure from wills, which in turn have a different structure from memos. So you would need to rigorously define what it means for each type of document to be valid. In SGML terminology, each of these is a *document type* and the formal definition that describes each type is called a *document type definition* (DTD) or *schema definition*. We use the word *document type* (or *schema*) to refer both to a vocabulary and the constraints on the vocabulary's use.

Once you have a document type worked out, you can describe for the computer how to print or display documents that conform to it with a *stylesheet*. So you might say that the address line in memos would be bold, or that there should be two lines between speeches in a court transcript. These processes can work reliably because documents are constrained by the document type definition. (See Figure 1-2.)

For instance, a letter cannot have a postscript ("P.S.") at the beginning of the document nor an address at the end. Because there is no convention for

Figure 1-2   Rule-based markup

formatting such a letter, a stylesheet would typically not do a good job with it. In fact, it might crash, as some word processors do when they try to load corrupted documents. The document type definition protects us from this.[3]

The rigor of a formal document type is just as important when the creator of the document is a computer (e.g. a purchasing system) and the receiver is also a computer (e.g. a delivery system). If your company lives and dies by its supply of widgets, you cannot afford for a miscommunica-

---

3. Of course, computer programmers will always invent new excuses for crashing software.

tion to cause a purchase to fail. You need both parties to know in advance what they should provide as requests and what they should expect back as responses. You need seamless interchange. As they say in the space exploration business, "Failure is not an option."

1.2 | XML markup

Enough hype about generalized markup! You probably want to know what it looks like. To mark up a letter, we could identify the components of the letter like this:

Example 1-2. A simple memo

```
<memo>
<to>Martha Mason</to>
<from>Joan Joplin</from>
<re>John Smith's will</re>
<p>John Smith wants to update his will. Another wife left him.</p>
</memo>
```

This text would be part of an XML document. The markup identifies components, called elements, of the document in ways that the computer can understand. The start-tag "<to>" marks the beginning of an element and the end-tag "</to>" marks the end of the element. Each element is an instance of an *element type*, such as to, from, re and p.

If you use an XML-aware word processor, you may never work with markup at the textual tag level, but you would still annotate sections of the document in this way (using the graphical interface that the tool provides).

Instead of each element type describing a formatting construct, each one instead describes the logical role of its elements – the *abstraction* it represents. The goal is for the abstraction to be descriptive enough and suitably chosen so that particular uses of the document (such as printing, searching and so forth) can be completely automated as computer processes acting on the elements.

For instance, we can search for a document that is "to" Martha, about ("re") John Smith's will. Of course the computer still does not understand the human interaction and concepts of sender and receiver, but it does know enough about the document to be able to tell me that in a "to" element of this particular document, the word "Martha" appears. If we expanded the letter a little to include addresses and so forth, we could also use an appropriate stylesheet to print it as a standard business letter.

1.2.1 *Documents and databases*

We can make our letter example even more precise and specific:

Example 1-3. Another letter

```
<memo>
<to>marthac@thelegaleagles.com</to>
<from>joanj@thelegaleagles.com</from>
<regarding>
<document-retrieval-request>will</document-retrieval-request>
<customer-name>John Smith</customer-name>
<customer-number>802-31348-5749</customer-number>
</regarding>
<comment>John Smith wants to update his will. Another wife left
him.</comment>
</memo>
```

XML does not require this level of detail, but it allows it. If you are familiar with databases, you might recognize that this looks database-ish in the sense that the customer number could be stored in a special index and you could easily search and sort this document based on customer numbers, document retrieval requests and so forth.

But you can only do this sort of thing if your letter processing system understands your company's concepts of customer-numbers and your documents consistently provide the information. In other words, you must define your own vocabulary of element types just as the IBM team did.

In fact, many people have noticed that XML documents resemble traditional relational and object database data in many ways. Once you have a language for rigorously representing documents, those documents can be treated more like other forms of data.

But the converse is also true. As we have described, XML documents have many features in common with databases. They can preserve the abstract data and prevent it from being mingled with rendition information.

Furthermore, you can actually use generalized markup to represent data that is not what we would traditionally think of as documents, but too complex to be directly handled in conventional databases. In this brave new world, DNA sequences are documents, and so are molecular diagrams and virtual reality worlds. A document is just an interchangeable form of data! In other words, generalized markup allows us to blow the doors off the word "document" and integrate diverse types of data. This database-ization of documents and document-ization of data is one of the major drivers of the XML excitement. Prior to XML, the Web had no standard data interchange format for even moderately complex data.

Only a few people could see 30 years ago that markup languages might one day change the entire world of databases and electronic commerce. But XML's unique usefulness as a data interchange representation is a direct consequence of the IBM team's three fundamental concepts:

- Markup as a common data representation
- Extensibility through document types (vocabularies)
- Verification that documents follow rules (document type/schema definitions).

XML isn't magic. Building XML-based systems can be easy or difficult, depending on the complexity of the problem at hand. XML eases the difficulty by allowing you to concentrate on the important aspects of your problem and ignore the irrelevant ones. Thanks to its common data representation, projects that use XML can avoid a tedious process of inventing a new data representation. That allows you to concentrate on choosing or creating a vocabulary tailored to your problem. Finally, XML has schema and DTD languages that allow you to clearly and precisely define the rules of your vocabulary.

Beyond XML, there are many related standards for stylesheets, transformations, linking and so forth. Each standard exists to help you to focus on the essential points that make your vocabulary unique. The associated standards allow you to avoid reinventing wheels.

1.3 | Road to XML

In 1969, the IBM team developed a language that could implement their vision of markup that would allow the construction of sophisticated, robust systems that integrate many applications on many different operating systems. They called it the *Generalized Markup Language* (which, not coincidentally, has the same initials as the names Goldfarb, Mosher and Lorie).[4]

However, it wasn't until 1974 that Goldfarb proved the concept of a "validating parser", one that could read a document type definition and check the accuracy of markup, without going to the expense of actually processing a document. As he recalls it: "At that point SGML was born – although it still had a lot of growing up to do."

Between 1978 and 1986, Goldfarb acted as technical leader of a team of users, programmers and academics that developed his nascent invention into the robust International Standard (ISO 8879) they called the *Standard Generalized Markup Language.*

That team, with many of the same players still involved, is now JTC1/SC34, which continues to develop SGML and related standards. Three of the most important are *HyTime*, which standardizes the representation of hyperlinking features, *Topic Maps*, which standardize the representation of information navigation features, and *DSSSL*, which standardizes the creation of stylesheets.[5]

The SGML standard took a long time to develop, but arguably it was still ahead of the market when it was created. Over those years, the basic concepts of GML were broadened to support a very wide range of applications. Although GML was always extensible and generalized, the SGML standard added many features and options, many intended for niche markets. But the niches had to be catered for: some of the niche users have document collections that rival the Web in size!

By the time it was standardized in 1986, SGML had become large, intricate and powerful. In addition to being an official International Standard, SGML is the de facto standard for the interchange of large, complex docu-

---

4. In fact, Goldfarb coined the term "markup language" for the purpose.
5. Knowing the full names probably won't help much, but just in case, HyTime is short for "Hypermedia/Time-based Structuring Language" and DSSSL (pronounced "dis-sal") is short for "Document Style Semantics and Specification Language". We warned you that it wouldn't help much.

ments and has been used in domains as diverse as programming language design and airplane maintenance.

1.3.1 *HTML and the Web*

In 1989, a researcher named Tim Berners-Lee proposed that information could be shared within the CERN European Nuclear Research Facility using hyperlinked text documents. He was advised to use an SGML-ish syntax by a colleague named Anders Berglund, an early adopter of the new SGML standard. They started from a simple example document type in the SGML standard[6] and developed a hypertext version called the *Hypertext Markup Language* (HTML).

Relative to the 20 year evolution of SGML, HTML was developed in a hurry, but it did the job well. Tim called his hypertext system the *World Wide Web* and today it is the most diverse, popular hypertext information system in existence. Its simplicity is widely believed to be an important part of its success. The simplicity of HTML and the other Web specifications allowed programmers around the world to quickly build systems and tools to work with the Web.

HTML exhibits some important strengths of SGML. With a few exceptions, its element types are generalized and descriptive, not formatting constructs as in languages like TeX and Microsoft Word. This means that HTML documents can be displayed on text screens, under graphical user interfaces, and even projected through speakers for the sight impaired.

HTML documents use SGML's simple angle bracket convention for markup. That means that authors can create HTML documents in almost any text editor or word processor. The documents are also compatible with almost every computer system in existence.

On the other hand, HTML only uses a fixed set of element types. As we discussed before, no one document type can serve all purposes, so HTML only benefits from the first of GML's revelations, that document representations must be standardized. It is not extensible and therefore cannot be tailored for particular document types, and it was not very rigorously defined

---

6. That DTD was based on the very first published DTD, from a 1978 IBM manual written by Goldfarb, derived in turn from work that he and Mosher had done in the early 70's.

until years after its invention. By the time HTML was given a formal DTD, there were already thousands of Web pages with erroneous HTML.[7]

1.3.2 *HTML gets extended – unofficially!*

As the Web grew in popularity many people started to chafe under HTML's fixed document type. Browser vendors saw an opportunity to gain market share by making incompatible extensions to HTML. Most of the extensions were formatting commands and thus damaged the Web's interoperability. The first golden rule – standardization – was in serious danger.

For instance the Netscape browser introduced a CENTER element that cannot be "pronounced" in a text to speech converter. A BLINK element cannot be rendered on some computers. Still, this was a fairly understandable reaction to HTML's limitations.

One argument for implementing formatting constructs instead of abstractions is that there are a fixed number of formatting constructs in wide use, but an ever growing number of abstractions. Let's say that next year biologists invent a new formatting notation for discussing a particular type of DNA. They might use italics to represent one kind of DNA construct and bold to represent another. In other words, as new abstractions are invented, we usually use existing formatting features to represent them. We have been doing this for thousands of years, and prior to computerization, it was essentially the only way.

We human readers can read a textual description of the meanings of the features ("in this book, we will use Roman text to represent...") and we can differentiate them from others using our reasoning and understanding of the text. But this system leaves computers more or less out of the loop.

For instance superscripts can be used for trademarks, footnotes and various mathematical constructs. Italics can be used for references to book titles, for emphasis and to represent foreign languages. Without generalized markup to differentiate, computers cannot do anything useful with that information. It would be impossible for them to translate foreign languages, convert emphasis to a louder voice for text to speech conversion, or do calculations on the mathematical formulae. Over time, the Web became more

---

7. Today there are tens of thousands with misleading or downright erroneous informational content, so perhaps bad HTML markup is not that big a problem in the overall scheme of things.

and more optimized for a single delivery platform: whichever Web browser had the most market share on a particular day. Handhelds, braille printers and other alternative devices became marginalized.[8]

1.3.3 *The World Wide Web reacts*

As the interoperability and diversity of the Web became more and more endangered by proprietary formatting markup, the World Wide Web Consortium (headed by the same Tim Berners-Lee) decided to act. They attacked the problem in three ways. First, they decided to adopt the GML convention for attaching formatting to documents, the stylesheet.

They invented a simple HTML-oriented stylesheet language called *Cascading Style Sheets* (CSS) that allowed people to attach formatting to HTML documents without filling the HTML itself with proprietary, rendition-oriented markup.

Second, they invented a simple mechanism for adding abstractions to HTML. We will not look at that mechanism here, because XML makes it obsolete. It allowed new abstractions to be invented but provided no mechanism for constraining their occurrence. In other words it addressed two of GML's revelations: it brought HTML back to being a single standard, more or less equally supported by the major vendors, and it allowed people to define arbitrary extensions (with many limitations).

But they knew that their stool would not stand long on two of its three legs. The (weakly) extensible HTML and CSS are only stopgaps. For the Web to move to a new level, it had to incorporate the third of GML's important ideas, that document types should be formally defined so that documents can be checked for validity against them.

Therefore, the World Wide Web Consortium decided to develop a subset of SGML that would retain SGML's major virtues but also embrace the Web ethic of minimalist simplicity. They decided to give the new language the catchy name *Extensible Markup Language* (XML). They also decided to make related standards for advanced hyperlinking and stylesheets.

The first, called the *Extensible Linking Language* (XLink), is inspired by HyTime, the ISO standard for linking SGML documents, and by the Text Encoding Initiative, the academic community's guidelines for applying SGML to scholarly applications.

---

8. Although, thanks to XML, that is starting to change, as we shall see.

The second, called the *Extensible Style Language* is a combination of ideas from the Web's Cascading Style Sheets and ISO's DSSSL standard. There have been many new XML-related standards added to the World Wide Web Consortium scripture since XML was published. We will discuss these as we go along.[9]

XML was specifically designed to enhance reliable interchange on the Web. At about the same time, the Internet became popular as a place to do business: to buy and sell things. People saw that in the future, computers would do the buying and selling completely independently of human beings. They would also need a robust, sophisticated information interchange language. In other words, electronic business needed XML.

1.4 | EDI, EAI and other TLAs

By 1998, many understood that XML was not just a tool for Web servers sending information to Web browsers. Many people who had previously considered their problem domains to be separate came to see them as really variations on the same things.

Each of these domains is known by a *Three Letter Acronym (TLA)*. When you combine these with the various XML-world specs and standards the result is a terminological alphabet soup. Pick up your spoon, we'll help you through!

1.4.1 *Electronic data interchange (EDI)*

One of the first groups to sense the coming convergence between documents and data was the electronic data interchange (EDI) community. EDI is the technology that large companies typically use to buy, sell and interchange information with each other.

---

9. This description necessarily presented as linear, straightforward, and obvious a process that was actually messy and at times confusing. It is fair to say that there were many people outside the World Wide Web Consortium who had a better grasp on the need for XML than many within it, and that various member corporations "caught on" to the importance of XML at different rates.

Most people agree that XML is easier to work with and more extensible. Where EDI only scratched the surface of the business world, XML-based e-commerce should penetrate down even to small companies. The thing that differentiates this sort of e-commerce from the kind you can find on any old website is that it is *integrated*.

With integrated e-commerce (IEC), your system is integrated directly or indirectly with your partner's system so that transactions can be verified and logged automatically in your internal systems. In contrast, buying a book (even this book!) from Amazon's website is not integrated e-commerce because there is no way that the purchase could be automatically entered into your local accounting system or sent to your boss for approval. Amazon, of course, uses a great deal of IEC when buying from *its* suppliers.

The venture capital world has chosen to embrace the somewhat confusing term "business to business e-commerce"(B2B) for this application. We consider the term confusing because one business could buy products from another business through a Web storefront and it would not typically be termed B2B, even though it was "business to business" and "e-commerce". What the pundits (fund-its?) really mean is *integrated* e-commerce.

So if buying from Amazon isn't IEC, what would be? Imagine if you bought a thousand widgets and your computer system automatically generated and delivered a purchase order and then updated your inventory while the receiving system automatically entered the order into its order system. Whew! That's a lot of automation! The opportunity to automate things is the fundamental strength of integrated e-commerce.

Integration wasn't invented with XML. Rather, XML allows corporations and consortia to rapidly negotiate standards that make it feasible to integrate disparate computer systems economically. Without standards, each business must negotiate with every other business individually and the costs quickly spiral out of control. A much more *scalable* solution is to negotiate a standard with all potential partners at once. XML provides the framework for this negotiation and thus for integrated e-commerce.

The integrated solution allows a new class of *Business Process Automation (BPA)* software. BPA software allows businesses to describe their business process workflows in terms of the steps necessary to complete the process. Where human oversight is necessary, BPA software routes the information to the right person and solicits approval or input. BPA extends the concept of workflow by allowing processes to go beyond the boundaries of an organization. Of course this depends on standards – and most of these standards will be based upon XML.

There will also be a role for intermediaries that help businesses find each other and conduct transactions. Depending on their features, you can think of them as brokers or exchanges. Fortunes will be made and lost in this new application domain.

1.4.2 *Enterprise Application Integration (EAI)*

The next TLA that we will tackle is Enterprise Application Integration (EAI). We have described how XML helps businesses to communicate with each other. It is just as good at helping the parts of a business to communicate. This area of XML use is termed Enterprise Application Integration (or just Application Integration).

EAI is important because it is necessary before integrated e-commerce can really begin to save money. The accounting system must be integrated with inventory. Inventory must be integrated with delivery systems. Deliveries must be integrated with billing, which is a part of accounting and so forth. "The thigh bone's connected to the leg bone, the leg bone's connected to the ankle bone..." XML is today's choice for the cartilage between the bones in your organizational skeleton.

XML can be directly generated by many large-scale enterprise accounting, Enterprise Resource Planning (ERP), Customer Relationship Management (CRM), Supply Chain Management (SCM) and related packages. Even systems that do not natively "speak" XML can be made to do so through third-party or in-house extensions. When the vocabularies do not exactly match up (in other words, before there is a widely adopted standard vocabulary for a particular task) we can *transform* XML from one vocabulary into another.

In a sense, EAI and integrated e-commerce are two sides of the same coin. EAI is a kind of integration within your corporate boundaries in order to present better information to employees and systems. Integrated e-commerce is a form of integration that spans corporate boundaries in order to improve the flow of information and products among partners.

1.5 | Conclusion

EAI, EDI, B2B, IEC, ERP: XML touches every acronym.

XML is likely to be the basis for most structured information interchange in the future. If you buy a car on the Web, your browser will signal your decision with an XML document in one vocabulary. The auto dealer will replenish its stock of cars from the car company through another XML document using another vocabulary. The auto manufacturer will buy parts from its suppliers by sending out an automated request for quotes in XML in an e-business auction vocabulary and suppliers will respond in XML. In other words, whenever two computers need to communicate with each other, there is a role for XML.

In many ways, none of this is new. Ancients used documents to communicate around their kingdoms and across centuries. Cavemen used documents (also known as wall paintings) to communicate their hopes and fears. XML allows computers to get into the conversation.

Analysis   Now we've seen the origins of XML, and some of its key ideas. Unlike lots of other "next great things" of the high-tech world, XML has solid roots and a proven track record. You can have confidence in XML because the particular subset of SGML that is XML has been in use for fifteen years.

Just enough XML

■ Elements

■ Entities

■ Markup

■ Document types

■ Parsers

■ Protocols

Chapter

2

In this chapter we will explore the fundamental concepts of XML documents and XML systems. If XML were a great work of literature then this chapter would be the Cliff notes. The chapter will introduce the ideas that define the language but will avoid the nitty-gritty details (the *syntax*) behind the constructs. As a result, some concepts may remain slightly fuzzy because you will not be able to work with them "hands on". Our tutorial chapters will provide that opportunity.

This early presentation of these ideas will allow you to see XML's "big picture". We will do this by walking through the design process for an XML-like language. Hopefully by the end of the process, you will understand each of the design decisions and XML's overall architecture.

Our objective is to equip you with "just enough" XML to appreciate the application and tool discussions in the following parts of the book, but being over-achievers we may go a little too far. Feel free to leave at any time to read about XML in the real world.

2.1 | The goal

First we should summarize what we are trying to achieve. In short, "What is XML used for?" XML is for the *digital representation* of documents. You probably have an intuitive feel for what a document is. We will work from your intuition.

Documents can be large and small. Both a multi-volume encyclopedia and an invoice can be thought of as documents. A particular volume of the encyclopedia can also be called a document. XML allows you to think of the encyclopedia whichever way will allow you to get your job done most efficiently. You'll notice that XML will give you these sorts of options in many places. XML can even represent the message from a police department's server to a police officer's handheld computer that reports that you have unpaid parking tickets.[1]

When we say that we want to *digitally represent* documents we mean that we want to put them in some kind of computer-readable notation so that a computer can help us store, process, search, transmit, display and print them. In order for a computer to do useful things with a document, we are going to have to tell it about the structure of the document. This is our simple goal: to represent the documents in a way that the computer can "understand", insofar as computers can understand anything.

XML saves money by allowing programmers to reuse a piece of code called an XML *processor* or *parser*. The former term is used in the XML spec, but the latter is more often used in discussions. The processor parses (interprets) the markup and passes the data to whatever application the programmer is writing. It figures out which parts of the document are there just to get the document from point A to point B and which are the real information that the programmer needs to deal with. There are processors available for almost every programming language on every platform and most of them are available freely on the Web!

XML documents can include pictures, movies and other multimedia, but we will not usually represent the multimedia components as XML. If you think of representation as a translation process, similar to language translation, then many multimedia components are the parts that we will leave in their "native language" because they have no simple translation into the "target language" (XML). We will just include them in their native formats

---

1. Sorry about that.

as you might include a French or Latin phrase in an English text without explicit translation.

Most pictures on the Web are files in formats called GIF or JPEG and most movies are in a format called MPEG. An XML document would just refer to those files in their native GIF, JPEG or MPEG formats. If you were transcribing an existing print document into XML, you would most likely represent the character-text parts as XML and the graphical parts in these other formats. XML is the glue that holds everything together and can even be used to handle the timing and sequencing of multimedia events.

On the other hand, there are some kinds of graphics that actually do make sense to represent right in XML. If a graphic is made up mostly of lines, boxes, arcs, fades and other, similar geometric shapes, we call it a *vector graphic*. In other words, vector graphics are graphics that are created in terms of structured components by a graphic artists. In contrast, many *bitmap graphics* are photographs of things in the real world. XML is often used to represent vector graphics but seldom used to represent bitmap graphics, recorded audio or movies. Nevertheless, XML can easily integrate those types of data by reference.

2.2 | Elements: The logical structure

Before we can describe exactly how we are going to represent documents, we must have a model in our heads of how a document is structured. Most documents (for example books and magazines) can be broken down into components (chapters and articles). These can also be broken down into components (titles, paragraphs, figures and so forth). And those components can be broken down into components until we get to the textual data itself – words and sentences. At this point we would typically stop breaking the document into components unless we were interested in linguistic research.

It turns out that every document can be viewed this way, though some fit the model more naturally than others. In fact all information can be viewed this way...with the same caveat!

In XML, these components are called *elements*. Each element represents a logical component of a document. Elements can contain other elements and can also contain the words and sentences that you would usually think of as the text of the document. XML calls this text the document's *character data*. This hierarchical view of XML documents is demonstrated in Figure 2-1.

Markup professionals call this the *tree structure* of the document. The element that contains all of the others (e.g. `Book`, `Article` or `Memo`) is known as the *root element*. This name captures the fact that it is the only element that does not "hang" off of some other element. The root element is also referred to as the *document element* because it holds the entire logical document within it. The terms *root element* and *document element* are interchangeable.

The elements that are contained in the root are called its *subelements*. They may contain subelements themselves. If they do, we will call them *branches*. If they do not, we will call them *leaves*.

Thus, the `Chapter` and `Section` elements are branches (because they have subelements), but the `Paragraph` and `Title` elements are leaves (because they only contain character data).[2]

Elements can also have extra information attached to them called *attributes*. Attributes describe properties of elements. For instance a `CIA-record` element might have a security attribute that gives the security rating for that element. A CIA database might only release certain records to certain people depending on their security rating. It is somewhat of a judgement call which aspects of a document should be represented with elements and which should be represented with attributes, but we will give some guidelines in Chapter 54, "Creating a document type definition", on page 788.

Real-world documents do not always fit this tree model perfectly. They often have non-hierarchical features such as cross-references or hypertext links from one section of the tree to another. XML can represent these structures too. In fact, XML goes beyond the powerful links provided by HTML. More on this in 2.9, "Hyperlinking", on page 47.

---

2. This arboreal metaphor is firmly rooted in computer science. However, markup experts have recently extended it with the term "grove". This term recognizes that a single document may best be viewed as multiple trees.

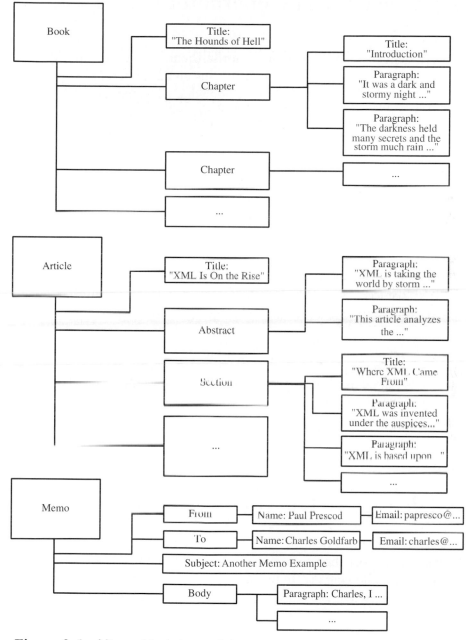

Figure 2-1   Hierarchical views of documents

2.3 | Unicode: The character set

Texts are made up of characters. If we are going to represent texts, then we must represent the characters that comprise them. So we must decide how we are going to represent characters at the bits and bytes level. This is called the *character encoding*. We must also decide what characters we are going to allow in our documents. This is the *character set*. A particularly restrictive character set might allow only upper-case characters. A very large character set might allow Eastern ideographs and Arabic characters.

If you are a native English speaker you may only need the fifty-two upper- and lower-case characters, some punctuation and a few accented characters. The pervasive *7-bit ASCII character set* caters to this market. It has just enough characters (128) for all of the letters, symbols, some accented characters and some other oddments. ASCII is both a character set *and* a character encoding. It defines what set of characters are available and how they are to be encoded in terms of bits and bytes.

XML's character set is *Unicode*, a sort of ASCII on steroids. Unicode includes thousands of characters from languages around the world.[3] However the first 128 characters of Unicode are compatible with ASCII and there is a character encoding of Unicode, *UTF-8* that is compatible with 7-bit ASCII. This means that at the bits and bytes level, the first 128 characters of UTF-8 Unicode and 7-bit ASCII are the same. As if by magic, every ASCII document is automatically a Unicode document. This feature of Unicode allows authors to use standard plain-text editors to create XML immediately.

2.4 | Entities: The physical structure

An XML document is defined as a series of characters. An XML processor (aka parser) starts at the beginning and works to the end. XML provides a mechanism for allowing text to be organized non-linearly and potentially in multiple pieces. The processor reorganizes it into the linear structure.

---

3. Some are quite esoteric. There are sections of Unicode dedicated to "Japanese dentistry symbols", "Dingbat ornamental brackets", "Recycling symbols" and "More recycling symbols". Even "Klingon" from *Star Trek*™ was considered, but eventually rejected.

The "piece-of-text" construct is called an *entity*. An entity could be as small as a single character or as large as all the characters of a book.

Entities have *names*. Somewhere in your document, you insert an *entity reference* to make use of an entity. The processor replaces the entity reference with the entity itself, which is called the *replacement text*. It works somewhat like a word processor macro.

For instance an entity named "sigma", might contain the name of a Greek character. You would use a reference to the entity whenever you wanted to insert the sigma character. An update in one place would propagate across all uses of the text. For instance you could define your company name as an entity and update all occurrences of it automatically by changing the entity text.

An entity could also be called "introduction-chapter" and be a chapter in a book. You would refer to the entity at the point where you wanted the chapter to appear.

The feature of XML that allows documents to be broken into many physical files is called the *external entity*. External entities are often referred to merely as entities, but the meaning is usually clear from context. An XML document can be broken up into many files on a hard disk or objects in a database and each of them is called an entity in XML terminology. Entities could even be spread across the Internet. Whereas XML elements describe the document's logical structure, entities keep track of the location of the chunks of bytes that make up an XML document. We call this the *physical structure* of the document.

The units of XML text that we will typically talk about are the entity and the document. Documents are composed of one or more entities. You may be accustomed to thinking about files, but entities do not have to be stored as files. For instance, entities could be stored in databases or generated on the fly by a computer program. Some file formats (e.g. a *zip* file) even allow multiple entities to reside in the same file at once. The term that covers all of these possibilities is entity, *not* file. Still, on most Web sites each entity will reside in a single file so in those cases external entities and files will functionally be the same. This setup is simple and efficient, but will not be sufficient for very large sites.

External entities help to break up large files to make them editable, searchable, downloadable and otherwise usable on the ordinary computer systems that real people use. Entities allow authors to break their documents into workable chunks that can fit into memory for editing, can be downloaded across a slow modem and so forth.

Without entities, authors would have to break their documents unnaturally into smaller documents with only weak links between them (as is commonly done with HTML). This complicates document management and maintenance. If you have ever tried to print out one of these HTML documents broken into a hundred HTML files then you know the problem. Entities allow documents to be broken up into chunks without forgetting that they actually represent a single coherent document that can be printed, edited and searched as a unit when that makes sense.

Non-XML objects are referenced in much the same way and are called *unparsed entities*. We think of them as "data entities" because there is no XML markup in them that will be noticed by the XML processor. Data entities include graphics, movies, audio, raw text, PDF and anything else you can think of that is not XML (including HTML and other forms of SGML).[4] Each data entity has an associated *notation declaration* that is simply a statement declaring whether the entity is a GIF, JPEG, MPEG, PDF and so forth.

Entities are described in all of their glorious (occasionally gory) detail in Chapter 55, "Entities: Breaking up is easy to do", on page 822.

2.5 | Markup

We have discussed XML's conceptual model, the tree of elements, its strategy for encoding characters, Unicode, and its mechanism for managing the size and complexity of documents, entities. We have not yet discussed how to represent the logical structure of the document and link together all of the physical entities.

Although there are XML word processors, one of the design goals of XML was that it should be possible to create XML documents in standard text editors. Most people do not own XML-based word processors and even those who do may depend on text editors to "debug" their document if the word processor makes a mistake, or allows the user to make a mistake. The only way to allow authors convenient access to both the structure and data of the document in standard text editors is to put the two right beside each other, "cheek to cheek".

---

4. Actually, a data entity could even contain XML, but it wouldn't be treated as part of the main XML document.

As we discussed in the introduction, the stuff that represents the logical structure and connects the entities is called markup. An XML document is made up exclusively of markup and character data. Both are in Unicode. Collectively they are termed *XML text*.

This last point is important! Unless the context unambiguously refers to data, as in "textual data", when we say "XML text", we mean the markup and the data.

Caution The term XML text refers to the combination of character data and markup, not character data alone. Character data + markup = text.

Markup is differentiated from character data by special characters called *delimiters*. Informally, text between a less-than (<) and a greater-than (>) character or between an ampersand (&) and a semicolon (;) character is markup. Those four characters are the most common delimiters. This rule will become more concrete in later chapters. In the meantime, Example 2-1 shows a small document to give you a taste of XML markup.

Example 2-1. A small XML document

```
<?xml version="1.0"?>
<!DOCTYPE Q-AND-A SYSTEM "http://www.q.and.a.com/faq.dtd">
<Q-AND-A>
<QUESTION>I'm having trouble loading a WurdWriter 2.0 file into
WurdPurformertWriter 7.0. Any suggestions?</QUESTION>
<ANSWER>Why don't you use XML?</ANSWER>
<QUESTION>What's XML?</QUESTION>
<ANSWER>It's a long story, but there is a book I can
recommend...</ANSWER>
</Q-AND-A>
```

The markup starting with the less-than and ending with the greater-than is called a *tag*.

You may be familiar with other languages that use similar syntax. These include HTML and other SGML-based languages.

2.6 | Document types and schemas

The concept of a document type is fairly intuitive. You are well aware that novels, bills of lading and telephone books are quite different, and you are probably comfortable recognizing documents that conform to one of these categories. No matter what its title or binding, you would call a book that listed names and phone numbers a phone book. So, a document type is defined by its element types. If two documents have radically different element types or allow elements to be combined in very different ways then they probably do not conform to the same document type.

A set of element types is called a *vocabulary* and every document type, of course, has one. Or perhaps more than one. Just as in English, there are no hard and fast rules in XML about where one vocabulary ends and another begins.

2.6.1 *Defining document types*

This notion of a document type can be formalized in XML. A *document type definition* (*DTD*) or *schema definition* consists of a series of definitions for element types, attributes, entities and notations.

The DTD declaration syntax is the original mechanism for doing this. DTDs are built into XML. Schemas are a newer, more sophisticated (and also more complicated) arrival to the party. Schemas and document types share concepts, so at a high level the terms can be used interchangeably. Of course when we get down to the details, schema definitions and DTDs look quite different, even though the underlying concepts are similar.

The DTD or schema definition declares which element types, etc., are legal within the document and in what places they are legal. A document can claim to conform to a particular DTD in its *document type declaration*.[5] There is also a mechanism for referring to a schema through a specialized attribute.

Other terms for document type include "message format" or "message layout." We don't use them because we believe that there is an important distinction between the term "document" and "message". A book is a docu-

---

5. The document type declaration is usually abbreviated "DOCTYPE", because the obvious abbreviation would be the same as that for document type definition!

ment. The information that the book conveys is its message. In other words, the message is the informational content of the document. According to this definition, a message cannot really have a layout or format.

DTDs and schemas are powerful tools for organizational standardization in much the same way that forms, templates and style-guides are. A very rigid DTD that only allows one element type in a particular place is like a form: "Just fill in the blanks!". A more flexible DTD is like a style-guide in that it can, for instance, require every `list` to have two or more `items`, every `report` to have an `abstract` and could restrict `footnotes` from appearing within `footnotes`.

DTDs are critical for organizational standardization, but they are just as important for allowing robust processing of documents by software. For example, a letter document with a `chapter` in the middle of it would be most unexpected and unlikely to be very useful. Letter printing software would not reliably be able to print such a document because it is not well defined what a chapter in a letter looks like.

Even worse is a situation where a document is missing an element expected by the software that processes it. If your mail program used XML as its storage format, you might expect it to be able to search all of the incoming email addresses for a particular person's address. Let us assume that each message stores this address in a `from` element. What do we do about letters without `from` elements when we are searching them? Programmers could write special code to "work around" the problem, but these kinds of workarounds make code difficult to write.

By taking on the entire responsibility for checking input validity, DTDs and schemas simplify the construction of software. This is very analogous to the way that XML processors take over responsibility for parsing!

DTDs and schemas also serve as a sort of agreement or contract between information creators and consumers. You can hammer them out using any reasonable mechanism (a consortium, an ad hoc meeting or even through old-fashioned coercion). Once you have a schema or DTD, you can use it as a very formal and objective definition of which documents are valid within the system and which are not.

2.6.2 *HTML: A cautionary tale*

HTML serves as a useful cautionary tale. It actually has a fairly rigorous structure, defined in SGML, and available from the World Wide Web Consortium. But everybody tends to treat the rules as if they actually came from the World Wrestling Federation – they ignore them.

The programmers that maintain HTML browsers spend a huge amount of time incorporating support for all of the incorrect ways people combine the HTML elements in their documents. Although HTML has an SGML DTD, very few people use it, and the browser vendors have unofficially sanctioned the practice of ignoring it. Workarounds are expensive, time consuming, boring and frustrating, but the worst problem is that there is no good definition of what these illegal constructs mean. Some incorrect constructs will actually make HTML browsers crash, but others will merely make them display confusing or random results.

In HTML, the `title` element is used to display the document's name at the top of the browser window (on the title bar). But what should a browser do if there are two titles? Use the first? Use the last? Use both? Pick one at random? The HTML standard does not allow this construct. It certainly does not specify a behavior! Believe it or not, an early version of Netscape's browser showed each title sequentially over time, creating a primitive sort of text animation. That behavior disappeared quickly when Netscape programmers realized that authors were actually creating invalid HTML specifically to get this effect! Since authors cannot depend on nonsensical documents to work across browsers, or even across browser versions, there must be a formal definition of a valid, reasonable document of a particular type.

In XML, the DTD or schema provides a formal definition of the element types, attributes and entities allowed in a document of a specified type. If this seems important for documents intended for human reading, consider the absolute importance of clear standards and tight validation in computer-to-computer e-commerce applications!

There is also a more subtle, related issue. If you do not stop and think carefully about the structure of your documents, you may accidently slip back into specifying them in terms of their formatting rather than their abstract structure. We are accustomed to thinking of documents in terms of their rendition. That is because, prior to GML, there was no practical way to create a document without creating a rendition. The process of creating a DTD gives us an opportunity to rethink our documents in terms of their structure, as abstractions.

2.6.3   *Declaring a DTD*

Example 2-2 shows examples of some of the declarations that are used to express a DTD. Example 2-3 shows the equivalent DTD as a schema definition.

Example 2-2. Markup declarations

```
<!ELEMENT Q-AND-A (QUESTION,ANSWER)+>
<!-- This allows: question, answer, question, answer ... -->
<!ELEMENT QUESTION (#PCDATA)>
<!-- Questions are just made up of textual data -->
<!ELEMENT ANSWER (#PCDATA)>
<!-- Answers are just made up of textual data -->
```

Example 2-3. Schema definition

```
<schema xmlns='http://www.w3.org/2001/XMLSchema'
        xmlns:qa='http://www.q.and.a.com/'
        targetNamespace='http://www.q.and.a.com/'>
 <element name="Q-AND-A">
 <complexType>
  <sequence minOccurs="1" maxOccurs="unbounded">
   <element ref="qa:QUESTION"/>
   <element ref="qa:ANSWER"/>
  </sequence>
 </complexType>
 </element>
<!-- This allows: question, answer, question, answer ... -->
 <element name="QUESTION" type="string"/>
<!-- Questions are just made up of textual data -->
 <element name="ANSWER" type="string"/>
<!-- Answers are just made up of textual data -->
</schema>
```

Caution   A document type or schema is a concept. A document type definition (DTD) or schema definition is the expression of that concept. The distinction is important because that expression can be created in several ways. You can use markup declarations (for DTDs), or any of several schema definition languages. However, the distinction is rarely made in normal parlance. In this book we make it only when needed for clarity.

Some XML documents do not have a schema definition or document type declaration. That does not mean that they do not conform to a document type. It merely means that they do not claim to conform to some formally defined document type definition.

If the document is to be useful as an XML document, it must still have some structure, expressed through elements, attributes and so forth. When you create a stylesheet for a document you will depend on it having certain elements, on the element type names having certain meanings, and on the elements appearing in certain places. However it manifests itself, that set of things that you depend on is the document type.

You can formalize that structure in a DTD or schema. In addition to or instead of a formal computer-readable DTD, you can also write out a prose description. You might consider the many HTML books in existence to be prose definitions of HTML.

Finally, you can just keep the document type in your head and maintain conformance through careful discipline. If you can achieve this for large, complex documents, your powers of concentration are astounding! Which is our way of saying: we do not advise it. We will discuss DTDs more in Chapter 54, "Creating a document type definition", on page 788 and schemas in Chapter 60, "XML Schema (XSDL)", on page 918.

2.7 | Well-formedness and validity

Every language has rules about what is or is not correct in the language. In human languages that takes many forms: words have a particular correct pronunciation (or range of pronunciations) and they can be combined in certain ways to make valid sentences (grammar). Similarly XML has two different notions of "correct". The first is merely that the markup is intelligible: the XML equivalent of "getting the pronunciation right". A document with intelligible markup is called a *well-formed* document. One important goal of XML was that these basic rules should be simple so that they could be strictly adhered to.

The experience of the HTML market greatly informed the development of XML. Much of the HTML on the Web does *not* conform to even the simplest rules in the HTML specifications. This makes automated processing of HTML quite difficult.

Because Web browsers will display ill-formed documents, authors continue to create them. In designing XML, we decided that XML processors should actually be prohibited from trying to recover from a *well-formedness* error in an XML document. This was a controversial decision because there were many who felt that it was inappropriate to restrict XML implementors from deciding the best error recovery policy for their applications.

The XML equivalent of "using the right words in the right place" is called *validity* and is related to the notion of document types. A document is *valid* if it declares conformance to a DTD in a document type declaration and actually conforms to that DTD.[6]

Documents that do not have a document type declaration are not really *invalid* as there is no known DTD for them to violate. But neither are they valid, because there is also no known DTD to which they conform.

If HTML documents with multiple titles were changed over to use XML syntax, they would be *well-formed* and yet *invalid* because they would not conform to the DTD (known as XHTML). If we remove the document type declaration, so that they no longer claim to conform to the XHTML DTD, then they would become merely well-formed but neither valid nor invalid.

> *Caution* For most of us, the word "invalid" means something that breaks the rules. It is an easy jump from there to concluding that an XML document that does not conform to a DTD is free to break any rules at all. This is not so. Well-formed documents are at least still XML even if they do not conform to the DTD.

You should think carefully before you decide to make a document that is well-formed but not valid. If the document is one-of-a-kind and is small, then making it well-formed is probably sufficient. But if it is to be part of any kind of information system (even a small one) or if it is a large document, then you should write a DTD or schema definition for it and validate whenever you revise it. When you decide to build or extend your information system, the fact that the document is guaranteed to be consistent will make your programming or stylesheet writing many times easier and your results much more reliable.

---

6. There is a similar concept for schemas.

2.8 | Namespaces

There is a problem that arises when you allow anybody to pick names as XML does. The problem is that different people in different places will invariably pick the same names accidentally. This makes it very difficult to build systems that work with documents from multiple independent sources because a publisher could use the element type name PAR to mean paragraph while a military vocabulary could use an element type with the same name to mean paratrooper. A mathematician might use an element type with that name to label paradoxes!

2.8.1 *The homonym problem*

Recall that a vocabulary is just a set of element types. XML has no formal construct for "vocabulary" that would allow a computer to resolve this homonym problem. Indeed, it is inherent in our human languages. A "trunk" is one thing to a baggage handler and quite another to an elephant keeper.

So even using full names as element types would not help to avoid name clashes. Two different e-business frameworks might mean slightly different things by the term purchase_order. This slight misunderstanding is just as dangerous to a computer program as a more drastic mistake. If an XML system misinterprets an element type then it will launch the wrong processing, expect the wrong elements to be in particular places and otherwise just mess up.

Yet it is becoming more and more necessary to mix and match element types invented by different groups in different places. If you need to include math formulas in your technical reports, it makes no sense to reinvent element types for them when you can use the MathML vocabulary. The problem is, how can you tell which names in your document come from MathML?

2.8.2 *Prefixes*

There is a standard that addresses this problem. It is known as "XML Namespaces". A *namespace* is an area within which a name has the same meaning whenever it is used. A vocabulary is a namespace and so is a document. The standard lets you mix vocabularies in a document by creating vocabulary nicknames that you can prefix to element type names.

For example, you might choose to prefix names from a meteorological information vocabulary with `met:`. So a document might have elements such as `met:temperature`, `met:humidity` and so forth. It could also have `health:temperature`, from a different vocabulary. To the computer, `met:temperature` and `health:temperature` are clearly different names.

Of course, this solution appears to create its own problem: How can you be sure that different XML designers will use `met` to refer to the same vocabulary? The short and happy answer is: They don't have to!

That's because within your document `met` — which, remember, is just a nickname — is associated with an unambiguous identifier of the vocabulary. That identifier is based on a URL and could look something like `http://www.weatherworld.com`. Other documents might use a different prefix for that vocabulary or use `met:` to prefix a different vocabulary. In practice, though, vocabulary developers recommend prefixes and people tend to use the recommended ones.

2.9 | Hyperlinking

You probably do not need to be convinced of the importance of hyperlinking. It is a cornerstone of the Web. One thing you might not know, however, is that the Web's notions of hyperlink are fairly tame compared to what is available in the best academic and commercial hypertext systems. XML alone does not correct this, but it has an associated standard called *XLink* that goes a long way towards making the Web a more advanced hypertext environment.

The first deficiency of today's Web links is that there are no standardized mechanisms for making links that are external to the documents that they are linking from. Let's imagine, for example that you stumble upon a Web page for your favorite music group. You read it, enjoy it and move on. Imagine next week you stumble upon a Web page with all of the lyrics for all of their songs (with appropriate copyrights, of course!). You think: there should be a link between these two pages. Someone visiting one might want to know about the other and vice versa.

What you want to do is make an *external link*. You want to make a link on your computer that appears on both of the other websites. But of course you do not have the ability to edit those two documents. XLink will allow this external linking. It provides a representation for external links, but it does not provide the technology to automatically publish those links to the world. That would take some kind of *link database* that would track all of the links from people around the world. Needless to say this is a big job and though there are prototypes, there is no standardized system yet.

You may wonder how all of these links will be displayed, how readers will select link sheets and annotations, how browsers will talk to databases and about other operational issues. The simple answer is: "nobody knows yet."[7]

Before the first Web browser was developed there was no way to know that we would develop a convention of using colored, underlined text to represent links (and even today some browsers use other conventions). There was also no way to know that browsers would typically have "back" buttons and "history lists". These are just conventions that arose and browser features that became popular.

This same process will one day occur with external links. Some user interface (perhaps a menu) will be provided to apply external link sheets, and there will probably be some mechanism for searching for link sheets related to a document on the Web. Eventually these will stabilize into standards that will be ubiquitous and transparent (we hope!). In the meantime, things are confused, but that is the price for living on the cutting edge. XLink moves us a notch further ahead by providing a notation for representing the links.

Another interesting feature of XML extended links is that they can point to more than one resource. For instance instead of making a link from a word to its definition, you might choose to link to definitions in several different dictionaries. The browser might represent this as a popup menu, a tiny window with the choices listed, or might even open one window for each. The same disclaimer applies: the XML Link specification does not tell browsers exactly what they must do. Each is free to try to make the most intuitive, powerful user interface for links. XML brings many interesting hypertext ideas from university research labs and high-tech companies "to the masses." We still have to work out exactly how that will look and who will use them for what. We live in interesting times!

---

7. But we've got some ideas. See Chapter 42, "Extended linking", on page 614.

2.10 | Stylesheets

To a certain extent, the concerns described above are endemic to generalized markup. Because it describes structure, and not formatting, it allows variations in display and processing that can sometimes disturb people.

However, as the Web has evolved, Web developers have become less and less tolerant of having browser vendors control the "look and feel" of their documents. An important part of all communication, but especially modern business communication, is the idea of style. Stylesheets allow us to attach our own visual style to documents without destroying the virtue of generalized markup. Because the style is described in a separate entity, the stylesheet, software that is not interested in style can ignore it.

For instance most search engines would not care if your corporate color is blue or green, so they will just ignore those declarations in the stylesheet. Similarly, software that reads documents aloud to the sight-impaired would ignore font sizes and colors and concentrate on the abstractions — paragraphs, sections, titles and so forth.

The Web has a very simple stylesheet language called *Cascading Style Sheets* (CSS), which arose out of the early battles between formatting and generalized markup in HTML. Like any other specification, CSS is a product of its environment, and so is not powerful enough to describe the formatting of documents types that are radically different in structure from HTML.

Because CSS is not sufficient, the World Wide Web Consortium has developed a complementary alternative called the *Extensible Stylesheet Language* (XSL). XSL has many features from CSS, but also borrows some major ideas from ISO's DSSSL stylesheet language. XSL is extensible, just as XML is, so that it will be appropriate for all document types and not just for HTML.

While we wait for XSL to gain widespread software support, an important subset of its functionality has become popular under the name XSLT (for XSL Transformations). XSLT can take any type of XML document and transform it into any other type. When XSLT is used as part of XSL, the output document is a rendered type. More often, though, when a rendition is wanted XSLT is used alone to generate HTML because it is compatible with today's Web browsers.

2.11 | Programming interfaces and models

This subject may seem intimidating if you are not a programmer – possibly even if you are! But we are just going to take a high-level view of a few constructs that will be helpful in understanding the chapters that follow. We'll cover the XML geek-speak Top Term List: Parsing, APIs, DOM, and SAX.

2.11.1 *Parsing*

Great as XML is for representing data, eventually that data has to be processed, which requires the use of one or more programs. One of the nice things about writing XML applications is that there is an abundance of reusable component and utility software available to help.

All great programmers try to reduce their work! If every programmer reinvented the wheel when it came to basic processing of XML, no programmer would ever get around to building applications that *use* XML. Instead of implementing basic XML processing over and over again, programmers tend to download or buy packages that implement various types of XML services.

The most basic reusable service is parsing. Parsing is about ripping apart the textual representation of a document and turning it into a set of conceptual objects.

For example, a processor looking at the document in Example 2-1 would recognize the characters <QUESTION> to be a start-tag, and would know that they signaled the start of a QUESTION element. The tag is part of the representation; the element is the conceptual object.

If the processor were also validating the document according to the DTD in Example 2-2, it would make sure that an ANSWER element followed the QUESTION element.

As a human being, you do parsing subconsciously. Because you've learned about elements and attributes, when you look at XML text you can think about the document in those conceptual terms.

But without an XML *processor*, a computer program can only see the characters. It's sort of the opposite of not seeing the forest for the trees. Without some form of parsing, an XML application cannot see the tree because of all of the characters!

2.11.2 *APIs*

There are many good XML processors ("parsers") out there for use with many different programming languages. There are so many that it is hard to choose. A software developer would hate to pick one and be wedded to it forever. The programmer might want to change some day to a faster or cheaper one, or from a non-validating processor to a validating one.

Switching processors is easy if the two "look" the same to the programmer. You can plug in different brands and types of light bulbs into the same socket because of the standardization of the socket. The equivalent concept in software components is the standardization of *Application Processing Interfaces (APIs)*.

2.11.2.1   The DOM

The World Wide Web Consortium has standardized an API for working with XML. It is called the *Document Object Model* and it has been available in Web browsers since version 5. If you write code for Microsoft's *DOM* implementation, it should be relatively easy to make that code also work on Netscape's DOM.

But the DOM is not only for use in browsers. It can also be used on the server side. You can use the DOM to read, write and transmit XML on your Web server. DOM-based programs can talk to some XML content management systems. The DOM is very popular for general XML processing. It has been implemented, for example, for use with Python and Perl scripts and with the C++ and Java™ programming languages, among others. In fact, Microsoft's DOM implementation is a built-in part of Windows 2000 itself.

2.11.2.2   SAX

The DOM is popular and useful but it is not the be-all and end-all of XML parsing APIs. It is a little bit like putting a plane on automatic pilot. You point your DOM-building processor at an XML document and it returns you an object tree based on the structure of the document.

But if the document is five hundred megabytes of text and resides on the "other side" of the Internet, your program will just wait. And wait. And wait. When you finally get the data it will fill your computer's memory and some of its disk space. If you are having a bad day it might fill up everything and then crash the computer.

In a situation like this, you would rather just get tiny bits of the data as they come in. An *event-based parser* allows this mode of operation. Event-based parsers let your application work on the bit of the data that the parser finds at each "event" in the document.

For example, each XML start-tag corresponds to a "start element" event. Each end-tag corresponds to an "end element" event. Characters and other constructs have their own events. The event-based XML parser tells the application what it sees in the document as if through a peep-hole. It does not try to describe the larger picture to the application. This sort of event-driven mode is more efficient even for small documents, but it is not as convenient as a tree-based parser.[8]

The most popular event-based API is the *Simple API for XML*. *SAX* was developed by XML processor users and developers in an open discussion group called *XML-DEV*. Despite the name, SAX is not actually much simpler than the DOM. It is much more efficient and low-level, however. The price for efficiency is convenience. The processor only provides you with a peep-hole view, so if your application needs more than that, you'll need to write your own code to understand the "big picture" of the parsed document.

These two APIs are pervasive in the XML processing world. There are many other services that we could envision for XML handling: link management, searching and so forth. It is likely that these will be built either on top of or as extensions to these two popular APIs.

2.11.3 *Protocols*

Computers are like humans in that they cannot communicate with each other except by dint of a shared language. Just like humans, they cannot communicate if both parties speak at the same time. There must be some concept of back and forth, send and receive, talk and listen. The specification of how this happens is termed a protocol.

---

8. If you concluded from this description that a DOM processor in effect uses an event-based parser as it constructs the DOM, you are right.

XML alone is not a protocol. XML helps you to define what the terms of discussion are. But XML does not itself say anything about who speaks first, what they may say, what is appropriate in response, and other requirements of transmission.

Once again we are visiting the domain of programmers, but we'll try to keep the conversation at a level that will be meaningful to others – a diplomatic protocol discussion, so to speak!

2.11.3.1 The protocol stack

You seldom just use one protocol. Protocols build on one another, as shown in Figure 2-2.

Document types   HTML, WebDAV, SOAP

Web communication   HTTP

Internet addressing   TCP/IP

Wire protocols   Ethernet, V.42

Figure 2-2 Protocol stack

At the lowest level, your computer's network interface card speaks the Ethernet protocol and your modem uses protocols with cryptic names like V.32, V.42, V.32bis, and V.42bis. Wireless devices use IEEE 802.11b. Protocols at this level just let the bits go back and forth. They are known as *wire protocols*, although nowadays the wires are optional!

Above this physical level of communication, protocols typically organize the bits into *packets* or *messages*. For example, to communicate over the Internet, the TCP/IP protocol directs packets of bits to specific "IP" addresses. However, it doesn't say anything about the meaning of the packets. For that, you need a higher-level protocol.

Those protocols come into play during activities like email or Web browsing. Email uses the POP and SMTP protocols. The Web uses the HTTP protocol, which transmits HTML documents. These protocols let you have a "conversation" about specific subjects; they define what is in the packets.

If you want two computers to have a new sort of conversation, you need to invent a new protocol. For instance to get computers to talk about network management, the Internet Engineering Task Force invented the Simple Network Management Protocol.

The HTTP protocol can also transmit XML documents. That provides a convenient base for creating more specialized protocols, simply by defining them as document types. We'll look at three such protocols: WebDAV, XML-RPC, and SOAP. We'll even explain what the acronyms mean![9]

2.11.3.2   Writing the Web (WebDAV)

The early Web allowed little more interactivity than following links. Later, it became possible to build real, interactive Web applications. This is a quantum leap but it still does not go as far as Tim Berners-Lee had hoped. He wanted Web publishing to be so easy that anyone could do it with any software package whenever they felt like it. We are not there yet.

The problem is that the protocol used to communicate between Web clients and servers (HTTP) is only really designed to retrieve information. The early Web designers never got around to finishing the half of the specification that would standardize writing back to the Web. A variety of half-solutions have arisen. Some people use the older File Transfer Protocol (FTP). Some use product-specific protocols like Microsoft's *FrontPage Extensions*. Neither of these is a true, standardized Web protocol.

Another half-solution is to allow publishing through a small "text entry box" on a Web page. Some bulletin-board websites use this technique. If

---

9. At least the most important and less-known ones; the rest are in Chapter 68, "Acronyms and initialisms in The XML Handbook", on page 1102.

you have ever edited more than a few lines in this environment, you will know how inconvenient it is – like mowing the lawn with hand-clippers.

Finally we have a real Web protocol for writing to Web sites. It is called *WebDAV* because it allows *Web-based Distributed Authoring and Versioning*.

WebDAV uses XML extensively to represent complex, structured values that can be associated with documents for searching and management. WebDAV is already supported by the Microsoft Office software products and the Apache Web server. That means it has already passed a significant milestone: most people buying new computers will have WebDAV-enabled content creation capability and most people deploying new Web servers will have free access to a WebDAV implementation. Even so, it takes time for these technologies to become ubiquitous and popular. WebDAV promises to one day correct a long-acknowledged limitation of the World Wide Web.

2.11.3.3   Remote procedure call

A procedure is a basic unit of program behavior. In many languages, computer programs are made by stringing together calls from one procedure to another. A *Remote Procedure Call (RPC)* protocol extends this paradigm to calls between computers.

You can do remote procedure calls in XML using a protocol called XML-RPC. Example 2-4 is the XML portion of an XML-RPC message that invokes a procedure called calculateTax. The methodCall element invokes the procedure. The methodName element names the procedure to be called. The param elements provide the information that the calculation requires.

Example 2-4. XML-RPC method call

```
<?xml version="1.0"?>
<methodCall>
  <methodName>calculateTax</methodName>
  <params>
    <param><value><i4>Alaska</i4></value></param>
    <param><value><i4>41</i4></value></param>
  </params>
</methodCall>
```

Example 2-5 shows the response to the remote procedure call in Example 2-4. The Alaskan sales tax is $1.87.

Example 2-5. XML-RPC method response

```
<?xml version="1.0"?>
<methodResponse>
  <params>
    <param><double>1.87</double></param>
  </params>
</methodResponse>
```

The primary virtue of XML-RPC is that the programmer does not need to think about this stuff at all. In many programming languages, one can just call a procedure, using traditional procedure call syntax, and all of the remote procedure stuff happens automatically.

Some programmers consider this approach heresy and would rather control the details of the transmission themselves. Neither side is right or wrong. Suffice to say that the right approach depends on a variety of factors including how fast and secure your network is and how much time you have available to solve a problem!

There is a subtle but important difference between WebDAV and XML-RPC. WebDAV is designed to do exactly one thing: allow you to manage content over the Internet. XML-RPC is more of a meta-protocol. Just as XML is a language for defining new computer-processable languages, XML-RPC is a protocol that allows you to define new protocols. In the example above, we invented a tax calculation protocol. We could use XML-RPC to create protocols that talk about anything we like – the price of tea in China or the odds in Vegas. XML-RPC is really more of a *protocol framework* than a single, domain-specific protocol like WebDAV. If Web-DAV were invented today it might be built on top of XML-RPC. Or more likely on top of the a newer specification that has more corporate backing, SOAP.

2.11.3.4   Simple Object Access Protocol (SOAP)

The dominant mode of thinking about software problems is in terms of *objects*. An object in a computer is just like an object in the real world. Each object has *properties* and *behaviors*. You can send messages to objects to ask them to do something. You can also update the properties.

2.11.3.4.1 *What is an object?*

Everything from a bank account to an entire bank can be represented as an object. You could add money to the bank account by sending it a message, or you could negotiate to open a new account with the bank object. Though religious wars still rage on, most programmers feel that working with objects is a little easier and somewhat more sophisticated than working only with procedures.

Most modern programming languages provide some way of building objects. Many operating systems provide ways of communicating between objects written in various languages. On Windows™ systems, there is the Component Object Model (COM). On Unix™, Linux and other systems, it is often CORBA.

These object communication specifications have never caught on for communicating between machines. Developers have shown a clear preference for text-based inter-machine communication mechanisms. Binary communication mechanisms are essentially made up of strings of bits. They are not easy to understand without special tools.

Inter-object communication mechanisms – known as *inter-object protocols* – can work well with XML. Since XML can represent any information, the inter-object protocols can be expressed as XML elements instead of in terms of raw bits. Complete structured information objects can even move from place to place represented as XML elements. This means that the messages can be inspected with standard textual tools and processed with any programming language.

2.11.3.4.2 *SOAP cleans up!*

The most popular specification in this category is *Simple Object Access Protocol (SOAP)*. SOAP is a derivative of XML-RPC with a little more support for object-oriented features. Despite its name, SOAP is not a great deal better than XML-RPC at "accessing objects". But it is much better than XML-RPC at moving complex hierarchical information such as "Employee Records" or "Invoices".

Like XML-RPC, SOAP is a meta-protocol; it allows you to define new protocols based on it. The big difference between the two is in how this is accomplished. XML-RPC is restricted to a fixed set of XML element types;

you customize by means of the data you put in their content. In contrast, SOAP messages can include element types that you define, even those with complex hierarchical structures.

SOAP also goes beyond XML-RPC in that it can be used in *asynchronous* systems. If you go to an ice cream store to ask for some ice cream, you expect to receive it immediately. On the other hand, if you order a tub of specialty ice cream over the phone (or the Internet!) you expect it to arrive later. That's an asynchronous situation. A protocol is *asynchronous* if the person making the request does not wait around for a response but rather expects it to arrive some time later. SOAP has specific support for these kinds of situations.

SOAP versions 1.0 and 1.1 were created by a group of companies led by Microsoft. Now version 1.2 is in a formal standardization process within the World Wide Web Consortium. SOAP is one of the few things that Microsoft, IBM and Sun all agree is useful. It is even becoming popular in the Linux world, which tends to be suspicious of Microsoft-sponsored technologies.

2.11.4 *Web services (WSDL, UDDI)*

It has become common to speak of XML-based protocols in breathless terms as a "revolution". We won't point fingers but the last time there was so much revolutionary talk in the air, there was also tea in Boston harbor. You can understand the hype if you look back at recent history. Before the Web, it was very difficult to distribute information so that anybody could access it using any computer system. The Web standards made computer-to-human communication easy and automatic.

Web services is a term for programs that use a new set of protocols designed to make computer-to-computer communications just as easy, standardized, and automatic. Note that these services are sometimes also known as "XML Web Services" or "e-services" to distinguish them from the general class of services available via the Web, such as online psychic readings. However, most people in information technology these days use the words "Web services" to mean these XML-based services exclusively, and so shall we.

The Web services protocols adopt many of the existing Web protocols and adapt them to a computer-to-computer context. They do so by using XML as the data representation and protocols such as HTTP as the mechanisms for moving information around the Internet. The new protocols add layers on top of XML and HTTP that are specific to computer-to-computer communications. XML-RPC and SOAP are notable in this group. So much so that many now think of them as Web services protocols, although they actually pre-date the Web services hype by several years.

Perhaps the most interesting idea underpinning Web services is that of *service discovery*. At present, humans generally decide with whom a program should share information. The purchasing agent for Miracle Cleanser tells his computer that the order for the "free if you act now" scrub brushes should be sent to the High-on-the-Hog Bristle Company.

With Web services, that won't be necessary. The purchasing program can search for a supplier using an elaborate directory system called *Universal Description, Discovery, and Integration (UDDI)*. The directory entries describe the potential suppliers using the *Web Services Description Language (WSDL)*.

For some this new convenience conjures up nightmare visions of computers taking over the world. For others it suggests extraordinary opportunities for universal commerce. Either way, you can see why it is arousing enormous interest. We discuss Web services at length in Part 13, "Web Services", on page 668.

2.12 | Conclusion

There are a lot of new ideas here to absorb, but we'll be repeating and re-emphasizing them as we move along. At this point, we're ready to look at the spectrum of XML usage in the real world.

The XML usage spectrum

Introductory Discussion

- Real-world concepts
- Documents vs. data
- Machine-oriented messaging (MOM)
- People-oriented publishing (POP)

Chapter

3

 ike the Jets and the Sharks, the factions never mixed.[1]
On the one hand there were the document-heads armed with
word processors and formatters. On the other, the data-heads
from the relational database world. It's time for a truce – no, an alliance.
XML finally makes clear an internal truth: documents and data are the
same thing. To be precise, documents are the interchangeable form of data!

3.1 | Is XML for documents or for data?

What is a document?
The dictionary says:

> "Something written, inscribed, engraved, etc., which provides
> evidence or information or serves as a record".

---

1. Depending on your cultural proclivities, these are either athletic teams or
the rival gangs in *West Side Story*.

Documents come in all shapes and sizes and media, as you can see in Figure 3-1. Here are some you may have encountered:

- Long documents: books, manuals, product specifications
- Broadsides: catalog sheets, posters, notices
- Forms: registration, application, etc.
- Letters: email, memos
- Records: "Acme Co., Part# 732, reverse widget, $32.50, 5323 in stock"
- Messages: "job complete", "update accepted"

An e-commerce transaction, such as a purchase, might involve several of these. A buyer could start by sending several documents to a vendor:

- Covering note: a letter
- Purchase order: a form
- Attached product specification: a long document

The vendor might respond with several more documents:

- Formal acknowledgment: a message
- Thank you note: a letter
- Invoice: a form

The beauty of XML is that the same software can process all of this diversity. Whatever you can do with one kind of document you can do with all the others. The only time you need additional tools is when you want to do different kinds of things – not when you want to work with different kinds of documents.

And there are lots of things that you can do.

3.2 | A wide spectrum of application opportunities

Sorry about that, we've been reading too many marketing brochures. But it's true, nevertheless.

Figure 3-1 Documents come in all shapes and sizes.

At one end of the spectrum we have the grand old man of generalized markup, *POP* – People-Oriented Publishing. You can see him in Figure 3-2.

At the other end of the spectrum is that darling of the data processors, *MOM* – Machine-Oriented Messaging. She smiles radiantly from Figure 3-3.

Let's take a closer look at both of them.

human
writes POP
document

wants one
style for print

another
for CD-ROM

the coolest
for the Web

Figure 3-2   POP application.

3.2.1 *People-oriented publishing*

POP was the original killer app for SGML, XML's parent, because it saves so much money for enterprises with Web-sized document collections.

POP documents are chiefly written by humans for other humans to read.

computer
generates
MOM
document

 data is
wrapped
in tags to
preserve
metadata

 to be utilized
by another
computer

Figure 3-3   MOM application.

Instead of creating formatted renditions, as in word processors or desktop publishing programs, XML POP users create unformatted abstractions. That means the document file captures what is *in* the document, but not how it is supposed to look.

To get the desired look, the POP user creates a stylesheet, a set of commands that tell a program how to format (and/or otherwise process) the document. The power of XML in this regard is that you don't need to choose just one look – you can have a separate stylesheet for every purpose.[2] At a minimum, you might want one for print, one for CD-ROM, and another for a website.

POP documents tend to be (but needn't be) long-lived, large, and with complex structures. When delivered in electronic media, they may be interactive. How they will be rendered is of great importance, but, because XML is used, the rendition information can be – and is – kept distinct from the abstract data.

3.2.2 *Machine-oriented messaging*

MOM is the killer app – actually, a technology that drives lots of killer apps – for XML on the Web.

The software that processes the messages is called *middleware*.[3] As you might suspect from the name, it is software that comes between two other programs. It acts like your interpreter/guide might if you were to visit someplace where you couldn't speak the language and had no idea of the local customs. It talks in the native tongue, using the native customs, and translates the native replies – the messages – into your language.

MOM documents are chiefly generated by programs for other programs to read.

Instead of writing specialized programs (clients) to access particular databases or other data sources (servers), XML MOM users break the old two-tier client/server model. They introduce a third tier, the "middle tier", that acts as a data integrator. The middle-tier server does all the talking to the data sources and sends their messages to the client as XML documents.

That means the client can read data from anywhere, but only has to understand data that is in XML documents. The XML markup provides the *metadata* – information about the data – that was in the original data source schema, like the database table name and field names (also called "cell" or "column" names).

The MOM user typically doesn't care much about rendition. He *does* care, though, about extracting the original data accurately and making

---

2. We know that all office suites offer some degree of stylesheet support today, but XML (well, GML) did it first, and still is the only way to do it cleanly.
3. In fact the MOM acronym has long been used in the industry – and in previous editions of this book – to mean *message-oriented middleware*. We prefer the new meaning because it puts the emphasis on the data, rather than the software, some of which still hasn't caught on to using XML.

some use of the metadata. His client software, instead of having a specialized module for each data source, has a single "XML parser" module. The parser is the program that separates the markup from the data, just as it does in POP applications.

And just like POP applications, there can be a stylesheet, a set of commands that tell a program how to process the document. It may not look much like a POP stylesheet – it might look more like a script or program – but it performs the same function. And, as with POP stylesheets, there can be different MOM stylesheets for different document types, or to do different things with message documents of a single document type.

There is an extra benefit to XML three-tier MOM applications in a networked environment. For many applications, the middle-tier server can collect all of the relevant data at once and send it in a single document to the client. Further querying, sorting, and other processing can then take place solely on the client system. That not only cuts down Web traffic and overhead, but it vastly improves the end-user's perceived performance and his satisfaction with the experience.

MOM documents tend to be (but needn't be) short-lived, non-interactive, small, and with simple structures.

3.3 | Opposites are attracted

To XML, that is!

How is it that XML can be optimal for two such apparently extreme opposites as MOM and POP? The answer is, the two are not really different where it counts.

In both cases, we start with abstract information. For POP, it comes from a human author's head. For MOM, it comes from a database. But either way, the abstract data is marked up with tags and becomes a document.

Here is a terminally cute mnemonic for this very important relationship:

Data + Markup = DocuMent

Aren't you sorry you read it? Now you'll never forget it.

But XML "DocuMents" are special. An application can use three different processing techniques with one:

- *Parse it*, in order to extract the original data. This can be done without information loss because XML represents both metadata and data, and it lets you keep the abstractions distinct from rendition information. Once extracted, the data can be manipulated as needed by the application.
- *Render it*, so it can be presented in a physical medium that a human can perceive. It can be rendered in many different ways, for delivery in multiple media such as screen displays, print, Braille, spoken word, and so on.
- *Hack it*, meaning "process it as plain text without parsing". Hacking might involve cutting and pasting into other XML documents, or scanning the text to get some information from it without doing a real parse.

The important revelation here is that data and documents aren't opposites. Far from it – they are actually two states of the same information. The real difference between the two is this:

- When data is in a database, the metadata about its structure and meaning (the schema) is stored according to the proprietary architecture of the database.
- When data is in a document, the metadata is stored as markup.

A mixture of markup and data must be governed by the rules of some *notation*. XML and SGML are notations, as are RTF and Word file format. The rules of the notation determine how a parser will interpret the document text to separate the data from the markup.

Notations are not just for complete documents. There are also *data object notations*, such as GIF, TIFF, and EPS, that are used to represent such things as graphics, video (e.g., MPEG), and audio (e.g., MP3). Document notations usually allow their documents to contain data objects, such as pictures, that are in the objects' own data object notations.

Data object notations are usually (not always) in *binary*; that is, they are built-up from low-level ones and zeros. Document notations, however, are frequently *character-based*. XML is character-based, which is why it can be hacked.[4]

Since databases and documents are really the same, and MOM and POP applications both use XML documents, there are lots of opportunities for synergy.

Figure 3-4   Dynamic servers: The MOM and POP store.

3.4 | MOM and POP – They're so great together!

Classically, MOM and POP were radically different kinds of applications, each doing things its own way with different technologies and mental models. But POP applications frequently need to include database data in their document content – think of an automotive maintenance manual that has to get the accurate part numbers from a database.

Similarly, MOM applications need to include human-written components. When the dealer asks for price and availability of the automotive parts you need, the display might include a description as well.

---

4. In fact, a design objective was to support the *desperate Perl hacker* – someone in a hurry who writes a script to scan XML without parsing it. Note that the term "hacker" had none of the "cracker" stigma implied by the popular press. The only security compromised by the desperate Perl hacker is his job security, for leaving things to the last minute!

With the advent of generalized markup, the barriers to doing MOM-like things in POP applications began to disappear. Some of the POP-like applications you'll read about later in the book appear to have invented the middle tier on their own. And now, with the advent of XML, MOM applications can easily incorporate POP functionality as well.

What is now emerging is a new generation of composite systems, dynamically serving both persistent POP information and dynamic MOM data. They use databases to store information components so they can be controlled, managed, and assembled into end-products in the same way as components of automobiles, aircraft, or other complex devices. Think of them as the MOM and POP store (Figure 3-4).[5]

In fact, we'd go so far as to say there is no longer a difference in kind between the two, only a difference in degree. There really is "an endless spectrum of application opportunities". It is a multi-dimensional spectrum where applications need not be implemented differently just because they process different document types. The real differentiators are other document characteristics, like persistence, size, interactivity, structural complexity, percentage of human-written content, and the importance of eventual presentation to humans.[6]

At the extremes, some applications may call for specialized (or optimized) techniques, but the broad central universe of applications can all be implemented similarly. Much of the knowledge that POP application developers have acquired over the years is now applicable to MOM applications, and vice versa. Keep that in mind as you read the application descriptions and case studies.

That cross-fertilization is true of products and their underlying technologies as well. All of the tool discussions in this book should be of interest, whether you think of your applications as chiefly being MOM or being POP. It is the differences in functionality and design that should cause you to choose one product over another, not their marketing thrust or apparent orientation. As you read the tool category discussions, you'll find remarkable similarities among tools that were developed for entirely different purposes.

---

5. Generations ago the Mom and Pop store (grocery, convenience, etc.) was the achievement of the entrepreneurial couple who'd lifted themselves out of the working class. Today they'd have an e-commerce website!

6. The relationship between documents and data is explored further in 6.10, "Documents and data", on page 115.

3.5 | Conclusion

We've covered the key concepts of XML itself and the spectrum of its uses. The next few chapters will zoom in on applications at both ends of the spectrum.

Better browsing through XML

- Beyond HTML

- Multimedia

- Metadata

- Content syndication

- Portals and personalization

- Alternative delivery platforms

Chapter

4

The XML effort is new ground in many senses. The Web has never before had access to the new features that XML offers. It will take a while for the Web culture to understand the strengths (and weaknesses) of the new language and learn how to properly deploy it. Still, XML is already becoming a building block for the next generation of Web applications and specifications.

4.1 | Beyond HTML

XML was originally conceived as a big brother to HTML. As its name implies, XML can be used to extend HTML or even define whole new languages completely unlike HTML.

For instance, a company might want to offer technical manuals on the Web. Many manuals have a formatting style for tables (e.g. a table listing a software product's supported languages) and repeat the formatting on several tables in the manual (perhaps once per program in a package). The formatting of these tables can be very intricate.

The rows, for example may be broken into categories with borders between them. The title of each column and row might be in a particular font and color. The width of the columns might be very precisely described. The final row ("the bottom line") might be colored. HTML could provide the formatting markup that the layout would require, but it would entail a lot of duplication. In fact, it would be such a hassle that most companies would choose to use a graphic or an *Adobe Portable Document Format* (PDF) file instead.

4.1.1 *An HTML table*

To demonstrate how XML can help, we will use a sample table from the specification for HTML tables, shown in Table 4-1. We will simplify the table somewhat, but the XML solution will still be shorter (in characters) and easier to read than the HTML source in Example 4-1.

If there are many of these tables the cumulative effort of doing this manual work can add up to a large burden, especially since it must be maintained as products change. Even with an HTML editing tool, you will probably have to do the layout manually, over and over again. As if this internal expense was not disturbing enough, every person who reads the annual report over the Web must download the same formatting information row after row, column after column, table after table, year after year. Right thinking Web page authors will understand that this situation is not good. The repetition leads to longer download times, congested servers, dissatisfied customers and perhaps irate managers.

4.1.2 *An XML table*

The XML solution would be to invent a simple extension to HTML that is customized to the needs of the manual. It would have table elements that would only require data that varies from table to table. None of the redundant formatting information would be included. We would then use a sophisticated stylesheet to add that information back in. The beauty of the stylesheet solution is that the formatting information is expressed only in one place. Surfers only have to download that once. Also, if your company decides to change the style of the tables, all of them can be changed at once

Table 4-1   Rendered Table

Code Page ID	Name	Windows NT 3.1	Windows NT 3.51	Windows 95
1200	Unicode (BMP of ISO 10646)	X	X	
1250	Windows 3.1 Eastern European	X	X	X
1251	Windows 3.1 Cyrillic	X	X	X
1252	Windows 3.1 US (ANSI)	X	X	X
1253	Windows 3.1 Greek	X	X	X
1254	Windows 3.1 Turkish	X	X	X
1255	Hebrew			X
1256	Arabic			X
1257	Baltic			X
1361	Korean (Johab)			X

Example 4-1. HTML markup for Table 4-1

```
<TABLE>
<COLGROUP align="center">
<COLGROUP align="left">
<COLGROUP align="center" span="3">
<THEAD valign="top"> <TR> <TH>Code<br>Page<br>ID<TH>Name
<TH>Windows<br>NT 3.1<TH>Windows<br>NT 3.51<TH>Windows<br>95
<TBODY>
<TR><TD>1200<TD>Unicode (BMP of ISO/IEC-10646)<TD>X<TD>X<TD>
<TR><TD>1250<TD>Windows 3.1 Eastern European<TD>X<TD>X<TD>X
<TR><TD>1251<TD>Windows 3.1 Cyrillic<TD>X<TD>X<TD>X
<TR><TD>1252<TD>Windows 3.1 US (ANSI)<TD>X<TD>X<TD>X
<TR><TD>1253<TD>Windows 3.1 Greek<TD>X<TD>X<TD>X
<TR><TD>1254<TD>Windows 3.1 Turkish<TD>X<TD>X<TD>X
<TR><TD>1255<TD>Hebrew<TD><TD><TD>X
<TR><TD>1256<TD>Arabic<TD><TD><TD>X
<TR><TD>1257<TD>Baltic<TD><TD><TD>X
<TR><TD>1361<TD>Korean (Johab)<TD><TD><TD>X
</TABLE>
```

merely by changing the stylesheet. Example 4-2 shows what that might look like.

Example 4-2. XML version of Table 4-1

```
<CODE-PAGE-TABLE>
<CP NUM="1200" NAME="Unicode (BMP of ISO/IEC-10646)"
    PLATFORMS="NT3.1 NT3.51"/>
<CP NUM="1250" NAME="Windows 3.1 Eastern European"
    PLATFORMS="NT3.1 NT3.51 WIN95"/>
<CP NUM="1251" NAME="Windows 3.1 Cyrillic"
    PLATFORMS="NT3.1 NT3.51 WIN95"/>
<CP NUM="1252" NAME="Windows 3.1 US (ANSI)"
    PLATFORMS="NT3.1 NT3.51 WIN95"/>
<CP NUM="1253" NAME="Windows 3.1 Greek"
    PLATFORMS="NT3.1 NT3.51 WIN95"/>
<CP NUM="1254" NAME="Windows 3.1 Turkish"
    PLATFORMS="NT3.1 NT3.51 WIN95"/>
<CP NUM="1255" NAME="Hebrew"
    PLATFORMS="WIN95"/>
<CP NUM="1256" NAME="Arabic"
    PLATFORMS="WIN95"/>
<CP NUM="1257" NAME="Baltic"
    PLATFORMS="WIN95"/>
<CP NUM="1261" NAME="Korean (Johab)"
    PLATFORMS="WIN95"/>
</CODE-PAGE-TABLE>
```

The difference between this XML version and the HTML version is not as dramatic as in some examples, but the XML version is clearer, has fewer lines and characters and is easier to maintain. More important, the stylesheet can choose to format this in many different ways as time goes by and tastes change. All the XML version represents is the actual information about Windows code pages, not the tabular format of a particular presentation of it. The markup is also clearer (to someone interested in code pages!) because the element type names (CODE-PAGE-TABLE, CP) and attribute names (NAME, PLATFORMS, NUM) relate directly to the world of code pages and not to the world of HTML tables. A table is just one way to display this data today! We may choose another way tomorrow.

You can already do this kind of client-side processing in some browsers. Internet Explorer has taken the lead in the XML race. Netscape's browser has XML support but it does not yet have the ability to run complicated

(XSLT) stylesheets on the client-side. Both support the simpler (and less powerful) CSS style language.

One thing to note is that the extra download of a stylesheet does take time. It makes the most sense to move formatting into a stylesheet when that formatting will be used on many pages or in many parts of the same page. The goal is to amortize the cost of the download over a body of text. A similar caveat applies to the time it takes to make the stylesheet and design the table elements. Doing so for a single table would probably not be cost effective. Our example above basically shifts the complexity from the document to the stylesheet, on the presumption that there will probably be many documents (or at least many tables) for every stylesheet. In general, XML is about short-term investment in long-term productivity.

4.1.3 *Extensible HTML (XHTML)*

What if you are not interested in the extra investment that XML usually requires? You can get some of its benefits "on the cheap" with XHTML. *XHTML* is a version of HTML that uses XML syntax. The element types are all identical to those in ordinary HTML, so you do not have to learn new ones.

XHTML's major benefit is the availability of XML parsers. HTML's definition has always been very loose. Major browsers do not offer a way to validate documents and often accept non-conforming HTML-like text as if it were really HTML. XHTML disallows this practice. XHTML documents must always be well-formed and valid. At least one browser can already validate XHTML documents and report errors. Because of this "cleanliness", XHTML is much easier to work with than old-fashioned HTML. Future versions of XHTML will be extensible so that you can add a few of your own element types to the standard XHTML mix.

4.1.4 *Specialized document types*

XHTML is fine as a generic Web display language but the real savings come when you move to a full-fledged industry- or company-specific XML document type. Once you have made that investment you can sometimes realize more radical productivity gains than you first intended. That's because your documents, like your database, now hold abstract data – not rendered, as in HTML.

Imagine that you use XML tables to publish the financial information in your company's annual report. Your accountants may be able to use their software's report writing feature to directly transfer accounting information into the XML table. This can save one more opportunity for typos between the accountants' printout and the Web author's keyboard. There might also be opportunities for automation at the other end of the spectrum. Other software might transform the XML table directly into a format required for submission to some government agency.

Of course none of this automation comes for free. You still need to actually connect XML based systems somehow (usually using Internet protocols). You still need to design or negotiate a DTD or schema. XML allows you to focus on these project-specific issues instead of on the more generalized issue of the nitty-gritty syntax.

4.2 | Database publishing

The last example hints at the way XML can interact with systems that are not typically associated with documentation. As documents become abstractions, they can become integrated with the other abstract data in an organization. Some of the same techniques can be used to create them (such as report writing software or custom graphical user interfaces) and some of the same software will be able to read them (such as spreadsheets and database software). One already popular application of XML is the publishing of databases to the Web.

Consider for instance a product database, used by the internal ordering system of a toy manufacturer. The manufacturer might want the database to be available on the Web so that potential customers would know what was available and at what price. Rather than having someone in the Web design department mark up the data again, they could build a connection between their Web server and their database using the features typically built into Web servers that allow those sorts of data pipes.

The designers could then make the product list beautiful using a stylesheet. Pictures of the toys could be supplied by the database. In essence, the Web site would be merely a view on the data in the database. As toys get added and removed from the database, they will appear and disappear from the view on the website. This mechanism also gives the website maintainer the freedom to update the "look and feel" of the website without dealing with the database or the plumbing that connects it to the Web server! Publishing information from a database to the Web is pretty well understood these days, but XML allows standardization, rigor and a separation of the tasks of programmers and Web designers.

XML is already becoming an important tool for interchange of database information. Databases have typically interchanged information using simple file formats like one-record per line with semi-colons between the fields. This is not sufficient for the new object-oriented information being stored and generated by databases. Objects must have internal structure and links between them.

XML can represent objects by using elements and attributes to provide a common representation for transferring database records between databases. You can imagine that one database might produce an XML document representing all of the toys the manufacturer produces. That document could be directly loaded into another database either within the company or at a customer's site. This is a very interesting way of thinking about documents, because in many cases human beings will never see them. They are documents produced by and for computer software.

One is shown in Example 4.3.

4.3 | Multimedia

XML can be a central component in a rich multimedia system. Consider the *Scalable Vector Graphics (SVG)* specification. This World Wide Web Consortium specification allows vector graphics to be represented entirely in XML, as shown in Example 4-4.

Vector graphics are described in terms of lines and shapes instead of individual points. This makes them relatively efficient (compared to bitmaps) and much easier to work with. Once the Web adopts this standard vector graphics notation, it will be easy to move these graphics between software products like *Adobe Illustrator*™ and *CorelDraw*™. SVG support is not yet built into browsers but is available through plug-ins. SVG can also support animations of structured objects.

The *Synchronized Multimedia Integration Language (SMIL)* is an XML document type for describing multimedia presentations. SMIL allows

Example 4-3. A products database in XML

```
<TOYS>
<ITEM>
<TITLE>GI John</TITLE>
<MANUFACTURER>War Toys Inc.</MANUFACTURER>
<PRICE>50.95</PRICE>
<IN-STOCK>3000</IN-STOCK>
</ITEM>
<ITEM>
<TITLE>Leggo!</TITLE>
<MANUFACTURER>Grips R US</MANUFACTURER>
<PRICE>64.95</PRICE>
<IN-STOCK>2000</IN-STOCK>
</ITEM>
<ITEM>
<TITLE>Hell On Wheels</TITLE>
<MANUFACTURER>Li'l Road Warriors</MANUFACTURER>
<PRICE>150.95</PRICE>
<IN-STOCK>3200</IN-STOCK>
</ITEM>
</TOYS>
```

Example 4-4. Diagram represented in SVG

```
<?xml version="1.0" standalone="no"?>
<!DOCTYPE svg PUBLIC "-//W3C//DTD SVG August 1999//EN"
  "http://www.w3.org/Graphics/SVG/SVG-19990812.dtd">
<svg width="4in" height="3in">
<desc>Two groups, each of two rectangles</desc>
<g style="fillcolor:red">
  <rect x="100" y="100" width="100" height="100" />
  <rect x="300" y="100" width="100" height="100" />
</g>
<g style="fillcolor:blue">
  <rect x="100" y="300" width="100" height="100" />
  <rect x="300" y="300" width="100" height="100" />
</g>
</svg>
```

sequencing of audio, video, text and graphic components. SMIL is used in the *RealPlayer G2*™ product.

4.4 | Metadata

There is a special type of data that interests owners and users of large information collections. It is called *metadata*: information about information. Metadata is starting to become crucial to Web searching and navigation.

4.4.1 *Platform for Internet Content Selection*

The first standardized metadata specification for the Web was developed before XML and is called the *Platform for Internet Content Selection (PICS)*. PICS allows the filtering of inappropriate material from computer screens based on external descriptions of content.

The "violent content" label on a video tape is a perfect example of metadata. The data provided, "violent content" describes the contents of the tape – it is data about data. PICS is an electronic version of that label.

Parts of the PICS family of standards are based upon XML. It took almost two years to get PICS into the XML world. This is because on the way to developing PICS the W3C created an intermediate layer called *Resource Description Framework (RDF)*.

4.4.2 *Resource Description Framework*

RDF is not a document type: it is a convention for designing XML documents so that they can more easily be interpreted as metadata.[1]

Metadata, as we have seen, is data about data. Having better access to it should make computer filtering, sorting and other processing easier.

RDF's central concept is the "property". An RDF document can associate many properties with documents on the Web. Some of those properties can be from the PICS vocabulary. However, there are other vocabularies used with RDF that are unrelated to content filtering, as illustrated by the (imaginary) "bibliography" vocabulary used in Example 4-5.

---

1. At least that is what it looks like from an XML user's point of view. A metadata user would say that RDF is a model for metadata and XML is a particular way of representing that model. We discuss RDF from that viewpoint in Chapter 44, "RDF: Metadata description for Web resources", on page 646.

Example 4-5. Describing the author of a document in RDF

```
<rdf:RDF xmlns:bib="http://bibliography.dummy.org">
  xmlns:rdf="http://www.w3.org/1999/02/22-rdf-syntax-ns#">
  <rdf:Description about="http://www.bar.com/some.doc">
    <bib:author rdf:resource="http://bibliography.dummy.org/author">
      <bib:name>John Smith</bib:name>
<bib:email>john@smith.com</bib:email>
<bib:phone>+1 (555) 123-4567</bib:phone>
    </bib:author>
  </rdf:Description>
</rdf:RDF>
```

In one sense, this sounds very complicated: PICS is based on RDF which is based on XML. But on the other hand, it will not be so complicated in practice. PICS will have a set of element types that you must learn to apply according to the XML syntax described in this book. RDF, the middle layer, will only be visible to the wizards who invent new ways of cataloging, describing and organizing information – the librarians of the future.[2]

RDF is discussed in Chapter 44, "RDF: Metadata description for Web resources", on page 646.

4.4.3 *Topic maps*

A related development comes from the *International Organization for Standardization (ISO)*. *Topic maps* are a specific type of metadata designed to allow the construction of logical "maps" of information. Topic maps are designed to help us navigate through the massive amounts of information on the Web. You can think of topic maps as a very sophisticated indexing mechanism for online information. We think of them as the GPS for the Web![3]

One aspect of topic maps' sophistication is the idea of *scoping*. With scoping, you can label a particular characteristic (roughly, an index entry) as only being applicable within a certain context.

---

2. Luckily, the librarians of the present are very much involved in these standardization efforts.
3. The exact relationship between RDF and topic maps is somewhat unclear to everybody concerned. Formally, they are unrelated but it seems like there is some opportunity for cooperation in the future. The experts are looking into this even as you read!

For example, if you label characteristics as being applicable only in a particular language, a query for information on a topic would only return occurrences in your native tongue. If you labeled characteristics as being either "biological" or "psychological", then a search for the word "evolution" would return only biological topics or only psychological ones, depending on your query.

> *Tip*   There is a friendly tutorial on topic maps in Chapter 43, "Topic maps: Knowledge navigation aids", on page 628.

4.5 | Content syndication

Content syndication is about using metadata to move documents, such as news articles, from place to place. It is a problem domain that is tailor-made for XML because when you put XML and the Internet together you have a powerful information distribution infrastructure.

The alphabet soup of competing and cooperating standards is too long to cover in depth, but we can name a few:

- *ICE* is the *Information Content and Exchange* specification from the vendor consortium of the same name. It is described in Chapter 24, "Information and Content Exchange (ICE)", on page 358.
- *PRISM* (Publishing Requirements for Industry Standard Metadata) is an extensible XML metadata standard for syndicating, aggregating, post-processing and re-purposing content from publications, news feeds, and similar sources. It also provides a set of controlled vocabularies with which to describe the content being interchanged. PRISM is illustrated in 18.3.1, "Associating metadata", on page 281.
- *RSS*, the *RDF Site Specification* is a lightweight standard from Netscape that has been embraced by the Open Source and Linux communities.
- *NewsML* is a packaging and metadata format for news content, similar to PRISM and RSS. NewsML is developed by

the International Press Telecommunications Council (IPTC), a consortium of news providers, mostly in the print or wire-service industries. Since it deals only with packaging and metadata, NewsML is complementary to syndication protocols like ICE.

4.6 | Science on the Web

Although the Web was originally invented in a physics laboratory for communication among physicists, it never developed into a great system for communicating mathematical formulae. Markup for mathematics is more complex than it seems at first to non-mathematicians.

The World Wide Web Consortium has created an XML-based language called *MathML*. Although the major browsers do not support MathML directly, you can get MathML support through Java applets, browser plug-ins and specialized browsers.

A rendition of a mathematical formula is shown in Figure 4-1. Its MathML markup is illustrated in Example 4-6.

$$x^2 + 4x + 4 = 0$$

Figure 4-1   Rendition of a mathematical formula

The *Chemical Markup Language* (CML) is an XML-based language for describing the management of molecular information on computer networks. Using a Java viewer, users will be able to view and manipulate molecules in 2 and 3 dimensions.

Bioinformatic Sequence Markup Language is a standard for representing DNA, RNA and protein sequence information. One day your doctor may download your DNA into XML and then upload it into a petri dish to make a mini-you. We hope you'll be well-formed!

Example 4-6. MathML markup for the formula in Figure 4-1

```
<mrow>
  <mrow>
    <msup>
      <mi>x</mi>
      <mn>2</mn>
    </msup>
    <mo>+</mo>
    <mrow>
      <mn>4</mn>
      <mo>&invisibletimes;</mo>
      <mi>x</mi>
    </mrow>
    <mo>+</mo>
    <mn>4</mn>
  </mrow>
  <mo>=</mo>
  <mn>0</mn>
</mrow>
```

4.7 | Portals and personalization

At the beginning of the Internet revolution, knowledge workers were like kids in a candy store. The information they needed became easily available. Now the stomach-ache is setting in. The information that they need is buried in gigabytes of information they do not need.

A portal is a website designed to help users find their way through information. The first portals only helped people to find other websites. Then public portals started to add interactive features such as stock quotes and weather reports. Later, they started to allow users to build customized "home pages" including their favorite stock quotes, local weather reports and other information specific to them. This is termed *personalization*. In addition to public portals like Yahoo™, there are also many portals used within large companies. These are termed *Enterprise Information Portals* (EIPs) or *digital dashboards*. We discuss EIPs in detail in Part 6, "Portals", on page 322.

XML serves as a fundamental building block for personalized portals. XML can be used to bring various information resources into one common structure. From there, XML tools such as parsers, search engines and transformation engines can slice and dice the information into bite-sized pieces applicable to the user. The vocabulary details of the information returned by various enterprise systems may vary, but they can be *transformed* into a common vocabulary using any programming language or the XSLT transformation language.

In a sense, an Enterprise Information Portal serves as a friendly user interface to the unified system that results from Enterprise Application Integration (see 1.4, "EDI, EAI and other TLAs", on page 26). EAI systems use XML because it is good for integrating various data sources. The EIP adds another feature of XML: XML documents can easily be formatted for presentation to a human being using stylesheets.

We'll say it again: XML brings the worlds of document and data processing together.

4.8 | Alternative delivery platforms

One of the original benefits of generalized markup was its ability to make information available to new delivery devices. When the Web was young, some of the first serious content providers were established SGML users. Information that predated the Web by years could easily be served as HTML through an automated conversion. Now the Web as-we-know-it is the legacy platform (not paper) and new devices such as electronic books and hand-held computers are the up and coming, new, new thing.

4.8.1 *XML goes wireless*

As you may have heard, desktop Web browsers are already passé. The next wave is wireless. And your new surfboard is the *Wireless Application Protocol (WAP)*. WAP is the term for the collection of standards that is driving the move to Internet access over handheld computers, mobile telephones, wrist watches and other go-anywhere technologies. Web browsing is not the only interesting application, either. Many people argue that hand-held instant messaging will be even more popular and important.

Not all of the WAP family of standards are based on XML. The main XML-specifications are *WBXML* and *WML*.

WBXML, is, as you might have guessed, a schema for television shows on the Warner Brothers Network. Okay, not really. WBXML is WAP Binary XML. The philosophy behind WBXML is that small machines typically have very slow connectivity to the Internet. WBXML documents are compressed XML files that can be more efficiently sent back and forth over tiny little Internet pipelines.

Wireless Markup Language (WML) is a markup language for small devices.

The central concept of WML is the *card*. Cards are to WML what pages are to the Web's HTML. One big difference is that many cards may reside in the same XML document. This means that the WML browser in the cell-phone or handheld computer does not have to constantly download new documents across the network.

Example 4-7 is an example of a document made up of two cards. The example is not very interesting: it just allows the user to bounce back and forth between the two cards.

Example 4-7. Two-card WML example

```
<?xml version="1.0"?>
<!DOCTYPE wml PUBLIC "-//WAPFORUM//DTD WML 1.1//EN"
    "http://www.wapforum.org/DTD/wml_1.1.xml">
<wml>

    <card id="card1" title="My Wap Page">
      <p>
       Hello world - welcome to my first wap card!
      </p>
      <p>
       <a href="#card2">Go to the second card</a>
      </p>
    </card>

    <card id="card2" title="Second Card">
      <p>
       Welcome to my second wap card!
      </p>
      <p>
       <a href="#card1">Go back to the first card</a>
      </p>
    </card>

</wml>
```

OpenWave™ has an application that allows testing of WAP applications on ordinary desktop computers. It actually emulates various kinds of cellular telephones. Figure 4-2 shows the rendered version of Example 4-7.

Figure 4-2   Two-card WML example rendered

WML also supports forms to send information back to the server, client-side scripts to add interactivity, hyperlinks to jump from card to card and document to document and so forth. Form fields are entered one at a time rather than in a screenful as in HTML. Example 4-8 is a single card with a form for subscribing to a service. It causes separate screens to be rendered for each field, as shown in Figure 4-3 and Figure 4-4.

Example 4-8. WML subscription card

```
<?xml version="1.0"?>
<!DOCTYPE wml PUBLIC "-//WAPFORUM//DTD WML 1.1//EN"
    "http://www.wapforum.org/DTD/wml_1.1.xml">
<wml>
  <card id="card1" title="Subscribe">
    <p>E-mail login:<br/>
     <input name="login" title="E-mail login"/>
    </p>
    <p>Password:<br/>
     <input name="pwd" type="password" title="Password"/>
    </p>
  </card>
</wml>
```

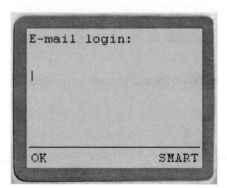

Figure 4-3   Rendered login screen

Figure 4-4   Rendered password screen

Not everyone believes that WAP is destined for great success. The first complaint about WAP was that it is designed to present the so-called "wireless Web" on cell phones. But many people claim that cell phone users do not want the Web as much as they want instant messaging. In other words, they are much more interested in using cell phones to communicate with each other than to browse Web sites. WAP supports this form of communication but not to the same extent as it does browser-style applications.

The other major issue with WAP is that it does not build strongly enough on Web standards. For instance WBXML is very much like XML, but it is not pure XML – it uses a WAP-specific compression mechanism.

The WAP specifications are controversial to some technologists but what concerns some business analysts are the business issues. Many WAP implementations are closed systems with no connectivity to other WAP systems. Many WAP implementations are very expensive and inefficient in terms of connection times. It is possible that these issues will be worked out over time.

While WAP allows the Web to be presented on cell phones in real time, there is a separate language called *SyncML* for synchronizing data between small platforms (such as mobile phones or PDAs) and desktop computers. SyncML would allow you to program your desktop calendar software to inform your cell phone about your meeting times. SyncML should also prove popular for moving contact information (electronic business cards) to, from and between handheld devices.

4.8.2 *Beyond voice mail*

It is all very well and good to surf the Web on a cell phone but that does not change the fact that there are some serious limitations to the reach of WAP technology. Not everyone has a cell phone. Not all cell phones are WAP enabled. Many people do not consider number keys and small LCD screens a good user interface. There is another technology that is well-established without any of these limitations. Press 1 if you know what technology we are speaking of. Press 2 if you do not. Then say your name after the tone.

The computers that answer telephones are known to most people as "answering machines" But they do not have much in common with the old tape-based devices. As you have probably noticed, the most interesting change is that it is now possible to navigate many of these services using your voice rather than the keypad. This is due to advances in a technology known as *speech recognition*. Speech recognition is maturing at exactly the same time that XML is gaining popularity and the Web is expanding to other devices. The merger of these technologies is known as *VoiceXML*.

VoiceXML is an emerging industry standard for building these so-called Interactive Voice Response (IVR) applications. What HTML is to Web pages and WML to the wireless Web, VoiceXML is to voice-based applications. Example 4-9 has an example.

Unfortunately we cannot show you the output of this example as easily as we could with WML but you can imagine one of those robotic generated computer voices. It would ask you to say one of the phrases "Sports", "Weather" or "Stargazer astrophysics news". Once you selected one, it would launch a new VoiceXML document and either ask you some more

Example 4-9. VoiceXML example

```
<menu>
  <prompt>Welcome home. Say one of: <enumerate/></prompt>
  <choice next="http://www.sports.example/vxml/start.vxml">
    Sports
  </choice>
  <choice next="http://www.weather.example/intro.vxml">
    Weather
  </choice>
  <choice next="http://www.stargazer.example/voice/astronews.vxml">
    Stargazer astrophysics news
  </choice>
  <noinput>Please say one of <enumerate/></noinput>
</menu>
```

questions or read you some information. Note that the tinny robotic voice is not a requirement. You can use VoiceXML with pre-recorded voices. VoiceXML is a whole new market for voice actors.

We let VoiceXML speak for itself in Part 11, "Voice", on page 588.

4.8.3 *Downloading the library*

Surfing your stock quotes is great while you are on the run, but what about when you want to curl up by the fire with a novella? Futurists have promised us electronic books for almost as long as they have promised us flying cars. Business interests are starting to believe that electronic books are now feasible and worth research and investment. We should all have one any day now. No word yet on the flying cars.

The Open eBook Forum creates and maintains standards relating to electronic books. The forum is made up of hardware and software companies, electronic book publishers and related organizations. A common standard for electronic books will allow those books to work on media as diverse as laptop computers, text-to-speech readers and palm computers.

The Open eBook specification is fairly simple in that it combines existing specifications into a single unified whole. The basic syntax for eBooks is XML. The "core" vocabulary is a variant of XHTML but the language is designed to be extensible to any XML vocabulary. Books are rendered using the Cascading Style Sheet (CSS) language. Metadata is represented using a vocabulary known as Dublin Core.

The Open eBook spec is not so much an invention as a standardized combination of specifications defined elsewhere. It is likely to drive the adoption of XML down into portable reading devices.

4.9 | Conclusion

XML is set to revolutionize the Web and all forms of information delivery. This will allow more sophisticated means of communication between computers and people and among people.

In the next chapter we'll talk about applications that dispense with people. Computers talk to one another to automatically accomplish tasks that have traditionally been labor-intensive and error prone.

Taking care of
e-business

Introductory Discussion

- Electronic business

- ebXML and BizTalk

- Electronic marketplaces

- Repositories

Chapter

5

At one end of the XML spectrum are the people-oriented publishing (POP) applications designed primarily for human consumption. XHTML, WAP and similar specifications will increase the availability and sophistication of online information in these sorts of applications. At the other end of the spectrum there are machine-oriented messaging (MOM) applications wherein computers talk to each other with minimal human intervention.

There is no requirement that MOM applications involve e-commerce, but as a notorious criminal said when asked why he robbed banks: "That's where the money is." It's also where most of the current research and energy are directed. Many people are working extremely hard to completely integrate commerce among organizations.

We discussed generic machine-to-machine protocols such as SOAP and XML-RPC in 2.11.3, "Protocols", on page 52. Now we'll look at the applications they support in the rapidly growing area of integrated e-commerce. There are many different standards under development in this area. They sometimes overlap, compete and maybe even contradict each other. That's merely a consequence of the fact that we are in the early days of XML-based e-business.

The dream of automated supply chain management is unmediated computer-to-computer, business-to-business integrated e-commerce. When you buy a television set, you are really buying a bundle of parts that one company bought from other companies to assemble for you. Those parts are made up of raw materials that were bought from somewhere else. Some company sold the service of removing the waste materials from these processes. Every company in this *supply chain* also had to buy desks, paper clips, and overhead projectors.

In the future the vast majority of these products will be bought over the Internet. A large subset will be bought automatically, without human intervention, through XML-based systems. When the warehouse runs low on staples, a computer will recognize this situation through the inventory and order more. Before a plant runs short of steel, it will order some from whichever supplier promises the best price that day.

XML does not do all of this by itself. There will be many pieces of sophisticated software that do the heavy lifting. XML-based Web Services protocols are the basis for all of the new standards that will allow these different programs to communicate with each other.

5.1 | History

Business-to-business electronic communication is not new. For 25 years big businesses depended heavily on electronic data interchange. EDI is wonderful for big businesses but it has never appealed to small or medium sized organizations for a variety of reasons. The first problem is that EDI is typically conducted over expensive private networks known as *Value Added Networks* (VANs). The EDI standards predate the public Internet by many years. VANs are in many ways still better than the public Internet. They are very secure and are better at quickly and reliably delivering information. But VANs are also too expensive and proprietary to appeal to small businesses.

The second problem with EDI is that it is typically always "customized" for every communication between two corporations. This is very expensive for a small corporation with many big partners. Each big partner will demand the small company use its own variant of EDI. Finally, EDI is considered to be too complicated because it uses a somewhat confusing pre-XML representation.

EDI would not have been successful with its large customers if it did not have some important features. Embedded within EDI is a great deal of knowledge about how businesses work in terms of processes and policies. The challenge of the new XML commerce frameworks is to take the virtues of EDI forward into a more open environment based on Web standards. Ideally the new XML-based specifications will be just as useful to a small emu rancher as to a large airplane manufacturer.

5.2 | Commerce frameworks

The word framework is deliberately vague. It is an environment in which to frame other work: not something directly usable by itself. XML itself can be considered a framework!

You cannot simply download an e-commerce framework and begin to work. Rather you use it as guidance in designing the particular details of your document types and software. If many document types adhere to the same framework then some portion of your implementation code can be reused between document types.

The electronic business frameworks we are about to discuss are based upon XML. They consist of a mix of vocabularies, best practice recommendations and markup conventions.

5.2.1 *ebXML*

Getting all of the world's computers to talk to and negotiate with each other will not be easy. There are many reasons why the problems are tricky and XML only provides a framework for solving them, not a solution in and of itself. Consider the variety of international human languages. Even within a country, there are huge variations in terminology and process between and within industries. Someone needs to standardize terminology, message structures and product and business codes.

The United Nations and OASIS have set up a joint project to tackle this problem. It is known as *ebXML*. Because ebXML has the formal support of the United Nations, it is likely to become a very important standard internationally. According to the founders:

The goal of ebXML is to facilitate open trade between organizations regardless of size by enabling XML to be used in a consistent manner to exchange electronic business data.

ebXML is composed of many different related specifications. The easiest way through them is to consider an example. The specifications address two key areas: discovery and messaging.

5.2.1.1   Discovery

Let us pretend that you are the president of Crazy Kazoos Incorporated. The first thing you need to do is try to find business partners such as customers and suppliers. There are two parts to this. First you want to publish your contact information and second you want to browse other companies' contact information to look for potential partners.

In either case you need some form of *registry*. ebXML contains standards for creating interoperable registries similar to those defined by UDDI (see 47.2, "Universal Description, Discovery, and Integration", on page 689). The exact relationship between these two specifications is not well defined yet. ebXML goes beyond UDDI in providing not just a registry but also a *repository*. Whereas registries hold only small bits of simple information with a known structure, repositories can hold more complicated informational files and freeform documents. The ebXML repository allows organizations to publish specifications, schema definitions and other business documents for public consumption.

Companies publish information about themselves in a *Business Profile*. The profile covers the business' contact information and industrial classification. It also describes the *Business scenarios* supported by the business. *Business scenarios* are XML descriptions of the business processes that a particular business supports. The business' technical capabilities are described by a *Collaboration-Protocol Profile (CPP)*. It describes what protocol the business intends to use, what URL to use as the end-point, what security features it uses, and so forth.

When two companies find each other through the registry, the two determine (either automatically or manually) what protocols they support in common. They do this by comparing their Collaboration-Protocol Profiles (CPPs) and merging them into a Collaboration-Protocol Agreement (CPA).

5.2.1.2 Messaging

Next they will want to start send messages back and forth. ebXML has a messaging infrastructure that is based upon SOAP. ebXML's messaging extends SOAP with features for guaranteeing the reliability of transmission.

The most important part of an ebXML message is the *payload* – a business document such as a purchase order or invoice. In ebXML terminology, these documents are decomposed into *core components*, which are defined in a part of the ebXML registry known as the *Core Component Library*.

The core components are among the trickiest parts of the ebXML system to get right because they are most directly linked to the wide variety of business processes in the real world. The core components specification will have to deal with the wide variance in terminology and practice around the world. Because of the complexity of this challenge, the Core Component Library is currently the least developed part of ebXML.

5.2.2 *Trading Partner Agreement Markup Language*

In order to trade with a new partner, you may need a formal agreement on the terms of your partnership. Collaboration-Protocol Agreements handle the technical details (which protocols, what URLs, and so forth) but they do not handle the higher-level legal issues. IBM has developed a language called the Trading Partner Agreement Markup Language (tpaML) for electronic contracts. IBM has submitted tpaML to the ebXML project for standardization.

Here is IBM's description of tpaML:

> The foundation of tpaML is the Trading Partner Agreement (TPA), which defines how trading partners will interact at the transport, document exchange and business protocol layers. A TPA contains the general contract terms and conditions, participant roles (buyers, sellers), communication and security protocols and business processes, (valid actions, sequencing rules, etc.).

In other words, TPA documents formalize the agreement required before two businesses can begin trading.

5.2.3 *BizTalk Framework*

BizTalk™ is a set of technologies from Microsoft. There is the BizTalk Framework (an electronic business framework), the BizTalk server (which is Microsoft's implementation of the framework) and the BizTalk repository.

The BizTalk Framework is a set of guidelines for XML best practices. The framework describes how to publish schema definitions in XML and how to use XML messages to integrate software programs together in order to build new solutions.

The framework includes a vocabulary for wrapping XML documents in an "envelope" that manages message routing, workflow and security. Biz-Talk has no pre-defined e-business document types such as Purchase Order or Request For Quotation. Those would be the contents of the envelope and would likely be defined by ebXML or an industry consortium.

The BizTalk envelope is a little more descriptive than the sort of envelopes we use in the paper world. It describes the sender and receiver of the message, how it should be delivered, whether a return receipt is required, what sort of processing deadlines are in force and other, similar *quality of service (QoS)* details.

5.3 | Going Vertical

In addition to generalized, common frameworks, there are dozens of organizations adapting XML to particular industries. These are termed *vertical* applications or *verticals*. It is not possible to discuss them all here.[1] Instead, we will focus on a few examples. These verticals seem to be achieving real success and can serve as models for other, similar activities.

5.3.1 *RosettaNet*

RosettaNet is an non-profit consortium that develops and deploys standard electronic business interfaces. RosettaNet exists to combat the problem of "supply chain misalignments" in the information technology industry. The

---

1. There's a helpful catalog, including website links, in Chapter 67, "Repositories and vocabularies", on page 1070.

supply chain is the path from raw materials to finished products. In the information technology business, this would include everything from silicon to chips to parts to software.

A supply-chain misalignment is an inefficiency caused by poor information flow between organizations in a supply chain. As a child you may have played the game "telephone" where information was relayed from person to person, getting more and more garbled as it traveled. A supply chain has the same problems. These problems are particularly severe in the computer hardware industry because things change so rapidly and margins are very thin. A small company that makes too many or too few computer chips may not have an opportunity to correct its mistake.

RosettaNet is the name of the organization and also of the electronic business framework developed by the consortium. Partners use RosettaNet specifications to "align" their internal business processes and create inter-company information flows. The RosettaNet framework describes dictionaries of common definitions for computer and business terminology. RosettaNet also defines many standardized business processes known as Partner Interface Processes (PIPs).

RosettaNet has developed a 3,600-word "dictionary" of IT products. The group has also created dozens of XML-based PIPs. These guidelines amount to dialogs between computers conducted entirely in XML. The PIPs enable manufacturers, distributors, resellers, customers and other supply chain members to execute those processes in a standard fashion. Existing PIPs cover basic supply chain functions such as distributing new product information, transferring shopping carts, managing purchase orders and querying technical information. Others are under development.

Examples of PIPs include "Request Quote", "Query Price and Availability" and "Change Basic Product Information". These standards form a common integrated e-commerce language. They align processes between supply chain partners on a global basis, rather than using individually or bilaterally developed methods.

RosettaNet has announced that it will support ebXML messaging in a future version of the standard. Members of the RosettaNet Board of Directors are typically vice-presidents or directors of large companies in the IT industry, so this is a big vote of confidence.

Judged by technical specification output, RosettaNet is advancing quickly. Corporations in the Information Technology (IT) industry have pledged support for the RosettaNet processes, and products that support these processes are now available.

5.3.2 *Open Financial Exchange (OFX)*

The Open Financial Exchange is the name of a technical specification created by Intuit, CheckFree and Microsoft. OFX allows financial institutions (banks, brokerages and billers) to communicate with one another and their clients about account transactions.

OFX is one of the most mature uses of markup languages in the consumer software world, having originated as an SGML application. It is supported on the client side by accounting packages such as *Microsoft Money* and Intuit's *Quicken*, and on the server side by numerous financial institutions.

OFX supports four major kinds of services: banking, bill presentment, bill payment, investment and tax forms.

5.3.2.1 Banking

Using the OFX Banking services, your client software (e.g. *Quicken*, *Microsoft Money* or *Peachtree*) could communicate directly with your bank. That means that your banking transactions can appear in your accounting software automatically. Bad news: covering up the trail left by transfers into the "poker money" account is about to get tricky.

Information can flow the other way also. Using an OFX-based accounting program, you could transfer money from account to account instead of through a separate website (or, heaven forbid, a branch office). Now your spouse can transfer the money back into the "university fund" account without leaving the house!

Customers can even schedule transfers in advance so that the disputed money is sent to the university account (or the university!) as soon as the paycheck clears. All of these features apply both to regular accounts and to credit card accounts. Spending money has never been so easy!

5.3.2.2 Bill presentment and payment

OFX-based bill payment is exactly as boring as it sounds. Accounting software can direct the bank to automatically pay your bills for you when they arrive. You can specify which bills should be paid automatically and which should be done manually. Bill presentment allows billers (typically utility companies) to deliver their bills directly to your accounting software.

5.3.2.3 Investment

Although OFX does not currently allow customers to buy and sell investments through their accounting software, it does allow you to download information about your transactions, open orders, balances and positions for entry into your accounting package. It is possible to manage 401(k) accounts as well as cash, margin and short accounts. OFX cannot guarantee that your investments grow but it can ensure that you are always aware of exactly where they stand.

5.3.2.4 Tax Forms

OFX version 2 allows accounting software to download 1099 and W2 Forms from financial institutions and payroll processors. These XML element types closely mimic the equivalent print forms. As the tax forms change, the XML specifications have to change to follow them. As this is the only part of OFX that is totally US-specific, all amounts are expressed in US dollars.

5.3.3 *Health Level Seven (HL7)*

Health Level Seven is the dominant industry consortium for health care. HL7 has been around since 1987 and is moving now to embrace XML. In September 2000, the HL7 membership ratified Version One of the Clinical Document Architecture, which defines an XML architecture for exchange of clinical documents

The most widely used HL7 specification is the Application Protocol for Electronic Data Exchange in Healthcare Environments. This is a messaging standard that enables various health care applications to exchange data within and between organizations. Version Three of the HL7 specifications will use XML extensively. The group has also announced that it intends to support ebXML Messaging.

HL7 reminds us that XML is used in life and death applications. It was specifically designed for systems that cannot be permitted to fail. Those of us that develop XML specifications and tools must take this responsibility seriously and keep reliability as a major focus.

5.4 | Repository stories

As you can see, there are hundreds of schemas, DTDs, frameworks and other specifications swirling around XML like leaves in a storm. This is as it should be. XML is a building block. There can never be one or ten or one hundred "definitive" XML document types. Actually, there are going to be new ones invented all of the time, as new situations arise.

As we come to understand the human genome, we will need genome markup languages. When we send robotic probes to other planets, NASA may well deliver the results of experiments to the Web in various appropriate markup languages. Believe it or not, there is already a Spacecraft Markup Language![2]

Fortunately, organizations have begun to establish repository sites on the Web to catalog vocabularies and schemas in process. We discuss them in Chapter 67, "Repositories and vocabularies", on page 1070.

5.5 | Conclusion

The first wave of the Internet revolution made access to information easier than it had ever been before. The second wave made commerce between individuals and businesses easier. Now the third wave will eliminate vast amounts of paperwork and inefficiency in processes that are conducted between businesses. XML is a key enabler of this more integrated business world. It serves as the foundation for industry-neutral frameworks and industry-specific vertical markets.

---

2. It might be presumptuous to predict that XML would be the basis for communication at Federation Headquarters. The aliens may already have their own Galactic Markup Language.

XML Jargon Demystifier™

- Structured vs. unstructured

- Tag vs. element

- Document type, DTD, and markup declarations

- Schema and schema definitions

- Notations and characters

- Documents and data

Chapter

6

One of the problems in learning a new technology like XML is getting used to the jargon. A good book will hold you by the hand, introduce terms gradually, and use them precisely and consistently.

Out in the real word, though, people use imprecise terminology that often makes it hard to understand things, let alone compare products. And, unlike authors,[1] they sometimes just plain get things wrong.

For example, you may see statements like "XML documents are either well-formed or valid." As you've learned from this book, that simply isn't true. *All* XML documents are well-formed; some of them are also valid.[2]

In this book, we've taken pains to edit the application and tool chapters to use consistent and accurate terminology. However, for product literature and other documents you read, the mileage may vary. So we've prepared a handy guide to the important XML jargon, both right and wrong. Think of it as middleware for XML knowledge.

---

1. We should be so lucky!
2. So does that mean a merely well-formed document is "invalid"? No, for the reasons described in 2.7, "Well-formedness and validity", on page 44. Hey, we didn't promise to justify XML jargon, just to explain it.

6.1 | Structured vs. unstructured

Structured is arguably the most commonly used word to characterize the essence of markup languages. It is also the most ambiguous and most often misused word.

There are four common meanings:

structured = abstract

XML documents are frequently referred to as structured while other text, such as renditions in notations like RTF, is called *unstructured* or *semi-structured*. Separating "structure from style" is considered the hallmark of a markup language. But in fact, renditions can have a rich structure, composed of elements like pages, columns, and blocks. The real distinction being made is between "abstract" and "rendered".

structured = managed

This is one of the meanings that folks with a database background usually have in mind. Structured information is managed as a common resource and is accessible to the entire enterprise. Unfortunately, there are also departmental and individual databases and their content isn't "structured" in quite the same sense.

structured = predictable

This is another alternative for relational database people. Structured data is captured from business transactions, comes in easily identified granules, and has metadata that identifies its semantics. In contrast, *freeform data* is normally buried in reports, with no metadata, and therefore must be "parsed" (by reading it!) to determine what it is and what it means. See 6.10, "Documents and data", on page 115 for more on this.

structured = possessing structure

This is the dictionary meaning, and the one used in this book. There is usually the (sometimes unwarranted) implication that the structure is fine-grained (rich, detailed), making components accessible at efficient levels of granularity. A structure can be very simple – a single really big component – but nothing is unstructured. All structure is well-defined and "predictable" (in the sense of consistent), it just may not be very granular.

These distinctions aren't academic. It is very important to know which "structured" a vendor means.

What if your publishing system has bottlenecks because you are maintaining four rendered versions of your documents in different representations? It isn't much of a solution to "structure" them in a database so that modifying one version warns you to modify the others.

You'll want to have a single "structured" – that is, abstract – version from which the others can be rendered. And if you find that your document has scores of pages unrelieved by sub-headings, you may want to "structure" it more finely so that both readers and editors can deal with it in smaller chunks.

Keep these different meanings in mind when you read about "structured" and "unstructured". In this book, we try to confine our use of the word to its dictionary meaning, occasionally (when it is clear from the context) with the implication of "fine-grained".

6.2 | Tag vs. element

Tags aren't the same thing as elements. Tags describe elements.

In Figure 6-1 the package, metaphorically speaking, is an element. The contents of the package is the content of an element. The tag describes the element. It contains three names:

- The *element-type name* (`Wristwatch`), which says what type of element it is.
- A *unique identifier*, or ID (`9842-3729`), which says which particular element it is.
- The name of an attribute that describes some other property of the element: `Manufacturer="Hy TimePiece Company"`.

When people talk about a *tag name*:

1. They are referring to the element-type name.
2. They are making an error, because tags aren't named.

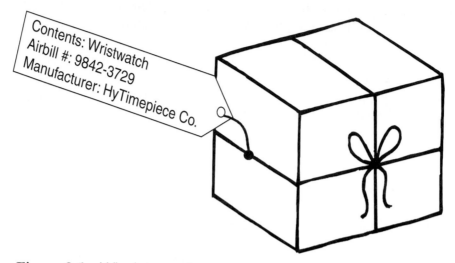

Figure 6-1   What's in a tag?

And when they talk about an *element name*:

1. They are referring to the element-type name.
2. They are making an error, because an element is named by its unique identifier.

6.3 | Document type, DTD, and markup declarations

A *document type* is a class of similar documents, like telephone books, technical manuals, or (when they are marked up as XML) inventory records.

A *document type definition* (*DTD*) is the set of rules for using XML to represent documents of a particular type. These rules might exist only in your mind as you create a document, or they may be written out.

Markup declarations, such as those in Example 6-1, are XML's way of writing out DTDs.

It is easy to mix up these three constructs: a document type, XML's markup rules for documents of that type (the DTD), and the expression of those rules (the markup declarations). It is necessary to keep the constructs separate if you are dealing with two or more of them at the same time, as

Example 6-1. Markup declarations in the file `greeting.dtd`.

```
<!ELEMENT greeting (salutation, addressee) >
<!ELEMENT salutation (#PCDATA) >
<!ELEMENT addressee  (#PCDATA) >
```

when discussing alternative ways to express a DTD. But most of the time, even in this book, "DTD" will suffice for referring to any of the three.

6.4 | Schema and schema definition

The programming and database worlds have introduced some new terminology to XML.

We now speak of a document type as a kind of *schema*, a conception of the common characteristics of some class of things. Similarly, a DTD is a *schema definition*, the rules for using XML to represent documents conforming to the schema.

Schema definitions are invariably written out in a notation called a *schema definition language*, or simply a *schema language*. And as with DTDs, the word "schema" can serve for all these purposes when there is no ambiguity.

6.5 | Document, XML document, and instance

The term *document* has two distinct meanings in XML.

Consider a really short XML document that might be rendered as:

Hello World

The *conceptual document* that you see in your mind's eye when you read the rendition is intuitively what you think of as the document. Communicating that conception is the reason for using XML in the first place.

In a formal, syntactic sense, though, the complete text (markup + data, remember) of Example 6-2, is the *XML document*. Perhaps surprisingly, that includes the markup declarations for its DTD (shown in Example 6-1).

The XML document, in other words, is a character string that *represents* the conceptual document.

In this example, much of that string consists of the markup declarations, which express the `greeting` DTD. Only the last four lines describe the conceptual document, which is an instance of a `greeting`. Those lines are called the *document instance*.

Example 6-2. A greeting document.

```
<?xml version="1.0"?>
<!DOCTYPE greeting SYSTEM "file://greeting.dtd">
<greeting>
<salutation>Hello</salutation>
<addressee>World</addressee>
</greeting>
```

That term gets flipped around when schema languages are involved. Unlike DTD declarations, schema languages are XML-based, so a schema definition must be stored as an XML document in its own right (a *schema document*). That means an instance of a schema definition is a separate document, so it is known as an *instance document*.

6.6 | What's the meta?

Nothing. What did you think was the meta?[3]

There are two "meta" words that come up regularly when computer types talk about XML: metadata and metalanguage.

6.6.1 *Metadata*

Metadata is data about data. The date, publisher's name, and author's name of a book are metadata about the book, while the data of the book is its content. The DTD and markup tags of an XML document are also metadata. If you choose to represent the author's name as an element, then it is both data and metadata.

---

3. Sorry about that!

If you get the idea that the line between data and metadata is a fluid one, you are right. And as long as your document representation and system let you access and process metadata as though it were data, it doesn't much matter where you draw that line.

Be careful when talking to database experts, though. In their discipline "metadata" typically refers only to the schema.

6.6.2 *Metalanguage*

You may hear some DTDs referred to as languages, rather than document types. HTML is a prominent example. There's nothing special about them, it is just another way of looking at the way a markup language works.

Remember that an XML document is a character string that represents some conceptual document. The rules for creating a valid string are like the rules of a language: There is a *vocabulary* of element type and attribute names, and a *grammar* that determines where the names can be used.

These language rules come from the DTD, which in turn follows the rules of XML. A language, such as XML, which you can use to define other languages (such as DTDs), is called a *metalanguage*. XML document types are sometimes called *XML-based languages*.

6.7 | Notations and characters

Normally, the characters in a document are interpreted one at a time. They are given the meaning assigned by the document character set, which for XML documents is Unicode. So the character a is interpreted as the letter "a" and the character < is interpreted as the mathematical symbol "less-than".

A character-based *notation* is a set of rules for interpreting a *sequence* of characters at once, and giving the sequence a meaning that is different from the character-set meaning of the individual characters. The HTML notation, for example, interprets <a name=b> as the start-tag of an "a" element.

Computer languages (including markup languages and languages defined by markup languages), document and data formats like RTF and JPEG, and the string representations of datatypes, are all examples of notations.

The distinction between various kinds of notations can be rather esoteric. The important thing is that characters don't have their usual meaning. You need a *parser* to figure out what that meaning is. But XML is simple enough that, after reading Part 15, "XML Core Tutorials" of this book, you should be able to parse XML documents yourself.

6.8 | Coding, encoding, and markup

People refer to computer programs as *code*, and to the act of programming as *coding*.

There is also the word *encoding*, which refers to the way that characters are represented as ones and zeros in computer storage. XML has a declaration for specifying an encoding.

You'll often see (in places other than this book) phrases like "XML-encoded data", "coded in HTML", or "XML coding".

But using XML isn't coding. Not in the sense of programming, and not in the sense of character encoding. What those phrases mean are "XML document", "marked-up in HTML", and "XML markup".[4]

6.9 | URL and URN and URI and URI reference

"U R kidding!", U might think, but we R not!

There really are four different things that look like URLs, and act like them as well. We explain the differences and their significance in 64.2, "Uniform Resource Identifiers", on page 1006. But unless we make a point of the difference in a specific context, you can safely treat them as equivalent when reading the book.

Now when you see *URI* in the text, you'll know that it isn't a typo.

---

4. Although dynamic HTML pages contain so much scripting that the phrase "HTML coding" is sometimes warranted.

6.10 | Documents and data

We presented the easy illustrated guide to the documents and data relationship in Chapter 3, "The XML usage spectrum", on page 60, but it's worth summarizing the high points here.

6.10.1 *It's all data!*

In an XML document, the text that isn't markup is data. You can edit it directly with an XML editor or plain text editor. With a stylesheet and a rendering system you can cause it to be displayed in various ways.

In a database, you can't touch the data directly. You can enter and revise it only through forms controlled by the database program. However, rendition is similar to XML documents, except that the stylesheet is usually called something like "report template".

The important thing is that, in both cases, the data can be kept in the abstract, untainted by the style information for rendering it. This is very different from word processing documents, of course, which normally keep their data in rendered form.

6.10.2 *Data-centric vs. document-centric*

Documents, data, and processes are sometimes characterized as "data-centric" in contrast to "document-centric". Since all XML documents (except empty ones) contain data, these terms are actually a misleading shorthand. Worse, they are applied in two very different contexts:

- how much the XML resembles relational data; and,
- whether you have to deal with the whole document at once.

6.10.2.1 How relational is it?

The *data-centric* misnomer is common among database hackers trying to describe structures that map easily onto relational tables and primitive datatypes. Structures that don't are called *document-centric*.

The intended meaning of data-centric is that the document structure – really element structure, since a document is essentially just the largest element – is *predictable*.

An element has a *strongly predictable structure* if it (and its subelements, if any) are constrained to contain either:

- type-sequenced elements (e.g., a sequence of elements of the types: `quantity`, `itemNum`, `description`, `price`),
- data characters only (i.e., #PCDATA), or
- nothing at all.

A business transaction document such as a purchase order is likely to be more predictable than a memo.

In addition to "data-centric", the misnomer *highly structured* is sometimes used. However, *highly predictable* would be a better term, particularly as many documents that don't meet our definition of "strongly predictable" are still much more predictable than they are freeform.

6.10.2.2   How granular is it?

Another (mis)use of *data-centric* is to characterize the storage and/or access of documents at the level of individual elements, rather than the entire document at once (*document-centric*). Once again, the usage is misleading because what it describes has nothing to do with data per se, and because it implies a contradiction between data and documents that does not exist.

6.10.3 *Comparing documents to data*

Since documents contain data, what are people doing when they compare or contrast documents and data?

They are being human. Which is to say, they are using a simplified expression for the complex and subtle relationship shown in Table 6-1. They are comparing the typical kind of data that is found in XML and word processing (WP) documents with business process (BP) transactional data, which usually resides in databases.

Table 6-1   (typical data in) **Documents and** (business process) **Data**

	XML data	**BP data**	**WP data**
Presentability	Abstraction	Abstraction	Rendition
Source	Written	Captured	Written
Structure	Hierarchy+ links	Fields	Paragraphs
Purpose	Presentation	Processing	Presentation
Representation	Document	Database	Document

Note that the characteristics in the table are typical, not fixed. For example, as we've shown many times in this book, XML data can be a rendition and WP data can be an abstraction. In addition, XML data could:

■ Be captured from a data entry form or a program (rather than written);

■ Consist of simple fields like those in a relational table (rather than a deeply nested hierarchy with links among the nodes); and

■ Be intended for processing (rather than presentation).

In casual use, the term "document" connotes the data characteristics shown in Table 6-1 for "XML data" or "WP data", whichever is being referred to.

When "data" is contrasted with "document", it means the "BP data" column of the table. However, in other contexts, it could refer to "XML data" or all data.

We are more specific whenever a different meaning is intended in this chapter (and elsewhere in the book).

Caution   The true relationship between documents and data isn't as widely understood as it ought to be, even among experts. That is in part because the two domains existed independently for so long. This fact can complicate communication.

6.11 | And in conclusion

The matrix in Figure 6-2 ties together a number of the concepts we've been discussing.

The top row contains two conceptual documents, as they might appear in your mind's eye. Actually, they are two states of the same document, the one we saw in Example 2-1.[5]

The left column shows the document in its abstract state, while the right column shows it rendered.

The bottom row shows the computer representations of the abstraction and the rendition. The abstraction uses the XML notation while the rendition uses HTML. The horizontal arrow indicates that the rendition was generated from the abstraction.

The diagram illustrates some important points:

- Abstraction and rendition are two *presentability* states that a document can be in. Renditions are ready to be presented; abstractions aren't.
- Renditions can be generated from abstractions automatically.
- Markup languages can represent both abstractions and renditions; "structuring in XML" is no guarantee that you'll get an abstraction.
- The *computer representation* of a document incorporates two ideas: presentability and notation. In other words, the

---

5. But for clarity only the second pair of QUESTION and ANSWER elements is shown here.

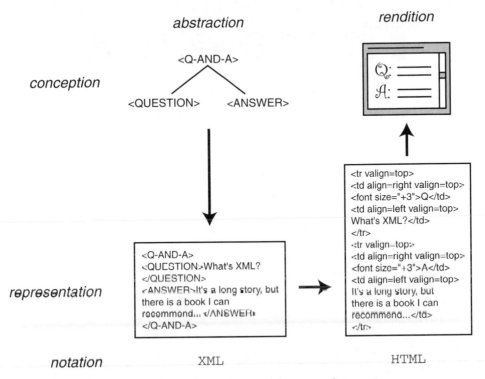

Figure 6-2   A rendition can be generated from an abstraction

representation of a document is either an abstraction or a rendition, and is either in an XML-based language or some other notation.

Hint   The road ahead diverges at this point. If your main interest is in what XML can do for you, rather than what makes it tick, proceed with the application and tool discussions in Part 2 through Part 14. On the other hand, if you took clocks apart as a child, you may want to read Part 15, Part 16, "Schema Tutorials", and Part 17, "Transform & Navigation Tutorials" before continuing.

Three-tier
applications

■ Content aggregation

■ Middle-tier servers

■ Data sources

Part Two

The advent of the personal computer (PC) popularized a two-tier networking model called *client/server*. Servers are typically large computers that control proprietary databases and act as *data sources*. They "serve" that data to end-users whose software, running on PCs (the "clients"), requests it.

Both client and server have to understand the proprietary representation in which the data is interchanged. And if a client needs data from several data sources, it has to deal with multiple servers and be able to understand the proprietary data formats of all of them.

XML is changing all that because it is a universal data representation. XML facilitates a *three-tier* model, in which a single *middle-tier* server can be an intermediary that aggregates data from multiple sources and presents all of it at once to the client.

In this part, we look at three-tier Web applications from all three sides. First we see the end-user's perspective from the client side, then take a closer look at how a middle-tier application works. Finally, we'll examine how remote data sources can deliver XML to the middle tier.

Personalized frequent-flyer website

Introductory Discussion

- Three-tier XML Web application

- What makes websites "hot"

- Client/server Web model has changed

- Website personalization

Contributing experts: Dianne Kennedy of XMLXperts Ltd., `http://www.xmlxperts.com`, and Bruce Sharpe of SoftQuad Inc., `http://www.sq.com`

Chapter

7

If the original frequent-flyer website model had been the ultimate in doing business on the Web, then business on the Web would never have taken off. This chapter explains how the middle tier gives a lift to those high-flying e-businesses.

f you travel by air, you have probably stopped by your favorite airline frequent flyer website. Let's consider how that experience would have been in the early days of the Web.

It might have been fun to find the site and to see all the last minute bargains offered for frequent flyers. Perhaps those specials were initially enough to motivate you to return to the site, if only to dream of taking a vacation in the middle of your biggest project!

7.1 | Client/server frequent-flyer sites

Beyond viewing the posted specials, perhaps you interacted with the site in a limited way, by entering your frequent flyer number to see your current point balance. But during heavy traffic hours on the Web, such interactions can take quite a long time.

And once you know how many points you've accumulated, what about the whole series of new questions it stimulates for which the website can't provide an answer. At that point, you must resort to calling the toll-free number to learn more about your award options and eventually book a flight.

Bottom line: once the novelty wears off, this Web experience, like countless others, is less than satisfying.

Figure 7-1   Three-tier XML processing architecture.

7.2 | What's wrong with this Web model?

The original Web model that we've described here is a "client/server" model. In this model, any personalized interaction takes place on the Web server you have contacted. As a result, there is little of it.

Instead, the Web pages you saw were static brochures rendered in HTML to provide eye-appealing display. In fact, some of the websites that were rated the "hottest" in that early market were those that provided multi-media sizzle – heavy on graphics, streaming media, animation, and sound. Personalized content, while an increasingly important consideration, had not yet become the primary distinguishing characteristic of a "hot" website. But as the Web continued its shift from simply providing entertainment value to facilitating business transactions, it became clear that personalization was the way to win customers.

In an airline frequent-flyer website, there is a great deal of HTML information that the customer can view. If this information and its associated links changes daily, the website becomes more interesting and is more likely to generate return visits. Likewise, interactivity generates more site traffic.

But in the two-tier client/server model, interactivity requires lengthy periods where the customer must be "connected" to remote servers. Queries from the customer go to the server, and resulting responses are shipped back to the customer for viewing in HTML. Unfortunately, a Web server can handle only a limited number of connections at one time.

Every time a new piece of information is requested, a transaction between the client's Web browser and remote Web servers is required. Sooner or later the number of transactions slows the server and the customer experiences lengthy time-outs when queries are processed and data is transferred back to the browser.

7.3 | A better model for doing business on the Web

Today, XML has enabled a new breed of Web server software, one that allows the Web developer to add a new "middle-tier" server to the Web model. This new three-tier Web architecture is illustrated in Figure 7-1.

Remember, in the old Web model, the customer using a browser on the client interacted directly with data sources on remote servers. The client maintained its connection throughout the interactive session. Each query was sent a response in HTML which could be directly viewed by the client browser. Maintaining the connection between the client and server was critical.

In the new three-tier Web model, the information that fits the profile of the customer is retrieved at once from remote data sources by software on the middle tier, either as XML documents or through an ODBC or similar database connection. From that point, continued interaction with the remote data sources is no longer required. The connection to the remote servers can be, and is, terminated.[1]

Once all information that fits the customer profile has been assembled by software on the middle tier, it is sent in XML to the client. Now the requirement for further interaction between the client and the middle-tier server is eliminated as well.

Figure 7-2   "Welcome to *Softland Air*"

Rich XML data, directly usable by client applications and scripting languages like *JavaScript*, has been delivered to the client. The connection

---

1. Incidentally, the term "three-tier" is a relative one. Any of the remote data sources could itself be the client of a three-tier application, so if you are actually counting tiers between the end user and the farthest data source, the number could be much higher than three. Nevertheless, the architectural model remains three-tiered.

between the client and middle-tier server can now be terminated. At this point, all computing becomes client-based, resulting in a much more efficient use of the Web and a much more satisfying customer experience.

To understand the new three-tier Web model better, one must understand the role XML plays as an enabling technology. One must also understand how efficient delivery of structured abstract data to the client makes all the difference.

7.4 | An XML-enabled frequent-flyer website

Initially, differences between the *Softland Air* XML-enabled frequent-flyer website shown in Figure 7-2 and those early sites may not be apparent. Both provide a pleasing HTML rendered site brochure. Both enable you to select the services you wish to use. But here the similarities end. New business functions, not possible with non-XML sites, quickly become apparent.

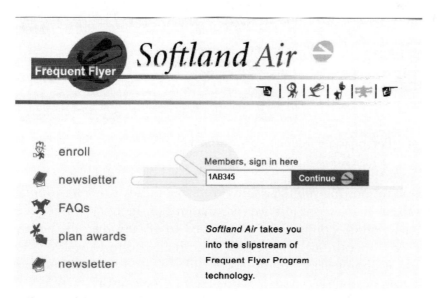

Figure 7-3 "Members, sign in here"

From the initial *Softland Air* screen you can select the "frequent flyer" option, which causes the page in Figure 7-3 to be displayed. The frequent-flyer page asks you to enter your membership identification number.

Once you have entered your membership number, a personalized, interactive Web experience begins. The next screen that is displayed (Figure 7-4) not only returns your number of frequent flyer points, but shows you destinations for which you have already qualified for awards. This screen will vary from member to member, based upon the points a member has in the frequent-flyer database and other personal information the database holds, such as city of origin.

Figure 7-4   Personalized frequent-flyer information

In addition to showing you the awards you have already earned, the *Softland Air* website enables you to select destinations of interest. You can see that you have 46,000 points and are qualified to go anywhere in North America in economy through first class. You can also go to Hawaii or the Caribbean by economy class. You do not qualify to go to Europe, but you can see that you nearly have enough points for a European trip.

Suppose you are interested in going to Europe. To learn more about options to get there, you would select a destination on the "Awards Specials" part of the screen. This destination information is added to your profile, along with your city of origin and the number of points you currently have. It will be used to personalize the ongoing transactions.

Once you have selected a destination, the Web page in Figure 7-5 shows you awards, both on *Softland Air* and on partner airlines, that fit the destination you have selected. From this screen you can see what destinations in Europe most nearly fit with the number of award points you hold. As you do not currently qualify for a trip to Europe, you can use the "Planned Trips" portion of the screen to determine what trips you can take by this summer in order to qualify for the award you want.

Figure 7-5   Trip planning

Using the screen in Figure 7-5, you can plan trips and even book tickets. In this way you can put enough miles in the bank to be able to earn the award to Europe.

Notice how the entire transaction is personalized for the client interacting with the website. It is also important to note that aside from logging on to enter your membership number and select the frequent-flyer transaction, all other transactions occurred on the PC in your home or office. Because the middle-tier server can aggregate data from remote sources, package it as XML documents, and send it to the client, a continuous connection to the data source servers is not required.

This model is one that leading business sites on the Web have striven for and can now achieve. And XML, working with an information server in the middle tier, is the reason.

7.5 | Understanding the *Softland Air* scenario

When you connect to the *Softland Air* website you first sign in with your membership ID. Your membership number is used to extract your name, the number of award points you have earned, and your city of origin from the "member information" database. This information is sent from remote data sources to the middle-tier server, which combines it into an XML document (see Example 7-1). Once the data is in XML, the member name, city of origin, and number of award points can be addressed and used by middle-tier and client applications.

Example 7-1. XML document generated from member information database

```
<CUSTOMER
  MEMBERID="1AB345"
  FIRST="Bruce"
  LAST="Sharpe"
  POINTS="46000"
  CITY="Vancouver"/>
```

At this point, the middle-tier software knows who signed on. It can request all relevant awards information from both its own awards database and the remote databases maintained by its partner airlines. Example 7-2 shows the XML data for award specials items from remote awards databases. Note that because this data is in XML, we can easily see the number of points required for each award, the partner airline name, the city of origin, the destination, and the dates the special runs. Again, this information is available for use by both middle-tier and client-side processing based on member queries.

Example 7-2. XML document generated from award specials database

```
<special_item
  economy="50000"
  business ="60000"
  first   ="70000"
  partner_name="Sperling Airlines"
  from_city="Vancouver"
  to_city="Paris"
  start   ="02/Apr/1998"
  end   ="Aug 30"/>
<special_item
  economy="52000"
  business ="62000"
  first   ="72000"
  partner_name="Sperling Airlines"
  from_city="Vancouver"
  to_city="Frankfurt"
  start   ="02/Apr/1998"
  end   ="Sep 30"/>
<special_item
  economy="50000"
  business="60000"
  first="70000"
  partner_name="Trillium Airways"
  from_city="Vancouver"
  to_city="London"
  start="01/Apr/1998"
  end="Jul 30"/>
```

The middle-tier server can also request all planned flight point earnings from all remote flight information databases, as shown in Example 7-3. We can easily see the number of points that would be earned from each flight, the partner airline name, the city of origin, the destination, and the date of flight and class of service. This information is available for use by middle-tier and client-side processing.

The information that is sent to the middle tier is compact, personalized, and precise. It differs from HTML because it contains the actual abstract data, not the look of the screen. Middle-tier software acts to assemble and deliver the right information at the right time, minimizing Web traffic and providing a higher degree of user interaction and satisfaction.

Example 7-3. XML document with flight point earnings

```
<flight
    points="10000"
    partner_name = "Sperling Airlines"
    from_city = "Vancouver"
    to_city = "New York"
    depart="Jun 01"
    flightclass="business"/>
<flight
    points="15000"
    partner_name = "Trillium Airways"
    from_city = "Vancouver"
    to_city = "New York"
    depart="Jul 21"
    flightclass="business"/>
```

7.6 | Towards the Brave New Web

The World Wide Web continues to evolve rapidly. Today the hottest websites are still those that provide multimedia sizzle. But as the shift continues from simply providing entertainment value to facilitating business transactions, dynamic personalized content is increasingly becoming hot.

Products like those described in this book allow the website developer to add a new middle-tier server to the Web model. It is this middle tier that enables business transactions in a way that was simply not possible before XML.

The *Softland Air* scenario shows how a middle-tier server, using XML as a structured information interchange representation, enables personalized data aggregation and organization from multiple remote data sources, and interactive delivery to client browsers based upon end-user requirements.

Building an online auction website

Application Discussion

▮ Three-tier Web application

▮ Dynamic generation of XML documents

▮ Extracting data from XML documents

▮ Creating a user interface

▮ Demo on CD-ROM

Sponsor: Microsoft Corporation, `http://msdn.microsoft.com/xml`

Contributing expert: Charles Heinemann

Chapter

8

An online auction is the epitome of a complex real-time interactive application – not to mention being the hottest business-to-consumer (B2C) business model on the Web! This chapter describes a realistic *Auction Demo* that shows that even complex applications can be based on straightforward use of the three-tier Web architecture.

T he *Auction Demo* is a three tier Web application that simulates an online auction using technologies that have been available since *Internet Explorer 5.01* (IE 5.01). It allows you to view the items available for auction, place bids on those items, and monitor the bids placed by fellow bidders.

Like other three-tier Web applications, the *Auction Demo* has data sources on the back end, a user interface on the client, and a Web server in the middle. We'll see how it was developed, using just three permanent Web pages:

userInterface.htm

This page uses *Dynamic HTML* (DHTML) to allow the Web browser to present the auction information to the user. It contains scripts that collect or update data on the middle tier by requesting *Active Server Pages* (ASP).

auction.asp

This page is an ASP file. When userInterface.htm requests this page, the scripts in it are executed on the server. The scripts generate auction.xml, an XML document that contains the latest auction data, which is delivered to the client.

makebid.asp

This page is requested by userInterface.htm when the user wants to make a bid. It is executed on the middle tier, causing the data source to be updated with the new bid information.

The user interface (UI) for the *Auction Demo* is shown in Figure 8-1. It is the rendition of the userInterface.htm *Dynamic HTML* page, which is downloaded to the client when the user clicks on a link to the auction.

That page has scripts within it that handle all the client-side activity. That includes requesting data from the middle tier in order to display the most current values of the items and bids. We'll see later how the UI page does its thing, but first let's look at how the middle tier collects and transmits the data. It does so by packaging the data as XML documents.

8.1 | Getting data from the middle tier

The role of the middle tier in a Web application is to gather information from data sources and deliver it in a consistent manner to clients. In the *Auction Demo* we start with a single data source, an ODBC-compliant database. (Later we'll see how multiple data sources of different kinds can be accessed.)

The "Auction" database used for the *Auction Demo* is a relational database with two tables, an "Item" table and a "Bids" table. The "Item" table contains data about each of the items up for auction. It is shown in Figure 8-2.

For the sake of clarity, we'll just cover the "Item" table in this chapter (the "Bids" are handled similarly). You can see the full demo in the Microsoft folder on the CD-ROM. We want to deliver the data in that table in the form of an XML document, so the client's user interface page won't have to know anything about the actual data source.

Figure 8-1   The *Auction Demo* user interface.

Title	Artist	Dimensions	Materials	Year
Vase and Stones	Linda Mann	20x30 inches	Oil	1996
Still Life / Onions	Linda Mann	20x30 inches	Oil	1997
Sandstone	Linda Mann	20x30 inches	Oil	1995
Jewelry Box	Linda Mann	20x30 inches	Oil	1994
Personal Objects	Linda Mann	20x30 inches	Oil	1995
Still Life / Sweets	Linda Mann	20x30 inches	Oil	1994
Bread and Apples	Linda Mann	20x30 inches	Oil	1995
Rabbits	Linda Mann	20x30 inches	Oil	1996
Risotto	Linda Mann	20x30 inches	Oil	1995

Figure 8-2   The *Auction Demo* item table.

8.1.1   *Defining the XML document structure*

The key to creating useful XML documents is the proper structuring of the data. For the *Auction Demo*, that means deciding how a record in the "Item" table will be represented as an ITEM element in XML. There is a straightforward mapping, shown in the data-less element in Example 8-1.

Example 8-1. Template for an ITEM element

```
<ITEM>
  <TITLE></TITLE>
  <ARTIST></ARTIST>
  <DIMENSIONS></DIMENSIONS>
  <MATERIALS></MATERIALS>
  <YEAR></YEAR>
</ITEM>
```

For each field in the "Item" table, there is a corresponding subelement of the ITEM element.

To generate XML documents with these ITEM elements, the *Auction Demo* uses ASP files.

8.1.2   *Using ASP files to generate XML documents*

XML can be generated on the middle tier using *Active Server Pages*. ASP offers an environment in which Web authors can create documents dynamically by intermixing markup languages with in-line scripts. The scripts can be written in a variety of scripting languages, including *JScript* and *VBScript*, and can invoke server-side components to access databases, execute applications, and process information.

When a browser requests an ASP file, it is first processed by the server, which delivers a generated Web page containing standard markup.

In an ASP file, commands and scripts are delimited by "<%" and "%>". Everything not so delimited is markup or data that will appear in the generated page. For example, consider the trivial ASP file in Example 8-2.

Example 8-2. Sample ASP file

```
<%@ LANGUAGE = VBScript%>
<%DIM Total = 2%>
<AMOUNT><%=Total%></AMOUNT>
```

The file, after establishing that the scripting language is *VBScript*, creates the variable "Total" with the value "2". The following line generates an XML AMOUNT element whose content is generated by executing the small script, which in this case retrieves the value of "Total".

When the browser requests this file, it will actually receive the XML document that is generated from the file, as shown in Example 8-3.

Example 8-3. XML document generated by sample ASP file

```
<AMOUNT>2</AMOUNT>
```

Note that the ASP syntax (<%...%>) does not cause an XML parsing error. That is because the ASP file is not itself an XML document. The ASP file is processed on the server and only the generated XML document is returned to the client.

In the case of the *Auction Demo*, the file auction.asp is used to access the "Auction" database and generate XML containing the data within the "Item" and "Bids" tables. The ability to generate XML on the middle tier makes it possible to provide the Web application with content that can be manipulated on the client and refreshed without having to refresh the entire user interface.

In Example 8-4, auction.asp begins like the ASP file in Example 8-2, by declaring the scripting language. The next two lines are the XML declaration and the start-tag of the root element (AUCTIONBLOCK) of the XML document to be generated, which we will call "auction.xml".

Example 8-4. Start of auction.asp

```
<%@ LANGUAGE = VBScript %>
<?xml version="1.0"?>
<AUCTIONBLOCK>
```

Next, a connection to the "Auction" database is established and that connection is opened:

Example 8-5. Connecting to the database

```
<%
Set Conn = Server.CreateObject("ADODB.Connection")
Conn.Open "Auction","Auction","Auction"
%>
```

A "record set" variable (ItemRS) is now established to contain each record of the "Item" table as it is accessed, and a "Do While" loop is begun to perform the access.

Example 8-6. Preparing to access the "Item" records

```
<%
Set ItemRS = Conn.Execute("select * from item")
Do While Not ItemRS.EOF
%>
```

Next, the template in Example 8-1 is used to create the XML ITEM element that will be generated. Just as in Example 8-2, a small script is inserted as the content of each subelement of ITEM within auction.asp. In this case, the script extracts the corresponding field's data from the record set.

Example 8-7. Markup and scripts to generate an ITEM element

```
<ITEM>
   <TITLE><%=ItemRS("Title")%></TITLE>
   <ARTIST><%=ItemRS("Artist")%></ARTIST>
   <DIMENSIONS><%=ItemRS("Dimensions")%></DIMENSIONS>
   <MATERIALS><%=ItemRS("Materials")%></MATERIALS>
   <YEAR><%=ItemRS("Year")%></YEAR>
</ITEM>
```

After an ITEM element is generated, the script moves to the next record in the record set. The loop is then repeated. Once all of the records have been run through, the root element is ended.

Example 8-8. Repeating the loop and ending the document

```
<%
   ItemRS.MoveNext
Loop
%>
</AUCTIONBLOCK>
```

The complete auction.asp file is in Example 8-9.

Example 8-10 is an abridged version of the XML document (auction.xml) generated by the auction.asp file in Example 8-9.

8.1.3 *Generating XML from multiple databases*

One powerful reason to generate XML documents on the middle tier is that they can contain data that is sourced from multiple independent databases. The technique is similar to what we've already seen. The only difference is that multiple database connections are made instead of one.

The ASP file in Example 8-11 does just this, generating a single XML document with data from the databases "Gallery1" and "Gallery2".

Example 8-9. The complete auction.asp file

```
<%@ LANGUAGE = VBScript %>
<?xml version="1.0"?>
<AUCTIONBLOCK>
<%
Set Conn = Server.CreateObject("ADODB.Connection")
Conn.Open "Auction","Auction","Auction"
Set ItemRS = Conn.Execute("select * from item")
Do While Not ItemRS.EOF
%>
  <ITEM>
    <TITLE><%=ItemRS("Title")%></TITLE>
    <ARTIST><%=ItemRS("Artist")%></ARTIST>
    <DIMENSIONS><%=ItemRS("Dimensions")%></DIMENSIONS>
    <MATERIALS><%=ItemRS("Materials")%></MATERIALS>
    <YEAR><%=ItemRS("Year")%></YEAR>
  </ITEM>
<%
  ItemRS.MoveNext
Loop
%>
</AUCTIONBLOCK>
```

Example 8-10. Abridged auction.xml document generated by auction.asp

```
<?xml version="1.0"?>
<AUCTIONBLOCK>
  <ITEM>
    <TITLE>Vase and Stones</TITLE>
    <ARTIST>Linda Mann</ARTIST>
    <DIMENSIONS>20 X 30 inches</DIMENSIONS>
    <MATERIALS>Oil</MATERIALS>
    <YEAR>1996</YEAR>
  </ITEM>
  <ITEM>
  . . .
  </ITEM>
  . . .
</AUCTIONBLOCK>
```

The XML generated by the ASP file in Example 8-11 looks structurally just like Example 8-10, an AUCTIONBLOCK element with multiple ITEM children. However, the data content originates from two different data sources.

Also notice that, for the DIMENSIONS, MATERIALS, and YEAR elements, the source fields in the "Gallery2" database are actually labeled differently from

Example 8-11. Generating one XML document from two databases

```
<%@ LANGUAGE = VBScript %>
<?xml version="1.0"?>
<AUCTIONBLOCK>
<%
'Connect to the Gallery1 database data source
Set Conn = Server.CreateObject("ADODB.Connection")
Conn.Open "Gallery1","Gallery1","Gallery1"
Set ItemRS = Conn.Execute("select * from item")
Do While Not ItemRS.EOF
%>
  <ITEM>
    <TITLE><%=ItemRS("Title")%></TITLE>
    <ARTIST><%=ItemRS("Artist")%></ARTIST>
    <DIMENSIONS><%=ItemRS("Dimensions")%></DIMENSIONS>
    <MATERIALS><%=ItemRS("Materials")%></MATERIALS>
    <YEAR><%=ItemRS("Year")%></YEAR>
  </ITEM>
<%
  ItemRS.MoveNext
Loop
'Connect to the Gallery2 database data source
Set Conn = Server.CreateObject("ADODB.Connection")
Conn.Open "Gallery2","Gallery2","Gallery2"
Set ItemRS = Conn.Execute("select * from item")
Do While Not ItemRS.EOF
%>
  <ITEM>
    <TITLE><%=ItemRS("Title")%></TITLE>
    <ARTIST><%=ItemRS("Artist")%></ARTIST>
    <DIMENSIONS><%=ItemRS("Size")%></DIMENSIONS>
    <MATERIALS><%=ItemRS("Medium")%></MATERIALS>
    <YEAR><%=ItemRS("Date")%></YEAR>
  </ITEM>
<%
  ItemRS.MoveNext
Loop
%>
</AUCTIONBLOCK>
```

the corresponding fields in "Gallery1." One benefit of consolidating the data on the middle tier is that the semantics can be identified consistently, and therefore made more easily accessible.

8.1.4 *Generating XML from both databases and XML data sources*

The middle tier can source data of different kinds, not just databases. In Example 8-12, the ASP file, as in previous examples, first accesses data from "Gallery 1", an ODBC compliant database. However, it then adds data from "Gallery 3", a source of XML documents.

The Gallery3 XML document is processed by the *MSXML* parser (details below), which allows access to the document's data content. Note that there is no way – and no need – to tell whether Gallery3 is a persistent document, or was generated by another middle-tier application.

8.2 | Building the user interface

The user interface is critical to the success of any application. It must allow the user to interact with the application in an efficient and straightforward manner. The user interface for the *Auction Demo* was built using DHTML.

DHTML is a set of features introduced in *Internet Explorer 4.0* for creating interactive and visually interesting Web pages. It is based on existing HTML standards and is designed to work well with applications, *ActiveX* controls, and other embedded objects.

With DHTML a developer can create a robust and efficient UI without additional support from applications or embedded controls, or even return trips to the server. A *Dynamic HTML* page is self-contained, using styles and scripts to process user input and directly manipulate the HTML markup and other text within the page.

Let's see how userInterface.htm creates the *Auction Demo* interface by using scripts and the W3C Document Object Model. Two basic techniques are employed: procedural scripts and descriptive binding.

8.2.1 *Using procedural scripts*

Internet Explorer 5.01 includes the *MSXML* parser, which exposes the parsed XML document as a Document Object Model. Once exposed, scripts can access the data content of the XML elements and dynamically insert the data into the user interface.

Example 8-12. Generating one XML document from a database and another XML document

```
<%@ LANGUAGE = VBScript %>
<?xml version="1.0"?>
<AUCTIONBLOCK>
<%
'Connect to the Gallery1 database data source
Set Conn = Server.CreateObject("ADODB.Connection")
Conn.Open "Gallery1","Gallery1","Gallery1"
Set ItemRS = Conn.Execute("select * from item")
Do While Not ItemRS.EOF
%>
  <ITEM>
     <TITLE><%=ItemRS("Title")%></TITLE>
     <ARTIST><%=ItemRS("Artist")%></ARTIST>
     <DIMENSIONS><%=ItemRS("Dimensions")%></DIMENSIONS>
     <MATERIALS><%=ItemRS("Materials")%></MATERIALS>
     <YEAR><%=ItemRS("Year")%></YEAR>
  </ITEM>
<%
  ItemRS.MoveNext
Loop
'Connect to the Gallery3 XML document data source
Set XML = Server.CreateObject("MSXML2.DOMDocument")
XML.setProperty("ServerHTTPRequest",true)
XML.load("http://datasource3/Gallery3.xml")
Set Items = XML.documentElement.childNodes
For I = 0 to Items.length - 1
  Set Item = Items.childNodes.item(I)
%>
  <ITEM>
     <TITLE><%=Item.childNodes.item(0).text%></TITLE>
     <ARTIST><%=Item.childNodes.item(1).text%></ARTIST>
     <DIMENSIONS><%=Item.childNodes.item(2).text%></DIMENSIONS>
     <MATERIALS><%=Item.childNodes.item(3).text%></MATERIALS>
     <YEAR><%=Item.childNodes.item(4).text%></YEAR>
  </ITEM>
<%
Next
%>
</AUCTIONBLOCK>
```

The userInterface.htm code in Example 8-13 applies *MSXML* to auction.xml, the XML document generated by auction.asp. That creates an *ActiveX* object representing the parsed document.

Example 8-13. Creating the auction document object

```
var auction = new ActiveXObject("MSXML2.DOMDocument");
auction.load("http://Webserver/auction.asp");
```

In Example 8-14, the script next retrieves the root element. It then navigates the tree until it locates the TITLE element within the first ITEM element of auction.xml. The innerText property is used to insert the data content of TITLE into the user interface as the value of the item_title attribute, which appears on a DIV element.

Example 8-14. Extracting data from the auction document object

```
var root = auction.documentElement;
var item0 = root.childNodes.item(0);
var title = item0.childNodes.item(0).text;
document.all("item_title").innerText = title;
<DIV ID="item_title"></DIV>
```

One of the benefits of using procedural scripts to display XML documents is that you can manipulate the data content of an XML element before you display it. For example, if you wanted to display the dimensions of each painting using the metric system, rather than feet and inches, your script could simply convert the content of the DIMENSIONS element from inches to centimeters.

8.2.2 *Using descriptive data binding*

The *XML Data Source Object* (XML DSO) is a declarative alternative to the procedural scripts described in the last section. It enables the data of XML elements to be bound as the content of HTML documents.

Example 8-15. An *XML Data Source Object*

```
<XML ID="auction" SRC="auction.asp"></XML>
```

An XML DSO is shown in Example 8-15. It is an XML element that assigns the ID "auction" to the data source "auction.asp", which causes auction.xml to be generated on the middle tier. A persistent XML data source could also have been used.

In Example 8-16, data binding is used to populate the part of the user interface that shows the painting and the caption beneath it. No scripting is needed. Instead, the SPAN elements identify the "auction" DSO as the pointer to the data source and the XML element type name as the DATAFLD to be bound.

Example 8-16. Data binding with the XML DSO

```
<TD>
  <DIV STYLE="margin-left:16px;margin-top:16px;margin-right:16px">
    <DIV ID=pict></DIV>
    <DIV CLASS="details">
      <SPAN DATASRC=#auction DATAFLD=MATERIALS></SPAN>,
      <SPAN DATASRC=#auction DATAFLD=YEAR></SPAN>,
      <SPAN DATASRC=#auction DATAFLD=DIMENSIONS></SPAN>
    </DIV>
  </DIV>
</TD>
```

One advantage of displaying XML with the XML DSO is that the XML document is processed asynchronously to the rendering of the page. Therefore, if the inventory of paintings were very large, the initial elements of the XML document could be displayed even before the last elements were processed.

8.3 | Updating the data source from the client

We have seen how userInterface.htm on the client obtained data to display to the user by invoking auction.asp on the middle tier. It can also enable the user to make his own bid by invoking another middle tier page, makebid.asp.

In the *Auction Demo*, the user bids by overwriting the price and bidder name in the first row of the bid table. A bid therefore consists of the "title" of the item currently displayed, the "price" of the new bid, and the name of the new "bidder".

These data items must be passed as parameters to makebid.asp, which executes a script to process them and update the database. The script returns to the client a "return message" XML document: a single element containing information about the status of the processing.

The script in userInterface.htm (see Example 8-17) begins by assigning the title of the current item up for auction to the "title" variable, the value of the "price" text box to the "price" variable, and the value of the "bidder" text box to the "bidder" variable.

It then creates the return message document object, which will state whether makebid.asp successfully updated the database. The three variables are passed as parameters to the ASP file when it is invoked.

Example 8-17. Sending a new bid to makebid.asp

```
var title = current_item.childNodes.item(0).text;
var price = price.value;
var bidder = bidder.value;
var returnMsg = new ActiveXObject("MSXML2.DOMDocument");
returnMsg.load("http://auction/makebid.asp?title=" +
  title + "&price=" + price + "&bidder=" + bidder;
```

In Example 8-18, makebid.asp (called by userInterface.htm in Example 8-17) assigns the values of the parameters "title", "price", and "bidder" to variables with the same names.

The "BidRS" record set object is then created and a connection to the "Auction" database is made. Note that the connection is made for both reading and writing. The "Bids" table is then opened and the new information is added to the record set, after which the connection is closed. The process is much the same as it was for auction.asp, except that the database is written to instead of just being read.

Finally, makebid.asp generates the return message document with the status of the update.

Example 8-18. The makebid.asp file updates the database

```
<%@ LANGUAGE = VBScript %>
<%
title = Request.QueryString("title")
price = Request.QueryString("price")
bidder = Request.QueryString("bidder")

Set BidRS = Server.CreateObject("ADODB.RecordSet")
connect = "data source=Auction;user id=sa;password=;"
BidRS.CursorType = 2
BidRS.LockType = 3  ' read/write
BidRS.Open "Bids", connect

BidRS.AddNew
BidRS("item") = title
BidRS("price") = price
BidRS("bidder") = bidder
BidRS.Update
BidRS.Close
%>
<STATUS>OK</STATUS>
```

8.4 | Conclusion

The entire *Auction Demo* was built using the methods described above. You can get a head start on building a similar Web application by modifying these scripts to suit your particular requirements.

XML enables Web applications by providing dynamic, accessible content that can be navigated and manipulated on the client. In addition, it enables the updating of content without having to refresh the entire user interface. This ability saves time by reducing round trips to the server for information that already exists on the client.

With XML, users can manage data over the Internet just as they presently do on their local machines. As a result, the Web is made a more interactive and interoperable medium. As the information superhighway has transformed itself into the data superhighway, Web applications similar to the *Auction Demo* are allowing far better utilization of the vast resources made available by the Web.

Analysis   The Auction Demo clearly illustrates the architecture of a three-tier application. It uses the middle tier as a transient data aggregator and normalizer. In the next chapter we take a closer look at how data sources can generate XML for use by middle-tier servers.

Enabling data sources for XML

Case Study

- ▌ InetPurchasing.Com
- ▌ Dynamic data sources
- ▌ Catalog creation and dissemination
- ▌ Software on CD-ROM

Sponsor: Vertical Computer Systems/Emily Solutions,
http://www.emilysolutions.com

Contributing expert: Jeff Davison

One of the toughest jobs for developers of middle-tier applications is accessing and converting data from a multitude of sources. XML helps, of course, but even with XML there are challenges of data conversion and dissimilar vocabularies. Here's how one company was able to shift that burden onto the data sources, with happy results for all concerned.

M iddle-tier servers deliver to clients information that the servers aggregate from multiple data sources. At some point in that process, the data is converted to XML if it wasn't that way from the start. Even if it was, it might have used a different vocabulary, in which case the aggregation process would include converting it to the vocabulary of the aggregated information.

9.1 | XML data sources

In our examples so far, the data sources have either been relational databases or XML documents. That tends to be true in the real world as well, but "XML document" offers a lot of scope for variety. That's because the document doesn't have to be a persistent one. It could be generated by the data source to deliver information produced in real time by a complex process.

9.1.1 *Dynamic data sources*

We've seen plenty of websites that present weather information to readers. But consider a situation where an application program needs to get the outside temperature in order to accomplish some particular function. For instance, a program that is supposed to shut down some piece of machinery if the outside temperature is too high or too low.

Traditionally, to get the current outside temperature into a program, the programmer would have to interface with a sensor of some sort. That would entail a direct hardware hookup, replete with interface cabling and driver software.

How much more convenient it would be if the application programmer could get the temperature in a similar way to the end user, with a URL. The program could just link to the network location of an XML document that contains the desired information, download it via HTTP, and parse it to get the temperature values.

Several websites actually provide such a service. They offer various XML documents describing real-time temperature, humidity, and forecasts for many cities and regions.

9.1.2 *Converting to XML*

There is no question that such services free the data consumer of a major effort, hooking up temperature and humidity sensors. The current temperature (along with any other XML data item on the Web) is available as a service to any program that wishes to use it (and if necessary, pay for it). The fact that the temperature data is maintained by a website in a different state, or even a different country, is immaterial to the consuming program. The only thing that is relevant is that an XML document containing the local area weather can be pulled from the Web and easily parsed.

That leaves just one critical question: How does the service provider convert the sensor data to XML in the first place? In most cases, the first step in this or similar data capture situations is to store the data in a relational database. The database would probably have a simple schema, with each sensor reading stored as a record with fields for `date`, `time`, `location`, `temperature`, and so on.

We saw in the previous chapter how a middle-tier application can convert such database records to XML documents by using scripts in a Web page. The process is called *data binding*. In this case, the provider of the weather service wants to make things easier for its customers by performing the data binding itself. It may also want to publicize the service so others can find it.

Many tools are available for these purposes; we'll look at one shortly. But first, let's consider a burning question.

9.1.3 *Is this a Web service?*

As the chapter started, we were discussing "the delivery of XML documents". At this point we're talking in terms of "a service of collecting weather data, which is delivered in the form of XML documents". We've shifted the focus to the creation of the documents, but in other respects there is no real difference.

A search engine like *Google*, for example, is similar in that it also offers a service, except that it delivers its output as HTML pages rather than XML. In other words, Web-based services are as old as the Web itself.

But *Web services*, the idea that is getting all of the hype of late, is slightly different. If you recall our introduction to the subject in 2.11.4, "Web services (WSDL, UDDI)", on page 58, the newer, hyped Web services concept involves more standardization of the way in which service providers and service requestors communicate. There is also more emphasis on the discovery of services through a third party, called a *service broker*, also by means of standardized descriptions and protocols.

The ultimate vision for the new Web services is universal discovery and purchase of services from previously unknown providers, a very different world from what we have today, on or off the Web. But even as the industry promotes and begins to implement that vision, the classic Web-based services continue. Other XML-based techniques are providing simpler deployment and access options for smaller companies and narrower communities of interest.

For these situations, the benefits of the new Web services standards – universal reach and service anonymity – aren't needed and don't justify their cost and complexity (not to mention the wait for stable technology and universal acceptance). We discuss the vision, and the underlying reality, in detail in Part 13, "Web Services", on page 668. But for now, let's look at simpler means to achieve a less ambitious – but sufficient – result. We'll use the experience of a real company to illustrate.

9.2 | InetPurchasing.Com

InetPurchasing.Com provides Web based buying services for state government agencies in the U.S. To do this, it collects product and pricing information for all sorts of stuff: from paper clips, to computer systems, to jet fuel. It is a Web-based service for buying things over the Web, tailored for the requirements of government purchasing.

9.2.1 *Data acquisition*

The company needs to acquire product information from large numbers of different types of vendors. It must aggregate this information into a single relational database so that product characteristics, prices, availability, and delivery options can be compared and alternatives presented to its end users: government buyers.

There is an obvious problem: How does it get all the product, price and delivery information from all suppliers into its database? This data must be acquired in near real-time since prices and availability are subject to change for each supplier. Suppliers were willing to cooperate to a fair degree, since it improved their chances of getting orders.

Three methods of getting the product information were considered. Let's look at them.

9.2.1.1   Email

One possibility was to have each vendor email its product catalogs in a specific file representation, such as a particular spreadsheet format. The idea was rejected because it would have required an army of people to load the spreadsheet data into the database. A system that utilized this approach would not even be close to a real-time system.

9.2.1.2   HTML

Another approach was to collect URLs of product catalogs in HTML that each vendor made available on its own website. So-called *screen scraping* programs would parse the HTML and extract the data.

This technique was actually implemented. It had the benefit of near real-time update, but suppliers had to conform to rigorous layout standards in constructing their HTML-based catalogs. For example, product data had to be entered as a five-column table and no other markup could be used. That's because InetPurchasing.Com's software needed *abstract* product data, while HTML is designed to describe *rendered* Web pages.

9.2.1.3   XML

Ultimately, the company asked suppliers to create XML documents describing their products, and to submit URLs for those documents. This approach achieved the same near real-time availability as HTML. However, instead of rendition-oriented elements like `table` and `row`, the XML documents contained meaningful abstract elements, such as `item`, `description`, and `price`.

9.2.2   *Implementing the middle tier*

InetPurchasing.Com needed XML middleware to aggregate the product information from the vendors and make it available to the buyers.

9.2.2.1   System architecture

Figure 9-1 shows the system architecture. There are three major components – aggregator, directory, and vendors – each implemented with a product from Emily Systems.

aggregator

> The content aggregator, implemented with the *XML Portal* product, is shown in the upper center. Its role is to search the directory for relevant URLs and retrieve the XML documents from the vendor data sources. In this particular application, the aggregator loads the aggregated XML documents into a relational database that the buyers' client software can manipulate directly. It also creates HTML renditions of the aggregated data.

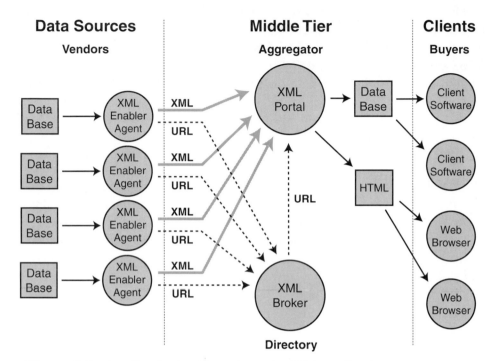

Figure 9-1   InetPurchasing.Com three-tier Web application

directory

> Vendors register the URLs of their product catalogs with a directory, shown at the lower center. The directory is implemented with *XML Broker*, a search engine that receives the URLs and performs some validation of the documents.

vendors

> Each vendor must create one or more product catalogs in XML, place them at a website, and submit the catalog URLs to the directory. To facilitate this, each vendor utilizes Emily's *XML Agent*, an adaptation of an HTTP server with tools for XML data binding and for registering URLs with directories.

9.2.2.2   System flow

To summarize the flow in Figure 9-1, multiple vendors convert database data into XML product catalogs and register the catalog URLs with the directory. The aggregator searches the directory for the documents, retrieves them directly from the vendors, and loads their data into a relational database. The net result is that many separate databases, under the control of different vendors, are aggregated into a single database.

Although the aggregator and the directory could have been implemented as a single program, there is value in their being distinct. The job of the directory is to collect URLs into a search engine database, whereas the job of the aggregator is to collect and process actual XML data. This division enhances scalability of the system.

Moreover, it is possible to mix-and-match directory sites and aggregator sites. Any directory can feed URL information to many different aggregators, and each aggregator can search the URLs from many different directories.

Finally, note that the aggregator produces two outputs:

- A relational database containing the aggregated data, to allow product comparisons and direct access by client software.
- HTML pages to display the aggregated data in a browser.

As a result, Emily's *XML Portal* simultaneously supports the aggregator as middleware for both a normal Web shopping portal and for specialized purchasing software implemented by the buyers on their own systems.

9.2.3 *Enabling the data sources*

The InetPurchasing.Com system is unusual in placing the burden of data binding on the vendors, rather than on the middle-tier aggregator. Each vendor is obliged to produce a catalog in XML that conforms to a DTD that the aggregator can accept. The vendors also have the responsibility of registering their catalog URLs with the directory.

The vendors are motivated to participate in the system because they want the increased business that will result. But there is a limit to the resources they can invest and, for smaller vendors, to the complexity they can handle. The process had to be as simple and inexpensive as possible for them.

The company's solution was to give each vendor a copy of *XML Enabler Agent*.

9.2.3.1   *XML Enabler Agent* functions

The vendor interface of the product is shown in Figure 9-2.[1] The vendors used it to perform the following functions:

Figure 9-2   *XML Enabler Agent* vendor interface

catalog creation
> The program accesses data from a relational database and generates an XML document, including a DTD and XSDL schema definition. A unique URL is assigned to the catalog document.

catalog registration
> A wizard guides the vendor in registering a catalog in the directory.

---

1. A copy of the program is available on the companion CD-ROM to this book.

catalog de-registration
> There is a tool for removing a registered ("published") URL from the directory.

support functions
> There are also tools to set up database drivers, authorize access to the system, and perform general-purpose queries on the database.

There was an added benefit for the vendors. The product is capable of creating multiple catalogs from the same database, each satisfying the requirements of a specific directory or aggregator, and each conforming to a different DTD. As a result, vendors could make their product information available to customers other than InetPurchasing.Com.

9.2.3.2   Conflict resolution

In some cases, vendor databases and the final aggregate database used different field names or datatypes. To resolve such conflicts, the *XML Enabler Agent* provides a Web-based client interface that allows InetPurchasing.Com employees to change the XML markup of catalogs generated for its use. Although the vendor continues to own the data, it does not need to get involved in data binding details for individual customers.

9.3 | Conclusion

The InetPurchasing.Com system is successful because its vendors find it simple enough to participate. They are willing and able to generate the necessary XML catalogs and publish them to the Web. Even small companies were able to take part, which allowed them to compete in the e-commerce arena along with their larger competitors. The result was increased choices for InetPurchasing.Com's customers and a higher perceived level of satisfaction with the service.

Tip   There is a personal edition of XML Enabler Agent on the CD-ROM. It will let you experience firsthand what the vendors experienced.

E-commerce

- Electronic data interchange (EDI)
- Business-to-business (B2B)
- Supply chain integration
- Trading exchanges
- Integrated e-commerce (IEC)

Part Three

E-commerce is all about the elimination of manual procedures among trading partners. The eventual goal is to have each partner's system exchange information directly with all the others.

The most visible manifestations of e-commerce are *Web storefronts* websites where an online catalog replaces a paper catalog and mailed-in order forms. These sites enter transactions directly into the vendor's system, but the purchaser must do everything manually.

Historically, though, business supply chain automation, in the form of electronic data interchange (EDI), has been the major driver of e-commerce. EDI is vital to those companies rich enough to have implemented it, but for smaller trading partners it is unattainable.

In the following chapters, we'll see why traditional EDI has reached its limit and how XML and the Web can help it realize its full potential. The key to the value of EDI is its *integration* into the business systems of all trading partners, something that the storefront does not accomplish. With XML-based EDI, a truly integrated e-commerce is now possible, for partners of all sizes.

From EDI to IEC: The new Web commerce

Introductory Discussion

▊ Electronic data interchange (EDI)

▊ Integrated e-commerce (IEC)

▊ Leveraging XML and the Internet for EDI

▊ Supply chains and supply webs

Contributing expert: Mike Hogan of POET Software Corporation,
http://www.poet.com.

Chapter 10

XML and the Internet are dramatically altering the electronic data interchange (EDI) landscape. By driving down costs and complexity, they are creating a revolutionary form of business-to-business integrated e-commerce (IEC) that complements EDI and vastly extends its reach. IEC is becoming a truly ubiquitous technology that is reshaping business as we know it. This chapter introduces EDI and explains its evolution to IEC.

O ver the past several decades, corporations have invested tril lions of dollars in automating their internal processes. While this investment has yielded significant improvements in efficiency, that efficiency is only beginning to be extended to external processes.

In effect, companies have created islands of automation that are isolated from their vendors and customers – their trading partners. The interaction among companies and their trading partners remains slow and inefficient because it is still based on manual processes.

10.1 | What is EDI?

Electronic data interchange (EDI) has been heralded as the solution to this problem. *EDI* is defined as the exchange of data between heterogeneous systems to support transactions.

EDI is not simply the exportation of data from one system to another, but actual interaction between systems. For example, Company B is a supplier to Company A. Instead of sending purchase orders, bills and checks in hard copy form, the two might connect their systems to exchange this same data electronically.

In the process they could benefit in many other ways, including faster turnaround on orders, better inventory control, reduced financial float, complete real-time information about orders and inventory for improved decision-making, reduced costs for manual data input, and more. Companies that have implemented EDI rave about the various benefits.

In fact, these benefits can be expanded to a chain of suppliers. For example, Company C might be a supplier to Company B above. If companies B and C implement EDI, then Company A gains the additional benefits of superior integration with its entire *supply chain* of suppliers.

10.1.1 *Extranets can't hack it*

There is a significant gap between the business benefits described above and the actual implementation of EDI. This is because the actual implementation of "traditional EDI" is fundamentally flawed. It is difficult and costly to implement and, even worse, it requires a unique solution for each pair of trading partners. This situation is analogous to requiring a unique telephone line to be wired to each person to whom you wish to speak.

Many people falsely proclaimed the Internet as the solution to this problem. By implementing EDI over a single network, our problems would be solved. This "solution" was so exciting it was even given its own name, the extranet. Unfortunately, a network with a common protocol is still only a partial solution.

This is because the systems implemented in each company are based on different platforms, applications, data formats (notations), protocols, schemas, business rules, and more. Simply "connecting" these systems over the Internet does not, by itself, solve the problem. To use the phone system analogy again, this is analogous to wiring each business into the global phone network, only to realize that each company's phone system is unique, and incompatible with every other phone system.

And given the trillions of dollars companies have invested in automation, they are not simply going to replace these systems with new "compatible" solutions, assuming such things existed.

10.1.2 *XML can!*

There are a number of reasons why XML provides a solution for EDI over the Internet. XML is a universal notation (data format) that allows computers to store and transfer data that can be understood by any other computer system. XML maintains the content and structure, but separates the business rules from the data. As a result, each trading partner can apply its own business rules. This flexibility is critical to creating a complete solution for EDI.

There are additional technologies that are also part of the complete solution. Security, for example, is critical to EDI. Transactional integrity, connection stability, authentication and other services are also critical to implementing a complete solution. These requirements are addressed by technologies that are layered on top of the Internet. We refer to them generically as *Internet-based services*.

The final piece of the EDI solution is data storage. XML introduces a unique set of requirements for hierarchical naming and structure. It also requires rich relationships and complex linking. XML's use in EDI adds further requirements for metadata and versioning. These requirements levy heavy demands on database technology

10.1.3 *Integrated e-commerce*

By combining XML, the Internet, Internet-based services and database connectivity, we have a complete solution for universal *integrated e-commerce (IEC)*. IEC, which complements and extends EDI, is changing our entire business landscape. EDI is metamorphosing from a handful of unique interconnections, defined by the supply chain, into a "supply web". The supply web is an intelligent common fabric of commerce over the Internet. Trading communities and exchanges are examples of supply webs.

According to Metcalfe's Law – formulated by Robert Metcalfe, the inventor of *Ethernet* – the value of a network is roughly proportional to the square of the number of users. Imagine what this means when your EDI "network" expands from a one-to-one proposition to a true network that encompasses practically every company in the world. Suddenly, the trillions of dollars companies have invested in internal automation increase in value by several factors. By the same token, this information can also be extended to customers, adding significant value to the vendor-customer relationship, thereby enhancing customer loyalty.

This is a pivotal time in the history of technology. With the emergence of XML, all of the pieces are available to create a universal mechanism for EDI. The Internet provides the transport. XML provides the flexible, extensible, structured message format. Various Internet-based services provide solutions for security, transactional integrity, authentication, connection stability, network fail-over and more.

Add to this sophisticated data storage and you have all of the pieces necessary to unite corporate islands of automation into a single coherent fabric of electronic commerce. IEC has already achieved dramatic improvements in efficiency, cost-savings, superior access to real-time data for analysis and decision-making, superior inventory management, and more.

Integrated e-commerce will have a profound impact on business-to-business (B2B) and business-to-consumer (B2C) relationships. The many problems with current implementations of EDI have relegated it to large enterprises and selected industries. However, the combination of the Internet, Internet-based technologies, and XML is opening up EDI – as enhanced by IEC – not only to small-to-medium enterprises (*SME*s), but also to individuals (Example 10-1).

IEC will experience growth and market penetration that will rival the email market. It has already begun to blossom on the Web and become an everyday part of our lives. It will eventually usher in a new era in computing. The Internet will complete its metamorphosis from a transport for Web pages into a ubiquitous and seamless foundation for every imaginable transaction. In the future, IEC will touch every aspect of computing.

We will be examining these propositions in detail, and the technology that makes them possible.

10.2 | The value of EDI

While traditional EDI is very costly and difficult to implement, the potential benefits are very significant. Companies that have implemented EDI rave about benefits like improved efficiency, vendor management, cost savings, superior access to information for decision making, tighter inventory control, customer responsiveness, and it is a competitive advantage that can be marketed to attract new customers.

Example 10-1. The value of data interchange.

Mike opens his company expense report, and in the microsecond it takes to launch, he reminisces about the old days when he had to fill out these things himself. Now the computer does it for him. Mike recently took a trip to Utah to close a major deal. In the process he purchased a plane ticket, a rental car and various meals. In the old days, he used to enter all of these charges manually into an expense program...not any more.

Mike uses a corporate American Express card for these purchases. When he opens the expense report, it automatically connects to American Express and presents a list of new charges. Mike selects the charges that are appropriate for this expense report.

American Express sends this data to Mike's computer, which automatically formats the data into his expense report. Mike then clicks the send button and the expense report is sent to his manager to approve. Then the company's bank instantly wires the money to Mike's bank account.

Behind the scenes, all these companies are establishing connections, as needed, to share information in a secure and reliable manner using XML and the Internet. But Mike doesn't concern himself with what goes on behind the scenes; he's off to close another big deal in Washington.

EDI was initially implemented to improve efficiency by enabling companies to eliminate costly and slow manual methodologies, like the processing of purchase orders and bills. It was thought that by allowing the computers of two or more companies to share this information, they could achieve dramatic improvements in efficiency.

However, the largest savings are derived from a complete shift to EDI that allows companies to completely eliminate their hard copy processes. The traditional 80/20 rule applies in reverse to EDI, meaning that it is the last 20% of your trading partners to convert to EDI who account for 80% of the potential savings.

This is because even with 80% of your trading partners using EDI, you must still maintain the same manual processes for the remaining 20% who don't. While most companies have not been able to completely convert from hard copy processes to EDI, the 20% savings companies have realized have still been very significant. With integrated e-commerce enabling companies to completely eliminate their manual processes, the savings will improve dramatically.

With EDI, companies are also able to manage their supply chains much more efficiently. Through EDI, companies have been able to reduce the average time from issuance of an order to receipt of goods from several weeks, to a matter of days. By improving inventory control, companies are able to minimize their investment in costly inventory, while still being able to address spikes in business. For industries where inventory costs are a significant part of their business, like manufacturing, this represents a significant cost savings.

EDI also reduces the financial float by eliminating the typical order generation, delivery and processing, by 5-7 days. By combining EDI with electronic funds transfer (EFT) companies can also reduce the financial float by 8-10+ days. Based on the amount of money involved, this can represent a significant savings.

EDI also provides companies with superior real-time information upon which to base decisions. Everyone recalls stories of companies who simply didn't have the data to realize how bad things were, until it was too late. With EDI, companies have access to complete data in real-time. The ability to collect, manipulate and measure information about your relationships with vendors and customers can be critical to your company's success.

Customer responsiveness is becoming increasingly important. Many companies have leveraged technology to dramatically improve customer responsiveness. A good example of this is Federal Express, who pioneered the concept of a website where customers can track the status of their packages.

The site is possible only because of FedEx's end-to-end dedication to EDI. By capturing information about the package status at each step in the process, and making this information accessible to customers, they have made themselves leaders in customer support. This is critical to building and growing businesses, especially in the Internet age.

Some companies who have implemented EDI with one customer, have gone on to market this capability to other potential customers, as a unique selling point. This has enabled them to grow their business. As IEC becomes more ubiquitous, the tide could even shift to the point where companies will not accept vendors who are not IEC-capable. That is because of the dramatic savings that vendors can achieve by a complete conversion to EDI.

10.3 | Traditional EDI: Built on outdated principles

EDI is a process for exchanging data in electronic format between heterogeneous applications and/or platforms in a manner that can be processed without manual intervention.

10.3.1 The history of EDI

EDI dates back to the 1970s, when it was introduced by the Transportation Data Coordinating Committee (TDCC). The TDCC created transaction sets for vendors to follow in order to enable electronic processing of purchase orders and bills.

At the time, the technology landscape was very different from what it is today. Lacking ubiquitous powerful CPUs, a common transport, and a file format that allows for flexibility, they defined strict transaction sets. These transaction sets addressed the needs for data content, structure and the process for handling the data. In other words, the business rules were embedded into the transaction set.

The incorporation of business rules into the definition of the transaction set causes many problems, because:

1. Business rules vary from company to company;
2. Business rules for one size company may be completely inappropriate for companies of another size;
3. Business rules are subject to change over time according to changes in market dynamics.

In short, the use of fixed and rigid transaction sets, while necessary at the time, have limited the value of EDI, and therefore stunted its growth.

10.3.2 EDI technology basics

Traditional EDI transaction sets are defined by standards bodies such as the United Nations Standard Messages Directory for Electronic Data Interchange for Administration, Commerce and Transport (*EDIFACT*), and the

American National Standards Institute's (ANSI) Accredited Standards Committee X12 sub-group.

Transaction sets define the fields, the order of these fields, and the length of the fields. Along with these transaction sets are business rules, which in the lexicon of the EDI folks are referred to as "implementation guidelines".

To actually implement EDI, the trading partners would follow these steps:

1. Trading partners enter into an agreement, called a trading arrangement.
2. They select a Value Added Network (VAN).
3. The trading partners typically either contract for, or build themselves, custom software that maps between the two data set formats used by these trading partners.
4. Each time a new trading partner is added, new software would have to be written to translate the sender's data set for the recipient. In other words, you start from scratch with each new trading partner.

Transaction sets are typically transmitted over expensive proprietary networks, which generally base charges on a mixture of fixed fees and message lengths. These fees can become quite substantial, but they are typically overshadowed by the cost to build and maintain the translation software. The VANs provide value-added services such as:

1. Data validation (compliance) and conversion
2. Logging for audit trails
3. Customer support
4. A secure and stable network
5. Accountability
6. Transaction roll-back to support uncommitted transactions

It is important to note that EDI is not simply the exportation of data from one system to another, but a bidirectional mechanism for interaction between systems. Because these disparate systems typically employ different file formats (data notations), schemas, data exchange protocols, etc., the process of exchanging data is very difficult.

10.3.3 *The problems of traditional EDI*

Traditional EDI suffers from many problems that have limited its growth. One of the most significant problems is the fact that it is based on the transfer of fixed transaction sets. This rigidity makes it extremely difficult to deal with the normal evolution necessary for companies to introduce new products and services, or evolve or replace their computer systems.

In addition, these transaction sets include strict processes for handling the data. These processes are not universally acceptable to companies in various industries and of various sizes. This problem is compounded by a standardization process that is too slow to accommodate the accelerating pace of business today.

In addition, the high fixed costs of implementation have been too much to justify for SMEs. In short, there are a host of problems which, despite the benefits of EDI, have prevented its universal adoption.

10.3.3.1 Fixed transaction sets

EDI is currently built on transaction sets that are fixed in nature. For example, a contact field might include the individual's name, title, company, company address and phone number. However, the company does not have the flexibility to add or subtract fields.

Why is this important?

Companies cannot be frozen in time by a fixed transaction set. This prevents them from evolving by adding new services or products, changing their computer systems and improving business processes. This inflexibility inherent in the current custom solutions required to map data between each trading partner pair is untenable, despite the significant benefits of EDI (Example 10-2).

10.3.3.2 Slow standards evolution

EDI standards are defined by standards bodies that are structurally ill-equipped to keep up with the rapid pace of change in the various business environments they impact, as illustrated by Example 10-2.

These standards accommodate many companies with very different needs. They also encompass not just the ontology, but the associated busi-

Example 10-2. Problems of traditional EDI: Healthcare

The transaction sets created for the healthcare system were defined for the traditional indemnity model, where the insurance company pays the doctor on a per visit basis. However, the movement toward managed care was not foreseen in this transaction set. Since managed care pays the doctor a set fee per patient, but does not reimburse on a per visit basis, the standard transaction set simply doesn't work.

The typical doctor sees a mixture of patients, some having managed care insurance and others with indemnity insurance. In order to accommodate this scenario, the doctor is forced to create a false "per visit" fee for managed care patients. This false fee, which is required in order to "complete" the transaction set, creates havoc with the doctor's other billing systems, which EDI was supposed to help.

Rigid transaction sets that enforce process as well as content are simply not flexible enough to address the ever-changing business environment.

ness processes. As a result, it is very slow and difficult, if not impossible, to develop one-size-fits-all solutions.

The current process for defining standards for transaction sets can take years. This simply will not work in today's business environment, which is characterized by accelerated change and increased competition. However, in an effort to jump-start the creation of industry ontologies in the form of DTDs for XML, the work of the traditional EDI standards bodies could be enormously valuable.

Historically, technology standards that are defined and managed in a top-down fashion, like EDI standards, have been replaced by bottom-up standards that allow for independent and distributed development. In other words, technologies like XML, that support greater flexibility and diversity, while providing compatibility between implementations, typically replace inflexible managed solutions like fixed transaction sets.

10.3.3.3   Non-standard standards

Despite the perception of standardization, there remains some flexibility in the interpretation of traditional EDI standards. The simple fact of the matter is that companies have unique needs, and these needs must be translated into the information they share with their trading partners.

In practical terms, the customer is at a significant economic advantage in defining these "standards", vis-a-vis the supplier. As a result, suppliers are forced to implement one-off solutions for each trading partner. In many of the industries where EDI is more prevalent, the suppliers also tend to be the smaller of the two partners, which makes the financial proposition even worse.

Because of the various informational needs of companies, it is impractical to expect that EDI standards can be a one-size-fits-all proposition. The variables of company size, focus, industry, systems, etc. will continue to create needs that are unique to each company. As evidence, consider the amounts companies spend on custom development and customization of packaged applications.

10.3.3.4   High fixed costs

While large companies tout the financial and operational benefits of EDI, these same benefits have eluded the SMEs. That is because of the high fixed costs of implementation, which must be balanced against savings that are variable.

Depending on the level of automation, implementing EDI for a large enterprise is not substantially more expensive than it is for SMEs. In fact, it can be more expensive for the SMEs. Larger companies can often implement a single EDI standard, while the SMEs must accommodate the various standards of their larger partners. This can be very expensive.

Yet, ironically, the benefits are variable. So, if savings are 2% of processing costs, this might not be a substantial number for the manufacturer of car seat springs, but it can be a huge number for GM, Ford or Chrysler. SMEs simply do not have the scale to compensate for the high fixed costs of traditional EDI.

Because of this some of the SMEs that claim to implement EDI are actually printing a hard copy of the data feeds and re-typing them in their systems. The reason they implemented this faux-EDI is to meet customer requirements, because they simply do not have the transactional scale to justify the investment in traditional EDI. Something had to be done to bring down those costs (Example 10-3).

Example 10-3. Problems of traditional EDI: Retail

One large retailer requires its vendors to implement EDI in order to qualify as a vendor. However, like all traditional EDI implementations, the data set is unique to the retailer.

For small companies, implementing this system can be quite an investment. Retail is a very fast-paced industry, because it is forced to cater to ever-changing customer demands. As a result, some suppliers to this retailer have implemented this costly technology, only to later lose their contract with the retailer. In fact, because of the significant investment in technology these companies were forced to make, they have sued the retailer.

If this technology were universally applicable, the vendor's investment in a single customer would be eliminated, as would the retailer's legal liability.

10.3.3.5   Fixed business rules

Business rules are encapsulated in the definition of the transaction sets as implementation guidelines. However, business rules are not something that can be legislated, nor can they be rigid.

Business rules that are applicable for a large enterprise, may be completely inappropriate for an SME. To make matters worse, business rules for a medium-sized enterprise may be wholly inappropriate for a small enterprise.

These business rules will also vary between industries. Even companies of the same size that are in the same industry will implement different business rules. What's more, business rules change over time. The earlier healthcare example demonstrates this point.

Traditional EDI focuses too much on process as an integral part of the transaction set. This is a fatal flaw. New technologies, like XML, support the separation of process, or business rules, from the content and structure of the data. Achieving this separation is critical to widespread adoption of EDI.

The linkage between transaction sets and business rules creates additional problems. The real-life implementation of EDI typically requires custom solutions for each trading partner pair. This creates havoc when trying to implement or modify global business rules.

For example, if your company changed business policy to begin accepting purchase orders, which you had refused to accommodate in the past, you would have to manually change the individual software for each trading partner. You could not make these changes on a global basis using traditional EDI.

This problem also impacts your ability to upgrade or replace your internal systems, since they are uniquely woven into the EDI software in place. In essence, you can become locked into systems that may become obsolete by the time you actually implement the total solution.

10.3.3.6   Limited penetration

EDI penetration has been very limited, when compared to the penetration rates of other automation technologies. Yet the majority of the value of EDI is derived by complete elimination of the hard-copy processes EDI is meant to replace.

As mentioned above, EDI benefits do not follow the 80/20 rule, because converting the first 80% of your vendors to EDI results in only 20% of the potential cost savings. The remaining 80% of the costs remain, since the company is forced to maintain all of the old manual process in tandem with the electronic processes. The most significant savings come only from completely replacing all manual processes with EDI.

The real value of any network is in its adoption by users. Remember Metcalfe's Law: The value of any network is roughly proportional to the number of users squared.

But EDI, in its current state, is *not* a single interlinked network. On the contrary it is a series of one-to-one chains of data flow. As a result, it is vulnerable to alternative "networked" solutions like those enabled by XML, the Internet, Internet-based services, and database connectivity.

10.4 | Leveraging XML and the Internet

Now that we've established the tremendous benefits of EDI, and the structural problems of traditional EDI, the obvious question is: "How can we fix the problems?"

Fortunately, new technologies are coming together to completely reshape the EDI landscape. Today, EDI is currently implemented in a 1-to-1 manner between trading partners. These partnerships can then be extended through tiers to create a supply chain.

This is all changing!

The new paradigm is the *supply web*. The supply web is based on utilization of XML, the Internet, Internet-based services and database connectivity to create a network, or "web", of trading partners.

Implementation and operational costs are plummeting, trading partners are able to implement one-size-fits-all solutions, and adoption is skyrocketing. And the benefits will not be limited to the trading partners, they will be driven down to end-users as well. EDI will become as commonplace as email.

In short, EDI will dramatically alter the business computing landscape, moving the world forward from our current islands of automation toward a single fabric of commerce tying together businesses and end-users.

Traditional EDI is based on the technologies that existed in the 1970s. Now it is time to build a new EDI architecture on current technologies like XML, the Internet, Internet-based services and database connectivity.

- XML provides the ability to separate the data and structure from the processes.
- The Internet provides the ubiquitous connectivity upon which a Web of interconnected trading partners can flourish.
- Internet technologies provide a layer of security, authentication, transactional support and more, to support the needs of EDI.
- Database connectivity means that XML data, and the business rules that interact with that data, can be communicated among disparate systems by means of middle-tier data filters and aggregators.

Together, these technologies are removing the barriers that prevented widespread adoption of EDI. By leveraging these technologies, EDI functionality is becoming more flexible, more powerful, and less expensive – and integrated e-commerce will ultimately become ubiquitous.

10.4.1 *XML*

XML is closely related to HyperText Markup Language (HTML), the original document representation of the World Wide Web, as both are based on SGML. While HTML enables the creation of Web pages that can be viewed on any browser, XML adds tags to data so that it can be processed by any application. These tags describe, in a standardized syntax, what the data is, so that the applications can understand its meaning and how to process it (Example 10-4).

For example, in HTML a product name and a price might be somewhere in the text. But the computer only knows that there is a collection of characters and numbers. It cannot discern that this data represents a product name and price. As a result, little can be done with the data.

With XML, however, the product name is tagged (e.g. `product_name`), as is the product price (e.g. `product_price`). More importantly, there is an association between the product price and the product name.

This information results in significant additional value. For example, a user can now search for the best price on a specific product.

Example 10-4. XML insulates applications from diversity: Customer record

The following example demonstrates one of the values of XML. Below are three different types of message documents from three different companies (A,B and C). Each describes its respective company's customer data:

Company A:
```
<Person name="Mike Hogan" phone="6502864640"
        email="mph@poet.com" />
```
Company B:
```
<Person name="Mike Hogan" street address="999 Baker Way"
        city="San Mateo" zip="94404" phone="6502864640"/>
```
Company C:
```
<Person name="Mike Hogan" phone="6502864640"/>
```
The XML parser parses, or disassembles, the messages to show the person element, which has associated attributes (`name`, `phone`, etc.). These attributes, as you can see, differ in content and organization.

However, if your application was written to extract a person's name and phone number, it could work equally well with each of these document types without modification. In fact, if these companies evolve their data to include additional information, your application continues to function without modification. This flexibility is one of the benefits of XML.

XML documents must be "well-formed", which means that most document-type information – grammar and hierarchy – can be embedded in the tags that "mark up" the individual document. There can also be an associated *document type definition* (DTD) or schema definition containing additional meta-information that describes the data.

In either case, XML is self-describing. As a result, applications can be very flexible in their ability to receive, parse and process very diverse sets of information. This enables companies to write a single application that will work with diverse sets of customers. In fact, such a system is even capable of processing information from new trading partners in an ad hoc fashion. This capability completely changes the dynamics of EDI.

Using XML, companies can separate the business rules from the content and structure of the data. By focusing on exchanging data content and structure, the trading partners are free to implement their own business rules, which can be quite distinct from one another. Yet, using templates, companies can work with legacy EDI, non-XML datatypes as well (as we will see in Chapter 11, "XML and EDI: Working together", on page 188).

10.4.2 *The Internet*

Many companies heralded the cost savings and ubiquity of the Internet as the death knell for VANs. However, this future has not come to pass...yet.

The boldest of these claims was based on the notion that the extranet would redefine the new computing paradigm. What these pundits failed to realize was that the Internet alone does not address the needs of the EDI community.

The EDI community is generally limited to the largest enterprises. EDI is mission critical, and requires a dependable network. It also requires a level of security that couldn't be found on the Internet. To put it simply, the savings were not sufficient to justify the switch.

Furthermore, connectivity is only a small part of the problem, the largest issue is the exchange of data in a universal fashion.

All these issues have now been addressed.

- Technology is now available to provide connectivity services to support the Internet in addressing up-time and throughput for mission critical information.
- Security has improved dramatically.

■ The use of XML has broadened the EDI customer base to include SMEs and individuals. This new group of customers is much more price-sensitive, so they are inclined to seek an Internet-based solution.

■ The ability to exchange data in a more democratic and ad hoc manner is causing an explosion in the average number of EDI connections.

The average number of traditional EDI trading partners, for those companies who utilize EDI at all, is *two*. Building EDI solutions based on XML, and operating this over the Internet, which offers a low-cost ubiquitous transport, is dramatically expanding the value of EDI, according to Metcalfe's Law.

10.4.3 *Internet technologies*

Internet technologies have improved, and continue to improve dramatically, now providing a critical mass of technologies that is capable of replacing the services of VANs. Consider the following list of VAN services, each followed by the Internet-based alternatives that offer greater functionality and flexibility:

Data validation and conversion
XML DTDs, XML validation, templates, and structure-based data feed interpretation.

Intermediary-based logging for audit trails
XML-savvy repositories employed by all trading partners enables rich logging for audit trails. Combining these with electronic signatures ensures system and company identification.

Consulting, customer service and customer support
This function could be handled by VANs capable of making the transition to Internet technologies, or by the other legions of consultants.

Security and accountability

Public key cryptography, certificate authorities, digital signatures can assure secure transactions.

Connection reliability, stability

New technologies in bandwidth allocation, general improvement in the stability of the Internet and alternative fail-over solutions like dial-up continue to move the Internet toward supporting critical real-time data flow. (Remember, it was originally designed to withstand nuclear attack!)

Trading partner negotiation

Directories (X.500, LDAP, NDS, Active Directory), certificate authorities, digital signatures, email, Internet versions of the Better Business Bureau, etc., can support this function.

Transactional support (roll-back, etc.)

The improvements in remote messaging systems and transaction processing monitors provide a layer of transaction support that is capable of adding transactional integrity even on unstable networks.

10.4.4 *XML data storage*

In other technological transitions, data storage has been a moot point, since the data could be mapped more-or-less directly into relational tables or file systems. More recently, object-oriented database management systems became available for this purpose.

XML data, however, is composed of self-describing information elements that are richly linked, and that utilize a hierarchical structure and naming mechanism. These qualities enable new data-access capabilities based on the tree structure, such as context-sensitive queries, navigation, and traversal.

XML-based support for these new capabilities can be provided by a content management layer above a relational DBMS, and by native XML databases.

10.4.5 *Data filtering*

The source of the vast majority of EDI-related information is currently in mainframes and relational databases. This data will be marked-up on the fly with XML tags. XML data will also come from data sources such as:

- XML content management systems
- Various Internet resources
- EDI-XML documents, both full documents like purchase orders and short inter-process messages
- Result sets from applications, also in XML

These diverse sources must be communicated with by a middle-tier "data filter" that can speak to each source in a manner that the source will recognize. The data must then be filtered in source-dependent ways, based on one's confidence in the data, application of consistent business logic, resolution of the various element-type name ontologies, response mechanisms, security, caching for performance, etc. Only then can the application address the data in a consistent manner and receive consistent responses from the middle tier, as shown in Figure 10-1.

The middle tier could maintain valuable meta-information that would add structure and context to the data stream. Such information could include:

- Routing for the query, response, etc.
- Source of the information (to indicate credibility, etc.)
- Time stamps
- Data, DTD, and tag normalization
- Context and navigation aids

Further details on XML content management and the use of storage systems in the management of XML data can be found in Part 5, "Content Management", on page 262 and Part 8, "Databases", on page 428.

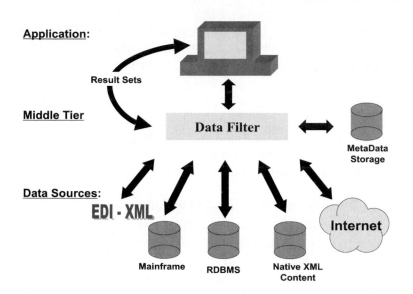

Figure 10-1   Data filter in an XML-based EDI system

10.5 | Conclusion

After decades of investment in corporate data centers, we have created islands of automation inside companies. Their isolation from trading partners limits the value companies can recognize from these systems.

EDI offers the ability to change all of this. EDI offers benefits like:

- improved efficiency
- supply chain management
- real-time data and metrics
- better planning
- superior execution
- control systems
- resource management
- cost savings
- superior access to information for decision making
- customer responsiveness

However, traditional EDI is very difficult and expensive to implement. Because of problems like rigid transaction sets that embed business rules, slow standards development, high fixed costs, and limited market penetration, EDI has not achieved broad adoption. Fortunately, XML-based technology is now available to address these problems and, in the process, reshape the use of EDI.

XML, the Internet, Internet-based services and database connectivity are combining to complement EDI and enhance commerce, in the form of integrated e-commerce. Instead of forcing companies to adapt their systems and business processes to the EDI data, this data can now adapt dynamically to the companies' existing systems.

Where traditional EDI was isolated to certain industries and to the largest enterprises, integrated e-commerce will become as ubiquitous as email. Trading communities have evolved from EDI's one-to-one supply chain to IEC's richly interconnected web of trading partners forming the supply web.

This supply web is resulting in dramatic improvements in efficiency. Companies are slashing costs, while improving access to critical information. This information will be pushed all the way to the end-user, providing superior customer support as well.

XML and EDI: Working together

Introductory Discussion

- Approaches to e-commerce

- Traditional-EDI and XML e-commerce compared

- Leverage existing EDI with XML

Contributing experts: Jeffrey Ricker and Drew Munro

Chapter

11

Large companies have invested millions in their existing successful EDI systems. XML can enhance that investment by extending them to a Webful of EDI-less trading partners. This chapter explains how traditional EDI and XML can work together.

In a few short years, the Internet has changed the fundamental rules for conducting business.

Now consider EDI: Large companies have been using it with their major trading partners for nearly 20 years. But, as we have seen, traditional EDI commerce has proven itself to be too complicated and expensive for most small and many midsize companies. As a result, EDI has never been adopted widely enough to cause any such fundamental change.

Now, however, there is an e-commerce that all companies can afford. The Internet and XML have lowered the barriers to e-commerce, in both cost and complexity. But they are not replacing EDI, they are extending it to bring e-commerce to small and midsize companies. XML complements EDI and, in so doing, finally turns the vision of EDI into the reality of integrated e-commerce.

11.1 | What is integrated e-commerce?

In traditional commerce, each customer and vendor may be automated internally, but they are individually isolated. They traverse the gulf between their systems by manual processes such as mail, email, fax, meetings and phone calls. This *manual gulf* between "islands of automation" is illustrated in Figure 11-1.

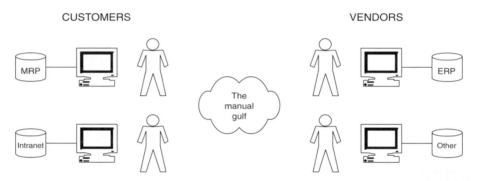

Figure 11-1   A manual gulf separates trading partners in traditional commerce

The objective of *integrated e-commerce (IEC)* is to bridge that manual gulf; that is, to eliminate manual trade processes by allowing the internal applications of different companies to exchange information directly.

Not all e-commerce is integrated e-commerce, but a lot of it is. At present, there are three major approaches, which vary in the extent to which they fully realize this goal.

11.1.1 *Web storefronts*

Web storefronts provide a Web interface to a vendor's catalog of products or services, as illustrated in Figure 11-2. Customers can place orders directly into a vendor's internal system through a Web storefront. Famous examples include Amazon.com and Dell Computer.

Web storefronts have proven immensely popular with customers, and they clearly can achieve economic and other objectives for vendors. How-

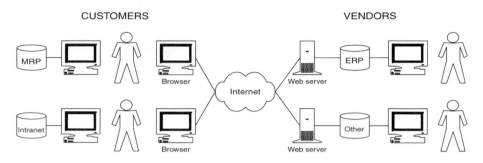

Figure 11-2 Web storefronts automate only one side of trading

ever, in terms of achieving the full potential of integrated e-commerce, they are unilateral.

Nothing is automated on the customer's side. He must go to each website separately and manually search through the catalogs. He must also enter orders manually through a Web form and simultaneously update his internal ERP system or intranet application.

For a large manufacturer with 40,000 suppliers, Web storefronts are not much of an improvement over printed catalogs and telephones.

11.1.2 *E-commerce portals*

Some companies have proposed *e-commerce portals* to automate both vendors and customers. With e-commerce portals, customers go to only one website – the portal website – to view vendor catalogs and place orders. Vendors go to the same portal to view and respond to orders (see Figure 11-3).

E-commerce portals bridge the manual gap better than Web storefronts, and can offer the convenience and quick ramp-up of an outsourced solution. However, there are tradeoffs to be considered in this approach:

- Both vendors and customers must update their ERP systems from the portal. Can this task be automated?
- A company's e-commerce data resides outside that company on the portal website. Is the security risk acceptable?
- E-commerce portals may charge a subscription fee and may also charge for every transaction. In essence, they are charging

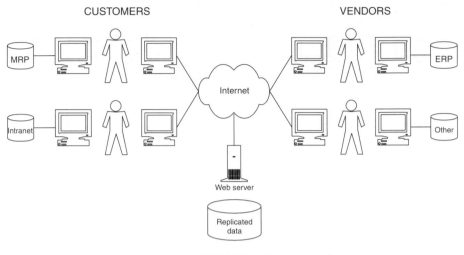

Figure 11-3   E-commerce portals rely on an intermediary

companies to access their own information. Would another approach be more cost-effective?

Caution   *E-commerce portals are a type of application service provider (ASP). They should not be confused with the popular types of information portal that are discussed in Part 6, "Portals", on page 322.*

11.1.3   *Integrated e-commerce*

EDI was the first attempt at integrated e-commerce. Although its users reap great benefits from it, there are only about 300,000 of them worldwide. The reasons for this were explored in Chapter 10, "From EDI to IEC: The new Web commerce", on page 166.

The basic premise of EDI, however, is right on track. EDI eliminates manual processes by allowing the internal applications of different companies to exchange information directly.

Today, thanks to XML, companies such as Vitria Technology can offer business-to-business e-commerce systems that accomplish the original goal of allowing the internal applications of trading partners to share information directly, as illustrated in Figure 11-4.

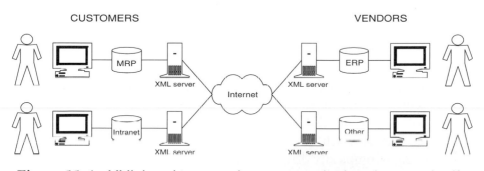

Figure 11-4   XML-based integrated e-commerce bridges the manual gulf

Intranets are ubiquitous today. Most, if not all, ERP systems have Web-based interfaces, which makes them intranets. Midsize and small companies that do not have ERP systems also have intranets. With XML-based EDI, any company can view its trading partners through its own corporate intranet, rather than through its hundreds of suppliers' individual websites or a third-party website.

The financial services industry has been a leader in bringing the benefits of integrated e-commerce to individuals. Its offerings reflect the approaches to e-commerce we have discussed here. When you go to your broker's website to execute trades and examine your statement, you are using a Web storefront. But when your broker sends the information to *Quicken* and you execute trades from your ledger, that's integrated e-commerce.[1]

---

1. We use the term "integrated e-commerce" in preference to "business-to-business (B2B)" e-commerce because not all B2B e-commerce is integrated into internal applications. Also, as seen in this example, integrated e-commerce isn't limited to businesses.

11.2 | Traditional EDI and XML compared

The stark differences between traditional EDI e-commerce and XML e-commerce stem from the basic characteristics of the two technologies, as compared in Table 11-1.

The creators of EDI were very concerned about size of their messages. Bandwidth for EDI networks is very expensive even today. EDI messages are therefore very compressed and use codes to represent complex values. For the same reason, all the metadata is stripped from the messages, which makes them very hard to read and debug.

The complexity of EDI makes EDI programmers hard to train and expensive to keep, which in turn makes EDI applications expensive to buy and maintain. Complexity drives cost.

Table 11-1   EDI and XML e-commerce solutions compared

Traditional EDI	**XML e-commerce**
Optimized for compressed messages	Optimized for easy programming
Requires dedicated EDI server costing $10,000 to $100,000	Requires Web server costing $0 to $5000
Uses value-added network (VAN) charging $1 to $20 per message or more	Uses your existing Internet connection
EDI message format takes months to master	XML message format learned in hours
Requires costly program development	Requires only scripts and stylesheets

11.2.1 *Message formats*

Example 11-1 and Example 11-2 provide a comparison between traditional EDI and XML. To demonstrate the difference to yourself, try to find the purchase order number in each document.

Example 11-1. Sample EDI purchase order

```
ISA*00*      *00*  *08*61112500TST        *01*DEMO WU000003
*970911*1039*U00302000009561*0*P?
GS*PO*6111250011*WU000003 *970911*1039*9784*X*003020
ST*850*397822
BEG*00*RE*194743**970911
REF*AH*M109
REF*DP*641
REF*IA*000100685
DTM*010*970918
N1*BY*92*1287
N1*ST*92*87447
N1*ZZ*992*1287
PO1*1*1*EA*13.33**CB*80211*IZ*364*UP*718379271641
PO1*1*2*EA*13.33**CB*80211*IZ*382*UP*718379271573
PO1*1*3*EA*13.33**CB*80213*IZ*320*UP*718379271497
PO1*1*4*EA*13.33**CB*80215*IZ*360*UP*718379271848
PO1*1*5*EA*13.33**CB*80215*IZ*364*UP*718379271005
CTT*25
SE*36*397822
GE*1*9784
IEA*1*000009561
```

11.2.2 *The different flavors of XML and EDI*

EDI comes in two distinct flavors, X12 and EDIFACT. X12 is the American standard that evolved over the years from the most basic attempts at exchange in the 1960s to full-blown billion-dollar networks. EDIFACT is the international standard, endorsed by the United Nations and designed from the ground up beginning in 1985. Both flavors have several version releases of their message formats. Compatibility between versions is not always straightforward.

XML e-commerce is currently even more diversified, with proposed standards that use XML only and others that are XML-EDI hybrids. Some of the most important are listed here.

Example 11-2. Sample XML purchase order

```xml
<?xml version="1.0" ?>
<?xml:stylesheet?>
<purchase-order>
<header>
   <po-number>1234</po-number>
   <date>1999-02-08</date><time>14:05</time>
   </header>
<billing>
   <company>XMLreSolutions</company>
   <address>
      <street>601 Pennsylvania Ave. NW</street>
      <street>Suite 900</street>
      <city>Washington</city>
      <st>DC</st><postcode>20004</postcode>
      </address>
   </billing>
<order items="1" >
   <item>
      <reference>097251</reference>
      <description>Widgets</description>
      <quantity>4</quantity>
      <unit-price>11.99</unit-price>
      <price>47.96</price>
      </item>
   <tax type="sales" >
      <tax-unit>VA</tax-unit>
      <calculation>0.045</calculation>
      <amount>2.16</amount>
      </tax>
   ...
```

- CommerceNet, a business consortium, is developing the eCo Framework.
- RosettaNet, another consortium, is working on XML standards for product catalogs.
- CommerceOne has created the common business library (CBL), in part funded by a government grant from the US National Institute for Standards and Technology (NIST).
- OASIS and UN/CEFACT are building industry consensus for a technical framework called *ebXML* that will enable consistent use of XML for the exchange of business data.
- Ariba has rallied several companies around commerce XML (cXML), a proposed standard for catalogs and purchase orders.

- Microsoft has loosely grouped many of these technologies under what it calls *BizTalk*.
- The XML-EDI Group has proposed a naming convention for representing EDI messages in XML. Essentially, they have built-on and preserved the hard-won consensus for the X12 taxonomy by using X12 names in XML tags.
- Still other groups, such as the Open Buying Initiative (OBI), are proposing standards for simply moving EDI X12 messages over HTTP.

11.3 | An XML-EDI trading system

Traditional EDI works. You can rely on it. There is no greater accolade for a technology. Large companies have spent millions on their EDI systems, which are mission-critical and unlikely to be abandoned. The objective now should be to leverage this sound base and extend it to more trading partners.

Simply sending EDI X12 or EDIFACT messages over HTTP – the Web transport protocol – won't do the job. Although EDI's transport system is primitive, it is not EDI's governing limitation.

The expense of EDI is rooted in its complexity, and its complexity is based in its compressed, cryptic message formats. XML can overcome this complexity by storing the metadata within the text of the message. And XML also happens to be designed for HTTP.

Traditional EDI users can extend their electronic trading base by installing XML-EDI translators on their Web servers, as shown in Figure 11-5. The translation must go both ways: XML to EDI for messages starting from the small company and EDI to XML for messages starting from the large company traditional EDI user.

Figure 11-5 An XML-EDI trading system

11.3.1 *XML to EDI*

XML-EDI translators are already available, many relying on proprietary technology and unique scripting languages. Others, including Vitria's *BusinessWare XEDI Translator* use XSLT to specify the transformation, as shown in Figure 11-6.

Although XSLT is most commonly used to transform XML into HTML for presentation, it is perfectly well-suited to transform XML into any representation, including EDI. And as it is an open standard, it is likely to benefit from the availability of free and open-source implementations and a large body of skilled developers.

11.3.2 *EDI to XML*

XSLT cannot be used directly for the inverse conversion, as it can only transform from XML. The problem is well-known from the long experience in SGML and XML systems of having to convert word processing documents to generalized markup. The solution is also well-known: an

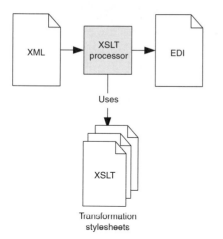

Figure 11-6   XSLT is well-suited for transforming XML into EDI

intermediate trivial translation from the foreign notation to the markup language. A translation, in other words, that changes only the representation of the document, not the meaning. Then XSLT can be applied to accomplish more powerful transforms.

This technique is illustrated in Figure 11-7, which shows an EDI parser as the intermediate translator. The EDI parser has an application programming interface (API) very similar to the XSLT processor (and the XML parser for that matter). The EDI parser makes an XML message out of the EDI message by replacing EDI codes with their full names and making XML elements out of the EDI segments and elements. This process follows the XML-EDI Group's concept of preserving the X12 taxonomy when translating to XML.

Once the EDI message is a well-formed XML document, XSLT can transform it into various XML-EDI message standards, such as cXML, RosettaNet or BizTalk.

Because there are many kinds of XML and many kinds of EDI, an XML-EDI translator is not a one-to-one system but rather a many-to-many system. Such a translator can therefore also serve as an XML to XML translator and an EDI to EDI translator.

Figure 11-7   Transforming EDI to XML requires an intermediate step

11.4 | The future of e-commerce

The objective of integrated e-commerce is to eliminate manual processes by allowing the internal applications of different companies to exchange information directly. Stated more generically, *integrated e-commerce* is systems integration that crosses the boundary of the enterprise.

That definition encompasses more than just the automation of supply chain paperwork. It envisions a future framework that also automates business processes and workflow between trading partners, and that accommodates those few trading partners that might never automate as well.

XML and EDI working together is the first step toward that future.

An information pipeline for petrochemicals

Case Study

- Petrochemical industry marketplace
- Integration with XML
- Enabling free information flows

Contributing experts: Kathleen House and John Evdemon

When does a supply chain become a supply noose? When a company is so dependent on its suppliers that market analysts won't evaluate it solely on its individual performance. That's the case in the petrochemical industry, where a slip from one primary vendor can create a logistical nightmare of missed and delayed communications for 50 other companies. What better reason to grease the skids for rapid adoption of integrated e-commerce!

 he petrochemical industry is a subsidiary of the oil and gas industry. As such, as well as in its own right, it is a huge and highly diverse horizontal market.

But it is also a complex vertical market!

12.1 | The petrochemical marketplace

Depending on the selling and buying position for a particular product range, business units within a large petrochemical company, like Shell or Exxon, compete against their corporate siblings. The product flows, both upstream and downstream from the refineries, often cross the traditional boundaries of competition.

12.1.1 Upstream flow

The upstream flow begins with OPEC and its control over the pricing of the crude oil flowing out of the ground. In the upstream flow we see the global purchase, transportation, and warehousing of the crude oil that eventually flows into the refineries.

The top-tier petrochemical companies and their oil and gas parents exert their own control over the industry by creating highly intertwined combinations of joint ventures, strategic partnerships, business unit ownerships, and non-disclosed horizontal agreements. Horizontal domination then occurs as petrochemical firms secure their production by entering into agreements with oil and gas supplier companies. To compete effectively, most large petrochemical companies own and control companies along the complete vertical industry chain – upstream as well as downstream.

12.1.2 *Downstream flow*

Once the crude has been refined, the downstream process occurs. It involves an amazing diversity of activities, including:

- Buying and/or retrieving refined oil products
- Transportation and warehousing
- Purchasing non-oil products
- Producing and selling half-finished products
- Manufacturing consumer products
- Ensuring quality and process control
- Pipelining
- Administration
- Product enhancement
- Product development

12.1.3 *The bottleneck!*

The critical bottleneck in this market is the information exchange among internal partners, outside vendors, distributors, and ancillary services. Data from one distributor's lab analysis of crude oil, for example, may enter the system in the form of a spreadsheet compiled by a customized (and usually non-standard) program. Yet the receiving ERP system might need the data in its own format to populate its back-end database.

Maintaining communications for a pair of such sending and receiving systems currently requires highly-experienced (not to mention highly-paid) computer programmers on each end. This labor-intensive process impacts negatively on companies' return on investment (ROI).

The petrochemical industry urgently needs a cost-effective means of utilizing these highly-segmented downstream information flows and connecting them to existing EDI, ERP, and legacy systems. It must be possible to pass data in a timely, efficient and standard manner, to and from varied sources, without reinvesting in another transactional, ERP-related system.

12.2 | Integrating with XML

After making an initial investment in their business software systems of choice, companies want to maximize their investment and use the technology long enough to realize positive ROI. Particularly on the downstream end of the petrochemical Industry, most companies do not make such a capital outlay lightly. To them, software has not been perceived as part of the core business model.

12.2.1 Coexistence with EDI

XML can be used to empower existing software without reinvesting in a new application. Integrating the petrochemical industry with XML means linking existing legacy applications, not reengineering the wheel. Supply chain logistics surrounding the flow of petrochemical products can be used to evaluate the ease of transferring data between companies.

For example, in the trading of chemical related products and services, such as logistics and packaging, the Internet delivers cost savings in materials alone of approximately 10-20%. The only way to offer these cost savings to small suppliers is to offer them via e-commerce capabilities, but *without* a full EDI implementation.

The benefit to the larger companies of doing so is that they gain the ability to expand their existing market share and reach markets more quickly. The key to survival in this industry is maintaining well-established networks for distribution and supplies.

Figure 12-1 illustrates the co-existence of EDI and XML-based systems within a supply web. The utilization of an already existing system leverages the investment in that system and does not throw away the years of effort involved in creating the EDI-system mappings to back-end legacy data.

Figure 12-1   EDI and XML-based systems within a supply web

12.2.2   *Significant information flows*

The petrochemical industry business processes with the most significant information flows are:

- Exchange of information regarding the selling and buying of crude oil
- Transportation, pipelining, and warehousing: internally and among business partners
- Quality and process control
- Quoting and selling of half-finished products and consumer products
- Customer support

It is logical to extract this information from existing EDI systems and simply extend the reach of that information over the Internet to smaller companies. In other words, to create an integrated e-commerce environment in which traditional EDI and XML-EDI coexist and complement one another.

12.3 | Achieving a free-flowing information pipeline

By examining the downstream business processes more closely, it becomes clear that XML can enable the internal and external flows of information to avoid critical blockages.

12.3.1 *Internal information flows*

A typical example involves a large petrochemical company with activities in various joint ventures, and in manufacturing of high quality finished products. This firm also needs to acquire half finished products from other large firms to produce other finished goods, outside of its core product line.

The interconnectivity within this company must encompass thousands of internal businesses and their individual data processing systems. There are multiple plants in multiple countries, each with vendors supplying systems tailored for those countries and their languages.

XML can enable communication among these diverse systems. Moreover, because of its use of Unicode, it can support multiple natural languages.

12.3.2 *External information flows*

Many companies force the constraints of industry standards organizations upon their suppliers. These companies can only assure on-time deliveries when information is readily available to all partners in their supply web – all the time!

For example, a supplier of jet fuel to the world's major airports cannot afford to have a late delivery. There would be a domino effect that could cause plane delays, resulting in major expenses to the airlines and other industries – not just petrochemicals.

A company's supply chain may be secure, but how reliable is the information feeding that chain? The key to survival is maintaining well-established networks for distribution and supplies – and for distributing accurate contemporaneous information to all trading partners. XML makes it easy for legacy systems to communicate both internally and externally.

12.3.3 *Mergers and acquisitions*

A merger of multiple companies does not necessarily equate to smooth, fast integration, nor realistic savings. In fact, most merged companies experience a period where the inability to share transactional data seamlessly (because of the technical complexity) causes breakdowns in what were once the most streamlined of business processes.

Consider two Fortune 500 petrochemical companies with ten to fifteen core legacy applications each. Both utilize EDI, e-commerce, and Web-based procurement processes. Imagine them trying to merge their data, hoping to leverage their core competencies to new levels.

Streamlining this process by conventional programming techniques is as likely as getting oil to flow back up the pipeline. XML gives companies the ability to utilize their existing applications to communicate with all vendors and business partners, without forcing costly implementations on those who cannot afford the capital investment.

12.3.4 *XML integration aids*

To communicate accurately with business partners while using XML, systems must maintain links between industry standards and company-specific standards. Tools for schema management, such as Vitria's *BusinessWare Schema Central*, can be helpful in this regard. They are discussed in Chapter 37, "Schema management", on page 558.

12.4 | Conclusion

Ancillary businesses surrounding the petrochemical industry are expected to grow to 25% of its size in the next 2 years. To accommodate this growth, the industry needs integrated e-commerce. Those petrochemical companies that adopt it can become well-oiled internal information exchanges. The others will likely become the fossils of the future.

Integration

- Enterprise application integration (EAI)
- Mainframe integration
- Integrated provisioning
- Unified business integration

Part Four

Integrating applications that know nothing of one another is a challenge, even when they are internal to a single enterprise. So it may seem strange that the earliest integration success – EDI – was external integration. (Perhaps it's because internal projects frequently abandon loosely-coupled application integration in favor of a tightly-coupled ERP system, an option not open to external trading partners.)

We saw in Part 3 how XML is changing EDI. In this part we'll see how XML message formats and inexpensive Web transport protocols are starting to change all forms of integration, even between websites and ancient mainframe applications.

We'll also explore a challenge introduced by the rapid relationship changes that integration causes: How can you integrate the provisioning of user resource access rights in order to manage the constant change?

Finally, we'll examine the convergence of external and internal integration into a single *business integration* problem space. Think of it as the integration of integration!

Application integration with Web and email

Case Study

- Legacy applications
- Integration of outsourced website with internal system
- Email as XML data transport

Sponsor: Infoteria Corporation, http://www.infoteria.com

Contributing experts: Tim Browne and Sasha Epstein

If your sales leads come from your outsourced website, and your sales tracking is done on your internal legacy system, how do you integrate the two? XML, as we have seen, solves the data representation aspects of the problem. But how will the XML documents be transported from the outsourced system to yours? For one company there was an easy answer: You get mail!

The long history of software development has left a legacy of ancient but vital applications, each written in a vacuum. Modern business needs require that these programs now cooperate, not just with one another, but with the newest programs and technologies. We'll explore how one company solved the problem, but first let's see where the problem came from.

13.1 | Legacy applications

In the 1950s, all the data that a program needed was represented in a manner that was integral to the program ("hard-coding"). Each computer system required its own special forms of program code and data representation. And each individual programmer was free to use these instructions and formats in a unique way.

By the 1960s, data was separated from programs and stored in ASCII flat files. However, there was still an integral tightness maintained between programs and their data, both input and output. While standardized languages and coding styles were starting to be established within the programming community, the data to be manipulated by the programs was still generally represented in completely arbitrary ways, according to the preferences of the programmer and not in conformance to any standardized rules.

By the late 1970s, nearly all newly-designed systems took advantage of data modeling techniques, along with storage and representation in formal database management systems. Languages, grammars, and program analysis methods coalesced as the foundation of a software engineering discipline. In particular, the relational model for representing and accessing data became the dominant approach and *Structured Query Language (SQL)* became the pervasive standard for formulating queries of data stored in the relational form.

Today, many of the programs and systems created in the 60's and 70's are still operating (!) and constitute the legacy applications that may comprise the vital core of an organization's daily activities. However, the competitive environment in most sectors has changed substantially over the past few years. Enterprises can – and, in fact, must – tolerate the existence of legacy applications because it is either too expensive or too risky to replace or rewrite them. However, they cannot tolerate the rigidity that was assumed when those legacy applications were originally written.

13.2 | Enterprise application integration (EAI)

Commercial applications of computing have evolved from straightforward production of payroll checks to the pervasive, and vital, role of controlling the enterprise central nervous system. It would seem obvious that "the right hand should know what the left hand is doing." Surprisingly, though, the central nervous system metaphor suffers a breakdown when subjected to that simple test.

Despite the fully fifty years of commercial computing, most intra-enterprise – and nearly all inter-enterprise – computing applications do not communicate effectively or efficiently with one another.

Today, businesses must adapt quickly to changing circumstances or they will die. Everything about modern business is volatile, from interest rates to technology innovations to competitor strengths and weaknesses. For example, among many other things, businesses need to:

- modify the partners in their supply chains,
- collaborate with their partners,
- limit or expand information provided to their distribution channel,
- modify the prices that they charge to customers as groups or as individuals,
- bundle or unbundle packages of products or services.

All of these activities require interaction among different computer systems, platforms and applications. These interactions proceed more or less smoothly as a function of the degree of communication among the various components.

Historically, enterprises attempting to improve this communication have seen it as two separate problem domains:

- Internal, or intra-enterprise;
- External, or inter-enterprise.

13.2.1 *Internal integration*

Intra-enterprise system integration projects have almost always resulted in the design and implementation of enterprise resource planning (ERP) or materials resource planning (MRP) systems. These are based on a single vendor's proprietary schemes for writing applications and representing data. Unfortunately, these efforts have not always produced the net economic benefits that, in the original investment analysis, justified going forward.

Moreover, many of these efforts were undertaken at different times, by different departments, and utilizing different vendors. At the end of the day, therefore, most corporations have an intra-enterprise computing system apparatus that resembles a Rube Goldberg contraption. This jumble of computing applications, with its *ad hoc* and jerry-built connections, is typically what is really meant by the euphemism "legacy applications".

13.2.2 *External integration*

The inter-enterprise integration and connectivity picture is hardly much prettier, if not actually worse. Typically, independent business partners who wish to share data electronically have to use either

- electronic data interchange (EDI);
- *ad hoc* electronic file transfer; or
- electronic mail.

EDI is both secure and predictable, but very expensive. As we saw in Chapter 10, "From EDI to IEC: The new Web commerce", on page 166, the realization of its potential benefits requires:

- a point-to-point real or virtual private network;
- compatible systems on both ends of the communication link;
- absolute compliance with X.12 or EDIFACT transaction and semantic rules; and
- custom programming for each document type to be transferred, on a per-business-partner basis.

To evaluate the other methods, we need to separate the media from the messages.

Ad hoc electronic file transfer and email are not as expensive as EDI, but neither are they as secure, reliable, or predictable.[1]

However, these weaknesses as transport mechanisms are surmountable, and are getting better all the time. The real problem is that both custom code and one-off translation/interpretation may be required to make sense of the data being transferred.

A thousand years ago, during the Middle Ages, crusaders and traders from many nations found themselves along the eastern shore of the Mediterranean Sea with a similar problem. They needed to communicate but had no common language. A kind of simplified pidgin language or jargon, called *lingua franca*, grew up to enable simple business transactions. In modern times, the term is applied to any common or commercial language or mechanism for communication among diverse peoples or systems.

---

1. Sneaker-net transmission of electronic files by manual delivery of tapes or disks may be, but just isn't fast enough, even with the coolest sneakers!

SQL is a modern *lingua franca*, but it has limitations. It assumes that the data to be queried, retrieved, or manipulated is stored and represented in conformance to the relational model.

XML, however, makes no such assumptions. It is rapidly becoming the *lingua franca* for everything else. Let's see how a company solved an external integration problem by combining XML with inexpensive transport mechanisms.

13.3 | Subject Software Company

Subject Software Company is a fictional name for a real software publisher. The company maintains a website on which it offers free trials of its products. Interested visitors complete a "trial software download form", which is an important source of sales leads

13.4 | The challenge

Like many companies, Subject Software manages its own internal system for sales force automation, customer support, order entry, and other business-unit applications, as well as enterprise email. However, its website is operated by its Internet service provider (ISP) and is not connected to its internal system.

As a result, the sales leads from the trial software downloads had to be imported manually from the outsourced website. This was done on a weekly basis, using a *comma-separated values (CSV)* text file. Subject Software needed to integrate its website with its internal system, as shown in Figure 13-1.

The company was able to accomplish this goal using Infoteria Corporation's *Asteria Components*. The new design is a message-oriented middleware solution. It uses XML documents and the Internet email infrastructure to move the sales lead information quickly from the website to the internal sales systems. Lead processing is now automatic, and occurs almost immediately after a person downloads trial software from the outsourced website.

Let's take a closer look at the new system.

Internet Service Provider

Prospect   Trial Software Form

Web Server

Internet

Sales Person   New Prospect Form

Lead-tracking System

In-house System

Figure 13-1   Integrating sales leads generated at an outsourced website

13.5 | The solution

The architecture of the new system is illustrated in Figure 13-2. An XML document contains information collected at the outsourced website. It is transmitted to the internal *Notes/Domino* sales-tracking system using the Internet email infrastructure as the transport.

The process consists of three parts:

1. Create and send XML email
2. Receive and verify XML email

3. Process XML email and update database

Figure 13-2   Lead-tracking system architecture

13.5.1   *One: Create and send XML email*

When a user fills out a form to download a trial version of software from the outsourced website, a `RegisterUser.CGI` script is invoked. That script calls the `Send_XML_Lead` subroutine, an excerpt from which is shown in Example 13-1.

Send_XML_Lead creates a `Download` XML document, like that shown in Example 13-2. It incorporates the document in an email message and calls the `SendMail` component of the Web server operating system to send the message to the lead-tracking inbox on the internal system's mail server.

Example 13-1. Excerpt from Send_XML_Lead subroutine

```
sub send_xml_lead {
  if ($FORM{'email'} ne '') {
  open (LEAD, ">$leadtemp") || die "Can't open $leadtemp!\n";
  print LEAD "To: SalesLeads\@infoteria.com\n";
  print LEAD "From: Infoteria <website@infoteria.com>\n";
  print LEAD "Reply-To: website\@infoteria.com\n";
  print LEAD "Content-Transfer-Encoding: 7bit\n";
  print LEAD "Content-Type: text/plain\n";
  print LEAD "Subject: $fullname ($product $edition) \n\n";
  print LEAD "<\?xml version=\"1.0\" encoding=\"UTF-8\"?>\n";
  print LEAD "<Download>\n";
  print LEAD "<Person>\n";
  print LEAD "  <FirstName>$FORM{'fname'}</FirstName>\n";
  print LEAD "</Person> \n";
  ...
  print LEAD "</Download>\n";
  close (LEAD);
  system("$convprog -SJ $leadtemp|$mailprog -t");
  }
}
```

Example 13-2. XML document created by CGI Script in Example 13-1

```
<?xml version="1.0" encoding="UTF-8"?>
<Download>
<Person>
  <FirstName>Robert</FirstName>
  <LastName>Blacken</LastName>
  <FullName>Robert Blacken</FullName>
  <MailAddress>rblacken@infoteria.com</MailAddress>
  <JobTitle>CIO</JobTitle>
</Person>
<Company>
  <CompanyName>Infoteria</CompanyName>
  <OfficeAddress>900 Cummings Center</OfficeAddress>
  <OfficeCity>Beverly</OfficeCity>
  <OfficeState>Massachusetts</OfficeState>
  <OfficeZip>01915</OfficeZip>
  <OfficeCountry>United States</OfficeCountry>
  <OfficePhone>978-922-4029</OfficePhone>
</Company>
<Other>
  <Comment>Evaluating software for new app</Comment>
  <Categories>Download - iPEX for Solaris</Categories>
</Other>
</Download>
```

13.5.2 *Two: Receive and verify XML email*

The second part of the process is handled inside the company's firewall, on its internal system. The `Download` XML documents containing the sales leads are stored in a mail queue on the company's Lotus *Domino* mail server.

Infoteria's *iMESSENGER*™ product pulls the email into a working directory, using the IMAP4 protocol. It verifies the sender's email address and the document type of the XML documents (in this case, `Download`). This information determines the subsequent processing, as we'll see shortly.

iMESSENGER is message-oriented middleware whose behavior is configurable by the configuration tool shown in Figure 13-3. That figure illustrates some of the settings that were used for this application. The program was set to run at one minute intervals and to use `D:\SalesLead\XML` as the working directory.

The configuration tool supports multiple categories of XML email in one or more email queues. It does so by allowing different behaviors to be specified for different XML document types and/or sender's email addresses.

13.5.3 *Three: Process XML email and update database*

After verification, the XML document is processed according to the business rules defined for the particular sender and document type. The rules can cause *iMESSENGER* to invoke DOS batch (.BAT) files or executable programs (.EXE). They also cause the internal system database to be updated with data extracted from the XML document.

Because Subject Software's internal system uses Lotus *Notes*, they were able to use Infoteria's *iCONNECTOR for Notes*™ to update the lead-tracking database. That tool includes *iRuleGenerator*™, a graphical interface for defining the rules for extracting data from XML elements and updating the corresponding database fields. The defined rules are represented in XML.

Example 13-3 shows a subset of the XML *rule* document used in this application. It maps the element types of a `Download` document onto the fields of the `Person` form in the *Domino* lead-tracking system.

Figure 13-3   *iMESSENGER* Configuration Tool

Although Subject Software's system uses Lotus *Notes* and *Domino*, the principles apply to any email system and to any database management system.

Example 13-3. Excerpt from rule document

```xml
<?xml version="1.0" encoding="UTF-8"?>
<rule:rule
  xmlns:rule=
    "http://www.xmlns.org/system/jp/co/infoteria/rule/"
  xmlns:notes=
    "http://www.xmlns.org/system/jp/co/infoteria/tdf/notes/"
  default-space="strip"
  indent-result="yes">
<rule:template
  match="/database/table[@name=&quot;Person&quot;]/record">
  <Download>
  <Person>
    <FirstName>
      <rule:apply-templates
        select="field[@name=&quot;FirstName&quot;]"
        mode="_Download_Person_FirstName_.text."/>
    </FirstName>
    <LastName>
      <rule:apply-templates
        select="field[@name=&quot;LastName&quot;]"
        mode="_Download_Person_LastName_.text."/>
    </LastName>
    ...
  </Person>
  ...
  </Download>
</rule:template>
</rule:rule>
```

Integrating the mainframe

Application Discussion

- Interface emulation

- Screen scraping

- IBM *Customer Information Control System (CICS)*

- XML-based host access

Sponsor: HostBridge Technology, http://www.hostbridge.com

Contributing experts: Russ Teubner and Michael Wilson

Chapter

14

Just in case you thought the mainframe was dead, brush away that tear. Tens of thousands of large enterprises rely on data stored on IBM-compatible mainframes, hidden behind applications that, by today's standards, are difficult to learn and use. These firms need to integrate that host data with Web applications, for use by employees, customers, and partners. XML lets you do it without reprogramming your mission-critical host applications.

iven that mainframe applications have evolved over five decades, it is not surprising that they come in numerous types and varieties. But one architecture that predominates is the classic transactional application, designed to interact with a user at a fixed-function terminal.

14.1 | The mainframe: *CICS*, but...

A substantial portion of those applications run under IBM's *Customer Information Control System (CICS)* and interact with a user at an IBM 3270 terminal.

How substantial?

According to IBM, there are approximately 20,000 large organizations using *CICS*. Among them, they process an incredible 30 billion transactions per day, with a commercial value of several trillion dollars per week.

But CICS applications are usually designed to interact with live users at dumb terminals, so for a Web application to share its data, the CICS application has to be fooled. That job is performed by a *host access solution*. It gets between the Web and CICS applications and must perform the following functions:

- Accept the request for host application access from the external application.
- Maintain a session, or the functional equivalent of a session, between the external application and the host application.
- Receive input data from the external application; process and transform the input data for presentation to the host application as input.
- Receive the output data sent from the host application; process and transform the output data for presentation to the external application.

The traditional approach to host access is to intercept the data to and from the terminal, but there is a newer method that takes advantage of XML. We'll compare the two, using *CICS* applications as examples.

14.2 | Display-oriented host access

The objective of this approach is to re-create the IBM 3270 terminal user interface in a Web browser. It is usually implemented with *Java* applets that communicate with the host using the TN3270 remote login protocol.

Figure 14-1 shows the rendition of a typical *CICS* transaction on a 3270 terminal.[1]

Several display-oriented strategies are possible. We'll consider the tradeoffs and then examine a fundamental problem with the whole approach.

14.2.1 *Design tradeoffs*

The fundamental design decision for display-oriented host access is whether existing 3270 application screens should be emulated without change, or whether they should be enhanced in some way.

---

1. They don't win a lot of design awards!

Figure 14-1 *CICS* transaction on IBM 3270 display

Strict emulation has several advantages:

- There is no need to design or maintain new user interfaces.
- The approach is scalable because it requires little or no software on the middle-tier server.
- There is no learning curve for users familiar with the applications on a real 3270.
- Changes to the real 3270 user interfaces can be reflected automatically in the Web interface.

The alternative to emulation is to use HTML and other modern technologies to create intuitive interfaces that will make host applications accessible to a broader range of users. New functionality can even be added to the applications by using Web page scripts to manipulate data on its way to or from the host.

For large applications, however, which can have thousands of screens, the cost of designing new Web interfaces can be prohibitive. Moreover, both large and small applications are subject to maintenance problems because of their dependency on 3270 data streams for communicating between the host application and the Web.

Information is extracted from the 3270 screen layout and data stream by means of a technique known as *screen scraping*. Row and column coordinates are used to locate the data areas that are processed as input or output. As a result, any change a *CICS* programmer makes to a host application must be communicated to the Web developer, who must make a corresponding change.

Fortunately, this dependency applies only to the 3270 screens, which are merely a rendition of the underlying abstract data. Changes to the actual application or business logic will not affect the Web application unless they also affect the user interface.

14.2.2   *End-user orientation*

Display-oriented host access methods serve the needs of organizations that want *end-users* to access the applications. Most Web-to-host products that support these methods convert host data into HTML so that it is readable through Web browsers.

Unfortunately, what works well for a browser doesn't work well for other applications. That's because browsers operate on *renditions* of data, which they present to human users. Other programs need to manipulate unrendered *abstract* data.[2]

For example, suppose a company needs to run a daily check with a distributor on parts availability. Using a display-oriented Web-to-host solution that translates the host application data to HTML, the results of a query to the host application might look something like Example 14-1.

When processed by a browser and presented to an end-user, as in Table 14-1, this page might make perfect sense. However, when processed as input data by another program it would make little sense. To parse this HTML and identify which of the table data (td) elements are part numbers, item descriptions, and available units is very complex. HTML merely describes the rendition of the data elements as cells in a table, rather than their abstract meaning.

---

2. Please review 1.1.4.3, "Abstractions and renditions", on page 13 if this distinction isn't clear. It is vital to understanding XML and recurs throughout the book.

Example 14-1. Inventory check in HTML

```
<html>
<table width="20* 40* 40*" border="0">
  <tr>
    <td>Part #</td>
    <td>Item description</td>
    <td>Available units</td>
  </tr>
  <tr>
    <td>123-ABC</td>
    <td>Component A</td>
    <td>12 </td>
  </tr>
  <tr>
    <td>456-DEF</td>
    <td>Component B</td>
    <td>5</td>
  </tr>
</table>
</body>
</html>
```

Table 14-1   Browser presentation of Example 14-1

Part #	Item description	Available units
123-ABC	Component A	12
456-DEF	Component B	5

14.3 | XML-based host access

A new generation of host access products is directed towards providing access to other software, as opposed to end-users. They solve the problems of screen scraping and data recognition by converting host data into XML.

And unlike HTML and the display-oriented techniques, the XML documents capture the abstract data. For example, Example 14-2 shows an XML alternative to the HTML document in Example 14-1. Note that it has distinct element types for part numbers (partnum), item descriptions(description), and available units (units).

Example 14-2. Inventory check in XML

```
<?xml version="1.0" ?>
<response>
  <catalog_item>
    <partnum>123-ABC</partnum>
    <description>Component A</description>
    <units>12</units>
  </catalog_item>
  <catalog_item>
    <partnum>456-DEF</partnum>
    <description>Component B</description>
    <units>5</units>
  </catalog_item>
</response>
```

As the 3270 data stream describes a rendered user interface, we have to look elsewhere to find the abstract data for the XML document. Fortunately, most *CICS* applications don't interact with the 3270 terminal directly. Instead they utilize a *CICS* component called *Basic Mapping Support (BMS)*.

BMS acts like a formatter for the 3270. The application works internally with abstract data items, called "fields". It also has a library of stylesheets, called "maps", for the transactions that it supports. The maps determine where on the 3270 screen the fields are to be placed.

A transaction calls BMS, specifying a map name and a set of field names and values to be used with it. BMS generates the appropriate 3270 data stream. BMS also accepts the 3270 terminal input and returns it to the program as values for the corresponding fields.

An XML application connector can use IBM's *3270 Bridge Interface* to replace BMS and handle the input and output for the application. Figure 14-2 shows the basic architecture.

Using this approach, a typical transaction would consist of the following steps:

1. The external application sends an HTTP request to the host, in the form of a query string or an XML document.

Figure 14-2   Integrating *CICS* with XML

2. The host receives the HTTP request and, if access is authorized, passes it to the XML application connector.
3. The XML application connector starts the transaction on the host, provides it the relevant input data, and receives the output from the transaction.
4. The XML application connector converts the output data to XML and sends it back to the external application as part of the HTTP response.

14.4 | A sample application

Take another look at the screen image in Figure 14-1. It shows how the output of a typical BMS-based *CICS* transaction would appear on a 3270 terminal.

14.4.1 *The XML representation*

Now look at Example 14-3 and Example 14-4. These show an XML representation of the abstract data that was sent to BMS by the application, before it was rendered. The XML was created by *HostBridge*, an XML application connector developed by HostBridge Technology.

Note what this XML document does and does not contain.

Example 14-3. XML representation of Figure 14-1 (1 of 2)

```
<hostbridge>
<!--  HostBridge Copyright 2000, 2001 HostBridge Technology,
      U.S. Patent Pending  -->
<token>73722b93</token>
<timestamp>20010702154224</timestamp>
<status> <response>0</response><desc>ok</desc></status>
<transaction facility="}AAB" next_tranid="TRAD">
 <status>
  <cics_resp>0</cics_resp><cics_resp2>0</cics_resp2>
  <cics_desc>ok</cics_desc><task_end>endtask</task_end>
  <abend_code/>
 </status>
 <parameters><tranid>TRAD</tranid><userid>DSI1</userid></parameters>
 <command>
  <send_map erase="y" erase_unp="n" unlock_kb="y"
           alarm="n" reset_mdt="n">
   <mapset>TRADBMS</mapset><map>T004</map>
   <data_indicator>map_and_data</data_indicator>
   <fields count="15">
    <field name="USER41" index="0"><name len="6">USER41</name>
     <value maxlen="20" len="4">RUSS</value>
     <attr byte="00" justify="l" disp="n" prot="n" num="n"
          int="n" mdt="n" /></field>
    <field name="COMP41" index="0"><name len="6">COMP41</name>
     <value maxlen="20" len="19">Casey_Import_Export</value>
     <attr byte="00" justify="l" disp="n" prot="n" num="n"
          int="n" mdt="n" /></field>
    <field name="SHRNOW" index="0"><name len="6">SHRNOW</name>
     <value maxlen="8" len="8">00079.00</value>
     <attr byte="00" justify="l" disp="n" prot="n" num="n"
          int="n" mdt="n" /></field>
    <field name="SELL" index="0"><name len="4">SELL</name>
     <value maxlen="12" len="3">007</value>
     <attr byte="00" justify="l" disp="n" prot="n" num="n"
          int="n" mdt="n" /></field>
    <field name="SHARE7" index="0"><name len="6">SHARE7</name>
     <value maxlen="8" len="8">00059.00</value>
     <attr byte="00" justify="l" disp="n" prot="n" num="n"
          int="n" mdt="n" /></field>
    <field name="SHARE6" index="0"><name len="6">SHARE6</name>
     <value maxlen="8" len="8">00063.00</value>
     <attr byte="00" justify="l" disp="n" prot="n" num="n"
          int="n" mdt="n" /></field>
```

It does *not* contain row/column references to data fields within a screen space; there is no screen scraping in the applications that process the document.

Example 14-4. XML representation of Figure 14-1 (2 of 2)

```
    <field name="BUY" index="0"><name len="3">BUY</name>
     <value maxlen="12" len="3">010</value>
     <attr byte="00" justify="l" disp="n" prot="n" num="n"
           int="n" mdt="n" /></field>
    <field name="SHARE5" index="0"><name len="6">SHARE5</name>
     <value maxlen="8" len="8">00065.00</value>
     <attr byte="00" justify="l" disp="n" prot="n" num="n"
           int="n" mdt="n" /></field>
    <field name="SHARE4" index="0"><name len="6">SHARE4</name>
     <value maxlen="8" len="8">00070.00</value>
     <attr byte="00" justify="l" disp="n" prot="n" num="n"
           int="n" mdt="n" /></field>
    <field name="SHARE3" index="0"><name len="6">SHARE3</name>
     <value maxlen="8" len="8">00072.00</value>
     <attr byte="00" justify="l" disp="n" prot="n" num="n"
           int="n" mdt="n" /></field>
    <field name="SHARE2" index="0"><name len="6">SHARE2</name>
     <value maxlen="8" len="8">00078.00</value>
     <attr byte="00" justify="l" disp="n" prot="n" num="n"
           int="n" mdt="n" /></field>
    <field name="HELD" index="0"><name len="4">HELD</name>
     <value maxlen="12" len="4">0500</value>
     <attr byte="00" justify="l" disp="n" prot="n" num="n"
           int="n" mdt="n" /></field>
    <field name="SHARE1" index="0"><name len="6">SHARE1</name>
     <value maxlen="8" len="8">00077.00</value>
     <attr byte="00" justify="l" disp="n" prot="n" num="n"
           int="n" mdt="n" /></field>
    <field name="VALUE" index="0"><name len="5">VALUE</name>
     <value maxlen="12" len="12">000039500.00</value>
     <attr byte="00" justify="l" disp="n" prot="n" num="n"
           int="n" mdt="n" /></field>
    <field name="MESS4" index="0"><name len="5">MESS4</name>
     <value maxlen="79" len="20">Request Completed OK</value>
     <attr byte="00" justify="l" disp="n" prot="n" num="n"
           int="n" mdt="n" /></field>
   </fields>
  </send_map>
 </command>
</transaction>
</hostbridge>
```

Nor does it contain the literal values on the screen (e.g., "Share Trading Demonstration"). This information may be important as part of a user interface, but the *CICS* application never sees or processes it. It is therefore superfluous for program-to-program communications.

On the other hand, it *does* contain the actual field name and value pairs that the application uses. Because the same names are also used in the BMS map and the XML document, a source of confusion among the developers is eliminated.

Finally, note that *HostBridge* uses a single XML document type for all transactions, which can simplify development.

14.4.2 *Invoking the application*

As we saw in Figure 14-2, the *CICS* transaction is invoked by the XML application connector in response to an HTTP request. For example, to invoke a transaction called TRAD using *HostBridge*, an application would send the following URI:

```
http://company.com:[port]/hostbridge?HB_TRANID=TRAD
```

To change the contents of the USER41 field from "RUSS" to "MICHAEL", the following would be appended to the URI:

```
&HB_TOKEN=73722b93&USER41=MICHAEL
```

The resulting full URI is shown in Table 14-2, along with an explanation of its components.

14.5 | Conclusion

Large organizations continue to exploit the power of IBM-compatible mainframes as part of their mission-critical IT infrastructure. For most of these organizations, their *CICS* applications must now be part of their Internet strategy. They must find ways to exploit the data and business logic contained in these applications.

To do so, they can utilize two approaches:

- Create end-user Web interfaces to the application by using techniques such as 3270 emulation and screen scraping.
- Integrate Web applications with host applications by using XML application connectors to access the host's abstract data.

Table 14-2   Explanation of URI for *CICS* access

This part of the URI...	Does this...
http://company.com:[port]	Identifies the address of the mainframe and the port assigned to *HostBridge*.
hostbridge?	Identifies this as a *HostBridge* request.
HB_TRANID=TRAD	Specifies the name of the *CICS* transaction to be invoked.
HB_TOKEN=f275ffa4	After initially connecting to the host application, *HostBridge* returns a session ID token (shown in Example 14-3 as `<token>73722b93</token>`). Subsequent transactions with the host include this token in the URI in order to be recognized as part of the same session.
USER41=MICHAEL	Specifies the field name and the data value to enter in the transaction. *HostBridge* interprets any name/value pair in the URI as input for a field, unless the name starts with "HB_" (e.g. HB_TOKEN).

Integrated provisioning

Application Discussion

■ Resource change management

■ Directories

■ Active Digital Profile (ADPr)

Sponsor: Business Layers, http://www.businesslayers.com

Contributing expert: Adrian Viego

Chapter 15

Congratulations! You've installed your integration server and joined an e-commerce marketplace. Suddenly you have business partners by the score and guess what? They need access to your inventory, employee contacts, catalogs, and more. Your applications may be integrated, but odds are their access rights provisioning is still a jumble of separate processes that can't keep up with the demand. They need some integration of their own!

Ebenezer Scrooge had it easy!
When he needed extra help for the Christmas rush, equipping the temp with the necessities was no big deal: a desk, a stool, some foolscap, quills, ink, blotting sand, a candle or two, and suddenly Bob Cratchit had an assistant.

That process is called *provisioning*, and today there's a lot more to it.

15.1 | Provisioning provides problems!

For a modern enterprise, provisioning a new business partner or employee means giving them access to a lot more than quills and ink, as Figure 15-1 illustrates. Substantial IT resources are involved.

Even as simple a situation as provisioning a contractor to deal with a temporary peak in business activity requires a lot of IT resources and services:

equipment
PC, telephone, pager, PDA, cell phone, etc.

Figure 15-1   Provisioning in a modern enterprise

data network resources

> user accounts, email accounts, etc.

security resources

> firewall "hole", VPN tunnel, RADIUS server, etc.

telecom resources

> extension number, voice mail, conference calling, international dialing, hunt group definitions, etc.

application resources

> groupware, task-specific applications, office applications, etc.

database access

> local sales databases, contact manager, etc.

The records of users of these resources and their access rights are called *profiles*. A large enterprise might have them spread among scores of databases, spreadsheets, and documents. Each might be in a different location, with different access and control features. The programs that manage them cannot interact with each other.

A single business event, like adding a new partner to an extranet, invariably involves multiple resource change tasks, like setting up accounts, configuring firewalls and PBXs, and granting database access. Because of the multiple incompatible profile systems, however, these tasks are not connected in the computer system. The situation presents a security exposure as there is no way to modify a single profile for a user and have it consistently affect all company resources.

Moreover, tracking and coordination among the various profile systems can require substantial time and attention from the IT staff. And this at a time when the demand for IT provisioning has increased dramatically, thanks to e-business and the integration we've been discussing in these pages. In many cases, business changes are happening faster than the infrastructure can support.

It would seem that the resource management on which enterprise integration depends could use some integration of its own!

15.2 | Resource directories

Network systems provide specialized databases for network resource management called *directories*. They also provide protocols that let programs access the profiles stored in the directories. Fortunately, most vendors support the IETF's *Lightweight Directory Access Protocol (LDAP)*.[1] As a result, directories and their associated LDAP directory services offer the promise of centralizing provisioning resources for every user on the network, while putting control in the hands of business management.

Such a centralized directory of enterprise resources is depicted in Figure 15-2. Creating one, though, can be a challenge.

The straightforward, brute force approach is to migrate all existing profile databases into a single LDAP directory. While that solves the management and security problems, it has a drawback.

In order to realize the full potential of a centralized directory, applications and network devices must be able to communicate with it directly.

---

1. LDAP works with directories whose data models conform to an international standard called *X.500*.

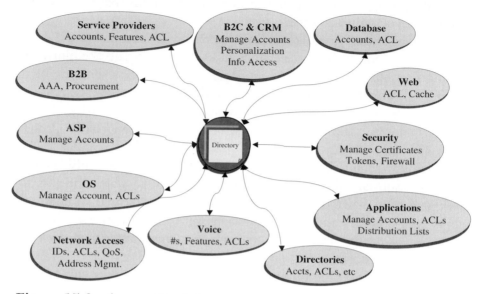

Figure 15-2   A centralized directory

Today, most applications and network devices do not have this capability; they are not yet "directory-enabled".

One way to deal with the temporary lack of directory-enabled applications and devices is to adopt a *meta-directory* approach. In this scenario, the LDAP directory still becomes the central user profile data repository, but the existing user directories and databases are left intact. To update and synchronize those legacy databases and directories, the meta-directory employs "connectors", much as integration servers do.

When a change is made to a user profile, the meta-directory translates the data and transmits it to the affected directories in formats that they understand. Applications and devices continue to access the legacy directories directly.

All major directory vendors are delivering meta-directory capabilities for their LDAP directories. However, like early application integration efforts, they are hampered by the proprietary nature of the legacy directories and the connector implementations.

Although LDAP provides a standard way to communicate with a directory, it does not standardize the form of the user profiles. XML is coming to the rescue here as it has done in other integration domains. The *Directory Services Markup Language (DSML)* is being developed as an industry standard representation for sharing data among disparate directories and database systems.

15.3 | Integrated provisioning

LDAP directories and meta-directories provide a centralized repository of user and resource information. However, that information is at a technical and physical level, unconnected to business activities.

In other words, directories alone cannot provide capabilities like:

business event translation
> Translating an activity from business terms, such as "hiring a contractor", to the specific resource changes that must occur to provision it: "what exactly does the contractor need to do his job".

workflow generation
> Creating a synchronized workflow to implement the provisioning tasks in the optimum order. For example, it is impossible to install the contractor's software before a computer is made available.

business-level resource coordination
> Maintaining a coordinated business view of resource allocations. For example, when a project is over, how can the company de-provision resources that were allocated to users specifically for that project.

Facilities like these require business-level (as opposed to IT-level) coordination of resource deployment across disparate legacy directories and databases. They require, in effect, a specialized form of application integration; a kind of "resource portal". Vendors offer a variety of such *integrated provisioning* systems.

Business Layers, for example, offers its *eProvision Day One*™ product. It performs the functions of a provisioning platform, as illustrated in Figure 15-3.

Let's step through a provisioning activity using the system. The last digits of the following subsection numbers correspond to the numbers in the diagram.

Figure 15-3   How integrated provisioning works

15.3.1 *Report a business event*

The system includes a Web-based GUI. When the system is deployed, managers use it to create resource access profiles for everyone connected with the enterprise, including employees, business partners and vendors. They also create profiles that associate business events with IT tasks. As business events occur, managers can use the interface to report the events to the system in familiar business terms. Events can also be reported by other systems, such as CRM, SCM, or HR.

A new contractor will be added to the marketing team in Dallas and will work as a copywriter on the Marley project.

15.3.2 *Generate list of resource changes required by the event*

The business event triggers the automatic creation of a list of resource changes that are necessary to support the event.

The contractor will need a standard PC with office and desktop publishing tools, an email account, access to marketing databases, a telephone extension with a speakerphone, and business cards.

15.3.3 *Create a workflow to execute the resource change tasks*

The provisioning platform creates a task sequence to implement the required resource changes for the business event.

Buy the PC, install the software, set up the user accounts and database access. In parallel, the telephone must be installed and set up, and the business cards ordered.

15.3.4 *Execute tasks requiring legacy system access*

APIs, scripts, and DSML-based connectors are used to interact with legacy directories and databases. The system initiates the completely automated activities.

Create user accounts, provide database access, and configure the departmental PBX.

For tasks that require human participation, the system generates notifications and escalations to employees and managers as needed.

Buy the computer. Order the business cards.

15.3.5   *Execute tasks requiring the centralized directory*

LDAP directory services perform the tasks associated with profiles stored in the centralized directory. To the extent that the directory is also a meta-directory, legacy systems are accessed as in the previous step.

15.3.6   *Log each task and action and generate reports*

Each completed resource change action is logged to a database. Provisioning activities are tracked, and historical information is maintained regarding the business event that triggered the action as well as the action itself. Managers use the generated reports to control provisioning activities and to connect resource change activities to the business events that triggered them.

   Project Marley is over; remove all its contractors from the system.

15.4 | Active Digital Profile (ADPr)

We've mentioned DSML, the emerging industry standard for communicating among directories. There is also a corresponding business-level standard in development by OASIS, for communication within and among provisioning systems.

   It is an XML document type called the *Active Digital Profile (ADPr)*. The development effort is intended to encompass all major resource categories, including, among others, human resources, operating systems, messaging, PBX, VoIP, security, database, directories, and PKI.

   Figure 15-4 shows the structure of an ADPr document.

15.5 | Conclusion

Advances in directory technology and recent product offerings are making it easier for organizations to manage resource deployment. However, there is no systematic connection of these resource changes to the business events

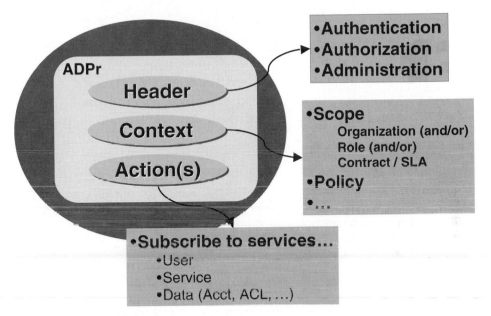

Figure 15-4   ADPr document structure

that initiate them, which makes coordination difficult and creates security exposures.

Integrated provisioning, by applying techniques of application integration to directories and resource profile databases, can provide that coordination. It offers the potential of keeping up with the increasing demand for resource changes induced by the ever-shifting relations of e-business.

Business integration

Application Discussion

- Partner connectivity

- Application connectivity

- Data transformation

- Process management

- Software and services

Sponsor: Peregrine Systems, http://www.peregrine.com

Contributing expert: Greg Olsen, Ph.D.

Chapter

16

In the quest for efficient operation and increased customer satisfaction, enterprises seek greater integration of their business processes with those of their partner suppliers and customers. Unfortunately, their independent software gets in the way. But thanks to XML, independent software can cooperate while remaining independent, and the desired business integration can be achieved.

P erhaps the earliest form of business integration is traditional *electronic data interchange (EDI)*, which allows members of a supply chain to conduct business electronically. With the rise of the Internet and the expansion of e-business, other areas have become targets for integration.

Caution   Acronym alert! This chapter contains an Alphabet Soup of Initialisms and Acronyms (ASIA). Please don't be put off by them. They're not for understanding the chapter, but to help readers who know them to see where they fit in the framework that the chapter describes. Any we don't explain here can safely be ignored, (Or you can look them up in Chapter 68, "Acronyms and initialisms in The XML Handbook", on page 1102.)

16.1 | Integration domains

Integration efforts have traditionally been categorized as either internal or external.

Internal integration occurs within an organization. Some examples are:

- Integration of application packages from different vendors.
- Integration of legacy systems with newer packaged applications.
- Coordination of data between business applications and data marts and data warehouses.
- Development of custom-distributed software applications.

External integration occurs among separate organizations. Domains include:

Supply chain integration
Sharing information with suppliers, customers, distributors, outsourced providers of fabrication or assembly services, etc.

Business unit integration
For example, post-merger coordination of independent business units.

Market integration
Procurement activities brokered through a market exchange would be an example.

For years, these two types of integration problem were considered independent of one another. Different groups within a company would manage the relevant activities separately and might apply completely different technology approaches to their solutions. Figure 16-1 shows an oversimplified view of the development of business integration.

E-business has progressed to the point where these separate integration efforts, which go by names like *Enterprise Application Integration (EAI)* and *Business to Business Integration (B2Bi)*, have converged into a single *business integration* problem space. The terms *eBusiness Integration (eBI)* and *Enterprise Business Integration (EBI)* are often used to describe the convergence.

Figure 16-1 A brief history of business integration

By "convergence" we mean that software and service providers are addressing these formerly independent problems holistically. It also means that the problem space can be described through a single set of layered components, the business integration stack.

16.2 | The business integration stack

Business integration is a complex activity that is built from several layers of technology. Figure 16-2 shows a high-level view of the business integration stack.

16.2.1 *Infrastructure*

The infrastructure technologies on which business integration relies are, of necessity, pervasive. They therefore tend to emanate from highly influential sources:

Figure 16-2   The business integration stack

- major software infrastructure vendors (e.g. IBM, Microsoft, Oracle, and Sun),
- open source initiatives,
- formal standards organizations (e.g. ISO, IEEE, ANSI), and
- industry consortia (e.g. W3C, IETF, OASIS, RosettaNet).

They fall into three major categories that we'll now examine.

16.2.1.1   System servers

Application servers have emerged as the focal point for runtime management and a variety of brokering functions used in integration solutions. Reliable messaging systems are also a fundamental component of nearly all integration solutions, as are information repositories.

While some products in the integration platform layer may incorporate facilities like these, developers increasingly expect them to be available as part of the infrastructure of a system.

16.2.1.2   Information representation

XML has emerged as the primary information representation for both internal and external integration requirements. It is an important ingredient in all the integration platform components at the next layer, as well as being employed in other infrastructure components.

In addition to the base XML 1.0 standard and related W3C standards such as XSLT and XLink, the infrastructure layer includes industry standards based on XML. Many consortia (e.g. RosettaNet and OAG) are developing common vocabularies that can be used in both internal and external integration contexts. While XML is clearly the preferred information representation approach some EBI vendors have yet to convert from proprietary information representations.

16.2.1.3   Security and communications

Recent years have seen a dramatic improvement in the technologies available in this category, for both internal and external integration needs. They include public key infrastructure (PKI), data compression, a diverse set of communication protocols (e.g. TCP/IP, HTTP, RMI, IIOP, SOAP), message and channel security standards, and directory infrastructure standards (e.g. LDAP, UDDI).

16.2.2   *Integration platform*

The integration platform layer builds upon the infrastructure just described. Its components are obtainable from a variety of integration product and service vendors.

It is important to keep in mind that the word "integration" refers only to the business result. At the software level, a better term would be "coordination". Individual application programs need not be rewritten; they can be totally unaware of one another.

Instead, the integration platform allows them to share data, and schedules their operation so as to achieve the desired result. Developers refer to this remote coordination of programs, when running on multiple computers, as *distributed computing*.

The integration platform components are shown in Figure 16-3. We'll discuss them in the following sections.

Figure 16-3   Integration platform components

16.2.2.1   Partner connectivity

Even with the advances in the available security and communications infrastructure, external communications (communications across organizational boundaries) are still a primary focus at the integration platform level. That is because of the diverse set of partners, and corresponding diverse partner connectivity requirements, that any good-sized organization is likely to have.

Typical requirements for partner connectivity include the need to support multiple communication protocols and security models, diverse approaches to message "envelopes", and multiple techniques for error recovery and other communication details.

16.2.2.2   Application connectivity

Integration platforms accomplish their magic by creating a "normalized" view of the applications with which they interact. This view includes the representation of the data that will be interchanged with the application, the protocols for requesting services from the application, and the means by which the application can initiate communications with the platform. This normalized view relies heavily on XML.

Unfortunately, the applications typically don't share this view. They have their own way of doing things that may have served them for years, even decades!

The primary method for bridging these conflicting views is through the use of software *adapters* (also called *connectors*). Adapters provide a bridge between the interfaces presented by applications and the normalized view of the integration platform.

Ideally, application adapters should require little or no custom coding. Vendors may supply wizards that can automatically configure an adapter by accessing a repository of application interface descriptions and metadata. This wizard-based approach not only simplifies initial installation but also provides significant advantages for long-term solution manageability.

16.2.2.3   Data transformation

Data transformation has probably the longest history as an integration function. Prior to XML it was inseparable from partner and application connectivity because there was no neutral representation technology. The structure and meaning of the information (semantics) could not be processed without understanding the proprietary notation (syntax) used by the originating application and/or external communication protocol.

XML, however, enables a clean separation. Connectivity adapters can transform the structure and semantics of the data to and from the XML notation. Data transformation functions can then operate on the data without regard to its origin or eventual destination. For example, a purchase order conforming to an internal DTD could be transformed to one that is used by a partner, which might require different element type names ("vendor" rather than "supplier") or a different sequence of elements.

An integration platform might increase efficiency for high-demand specialized transformations (e.g. among XML, X12, and EDIFACT) by retaining tight coupling between the semantics and syntax.

16.2.2.4   Process management

Coordination of activity can take many forms, from complex sequencing of interactions among applications and business partners to simple routing rules. Workflow and rules-based solutions allow high-level representation of dependencies and other logic.

An integration platform typically uses a process engine as a master controller. It reads the rules and controls the invocation of other platform components, such as data transformation components and adapters.

It is important for a platform to distinguish between external (public) processes that span multiple organizations from internal (private) processes. Doing so facilitates lifecycle and change management, which are ultimately the most difficult challenges facing large-scale integration solutions.

16.2.3   *Integration utilities and applications*

An integration platform, in addition to performing its primary function of coordinating independent applications, can support a variety of additional facilities. These include utilities that provide information about the system, portals that allow human access to data processed by the system, and applications built on top of the integration platform.

16.2.3.1   Monitoring and analytics

Much useful information can be gleaned from watching and recording the behavior of an integration platform. Metrics can be supplied to support a range of activities.

For vital signs monitoring, for example, data could include system load, throughput, and similar health metrics. For business-oriented analysis, data could help answer questions like:

- Which partners are performing best?
- Where are supply chain bottlenecks?
- What are the highest-value activities?
- What processes are most error prone?

16.2.3.2   Portals

Integration platforms may need to support user interaction, not just for the operation and monitoring of the system, but for access to the data processed by the applications under its control. Interaction among users, as well as between users and the system, may be supported.

The systems that provide such access are called *portals*. They can be thought of as being attached to the integration platform, rather than on top of it, as they may share the platform's infrastructure components (e.g. application server, information repository, and security infrastructure).

16.2.3.3   Integration applications

In the same way that business applications are built on relational database infrastructures, new categories of software are being built on top of integration platforms. These *integration applications* are actually composite applications, in the sense that they are built from the applications controlled by the platform.

As composites, integration applications tend to focus on inter-organizational tasks. Some examples are collaborative order management, collaborative forecast management, and collaborative design management.

16.3 | Deploying business integration

Business integration solutions can be implemented in the obvious manner by installing and configuring the appropriate software components at a customer site. However, it is also possible to obtain full business integration capabilities through service providers, such as Peregrine Systems.

A combination of the two can also be employed. Some possible scenarios are shown in Figure 16-4, Figure 16-5, Figure 16-6 and Figure 16-7.

The classic integration service provider is the *Value-Added Network (VAN)* that supports traditional EDI. The idea behind the VAN is that integration capabilities are provided in the network, outside the firewall, instead of within a company's own IT environment.

Integration service providers today are known by a variety of other names as well, such as *Managed Service Provider (MSP)*, *Application Service Pro-*

Figure 16-4   Integration solution: Connectivity

vider (ASP), or *Business Service Provider (BSP)*. In the following sections we'll look at their offerings for the components of an integration platform.

16.3.1 *Partner connectivity services*

The original EDI VANs provided basic connectivity prior to the existence of Internet-based options. These private networks continue to be used today and new forms of private networks, built on Internet infrastructure, have arisen. The range of external communications services that can be provided is broad and includes:

- basic data movement;
- guaranteed levels of service;
- numerous security services; auditing, tracking, and monitoring; and

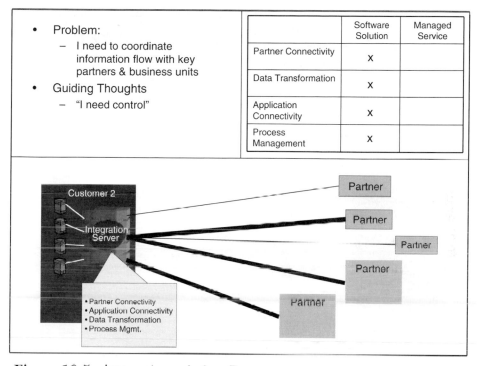

	Software Solution	Managed Service
Partner Connectivity	X	
Data Transformation	X	
Application Connectivity	X	
Process Management	X	

- Problem:
  - I need to coordinate information flow with key partners & business units
- Guiding Thoughts
  - "I need control"

Figure 16-5 Integration solution: Process management

- partner directory services.

Service providers can bridge diverse and asymmetric external communications requirements on a very large scale. The partners of any single company may collectively employ a great many security and communication options. These can include traditional EDI VAN traffic, batch direct dialup, SNA networks, and a wide variety of Internet-based protocols and security approaches. A service provider can consolidate support for large numbers of communications options in one place and can gateway customers from one communication method to another.

16.3.2 *Application connectivity services*

It is less common for service providers to supply application connectivity than other components of an integration platform. However, companies

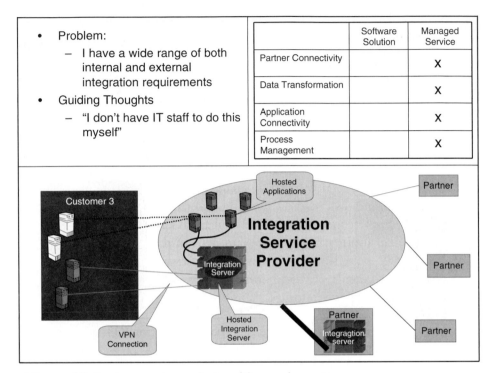

	Software Solution	Managed Service
Partner Connectivity		X
Data Transformation		X
Application Connectivity		X
Process Management		X

- Problem:
  - I have a wide range of both internal and external integration requirements
- Guiding Thoughts
  - "I don't have IT staff to do this myself"

Figure 16-6   Integration solution: Managed service

can grant application access to a provider over a virtual or physically private network, and let the service provider develop and maintain the adapters. This strategy allows application connectivity expertise to be consolidated by the provider, who can then offer client companies a very low maintenance solution.

16.3.3 *Data transformation services*

Service providers can enable very high performance bulk data transformation through access to high-end hardware environments.

A service provider can also centralize creation and maintenance of the maps used in transformations from one data representation vocabulary to another (as discussed in 16.2.2.3). These could include, for example, transformations from one DTD to another or between a data dictionary and a DTD.

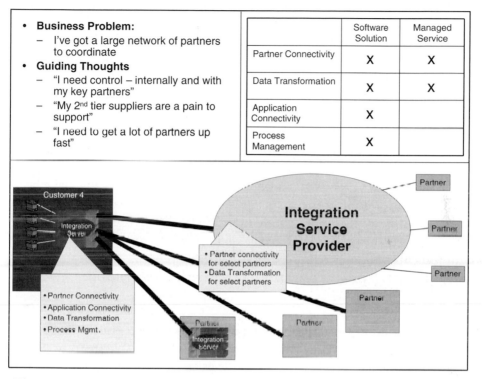

	Software Solution	Managed Service
Partner Connectivity	X	X
Data Transformation	X	X
Application Connectivity	X	
Process Management	X	

- **Business Problem:**
  - I've got a large network of partners to coordinate
- **Guiding Thoughts**
  - "I need control – internally and with my key partners"
  - "My 2nd tier suppliers are a pain to support"
  - "I need to get a lot of partners up fast"

Figure 16-7   Integration solution: Network management

16.3.4 *Process management services*

Many smaller companies are not equipped to maintain process management software on their sites. Service providers can help companies manage both internal and external processes. To do so, simple stateless linkages are maintained between the customer and the service provider, and the service provider is responsible for the management of state coordination and failure recovery.

16.4 | Conclusion

Many factors have led to the convergence of independent integration activities into the unified domain of business integration that we have been discussing. However, the emergence of the Internet and XML are the most significant. Unlike data representations such as ANSI X12, ASN.1, and SQL, XML has succeeded in providing a data model of sufficient flexibility and ease of use that it can be used as a common foundation for a broad spectrum of integration problems.

Of all the integration platform components, process management has emerged as the major differentiator among integration solutions. It is primarily in the definition of process rules that the business logic of integration is captured, and there that difficult change and lifecycle management issues are most visible.

Although generic workflow and process management systems have been in existence for some time, it is only recently that they have begun to address complex integration requirements such as internal and external process support, distributed lifecycle management, and failure recovery requirements. Though all integration platform vendors use process terminology and show process diagrams, the capabilities they provide can vary.

Analysis   Like content processing, business integration – and its counterpart, application coordination – is the dominant motivation of many XML applications and tool categories. And, as also occurs with content processing, that fact may not be explicit and the term "integration" may not even be used.

Content Management

- Multi-national translation and distribution
- Content systems in detail
- Component management for text and graphics

Part Five

Content is king!

Whether it's a website, your car's owner's manual, or a newspaper, the style may get your attention but the content is why you are there and why you will (or won't) return.

And the demand for new content – and new ways of packaging and delivering it – is growing by leaps and bounds. This calls for increased efficiency in the creation, processing, and delivery of content.

As a result, enterprises are increasingly realizing that content is a valuable corporate asset, one that needs to be managed with the same care as other valuable property.

In this part we'll look at the systems that have been developed for content management. We'll set the stage with a classic application, then look at the full scope of a content system that is built around a content management. Finally we'll look at the key XML value-add: component management, for both text and graphics.

"World" class content management

Case Study

- Tweddle Litho Company
- Automotive manuals in 30 languages
- XML content management
- Natural language translation

Sponsor: XyEnterprise, http://www.xyenterprise.com

Contributing experts: Jon Parsons and Judy Cox

Chapter

17

For the perfect introduction to content management and its benefits, you need look no further than the glove box of your car – and the manuals in the language of whichever of 60 countries you bought it in. It is literally a "world" class application. This chapter will show you how that miracle of logistics is accomplished.

hen you lease or buy an automobile, you become dependent on documentation.

You know that the glove box will contain an owner's manual, a maintenance schedule, a warranty maintenance book, and a book that describes your radio and/or CD player. You expect them to completely and accurately describe the car you are in. What's more, when you take the car in for service, you rely on the service technician having the information needed for the model and year of your car in a language he or she can read – no matter where in the world you are.

Ensuring that the information is there and available when needed is literally a "world" class task, a task made achievable by XML and a content management system. Let's look at how that task is accomplished at Tweddle Litho Company, producer of more than half of the world's automotive owner and glove box documentation.

17.1 | Auto manufacturing is large-scale publishing

For a successful worldwide launch of a new car, the manufacturer needs a full range of publications. The owner's guide, audio guide, and warranty material must be present in each vehicle. A service manual must be available to the service providers in every country.

These documents must be translated into as many as 30 different languages. Each document must be modified to conform to the national regulations for each country that imports the car. Cars shipped to Mexico, for example, must include jumper cables, and the documentation must reference this.

Producing those documents for a single new vehicle launch is a huge undertaking. Producing them for all of a manufacturer's models is a monumental one.

And one that compounds over time, because each model changes to a greater or lesser degree each year. And for each of the models, in each of the years, in each of the languages, the information must be available in print, on the Web, and on CD-ROM. Figure 17-1 illustrates the complexity.

Many auto manufacturers choose to outsource these projects to a full-service technical publishing house such as Tweddle Litho Company of Clinton Township, Michigan.

Founded in 1954 as a small printing company, Tweddle Litho pioneered computerized photocomposition and typesetting. As technologies changed, the company seized the opportunity to move further upstream from publishing to encompass the entire data management cycle, including writing, translation, and other related services.

Today, with customers such as Ford Motor Company, General Motors, Chrysler, Nissan, and Volvo, Tweddle Litho produces approximately 55 percent of all the automotive owner's literature worldwide.

Figure 17-1 Auto documentation for multiple models, model years, languages, and delivery formats

17.2 | Global markets, global information

As Tweddle's business grew, so did the requirements for internationalizing the information it managed for its customers. It soon became acquainted with the difficulties of the translation process:

- Passing information to translation houses, communicating about what was really meant, and answering questions about context
- Tracking the status and progress of the translations underway – and what had been returned
- Retranslating what had already been translated – and hadn't changed – when only a small portion of a document was modified

Managing the process manually was time consuming and prone to error. It also required a large editorial staff.

As a result, Tweddle undertook to find and apply a technology that would strategically position it to solve the large-scale problems of its customers. Tweddle knew it had to be prepared to support a vehicle release in 30 languages in 60 countries simultaneously. It needed to support 40 vehicle lines with a total of 6000 books. The information management team defined a number of objectives:

- Designing a friendlier more appealing visual style for the owner's manuals
- Creating a global, culturally neutral style
- Meeting local regulations (engineering, regulatory, safety, environmental)
- Reducing time to produce the information
- Reducing overall cost
- Increasing usability of the information
- Anticipating future uses of the information
- Managing artwork

Not everything on their list could be addressed by software, but the issues of time, cost, and reuse of the information could. They concluded that proper management of their information assets required generalized markup and a component-based information management system that could handle it.

17.3 | Needed: An XML component management system

By delimiting and labeling each of the individual elements of a document, XML enables both people and software to manipulate information as units useful for the purpose at hand. No longer is it necessary to deal with a whole document or even a complete chapter when only a small piece – perhaps only one or two paragraphs, a table, or step or two in a procedure – changes.

These units of information are called *components*. Figure 17-2 shows how XML identifies them.

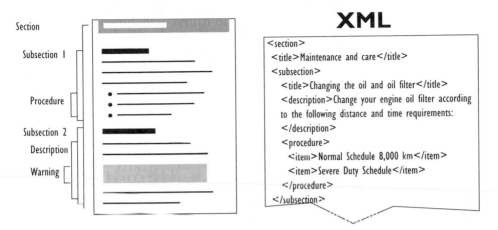

Figure 17-2 XML supports the use of document components

By managing these units separately and combining them into larger chunks of information – sections or chapters or books – only when needed, Tweddle could give only those units that changed to the translators. That level of precision enormously reduces redundant work.

In addition to providing the focus they needed for translation, a component management approach also let them reuse information in multiple documents. They could write a piece once, use it in several different places, and when changes occurred, update the component only once and have the changes replicated in each place it was used.

Even more, a component-based management system allowed them to build different views of the data. For example, a technical writer may be focusing on air conditioning or braking systems for a given auto model. The writer can look into the database and find all the procedures for that kind of system. Another writer, creating a view for a different model, might find that it included many of the same procedures because the systems were similar in both autos.

Tweddle developed its solution using *Content@*, a content management system from XyEnterprise. The architecture for component storage is shown in Figure 17-3.

Figure 17-3   Content storage with *Content@*

17.4 | Improving the translation process

Component management allowed translation to be focused on revised components only, a concept illustrated in Figure 17-4.

The translation workflow at Tweddle is based upon the use of in-country translators; that is, native speakers of a language living in the country for which the information is destined. In this workflow, there is a significant exchange of information at arm's length between Tweddle and the translators. A key aim in managing the translation process is to preserve context so that the translator has sufficient information to make sound decisions about which word to choose in rendering one language into another.

When changes are made to a previously translated document, *Content@* creates a translation package for the translator that includes a proof version that shows how the component looked in the last printed book, the previous XML source file for the component, the revised XML source file, and a list of differences. The package provides the context the translator needs.

The system creates the translation package automatically, triggered by the changes made when the revised component is returned to the repository. It is checked out for translation and the translation package is delivered electronically to the translator. Once the translation is complete, the revised translation component is checked back into the database and its status is automatically noted by the workflow manager.

Figure 17-4   Only revised components are sent to the translator.

A further advantage of component management is the ability to coordinate parallel work on the same document. For example, one of the European car manufacturers writes some parts in German while Tweddle continues to write other parts in English. They can still maintain the common use of data.

17.5 | One source, multiple delivery formats

A key advantage of using XML is that markup reflects the structure of an element, totally apart from how it is to be rendered. This separation of abstract content from rendered format allows delivery of the information in multiple formats from a single source.

17.5.1 *Printed delivery*

When all revisions and translations are complete, *Content@* assembles a complete version of the book from its components. This XML instance is then sent to *XML Professional Publisher (XPP)*, an XML publishing solution from XyEnterprise. *XPP* automatically composes and paginates the XML instance into finished documents.

Where it had taken up to six months to deliver a translated book, Tweddle is now getting the same results in three weeks and is even able to support the release of a foreign language document prior to release of the domestic English version.

Tweddle has been setting up remote printing facilities around the world in response to a growing need for on-demand printing. One of its European customers routinely has it prepare service literature in 22 languages and then prepare deliverables in both print and CD-ROM formats. Instead of shipping a large quantity of bulky books, Tweddle sends the files electronically to be printed in Belgium for European distribution, in Singapore for Asian distribution, and so on.

17.5.2 *Online delivery*

Owner's literature may stay a paper-based product for some time because inside a car, at present, there are few practical alternatives for viewing it electronically. However, with the advent of more on-board electronics and touch screen panels, the ability to deliver owner information in an electronic form as well as in print will become essential. XML provides the way. A few of the auto manufacturers have already eliminated paper deliverables completely for documents other than the owner's manuals.

Another big trend is the move away from paper toward electronic files for customer assistance representatives. Rather than sorting through one hundred manuals, each 1,400 to 2,000 pages long, the customer service representative is able to access a searchable database to find the appropriate procedure for a specific problem.

17.6 | Conclusion

XML enables solutions to complex information management problems such as Tweddle's because:

- XML can enforce the strict separation of abstract content from rendered format.
- XML enables the management and manipulation of small units of data that can be reused and assembled into multiple documents.
- XML can represent the structure of the abstract content, which is the same regardless of the natural language of the text.

Together with a component management system that supports and uses these advantages, XML solves immediate business problems while preserving a flexible and open foundation for whatever changes technology may bring.

Content systems

Application Discussion

- Acquisition
- Enrichment
- Management
- Collaboration
- Distribution

Sponsor: Interwoven, Inc., http://www.interwoven.com

Contributing experts: Mark A. Hale, Ron Daniel Jr., and Jack Jia

Chapter

18

> As businesses move more of their operations to
> the Web they become increasingly aware of the
> importance of their multitude of information content
> assets. These must now be made available as website
> content, in addition to their conventional use in
> reports and printed publications. To do it right, you
> need a robust content system, with content
> management at its core.

 large enterprise can have millions of information content assets, routinely produced by thousands of people. Those assets include everything from the graphs and figures that go into your year-end analysis report, to the operating instructions in your product manuals, to the business process data captured in your ERP or legacy systems.

As the Web looms ever larger in the business world, there is an increasing need to aggregate and exploit that content. And there is also an increasing recognition of just how complex and difficult a problem it is.

18.1 | The content challenge

All businesses, regardless of size, begin to appreciate the broad scope of content in day-to-day operations when they attempt to collect content for their first website. Even a single Web page may display information assets from many sources, as we see in Figure 18-1. That page contains graphics and text from the file system, output of applications, and data from databases. Clearly, many people contributed to this one Web page alone. Moreover, the form of the content varies significantly, ranging from static text strings to data generation on-demand.

Figure 18-1   Content of a Web page

This diversity of content types and sources is now the norm for production websites. It presents a challenge to the Web designers who must integrate the content to produce the final pages. They must cope with:

- Large numbers of interdependent contributors and information assets.
- A wide variety of continuously revised assets, from sources such as office applications, data collection forms, databases, and internal communications.
- Content delivery not just on the company website, but via printed documentation, wireless phones, handheld PDAs, portals, syndication, and other means.

These requirements can be met by aggregating and processing content as an enterprise resource, independently of its original sources or the uses to which it may eventually be put. XML makes this approach possible. You can think of it as building an XML-based *content infrastructure* for the enterprise. It would support five functional areas:

- Acquisition: Collecting content from diverse sources
- Enrichment: Adding value to content to maximize returns
- Management: Storage, versioning, and access control
- Collaboration: Working on content with other contributors
- Distribution: Making content available to users

Although it is convenient to speak of these areas as sequential processing steps, in practice there is overlap, concurrency, and recycling among them.

Let's look more closely at each area, using a media relations application as an example. We'll develop a simple press release.

18.2 | Acquisition

In order to maximize the use of content, it must be represented in XML. However, that phrase accommodates a number of approaches:

- Create an XML document from scratch.
- Convert a non-XML document to XML.
- Encapsulate a non-XML document in an XML wrapper.

Regardless of the approach, consideration must be given to the circumstances of acquisition and the skills and culture of the people involved. User interfaces should be provided that allow contributors to contribute content in the manner that is least obtrusive in their day-to-day work.

18.2.1 *Creating XML documents*

XML application designers may be willing to face XML markup head-on. They may even prefer it, because it guarantees that no software is distorting what they see. Such folks can use ordinary text editors or specialized XML development tools to create their XML documents.

For other document creators, XML-aware publishing and word processing tools may be best. These usually provide a rendered view of the data that conceals the XML markup. However, the markup can be examined when desired. These tools can support richly-structured complex documents.

However, for capture of structurally-simple business process data, the long-standing favorite user interface has been the form. Unlike the forms in HTML, though, a form in an XML content system is actually a rendition of an XML template. That is, an XML document with markup but no data.

Figure 18-2   Rendered XML template capturing press release in Example 18-1

Figure 18-2 shows the XML template for our press release rendered into a form by the Interwoven® *TeamSite*® content infrastructure system. A contributor has entered data into the form fields, which causes creation of the XML document shown in Example 18-1.

Example 18-1. Press release in XML

```
<PressReport>
  <Headline>
    Alliance Consulting finds a content infrastructure
    essential to its eBusiness
  </Headline>
  <ReleaseDate>
    Mon Jan 8 09:00:00 Eastern Standard Time 2001
  </ReleaseDate>
  <Body>
    Alliance Consulting announced today...
  </Body>
  <CorporateInfo>
    Alliance Consulting is a Fortune 500 company...
  </CorporateInfo>
</PressReport>
```

18.2.2 *Acquiring non-XML documents*

All content will undergo transformations in a content system as it is prepared to be placed on a website. XML content is easiest to operate on because its structure is explicit and its notation is standardized. However, there is a significant amount of content in non-XML form that businesses use every day that must be acquired for the content system.

Both document representation issues and user interface issues should be considered when planning this aspect of a content system.

18.2.2.1   User interface considerations

Contributing content should be made as unobtrusive as possible for the many content creators. They should be allowed to focus on what they do best: create meaningful content.

To achieve this goal, a content system could support transparent access from popular document creation tools such as *Microsoft Office*® and *Adobe*® *Acrobat*®. For example, on systems that use the WebDAV protocol, users could create documents in these applications and upload them to a content system straightforwardly by using the standard File Save function.

A content system could also allow users to import and export through a virtual file system view. Such a facility would allow users, for example, to import pictures from a photo CD by simply dragging them into a folder on the desktop. The cost-effectiveness is compelling, considering the number of users who create files and who are familiar with this common user interface.

18.2.2.2   Document representation

The basic distinction here is between converting data to XML or merely encapsulating it in an XML tracking document.

18.2.2.2.1   *Conversion*

Acquiring legacy content is an important component of publishing large catalogs in electronic commerce. Businesses find that they are exchanging a large number of content assets with their partners and customers. Conversion to XML provides a mechanism for automating catalog content generation and reuse for channel delivery.

Many tools are available for automatically or semi-automatically converting from non-XML notations to XML. There are also outsourcing services with specialized expertise and the capacity to handle large-volume projects that might be burdensome for in-house resources.

Some conversions are relatively trivial. Simple data structures such as comma-delimited text files exported from database systems, for example, can easily be converted using XSLT.

18.2.2.2.2   *Encapsulation*

Encapsulation is the simplest technique for implementing the file system interface. An XML tracking document is created for each non-XML asset, with elements that record metadata about its representation, access rights, external links, etc.

The non-XML document could physically be encapsulated as a CDATA section within the tracking document. More conveniently, it could be associated logically as an external unparsed data entity.

18.3 | Enrichment

In producing a website or other final publication, designers aggregate content collected from XML templates, office applications and other sources.

These designers aren't necessarily domain experts for the content they manipulate. To guide them in using content effectively and accurately, creators can associate metadata with content.

Example 18-2. PRISM metadata for press release

```
<rdf:RDF xmlns:prism="http://prismstandard.org/1.0#"
  xmlns:rdf="http://www.w3.org/1999/02/22-rdf-syntax-ns#"
  xmlns:dc="http://purl.org/dc/elements/1.1#">
  <rdf:Description about="release22.xml">
    <dc:title>Alliance Consulting finds a content infrastructure
              essential to its eBusiness</dc:title>
    <dc:creator>Alliance Consulting</dc:creator>
    <prism:releaseTime>2001-01-08T09:00:00Z-05
    </prism:releaseTime>
    <prism:creationTime>2001-01-05T10:51:17-08:00
    </prism:creationTime>
    <prism:modificationTime>2001-01-05T10:51:17-08:00
    </prism:modificationTime>
    <dc:format>text/xml</dc:format>
    <prism:category rdf:resource="#pressRelease" xml:base=
      "http://prismstandard.org/vocabularies/1.0/category.xml"/>
  </rdf:Description>
</rdf:RDF>
```

18.3.1 *Associating metadata*

Metadata consists of information like:

asset metadata
> Description of a content asset. It includes familiar properties such as file permissions, creation dates, etc.

subject metadata
> Controlled vocabularies of descriptive properties of the content, such as film type for photographs and drug classifications for prescriptions.

similarity metadata
> Information applicable to multiple content assets, such as similarity of subject matter or color.

usage metadata

Content performance measures, such as number of downloads and geographic locations.

link metadata

References to related content. For example, a paint selection guide could have link metadata that references home improvement and interior decorating catalogs that use the guide.

Example 18-2 is an RDF description of our press release utilizing metadata properties from the PRISM vocabulary. PRISM itself incorporates element types from other vocabularies, identified by the namespace prefix in the tags: rdf for RDF itself and dc for Dublin Core.

18.3.2 *Automated metadata creation*

A content system could supply tools that simplify a contributor's creation of metadata by generating it automatically from the asset. Such software is aware of appropriate metadata vocabularies and analyzes content for relevant data.

For example, in our press release, software could determine that Alliance Consulting is listed on the New York Stock Exchange. From the listing record, the company's Standard Industry Classification (SIC) code, 8748, could also be determined. Using the SIC code, further metadata about the industry classification could be obtained, as shown in Example 18-3. The pcv namespace prefix indicates that the PRISM Controlled Vocabulary is used.

Example 18-3. Generated metadata for the press release (excerpt)

```
<rdf:Description
  about="http://www.osha.gov/cgi-bin/sic/sicser2?8748">
  <pcv:label>Business Consulting Services,
          not elsewhere classified</pcv:label>
  <pcv:code>8748</pcv:code>
  <pcv:vocabulary>Standard Industry Classification</pcv:vocabulary>
  <pcv:definition>Establishments primarily engaged in
    furnishing business consulting services, not elsewhere
    classified, on a contract or fee basis.
  </pcv:definition>
</rdf:Description>
```

18.3.3 *Retrieving metadata*

There are a number of means by which a content system could allow metadata properties to be retrieved. Example 18-4 shows how the WebDAV protocol could be used for this purpose. The HTTP protocol header is shown at the beginning of the listing and the property request follows in XML. The `prop` element contains an empty element for each requested metadata property.

Example 18-4. WebDAV client request for press release metadata

```
PROPFIND /pressreleases/alliance.xml HTTP/1.1
Content-Type: text/xml
Depth: 1

<propfind xmlns="DAV:">
  <prop>
    <href/>
    <displayname/>
    <creationdate/>
    <getlastmodified/>
    <getcontenttype/>
  </prop>
</propfind>
```

The response from the server is shown in the listing in Example 18-5. Content has been supplied for the requested metadata property elements.

18.3.4 *Finding content*

In addition to finding metadata, a content system needs to provide tools for finding content assets themselves. It is particularly helpful for a contributor to know about related content during preparation of an asset, as it could improve the quality and accuracy of his work.

Metadata can make this possible. For example, consider a content system containing drug description documents. A user interface could be created for a doctor with two forms side-by-side. As he entered prescription information in one, related drugs could be shown in the other so that drug interactions can be assessed. The relationships, of course, are captured in the metadata in the drug descriptions.

Example 18-5. WebDAV server response to Example 18-4

```
HTTP/1.1 207 Multi-Status

<multistatus xmlns="DAV:">
  <response>
    <propstat>
      <prop>
        <href>/pressreleases/alliance.xml</href>
        <displayname>/alliance.xml</displayname>
        <creationdate>2001-01-05T10:51:17-08:00</creationdate>
        <getlastmodified>2001-01-06T18:51:17-08:00</getlastmodified>
        <getcontenttype>text/xml<getcontenttype/>
      </prop>
      <status>HTTP/1.1 200 OK</status>
    </propstat>
  </response>
</multistatus>
```

Such interfaces are called *recommendation systems*. While a user is work-ing in one part of the user interface, queries are executed in one (or more) other parts. Systems can allow users to create such queries explicitly. They can also "learn" from a user's previous activities and generate appropriate queries automatically.

18.4 | Management

Management facilities are responsible for ensuring across-the-board consis-tency of all assets, users, platforms, applications, and storage facilities within a content system. They must be scalable to cope with potentially enormous numbers of assets, and reliable to assure high availability.

Management functions include:

- Providing a repository for storage of assets
- Maintaining multiple versions of assets and editions
- Asset-locking for safe collaboration
- Asset comparison to determine differences among assets or versions
- Conflict resolution through merger of jointly-created content
- Providing user and role-based access control and user authentication

- Maintaining relationships for document composition
- Managing risk: backup, archiving, maintenance, etc.

Content management is the heart of a content system. Let's look at two key aspects in detail: storage and versioning.

18.4.1 *Storage*

A content repository holds all of the assets acquired for the system, whether original or converted XML, or encapsulated non-XML data. Once assets are brought into a repository, they are subsequently managed uniformly using the functions just described, such as versioning, merging, and locking.

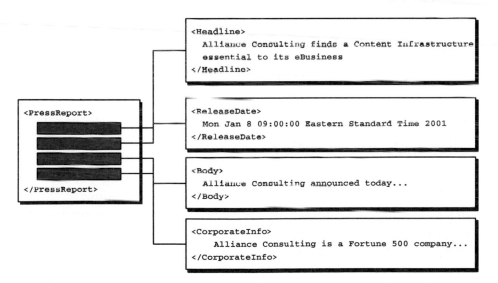

Figure 18-3 Components of press release

XML documents offer the added capability of being stored in *components*. That is, each of the document's constituent elements and fragments of data can be stored as individual assets. In Figure 18-3, our press release is divided into the components Headline, ReleaseDate, Body, and CorporateInfo, each consisting of an element of the original document.

18.4.2 *Versioning*

Version management is the content system facility that tracks and accesses the revision history for the assets managed by the system. The benefits and capabilities of versioning include:

- Tracking of individual assets

  All operations a user performs with respect to an asset are tracked. Content changes are therefore always accountable.

- Navigation of asset history

  Users can manage content development and revert to previous versions if needed.

- Parallel development and update of assets

  Users can try new ideas or start a new project from an existing one.

- Persistence in the event of system failure

  Content always keeps its integrity.

18.5 | Collaboration

As content is acquired from various sources, attention must be given to how the numerous interactions with the content can be coordinated. Some issues are the degree of interactivity of creators with their content and the relationship among diverse users.

The keys to managing this complexity are:

- organizing the content;
- coordination through workflow; and
- virtualized testing.

18.5.1 *Organization of content*

One approach is to organize the content by projects, each corresponding to a significant deliverable publication, such as a library of manuals for a product, a top-level feature on a website, or even a complete website. For example, one project could be created for a company's website on the public Internet and a separate project for its internal intranet, which would allow contributors to easily distinguish which information will be published inside or outside the corporate firewall.

Figure 18-4   Content organization for collaboration

Figure 18-4 shows a project in the Interwoven *TeamSite* content infra-structure system. At the left are work areas for each contributor to the project. Contributors can be individual contributors and/or departments, such as marketing, engineering, and sales. A work area is a directory in which a contributor collects content for the portion of the project for which he is responsible. That content could contain links to content outside the work area.

Content ultimately works its way from the work areas into deliverable publications. To facilitate this process, content is first collected from contributors in a "staging area", where a designer can merge contributions together and sort out conflicts.

Because content can change over time, the publications change as well. At the right the project diagram shows successive editions of the publication. The latest, at the top, is deployed on the production server for distribution.

Figure 18-5   Workflow coordinating press release

18.5.2 *Coordination through workflow*

Workflow is used to coordinate contributor activities as they collaborate to publish an edition. In our press relations example, the activities range from entering press contacts to publishing final releases to syndicates. Figure

18-5 depicts the workflow that governs a reporter ("Contributor") and manager ("Approver") in the tasks of approving a press release and submitting it for distribution.

Workflow can be represented in XML, as shown in Example 18-6. The elements corresponding to the various task types (user, submit, email, etc.) are easily identified in the listing.

Example 18-6. XML representation of workflow in Figure 18-5

```
<workflow name="AuthorAssignmentWithEmail">
  <usertask name="Contributor" >
    <successors>
      <succ v="JobDone"/>
    </successors>
  </usertask>
  <emailtask name="JobDone">
    <successors>
      <succ v="Approver"/>
    </successors>
  </emailtask>
  <usertask name="Approver">
    <successors>
      <succ v="reject"/>
      <succ v="Submit"/>
    </successors>
  </usertask>
  <emailtask name="reject" >
    <successors>
      <succ v="Contributor"/>
    </successors>
  </emailtask>
  <submittask name="Submit">
    <successors>
      <succ v="EndTask"/>
    </successors>
  </submittask>
  <endtask name="EndTask"/>
</workflow>
```

18.5.3 *Virtualized testing*

There is an underlying complexity that businesses face when accommodating a large number of contributors. A contributor only has control over a single work area, but the final publication incorporates content from other work areas as well. How then can a content contributor test individual content modifications before they have been deployed to a production server?

Consider for example, a standard corporate statement appended to the end of our press release example. This XML element may belong to the legal department and exist in that department's work area. However, the press release is in the work area of its author.

The solution lies in *virtualization*, automatically resolving references to content assets located outside the work area. During test, a contributor proceeds to aggregate content as though constructing a new edition of the final publication. As it would be prohibitive to replicate complete databases for individual testing needs, the current version of the specific content referenced is displayed from the staging area.

18.6 | Distribution

The final step in content development is to deploy the edition whose content has been tested and approved in a production environment. This process is shown in Figure 18-6.

In our media relations example, the press releases are frozen as an edition and distributed to a syndicate. In turn, the syndicate caches the releases for high volume distribution to news agencies. If a database provides some of the content, the database is also distributed.

All references are resolved for the published edition and optimized for delivery performance on production sites. For XML content, this includes reconstructing XML documents from their stored components.

The figure also shows some of the advanced capabilities of a distribution network. Distribution networks can be configured so that content can be distributed worldwide and replicated in server farms for fast access. Syndication permits rules, schedules, profiles, and transformations to be defined on the server so that subscriptions can effectively be managed for content delivery to users, partners, and suppliers.

18.6.1 *Preparing content for delivery*

Content today must be distributed not just in printed form or conventional website delivery, but through such means as Web services, personalization,

Figure 18-6   Content distribution and syndication

portals, wireless devices such as PDAs and cellular phones, and syndicates. This is called *multi-channel delivery* and businesses that adopt it are preparing their content for new products and markets.

As channels differ in their physical presentation capabilities, the content must be rendered appropriately for each one. A formatting program will process the edition and a suitable stylesheet to produce a rendition. Depending on the channel, the rendition may be represented in XML, as for many wireless devices, or may be in other notations, such as electronic data interchange (EDI).

For example, Figure 18-7 shows how a summary of our press release might appear on a cellular phone. Data is delivered to the phone using the Wireless Markup Language (WML), an XML document type.

To produce the summary, the XSLT stylesheet in Example 18-7 is used to govern the processing of the press release in Example 18-1. Elements in

Figure 18-7   Press release on a wireless device

the xsl namespace are instructions to the processor. The other elements are included unchanged in the generated output.

Note that if an instruction element returns data, the data is also included in the generated output. In our example, the first xsl:value-of instruction generates the data of the press release Headline element. The second generates the data of the ReleaseDate element.

18.6.2 *Distribution protocols*

Many of the emerging distribution channels use XML to transport content over many of the Internet protocols. We discussed the benefits of using XML in this way in 2.11.3, "Protocols", on page 52. In Example 18-8, you can see how our press release could be transmitted as email using ebXML (namespace prefix eb) for the routing header and manifest. ebXML in turn uses a SOAP envelope (namespace prefix SOAP-ENV).

Example 18-7. Stylesheet to generate press release summary in WML

```
<xsl:stylesheet
  xmlns:xsl="http://www.w3.org/1999/XSL/Transform"
  version="1.0">
  <xsl:output omit-xml-declaration="yes"/>
  <xsl:template match="/">
  <wml>
    <card id="card1" title="Alliance Press Release">
      <p>
        <b>Headline: </b>
        <xsl:value-of select="PressReport/Headline" /><br/>
        <b>Date: </b>
        <xsl:value-of select="PressReport/ReleaseDate" /><br/>
      </p>
    </card>
  </wml>
  </xsl:template>
</xsl:stylesheet>
```

Email is represented in a non-XML notation called MIME. In a multi-part email such as this one, the parts are separated by a boundary string ("111Boundary" in the example), much as XML uses tags to bound elements.

18.7 | Conclusion

We've seen our sample press release work its way through all parts of a content system. XML was critical in each step of the process. Some of the highlights:

- The press release was captured in XML without the user having to mark up the XML explicitly.
- Metadata about the release was captured in XML.
- The press release was stored in components that can be maintained and reused independently.
- XML documents represented and drove the workflow by which the release was eventually sent for publication.
- XSLT stylesheets were used to format the press release for multi-channel delivery.

Example 18-8. ebXML message to distribute press release

```
Content-type: multipart/related; boundary="111Boundary";
              type="text/xml"; start=" <ebxmlheader@interwoven.com>"
--111Boundary
Content-ID: <ebxmlheader@interwoven.com>
Content-Type: text/xml;
<SOAP-ENV:Envelope
  xmlns:SOAP-ENV='http://schemas.xmlsoap.org/soap/envelope/'
  xmlns:eb='http://www.ebxml.org/namespaces/messageHeader'>
  <SOAP-ENV:Header>
    <eb:MessageHeader SOAP-ENV:mustUnderstand="1" eb:version="1.0">
     ...
    </eb:MessageHeader>
  </SOAP-ENV:Header>
  <SOAP-ENV:Body>
    <eb:Manifest SOAP-ENV:mustUnderstand="1" eb:version="1.0">
     ...
    </eb:Manifest>
  </SOAP-ENV:Body>
</SOAP-ENV:Envelope>
--111Boundary
Content-ID: <ebxmlheader@interwoven.com>
Content-Type: text/xml
<PressReport>
  <Headline>
    Alliance Consulting finds a content infrastructure
    essential to its eBusiness
  </Headline>
  <ReleaseDate>
    Mon Jan 8 09:00:00 Eastern Standard Time 2001
  </ReleaseDate>
  <Body>
    Alliance Consulting announced today...
  </Body>
  <CorporateInfo>
    Alliance Consulting is a Fortune 500 company...
  </CorporateInfo>
</PressReport>
--111Boundary--
```

Components:
Key to content
management

Application Discussion

▊ Content management defined

▊ Document components

▊ Information reuse

▊ Custom document assembly

Sponsor: Chrystal Software, `http://www.chrystal.com`

Contributing experts: Sean Baird, Wil Shaw, Carol Houtz, Brad Chang, Willie Lim, Grant Vergottini, and Frazer Robinson

Chapter

19

> Document management is about managing documents as a whole, regardless of what is inside them. *Content* management, on the other hand, gets deep down inside and so is far more powerful. The key to content management is XML's ability to let you work with the bits and pieces of a document – its *components*.

Technical publications are critical in today's corporation. Behind these documents are the writers, artists, and editors who develop and maintain the massive amounts of documentation that keep a company running. Now, both publication managers and corporate directors are looking for better ways to exploit this wealth of data for higher returns throughout the enterprise.

Many enterprises benefit from managing document content as *components*, rather than as entire publications. This practice is called *content management*, in contrast to *document management*. Middle-tier Web applications, in particular, benefit from the ability to assemble components with other data for delivery to the client.

19.1 | Components are everywhere

From new cars to software, components are the way we make things today.

In manufacturing industries as much as 80% of products now consist of components drawn from a company's parts library or purchased from suppliers. Product designers routinely tap into internal databases and online parts warehouse services in the course of drafting and specifying new models.

In software, most new code is being written as objects, self-contained bundles of information and operations with the ability to send and receive messages in standard ways. Programs can be created by assembling a bunch of these object components and making them exchange information and services with each other.

19.1.1   *Components in publishing*

And now components are becoming the trend in publishing as well. That's because in publishing, as in other endeavors, components simplify complexity and increase flexibility for adapting to change. Consider these general advantages of components and how they come into play in a content management publishing environment.

19.1.1.1   System simplification

Components make it possible to break down complex systems into pieces that are easier to understand and work with. For publishing groups this means that teams of writers and editors can work on components for the same document simultaneously. Users can more easily locate specific information since components can be searched for individually.

19.1.1.2   Easier revision

When something needs to be revised or customized, changes can be made to just the components affected, without having to redesign the whole document. If a single paragraph in a document needs to be revised, the author can check out just that paragraph from the content management system rather than the whole document. Or, if it's important to see the change in context, the author can check out the section the paragraph appears in. After editing, when the section is checked back in, versioning information is applied only to the paragraph that has changed.

19.1.1.3 Efficient collaboration

Studies show that at least 30% of the content created by technical publishing groups is reusable – or would be, if people could find the information. Typically, it's buried in documents, scattered here and there in file systems on various desktop systems and servers. Content management eliminates the need to redo work by providing a universal repository for managing published and in-progress documents. The ability to unlock content from structured documents so that individual components of information can be independently accessed, tracked, and versioned enables writers and editors to immediately focus on exactly what they're looking for. With larger documents, since authors are able to work on small sections, multiple authors can work simultaneously on the same document.

19.1.1.4 Less routine editing

A huge amount of the editing process involves checking documents for consistency and correcting them to maintain a standardized style. Content management minimizes editing time and tedium by enabling editors to maintain glossaries as collections of components. This information can be added to or revised rapidly, every day if necessary, with the new material instantly available to all users.

19.1.1.5 Automated assembly and delivery

Component-level management means that new documents may be created and customized by changing only what is unique about them. This approach allows content management systems to automate the assembly and delivery of highly personalized documents, specific to new market or customer, based upon specific interests and requirements. By automating these processes, content management systems are able to deliver this level of personalized content delivery through dynamic Web sites.

19.1.1.6 Universal updates

Each information component exists in the content management repository as a single object. When authors want to reuse a component, instead of copying it, they simply create a pointer to the object. This approach eliminates the redundant work of trying to find all places where the information appears and updating them independently. Instead authors can revise the component in the repository once, and it will be automatically updated in all documents that incorporate it.

19.1.1.7   Streamlined translations

Translators typically work with a moving target, a source document that continues to change while translation is occurring. Translated versions then have to be returned to translators for a laborious manual process of identifying, changing, and checking new material. Content management can speed this process by providing translators with only those document components that are new, along with information about what has changed and exactly where the revisions should be inserted in the document.

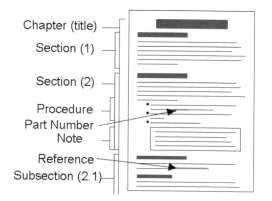

Figure 19-1   Document components described with XML

19.1.1.8   Flexible distribution

Content management makes it easy to reuse content for different media. Users can assign custom attributes to a particular component. For example, an attribute of an element could tell the software whether or not the element should be included when exporting a document for the Web, as opposed to printing it. Users can therefore automate document assembly, including adjustments for target media.

19.1.2 *XML makes components*

XML allows information to be broken into small components. The smaller and more specific the component is, the more addressable and reusable it is.

For example, the document in Figure 19-1 uses descriptive element type names to identify the components and structure of the document. A component is a piece of information that can be used independently, such as a paragraph, chapter, instructional procedure, warning note, part number, order quantity, graphic, side-bar story, video clip, or one of an infinite variety of additional information types.

When managed by a content management system (Figure 19-2), these pieces can be controlled, revised, reused, and assembled into a variety of new documents.

Figure 19-2 Hierarchical structure shown in content management system

Another way XML adds value to information is through attributes that describe additional metadata. The attributes let users describe the information more richly for reuse.

A user can assign an attribute to a particular component, for example, to specify whether or not to include it when publishing the document for the Web, as opposed to printing it. When the document is published, the content management system will make the proper adjustments for the target medium.

Metadata can also be used to identify the intended audience for specific components. In Example 19-1, for example, a "beginner" requires more information than an "expert". Multiple attributes may be used to create a matrix of possible document combinations. The content management system can then assemble and publish a document that matches these criteria.

Example 19-1. Metadata can identify the intended audience

```
<step audience="beginner">
Keep the engine running and park car on level ground.
</step>

<step audience="expert">
Keep the engine running.
</step>
```

19.1.3 *Applications for content reuse*

Reuse, the most compelling feature of content management, allows content within any document to be used elsewhere in the repository. Reuse means writing the information once and linking to it from other documents. This can be very useful when multiple documents contain standard "boilerplate" information. This reuse of information saves users rework and duplication of effort, as shown in Figure 19-3.

Applications for information reuse are everywhere. Reuse can be as simple as finding a description from one document and linking it into a new document. Common content creates an "information pool" of reusable pieces available to individuals or groups inside the company. Linked reuse, instead of copying, ensures consistency of information, makes updates more efficient and reduces redundant storage.

Organizations that maintain common glossaries of business terms can benefit from reuse. When glossary information stored in a content manage-

Component is checked out,
edited, and checked back in.

Tighten bolt A14 B12

**Content Management
Repository**

Components stored
as single objects

Tighten bolt A14 B12

Component is updated
automatically wherever used

Tighten bolt A14 B12

Tighten bolt A14 B12

Figure 19-3   Component reuse

ment system changes, the information is revised only one time. All of the documents incorporating that information are automatically updated.

Because commonly-used procedures, warnings, and cautions usually require careful wording, organizations strive for uniformity across all documents. Manually locating and changing dozens of these elements in hundreds of contexts can consume countless hours and is error-prone. Content management solves that problem by allowing XML documents to reuse content across documents.

For global business processes, linked reuse simplifies the translation process, helping organizations get to market faster around the world. By identifying the newly revised information in a repair manual, only the new information will be translated into the target languages, saving valuable time and money.

19.2 | A content management implementation

To better understand what content management systems provide, it is helpful to look at an actual product in action.

Chrystal Software's *Astoria* and *Eclipse* combination, like other component-based *content* management systems, attempts to provide value beyond that of generalized *document* management systems. It does so by managing the content of the document as a set of components (see Figure 19-4).

Figure 19-4   The *Astoria* repository

Some of the product combination's off-the-shelf capabilities are described in the following sections. Customization for specialized requirements is possible through public C++ and Java APIs.

19.2.1 *Revision tracking*

Astoria automatically collects revision information at each check-in, indicating time, date, author, revision number, and an optional comment. Past versions are available for republishing or to provide an audit trail (see Figure 19-5).

For XML documents, revision history is detected and maintained at the component level, not just at the document level. A sophisticated differencing engine is used to apply revision information to only the content that changes during an editing session.

Figure 19-5   Revision history of a paragraph

At important milestones such as release dates and the beginning of review cycles, users can formalize document versions into editions. The document state can then be recreated for that point in time by opening the appropriate edition.

19.2.2 *Search*

Astoria's search options let users locate documents created in more than 50 common applications. Advanced indexing enhances search by looking for various forms of the word (e.g., plural, tenses, root). Matching documents can be selected for viewing and editing.

Custom attributes can automatically be created from XML metadata. In addition to custom attributes, document structure, data content, and version information can be used in queries (see Figure 19-6).

Figure 19-6 Search results refined with XML structure and metadata

Another form of search, where-used queries, locates content that is reused in multiple XML documents. Users can determine whether changes to that content are appropriate in all contexts before committing to the change.

19.2.3 *Dynamic content assembly and delivery*

One of the compelling benefits of managing documents at the component level is that users can effectively create an information pool from which new documents may be created. For example, *Eclipse* works in conjunction with *Astoria* to assemble components of information from the repository into custom documents for delivery to Web browsers and other destinations.

Content creators define the associations between the attributes of individuals visiting the Web site and the metadata stored within the content. As visitors log into a Web site, *Eclipse* creates and delivers personalized Web pages to them, as shown in Figure 19-7.

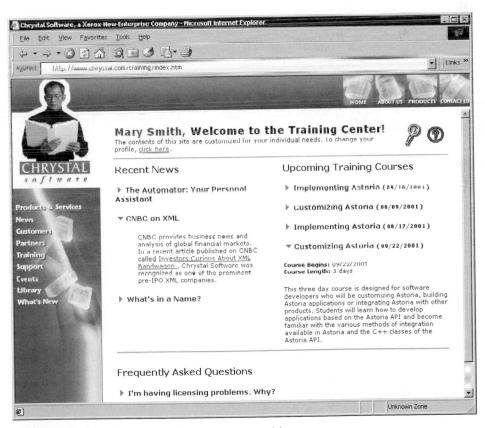

Figure 19-7   A custom document assembly

Components for graphic content

Application Discussion

▌ Computer graphics notations

▌ Graphic components

▌ WebCGM

▌ Hyperlinking graphic components

Sponsor: Auto-trol Technology Corporation,
http://www.auto-trol.com

Contributing expert: Kevin O' Kane

> There is a widely used graphic image notation called *TIFF*, for *Tagged Image File Format.* Unfortunately, its tags are binary and are meaningful only to TIFF processors. But what if graphics could be tagged with XML, organized into components, and hyperlinked to and from the text of documents? That pretty picture is the subject of this chapter.

raphics are more like text than you might think.

Consider Figure 20-1 for example. Unless you're an auto mechanic, it's probably not the kind of picture you customarily look at. But even a non-mechanic can see that the suspension assembly it depicts is made up of many different components.

Interestingly, that is true of the computer representation of the picture as well. In fact, it is possible to use XML to represent the component structure, thereby bringing to graphics the benefits of component management that we have been discussing. Before we look at how to accomplish that, we need a quick course in graphic representation.

20.1 | Computer graphics notations

The concepts of abstraction and rendition are critical to XML and have been discussed throughout this book.[1] It is relatively easy to see how they

---

1. For a refresher, see 6.11, "And in conclusion", on page 118.

Figure 20-1   Automobile suspension assembly

apply to text (formatted vs. unformatted). What is less obvious is that graphics have abstract and rendered representations as well.

The abstract notations use rich geometric formulas and are typically termed *vector graphics*. Some examples are CGM and EPS.

The rendered notations use arrays of points and are usually called *raster graphics* or *images*. Some image notations are JPEG, TIFF, and GIF.

20.1.1 *Raster is for rendition*

When you see a graphic on a physical medium, such as a printed page or computer screen, you are viewing a presentation of a raster rendition of the graphic.

Technically speaking, a raster image is actually another geometric representation, and the process of generating it is a geometric transformation. However, the geometric model of a raster image is rather impoverished. It is limited to points, called *pixels* (picture elements), which are X, Y coordinates in two-dimensional space.

Just as with text, the rendition of graphics loses abstract information. Consider the magnified image in Figure 20-2, in which each square represents a pixel. The image is round, but because the abstract information is lost, it is no longer possible to determine if the content was a circle, the number "0", or the letter "O".

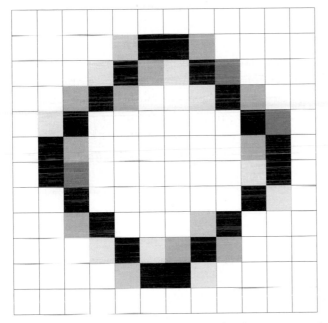

Figure 20-2   Raster rendition of unknown round abstraction

The raster geometric representation is almost identical to the model used by a computer display system. It can therefore be presented on a computer screen very quickly, which is why JPEG and GIF are so much favored for Web pages. But this speed comes at a price:

■   There is no abstract content, as we just saw, nor is there abstract structure.

■ A high quality image has a large memory footprint.

For example, 500 characters of text might require as much as 7KB when rendered as a JPEG.

■ Images are not easy to edit, which limits reuse.
■ The scale of an image cannot be changed without introducing visual distortions.

20.1.2   *Vectors allow variation*

Vector graphics employ a much richer geometric model.

In addition to points, a vector graphic document may contain geometric elements, such as lines, circles, ellipses, curves, and shapes – possibly in a three-dimensional coordinate system to represent solid objects.

A vector graphic, using equations for these geometric elements, is an abstract representation of graphic objects. Rather than representing a circle with a list of pixels, we can specify the center point and a radius for a circle element. When it is time to render the circle, the computer, either in software or hardware, can apply a transform to generate the list of pixels that would be "covered" by the circle, and would then color the pixels accordingly.

A vector graphics representation does not have the limitations of a raster image:

■ By applying a scale factor to the radius of the circle we can dynamically zoom in or zoom out of an image without distortion.
■ If we change the coordinates of the center point, we can easily edit the circle to change its location in the picture.
■ The number of bytes required to store the circle remains relatively constant, no matter how big or small the circle becomes.

20.1.3   *Structural elements*

If you've used a vector graphics drawing program, you may be familiar with the grouping command, which allows you to combine several geometric elements into a larger object. Groups may themselves be grouped, and so on.

A group is an example of a graphic *structural element*. Whereas a *geometric element*, such as a circle or polygon, contains the formula for drawing the shape, a structural element combines geometric elements and other structural elements but does no drawing of its own.

Most modern graphic notations include structural elements to model the abstract structure; for example, a circle and some lines might be grouped to form a wheel. A graphics notation with a structural element can be modeled using XML and integrated into the component structure of an XML document.

20.2 | Representing graphic components

XML-based content management systems typically support graphics, but they treat an entire graphic as a single component. This approach is less than optimal, since a complex graphic like that in Figure 20-1 is made up of multiple components. It would be desirable to manage those components in the same way as text components, with individual versioning, checkin/checkout, reuse, and other content management facilities. It would also be useful to have hyperlinks among the graphic components and between them and the text components.

In a nutshell, what is needed is the integration of graphics at the component level into the XML document, as shown in Figure 20-3.

The key to component management for graphics is the use of XML. Two approaches can be taken:

■ Use an XML-based graphics notation to represent geometric and structural elements.

The W3C is developing Scalable Vector Graphics (SVG) for this purpose. As it is an XML document type, utilization is straightforward and won't be discussed further here.

■ Use a binary graphics notation that has a structural element, but echo its structure in XML.

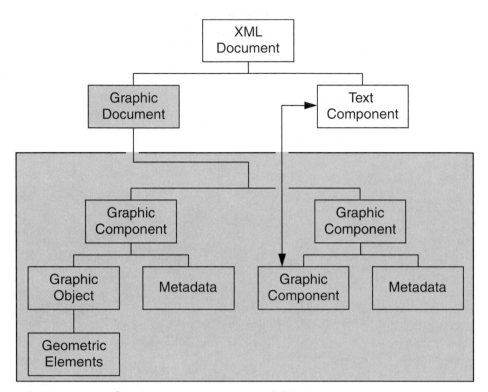

Figure 20-3   Graphic components in an XML document

The W3C has created WebCGM – a Web-optimized profile of the Computer Graphics Metafile (CGM) International Standard – that can be used in this way. It is of particular interest because it is compatible with the vast majority of existing CGM graphics, which therefore have a high probability of being rendered accurately in WebCGM-enabled software.

20.2.1   *WebCGM*

CGM is a stable graphics format of long standing.[2] The WebCGM profile supports almost all CGM graphic elements, plus several raster image notations, including JPEG and PNG.

Most importantly, WebCGM uses *CGM Application Structures (APS)* as a structural element for creating graphic components.

20.2.2 *Inside a graphic component*

It is common for XML content management systems (CMS) to create an XML tracking document for a non-XML component, such as a graphic. The graphic component document includes a pointer to the actual graphic object, plus metadata that describes access rights and other properties.

Systems for XML graphic content management take a similar approach, except that their graphic component documents have a detailed internal structure. It echoes the structure of graphic objects right down to the geometric element level.

Example 20-1 shows the WebCGM definition of a grobject, what we've been calling a *graphic component*.

Example 20-1. WebCGM definition of graphic component (grobject)

```
<!ELEMENT grobject (grobject | para | gdata)* >
<!ATTLIST grobject
  id            ID        #REQUIRED
  region        CDATA     #IMPLIED
  viewcontext   CDATA     #IMPLIED
  linkuri       CDATA     #IMPLIED
  screentip     CDATA     #IMPLIED
  name          CDATA     #IMPLIED
>

<!ELEMENT gdata EMPTY >
<!ATTLIST gdata
  cgmprim       ENTITY    #REQUIRED
>
```

A component can exhibit several attributes. They specify metadata for:

---

2. CGM's history parallels that of markup languages. It became an ISO standard in 1987, the year after SGML. Its WebCGM profile for the World Wide Web became a W3C Recommendation in 1999, the year after XML, which is SGML's profile for the Web.

identification
id and name

description
screentip

viewer control
region and viewcontext

hyperlinking
linkuri

The structure of a component is hierarchical because it can include other components. It can also include para and gdata elements, which have no data content; they serve as references to the graphic objects of components, which we'll examine next.

20.2.3 *Graphic objects*

A *graphic object* is created when a structural element is used to group geometric elements. Collectively, the geometric elements form the geometric representation of an object, such as the objects in the four components shown in Figure 20-4.

Example 20-2 shows a graphic object as it might be represented in an XML-aware component-based graphic drawing product; in this case, Auto-trol Technology's *Tech Illustrator*.

It is possible for a component's object to have several geometric representations, each referenced by a separate gdata element. For example, the representation of a manufactured object can start as a 3-D solid model, be transformed into a 3-D polygon mesh, and collapsed to a 2-D view using shapes. All of them would be managed together as part of the component.

20.3 | Reusing graphic components

Reusing graphic components offers the same benefits as reusing text components, but introduces some unique technical considerations.

Figure 20-4 Components of an automobile suspension

Example 20-2. Graphic object represented in XML

```
<graphic_object>
  <circle>....</circle>
  <spline>....</spline>
  <rect>......</rect>
</graphic_object>
```

Consider the graphic in Figure 20-5, which was produced using *Tech Illustrator* and its *Master Component Library*. It contains several instances of the graphic components from Figure 20-4, but note that they have different sizes and orientations.

The product was able to use the component's metadata to reconcile the rotation and scale of the component with respect to those of the full graphic.

Figure 20-5   Assembly with rotated and scaled components from Figure 20-4

Full reuse and integration of graphic and text components requires a suitable content management system, such as Auto-trol's *CENTRA 2000®*. Figure 20-6 shows its interface for managing the hierarchy of objects.

20.4 | Hyperlinking graphic components

Hyperlinking is possible both to and from graphic components. Hyperlinking *from* a component is done with the `linkuri` attribute of the `grobject` element. Hyperlinking *to* a component is done with a *URI reference*, which can address file fragments, as shown in in Example 20-3.

The URI portion of the reference addresses the "auto13.cgm" file. The fragment identifier portion begins with the #. It is an XPointer that addresses the graphic component named "123" within that file. The viewer

Figure 20-6   *CENTRA 2000* management interface

Example 20-3. URI reference to a WebCGM graphic component

```
<a xlink:href="auto13.cgm#name(123)">
  <text x="12" y="437" style="fill:blue">
    Automatic Transmission Drive Chain Assembly
  </text>
</a>
```

would normally center and zoom into the view window defined by the component's viewcontext attribute.

In Figure 20-7 the graphic components are both sources ("hotspots") and targets of hyperlinking. They are bi-directionally linked to the parts list on the left of the HTML page in which both the list and graphic are framed.

Figure 20-7   Parts list hyperlinked to graphic components of assembly

Figure 20-8 shows the result of navigating from the parts list to the "chain" component of the WebCGM graphic. The graphic was scaled and positioned to the view region specified by the component's `view_context` attribute.

20.5 | Conclusion

It is possible to integrate reusable graphic components into an XML document by using XML to model the abstract structure of graphic documents represented in a binary notation. The graphic notation must have a structural element that can group geometric elements and metadata in a hierarchical structure; WebCGM has this facility.

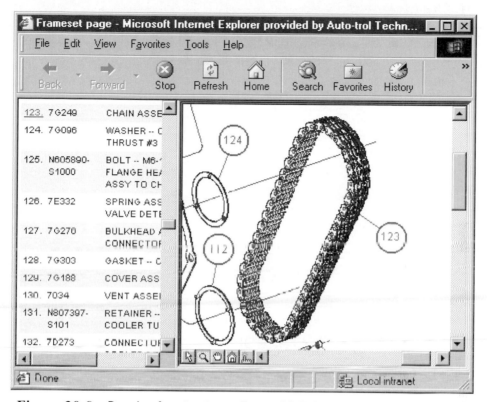

Figure 20-8   Result of navigating in Figure 20-7 from a part number to its graphic component

Once the abstract structure is modeled, the components of the graphic document can be used in bi-directional links among themselves and non-graphic components of XML documents.

Portals

- Doorways to information
- Enterprise information portal (EIP)
- Digital dashboards
- Content processing for portals
- Managing content feeds

Part Six

A portal is a doorway, and in the language of the World Wide Web, a "portal site" is one that users visit first. It acts, literally, as the user's doorway to all of the resources of the Web.

Now organizations are constructing their own portals – not all-encompassing sites for the masses, like traditional Web portals, but *enterprise information portals* (EIP). An EIP is a doorway to a focused set of resources, intended for a specific audience, like the employees, customers, and suppliers of a business. Most importantly, an EIP can serve as a single coherent view of information aggregated from disparate sources by e-commerce systems and integration servers.

In this part, we'll explore the reasons for EIPs and the systems needed to build them. We'll look at an EIP in detail: an imaginary but possible portal that you'll wish your doctor had. Finally, we'll examine a standard for managing the dynamic content feeds that portals thrive on.

Portal servers
for e-business

Tool Discussion

- Portal server requirements
- Architecture of an e-business portal server
- Other portal server facilities

Sponsor: Sequoia Software Corporation,
http://www.sequoiasoftware.com

Contributing expert: Bryan Caporlette

In today's e-business environment, an enterprise information portal is literally a "digital dashboard" that allows employees, suppliers, and customers to interact with an enterprise. The EIP accepts and delivers information, ranging from formal publications to dynamic business process data, anywhere the Internet can reach — with or without wires! The resulting requirements for portal servers are quite demanding, as this chapter reveals.

To meet the needs of today's interactive e-business portals, a portal server must do many things. It combines the functions of an application server, workflow manager, content manager, end-to-end publishing system, and database – either as a single product or a set of interconnected ones. But however they are implemented, the requirements are the same.

21.1 | Portal server requirements

The requirements for interactive e-business portals can be divided into three categories: performance, content distribution, and business process integration.

21.1.1 *Performance*

Performance, for a portal server, means reliability, availability, and scalability. An application server is required that can provide sophisticated load distribution and communication capabilities that allow an enterprise to scale its portal in multiple directions. It must be possible for administrators to add hardware to stress points as they expand the reach of the portal to new users and data sources.

21.1.2 *Content distribution*

It is no longer feasible to require that a portal user have access to a powerful PC and a large monitor. The reach of the EIP has extended to network PCs, thin clients, and mobile devices – including phones and personal digital assistants (PDA).

Content sources are also expanding. They now include ERP and MRP systems, legacy business applications, Internet sites, syndicated information sources, and information services integrated within the portal. To cope with the increasing variety of content, the server must offer a quickly extensible environment for adding new content sources.

A further requirement for content distribution is personalization. Users must be able to filter the content to satisfy personal profiles, and at the same time be able to specify a rendition style that best suits their personal needs and the capabilities of the delivery device.

21.1.3 *Business process integration*

The portal server must allow an enterprise to define complex business flows in a modular and flexible way. These modules can be thought of as *integration agents* because their individual small actions can have the combined effect of implementing a large and complex process.

For example, Figure 21-1 shows the workflow for an expense report that is submitted to the portal as an XML document. The first integration agent validates the report against the company expense report schema. The next agent interrogates the amount and, depending on the dollar value, either sends the report directly to the accounting department for processing, or else routes it to the manager's inbox for review and approval.

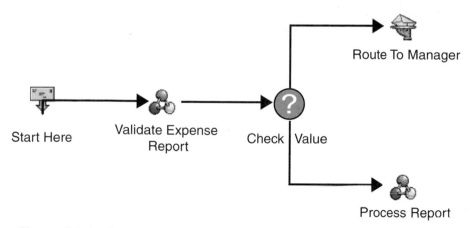

Figure 21-1   Expense report flow

21.2 | Architecture of an e-business portal server

To understand the workings of portal servers and discuss their requirements, it is helpful to have an architectural model in mind as a frame of reference. Figure 21-2 depicts the architecture of an XML based portal server at a level where the components relate directly to the requirements categories we have been discussing.

There are three major components, and XML plays a significant role in each of them:

- The *XML Application Server (XAS)* addresses performance issues by providing the necessary reliability and scaling. All data is packaged in XML "envelopes", thereby creating a messaging architecture that is easily connected to other systems, both internal and external.
- *Content Delivery Services* (CDS) brokers end-user requests for information and generates the appropriate response. Because the XML representation separates the abstract data from any specific presentation format, the data can easily be reformatted for multiple delivery devices.

Figure 21-2　Portal server architecture

- *Business Integration Services* (BIS) automates work processes within the portal. A sophisticated rules engine can interrogate the XML envelopes in order to make routing decisions.

We will examine each of these components in detail in the following sections. Bear in mind that we are discussing an architecture, not a specific implementation. Although we use a single integrated product to illustrate the functionality, it would also be possible to satisfy the requirements by using several intercommunicating dedicated products.

21.2.1　*XML application server*

The XML application server provides load balancing and a messaging architecture.

21.2.1.1　Portal clusters

The load balancer distributes work among sets of portal servers known as *portal clusters*. Each cluster has a *cluster server*, which stores information about the portal cluster's configuration. That information is stored persistently in a relational database, which provides backup and replication capabilities.

The cluster environment provides fail-over capabilities that ensure that the portal is always available. When a message is sent to a load-balanced server, the XAS awaits a response from it. If that machine does not respond in a timely manner, the application server may re-submit the request to the next available portal server, or enter a failure event into the auditing system. The administrator can set a threshold for failures, which will determine the number of negative responses a given machine can have prior to becoming deactivated within the cluster.

21.2.1.2   Messaging architecture

XML messages are the interface between the portal server and external systems. All communications with the XAS, whether business objects (e.g. documents) or remote procedure calls (e.g. search requests), are encapsulated in XML envelopes.

21.2.1.2.1   *Messaging protocols*

The application server abstracts the notion of envelopes through the definition of *message types*. Message types provide the routing and metadata information necessary to transmit data between an application and the portal by means of a *message protocol*. There are several industry initiatives for message protocols, including Microsoft's *BizTalk*, *ICE*,[1] and *RosettaNet*. As the XAS abstracts the message types, it is not limited to a single protocol.

There are two directions a message might take, depending on the message type. Presentation requests coming from a browser or Wireless Application Protocol (WAP) gateway are routed to the *Content Delivery Services* component. Business objects, such as documents and business interactions, are routed to the *Business Integration Services* component.

21.2.1.2.2   *Receivers and senders*

Receivers and senders are modules that provide access to the portal. They are shown at the bottom of Figure 21-2.

---

1. ICE is discussed in Chapter 24, "Information and Content Exchange (ICE)", on page 358.

Receivers listen for new messages coming into the portal. Senders transmit messages to external applications. The modular design allows the XAS to provide support for any data communications protocols, including HTTP, MSMQ, SMTP, COM, FTP, and directory polling.

This flexible support for data communications protocols allows the portal server to interoperate with enterprise application integration (EAI) tools. The portal server is thereby able to leverage corporate experience and expenditures on existing EAI applications.

21.2.1.3   Load balancing

As messages flow into the portal, a message processor communicates with the load balancer to distribute the processing across the known load-balanced servers within the cluster.

Once a load-balanced server is selected, XAS instantiates a new transaction to process the message. Depending on the success or failure of the transaction, XAS will log one or more events into the auditing component. The auditing component provides system monitoring and health status for all portal services.

21.2.1.4   Rules engine

The XAS dispatcher routes messages to the appropriate services, such as integration agents. It has a sophisticated rules engine that interrogates the Document Object Model (DOM) of the XML envelope.

Rules are test conditions that are evaluated to determine the route a message will take through the portal. The rules include XML Path Language (XPath) expressions that address values in the DOM.

For example, the rule in Example 21-1 might be used at the `Check value` decision point in Figure 21-1 to route the expense report. It compares the `value` attribute of the `total` element of an `expense-report` document to "500.00".

Example 21-1. Rule containing an XPath expression

```
%/expense_report/total/@value% > 500.00
```

21.2.2 *Content delivery services*

The *Content Delivery Services* component controls the delivery of data to an end user. It allows for personalization of the rendered information, the portal desktop, and individual content sources.

21.2.2.1 Rendition

CDS exploits the fact that XML allows abstract information content to be separate from formatting style, so data can be rendered in the needed form on delivery.

This separation enables the portal to service requests coming in from Web servers or Wireless Access Protocol gateway servers. CDS dynamically associates an XSLT stylesheet with each XML document, based on the type of device on which it will be presented (e.g. Web browser, cellular phone, personal digital assistant). It then generates HTML or Wireless Markup Language (WML), as appropriate.

The rendering engine is controlled by rules that establish a one-to-many relationship of XSLT stylesheets to XML schemas. When a user requests a document, the rendering engine uses the rules to select a stylesheet, apply that stylesheet to the XML document, and deliver the result. The rules that select the stylesheet can be based on the user's name and/or role within the portal (explained later), as well as the type of requesting device.

In fact, rendition rules can also specify selection criteria based on the content of the document. For example, a rule might test for the payment method of an order, represented by the content of the `payment.method` element. The rules could apply different style sheets to the document depending on whether the payment method is Visa, Mastercard, or American Express.

21.2.2.2 Personalization

The essence of a portal is the personalized aggregation and delivery of information from multiple sources. The delivery point is the desktop, which is populated with information by means of *content delivery agents (CDA)*.

21.2.2.3   Personalized desktop

Figure 21-3 shows an example of a portal desktop, as generated by Sequoia's *XML Portal Server (XPS)*™. The tabs at the upper left allow different pages to be selected.

Figure 21-3   Desktop in Sequoia's *XML Portal Server*

The portal desktop is controlled by a template, which specifies the content and layout. Customization of the template occurs at two levels: roles and individual personalization.

21.2.2.3.3   *Roles*

The types of pages and CDAs available to a user are controlled by assigning each user to one or more "roles". A role corresponds conceptually to a mode of use of the portal, such as engineer, manager, administrator, etc.

In system terms, a role is a collection of pages, CDAs, and a default theme (i.e. a color scheme and background). As users log into the portal, their roles are used to generate the original desktop.

21.2.2.3.4 *Individual personalization*

The rightmost tab in Figure 21-3 allows the desktop to be personalized. With it the user can change the layout of any page. Content source windows can be moved around, added, and hidden. In addition, the user can select from a set of pre-configured themes that control the color and background images of the desktop.

21.2.2.4   Content delivery agents (CDA)

The portal administrator can associate content delivery agents with pages. A CDA is a program or script that creates a window for communicating with a data source. These include:

- Internet content providers (e.g. *Hoovers, CNBC*, etc.).
- Application programs (e.g. *Exchange, Lotus Notes*).
- Internal integration agents (see 21.3.1, "Integration agents", on page 334).

A CDA can provide a personalization option to elicit property settings for the data source, such as news categories, mail servers, or stock symbols. The CDA tailors the content delivered based on the user's current preferences.

21.2.3 *Business integration services*

The *Business Integration Services* component enables the administrator to automate business processes within the portal. The dispatcher controls the path through which a message flows.

Message paths could be simple, routing a message to an index server or content repository. However, they could also follow complex alternative routes among integration agents and decision points that must be resolved by use of the rules engine.

In BIS, unlike XAS, the rules can test not just the XML envelope, but the contained business object itself. If the object is an XML document, its content can be tested to determine the path.

A flow design tool enables the portal administrator to define routes graphically, using icons for integration agents and decision points, as in Figure 21-1. Icons for subflows allow the reuse of common business processes.

21.3 | Other portal server facilities

Sequoia's *XML Portal Server (XPS)* implements the architecture we have been discussing in a single integrated product. In addition to providing the three core architectural components, it comes packaged with a set of integration agents and an administration tool.

21.3.1 *Integration agents*

Integration agents can provide the following functions:

taxonomy
>   This agent provides a mechanism for organizing relevant information into a hierarchical view.

content management
>   The content management agent provides persisten local storage of information, including configuration management features.

smart summary
>   This agent provides summary views of data aggregated within the portal.

transformation
>   The transformation agent uses XSLT to map data from one schema to another.

data entry
>   This agent maps HTML form designs to XML schema definitions in order to generate XML documents from the completed forms.

Indexing

The indexing agent creates both XML-based contextual indices and full-text indices of information flowing through the portal.

scripting

The scripting agent provides a mechanism for extending the functionality of the portal through scripts written in a variety of languages.

21.3.2 *Administration and configuration*

The sheer number of components and configuration options available within a portal server can be daunting even to contemplate, let alone to deal with in a production environment. The interface provided by a server implementation is therefore as important a consideration as the functionality.

Product vendors are aware of this fact. Sequoia's *XML Portal Server*, for example, includes a *Portal Management Console* that provides a single point of administration and configuration for the entire portal environment.

Content systems for portals

Tool Discussion

- Enterprise content systems

- Structuring non-XML content

- High-volume auto-linking

- Organizing portal content

Sponsor: eidon GmbH, http://www.eidon-products.com
Contributing expert: Lothar Simon

22

When you conduct a search at a Web portal, you may be offered links to thousands of documents from hundreds of sources. You don't really expect them to be consistent in any way, let alone hyperlinked together. But when you go to an enterprise portal, consistency and integration are things you might well expect, even when the documents are independently created with word processors, spreadsheets, and presentation programs. Here's how it can be done!

The content management systems (CMS) we discussed in Part 5, "Content Management", on page 262 are designed to support the development of document content based on elements or other components. Reuse, checkin/checkout, versioning, access control, variants, translation support, etc. on a component level are key functions of such systems.

For portals though, both content management and something more are required.

22.1 | Beyond content management

A major benefit of a CMS is that you can write a source once, reuse it often, and publish it to different media. A typical system allows you to create customized environments for developing a structured information set to support a business objective. Typical applications include the technical documentation for a machine manufacturer, or the articles, magazines and books for a legal publisher.

However, system requirements change when information reuse and multiple-source publishing are scaled up from the "department creating manuals" to the inter-enterprise B2B level. Now we must deal with an open, asynchronous, and dynamic information environment. Different collections of (partially) homogeneous, structured content, designed for different objectives, must be integrated to form a common component-based information pool.

On this level, functions beyond basic content management are required. Manual *document-based* editing yields priority to automatic *collection-based* mass transformation, homogenization, and integration of content.

For example, consider a machine installed in a plant along with hundreds of others from different manufacturers; the service technicians need efficient access to a common "plant manual". Similarly, a lawyer working on a case needs all relevant information scattered among laws from the government, decisions from courts, articles from different publishers, and previous briefs created by his own firm.

These integrated information collections are what we look to enterprise information portals (EIP) to provide.

22.2 | Requirements of enterprise portals

Typical Web portals offer widespread information from different sources to a large audience – the larger the better – with some personalization and groupware features. Access to the information is supported by categorization and full-text search. The original information is either presented unchanged, or just converted to a rendered format like HTML or PDF. Separate information sources stay separate.

In contrast, the enterprise information portals that we have been discussing aim at a clearly defined target audience – typically a business and its partners – and deliver a homogeneous information pool taken from disparate sources. The original information is frequently hyperlinked across sources and available in a consistent uniform structure.

To address these requirements, content systems for portals must provide functions beyond the usual content management. These include:

structuring non-XML content

In an enterprise-wide information pool one cannot expect all sources to be in XML. How can content in rendition-oriented notations, such as *Word* or *PowerPoint*, be integrated with the XML content?

managing production flow

To satisfy the volume demands of a portal, some sort of guided batch processing of document collections is needed. How can production environments be made to encompass features of a development environment and a production control center alike?

high-volume link management

Relationships among content from disparate information sources need to be identified and made explicit. How can these links be generated and managed in a high-volume portal system?

organizing portal content

Content in portals must be associated with business processes, such as procurement or customer service. How can content be organized to facilitate such connections?

22.3 | Structuring non-XML content

As we point out in 6.1, "Structured vs. unstructured", on page 108, the term "structured" is commonly used as a synonym for "abstract". XML documents are frequently characterized as "structured" and non-XML documents as "unstructured".

These characterizations are, of course, incorrect. XML can be used to represent renditions, not just abstractions. Consider XSL-FO or XHTML, for example.

Similarly, and more importantly for this discussion, the term "unstructured" is given two meanings: "not abstract" and "lacking in structure". That is, a non-XML document is not only a rendition, but there is the implication that it is structureless in the dictionary sense of the word.

In fact, renditions do have structure, reflected in "paragraph styles" (e.g. "warning", "procedure", or "definition"), chapters and sections, tables, etc.

For legacy content, it would be simple enough to convert this structure to XML, as we discuss in Part 9, "Content Acquisition", on page 490.

But in an enterprise portal, these documents may well arrive in a recurring feed of syndicated content. And you probably have no control over the tool used to create them: Try to convince the marketing department to use an XML editor for letters or reports, or the sales force to abandon *PowerPoint!*

What is needed is the ability to deal with non-XML text on a component level, just as we discussed for binary graphics in Part 5.

Figure 22-1 shows one solution, implemented in the portal content system *eidonXportal*. It is called "FIDOM", for "Format-Independent DOM", and is based on concepts from the HyTime International Standard.

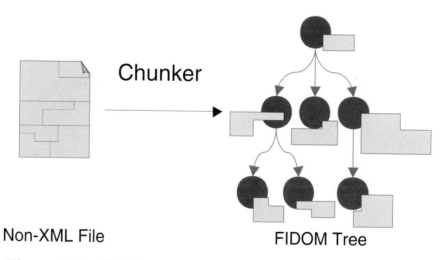

Chunker

Non-XML File   FIDOM Tree

Figure 22-1   FIDOM tree

A FIDOM tree represents the structure information of a non-XML file in much the same way that a DOM tree does for XML. However, the content of the FIDOM tree elements is that of the non-XML document's components.

The "chunker" shown in the diagram is a parser for a file format such as *Word, PowerPoint, Excel,* or *Interleaf;* it creates FIDOM trees from those files.

The resulting structure provides component-level access to the non-XML document. It offers possibilities ranging from enterprise-level *PowerPoint* slide management to hyperlinking non-XML components.

22.4 | Managing production flow

A key component of a content management system is a workflow manager that guides individual documents and their authors through a predefined sequence of processing steps. Content systems for portals also require such a component, but because of the enormous volumes involved, it is just a sub-component of a production system for mass content transformation.

A portal's production flow manager must integrate the tools for multiple processing steps, to be applied to large numbers of documents concurrently – perhaps thousands at a time. Moreover, it must be capable of customization for the specific task at hand in order to achieve maximum efficiency and simplify user training.

As a content management system is designed to manage changes to documents, a logical approach to meeting these customization needs is to define user interfaces as XML documents. *eidonXportal*, for example, is built on the CMS *eidonXbase*. Its user interfaces, called "desktops", can be displayed and revised like any other XML document. There is even a desktop for creating desktops, which is illustrated in Figure 22-2.

The left pane is opened at the desktop document hierarchy, and the TABS component is highlighted. In the right pane, the text of the TABS element is shown, and rendered tabs can be seen at the top of the pane. As the component structure indicates, it is also possible to define menus, buttons, and folders.

The latter include so-called "dynamic folders", to which a script can be attached. Opening the folder executes the script and the result is shown as the contents of the folder.

The scripting language processes lists of objects, such as documents, versions, variants, content components, users, etc. In doing so, the scripts can access all of the product's capabilities, from administration, workflow, and import/export through search, structure navigation, link manipulation, and content processing.

Figure 22-2   Editing a desktop definition

22.5 | High-volume link management

An EIP, unlike a typical Web portal, integrates the content that it aggregates. Given the large volume of documents involved, a high degree of automation is necessary, so some form of *auto-linking* software must be used.

In principle, implementing auto-linking seems quite simple, given something like a FIDOM tree: Write a script to detect references in the rendered content and turn them into XML link elements. The problem is that links have more than one anchor!

At the time the scanning program detects a reference, it does not necessarily know where the object of the reference can be found. In consequence, it cannot insert a link right away. A three step process is required, as depicted in Figure 22-3.

The three steps are:

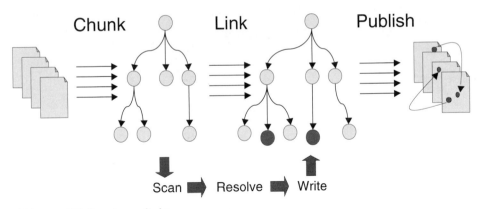

Figure 22-3 Auto-linking process

scan

Based on rules established for the various types of link, scan the content of a document collection for references and referenced objects.

resolve

Resolve all found references and referenced objects to create a link data structure for each resolved reference. Report dangling references; i.e. references or referenced objects whose counterpart could not be found.

write

Based on the link type rules, insert the appropriate link markup into the documents.

Auto-linking a portal's complete document collection may be impractical if the collection is extremely large, or even impossible if it is based on constantly changing dynamic feeds. In these cases, it is possible to implement an incremental approach, in which only the changed parts of the document collection are processed.

This can be accomplished by implementing a "link manager", as shown in Figure 22-4. It stores link information in a dedicated repository, separate from the documents. During incremental auto-linking, the link manager can be queried to determine what must be changed.

Figure 22-4   Link manager

In combination with the ability to process structured non-XML documents, auto-linking enables the creation of a homogeneous information pool from heterogeneous document formats. As a result, related content is only a click away, even among, for example, *Word, Excel, Interleaf,* and XML documents.

22.6 | Organizing portal content

As part of the integration required by an EIP, content must be associated with relevant business processes and systems. The information should therefore be organized in categories that derive from the processes themselves. For example, product line documentation might reflect:

1. product structure, based on a parts list or bill of materials;
2. information type, such as marketing, service, or engineering;

3. natural language; and
4. target audience, such as users, service technicians, etc.

Content management allows us to create independent components that convey exactly one piece of information, so one component in this scheme might be:

1. for the motor;
2. maintenance information;
3. in Chinese;
4. for service technicians.

One can imagine this information organization as a multi-dimensional (in this case four-dimensional) array whose cells are folders in which the components are stored.

Figure 22-5 shows how a content system for portals, in this case *eidonX-portal*, can offer a built-in two-dimensional filtered view into such a multi-dimensional structure. The product structure is shown in the left-most column and there are separate columns for each information type. Icons in the intersecting cells indicate whether information exists for the combination of product component and information type.

Figure 22-5   Filtered view showing product structure and information type

RxML: Your prescription for healthcare

Case Study

- Health portal system
- Dynamic patient summary
- Information aggregation
- Supply chain automation

Sponsor: Sequoia Software Corporation,
http://www.sequoiasoftware.com

Contributing expert: Bryan Caporlette

Chapter 23

> When it comes to electronic information processing, the U.S. medical system is "terminally" ill, so to speak. Systems rarely share data, even in the same medical organization, and there is little chance that your doctor can usefully access all your records for a diagnosis. This chapter prescribes a cure.

I magine you're feeling under the weather, so you make an office visit to your primary care physician.

Dr. Caps enters the examination room with a portable device instead of a clipboard. From that device he can access a patient summary record that contains your complete medical history, follow-up visits, current medications, and your favorite pharmacy. This information has been pooled together from various sources in the ABC Medical Center to create a single integrated logical view.

After an initial evaluation, Dr. Caps orders a throat culture to check for streptococcus bacteria. A laboratory order request, in the form of an XML document, is transmitted to the microbiology department. A culture is obtained by the nurse and sent to the lab. The culture results will be sent directly to the doctor's electronic in-basket, where he can evaluate them to determine the appropriate course of action.

Until determination of the culture result, he prescribes Keflex for coverage. He chooses Keflex, rather than amoxicillin, because the patient summary indicates that in a previous "encounter" (office visit, etc.) you reported an adverse reaction to amoxicillin.

The prescription is sent electronically to your local pharmacy, where it will be awaiting your arrival as you head home for some much needed rest. Following your departure, the billing department will automatically generate an XML invoice that is electronically submitted to Blue Triangle, your healthcare provider.

That all-important patient summary is made possible for Dr. Caps through a collection of electronically stored medical information, aggregated and distributed through a *health portal system*, as shown in Figure 23-1. It enables you, as a patient, to receive the best service, and clinicians to make the most informed decisions regarding your care.

Figure 23-1   Health portal system

23.1 | Doing as well as can be expected – Not!

As you have probably noticed, real-world experiences with the healthcare industry do not resemble the integrated environment we've portrayed. Let's say you were born in upstate New York, went to school in Ohio, and now live in Silicon Valley. More likely than not, you have had to receive medical attention at each of these locations.

Most of us have been asked repeatedly to fill out the same forms, with our demographic and medical histories. The onus has been on us to remember our doctors' names, dates of injury and illness, arcane names of medications we are taking, and allergies that have been discovered over a lifetime. This information has been stored multiple times, in multiple systems, in multiple geographic locations.

Unless you have been fortunate enough to have the same doctor your whole life, your physicians probably haven't had all the information necessary to render the best diagnosis. Stories of duplicate laboratory tests, negative reactions to unknown medical allergies, and misdiagnosis due to missing or incorrect information abound within the industry.

There are many reasons the care we receive falls short of our expectations. Organizations have to deal with a copious amount of information. However, providing access to this information to the correct person at the correct time is often impossible.

The typical healthcare organization information system deploys between 30 and 70 applications. These applications are spread across multiple functional departments, hardware platforms, and geographical locations, which impedes effective use of their information. Other barriers include security considerations and the cost of software licenses.

23.2 | The prescription: a health portal system

Fortunately, there is a cure for this condition. Health portal systems like the one used by Dr. Caps in our example can exist. They are just examples of Enterprise Information Portals, which organizations can build using products like Sequoia's *XML Portal Server*.

A *health portal system* provides a single point of access for all your medical information. Clinicians log into the portal, after which they have sophisticated search and navigation capabilities to access a comprehensive library of information.

These capabilities enable the clinician to locate your patient summary record quickly. The patient summary is an aggregate view of your complete medical history, made up of information components extracted from the numerous systems deployed by the health enterprise. Figure 23-2 depicts what Dr. Caps saw in our example.

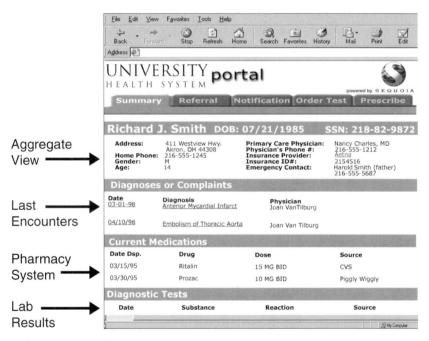

Figure 23-2   Rendition of patient summary

In addition to those internal systems, the portal provides access to medical libraries and external systems, such as laboratory results and pharmaceutical ordering systems. Its all done by the portal system's acquisition component and its connectors.

23.3 | Connectivity counts

The portal software in Figure 23-1 is Sequoia's *XML Portal Server*; its acquisition component is labeled *iAcquire* and it uses senders and receivers to communicate with connectors that tap into various disparate systems. The connectors communicate with software applications, extract data from them, and package that data in XML messages that are passed on to the XML data server.

The connectors are a flexible bunch. One might be communicating directly with a radiology system, capturing the images and routing them into the portal. Another connector could be listening through a TCP/IP port for health industry standard (HL7) messages being transmitted from the "admit, discharge, transfer" application.

Yet another connector might poll an FTP directory that has been set up for our transcription service company to submit operative reports and other transcribed documents. As the documents are sent into the directory, the connector grabs them and converts the information into XML.

This functionality doesn't just happen. The portal administrator must train the system to perform the transformations by defining connectors. Systems typically provide a graphical user interface (GUI) that enables easy mapping of source data elements into their target XML documents. Some, like Sequoia's *XML Portal Server*, provide other features that make the administrator's life easier, such as DTDs that allow automatic import of standard HL7 messages. Once defined, the connectors are deployed across the enterprise to begin collecting the data needed by Dr. Caps.

But these connectors are not just one-way data pumps. The administrator can also enable connectors to dynamically query data stored in an electronic medical records (EMR) application. When Dr. Caps needs to find out if you have had streptococcus recently, the data server can formulate a search request. This request is serviced in real-time by the connector, communicating to the EMR application through an ODBC interface. Perhaps he will recommend a vitamin C supplement to your diet.

Figure 23-3 illustrates the acquisition component of Sequoia's *XML Portal Server* and its connectors, which are labeled *Accessor* in the diagram.

Figure 23-3   Sequoia's *XML Portal Server* and its *Accessor* connectors

23.4 | Aggregation adds value

As information flows into the portal's XML data server, it must be organized in a way that facilitates easy, intuitive access by Dr. Caps.

Information overload could become a problem, if information is not properly presented to the physician. The obvious first step is to provide a categorization facility to help organize the data into folders. XML provides the ability to define element types such as patient name, encounter date, and attending physician that can be used to place documents into a particular folder.

However, the unique capability of a true enterprise information portal is that it can aggregate data from disparate sources to create a comprehensive view of your overall health. This is where XML really plays a significant role.

Imagine trying to assimilate information from a proprietary ASCII format, the results of an SQL query, and an operative report in some word processor format. But, if the connectors are doing their transformation job properly and sending only XML into the portal, a new breed of aggregate XML objects can be built dynamically from these sources.

The aggregate XML object in this case is a patient summary. The template that causes it to be created is shown in Figure 23-4. The template is an XML document with no data. The empty elements act as queries that retrieve the data of the same element types in other documents – the "data sources".

Actual patient summaries are constructed by filling in copies of the template with data extracted dynamically from the data sources as they enter the system. The patient summary becomes the universal access point for all information, with hyperlinks into the original data source documents supplementing the summary where appropriate.

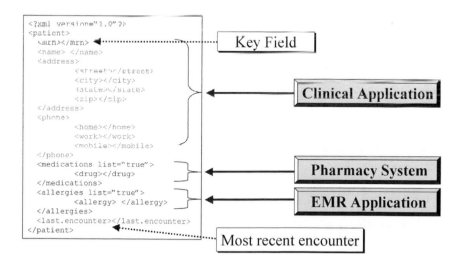

Figure 23-4   Template for patient summary

23.5 | Personalization assures usability

Not everyone needs to see, or should see, all the information flowing into the system. The portal can deliver personalized renditions of the XML information to the clinicians by using XSLT stylesheets. These provide very granular personalization, applying transformation rules at the element level.

The portal applies XSLT on the server-side, where it can employ a powerful rules engine to associate multiple stylesheets with the same document. Users can define profiles that choose their preferred stylesheet.

Personalization doesn't only apply to the presentation. Access and document routing can be controlled through XML documents so that physicians can automatically be sent a "today's appointments" report listing the day's schedule.

The portal can also limit access to patient records to their own doctors. For example, the access rule in Example 23-1 ensures that only Dr. Caps has access to the lab report in Example 23-2, where he is identified as the attending physician. The %doctor_name% variable accesses the user's login identity.

Example 23-1. Access rule for lab reports

```
Access Rule: Grant Read where
   Lab.report\attending.physician$eq$%doctor_name%
```

Example 23-2. Lab report

```
<lab.report>
<patient>
<name>John Smith</name>
<mrn>ID939393</mrn>
</patient>
<attending.physician>Dr. Caps</attending.physician>
<result>
<test>
<name>Throat culture</name>
</test>
</result>
</lab.report>
```

23.6 | Linking up the supply chain

Healthcare enterprises struggle constantly with managing all their external suppliers. The typical organization must deal on a daily basis with laboratories, physicians, transcription services houses, and most importantly, the benefit providers (Blue Triangle in your case).

The portal's ability to automate the relationship with provider organizations is one of the key benefits to the healthcare facility. The billing department will extract XML information from the portal to create an electronic billing invoice, passing it through an XML-enabled transaction server for transmittal over a secure extranet connection to Blue Triangle. Blue Triangle, in processing the invoice, verifies your benefits eligibility with Healtheon prior to transmitting a payment voucher back to ABC Medical Center.

Internet banking services will also impact the payment system. Soon you might be able to authorize electronic payment of your co-pay amount directly from your checking account.

23.7 | Conclusion

XML-powered health portals with dynamic patient summaries transform the healthcare experience. Patients receive better, faster healthcare service while clinicians gain greater access to information that enables them to make the best decisions.

Healthcare organizations also realize significant benefits. Their service reputation improves even while they cut costs because doctors don't order the same tests multiple times. In addition, automated billing lowers costs further while improving cash flow.

Hint   *You can learn more about building enterprise information portals with Sequoia's XML Portal Server in Chapter 21, "Portal servers for e-business", on page 324.*

Information and Content Exchange (ICE)

Application Discussion

▌ The new role of syndication

▌ Managed content interchange

▌ An ICE scenario

Sponsor: ICE Authoring Group, http://www.icestandard.org

Contributing experts: Lucien Rhodes, Linda Burman, Daniel Koger, Richard Martin, and Laird Popkin

Chapter

24

Portals feed on *feeds* – automated recurring content flows: technical and marketing information from business partners, product manuals from your company's divisions, and publications from traditional media sources. Negotiating and managing the syndication of content feeds used to be time-consuming and expensive, but now there's a cool way to do it!

 ou may not realize it, but syndication is part of your business even if you have nothing to do with the media industry. To see why, let's have a brief history lesson.

24.1 | Beyond the newswire

Syndication – historically, the delivery of content to multiple subscribers simultaneously – began in the earliest days of the newspaper business. It was automated by the telegraph, with reporters and local newspapers transmitting articles to big city newspapers.

Syndication drove the growth of a media industry that is now dominated by giant content providers – the *syndicators*. They deliver everything from news articles to television programs, and they deliver them to a legion of newspapers, networks, and TV stations – *subscribers*.

In fact, that first syndication – the newswire – is perhaps the oldest example of an automated supply chain. Unlike the EDI supply chain, however, which delivers only data about commercial transactions, the newswire delivers the actual goods – the news articles.

The Internet has redefined and expanded the concept of syndication. Today, *syndication* means *managed content interchange*, and it goes far beyond the newswire, or even the media industry. As business integration becomes pervasive, ordinary enterprises need to syndicate and subscribe to such content as supplier catalogs and maintenance manuals – even customer profiles and transaction records!

Two trends in particular are creating this demand: the growth of value networks, and the increasing number of intermediaries serving as market makers.

24.1.1 Value networks

A *value network* is a group of businesses that cooperate to create and deliver products and services. Content syndication can be a valuable tool for coordinating and managing the activities of such a network.

For example, consider a high-tech manufacturer. The manufacturer may design new products but outsource the actual manufacturing. The manufacturer needs to manage the set of manufacturing documents its outsourcing partners are using, such as work instructions, assembly procedures, and engineering drawings.

As new manufacturing documents are distributed, effective dates and expiration dates need to be assigned to them. The manufacturer also needs to be assured that all documents are successfully delivered. It also needs notification of any problems as they arise, so they can be resolved promptly.

The manufacturer also needs to supply marketing collateral to its distributors. Marketing documents could include a mix of descriptive text, graphics, and business data, with each document having its own effective date and expiration date. The documents might also need to incorporate each distributor's unique branding.

While manufacturing and marketing documents are certainly not editorial news content, this B2B syndication process shares many of the characteristics of news syndication.

24.1.2 Intermediaries as market makers

In the case of value networks, syndication supports the efficient coordination of business partners who have already developed a close working relationship. In other, more fragmented markets, syndication can play a role in helping potential buyers and vendors to find one another in the first place.

In such markets, intermediaries have a key role to play. They aggregate many vendors' marketing collateral, product specifications, data sheets, catalogs, and the like at a single website, so buyers can more easily find what they want. Syndication is used to keep the website current.

In addition, the site can offer subscriptions for buyers who are interested in a specific product. New content is syndicated to the buyer as soon as it becomes available.

24.2 | Syndication requirements

The purpose of syndication is automated delivery of recurring content to subscribing business partners.

However, just as with traditional EDI, sharing online information among a network of partners can be problematic, as adding a new partner requires time-consuming, customized, error-prone, manual processes. The syndicator must negotiate special requirements with each new subscriber, such as delivery times and frequency, notification, reporting, and monitoring. For example:

flexible delivery
To operate properly and scale across a wide range of relationships, content syndication must support several delivery techniques. Some subscribers can accept delivery of content at any time, others only at specified times – for instance, off-peak hours. Some subscribers may request specific data at agreed-upon times; others will be set up to receive "pushed" data asynchronously.

delivery guarantees
Some content items, such as press releases, are withheld until a certain date and should not be accessible until that date. Also, most content has a shelf life and should be subject to expiration.

time value
Some content has a time value for delivery. For example, subscribers to a financial service that delivers stock quotes every ten minutes need a guarantee that the quotes will either arrive on time, or that the subscribers will be advised of failure.

24.3 | ICE: A cool and solid solution!

These requirements and other needs of Internet-based content interchange are addressed by the *Information and Content Exchange (ICE)*. ICE is an XML-based protocol that defines and negotiates the business rules and processes needed for reliable content syndication among Web servers. It was developed by a consortium of more than 80 software developers, technology suppliers, content owners, and publishers.

24.3.1 *ICE capabilities*

The ICE protocol defines a model for the ongoing management of syndication relationships, including the roles and responsibilities of syndicators and subscribers. Here are some key capabilities that ICE-based tools can offer:

- Syndicators can describe business rules, such as usage constraints and intellectual property rights.
- Syndicators can create and manage catalogs of subscription offers. These can be accessed by content type, source, and other criteria.
- ICE uses XML to represent the messages that syndicators and subscribers exchange. The ICE message structure keeps the content payload independent of the protocol itself, so virtually any data can be exchanged – from text to streaming video. ICE accommodates data conforming to industry specifications such as RosettaNet and Publishing Requirements for Industry Standard Metadata (PRISM).
- Subscribers can specify a variety of "push" or "pull" delivery modes, as well as delivery times and frequency.
- Subscribers can specify content update parameters, such as incremental or full updates.
- ICE-based tools allow content to be obtained from, and delivered to, a wide variety of content repository types. These include databases, content management systems, file directories, Web servers, PDAs, and Internet appliances.
- ICE can work with any transport protocol. The standard HTTP POST "request/response" transport model, for

example, allows fully symmetric ICE implementations in which both syndicators and subscribers can initiate requests.

24.3.2 *An ICE implementation*

Figure 24-1 shows the architecture of an ICE implementation.

Figure 24-1   Architecture of an ICE platform

In this particular ICE platform, there are two separate software components named – logically enough – the *Syndication Manager* and the *Subscription Manager*.

24.3.2.1   Syndicator functions

The *Syndication Manager* lets syndicators manage the packaging and syndication of content, including such essential tasks as:

creating subscription offers

Syndicators can identify content types and content sources, such as local directories and databases or remote locations, and package the content as subscription offers. They can also define management information, such as security, availability, and shelf life.

defining subscribers

Syndicators can identify subscribers and the addresses of the receiving computers. They can also provide passwords and other administrative information.

turning subscription offers into subscriptions

Syndicators provide a catalog of offers and define the terms that can be negotiated. These can include times of delivery and the right to customize the delivered material. Subscribers select offers and negotiate the specific terms of a subscription.

distribute subscription content to subscribers.

The *Syndication Manager* maintains records of subscriptions, offers, and subscribers and uses these records to control the delivery of the appropriate content using the ICE protocol. Configurable logging tracks management and transmission events at the appropriate level of detail, and can automatically report anomalies and problems.

24.3.2.2 Subscriber functions

The *Subscription Manager* provides tools and processes to manage content delivery, including:

defining subscriptions
Subscribers choose an offer from the syndicator's catalog and negotiate terms of delivery, customization, etc.

transforming received content
Subscribers can customize and transform downloaded content to the extent permitted by the negotiated subscription terms. For example, a company might insert its own branding and ads in the content before posting it on its website.

monitoring content
Subscribers can control event logging and notification priorities.

24.3.2.3 User interface

GUIs are not required by the ICE protocol and ICE transactions can be completed without them, but the appeal of a user-friendly interface is obvious. Interfaces can be tailored to particular content types or audiences, as illustrated in Figure 24-2. The interface code automatically generates ICE XML message documents from the data provided by the user.

24.3.2.4 ICE messages

An ICE message is a valid XML document whose document type is `ice-payload`; subordinate element types describe ICE operations and data, including requests and responses.

ICE does not restrict the type of content that is the subject of a transmission; the ICE message is effectively an envelope. The content can be incorporated as a subelement of the ICE message if doing so won't cause the document to be invalid XML. Alternatively, a URI to the actual content can be incorporated.

Offer Description

Offer Name   [Golf News and Reviews]

Description Shown to Subscribers

> Latest information on tournaments
> and in-depth reviews of courses
> and equipment.

Content Source   [Local Directory ▼]

Start Date   [3/24/2000]
Calendar

Stop Date   [3/24/2001]
Calendar

Needs Confirmation   ☑

Rights Holder   [World Golfing News Syndicate]

Usage Requirements
☐ Atomic Use
☐ Not Editable
☐ Show-Credit
☑ Usage-Required

Intellectual Property Status   [FREE-WITH-ACK ▼]

Figure 24-2   One possible interface for ICE transactions

24.4 | An ICE scenario

Let's look at a step-by-step example of a simple transaction between a syndicator and a subscriber in a familiar industry. The syndicator, the Best Code Company, a software developer, sets up and delivers a subscription to Tech News, a trade journal for the high technology industry.

24.4.1 *Syndicator and subscriber set up a business agreement*

Syndication relationships begin with a business agreement. Best Code and Tech News agree on such terms as payment issues, usage rights, and subscription lifetime. The business agreement negotiation typically happens outside ICE and can involve person-to-person discussion, legal review, and contracts.

24.4.2 *Syndicator and subscriber set up a subscription*

Once the business agreement is in place, ICE comes into play as Best Code and Tech News start exchanging ICE messages to negotiate a subscription and begin content delivery.

24.4.2.1 Subscriber requests catalog of subscription offers

Example 24-1 shows an ICE message in which Tech News uses `ice-get-catalog` to request a subscription catalog from Best Code. Tech News identifies itself to Best Code using a Universal Unique Identifier (UUID), as defined by the Open Group.

24.4.2.2 Syndicator responds with catalog containing one offer

In Example 24-2, Best Code uses `ice-offer-type="subscription"` to tell Tech News that the catalog contains a single subscription offer for press releases. `ice-delivery-rule mode="pull"` tells Tech News that this particular subscription offer will be delivered by the "pull" delivery method. (For simplicity, the detailed negotiation of delivery and other terms is not shown.)

Example 24-1. Request for a catalog of subscription offers

```
<?xml version="1.0"?>
<!DOCTYPE ice-payload SYSTEM "http://www.ice-ag.org/ICE.dtd">
<ice-payload ice.version="1.1"
             payload-id="74"
             timestamp="2000-09-22T04:37:00">
<ice-header>
  <ice-sender sender-id="37AB3FD0-D2CA-11d3-BBE9-723B75000000"
              name="tech news"
              role="subscriber"/>
  <ice-user-agent>Kinecta Subscriber 3.0</ice-user-agent>
</ice-header>
<ice-request request-id="74">
  <ice-get-catalog/>
</ice-request>
</ice-payload>
```

Example 24-2. Catalog containing one offer

```
<?xml version="1.0"?>
<!DOCTYPE ice-payload SYSTEM "http://www.ice-ag.org/ICE.dtd">
<ice-payload ice.version="1.1"
             payload-id="74"
             timestamp="2000-09-22T04:37:03">
<ice-header>
  <ice-sender sender-id="37AB3FD1-D2CA-11d3-BBE9-723B75000000"
              name="best code"
              role="syndicator"/>
  <ice-user-agent>Kinecta Syndicator 3.0</ice-user-agent>
</ice-header>
<ice-response response-id="74">
  <ice-code numeric="200" phrase="OK"/>
  <ice-catalog>
    <ice-contact description="Call her if something crashes."
                 name="Marcia Programmer, CEO, Code Co.">
Marcia Programmer mprog@bcode.com
(123) 456 7890
    </ice-contact>
    <ice-offer type="subscription"
               description="code co. press releases">
      <ice-delivery-policy>
        <ice-delivery-rule mode="pull"/>
      </ice-delivery-policy>
    </ice-offer>
  </ice-catalog>
</ice-response>
</ice-payload>
```

24.4.2.3   Subscriber sends a request to subscribe to the offer

Tech News thinks the press releases are exciting stuff and promptly asks to sign up for the subscription offer. It agrees to pull the content from Best Code's site and with `minfreq="P300S"` requests 5 minute intervals at most (Example 24-3.

Example 24-3. Request for a subscription

```
<?xml version="1.0"?>
<!DOCTYPE ice-payload SYSTEM "http://www.ice-ag.org/ICE.dtd">
<ice-payload ice.version="1.1"
             payload-id="75"
             timestamp="2000-09-22T04:40:00">
<ice-header>
  <ice-sender sender-id="37AB3FD0-D2CA-11d3 BBE9-723B75000000"
              name="tech news"
              role="subscriber"/>
  <ice-user-agent>Kinecta Subscriber 3.0</ice-user-agent>
</ice-header>
<ice-request request-id="75">
  <ice-offer type="subscription"
             description=" code co. press releases">
    <ice-delivery-policy>
      <ice-delivery-rule mode="pull" minfreq="P300S"/>
    </ice-delivery-policy>
  </ice-offer>
</ice-request>
</ice-payload>
```

24.4.2.4   Syndicator accepts request and responds with subscription

Best Code indicates that a subscription has been established by enclosing the agreed-upon offer within an `ice-subscription` element. Best Code gives Tech News an ID number of "1" for the subscription and also confirms the delivery method and "pull" time (Example 24-4).

Example 24-4. Acceptance of subscription request

```
<?xml version="1.0"?>
<!DOCTYPE ice-payload SYSTEM "http://www.ice-ag.org/ICE.dtd">
<ice-payload ice.version="1.1"
             payload-id="75"
             timestamp="2000-09-22T04:40:03">
<ice-header>
  <ice-sender sender-id="37AB3FD1-D2CA-11d3-BBE9-723B75000000"
              name="best code"
              role="syndicator"/>
  <ice-user-agent>Kinecta Syndicator 3.0</ice-user-agent>
</ice-header>
<ice-response response-id="75">
  <ice-code numeric="200" phrase="OK"/>
  <ice-subscription subscription-id="1">
    <ice-offer type="subscription"
               description="best code press releases">
      <ice-delivery-policy>
        <ice-delivery-rule mode="pull" minfreq="P300S"/>
      </ice-delivery-policy>
    </ice-offer>
  </ice-subscription>
</ice-response>
</ice-payload>
```

24.4.3 *Subscriber receives content*

Once the subscription is set up, Tech News is ready to receive content. Tech News starts by asking for new content. Best Code responds with a message describing the changes to the content in the subscription. These changes can include new content and can also include requests to delete existing content. In this way, Best Code can control the precise content for that subscription on the Tech News site. Together with the actual content, the messages may also specify other subscription parameters such as effective date and expiration date.

24.4.3.1 Subscriber requests initial subscription content

Tech News uses `ice-get-package` to ask for subscription content. `current-state="ICE-INITIAL"` indicates that this is an initial request for this subscription, which alerts Best Code to download the full content (Example 24-5).

Example 24-5. Request for initial subscription content

```
<?xml version="1.0"?>
<!DOCTYPE ice-payload SYSTEM "http://www.ice-ag.org/ICE.dtd">
<ice-payload ice.version="1.0"
             payload-id="951723923006951723922044"
             timestamp="07:45:22,044">
<ice-header>
  <ice-sender sender-id="37AB3FD0-D2CA-11d3-BBE9-723B75000000"
              name="tech news"
              role="subscriber"/>
  <ice-user-agent>Kinecta Subscriber 3.0</ice-user-agent>
</ice-header>
<ice-request request-id="951723923012951723922044">
  <ice-get-package current-state="ICE-INITIAL"
                   subscription-id="1"/>
</ice-request>
</ice-payload>
```

24.4.3.2 Syndicator responds with full content of subscription

In Example 24-6, Best Code delivers the content of its subscription, consisting of an `ice-package` with two press releases. The first release is part of the message — the content of an `ice-item` element. The second release, however, is not actually in the message. Instead, its location is given in the `url` attribute of an `ice-item-ref` element.

The `ice-package` element also conveys other information. `editable="true"` gives Tech News permission to edit the content, while `new-state="2"` establishes the state of the subscription. The next time

Example 24-6. Delivery of subscription content

```xml
<?xml version="1.0"?>
<!DOCTYPE ice-payload SYSTEM "http://www.ice-ag.org/ICE.dtd">
<ice-payload ice-version-"1.1"
             payload-id="95341031058775195172429302"
             timestamp="07:50:29,743">
<ice-header>
  <ice-sender sender-id="37AB3FD1-D2CA-11d3-BBE9-723B75000000"
              name="best code"
              role="syndicator"/>
  <ice-user-agent>Kinecta Syndicator 3.0</ice-user-agent>
</ice-header>
<ice-response response-id="9534084755799519172429302">
  <ice-code numeric="200" phrase="OK"
            message-id="9517239230129517239220044" />
  <ice-package editable="true"
               new-state="2"
               old-state="ICE-INITIAL"
               package-id="9537749528919519172429302"
               subscription-id="1">
    <ice-item item-id="1" name="press release 1"
      subscription-element=
        "http://10.10.1.53:8891/1762994087/PressRelease1.DOC"
      content-filename="PressRelease1.DOC">
Press Release 1
Latest news: we've released our first press release!
    </ice-item>
    <ice-item-ref
      item-id="2-951719746000"
      name="press release 2"
      subscription-element=
        "http://10.10.1.53:8891/1762994087/PressRelease2.DOC"
      url="http://10.10.1.53:8891/1762994087/PressRelease2.DOC"
      content-filename="PressRelease2.DOC"/>
  </ice-package>
</ice-response>
</ice-payload>
```

Tech News requests content, it will receive only content added or changed since this delivery, instead of receiving the entire content load all over again.

Tip   This example showed a basic ICE transaction in a single industry. The protocol is industry-neutral and is capable of far more complex negotiations, as you can learn by visiting http://www.icestandard.org/. The site includes information on available implementations and content syndicators who use ICE.

There are copies of the ICE spec and the ICE Cookbook on the CD-ROM that accompanies this book.

Publishing

- Online and offline from single source
- Extranet delivery of high-quality printing
- Business data reporting
- Developing and publishing reusable content

Part Seven

Publish or perish!

For decades that has been the mandate for academics seeking an assured career path. Today it is the mandate for enterprises of all kinds that are hostage to documentation requirements. If the manuals, reports, and marketing materials aren't ready, it is the products and business opportunities that will perish – not the career of some assistant professor.

And publishing today doesn't necessarily mean just a uniform static message on the corpses of dead trees: It means websites, CD-ROMs, multimedia, wireless, personalized delivery, and – yes – paper as well.

In this part we'll see how a leading financial management firm used XML to meet the demands of this new publishing environment, and a methodology for high-volume business data reporting.

We'll also look at the chief challenge in developing reusable content: How can you write it when you don't know what it's for?

Personalized financial publishing

- Frank Russell Company

- Business and technical requirements identification

- Structure-driven style

Sponsor: Synth-Bank LLC, http://www.synthbank.com

Contributing experts: Bryan Bell of Synth-Bank LLC and Randy Kelley of Frank Russell Company

This chapter is the chronicle of an extraordinary project: demanding requirements, ambitious goals, leading-edge technology, business school management techniques, and – did we mention "mission-critical"? a trillion dollars riding on the outcome. And XML figures in it as well.

F rank Russell Company is the investment management and asset consulting firm that is known for its *Russell 3000®* market index, the hallmark by which the performance of many investment advisors and mutual funds is judged. Russell provides investment solutions for institutions and individuals, guiding the investment of more than $1 trillion for clients in more than 25 countries.

25.1 | Background

During the eighties, Russell pioneered the use of high quality color presentations and "high touch" relationship management with its clients. Emblematic of this style were the beautifully printed portfolio performance reports known as the "client books".

Recently, Russell's investment management division experienced explosive growth, marketing private mutual fund products to the institutional marketplace, and retail funds through a group of selected distribution partners. This growth threatened Russell's ability to maintain its customer relationship style. It needed a way to address the increasing production volume demands for client books without sacrificing quality or profit margins.

The company engaged Synth-Bank LLC® to develop and implement a strategy for automating the process. A team of Synth-Bank and Russell employees was formed.

Russell had traditionally viewed its printed client books as products. The project team, however, realized that the real product was Russell's content, and that the book itself was merely one possible rendition.

Russell had been using the "print, then distribute" metaphor for decades. But as the newer digital technologies and communication processes were taking hold, and the World Wide Web's popularity became undeniable, the team began an effort to evangelize, design, produce and deliver a new metaphor: "distribute, then print".

Along with this shift in metaphors come real quality control issues, especially revolving around color printing. Not only were the traditional problems of re-purposing content for different media (i.e. for paper, CD-ROM, electronic, fax, and email) an issue, but also an entirely new set of workflow and editing issues was recognized with respect to the reuse of component objects from within the created documents.

Also, the trend to customizing the content product – moving from generic content to a specialized product for an individual information consumer, a "market of one" – was extremely interesting to Russell.

This chapter chronicles both the team's journey and the Russell solution that is currently in production.

25.2 | Project strategy considerations

Russell has steadily been increasing its own awareness that it truly is a large publishing concern, producing millions of pages of color and black and white output for its clients every year. And as a major financial intellectual property publisher, it is also realizing that printing and electronic delivery systems play a very strategic role in its continued growth and success.

There were five principle strategic considerations for the conduct of the project:

■ Proceeding from a theoretical abstraction to practical applications.

- Phasing deliverables with measurable return on investment.
- Continuing research in parallel with focused development projects.
- Alignment with overall corporate strategies.
- Executive sponsorship.

25.2.1 *Proceeding from a theoretical abstraction to practical applications*

The project team, though capable of grasping both the short- and long-term objectives for the enterprise, required a methodology to manage scope creep. It chose to divide the tasks into two clear groups:

- the theoretical research and related effort towards general solutions; and
- day-to-day development.

The team was always able to have discussions from the abstract down to the practical by mapping them onto the architecture and life cycle models When new technologies or vendor products came onto the radar, it was able to discuss them in the context of both the theory and practical project impact using a systematic method.

25.2.2 *Phasing deliverables with measurable return on investment*

This concept may sound similar to the concept of milestones, but is really quite different. This method assumes that there is *no* other project beyond the goals of this one.

It also assumes that this project must justify its own return on investment and bear management review based on its own merits.

Another key element is the openness of each phase's architecture, so that later phases can be bolted on seamlessly with very little trauma to users or developers.

25.2.3 *Continuing research in parallel with focused development projects*

Scope creep is an ever-present danger in technology. Change is a constant. Managing new inputs from press, rumors, research, and outside influence is a constant pressure on fixed milestones and deliverables.

The project team chose discretion as the better part of valor by separating the tasks of research and development into two distinct activities. The development tasks have clearly documented milestones, schedules, and budgets, with methodology in place to monitor their success weekly.

The research tasks are managed more loosely, with overall topics of interest. They use annual funding, rather than project-based funding, and measure deliverables by the published output from the team.

The team believes that this separation keeps developers on the hook for cleaner deliverables and return on investment, while still allowing a response to the crucial happenings that are a day-to-day part of the technology world.

25.2.4 *Alignment with overall corporate strategies*

Any technology project can be fraught with risk. Any technology project can solve a specific technical application and add value if properly executed. Russell's experience was that the real grand slam winner projects are the ones that support the overall mission, culture, vision, and business objectives of an enterprise.

In theory every part of an enterprise is supposed to be working on things that contribute to the goals of the entire enterprise. Straying too far from this principle increases risk and confuses observers, whereas following this principle makes a project's justification much easier to defend and publicize.

25.2.5 *Executive sponsorship*

For several reasons, this is the most powerful thing you can do to enhance a project's chance for success:

- Executives are generally seasoned professionals who have earned a place of authority by knowing how to exploit strengths and manage around weaknesses.
- Executives are generally the best funded portion of an enterprise.
- Executives generally have a clear understanding of the long-term objectives of the enterprise.
- Executives generally have a feeling for the short-term pressures on operations.

These executive qualities enhance a group's ability to make sure their work is done with the support and point-of-view of the senior management and shareholders.

25.3 | Identifying the needs

Russell began to realize the extremely high importance of publishing to the company when it found out the cost. A study determined that almost 1/3 of every expense dollar worldwide was attributable to documents and their production, printing and distribution.

25.3.1 *Business requirements*

The question then became: "How to distribute financial services publications better to a geographically diverse audience, while maintaining premium typographical quality, data integrity, security and compliance?"

Compliance
Russell operates in a heavily regulated environment. There is a legal requirement to reproduce documents related to a customer from many years in the past.

Premium typographic quality
Russell customers typically evaluate large amounts of financial information in a limited time. Russell adds tremendous value for

their customers by simplifying and clarifying these numbers through the use of text, graphics, charts, and color.

Data integrity

It is extremely important that the document received by a customer is identical to the one that was sent to it.

Security

Because of the confidential nature of financial information, it is imperative that only the appropriate people can view these files.

25.3.2 *Technical requirements*

There were significant technical requirements to be met in addition to the business requirements.

Scalability

At Russell, a *Quarterly Investment Review* (QIR) runs from 20-125 pages, averaging around 50 pages. There are hundreds of clients who each get a customized QIR each quarter. Multiple writing, editing, assembly, and compliance steps are required throughout the process.

Low licensing impact for reader software

The problem with end-user licensing of software is that it penalizes a business for the success of a document.

Ease of use

The team felt ease of use to be the single most important factor in the true success of a product.

Cross-platform

Russell cannot control the platforms that its customers use. It has to provide its information in an easily accessible form on virtually every platform available.

Multilingual capability

Russell has offices in London, New York, Winston-Salem, Paris, Hong Kong, Toronto, Tokyo, Sydney, and Auckland. Russell has clients in 25 countries.

25.4 | Create an abstract architecture

The Synth-Bank/Russell team set off to learn about the state of the art in publishing systems, SGML, PDF, and document delivery systems.

Russell had been a pioneer of Postscript assembly and color graphics in the financial services industry. Now the team desired to modernize Russell's publication capabilities to support lower than page granularity and the "distribute then print" metaphor. The team felt that this type of system could meet Russell's business objectives.

The team, working with consultants, created a "Request For Information and Statement of Direction" for a system to purchase (Figure 25-1).

Architectural Model

Figure 25-1 Architectural model of desired system.

The team also performed research on document life cycles and included the life cycle requirements shown in Figure 25-2.

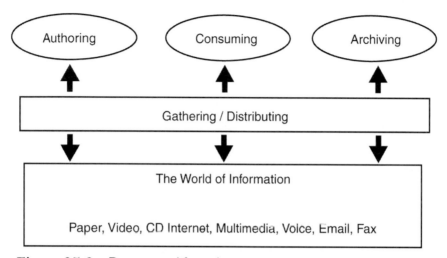

Figure 25-2   Document life cycle requirements.

Russell searched the SGML community for a publishing solution to meet its requirements and found no single commercial product in the marketplace. It then asked the big question: "Why isn't there one already"? The team felt that there were many companies and institutions with document problems similar to, if not more complex than, Russell's.

So the team spent several more months analyzing vendor capabilities and mapping them onto the life cycle graphic until it finally found what it felt was a possible reason. Namely, that the creating, consuming, and archiving stages of a document's life require different system capabilities and orientations: component management, document management, and records management, respectively (Figure 25-3).

Armed with this insight, the team developed the knowledge management model shown in Figure 25-4.

Russell's management and the Synth-Bank team then decided to build and integrate a solution out of *commercially available off-the-shelf* (*COTS*) products. The team decided to break the deliverables into different phases that would be integrated upon completion.

Figure 25-3   Document system orientations.

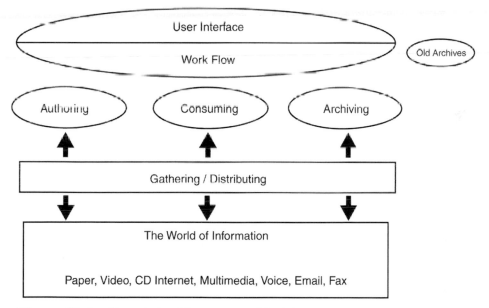

Figure 25-4   Knowledge Management Model

25.5 | Implement applications

The team's initial choice for an application was the *Quarterly Investment Review*. The QIR is representative of many of Russell's publications because it consists of a combination of generic, proprietary, customer-specific, and reusable components.

25.5.1 *Real-world design issues*

In order to apply the theoretical architecture to specific application designs for the QIR publications, the team had to come to grips with real-world issues of internetworking and document representation (file format) standards, to name a few.

25.5.1.1 Internetworking

The WWW family of technologies was chosen for its popularity. Its open-standard nature met the team's basic technical requirements for global electronic delivery, easy access, cheap per-seat licensing costs, cross-platform availability, and security.

The extranet model best served Russell's clients in this application. That is, WWW technologies connected, via public and/or private networks, to a restricted website.

25.5.1.2 Document representation

Synth-Bank firmly believes that document representation is the key to an organization's success with knowledge management. In the *SGML Buyers Guide* (1998), the authors clearly express this point: *"Don't let the software you buy determine the representation. Let the representation you need determine the software you buy"*.

In Russell's case, they needed to choose document representations for all three stages of the document life cycle.

During the creation stage, documents are most useful in an abstract unrendered representation, in which the data can easily be reused and reprocessed. During the consumption and archiving stages, however, the document must be in a rendered form so that it can be presented and displayed quickly and consistently.

25.5.1.2.1 *Abstract document representation*

At the time the work began, SGML was the only document representation that preserved the abstract data and had the "industrial strength" for Russell's requirements. So Russell used it.

XML, as a streamlined subset of SGML, is by definition, not as feature-rich. However, like its parent it preserves the abstraction, and it proved sufficient for Russell's purposes when they eventually converted to it.

25.5.1.2.2 *Rendered document representation*

Portable Document Format (PDF) was chosen for the rendered document representation. The archiving requirement, that it must be readable for a minimum of ten years time, was the dominant deciding criterion.

Large document collections have been faced with this need for some time; for example, those of the Library of Congress and Department of Defense in the U.S. At Russell and many other enterprises, the final formatted image of a document must be retrievable to meet business needs for compliance and reference. Russell's strong desire to use electronic documents to meet its goals was dependent upon a satisfactory decision in this single topic.

Synth-Bank first considered using SGML to meet Russell's archiving requirements. It has successfully been used for simple partial renditions (e.g., HTML), but fully rendered final-form and graphics are outside its design objectives. Although it is undeniably the best representation for long-term preservation of text, that is not what Russell meant by archiving. To be compliant, from Russell's archive it must be possible to retrieve exactly what the client printed originally.

The team made the choice to use PDF because it met the rendered image requirement for both text and graphics, was widely used across many platforms, had a publicly specified format, and supported a large set of the world's languages. It was also attracted to PDF's usability for email distribution and on-screen display.

PDF supports full text search, linking, and page by page loading. It has a development kit available, a compressed file size, interactive forms, cheap seats, and also prints extremely well.

25.5.2 *Phased implementation plan*

The work involved some parallel processing, with secondary teams doing research and advanced studies on upcoming phases. The implementation teams, however, focused on the deliverables.

One team was assigned to create archiving requirements for the corporation. Another team worked on object databases and SGML abstractions.

A third team worked on graphical design. Its goal was to constrain the number of presentation layouts in order to optimize for batch processing. Finally, a fourth team had the task of tracking and understanding key standards like SGML, XML, HyTime, and various related W3C activities.

25.5.2.1   Phase I: Records management business study

The technical work on this phase was deferred. The main candidate for an archiving product was in the middle of an acquisition, which created an unacceptable business risk.

However, Russell did conduct a two-year study on document archiving requirements for its Investment Management Business. Once the business case for records management was made, Russell hired a full-time professional archivist to champion the deployment of the technology.

25.5.2.2   Phase II: Document management of PDF files

Russell's corporate Information Technology department had previously deployed a document management system. The project team used it in the interests of corporate harmony, and worked with its vendor's R&D department on the beta version of an application to make documents available over the Web.

This product allows you to build a query on a Web-based form (Figure 25-5), which can be tailored to meet application requirements.

Figure 25-5   Document management search screen.

The query results are delivered as an HTML frame (Figure 25-6), the form of which can also be customized. Russell's users found that it made the interface to the product's library services, particularly document check-out, much more appealing than it had been.

25.5.2.3   Phase III: Document assembly and formatting

The objective of this phase was to create structured documents in SGML that could be auto-assembled, and to implement auto-check-in to the document management system.

As the assembly and formatting phase of the project began, the team focused on the issues of: How much structure is needed?, What are the quality levels required for the publication in its final form? What should the user interface experience be like for editing sections, book assembly and releasing books to the document management system?

Figure 25-6   Document management search results.

Russell decided to purchase a product that supported integrated structured editing, layout, and typographic control.

The users for this phase are a small group of document editors who compile and author the QIR documents for clients at Russell. Their typical quarterly work cycle involves revising the previous quarter's document files, graphics, and tables, and launching a new composite book for each client. New document pages are created approximately 10% of the time.

The users are trained in popular word processors, spreadsheet, and graphics packages, but have no experience in SGML. They are accustomed to setting the indents, font style, size of a page, and common typography settings. They are often under the spotlight to make a production deadline in hours and therefore must be able to make edits quickly with minimal amount of new steps. They are only interested in software that makes their life easier.

The team quickly found that the system must make the SGML transparent to the user, that the layout must be WYSIWYG, and that the application should assist in the creation of a consistent layout throughout the book.

25.5.2.3.3 *How structure was used*

The approach taken was to replace the use of paragraph style codes with meaningful SGML element-type names. The document was then formatted in real time, based on the element types, thereby giving the users their customary WYSIWYG effect.

A welcome side-effect was that the list of element-type choices was much smaller than the full list of paragraph styles typically presented by a WYSIWYG editor, because of the context enforced by the DTD. In addition, the product has a guided creation feature, which automatically inserts required elements. It allowed us to lay out a typical page easily, and still allowed deviations by making choices permitted by the DTD.

One area of improvement to the overall professionalism of the book was in the consistency of format and layout. In the old system, each page was laid out individually and it often deviated slightly as editing continued over several quarters of revisions.

The new system, however, used a series of matched templates created by a professional typographer, and it used structure to drive the formatting of the text. The resultant books were consistent, and compliant with corporate guidelines. This achievement was a significant win since "document police" (people trying to enforce style quality control issues from a corporate perspective) are not often welcome.

25.5.2.3.4 *Document editing*

With all of these facilities available, the team found that it needed to simplify the application menus. Doing so would limit access to designer pallets and provide users with a simpler interface to this complex and powerful tool.

Simplifying was done by using the application's custom user interface feature. It required no programming, although some developer expertise is required.

Training the users on the new system consisted of five sessions of one day in length, including hands on lab sessions. The editing tool took 50% of the training time, with the remaining time being spread on a general introduction, graphics, book building, and lab sessions. The users quickly grasped the system's capabilities and found it to be a huge improvement over the previous system.

Figure 25-7   Fund page example in editing system.

25.5.2.3.5   *How much structure is needed?*

Once the decision was made to use a structured representation of its publications, the challenge became to decide how much structure was appropriate and for what reasons. The team approached this from two viewpoints: long-term and short-term.

The long-term objectives of using structure were to add value to the intellectual property and aid with reuse, navigation, automation and archiving.

The short-term goals were to enforce consistency in the typography, assure better quality control, and facilitate the aggregation of disparate content sources into single publications with a high degree of automation. Other short-term goals were to facilitate document assembly with automation, and to improve the user's experience.

25.5.2.3.6 *Final-form quality requirements*

Russell's output quality requirements are extremely high (Figure 25-7). When it looked at the commercially available database-driven publishing systems and dynamic Web page assemblers, none were capable of presenting publications as well as Russell's legacy systems. Also, although the Web publishing systems were great for producing pages from the current state of the database, they were not capable of satisfying Russell's compliance requirements.

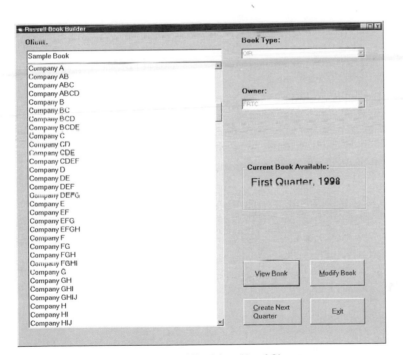

Figure 25-8   Russell BookBuilder (1 of 2)

25.5.2.3.7 *Book assembly*

The team wanted to make the user experience during book building as straightforward as possible by presenting only immediately relevant infor-

Figure 25-9   Russell BookBuilder (2 of 2)

mation. It built a simple windowing scheme, based on a customer database, that presented the bookbuilding experience on two screens (Figure 25-8 and Figure 25-9).

Along with the customer name and the component bill of materials list selections, the book building interface also gathers the metadata required for check-in to the document management system and stores it for later use. This may seem trivial, but it completely removes the user pain from the document management check-in process.

25.5.2.3.8 *Releasing books to the document management system*

Final preparation of a book for review and release is invoked by a single custom menu item, `Publish`, on the *File* menu. The `Publish` command creates a PostScript file of the book, which is then distilled into a PDF file (Figure 25-10). During this process, the PDF file is updated with the document management system check-in metadata that was gathered during the book building.

The `Publish` command eliminates a large number of print and configuration item choices for the user and controls the way PDF files are created. This plug-in also automatically generates bookmark hyperlinks for the PDF table of contents from the SGML structural element hierarchy.

Figure 25-10   Fund page example in PDF book.

25.5.2.4   Phase IV: XML and the future

In 1995 Synth-Bank began a pure research project for Russell into the notion of "Knowledge Management Systems". These are automated systems that would be the next logical extension for publishing, collaborative creation, and electronic delivery.

Because of the importance of the Internet in such systems, XML seemed better for the purpose than full SGML. The SGML to XML conversion took one developer three days.

25.6 | Conclusion

In the past, internetworking of systems was complex. Now, with the World Wide Web and TCP/IP, internetworking is routine and affordable. The next frontier is content interoperability.

And the key to content interoperability is open standards for data representation. Not the proprietary data formats used by most popular word processing and publishing tools, but true open standards like XML. The power and future of information technologies is determined by the degree of vendor and platform independence that they offer for the long term.

The system developed by Synth-Bank for Frank Russell Company is well-positioned for that future.

High-volume data reporting

Tool Discussion

- Characteristics of data reporting

- The data reporting stack

- Data reporting examples

Sponsor: Four J's Development Tools, http://www.4js.com

Contributing expert: Alex Geller

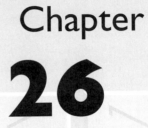

Chapter

26

Markup isn't just for long complex documents any more! Long simple ones, like inventory and sales reports, are no longer locked into restrictive dedicated programs in order to get the speed they need. XML can provide POP flexibility to MOM data reporting without compromising performance. The secret is stacked, speedy, stylesheets!

The traditional domain of markup-based publishing has been technical manuals and other long documents with complex structures. Data processing reports – inventory, sales, personnel – have rigid formats and couldn't afford the performance hit that flexibility entails: parsing markup, interpreting stylesheets, etc.

But while individual report forms are indeed simple and rigid, the set of reports as a whole is really a multitude of variations on just a few themes: a list is a list is a list, although the customer list is slightly different from the product list. Think of each report type and its variations as an XML document type with a variable structure and reports start to look more like POP documents.

As for the performance, there is no law that says all stylesheets have to be interpreted by the same general purpose processor. What if a "stylesheet" were a program, specialized for a report type and a specific task, and customizable by run-time parameters?

Let's keep these alternative ways of looking at the problem in mind as we consider the unique characteristics of data reporting.

26.1 | Characteristics of data reporting

Business data reporting has characteristics that distinguish it from general publishing.

26.1.1 Document patterns

The reports typically created by data processing applications exhibit strong similarities in data structure, document structure, or both. For example, a list of inventory items grouped by "classes of goods" is based on the same data structure as a list of customers grouped by "lines of business".

Similarly, an order confirmation form and an invoice form have similar document structures (e.g. address, item number, item description). As a result, a high percentage of reports can be handled by a small number of templates for these commonly used report forms.

26.1.2 Optimization for speed

Because of the volume of reports created, they must be optimized for speed. For example, a billing batch may create thousands of documents, spooled on a laser printer that prints 250 pages per minute.

26.1.3 Variety of target formats

Like other documents, rendered reports must be delivered on multiple printers and other devices. However, they must also be delivered as documents in proprietary formats (e.g., Excel worksheets), for access through other applications.

26.1.4 Special composition needs

Business reporting requires features not commonly needed for word processing or general publishing. These include decimal number alignment and page-dependent totals.

26.2 | The data reporting stack

In 2.11.3.1, "The protocol stack", on page 53 we introduced the common computer metaphor of the stack, wherein a process is modeled in layers to divide it into sub-processes with well-defined interfaces. The sub-processes pass data from one layer of the stack to another.

It is also possible to use a stack to represent states of the *data*, in which case it is the *processes* that occur between the layers.

It is possible to model the XML-based publishing of a database report as a data-oriented stack in which the information passes through several transformations. A possible layering is shown in Figure 26-1. Let's look at each layer, starting, as usual, from the bottom.

Figure 26-1   The data reporting stack

26.2.1 *Database layer*

This layer is an XML document that captures the data to be reported when it is initially extracted from a database. The document reflects the database structure; its element types are chiefly records and fields.

Example 26-1. XML document in database layer

```
<FGLDATA>
<SCHEMAPROLOG>
<RECORDDESCRIPTION name="record0">
 <FIELDDESCRIPTION name="customerid" alias="No." type="integer"/>
 <FIELDDESCRIPTION name="fname" alias="FirstName" type="char(15s)"/>
 <RECORDDESCRIPTION name="record0record0">
   <FIELDDESCRIPTION name="orderid" alias="No." type="integer"/>
 </RECORDDESCRIPTION>
 <REFDESCRIPTION name="ref0" refrelation="states"
                 refproc="maintenance/States">
   <REFFIELD name="state"/>
 </REFDESCRIPTION>
</RECORDDESCRIPTION>
</SCHEMAPROLOG>
<LIST>
  <RECORD type="record0">
    <FIELD type="customerid" value="100"/>
    <FIELD type="fname" value="Raymond Vector"/>
    <LIST>
      <RECORD type="record0record0">
        <FIELD type="orderid" value="1000"/>
      </RECORD>
      <RECORD type="record0record0">
        <FIELD type="orderid" value="1010"/>
      </RECORD>
    </LIST>
  </RECORD>
  <RECORD type="record0">
    <FIELD type="customerid" value="101"/>
    <FIELD type="fname" value="Margaret Lawson"/>
    <LIST>
      <RECORD type="record0record0">
        <FIELD type="orderid" value="1020"/>
      </RECORD>
    </LIST>
  </RECORD>
</LIST>
</FGLDATA>
```

Example 26-2. SQL query that extracted the data for Example 26-1

```
SELECT customer.customerid,
       customer.fname,
       order.orderid
from   customer,
       order
where  customer.customerid=order.customerid;
```

Example 26-1 shows an example. The SQL query that extracted the data is shown in Example 26-2.

The document begins with a SCHEMAPROLOG element that contains descriptions of the records and fields derived from the database schema. The LIST element contains the records returned in response to the query.

Processes, such as stylesheets, can transform documents in this layer to reports at the next. For example, documents derived from customer and inventory databases can be transformed into invoices.

26.2.2 *Report layer*

There is a small number of document types in the report layer that correspond to the templates for common data processing reports. In XML terms, these are abstract. Although they are organized like the final reports, they are not yet rendered and lack style information (fonts, margins, etc.).

This layer serves as a consolidation point, as multiple combinations of database documents are reduced to a small number of report types. It also serves as an interface to different formatting systems and devices, as well as to applications that want to use the reporting system; they do so by generating documents that conform to a report type.

Stylesheets that operate on documents in this layer may created modified versions within the same layer. For example, Example 26-1 might originally have lacked the alias attributes. A stylesheet could have supplied them by performing a table lookup.

Eventually, a stylesheet will format a database document into a rendition or directly into the device layer.

26.2.3 *Rendition layer*

This layer contains rendered documents, either in a markup language such as HTML or XHTML, or as full-blown page descriptions. They are processed by imaging software that creates device-specific data streams.

26.2.4 *Device layer*

This layer contains data streams for output devices. These can be physical devices, such as printers or displays, or virtual devices, such as input files for other applications.

26.3 | Data reporting examples

Let's look at some examples of high-volume data reporting based on the stack. We will illustrate them with the *XML Publication System* from Four J's Development Tools.

26.3.1 *System characteristics*

The system is a component of the *Four J's Business Development Suite* and has some special characteristics that are relevant to the examples.

26.3.1.1   Parameterized stylesheets

The system provides a basic set of stylesheets that are actually Java classes. They are specialized for particular document types and their actions are triggered from SAX events. The stylesheets are parameterized to provide runtime processing options. Additional stylesheets can be developed by deriving them from the basic classes, but other stylesheet processors can also be used.

26.3.1.2   Pipe support

To obtain a report, data is processed through a sequence of stylesheets, utilizing operating system pipes.

Pipes are a means of directing the output of one program to be the input of another. In principle, this is done on an incremental basis, rather than the first program running to completion and passing on all of its output at once. That is especially important when high volumes are involved, as is the case with most data reporting.

The publication system includes a small framework, written in Java, that offers additional piping features and addresses some problems with OS pipes.

26.3.1.3   Built-in document types

The product includes several DTDs and stylesheets for processing them.

database layer
> File Generic-List Data (FGLDATA) is the document type for data extracted from databases. It closely follows the database structure, as it consists of lists of records of various types, each made up of fields. Database schema information describing the record and field types is also captured.

report layer
> Several document types are available at this layer, representing the typical forms in which database data is organized for presentation. They include lists, labels, letters, invoices, etc. The number can be kept small because of the configurability provided by the stylesheets that generate and process them.

rendition layer
> Page XML (PXML) is an elementary page description language. Its descriptive capabilities range from specifying the coordinates of individual characters to adjusting paragraphs in arbitrary shapes.

26.3.1.4   `PxmlLayouter` stylesheet

`PxmlLayouter` is a special stylesheet that transforms PXML page markup into a DOM-like tree of drawable objects. The objects receive final processing by printer or viewer stylesheets, which transform them into device data streams.

26.3.2 *Examples*

These examples use database layer documents generated from two sources, a customer database and an inventory database. From them we will produce a customer contact list, a sales report, and form letters addressed to the customers.

Figure 26-2   Preview of customer contact list

26.3.2.1   Customer contact list

We begin by using an SQL query or other means to extract contact information from the customer database. The result is the FGLDATA document shown in Example 26-3.

Figure 26-2 shows the *Pxml Previewer* displaying the result of processing. Once a report is debugged, a printer would typically replace the *Pxml Previewer* as the output device.

Example 26-3. Customer database document

```
<!DOCTYPE FGLDATA PUBLIC "-//HST//DTD Specification::19990423//EN"
                          "file:fgldata.dtd">

<FGLDATA>
<SCHEMAPROLOG>
<RECORDDESCRIPTION name="label_record">
 <FIELDDESCRIPTION name="fname" alias="First Name" type="char(15)"/>
 <FIELDDESCRIPTION name="lname" alias="Last Name" type="char(15)"/>
 <FIELDDESCRIPTION name="company" alias="Company Name"
                                   type="char(20)"/>
 <FIELDDESCRIPTION name="address1" alias="Address" type="char(20)"/>
 <FIELDDESCRIPTION name="address2" alias="Address" type="char(20)"/>
 <FIELDDESCRIPTION name="city" alias="City" type="char(15)"/>
 <FIELDDESCRIPTION name="state" alias="State" type="char(2)"/>
 <FIELDDESCRIPTION name="zipcode" alias="Zipcode" type="char(5)"/>
 <FIELDDESCRIPTION name="accountNo" alias="Account number"
                                     type="char(20)"/>
</RECORDDESCRIPTION>
</SCHEMAPROLOG>
<LIST name="main list">
  <RECORD name="rec0" type="label_record">
    <FIELD name="fname" value="Raymond"/>
    <FIELD name="lname" value="Vector"/>
    <FIELD name="company" value="Los Altos Sports"/>
    <FIELD name="address1" value="1899 La Loma Drive"/>
    <FIELD name="address2" value="" isnull="1"/>
    <FIELD name="city" value="Los Altos"/>
    <FIELD name="state" value="CA"/>
    <FIELD name="zipcode" value="94022"/>
    <FIELD name="accountNo" value="4711123"/>
  </RECORD>
  ...
</LIST>
</FGLDATA>
```

The large pane on the right shows the document as it will eventually be printed. The two panes on the left are there for debugging. The top one shows the document tree while the pane below shows the stylesheets used in the pipe and their configuration options. The lower pane information comes from the file shown in Example 26-4, which has the instructions for the task.

The file has two parts, as indicated by the comment declarations. The first part has seven processing instructions that define the piped sequence of the eight stylesheets. The pipe begins with LoaderStyleSheet, which extracts the data and creates the FGLDATA document shown in Example

Example 26-4. Instructions for customer contact list

```
<!-- Establish pipe sequence of stylesheets -->
<?LoaderStyleSheet command="outputto" processorName="FglData2List"?>
<?FglData2List    command="outputto" processorName="List2Pxml"?>
<?List2Pxml       command="outputto"
                  processorName="MarginStyleSheet"?>
<?MarginStyleSheet command="outputto"
                  processorName="MapperStyleSheet"?>
<?MapperStyleSheet command="outputto"
                  processorName="PrettyPrinterStyleSheet"?>
<?PrettyPrinterStyleSheet command="outputto"
                          processorName="PxmlLayouter"?>
<?PxmlLayouter    command="outputto" processorName="Viewer"?>
<!-- Configure stylesheet parameters -->
<?FglData2List    command="configure"
  whichList="main_list" whichRecord="label_record"
  whatTitle="Customer Report"?>
<?List2Pxml       command="configure"
  fixed-column-width="true" table-style="plain" titleFontSize="16"
  colTitleFontSize="15" rowFontSize="10"?>
<?MarginStyleSheet command="configure"
  topMargin="1cm" bottomMargin="1cm"
  leftMargin="1cm" rightMargin="1cm"?>
<?MapperStyleSheet command="configure" pathPattern="*PAGENOBOX"
  attributeNamePattern="*" attributeValuePattern="*"
  mapName="pageNoFormat" mapValue="UpperRoman"?>
<?MapperStyleSheet command="configure" pathPattern="*PAGENOBOX"
  attributeNamePattern="*" attributeValuePattern="*"
  mapName="pageNoOffset" mapValue="100"?>
<?PrettyPrinterStyleSheet command="configure"
  writeTo=".\\debug.pxml" docTypeName="PXML"
  publicID="-//HST/DTD/ Specification::19990423//EN"
  systemID="file:pxml.dtd?>
<?PxmlLayouter      command="configure"
  pageWidth="2*a4length" pageHeight="a4width" topMargin="1cm"
  bottomMargin="1cm" rightMargin="1cm" leftMargin="1cm" minPages="0"
  maxPages="-1" maxPageTimeout="60000"?>
<?Viewer            command="configure"
  showTree="true" showStyleSheets="true"
  antialiasShapes="true" antialiasFonts="true"?>
```

26-3. It ends with Viewer, which generates the data stream for the *Pxml Previewer.*

The second part of the file is where the configuration of the stylesheets takes place. Each processing instruction specifies parameter values for one of the stylesheets. The principal ones are FglData2List and List2Pxml.

FglData2List, as its name suggests, transforms the FGLDATA document to the report document type LIST. In order to perform the transformation, it needs the parameters which_list and which_record, since fgldata.dtd allows more than one list per document and more than one record type per list. The parameter what_title is also required in order to supply required data for the LIST TITLE element.

The List2Pxml stylesheet renders the LIST document into PXML under the control of some parameters. The table-style parameter, for example, can accept the values "plain" or "fancy".

The next four stylesheets also affect the PXML document, while the last two generate the data stream for the *Pxml Previewer*.

Figure 26-3   Preview of sales report

26.3.2.2   Sales report

Figure 26-3 shows the preview of a sales report created by processing the inventory FGLDATA document in Example 26-5.

Example 26-5. Inventory database document

```
<!DOCTYPE FGLDATA PUBLIC "-//HST//DTD Specification::19990423//EN"
                         "file:fgldata.dtd">
<FGLDATA>
<SCHEMAPROLOG>
<RECORDDESCRIPTION name="stock_record">
  <FIELDDESCRIPTION name="stock_no" alias="Article No."
                                    type="char(10)"/>
  <FIELDDESCRIPTION name="description" alias="Description"
                                       type="varchar"/>
  <FIELDDESCRIPTION name="quantity" alias="Amount" type="smallint"/>
  <FIELDDESCRIPTION name="price" alias="Price" type="money(8,2)"/>
  <FIELDDESCRIPTION name="total" alias="Total" type="money(10,2)"/>
  <FIELDDESCRIPTION name="grand_total" alias="Grand Total"
                    type="money(10,2)" aggregate="true"/>
</RECORDDESCRIPTION>
</SCHEMAPROLOG>
<LIST name="main_list">
  <RECORD name="rec0" type="stock_record">
    <FIELD name="stock_no" value="1001 HRO"/>
    <FIELD name="description" value=
      "Brown leather. Specify first baseman's or infield/outfield
       style. Specify right- or left-handed. Your First Season's
       Baseball Glove"/>
    <FIELD name="quantity" value="1,5"/>
    <FIELD name="price" value="2500,00"/>
    <FIELD name="total" value="2500,00"/>
    <FIELD name="grand_total" value="2500,00"/>
  </RECORD>
  ...
</LIST>
</FGLDATA>
```

This report, like the customer contact list, is based on the LIST document type and was created using the instructions in Example 26-4, with one exception. The FglData2List parameters are different, as shown in Example 26-6.

Example 26-6. Instruction change for sales report

```
<?FglData2List command="configure"
  whichList="main_list" whichRecord="stock_record"
  whatTitle="Sales Report"?>
```

26.3.2.3 Customer form letters

Figure 26-4 depicts the viewer showing one of a set of form letters to be sent to customers.

The instructions for generating these form letters from the customer `label_record` document are contained in the instruction file, which is shown in Example 26-7.

Figure 26-4 Preview of customer form letters

Example 26-7. Instructions for customer form letters

```
<!-- Establish pipe sequence of stylesheets -->
<?LoaderStyleSheet command="outputto" processorName="Label2Letter"?>
<?Label2Letter    command="outputto" processorName="Letter2Pxml"?>
<?Letter2Pxml     command="outputto" processorName="PxmlLayouter"?>
<?PxmlLayouter    command="outputto" processorName="Viewer"?>
<!-- Configure stylesheet parameters -->
<?Letter2Pxml     command="configure" text="wetter.pxml"?>
<?PxmlLayouter    command="configure" pageWidth="a4width"
  pageHeight="a4length" topMargin="1cm" bottomMargin="1cm"
  rightMargin="1cm" leftMargin="1cm" minPages="0" maxPages="-1"
  maxPageTimeout="60000"?>
<?Viewer          command="configure"
  showTree="false" showStyleSheets="false"
  antialiasShapes="true" antialiasFonts="true"?>
```

The return address is fixed by the `Letter2Pxml` stylesheet. However, the body of the letter is imported using that stylesheet's `text` parameter, which identifies a file containing the already formatted body.

Note that the `Viewer` parameters suppress the two debugging panes.

Developing reusable content

Application Discussion

- The content developer's dilemma

- Content development strategy

- Editing XML abstractions

- Linking and navigation

Sponsor: Adobe Systems Incorporated,
http://www.adobe.com/products/framemaker

Contributing expert: Doug Yagaloff and Lani Hajagos

How do you develop content when you have no
idea how it will be used? When you create a rendered
document with a word processor, what you see is all
you've got, but at least you've got something you can
see! When you create an XML abstraction, you've got
a lot more, but only if you've done it right. This
chapter will show you how.

I n the wonderful way that often occurs with high-tech solutions,
XML has become a requirement in its own right for content developers. As a result, authors and publishing groups find themselves rushing to implement XML in their writing and delivery solutions,
often without clear objectives and requirements for XML use. This tendency can throw a content development plan into a tailspin, as developers
chase ever-changing and poorly defined requirements.

27.1 | The content developer's dilemma

Have you ever been involved in a construction project? The excited anticipation of the first step – clearing the ground for the foundation – can easily
blur the details of the steps that must follow. If you have mapped out all of
the steps before you begin, you will forge ahead with confidence. If not, you
may find your project faltering after that first step.

Many content developers have had similar experiences with their XML
projects. The anticipation of developing and deploying an XML-based

publishing solution is so great that only after completing the first few steps do they take time to fully understand the complexity of the project.

The first component of the solution – content creation – is easy to plan, since it is the primary function of the content developer. The second component – determining who will use the information and making it suitable for their intended uses – may be difficult or impossible to accomplish.

27.1.1   *What do solution developers want from XML?*

XML is deployed in a wide range of application solutions involving the control and delivery of data, from simple online help systems to complex integrated e-commerce systems. You've been getting some idea of the scale and diversity from this book, but XML is undoubtedly being put to use in still more ways even as you read this.

These applications may be conceived and defined independently of the developers of the content, usually without consideration of writing workflow constraints or packaging of content deliverables. This singular focus on deployment can create conflict between the needs of the XML-using solution developer and the requirements of the content creator.

27.1.2   *What do content creators need from XML?*

Content creators look to XML to improve the process of writing and managing content from the beginning of a writing project to the delivery. They rely on specific XML facilities:

- *Schemas and DTDs*, which define rules for organizing and validating information content.
- *Attributes*, which provide a means of annotating the information content with descriptive metadata.
- *Abstraction preservation*, which allows the information content to be kept separate from rendition style so that the information can be reused in multiple ways.

The attention of the content creator is on creation and management, not necessarily deployment – which can create a conflict with the solution developer's requirements.

27.1.3 *Creation and deployment requirements may not conform*

In addition to the differing goals and needs of the content creator and the solution developer, there are other reasons why the requirements for creation and deployment may conflict:

- The content creator and solution developer may have little or no interaction.
- The requirements for the content creator may not be known, or may not even exist, when the solution is being developed.
- The requirements for the solution may not be known, or even exist, when the content is being created.
- The requirements for each may be affected by differing business objectives and constraints.

These factors can hinder the content creator from implementing a development strategy that delivers reusable XML abstractions. He will be hard put to deliver anything but well-defined renditions, like printed pages, HTML pages, or online help files.

To overcome these hindrances, the content creator needs a strategy for reusable content development, the ability to create abstract XML documents, and facilities for creating portable and reusable hyperlinks and other navigation aids. We'll discuss these points in the next few sections.

27.2 | Content development strategy

For the content creator, the basic development strategy of design, create, validate, and deploy has worked well for delivering renditions (Figure 27-1). The process is easy to manage and the deployment expectations are well-defined. If the rendition requirements change, the process can easily be modified. The representation of the information can be optimized for the particular rendition because it will not be reused for other purposes.

Figure 27-1   The basic content development strategy

Today's deployment requirements affect each of these stages, making the process more dynamic and complex. The process must utilize tools and methods that allow the development of content that can be reused and processed by tools and applications unknown to the content creators.

27.2.1   *Beyond the basic*

As the deployment requirements of solution developers are ever-changing, there must be a step added to the current content development process (Figure 27-2).

Figure 27-2   The basic content development strategy extended

The more detailed a document's structure and the richer its set of attributes, the more likely that applications will have the data they need. However, as each data point adds development cost, and as it is impossible to predict all future deployment requirements, it is important to design for future extensibility.

Consider the following suggestions:

- Design DTDs and schemas that can be expanded. Identify and document aspects of the design that you know cannot possibly be complete until deployment requirements are defined. Return to these areas periodically to determine when and if they can be completed.

- Expect that information created and maintained today may never be "rich" enough for some future deployment requirements. Regularly survey users to help anticipate requirements.

- Research current and developing XML facilities like namespaces, topic maps, extended linking, and XSL stylesheets. Consider whether and how those facilities might improve your content development strategy. There are tutorials on all of them, and others, in this book.

There are also specific techniques to employ in schemas and DTDs that will enhance reusability by improving both the quality of the content and the extensibility of the schema:

- Provide attributes that are solely for management and classification: keywords, references, purpose, source, etc.
- Design element types that can be extended with newly-developed subelements.
- Provide "annotation" element types for describing the context and content of other elements. The descriptions could occur in the attributes or content of the annotation elements.
- Model schemas with a database to identify relationships, expose limitations, and test reusability.
- Be clear and precise regarding the naming and usage of element types and attributes.
- Create a well-defined syntax for complex attribute values and a parser for extracting their data. Better yet, express complex properties as multiple attributes (perhaps in "annotation" subelements) and let XML do the parsing.

27.3 | Editing XML abstractions

Writing and editing an abstract XML document is different from creating a rendered document in a word processor. You are capturing a lot more information that will maximize the potential uses of the document, but you can't normally see this information in a rendition and so you lack the conventional visual confirmation that it is being created accurately.

Fortunately, XML editing tools offer capabilities to overcome these difficulties, and to take advantage of the strengths of abstract documents. We'll discuss a few of the key points and illustrate them with Adobe *FrameMaker+SGML*, an integrated XML editing and composition product.

The tool is designed to shield the user from the technicalities of XML and to support a workgroup environment. It includes a robust composition capability that can handle complex page layouts with a high degree of automation, even such professional graphic arts requirements as spot and process color separations.

27.3.1   *Guided editing*

Guided editing features help authors create documents that conform to the rules for a document type. In Figure 27-3, the element-type catalog shows which element types are valid for the current location in the document. The interactive structure view lets the author manipulate the structure of the document. It graphically advises whether a proposed move will invalidate the structure. These devices make it possible to create and manipulate the structure of the document without ever working directly with, or even looking at, a markup tag.

27.3.2   *Editing non-valid documents*

When creating type-valid XML documents, an editing tool might require that the document be valid at all times, even if that means putting in empty elements when information is not yet available. Maintaining validity in this way means that the author has to start at the beginning of the document, and write everything in order, not skipping any required elements.

However, this isn't what happens in the real world. All too often, the information a writer needs simply isn't available. So the writer may skip some parts of the document and write others out of order. As more and more of the information becomes available, the gaps are filled in and eventually the document is complete. This is easy to do in a word processor, but difficult if your editing tool insists that validity must be maintained.

Figure 27-3   Structure view and element-type catalog.

Some editors address this requirement by allowing information to be entered in any order and allowing required information to be skipped. The document can be saved as a work in progress even if it is not valid. The software keeps track of what is missing and what is in the wrong place, and helps the writer fix things. So the end result is a valid, complete document, without the hassle of having to fight with an inflexible editing tool.

With *FrameMaker+SGML*, when working in the guided editing mode, the element-type catalog shows only those element types valid at the current location in the document. However, as shown in Figure 27-4, the element-type catalog can also be set to display all element types, or any element type that may be valid within a parent element, even further down in the hierarchy. The valid element types are indicated by a checkmark.

This facility is also helpful when editing merely well-formed XML documents.

monde change et nous changeons avec lui.

rld is changing, and we are changing with it.)

ı this repor̩t, the Office of Technology Assessment (OTA) evaluates the
erformance and cost of a range of advanced vehicle technologies that ar
) be available during the next 10 to 20 years. Consistent with the CCI's ¿
nproving fuel economy while maintaining performance, a central empł
)TA's analysis is the potential to improve fuel economy.

ocus

Vith the exception of nitrogen oxide (NOx) catalysts for lean and more
engines, technologies whose primary function is to reduce tailpipe
ocus of this study.

Time Factor

is less with the process by which advanced technologies may enter the
the questions of how soon and to what extent these technologies could
goals. It is the hope of the CCI that attractive, affordable, fun-to-drive
be developed during the next five years that will attract a loyal following and
on industry. See "Detailed Outcomes" on page 7.

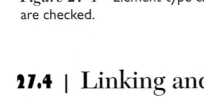

Figure 27-4   Element-type catalog displaying all element types; valid ones
are checked.

27.4 | Linking and navigation

In an XML document, the links and indexes can be developed as abstractions, which enhances their reusability. They can even be developed on the
principles of topic maps, which can make them extensible and portable as
well.

27.4.1 *Abstract links*

A link is a representation of a relationship. Let's look at two of the most
common kinds and see how an XML editor can support them as abstractions. We'll again use *FrameMaker+SGML* to illustrate.

27.4.1.1 Cross-references

The cross-reference tool makes it easy to link pieces of information, either within a document or across documents, using standard XML methodology. The user inserts a cross-reference element, and selects a target element type from a list. The tool (Figure 27-5) shows all the instances of that element type in the document.

Figure 27-5 Cross-reference interface.

The user selects the appropriate element and the format of the generated text (e.g., "See Section 5 on page 23"), and the generated string is placed in the displayed rendition of the document. For the XML markup, a unique ID value is automatically generated and placed in the ID attribute of the target element, as well as in the IDREF attribute of the referencing element.

Users can control the generated text by editing the cross-reference format in the stylesheet. As table, paragraph, and page numbers are similarly generated only for rendition, they are automatically updated in the display as content is inserted into or removed from the document.

27.4.1.2   Indexing

An index is a form of topic map that links subjects to page numbers. Think of it as a bunch of cross-references, taken out of context and sorted alphabetically. As with cross-references, the page numbers are generated automatically when the document is rendered.

FrameMaker+SGML can handle complex, multi-level indexes like the following example:

Example 27-1. Multi-level index entry

Continental drift
  Fossil evidence, 57
  Rock structures, 62, 80

Users enter index entries in proximity to occurrences of the subject in the document. Doing so also implicitly associates the entries with the numbers of the pages on which the subjects will occur when the document is rendered. These entries are used to compile the indexes automatically, either for a single document or a group of documents.

27.4.2   *Extensible and portable links*

Because all possible deployments of a document cannot be predicted, content developers are not always able to determine all of the links they need at the time they are developing the content. There are several reasons for this:

- The scope of references (i.e., the set of potential anchors) cannot be determined until the document is rendered and deployed.
- The actual addresses of anchors are subject to change, even after deployment, as websites move or cease to be.

Nevertheless, the relationships that the links will represent can be defined during content development. It is just the related objects that are unknown. Topic maps, which are described in Chapter 43, "Topic maps: Knowledge navigation aids", on page 628, are a generalized application of this principle.

The links, like the cross-references and index entries we have already seen, are forms of metadata. They are represented by element types and attributes that are defined for a given document type. For each link, a set of queries is developed that will address all available objects that are anchors of the link.

When a document is deployed, the queries are executed and the addresses of the result set objects are obtained. These are inserted in the deployed document in the form of XPointers.

27.4.3 *Extensible tools*

In order for your content development strategy and your content to be extensible, your tools should be extensible as well. For example, you might want to provide support for creating the extensible and portable links just described.

XML editing and composition products may offer scripting or programming languages for this purpose. A proprietary language usually offers the advantage of product-specific functions, while a standard language can be utilized more easily by a large body of developers who are already familiar with it.

For example, further customizing or extending the functions of *FrameMaker+SGML* can be accomplished by developing a "plug-in" using a C-based application programming interface (API). The API is accessed through a developers kit that provides an application development environment incorporating a library of function calls and makefiles. It was used to create the *Knowledge Chain™ Builder* plug-in shown in Figure 27-6.

The plug-in uses document properties such as content data strings to help users construct links. At deployment time, it parses the XML docu-

Figure 27-6   *Knowledge Chain Builder* plug-in

ment and builds the queries for locating potential link anchors. It also validates the anchors and constructs the XPointers that address them.

Analysis   Here's an interesting contradiction. One of the most important aspects of XML is that it can preserve data in the abstract; that is, it won't accidentally intermingle your data with rendition information. On the other hand, the style of a rendition is important, because that is what makes communication of the data effective.

This chapter illustrated an approach to XML editing that seeks to resolve that contradiction. The product is structure-driven, but provides a WYSIWYG rendered view and sophisticated graphic arts functionality. Other XML editors make different tradeoffs. Understanding them all will help you determine your own requirements more accurately.

Databases

- The XML data model
- XPath and databases
- Native XML databases
- XML in relational database management systems

Part Eight

Documents are humanity's database!

The very word "document" means "to make a record of", with no restrictions on the size or complexity of the record, whether stored on a cave wall or in a bound book. But computers, as you may have observed, aren't human. They like their records to be predictable and manageable for efficient processing, something that wasn't true of documents until markup languages came along.

So computer scientists developed their own *data models* for predictable and manageable records. In fact they developed several – *relational* and *object-oriented* being two – and they've been fighting ever since over which is best. Which hasn't stopped them from building powerful database management systems (DBMS) on which virtually every enterprise depends!

In this part we explore the impact of the XML data model on the DBMS world. We look at native XML databases, including a system based on XPath, and at the way that traditional DBMSs have adapted to XML.

XML and databases

Tool Discussion

- What is a database?

- Database management system (DBMS)

- XML DBMS requirements

- Designing an XML database

- Native XML DBMS (XDBMS)

Sponsor: Software AG, http://www.softwareagusa.com
Contributing expert: Michael Kay

28

Look inside XML portals and content management systems and you'll find XML databases. They may be native XML, an XML layer built on a relational platform – or something else. They vary in their query languages, indexing structures, and many other ways. In short, there's a large database of information you need to learn about them. This chapter will get you started.

f you've been with us all the way, you've gotten a good idea of the sheer breadth of XML's MOM-to-POP usage spectrum.[1] As you go from one end of the spectrum to the other, one of the characteristics that changes is the need for permanent storage of XML documents.

28.1 | Who stores XML documents?

At the people-oriented publishing (POP) end, permanent storage is an unquestioned requirement. The management of long-lived reusable content is at the heart of these applications. As we have seen, XML content management systems are available to satisfy those requirements.

But in the machine-oriented messaging (MOM) world, XML is chiefly used as a transient medium, for sending messages from one application to

---

1. In fact, you might want to read about it again in the light of your newly-acquired knowledge. You can do so in Chapter 3, "The XML usage spectrum", on page 60.

another. The message documents might be exchanged in an infrastructure for enterprise application integration, or represent e-commerce transactions between customers and suppliers.

However, as MOM users have gained experience with XML, they have also begun to see it as a vehicle for long-term data storage. There are three main reasons:

- The XML notation is not locked into any particular vendor, platform, or software product.
- XML documents provide a more flexible representation than relational tables for complex business process data and its related publication-like data (invoices, spreadsheets, etc.).
- An application might require the data to be in XML anyway. If it is received as XML or needs to be delivered in XML, it makes sense to store it as XML as well.

In fact, wherever XML is used for transient messages, there is often a need for those messages to be archived to provide a traceable record of the transactions that took place. There is then a very strong argument for storing the XML message in exactly the form it was transmitted.

28.2 | What is a database?

The term "database" has become somewhat degraded in popular usage, to mean almost any collection of data. We'll try to be more precise: a *database (DB)* is a collection of information managed as an asset for the benefit of a community of users.

You may have heard of – or participated in – the debates among fervent adherents to a particular database *data model*: relational, object-oriented, object-relational, etc., and lately, XML. But the definition applies to all of them; let's examine its two key ideas:

managed

This means there are policies in place defining what information is to be held, and for how long; defining who has access to it, and how its quality and integrity is to be maintained. And there are operational procedures in place to ensure that these policies are implemented.

community of users

Information is retained to meet the requirements of recognized user roles. Different users will have different requirements and the exact information needs will not always be known in advance. This leads to a requirement for ad-hoc query and reporting facilities, multiple views, and of course online concurrent access.

28.2.1 *Database management systems (DBMS)*

Databases don't exist in a vacuum. In order for them to be managed for a community of users, they must exist in a *database management system (DBMS)*.[2] A DBMS provides services such as caching, space management, locking, backup and restore, transactions, and logging.

All databases, regardless of their data model persuasion, benefit from these services, so it is sensible for XML DBMSs, which are relatively new, to take advantage of existing code in these areas. Software AG's *Tamino*, for example, which is a native XML DBMS, utilizes many of the same internal components as the company's longer-established *ADABAS* DBMS, which is "post relational".

Other companies have simply built an XML DBMS as a layer on top of an existing relational or object-oriented platform. Doing so gives the vendor a head start in bringing the product to market. It also benefits users by providing management services that are more likely to be robust, mature, and stable.

---

2. There is a confusing tendency to use the word "database" for both those things, although usually the context makes the meaning clear. But in this chapter, at least, we'll try to be scrupulous about minding our DBs and DBMSs.

28.2.2 *Alternatives to a DBMS*

Documents have been around far longer than databases, so there are clearly other ways to store and retrieve them.

28.2.2.1   Integral storage systems

A content management system or XML DBMS typically maintains XML documents in *dispersed storage*; that is, the documents are parsed and their data content, attribute values, and other components are stored in separate records and fields.

An alternative is *integral storage*, which normally keeps the unparsed document intact and stores it as a BLOB in a database or as a file in the operating system file store.[3]

Integral files are typically supplemented with an index database that allows searches based on metadata, such as descriptors, creation and modification dates, authorship, access rights, etc. But if the file store is unmanaged, users can access the files directly and change them. As a result, it can be difficult to maintain the integrity of the index and its consistency with the document files.

There are several products that overcome this problem. They support integral storage by providing managed access and specialized query facilities, either in OS file store or in dedicated repositories.

28.2.2.2   Full-text search systems

Another approach to XML document storage and retrieval is the full-text search system. These products focus on searching for documents based on their textual content. If you've used a Web search engine, you have some idea of how they work.

These products may offer management services. Some are even XML-aware and can take advantage of structural knowledge gained from the DTD or schema. It is in the nature of the queries they support that they differ from a mainstream DBMS.

---

3. A *BLOB* is a "binary large object". XML, of course, is character-based and not binary, but BLOBs were invented for graphics and only later became a catch-all for anything that isn't relational. Now there are CLOBs as well.

With a relational database, you ask questions such as "How many tons of tomatoes were exported by Uruguay in 1987?". With a typical *full-text search*, however, you would ask "Find me documents that talk about exports of tomatoes from Uruguay, listed in order of likely relevance".

Chances are that some of the documents you find will talk about exports *to* Uruguay, and one of them might mention that tomatoes were thrown at the leader of the Uruguay trade delegation when he threatened to boycott the export of cotton socks (Figure 28-1).

Figure 28-1   Is this what you were searching for?

For information that is weakly structured and already rendered, which is the usual case with HTML Web pages, that may be all that is possible. But a key benefit of XML is its ability to represent as much structure and abstract semantics as the document creator wishes.

If your data is an archive of XML e-commerce transaction messages, you can do better than finding all the messages that mention cucumbers and Peru. You can ask what the total shipments of cucumbers to Peru were, in each of the last five years, broken down by country of origin. Full-text search is not designed to support that kind of query.

28.3 | XML DBMS requirements

A DBMS must offer more than the generic services we've discussed if it is to support XML. An XML DBMS has requirements that a typical relational DBMS does not. These stem primarily from differences in:

- data models,
- applications,
- update policies, and
- schema management.

28.3.1 *Data models*

In the relational model, data is organized into tables with rows and columns. A row is a data record, made up of data element cells, one per column of the table. All the cells in a given column have identical properties (datatype, semantics, etc.). The definition of those properties is the metadata of the table, its *schema*.

In XML, as we have seen, data can be organized in more complex and less rigid ways. An XML document's schema is its document type, expressed as a DTD or in another schema language. Unlike the relational model, however, there can be more metadata than just the schema; individual elements can have metadata, represented by attributes. There is also relationship metadata, represented by the hierarchical structure.

These differences result in unique requirements for several aspects of an XML DBMS.

28.3.1.1   Query language

The query language used to retrieve information needs to be closely aligned with the data model. So too must the indexing structures used to support efficient queries, and the query optimization strategies used to take advantage of these indexing structures.

The W3C is developing such a language, which is discussed in 61.5.2, "XML Query Language (XQuery)", on page 967. It is based on XPath, and products such as *Tamino* have developed indexing structures and optimization algorithms to handle it.

28.3.1.2   Validation and integrity

The specification of validation processes and integrity constraints must be aligned with XSDL schema definitions and DTDs.

28.3.1.3   External relationships

XML has a well-defined data model for what happens inside a document, but there is no similar standard specifying how the documents within an XML database are related to each other. Most XML DBMSs will have some kind of concept of a document type, related to DTDs or schema definitions, and some kind of concept of a document collection or folder. However, the way in which document types and document folders are related to each other, and to URIs or unique document names, can vary from one product to another.

Many sorts of models are possible, for example:

- hyperlinking models in which documents refer to each other by URI;
- hierarchic structures, like file stores, in which documents are organized into named folders within folders; or
- structures like the WebDAV model, in which documents are not only arranged in a hierarchy, but also have external properties (metadata); the latter can be used to retrieve them, as an adjunct to content-based retrieval.

28.3.2 *Applications*

In Chapter 67, "Repositories and vocabularies", on page 1070, we listed over 350 XML vocabularies in 77 categories. By the time you read this there will be even more. Software AG, based on its experience with *Tamino* users, has attempted to classify this overwhelming diversity of XML applications as follows:

document management applications
> Storage and retrieval of business documents, such as records of safety inspections, job applications, or insurance quotations.

archival applications
> Long term storage of operational information. XML is preferred because the operational data is in the form of XML messages, and the audit value is maximized if it is kept unchanged. Also, an accepted vendor-independent standard representation like XML is safest for data whose lifetime is likely to exceed that of any particular DBMS product.

complex data applications
> Databases of information whose structure is too complex to store conveniently as rows and columns in a relational database. Examples are geographical information, biochemical information, engineering project plans, and medical records.

publishing applications
> information intended primarily for human consumption, but organized to keep the information content separate from considerations of how it is displayed. Content management for the Web is of course part of this story, but many of the most interesting DBMSs are those concerned primarily with print publishing, and especially with information designed to be reused in different media.

28.3.3 *Update policies*

XML users require support for multiple update policies. Some examples:

- Data once in the system can never be updated or deleted; it can only be superseded by later versions.
- Users check out a document, work on it for a while, then return the revised document to the database.
- Users can append data to individual documents, such as a patient's medical history, but the previous content of the document must be immutable.

28.3.4 *Schema management*

Document schemas normally evolve with time. For example, a new employee appraisal form might be introduced that asks a different set of questions, perhaps mandated by changes in employment laws.

But whereas a typical relational DB might be restructured to conform to the new schema, it is often a requirement that existing documents should be unaffected by a schema change. They should be held in their original form, using the schema that was current at the time they were created.

Queries that span different generations of the document type can be difficult to formulate, and even more difficult to execute efficiently.

28.4 | XML DBMSs and the Internet

One way in which an XML DBMS differs from previous generations of DBMS technology is that it is typically designed for the Internet.[4]

This is more than a marketing claim. Many details of the product architecture are affected, including:

- the communications protocols by which applications talk to the DBMS server;
- the use of URIs as globally unique identifiers;
- the way that users are authenticated and authorized;

---

4. XML DBMS adherents say that hierarchic and network DBMSs were designed for the mainframe, relational DBMSs were designed for client-server, object DBMSs for distributed computing, and XML DBMSs for the Internet. Of course, they are careful to whom they say it!

- the way that user sessions are managed and time-outs are handled;
- the design of user interfaces that reduce expensive and time-consuming interactions between client and server; and
- the support of open standards at every level of the system, because universal interworking is the goal of the Internet.

In fact, the requirements of running an Internet-based round-the-clock electronic commerce service have more in common with mainframe applications, such as airline reservation systems, than with the typical departmental applications of the client-server era. XML DBMS products are even offered for IBM mainframe operating systems; *Tamino* is an example.

28.5 | Designing an XML database

XML database design follows the traditional three-stage design process: conceptual modeling, logical design, and physical design.

28.5.1 *Conceptual modeling*

Conceptual modeling consists of analyzing the objects, properties and relationships that exist in the domain of interest.

Techniques such as the *Unified Modeling Language (UML)* are used. Just as with non-XML databases, you can start either by studying the way things are now – for example, the paper documents that are in use – or by creating a model of the way you want things to be in the future.

Perhaps because of the difference in applications, the models used for XML DBs are more closely related to business processes. Many of the objects that appear in the object model relate to dynamic entities, such as purchases or promotions or orders, rather than the traditional permanent entities, such as products and customers and employees.

28.5.2 *Logical design*

Logical design is the task of translating the conceptual model into the terms of the data model.

For XML, that means a DTD or schema, and designing one is still a craft. There aren't any standard recipes, like the use of normalization in the relational database world.

Newcomers are sometimes bewildered by the amount of choice available. Should I use elements or attributes? Should I represent relationships by nesting, or by ID/IDREF links, or by URI hyperlinks? The right answer usually comes naturally with experience.

The golden rule is to take advantage of the flexibility that XML gives you: don't try to structure the data in rows and columns because that's the only way you've been able to do it in the past. One good approach is to imagine the information on paper as a form or report, and then work back from the structure of the paper document to the abstract structure of the XML document.

Which raises a key question for logical design: what *is* a document?

The answer may be obvious for POP applications, or when dealing with data for which there is an associated form of manageable size (invoices, incident reports, etc.). But if your information is a rail timetable, the "right" level for a document is somewhere between the national timetable and the timetable for a single train.

The choice of what to represent as a single document is important. It will have a significant bearing on the usability of the database, as well as its performance characteristics.

28.5.3 *Physical design*

Physical design consists of deciding what data will be held where, how it will be organized, and what indexes are needed.

For an XML database, as with any other database, the task demands intimate knowledge of the implementation details of a specific product. Key factors are:

- the allocation and partitioning of space to hold different classes of document,
- the choice of storage and indexing options, and

- the design of a database loading strategy.

Database loading involves setting up the indexes and access structures to support efficient queries. For a database of several gigabytes, it can require a lot of time and storage space.

The indexing structures provided by an XML DBMS are highly specialized.[5] *Tamino*, for example, offers essentially three kinds:

structure index

It records the elements that are present in the document, and their nesting, but not the data content. When a query references a particular element type, a structure index quickly eliminates from the search all documents that don't use this element type, or that don't use it in the right context.

value index

It indexes the values – that is, the data – of selected elements or attribute values in much the same way as a conventional index in a relational database. This is useful for queries that require a specific value to be present; for example, finding all the transactions processed on a particular date.

word-level index

It indexes individual words or phrases in the document data content, in the manner of a full-text search product. This is useful for queries that look for documents that mention particular words. This sort of indexing is typically the most expensive.

As always, the more indexes you choose to build, the faster your queries will run, but the longer it will take to load new documents or update existing documents, and the more space will be taken up on disk. Space on disk, of course, is cheap: but the bigger the database, the less of it will fit in cache, and the longer it will take to do operations such as backup.

---

5. New structures are still being invented. Their techniques are often closely-guarded secrets – either because they are very clever, or because the vendor would like you to think they are.

28.6 | Native XML DBMS (XDBMS)

Some XML DBMS products (*Tamino*, for example) are promoted as *native XML databases*. The term is used to distinguish a DBMS that uses XML as its data model, meaning that its primary storage structures and indexing techniques are designed specifically to support XML.

In contrast, a relational DBMS (RDBMS) might store an XML document as a BLOB, while a *universal DBMS* would provide XML storage, indexing and query as one of several plug-in modules for various data representations.

Native XML DBMS vendors argue that, because it is designed to do one job well, a native XML DBMS (XDBMS) is inherently superior to a DBMS that was designed for a different job and subsequently adapted to support XML.

Other DBMS vendors argue back![6]

28.7 | Conclusion

XML DBMSs are still in their infancy, and the understanding of their requirements is still evolving. But XML is, after all, SGML, and SGML DBMSs have been in use for many years. They provide experience on the performance trade-offs between fast document loading, fast retrieval, and economical use of space.

Object-oriented DBMSs are another source of knowledge in relevant areas, such as management of long transactions, version control, and efficient storage of fine-grained complex data structures. All this knowledge is finding its way into new generations of XML DBMS products.

---

6. As we'll see in subsequent chapters.

XPath-based XML DBMS

Tool Discussion

▌ XPath primer

▌ Dispersed storage vs. integral storage

▌ Component-level access vs. document-level

▌ Variable information views

▌ Access and other controls

Sponsor: NeoCore, http://www.neocore.com

Contributing expert: Chris Brandin

> Most information is complex; it rarely comes in neat arrays. We try to make it look regular because it's so easy to address a cell in a relational table – a row number and a column number and you're there. Easy addressing makes for efficient processing, which is why we spend so much time and money fitting round information pegs into those square holes. But there is another path to finding information in databases, one that can free data from its cells!

n some sense there is a fundamental conflict between XML and databases. XML derives a lot of its power from its *flexibility*: elements are easily added and deleted, even for valid documents. Schemas and other metadata are easily changed.

Databases, though, derive their power from their *predictability*: their rigid predefined structures and indexes make it easy to address data and optimize performance.

For a native XML DBMS (XDBMS), XPath offers the possibility of getting the best of both worlds: flexible data and metadata, plus efficient addressing. However, you need to make the right decisions regarding document storage and access.

29.1 | Document storage and access

The storage and access issues for XML are not as simplistic as a choice between "document-centric" and "data-centric". In fact, as we'll see shortly, those terms are ambiguous. There can be a big difference between how a document is stored and how it is accessed. Let's look at what is really going on.

29.1.1 *Storage approaches*

Unlike relational data, which exists as such only within a relational DBMS (RDBMS), XML data exists independently in the form of documents. Content management systems and DBMSs use a variety of techniques for storing XML documents, but they boil down to combinations and variations of just two approaches: dispersed and integral.

Dispersed storage

Dispersed storage typically involves parsing the document and storing the parsed data content, attribute values, and other components in multiple fields of a database. Both relational and object DBMSs have been used successfully for this purpose, as well as hybrid object-relational. Indexes and maps are used to maintain the relationship between the element structure of the document and the underlying database schema. A variation of this approach stores the components as unparsed text.

Integral storage

Integral storage effectively keeps the unparsed document intact and stores it in a single field of a database or as a file in a file system. The document is parsed, however, in order to build indexes that facilitate searching the document base and locating individual components within their documents.

Proponents of integral storage claim that dispersed storage does not scale well. They say that adding documents makes the database structure grow in complexity – not just in size – which slows performance.

29.1.2 *Access and retrieval*

In any document management system, documents can be addressed, and therefore retrieved, by properties of the document as a whole. Such properties typically include a unique document identifier (e.g. a catalog number or ISBN) or a location (e.g. a file identifier or URL).

In a component-based CMS, as we have seen, addressing and access are possible at the level of individual elements or other components.

However, even when documents are stored and accessed as whole objects, addressing the document need not be based solely on properties of the whole document. Most systems allow searches on the text of a document, for example. Plain text and word processing documents can be searched in this way (although spurious hits can occur if the system doesn't understand – and ignore – the word processing markup).

When a document is represented in XML, an XML-aware system can support addressing of properties of the whole document or any part of it. The XPath specification provides a standardized notation for expressing those properties. It is very powerful, as we shall see, as it is the basis for *XSL Transformations*, extended linking, and other sophisticated accessing of XML documents.

29.1.3 *Words to watch out for: document-centric and data-centric*

XML products and applications are sometimes characterized as *component-centric* or *data-centric*, in contrast to *document-centric*. Several possible meanings could be intended:

- distributed storage in contrast to integral storage,
- component-level access as opposed to whole-document access, or
- both of the above.[1]

We avoid these terms in this book because it is so important to distinguish clearly between storage and granularity of access. A system that uses integral storage can still offer component-level access, just as a distributed storage system can provide access to complete documents.

---

1. Data-centric vs. document-centric is also used in a totally different context: data that fits the relational model easily vs. everything else. This usage is particularly confusing because all XML documents contain data; see 6.10.2, "Data-centric vs. document-centric", on page 115.

In fact, there is a novel form of integral storage DBMS that provides full access to components with no need to create a physical schema. It is based on XPath, so before we look at it, let's have a quick introduction to XPath.

29.2 | XML Path Language (XPath)

XPath is a notation for addressing information within a document. That information could be:

- An "executive summary" of a longer document.
- A glossary of terms whose definitions are scattered throughout a manual.
- The specific sequence of steps, buried in a large reference work, needed to solve a particular problem.
- The customized subset of information that a particular customer subscribes to.
- All the sections and subsections of a book that were written by a particular author or revised since a specific date.
- For documents holding information from relational databases, all the typical queries made of relational databases: a particular patient's medical records, the address of the customer with the most orders, the inventory items with low stock levels, and so on.
- For documents that are containers for document collections, all the typical queries made in a library catalog or on a website: articles about Abyssinian cats, essays on the proper study of mankind, etc.

A programmer working with an XML-aware programming or scripting language could write code to search the document for the information that meets the specified criteria. The purpose of XPath is to automate this searching so that a non-programming user can address the information just by writing an expression that contains the criteria.

29.2.1 *Location paths*

In order to retrieve something, you need to know where to find it – in other words, its *address*.

An address doesn't have to be an absolute location; you can address things relatively ("two doors down from 29 Jones St."). It doesn't have to be an explicit location at all: you can address things by name ("Lance") or description ("world's greatest athlete").

You can address several things at once ("Monty and Westy"), even if you don't know exactly what they are or whether they even exist ("inexpensive French restaurant downtown").

All those forms of address can be used to locate things in XML documents, by means of an *XPath expression*.

The most important form of XPath expression is called a *location path*. If you use UNIX or Windows, you may already be familiar with location paths because they are used to address files by specifying the path from the file system's root to a specific subdirectory. For example, the path /home/bob/xml/samples identifies a particular one of the four samples subdirectories shown in Figure 29-1.

Figure 29-1 File system directory structure

29.2.2 *Addressing multiple objects*

A location path is capable of addressing multiple objects. For example, the expression in Example 29-1 addresses all `caption` elements within `figure` elements that are within `chapter` elements within `book` elements.

Example 29-1. Location path

```
/book/chapter/figure/caption
```

In the book whose structure is shown in Figure 29-2, the expression in Example 29-1 would address the first two `caption` elements, because they are children of `figure` elements. It would not address the third, which is the child of an `example` element.

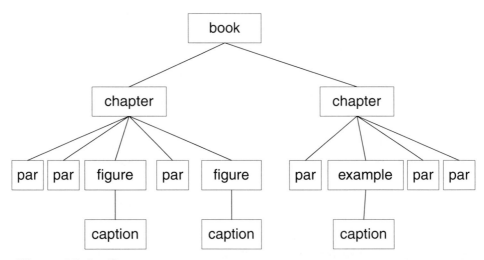

Figure 29-2   Document structure

Example 29-2 shows the XML representation of the book.

Example 29-2. A short book in XML

```
<?xml version="1.0"?>
<book>
  <chapter>
    <par author="bd">First paragraph. <emph>Really.</emph></par>
    <par author="cg">Second paragraph.</par>
    <figure picfile="one.jpg">
      <caption>The first figure's caption</caption>
    </figure>
    <par>Third paragraph.</par>
    <figure picfile="two.jpg">
      <caption>The second figure's caption.</caption>
    </figure>
  </chapter>
  <chapter>
    <par author="pp">Chapter 2, first paragraph.</par>
    <example>
      <caption>The first example.</caption>
    </example>
    <par>Chapter 2, second paragraph.</par>
    <par author="bd">Chapter 2, third paragraph.</par>
  </chapter>
</book>
```

29.2.3 *Children and descendants*

The /book/chapter/figure/caption expression addresses two elements with no children other than data. The expression /book/chapter/figure, however, addresses the figure elements with their caption children, as shown in Example 29-3.

Example 29-3. Figure elements with their caption children

```
<figure picfile="one.jpg">
  <caption>The first figure's caption</caption>
</figure>
<figure picfile="two.jpg">
  <caption>The second figure's caption.</caption>
</figure>
```

The location path /book addresses the entire document.

In a location path, the slash character (/) means "child of." A double slash (//) means "descendant of," which is more flexible as it includes children, grandchildren, great-grandchildren, and so on. For example, `/book//caption` addresses any `caption` element descended from a `book` element. In the book shown in Figure 29-2 it would address the `example` element's `caption` from the book's second chapter along with the figure elements' two `caption` elements:

Example 29-4. Caption elements descended from the book element

```
<caption>The first figure's caption</caption>
<caption>The second figure's caption.</caption>
<caption>The first example.</caption>
```

29.2.4 *Attributes*

An address in XML document navigation is not a storage address like a file system path, despite the similarity in syntax. An XPath expression locates objects by their position in a document's structure and other properties, such as the values of attributes.

A diagram like Figure 29-2 should not present an attribute's information as a child of the element exhibiting the attribute. To do so would be incorrect, because attributes are not siblings of subelements. For this reason, XPath uses `/@` to show the element/attribute relationship.

For example, the expression in Example 29-5 addresses all the values of the `par` elements' `author` attributes.

Example 29-5. Expression with an attribute

```
/book//par/@author
```

Example 29-6. Objects addressed by Example 29-6

```
bd
cg
pp
bd
```

29.2.5 *Predicates*

A *predicate* is an expression that changes the group of objects addressed by another expression that precedes it. A predicate expression is delimited by square brackets and is either true or false. If true, it adds to the objects addressed; if false, it removes objects.

For example, the expression in Example 29-7 addresses all chapters that have a `figure` element in them.

Example 29-7. Addressing chapters with a `figure` element

```
/book/chapter[figure]
```

The predicate expression `figure` is true for any `chapter` that contains a `figure`. If true, that `chapter` is included among the addressed objects. Note that the `figure` itself is not among the objects addressed (although it is contained within the addressed `chapter` object).

A predicate expression can be a comparison. For example, `.–` lets you address an element by comparing its content data to a specific character string. Example 29-8 uses this technique to address all the `par` elements that have "Second paragraph." as their content data.

Example 29-8. Addressing par elements with specific content data

```
/book//par[.="Second paragraph."]
```

Example 29-9. Objects addressed by Example 29-8

```
<par author="cg">Second paragraph.</par>
```

> *Tip*   An advanced tutorial on XPath can be found in Chapter
> 61, "XML Path Language (XPath)", on page 940.

29.3 | XPath and databases

XPath's ability to address an XML document at any level of granularity has interesting implications for a DBMS. It allows capabilities that have been difficult or impossible for a conventional relational DBMS.

To illustrate, let's look at examples of using an XPath-based DBMS for the basic DBMS processes: storing, retrieving, and controlling information.

29.3.1 *Storing information*

The first step in using a DBMS, of course, is getting information into it. Traditionally, this has been a big deal. With an RDBMS, for example, a logical schema of data elements must be established that organizes them into rows and columns. Search criteria and indexing parameters have to be designed as well. Only after all this has been completed can data be posted.

It is possible to create an XPath-based DBMS in which none of this is necessary. In the *NeoCore XML Information Management System (XMS)*, for example, you simply start posting XML documents. There is no need to post schema definitions or DTDs (although it is always desirable to check validity before posting a document). You can try it yourself with the software on the CD-ROM.

The benefit of having to do, well... nothing... to be able to start storing information is obvious; but it begs an interesting question: If you have not defined any structure or indexing parameters, how will you know how to access any of the information?

That is where XPath comes into play.

NeoCore XMS locates information by matching patterns in queries – XPath expressions – with the structural patterns of the stored documents. The patterns are converted to numbers by a patented technique. As a result, comparisons require the same amount of time regardless of the length of the pattern or the size of the database.

This approach is equivalent to always indexing everything, so no decision about what to index has to be made. This means you can decide how to access information when you use it, instead of when you store it.

29.3.2 *Retrieving information*

Information represented in XML is organized into documents. Each document is presumably a convenient set of information for some purpose.

However, a complete document is rarely the right level of granularity for all purposes. For some tasks, a user may want a single fragment of information – a component of the document – or fragments of information from multiple documents.

XML lends itself well to these requirements because of its recursive element structure. Conceptually, a document is just an element that contains all the other elements and their data. Any element can be extracted from a document and made a document in its own right. The top-level element is called the "document element"; the subelements, data, and attributes are its components.

Some CMSs and DBMSs require you to define the accessible components when establishing a database. In an XPath-based XDBMS, however, you can make that decision dynamically, whenever you search for information.

To demonstrate this point, we will look at three different searches of the same database, using *NeoCore XMS*. The searches return:

- All documents of a type
- A single selected document
- Components from multiple documents

A *NeoCore XMS* database is treated as a single large document whose document type is ND. The documents stored in the database are actually its children, but we'll speak of them as documents nevertheless.

Now for the three searches!

29.3.2.1 Dumping the database

Let's say that there are 100GB of documents in the database and among them are a number of music CD catalog listings. To dump the contents of the music CD listings we enter the XPath expression seen in Example 29-10.

Example 29-10. Retrieving all documents of a type

```
/ND/CD
```

Note that the first element type name in the expression is that of the database document, ND. Although we *talk* about CD as "the document", we have to be quite precise with XPath.

The results are shown in Example 29-11. The CD documents in the result set are returned as components of a single Query-Results document.[2]

Example 29-11. Results of Example 29-10

```
<Query-Results>
<CD>
  <TITLE>Empire Burlesque</TITLE>
  <ARTIST>Bob Dylan</ARTIST>
  <COUNTRY>USA</COUNTRY>
  <COMPANY>Columbia</COMPANY>
  <PRICE>10.90</PRICE>
  <YEAR>1985</YEAR>
</CD>
<CD>
  <TITLE>Hide your heart</TITLE>
  <ARTIST>Bonnie Tylor</ARTIST>
  <COUNTRY>UK</COUNTRY>
  <COMPANY>CBS Records</COMPANY>
  <PRICE>9.90</PRICE>
  <YEAR>1988</YEAR>
</CD>
<CD>
  <TITLE>Dolly's Greatest Hits</TITLE>
        ...
</Query-Results>
```

29.3.2.2   Finding a CD by its title

Example 29-10 is an example of a single query that returns several complete documents. To return a single document based on a unique selection parameter, the XPath expression seen in Example 29-12 is used.

---

2. If you are getting the idea that everything in this native XML DBMS is a document, you are correct. The same is true for other data models: a relational result set, for example, is usually returned as a table.

Example 29-12. Selecting a single document

```
/ND/CD[TITLE="Dolly's Greatest Hits"]
```

The predicate addresses only CD elements with a TITLE subelement whose value is "Dolly's Greatest Hits".[3]

The results are shown in Example 29-13. As you would expect, there is only one CD returned.

Example 29-13. Results of Example 29-12

```
<Query-Results>
<CD>
  <TITLE>Dolly's Greatest Hits</TITLE>
  <ARTIST>Dolly Parton</ARTIST>
  <COUNTRY>USA</COUNTRY>
  <COMPANY>RCA</COMPANY>
  <PRICE>9.90</PRICE>
  <YEAR>1982</YEAR>
</CD>
</Query-Results>
```

29.3.2.3   Selecting some of the artists

Now for something completely different: a query whose result is neither defined nor constrained by documents, and which uses a complex predicate to boot.

The XPath statement shown in Example 29-14 requests the artist name for any CD whose title contains "night only" and costs $9.90, or was produced in the UK in 1990 and costs $10.20.

Example 29-14. Retrieving fragments from multiple documents

```
/ND/CD[(TITLE=*"night only"* AND PRICE="9.90")
     OR (COUNTRY="UK" AND YEAR="1990" AND PRICE="10.20")]/ARTIST
```

The results are shown in Example 29-15.

---

3. In an RDBMS, TITLE might be defined as a "key" and an index of titles created to optimize searches. In this XDBMS, that isn't necessary.

Example 29-15. Results of Example 29-14

```
<Query-Results>
  <ARTIST>Bee Gees</ARTIST>
  <ARTIST>Gary More</ARTIST>
</Query-Results>
```

In conventional database terms we've accessed the same XML information according to two different views. The first two queries produced coarse-grained document-level results; the third produced fine-grained component-level results.

But because of the *NeoCore XMS* database organization, there really aren't two different views. Neither CD nor AUTHOR is really a document; they are both components of ND. There is really only a single XML view, capable of emulating an unlimited number of conventional database views. You could think of this as a *variable view* capability.

29.3.3 *Modifying information*

For the next two examples we will use contact lists, as seen in Example 29-16, to illustrate two things: modifying part of a document, and adding elements to selected documents.

29.3.3.1   Changing an address

To change a document, we need to access it, just as if we were searching. However, we need to provide the system with more than the XPath expression; we must supply the replacement information as well. An application program, built on the XDBMS, would normally provide an interface for entering both these things.

Example 29-17 shows the XPath expression. It locates the Address of the Contact with the last name "Aardvark".

The revised Address is shown in Example 29-18.

This common type of operation demonstrates a benefit of component-level access. It avoids the need to download and re-post the entire ContactList just to change one address.

Example 29-16. A contact list

```
<ContactList>
  <Contact>
    <Name>
      <Last>Aardvark</Last>
      <First>Jerry</First>
    </Name>
    <Address>
      <Number>818</Number>
      <Street>Main Street</Street>
      <City>Colorado Springs</City>
      <State>CO</State>
      <ZIPcode>80907</ZIPcode>
    </Address>
    <PhoneNumber>
      <AreaCode>719</AreaCode>
      <Number>555-3403</Number>
    </PhoneNumber>
  </Contact>
  . . .
</ContactList>
```

Example 29-17. Locating Mr. Aardvark's Address

```
/ND/ContactList/Contact[Name/Last="Aardvark"]/Address
```

Example 29-18. Mr. Aardvark's new Address

```
<Address>
  <Number>2024</Number>
  <Street>West Street</Street>
  <City>Green Bay</City>
  <State>WI</State>
  <ZIPcode>54304</ZIPcode>
</Address>
```

29.3.3.2 Adding some ZIP+4 codes

Let's say that some of our contacts are in an area where we can speed up postal delivery by heeding the US Postal Service's admonition to add a 4-digit extension to the ZIP postal code.[4] In XML terms, we want to insert a new ZIPExtension element after specific ZIPcode elements.

---

4. Not to be confused with the ZIP archival file format!

The XPath expression is in Example 29-19. It locates all 80907 ZIP codes.

Example 29-19. Locating ZIP codes to which extensions will be added

```
/ND/ContactList/Contact/Address/ZIPcode[.="80907"]
```

The `ZIPExtension` element we are adding is shown in Example 29-20. It follows the `ZIPcode` element within the parent `Address` element.

Example 29-20. Adding an empty `ZIPExtension`

```
<ZIPExtension></ZIPExtension>
```

The new element is empty because we have added it to many `Address` elements. Over time, as those addresses are revised, ZIP+4 data will be inserted into the content of the `ZIPExtension` elements.

This kind of operation illustrates the flexibility of the XML data model. The validity of the documents can be preserved by a simple change to the DTD: adding an optional `ZIPExtension` element type to the content model of `Address`.

In contrast, the relational model would require adding a new column, which would cause the new data field to be added to all addresses, not just those with a `ZIPcode` of 80907. For a typical RDBMS, that would require reorganizing the database.

29.3.4 *Controlling information*

XPath can be used for controlling information as well as accessing and modifying it. By "controlling" we refer to functions such as access control, asynchronous triggers, and referential integrity checks. To show how this works we will use an access control example.

Look again at the CD catalog listing in Example 29-13. Suppose we want certain users to see only CDs from the United States, but not see the prices of RCA CDs.

In other words, for these users – let's call them the "US-only" group – we want the results from the query in Example 29-12 to look like Example 29-21.

Example 29-21. Access-controlled results of Example 29-12

```
<Query-Results>
<CD>
   <TITLE>Dolly's Greatest Hits</TITLE>
   <ARTIST>Dolly Parton</ARTIST>
   <COUNTRY>USA</COUNTRY>
   <COMPANY>RCA</COMPANY>
   <YEAR>1982</YEAR>
</CD>
</Query-Results>
```

We accomplish the access control by means of the document shown in Example 29-22. It filters all queries made by any user who is a member of the "US-only" group.

Example 29-22. Access control document for "US-only" users

```
<NeoCore>
<AC user="US-only" type="All">
   <CD>
     <show>COUNTRY="USA"</show>
     <PRICE>
        <hide>/ND/CD[COMPANY="RCA"]</hide>
     </PRICE>
   </CD>
</AC>
</NeoCore>
```

The NeoCore, AC, show, and hide elements are the control information; the other elementss are from the documents being controlled. The show and hide elements determine whether the content of the elements in which they occur will be shown or hidden. They each contain an XPath expression that, if true, will cause the showing or hiding to occur.

This approach makes it possible to implement very flexible access control rules. In Example 29-22 we hid a fragment of information based on the contents of a different field, according to rules assigned to an arbitrary group of users. Write, modify, and delete permissions can be handled similarly.

Control documents can be set up for processes as well as for human users. In this way, if you've added data elements to support new applications, you can hide the new elements from legacy programs that don't expect them.

NeoCore XMS uses its patented pattern-matching technology to implement control functions. When a document is accessed that satisfies XPath expressions in the user's control document, a behavior is invoked that causes the control module to do something. In our example, the behavior caused the search results to be filtered.

Storing XML in a relational DBMS

Tool Discussion

▌ Choosing a DBMS

▌ RDBMS requirements for XML

▌ Storing XML hierarchies in tables

▌ Storing XML documents as CLOBs

Sponsor: IBM Informix, http://www.informix.com

Contributing experts: Martin Herbach and Paul Brown

Chapter

Some say that using XML as a data model "ignores the years of investment in relational database technology". Others say that Galileo heard the same argument applied to Copernican mapmaking technology! But if your world revolves around MOM applications more than POP, you'll want to see how XML documents can be handled by a non-XML DBMS.

ML documents are currently stored in DBMSs with both XML and non-XML data models, so choosing between them is not a cut-and-dried decision.

30.1 | Choosing a DBMS

Like many high-tech issues, choosing a DBMS depends on a mix of technical, practical, and quasi-theological criteria, such as:

- Do you use XML primarily for messages in business transactions, or for publications intended for human consumption?
- Are your documents stable, or in a constant state of revision?
- How large are they? Do you work with pieces or with the whole thing at once?
- How many documents are there? How many users?
- What are your passionate beliefs about the "rightness" of keeping XML documents in their official standardized representation?

- What are your passionate beliefs about the value of keeping XML documents together with all your other information in a managed, centralized data store?
- How much does your management care about your passionate beliefs?
- Do you need to ask combined XML/SQL queries, like: "show me all XML documents that have passed through the system this month for my five largest customers?"
- Do the products you are evaluating work well with your existing systems? Do they work at all?
- Can your staff cope with the complexity of the proposed solution? How will their passionate beliefs affect their efficiency?
- What is the cost of the solution?

In previous chapters we've looked at native XML databases. But since XML is widely used to interchange data to and from relational and object-relational databases, we'll now look at the way a relational DBMS handles XML.

30.2 | RDBMS requirements for XML

In earlier parts of this book we examined at length the role of XML in business integration and e-commerce. A key aspect is XML's use as an interchange representation, as shown in Figure 30-1.

The need for a DBMS to receive and send XML is obvious; that is the essence of using XML as an interchange representation. However, the reasons for storing the XML messages are worth reviewing:

- XML documents that convey information about orders and other business transactions become legal documents that must be retained as a "statement of record," meaning that the original source document may need to be examined at some future date.
- There may be elements of the XML exchange messages for which no corresponding place exists in the enterprise data schema.

Figure 30-1 XML in machine-oriented messaging (MOM) applications

- Early adopters of XML-based integration may be using non-standardized messages without DTDs or mappings to relational schemas.
- Storing XML messages allows them to be included with operational data in the search domain for SQL queries.
- A single store for XML documents and operational data permits uniform administration and recovery.

RDBMS vendors are addressing these requirements. For example, Informix® is pursuing a strategy, through its own products like *Informix Dynamic Server*[TM] and *Informix Internet Foundation*, and with partners who augment these products, of providing at least the following capabilities:

acting as receiver
Translating data from XML documents into relational tables.

acting as sender
Translating data from relational formats into appropriate XML message documents.

storing and manipulating XML documents
Preserving XML data in close to native form, at least on a temporary basis, while allowing it to be combined with relational data sources.

In the remainder of this chapter we'll look at two strategies for storing XML: storing XML hierarchies in tables and storing XML as a CLOB.

30.3 | Storing XML hierarchies in tables

Before we discuss XML specifically, lets look at the general techniques for modeling hierarchies in a relational database.

30.3.1 *Trees in general*

The hierarchy, or tree, is a common pattern in computer programming. We've seen many examples so far in this book. Mathematically, it is a special type of graph.

30.3.1.1   A little graph theory

A *graph* is formally defined as a set of nodes, a set of edges, and a set of relationships between nodes along edges.

Additional rules can be superimposed on this basic definition that restrict the construction of the graph. Impose enough rules, and you arrive at the kind of graph we call a hierarchy.

Why bother with the formalism? Well, it turns out that graph theory is a very well studied field. Over the years, techniques have been developed for working with graphs and they have found their way into commercial products. For example, Informix's approach to modeling hierarchies borrows from this body of knowledge.

30.3.1.2   The Node datatype

Extensible databases allow developers to augment their data models by introducing new datatypes into the SQL query language. We can model hierarchies by introducing a datatype whose value represents the position of a node within a hierarchy, and a set of methods for computing common hierarchical operations on that datatype.

These would include queries like:

- Is A under B in the hierarchy?
- Is C a sibling of D?

30.3.2 *Modeling a DTD*

A graph that models a tree is sometimes called a *holarchy*. An XML DTD can be represented by a holarchy. Example 30-1 shows the DTD for a business card.

Example 30-1. Business card DTD

```
<!ELEMENT business_card (name, title, address, contact)>
<!ELEMENT    name          (surname, given, other?)>
<!ELEMENT       surname     #PCDATA>
<!ELEMENT       given       #PCDATA>
<!ELEMENT       other       #PCDATA>

<!ELEMENT    title         #PCDATA>

<!ELEMENT    address       (street, city, state, zip)>
<!ELEMENT       street      #PCDATA>
<!ELEMENT       city        #PCDATA>
<!ELEMENT       state       #PCDATA>
<!ELEMENT       zip         #PCDATA>

<!ELEMENT    contact       (phone*)>
<!ELEMENT       phone       #PCDATA>
```

30.3.2.1 Creating a holarchy

Figure 30-2 shows the holarchy for the business card DTD.

Each node of the holarchy can be labeled with its position relative to the other nodes in the same holarchy. By implementing a new datatype to model these holarchy labels, it becomes possible to represent DTDs using relational constructs and to "shred" an XML document into a tabular form that is more amenable to queries.

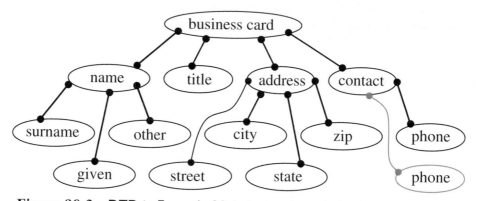

Figure 30-2   DTD in Example 30-1 depicted as a holarchy

We'll call this "node position" datatype Node.[1] It consists of a sequence of integers. When displaying a Node value it is customary to separate the integers with periods.

For example, the holarchy for the business card DTD introduced in Table 30-1 would be enumerated as in Figure 30-3.

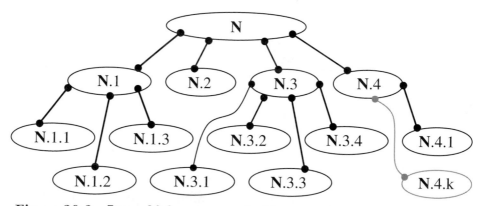

Figure 30-3   Figure 30-2 enumerated with Node values

---

1. It has other uses besides DTDs. Holarchies are useful in any application with hierarchies, such as manufacturing management or chains of command.

The document type is the root of the holarchy, designated "N". (It will become an integer momentarily!) The position of each node within the holarchy is represented by the sequence of integers following the root.

30.3.2.2 Generating a relational table

Using an enumerated holarchy, a DTD can automatically be transformed into a relational table. The table for the business_card DTD is shown in Example 30-1. Of course, in practice a system would have multiple DTDs, so the "N" would be replaced by an integer that uniquely identifies the DTD.

Table 30-1 Relational table for DTD in Example 30-1

Node Id	Element Type	Datatype	Cardinality
N	business_card	Root Node	1
N.1	name	Structural Element	1
N.2	title	#PCDATA	1
N.3	address	Structural Element	1
N.4	contact	Structural Element	1..k
N.1.1	surname	#PCDATA	1
N.1.2	given_name	#PCDATA	1
N.1.3	other	#PCDATA	0..1
N.3.1	street	#PCDATA	1
N.3.2	city	#PCDATA	1
N.3.3	state	#PCDATA	1
N.3.4	zip	#PCDATA	1
N.4.1	phone	#PCDATA	1

30.3.3 *Modeling a document instance*

Example 30-2 is an excerpt from an XML document received from an
Internet employment service. It is a list of candidates looking for work, in
the form of business_card elements.

Example 30-2. Two business_card elements

```
...
<business_card>
  <name>
    <surname>Brown</surname>
    <given>Paul</given>
    <other>G</other>
  </name>
  <title>Chief Plumber</title>
  <address>
    <street>20th Floor, 300 Lakeside</street>
    <city>OAKLAND</city>
    <state>CA</state><zip>94612</zip>
  </address>
  <contact>
    <phone>510 628 3999</phone>
  </contact>
</business_card>
<business_card>
  <name>
    <surname>Immanuel</surname>
    <given>Kant</given>
  </name>
  <title>Chief Philosopher</title>
  <address>
    <street>Ground Floor, 20 Leibenstrasse</street>
    <city>Konigsberg</city>
    <state>PRUSSIA</state><zip>12-A</zip>
  </address>
  <contact>
    <phone>4 343 2854 34</phone>
    <phone>4 343 2385 33</phone>
  </contact>
</business_card>
...
```

In the *Informix Dynamic Server*, the document can be parsed with a standard XML parser, either embedded within the product run-time or execut-

ing in an outside application server. It can then be transformed into the relational table shown in Table 30-2.

Table 30-2 shows how the Node type can be used to "shred" and store an XML document so that it can be retrieved and updated efficiently using SQL. Restoring the document to its original form is also straightforward. To understand why, we need to examine the Node values in more detail.

30.3.3.1 Understanding Node values

You can tell a lot about the relationships among nodes by examining their Node position values. For example:

- If the first integer of two Node values is the same, but the remaining integers are different, the nodes occupy different positions in the same hierarchy. For example, the values "70123.1.4" and "70123.1.5" tell us that both nodes come from the XML document or DTD numbered "70123".
- You can also tell that those two nodes are siblings; they share the parent that has Node position "70123.1.4".
- A third node, with Node value "70123.1.4.1", is underneath "70123.1.4"; correspondingly, the node at "70123.1.4" is above "70123.1.4.1".

30.3.3.2 Creating a B-tree index

Comparing Node positions is important in queries that, for example, find the number of distinct cities in the entire document, or the phone number of a person identified by his or her surname. A database designer would typically want to create a B-tree index of the Node column to optimize such queries.[2]

DBMSs differ in their approach to indexing user-defined datatypes. Many require the developer of a new type to create a user-defined function that converts an instance of the type into one of the SQL built-in types. However, it is unclear how that could work for the Node type.

---

2. A *B-tree index* is an index that has been optimized using the B-tree algorithm, which favors rapid search in preference to quick revision.

Table 30-2   Relational table for document in Example 30-2

Doc_Node	DTD_Node	Value
. . .	. . .	. . .
M.K.1.1	N.1.1	Brown
M.K.1.2	N.1.2	Paul
M.K.1.3	N.1.3	G
M.K.2	N.2	Chief Plumber
M.K.3.1	N.3.1	20th Floor...
M.K.3.2	N.3.2	OAKLAND
M.K.3.3	N.3.3	CA
M.K.3.4	N.3.4	94612
M.K.4.1	N.4.1	510 628 3999
M.(K+1).4.1	N.1.1	Immanuel
M.(K+1).1.2	N.1.2	Kant
M.(K+1).2	N.2	Chief Philosopher
M.(K+1).3.1	N.3.1	Ground Floor...
M.(K+1).3.2	N.3.2	Königsberg
M.(K+1).3.3	N.3.3	PRUSSIA
M.(K+1).3.4	N.3.4	12-A
M.(K+1).4.1	N.4.1	4 343 2854 34
M.(K+1).4.2	N.4.2	4 343 2385 33
. . .	. . .	. . .

In the *Informix Dynamic Server*, though, indexing support is achieved by embedding a `compare` method that the B-Tree and data sorting algorithms use. The method supports >, <, and = operators, as shown in Example 30-3.

Note the last two lines of the example. They restrict the query to rows underneath the root node identified as "103". Because the DBMS was able to create a B-Tree index of the `Node` type, it can perform this "hierarchical" operation as it would a normal table operation.

Example 30-3. SQL Query using `Node` type

```
REM     How many people listed in XML Document #103
REM     are from "Oakland"?

SELECT COUNT (DISTINCT Root_Value (T.Doc_Node))
  FROM Shred_XML_Table T, XML_DTD_Table D1
 WHERE T.DTD_Node      = D.Node Id
   AND D.Element_Type  = "city"
   AND T.Value         = "OAKLAND"
   AND (
         T.Doc_Node > "103"
   AND   T.Doc_Node < Node_Incr("103")
       )
;
```

30.4 | Storing XML documents as CLOBs

Perhaps the most common approach to managing XML in a relational or object-relational DBMS involves storing entire XML documents as binary or character large objects (BLOBs or CLOBs). Text indexing techniques are employed to speed up access to the document's contents. SQL can then be used to manipulate the XML documents.

This technique was widely used for other text before XML came on the scene, and still is. Some examples are product information, employee resumes, etc.

Example 30-4 contains SQL statements for the following functions:

■ Create a table to hold XML documents.
■ Insert a new document into the table.

- Build an index over the entire set of XML documents stored in the table.
- Query for documents with a VEGE_TYPE element containing "potato".

Example 30-4. SQL statements using text indexing to manage XML documents

```
CREATE TABLE XML_Docs (
      id         SERIAL       PRIMARY KEY,
      supplier VARCHAR(32) NOT NULL,
      xml_doc  CLOB         NOT NULL
);
INSERT INTO XML_Docs (supplier, xml_doc)
      VALUES (
          'ABC Inc',
          FileToClob('d:\xml\order_abcinc.xml','server'
      )
);
CREATE INDEX idx1 ON XML_Docs (xml_doc vts_clob_ops) USING vts
;
SELECT supplier FROM XML_docs
 WHERE vts_contains(xml_doc, '(potato) <IN> VEGE_TYPE')
;
```

On the surface, the CLOB strategy might seem inferior to component-level access because the entire document is retrieved at once, preventing others from working on it. Even if a system did allow concurrent access to the complete document, there would be a danger of concurrent update as well.

The *Informix Dynamic Server* addresses this problem by providing *transactional guarantees* for large object storage. Multiple users can read and update different regions of a single large object, and the DBMS' underlying disk storage algorithms will ensure the integrity of their actions.

30.5 | Conclusion

In order to support XML messaging, a DBMS must do more than be able to convert data to and from XML. Increasingly, there is also a need to store the messages in native form as XML documents. –>

XML, SQL, and XPath: Getting it all together

Tool Discussion

- Combining relational and text storage
- XPath in SQL statements
- SQL in XML documents
- Functional and text indexing

Sponsor: Oracle Corporation, http://www.oracle.com/xml

Contributing expert: Claire Dessaux and Mike Lehmann

The world runs on relational DBMSs. Then again, as we showed in the Preface to this book, it also runs on markup languages, a necessity for documenting things as complex as RDBMSs. When titans meet they can easily clash, but this chapter shows a better way. There can be many paths to successful database management: only one has to begin with "X"!

atabases and XML documents are both ways to represent data, but they do so differently. In a DBMS, the metadata is kept in proprietary form; in XML, it is interspersed with the data in the form of tags, and may also be included in a DTD or schema definition. RDBMS data is stored in tables; XML data is organized in hierarchies.

The primary languages for accessing data in these two representations – SQL and XPath – reflect these differences. In an RDBMS environment in which XML has become an essential part, it makes sense to be able to use both languages, separately and together.

In this chapter, we'll show examples of doing just that for the key processes of a DBMS:

writing XML into a database
Parsing an XML document and storing its components in a database, without losing the metadata that describes the properties of the components and the relationship among them.

reading XML from a database
Exporting database objects and representing them as XML documents.

Indexing and searching
Building indexes to optimize searches for XML data.

Let's begin by looking at the schema and sample data that will be used in all the examples.

31.1 | An insurance claim example

Figure 31-1 depicts part of an insurance schema in a relational database. It shows the table for an insurance Claim, together with tables referenced from it.

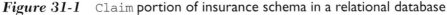

Figure 31-1   Claim portion of insurance schema in a relational database

An instance of a Claim can be represented as the XML document shown in Example 31-1, which preserves the data relationships and metadata set up by the database schema.

Field (column) names appear as element type names; some table names do as well: Claim because it is the root and Payment because there could be more than one of them.

Example 31-1. XML representation of a `Claim` **instance**

```
<Claim>
  <ClaimID>123456</ClaimID>
  <Filed>1999-01-01 12:00:00.0</Filed>
  <ClaimPolicy>
    <PolicyID>8895</PolicyID>
    <PrimaryInsured>
      <CustomerID>1044</CustomerID>
      <FirstName>John</FirstName>
      <LastName>Doe</LastName>
      <HomeAddress>
        <Street>123 Cherry Lane</Street>
        <City>San Francisco</City>
        <State>CA</State>
        <Zip>94100</Zip>
      </HomeAddress>
    </PrimaryInsured>
  </ClaimPolicy>
  <DamageReport>
    The driver lost control of the vehicle. This
    was because of <Cause>faulty brakes</Cause>.
  </DamageReport>
  <Settlements>
    <Payment id="0">
      <Approver>JCox</Approver>
      <Amount>7600</Amount>
      <PayDate>1999-03-01 09:00:00.0</PayDate>
    </Payment>
  </Settlements>
</Claim>
```

The hierarchy reflects the relationships among the tables. In the database, for example, `ClaimPolicy` is a *foreign key* that points to the `Policy` table. In the XML document, it appears as an element whose content is the fields of the `Policy` table. There are several others like this, shown by the nesting levels of the document.

The `DamageReport` field, although it contains XML markup, is different. We'll explain it in one of the examples.

This equivalence between the database and XML representations of data it important. It means, among other things, that XPath can be used to address the database!

There are potentially profound implications to this, such as direct hyperlinking between relational databases and Web pages. The *Oracle9i Database™* DBMS even provides two SQL types for the purpose: `DBURItype` for linking within a database, and `HTTPDBURItype` for linking to and from the Web.

31.2 | Writing XML into a database

In previous chapters we've seen examples of the two basic strategies for storing XML documents: integral storage with markup intact, and distributed storage across a set of tables. Integral storage preserves the unparsed text[1] while distributed storage normally parses the document and discards the markup.

However, it is also possible to store some elements as text while storing others as relational data.

31.2.1 *Combining relational data and XML text storage*

You can store as relational fields those elements whose data content conforms to a primitive datatype, while storing those with mixed content (character data with interspersed subelements) intact. *Oracle9i Database* supplies an SQL type called `XMLtype` for the purpose; Example 31-2 shows how it can be used when storing our insurance claim.

31.2.2 *Generating SQL* INSERT *statements*

Creating an SQL `INSERT` statement for every record you need to add is laborious. You can use SQL in combination with XPath to reduce the work, by creating a stylesheet to act as a program generator.

Example 31-3 shows the fragment of an XSLT stylesheet that would generate values for the `Payment` table.

The fragment would be iterated over all the `Payment` elements within all the `Claim` elements.

Note that the stylesheet does not load the database by itself. It merely generates the necessary SQL statements.

---

1. Markup plus data characters, remember!

Example 31-2. Document storage using XMLType

```
REM     Create the Claim table

CREATE table Claim (
        ClaimID      number(3),
        Filed        date,
        ClaimPolicy  sys.XMLType,
        DamageReport sys.XMLType,
        Settlements  sys.XMLType
);


REM     Insert a claim

INSERT INTO Claim VALUES (
        123456,
        sysdate(),
        sys.XMLType.createxml('
          <ClaimPolicy>
            ...details omitted for brevity...
          </ClaimPolicy>
          ')
        sys.XMLType.createxml('
          <DamageReport>
            The driver lost control of the vehicle. This
            was because of <Cause>faulty brakes</Cause>.
          </DamageReport>
          '),
        sys.XMLType.createxml('
          <Settlements>
            <Payment id="0">
              <Approver>JCox</Approver>
              <Amount>7600</Amount>
              <PayDate>1999-03-01 09:00:00.0</PayDate>
            </Payment>
          </Settlements>
          ')
);
```

Example 31-3. Generating SQL with XSLT

```
INSERT INTO Payment VALUES ('
  '<xsl:value-of select="Claim/Settlements/Payment/Approver"/>',
  <xsl:value-of select="Claim/Settlements/Payment/Amount"/>,
  <xsl:value-of select="Claim/Settlements/Payment/Paydate"/>
);
```

31.2.3 *XML SQL decomposition*

As an alternative method of storing XML, RDBMS vendors may offer a facility for *decomposing* (aka "shredding") an XML document. For example, Oracle's *XML SQL Utility* is illustrated in Figure 31-2.

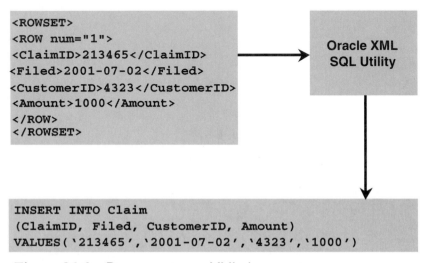

```
<ROWSET>
<ROW num="1">
<ClaimID>213465</ClaimID>
<Filed>2001-07-02</Filed>
<CustomerID>4323</CustomerID>
<Amount>1000</Amount>
</ROW>
</ROWSET>
```

Oracle XML
SQL Utility

```
INSERT INTO Claim
(ClaimID, Filed, CustomerID, Amount)
VALUES('213465','2001-07-02','4323','1000')
```

Figure 31-2   Decomposing an XML document

The product decomposes an XML document into any database table or view. Element type names are mapped to column (field) names in the table. Elements with data content only are mapped to scalar columns, and elements containing sub-elements are mapped to object types. Lists of elements are mapped to collections.

31.3 | Reading XML from a database

An RDBMS may offer several techniques for exporting database objects as XML. We'll look at the *Oracle9i Database* offerings: XSQL and three built-in functions.

31.3.1 *XSQL*

XSQL is a simple vocabulary for representing SQL statements in XML documents.

Example 31-4 is an example. It contains a query that looks for Doe's insurance claims. As there is only one such claim in the database, the document in Example 31-1 is generated.

Example 31-4. XSQL document that generates Doe's claims

```
<?xml-stylesheet type="text/xsl" href="claim.xsl"?>
<query connection="xmldemo">
  SELECT VALUE(c) as Claim
  FROM    insurance_claim_view c
  WHERE   c.ClaimPolicy.PrimaryInsured.LastName = 'Doe'
</query>
```

The XSQL document is processed in several steps:

1. It is parsed by an XML parser.
2. XSLT instructions, such as those in the associated "claim.xsl" stylesheet, are passed to an XSLT processor.
3. The attributes and data content of the query element are processed by the DBMS.

31.3.2 *Built-in XML generation functions*

The three built-in functions are:

dbms_xmlgen
> Generates XML documents from the results of SQL queries.

sys_xmlgen
> Generates XML documents by converting scalar value, object type, and XMLType instances.

sys_xmlagg
> Generates XML documents of arbitrary complexity by aggregating (concatenating) multiple XML documents.

Example 31-5 uses `dbms_xmlgen` to produce the same result as Example 31-4.

Example 31-5. Built-in function that generates Doe's claims

```
qryCtx := dbms_xmlgen.getContextHandle('
   SELECT VALUE(c) as Claim
   FROM   insurance_claim_view c
   WHERE  c.ClaimPolicy.PrimaryInsured.LastName = 'Doe'
');
result := dbms_xmlgen.getXMLClob(qryCtx);
```

31.4 | Indexing and searching

Database designers spend considerable effort on indexing, in order to optimize the performance of searches. XML, because of its different data model and mixed content, presents unique challenges in this area.

Let's examine how a DBMS can support indexing and searching for XML, using *Oracle9i Database* as an example. It provides two types of indexing for XML documents: functional indexes and textual indexes.

31.4.1 *Functional indexes*

A *functional index* is created by executing a function on a column (i.e., on all the elements of the same type) and indexing the result.

For example, it may be desirable to speed up searches for particular causes in damage reports, like that shown in Example 31-6.

Example 31-6. Search for specific `Cause` content

```
SELECT Filed
FROM   Claim c
WHERE  c.DamageReport.extract(
          '/DamageReport/Cause/text()'
       ).getStringVal() = 'faulty brakes'
```

A functional index can be created by using XPath to extract the data of all `Cause` elements, as shown in Example 31-7.

Example 31-7. Create functional index for `Cause`

```
CREATE INDEX cause_index ON Claim (
    DamageReport.extract(
        '/DamageReport/Cause/text()'
    ).getStringVal()
);
```

31.4.2 *Text indexes*

A *text index* is created from the words in a document or some portion of it. Searches on text can be used in combination with standard SQL query predicates, as shown in Example 31-8.

Example 31-8. Search for text in `Cause` content

```
SELECT  ClaimID
FROM    Claim c
WHERE   c.Filed > '04-01-2001'
  AND     CONTAINS(
            DamageReport,
            '"faulty brakes" INPATH (/DamageReport/Cause)'
          )
        >0
;
```

The SQL statement searches for all damage reports filed after April 1, 2001, that have a `Cause` containing the phrase "faulty brakes". It uses the `CONTAINS` function in conjunction with the XPath query operator, `INPATH`, to accomplish this.

Note the distinction between searching on the value of a field and searching for text within a field. The search in Example 31-6 is satisfied only if "faulty brakes" is the *complete* data of the `Cause` element. In Example 31-8, though, the search is satisfied if "faulty brakes" occurs *anywhere* in the data.

31.5 | Conclusion

RDBMSs are the leading infrastructure for application support, because of their flexibility and broad applicability. RDBMS users have adopted XML for largely the same reasons. Facilities like those we have discussed (Figure 31-3), let them do so without changing existing systems or databases.

And their developers don't have to abandon proven tools while learning the new possibilities of the XML data model. They can use both SQL and XPath, independently and in combination.

Figure 31-3   XML support in an RDBMS

Content Acquisition

- Converting legacy documents
- Large-scale conversion
- Accessing transactional data
- Acquiring reusable renditions

Part Nine

Content is king!

Yes, we said that before, but now we can tell the whole truth.

Actually, content is a royal family. There is the content of published documents, intended for people to read, and the content of machine-oriented transactions, which is a by-product of business processes. Ideally, we want the published content to be stored as unrendered abstractions, represented in XML, just as we want the transactional content to be in sharable enterprise databases.

But much of the time, the publications are *legacy documents* either rendered or not XML (or both!) – and the transactions are *legacy data*, usable only by the application that created it.

In this part, we look closely at several ways of acquiring reusable content for XML systems.

We consider the formidable problem of converting vast quantities of legacy documents to XML, both the software that is needed and the facilities required. We also see how XML can make legacy data an integral part of the enterprise's information resources.

Finally, we examine how renditions can be reused without converting them to abstractions.

XML
mass-conversion
facility

Tool Discussion

▌ XML content: why it is different

▌ Automating for markup consistency

▌ Value-added editorial services

Sponsor: Innodata Corporation, http://www.innodata.com

Contributing expert: J. Sperling Martin and John Chelsom

Chapter

32

In the musical *Ragtime*, Henry Ford sings "Speed up the belt, speed up the belt!" He refers to what is arguably the first complex mass-production system – his automobile assembly line. In today's XML conversion assembly lines, the system is equally complex but the "belt" is virtual and the control methods are a lot more sophisticated.

he demands of e-business and Web publication are creating an overwhelming demand for XML conversion and enrichment services. For many projects, the volumes are such that results can only be achieved by systematized mass-production facilities.

In other words, there is a requirement for a very special category of tool – the high-volume XML conversion facility. As an example of the scale involved, consider Innodata's dedicated facility for XML conversion, which it calls its *XML Content Factory.*™ It is a 54,000 square foot building with 2,500 computer workstations networked to a fully-clustered system of data center servers.

If this "tool" were packaged like most of the others in this book, it would need 142,833 square feet of shrink wrap!

32.1 | The challenge

Of course document conversion – even mass conversion – is nothing new. But creating XML content presents a very special challenge.

32.1.1 *Why XML is different*

Before generalized markup, document conversion was either from a paper rendition to a machine-processable rendition, or from one machine-processable rendition to another.

In creating XML data, however, a conversion facility is undertaking what are conceptually two different tasks. The first task is the classical one of capturing the text in digital form.

The second task is the difficult one: metadata must be associated with the captured textual data in the form of XML markup, distinguishing the style information from the real information content. Unlike conventional data conversion, XML conversion requires separating the true abstract data and its structure from the rendered form.

Performing this second task in a mass production environment is where the challenge arises. Let's look at some of the issues involved.

32.1.2 *Tagging consistency*

Large-scale projects that seek maximum value from XML are typically driven by complex DTDs. Project specs therefore call for richly-structured metadata and detailed hyperlinking.

Given the scale of the effort required for such large volumes, and the inherently subjective nature of operator-level decision-making, the many operators involved in complex tagging would likely compromise internal consistency. A conversion facility needs to overcome this problem.

32.1.3 *Diversity of project types*

Because XML applications are expanding into every sphere of business, a conversion facility must be able to handle a wide variety of project types. The facility must be able to build everything from e-commerce catalogs to electronic libraries, and anything else that can benefit from XML. There is diversity in all aspects, from the type of content, to the varying input data formats, to the set of output products produced.

The workflow for an XML conversion facility therefore needs to be independent of project type, yet capable of seamlessly integrating a variety of highly specialized content editors into the production process.

32.1.4 *Text accuracy*

XML conversion projects almost invariably produce abstractions, rather than renditions. That is because the data is intended for processing by computers, rather than simply being presented to humans.

As a result, the conversion facility must be capable of producing output that conforms to the highest industry standards for character accuracy. Producing 99.995% accurate data means one error in 20,000 characters.

32.2 | The solution

Meeting the challenge of mass-producing complex metadata requires a conversion facility whose design reflects the experience of conventional conversion projects, plus a technology-driven workflow that incorporates processes optimized for XML.

32.2.1 *Applicable lessons from the past*

Experience shows you can never have enough storage, planning, or quality assurance.

32.2.1.1 Employ large scale, fully redundant data storage

As enterprises embrace e-business they generate massive data conversion requirements. Such projects require equally massive data storage in the conversion facility.

The *XML Content Factory*, for example, was designed for a monthly output capacity of 15 gigabytes. To accomplish this, its 2,500 workstations are connected to a fully-clustered system of data center servers. To achieve high levels of redundancy as well as performance, each data center server has parallel CPUs and redundant storage and is connected to a fiber-optic backbone network.

32.2.1.2   Planning precedes production!

All projects should undergo detailed requirements studies, proof-of-concept, analysis, design, and engineering before going into production. This ensures, to the greatest extent possible, that all kinks are worked out of the process well in advance of the project going into full production.

32.2.1.3   Employ ISO-compliant quality assurance methodologies

ISO-compliant quality assurance methodologies should be fully integrated, including methodologies in respect of statistically valid sampling and auditing. In addition, quality circles should be integrated into the assembly line, with automated quality gates installed after each major phase in the production process.

32.2.2   *Technology-driven workflow*

To meet the throughput demands of mass conversion while at the same time applying metadata accurately requires a technology-driven workflow that incorporates processes optimized for XML.

Figure 32-1 illustrates a workflow for document conversion. It shows just seven processes, at a high level and quite generic. In contrast, the real-world workflow of the *XML Content Factory*, for example, involves over 45 distinct concurrent and serial processes, including six separate quality gates.

Nevertheless, we can use Figure 32-1 to show the basic sequence of processing, and to show where some of the optimization for XML takes place.

Before we do, however, let's take a quick refresher course in workflow.

32.2.2.1   Workflow explained

A business process that is organized or automated by a computer system is called a *workflow*. The software that defines and controls a workflow is called a *workflow management system*. A typical workflow can be decomposed into a set of sub-processes which may themselves consist of further sub-processes.

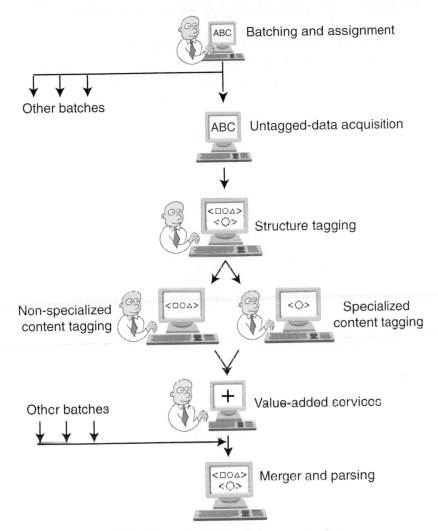

Figure 32-1   Workflow for high-volume conversion

At the lowest level, a process consists of an activity performed by one of the participants in the workflow. The overall process can therefore be thought of as a set of activities, and is complete when all the activities have been completed successfully.

An activity can be manual (performed by one or more humans) or automated, in which case one or more software applications is invoked to perform it. Of course these applications may or may not involve manual intervention.

A participant interacts with the workflow management system to find the list of activities assigned to him. When he selects an activity to perform, the workflow management system "acquires" the activity on his behalf, thereby removing it from the activity list of all the other participants in the workflow. It then delivers the required data to the participants desktop, launches any applications that are needed to perform the activity, and monitors the status of the activity until it is complete.[1]

32.2.2.2   Batching and assignment

In this, the first step of the workflow in Figure 32-1, a project begins. In the *XML Content Factory*, a project is broken into "batches" for assignment to different departments. There are two considerations in the batching decisions:

load balancing
> Batches are created and assigned based on available capacity in order to maximize throughput.

content-based routing
> Batches reflect the nature of the tagging that is required and are routed to content editors who possess the necessary skills.

The workflow system tracks the exact status of each batch, allowing bottlenecks to be identified early. Production managers know the upcoming load for each workgroup. Capacity is therefore deployed in an optimal way.

32.2.2.3   Untagged-data acquisition

There are several ways that untagged data can be acquired. Hardcopy documents can be scanned to produce images. The images are processed by

---

1. This description of workflow used the terminology of the Workflow Management Coalition (WfMC), a vendor-sponsored body set up in 1993 to develop industry standards for workflow management products.

rules-based optical character recognition (OCR) software and then edited to produce untagged character data.

Other paths to this point are possible. For example, some OCR software is capable of using page-layout patterns as a basis for automatic tagging.

Data can also be acquired from word processing files or other forms of legacy electronic data. Their rendition markup can be stripped, or else partially converted to XML tags by automated means.

32.2.2.4 Structure tagging

The workflow differentiates "structure" tagging from "content" tagging — more precisely, "element-content" tagging from "mixed-content" tagging. The principal reason for the distinction is that it is only when the higher levels of a document are tagged that a context is established for the mixed-content tagging.

Another reason is that different skills are required for the two. It is easier to train operators to perform element-content tagging, while mixed-content tagging often requires knowledge of the document's subject matter.

32.2.2.5 Content tagging

This step is divided into two paths because even at the mixed-content level, varying skills are required. Non-specialized mixed content only requires the ability to recognize citations, emphasized phrases, and other generic element types.

Specialized mixed content, on the other hand, can require domain knowledge. That requirement varies widely, depending on the specific project, from training in recognizing a few phrases that occur in specific element types, to detailed, substantive knowledge of the subject area.

In both cases, the mixed-content tagger is also the one to flag text that needs value-added services such as enriched indexing or the application of links. We discuss these shortly.

We now consider some aspects of tagging to keep in mind for both element content and mixed content.

32.2.2.5.1 *Prevent data modification*

One risk of XML conversion is that of inadvertently modifying the data when adding markup. The system should be able to take measures to prevent this.

For example, in the *XML Content Factory*, as a safety measure, the software does not allow the content editors to delete or modify data when their assignment is to add tags.

32.2.2.5.2 *Assisted markup*

The editing software can assist the operator by using its knowledge of the DTD and the partially-tagged structure to propose only valid tags at any given point in the document.

This capability is more complex than it might seem, given that the batching and assignment process makes only a portion of the document available. For example, the start-tag for a book will only occur in the first batch and its end-tag will only occur in the last. As a result, the workflow system must generate a DTD fragment that applies to the portion of the document that is the subject of the operator's assignment.

The editing software can suggest the most likely markup for specific words and phrases in the data. The suggestions are motivated by rules created when the project content was analyzed and serve to minimize errors of contextual interpretation.

Markup accuracy can be checked during assisted markup by means of a validating parser. Doing so allows errors to be caught while an individual batch is being processed and the error is easier to isolate and correct.

The workflow system can supplement assisted markup by invoking processes that apply markup automatically.

32.2.2.6   Value-added services

Conversion to XML presents an excellent opportunity to add value to documents through editorial processes. As part of the conversion planning, documents will be given careful scrutiny and analysis, which will help in defining the value-adds. It should also prove less expensive to do the editorial work at the same time as markup is added, as the document will need to be processed only once.

Typical value-added services are indexing, creating abstracts, classification with a taxonomy or thesaurus, attaching multimedia content, imbedding hyperlinks, developing topic maps, and so on.

Innodata's *XML Content Factory* extends the concept to include a full-service professional services section that works with clients on-site or at their locations to build DTDs and perform other data architecture-related services. There is even a research and development team that keeps current on XML developments and tools.

Let's take a look at an example of value-added services.

32.2.2.6.3 *A converted document*

Example 32-1 shows a document that has been converted to XML. The workflow system has delivered it to a value-added editing workstation.

Example 32-1. XML document extract

```
<data>
<recordset rowcount="3"
           fieldnames="Results-url, Test-ID, Index">
  <field name="Results-url">
    <string>http://***********</string>
    <string>http://***********</string>
    <string>http://***********</string>
  </field>
  <field name="Test ID">
    <string>95-002367A</string>
    <string>95-008856H</string>
    <string>97-017834C</string>
  </field>
  <field name="Index">
    <string>DAB, DAJ</string>
    <string>DA, DBA, DAHA</string>
    <string>DAAB, DBB, DC</string>
  </field>
</recordset>
</data>
```

The document has three `field` elements with different `name` attributes:

Results-url
> The `string` subelements each contain a URL for test data details posted on the document owner's intranet.

Test-ID

The `string` subelements identify motor vehicle brake test reports.

Index

These `string` subelements are initially empty. They are to be completed as part of the value-added processing.

32.2.2.6.4 *Data gathering and indexing*

The workflow system presents the operator with two windows: the document in Example 32-1 and the taxonomy shown in Example 32-2.

Example 32-2. Taxonomy extract

```
D Testing -- Evaluation
  DA . Vehicle testing
    DAA. . Brake systems tests
      DAAA . . Effectiveness of systems tests
      DAAB . . . Fade/recovery tests
      DAAC . . . Spike stops
      DAAD . . . Parking brake tests
    DAB. . Durability testing during vehicle tests
    DAC. . Brake component tests
    DAD. . Procedures for performing brake tests
    DAE. . Assembly line testing -- brakes
    DAF. . Hydraulic brake systems
    DAG. . Skid checks
    DAH. .Testing of safety vehicles
      DAHA . . . Evaluation of safety vehicle principles
    DAJ. . Vehicle inspections/test by local governments
  DB . Laboratory testing of brakes
    DBA. . Dynamometer brake tests
    DBB. . Bench tests of brake components
    DBC. . Durability testing in laboratory
    DBD. . Procedures for laboratory tests
  DC . .Test methods
```

The operator first gathers the three motor vehicle brake test reports identified in the `Test-Id` field. As part of his training for the project, he has been taught enough about the subject area to recognize the contextual cues and other indicators that will dictate which taxonomy codes apply to each report. He enters those codes in the `string` elements of the `Index` field.

32.2.2.7   Merger and parsing

This is the final step, in which the separate batches are recombined into a single document and parsed and validated. As the workflow system created the batches in the first instance, and has been tracking them through the conversion process, this step can be automated.

32.3 | Conclusion

Converting vast amounts of information to XML requires a new kind of "tool" – the high-volume XML conversion facility. Such a facility must do more than apply techniques that worked for other kinds of conversion, because XML has unique requirements.

Content that fully exploits XML usually has complex DTDs, which means that operators must apply significant editorial judgment. With ultra-large projects, maintaining consistency can be a challenge.

Automated mass-conversion facilities, such as Innodata's *XML Content Factory*, meet the challenge with technology-driven workflows that combine experience from conventional conversions with processes optimized for XML.

These "tools" may not lend themselves well to shrink-wrap, but they can undertake large XML tagging projects without compromising consistency or production speed.

Do-it-in-house mass conversion

Tool Discussion

- Predictable and unpredictable structures
- Systems for in-house mass-conversion
- Automatic tagging

Sponsor: XMLCities, Inc., http://www.XMLCities.com
Contributing expert: Dr. Evan Huang

Chapter

33

There are only two ways to convert to XML: convert documents or convert their authors! In a high volume environment, converting authors is highly unlikely. You can outsource the conversion of documents, but if you have an ongoing requirement and security and cycle times matter, you may want to do it in-house. This chapter tells you how.

Despite XML's widespread adoption and proven track record, introducing it remains a significant challenge for many corporations, governments, educational institutions, service bureaus, and other high-volume content environments.

33.1 | The high-volume content challenge

Some of the real world barriers to high-volume use of XML are:

- converting huge amounts of paper and legacy document files,
- integrating XML tools into the content creation process, and
- managing work flow in mass-conversion environments.

Most of these and other obstacles, though, come from the structure of the documents.

33.1.1   *Structure affects conversion*

At the heart of these barriers is the difficulty of adding markup to documents. How difficult depends on the structure; it is common to say that "highly-structured" documents are easier to tag than "semi-structured" or "unstructured" ones.

But why should a document with many levels of structure be easier to tag than a document with just a few? The simple answer is that "highly-structured", in this context, means something else entirely.

Unfortunately, *structured* is perhaps the most misused and misunderstood word in the entire XML vocabulary. We discussed why in 6.1, "Structured vs. unstructured", on page 108 and we won't repeat all of that here. But to make informed decisions about conversion issues, there is a key point worth emphasizing.

All documents are *completely* structured. The real questions are:

- Is the document abstract (unstyled), as are most XML documents and all databases, or rendered, as are HTML and most WP documents?
- Does the structure have an easily recognized representation, as do XML and business forms, or is it difficult to determine?
- Is the structure predictable?

The last question requires some explanation. Since the structure of any document (once you determine what it is) can be represented in XML, we can safely confine the discussion to XML.

The content of an XML element, in either valid or merely well-formed documents, can be one of the following:

- Nothing at all (*empty element*).
- Data characters (*data content*) only.
- Elements only (*element content*) in any order.
- Data characters with elements intermixed among them (*mixed content*).

In a valid document, there is another possibility:

Elements only, their order constrained by a predefined sequence of element types (*type-sequenced* elements).

Now we can explain what it means for an element – or document, since a document is essentially just the largest element – to be predictable.

An element has a *predictable structure* if it (and its subelements, if any) are constrained to contain either:

- type-sequenced elements,
- data characters only, or
- nothing at all.

Relational database hackers love predictable structures because they map so easily onto relational tables and primitive datatypes. An RDBMS can handle the less predictable as well, but with more effort, as we saw in Part 8, "Databases", on page 428.

It is unpredictable structure that causes the most grief for document conversion, as well.

Business process documents, for example, tend to be abstract and have predictable structures. For them, markup can largely be automated through data capture forms, scripts, and other techniques.

But tagging documents with unpredictable structures typically requires human involvement, either at the time of writing or later with a conversion tool.

33.1.2 *Authors aren't always the best taggers*

It can be argued that tagging elements in a document is fundamentally a separate exercise, distinct from writing the content.

Authors may intuitively know what the elements are – a "phone number", "chapter heading", "ingredient", or "customer-type" – but it takes more to mark them as elements. To identify an element requires a start-tag and an end-tag, each with an element type name, and both delimited by angle brackets.

This process can be simplified and accelerated, but it can't be eliminated. Tag selection menus, template support, advanced scripting, macros, and other modern enhancements to XML editing systems still require manual tagging.

Expecting content creators – knowledge workers such as technical writers, paralegals, insurance adjusters, law enforcement personnel, research professionals, and lab technicians – to perform manual tagging on original content may be unrealistic. XML editing tools are typically less appealing to users accustomed to familiar word processing or desktop publishing software.

33.2 | A do-it-in-house solution

Because of the difficulty of persuading content authors and subject matter experts to use XML editing tools, organizations have come to rely on outsourcing for mass conversion. However, a mass-conversion system that can be used in-house may be preferable because of cost, cycle time, and information security reasons, especially if the need for conversion is ongoing.

A functional diagram of one such system, the *XMLCapture™ Suite* from XMLCities™, is shown in Figure 33-1.

Figure 33-1   Functional diagram of a mass-conversion system

We'll use the diagram to guide our discussion, starting with the two legacy conversion functions at the left: converting digital files and capturing paper documents.

33.2.1 *Legacy document conversion*

Events that motivate a project that creates new XML information – such as mergers and acquisitions, new document management procedures, government regulations, or new business initiatives – frequently require a large volume of legacy documents to be converted as well.

Legacy documents can occur in paper or electronic form. There are organizations for which an XML conversion project could involve warehouses of paper in bankers' boxes, thousands of pounds of microfilm and microfiche, and terabytes of PDF files.

Two functions are shown in the diagram:

document capture

> Capturing text and graphics from scanned documents is an independent process that may require varying degrees of proofing and quality control. The resulting files are fed into the mass-conversion process.

convert digital files

> This process converts file formats such as *MS Office Suite*, *PageMaker*, RTF, and PDF. It requires less proofing and quality control than scanning. Some products cope with the variety of existing formats by supporting extensible interfaces. Others, like *XMLCapture Suite*, accept a single high fidelity representation like PDF, and recommend that the original editors or conversion tools be used to generate it.

33.2.2 *Tagging*

Adding markup is the heart of an XML conversion process. Ideally, most of it will be done automatically. To make that possible requires preparation.

33.2.2.1   Preparing for tagging

Preparation for tagging is shown in the bottom row of the diagram, where there are blocks for creating DTDs and defining pattern rules for auto-tagging.

33.2.2.1.1   *Create and edit DTDs*

The usefulness of an XML document depends directly on the suitability of its DTD or schema. The DTD should be designed to satisfy the information needs of the users and applications that work with the documents. Ideally, it should not be constrained by the limitations of editing tools, production platforms, or operator skills.

However, the schedule demands, high volumes, and cost considerations of mass conversion frequently compromise that ideal by compelling the use of standardized or simplified DTDs. Sacrificing optimal DTDs to reach cost or productivity goals is a short-term strategy that may negatively impact the long-term knowledge management goals of the organization.

A mass-conversion system can reduce the need to compromise the DTD by automating most of the markup. It can also provide DTD editing tools that make it easier to decide where to break up documents for parallel handling during mass conversion.

33.2.2.1.2   *Define pattern rules*

Pattern rules are what make automated tagging possible. They associate patterns of text in the unconverted document with element types and attributes in the DTD. When a pattern is recognized, the markup for the associated XML construct is added to the document.

The patterns can be more than simple string occurrences. They can be based on, among other things:

- keywords,
- phrases,
- document location,
- datatypes (numeric, alphanumeric),
- whitespace, and
- font characteristics.

Conditional and Boolean logic can be used to construct complex pattern rules.

Figure 33-2 illustrates a tool for pattern rule development. Fully marked-up representative sample documents are used to identify the source patterns and corresponding markup. Drop-down menus list the possible components (like those mentioned above) that may be grouped to form a rule.

Figure 33-2   Pattern rule definition tool

Pattern rules can be tested, refined, and optimized iteratively with sample documents during the pre-production phase. Doing so will identify additional rules, exceptions, anomalies, and other factors that can be accounted for in the full production run.

Rule libraries can be developed for similar element types that occur in a variety of document types.

The objective of all this preparation is to automate as much tagging as possible, thereby reducing the need for manual markup.

33.2.2.2   Adding the markup

Manual and auto-tagging occupy a single block in the center of Figure 33-1.

33.2.2.2.3   *Auto-tagging*

The key feature that enables non-technical personnel to perform high-volume XML conversion is automatic tagging. It can also be used to convert existing XML documents when a DTD is modified.

The degree to which auto-tagging can be accomplished depends upon the type of document being converted and the complexity of the target DTD. Where there the structure is predictable, a system like *XMLCapture Suite* can credibly claim to automate as much as 90% of the tagging. But even when circumstances allow only 50% of the markup to be automated, it can make a significant impact on the cycle time and cost of XML conversion.

33.2.2.2.4   *Manual tagging*

In a high-volume conversion system utilizing manual markup, some tagging can be performed by operators who can recognize only generic element types like citations and quotations. Other tagging requires domain knowledge.

In contrast, in a conversion environment that relies on automated markup, an attempt is made to capture all of the domain knowledge within the pattern rules. That is why iterative testing and optimization of the rules is so important.

When the rules are formulated accurately and completely, manual tagging becomes chiefly a matter of exception handling and does not require the operator to possess domain knowledge.

Even so, a tagging tool can make an operator more efficient by means of techniques like color-coding content to make exceptions stand out. Such a tool is illustrated in Figure 33-3.

Figure 33-3   Manual tagging tool

33.2.3 *XML quality assurance*

Quality assurance is shown to the right of tagging in Figure 33-1.

XML well-formedness and validation checks are performed on the converted documents. They are then delivered to the file destinations assigned by the content administrator.

33.2.4 *Workflow*

High-volume XML conversion requires workflow management, represented by the file dispatching block in the top center of Figure 33-1.

Content administrators need to distribute separate production tasks among operators to maximize output, balance workloads, and ensure quality. The workflow design must also provide effective management oversight, enabling monitoring, notification, approvals, and audit trails.

In most applications, the production system will also require policies and procedures to ensure appropriate information security, and workstation statistics logging for production control.

33.2.4.1   Work-in-process dispatching

To accomplish these objectives, workflow management must be integrated into the mass-conversion process.

The controller module in *XMLCapture Suite*, for example, automatically dispatches work-in-process files to work stations based upon a predetermined design established by administrators. The dispatching system is integrated with the scanning, auto-tagging, manual tagging, and quality assurance tools and requires no special operator action.

Administrators can determine throughput and work-in-process status at any time.

33.2.4.2   Workflow design

Workflow design for mass-conversion based on automated markup differs from workflow for manual markup.

In manual markup processes, workflow is typically driven by DTD complexity. Specialized tagging tasks are distributed to operators specifically trained in a subset of the content.

In projects that depend on automated markup, however, the subject matter of the project does not affect workflow. The workflow design can therefore be simpler, and potentially reusable for a variety of projects.

Figure 33-4 shows part of an overview of a typical workflow for automated mass-conversion.

The number of workstations deployed for a given function is determined by operational aspects of the project. These include expected accuracy of the OCR process and the breakdown between paper and electronic documents to be converted.

Figure 33-4   Workflow segment for tagging and quality assurance

Integrating legacy data

Application Discussion

- Legacy data defined

- Profiting from the Y2K problem

- Legacy data flow

Contributing expert: Sowmitri Swamy

Chapter

34

The infamous Y2K problem had a secret good side. Because of the efforts made to solve it, enterprises have better knowledge of their legacy data than ever before. This chapter shows how that knowledge can produce valuable XML data and metadata.

The overwhelming fact of legacy data is that there is a lot of it, and it is critical to the operations of the enterprises that own it. It has been a dominant theme in this book, as we have examined the task of dynamic data acquisition in the context of middle-tier servers, e-commerce, portal systems, and publishing.

34.1 | What is legacy data?

Legacy data is data that is generated and used by specific business processes that don't employ the enterprise's current technology. For that reason, the data is not directly available to other processes. The shared data in enterprise databases is *not* legacy data, although it is business process data.

 Caution   Legacy data is not the same thing as legacy documents, which are documents that are either renditions, or are not represented in XML, or both. However, legacy documents usually contain legacy data, which is why there is such interest in converting them to XML abstractions.

34.1.1 *Unlocking legacy data*

Legacy data is a critical revenue-generating asset in many corporations, but for reasons that are largely historical and technological, it is not easily accessed by any application but the one that created it.

Web-enabling of legacy applications and data is a goal of many companies, who look forward to leveraging their legacy data assets by migrating to a Web-based communication paradigm. However, although Web-enabling provides access, it does not necessarily provide knowledge of what the data means. Knowing what the data means leads to methods to transform and use it effectively.

The correct enterprise goal should be to *unlock* legacy data – not only provide access, but also an idiomatic understanding of the data for both human and computer use. Synergy is achieved when legacy data can be accessed, understood and utilized throughout the enterprise in a timely manner.

34.1.2 *The benefit of Y2K*

Such sharing of legacy data as exists in an enterprise is often in a specific context, such as a report, memo, or other document. Documents, however, are usually summaries or extracts from larger data sources and they tend to be formatted to suit the reporting context. Extracting complete data from a rendered document is often difficult or impossible. When it is possible, the data may not be current because of the lead time to produce and distribute the document.

So the only completely reliable means of utilizing legacy data is to go directly to the data itself, which in effect means analyzing the legacy applications that understand its structure and semantics. Fortunately, as a result of the otherwise completely unfortunate Year 2000 (Y2K) bug, enterprises have recently expended vast resources to do just that.

This valuable knowledge is being applied a second time – to making legacy data a sharable enterprise resource through the use of XML. Consultants with extensive Y2K backgrounds are leveraging their Y2K experience to offer a systematic approach to legacy data integration. Their model, called *legacy data flow*, provides conceptual underpinnings and heightened potential for dynamic data acquisition and EDI (see Chapter 11, "XML and EDI: Working together", on page 188).

34.2 | E-commerce with legacy data

Unlocking legacy data for use in e-commerce is valuable for business growth because it provides timely information on products, pricing, policy, and availability. Let's examine some e-commerce applications with an eye towards developing a model of automated legacy data flow.

Figure 34-1 provides a capsule view of the enabling architecture. Two legacy applications are interfaced to an XML-based e-commerce network implementation through special modules, identified in the figure as *metadata engines*.

Figure 34-1   XML-based e-commerce integrates legacy data

The e-commerce network uses XML to convey data and metadata between two XML servers anchoring the e-commerce implementation at either end (represented by the two stubs protruding from the e-commerce box).

The roles played by the metadata engines are critical in the proper functioning of the scheme because their role is to convert between XML metadata and legacy data so that the legacy applications can perform their normal processing.

We will use three simple examples to illustrate the functionality of the metadata engine: Year 2000 compliant dates, euro currency conversion, and inventory part numbers. In all three examples, legacy data is changed in an anonymous manner. That means the legacy applications process data in the formats that they are familiar with; they are unaware of the intermediate transformations into and out of XML.

34.2.1 *Y2K-compliant date exchange*

The solution for bringing legacy systems into Year 2000 compliance involves two major techniques: date expansion and windowing. The "expansion" part of the solution involves prefixing the two-digit year with a two-digit century whenever a date is accessed; the "windowing" part determines which century. A common window is "1930-2029", meaning that two-digit years lower than 30 are treated as occurring in the 21st century.

Note that the "compliance" occurs dynamically in the application software. The storage representation of the date is still two digits.

Consider the case of two compliant insurance applications with different internal date representations that need to communicate with one another. One application uses a flat file to store a policy record with the date in MMDDYY format, as shown in Example 34-1.

Example 34-1. Date stored in legacy flat file

```
...052998...
```

This application is written in COBOL. The code declares the date in the POLICY-ISSUED field of the POLICY-RECORD structure that is partly shown in Example 34-2.

Example 34-2. Legacy COBOL structure for date

```
01 POLICY-RECORD
   ....
   05 POLICY-ISSUED
      10 MM PIC 9(2)
      10 DD PIC 9(2)
      10 YY PIC 9(2)
   ....
```

The two applications interchange dates using the XML representation shown in Example 34-3.

Example 34-3. XML representation of Y2K-compliant date

```
<POLICY>
   ....
   <ISSUE_DATE FORMAT="ISO-8601">19980529</ISSUE_DATE>
   ....
</POLICY>
```

Example 34-4 shows the transformation rules by which the COBOL application's metadata engine produces the date in Example 34-3 from the COBOL record, prior to its transmittal over the XML-based e-commerce network. Note that CC refers to the calculated century prefix.

Example 34-4. Semantic transformation rules

```
<POLICY-ISSUED> => <ISSUE_DATE>
<FORMAT ISO-8601> <= CC&&YY&&MM&&DD
```

The metadata engine for the other application uses similar rules (not illustrated) to convert the XML data into a representation that its legacy application can process.

34.2.2 *International invoicing*

With the advent of the euro, a fourth reserve currency has been added to the current three widely-used reserve currencies: the dollar, the pound sterling and the yen. The XML-based techniques we have been examining can be used to enable legacy applications to handle e-commerce in euros.

Consider a U.S. vendor that must invoice a French customer. In addition to the normal conversion between legacy data and XML, the French metadata engine must convert to euros and add French value-added tax (VAT). The scenario would proceed as follows.

The metadata engine for the U.S. invoicing application converts the legacy invoice to the XML document partly shown in Example 34-5, prior to sending it over the e-commerce network.

Example 34-5. U.S. invoice in XML

```
<INVOICE>
....
<INVOICE_DATE format="ISO-8601">19990621</INVOICE_DATE>
<AMOUNT currency="USD">12000</AMOUNT>
<AMOUNT_DUE currency="USD">12000</AMOUNT_DUE>
....
</INVOICE>
```

The metadata engine for the French accounts payable application first transforms the U.S. XML invoice into the French XML invoice shown in Example 34-6 by applying the following semantic transformations:

- Convert U.S. dollars to euros.
- Compute French VAT tax payable.
- Calculate the total amount due in euros.

Example 34-6. Invoice created by French metadata engine

```
<INVOICE>
....
<INVOICE_DATE format="ISO-8601">19990621</INVOICE_DATE>
<AMOUNT currency="EURO">12600</AMOUNT>
<VAT country="FR" currency="EURO">2520</VAT>
<AMOUNT_DUE currency="EURO">15120</AMOUNT_DUE>
....
</INVOICE>
```

The French metadata engine then converts the French invoice data in Example 34-6 into legacy form (not shown) by applying other transformations, similar to those in Example 34-4.

34.2.3 *Automated bid response*

In this e-commerce scenario, a customer puts forth a list of parts on which it invites suppliers to bid. A vendor chooses from the list only those items that it can supply and submits bids on them.

Example 34-7 shows excerpts from the customer's consolidated list of bid requests. It requests bids on three different sizes of the part numbered "12T20-2".

Example 34-7. Customer's bid request

```
<BID_REQUEST>
<UNIT>MD-STLOUIS</UNIT>
<DEPARTMENT>EN</DEPARTMENT>
<CONTACT>J.DOE</CONTACT>
<TEL>8001111111</TEL>
<EMAIL>JDOE@MD-STLOUIS.COM</EMAIL>
<BID_OOB format="ISO-8601" >19990821</BID_OOB>
....
<ITEMNO>24</ITEMNO>
   <PARTNUM dimension="124">12T20-2</PARTNUM>
   <QUANTITY>2000</QUANTITY>
....
<ITEMNO>52</ITEMNO>
   <PARTNUM dimension="28">12T20-2</PARTNUM>
   <QUANTITY>3000</QUANTITY>
<ITEMNO>53</ITEMNO>
   <PARTNUM dimension="52">12T20-2</PARTNUM>
   <QUANTITY>3000</QUANTITY>
</BID_REQUEST>
```

The vendor's metadata engine extracts the PARTNUM content and dimension attribute value of each item to determine the part numbers and sizes requested. It queries the legacy application to determine which ones the vendor can supply. The application's response is used to prepare the XML bid document shown in Example 34-8.

The vendor uses the same BID document type for all its bids to all its customers, which allows it to use the bid data effectively. As a result, some ele-

Example 34-8. Vendor's bid document

```
<BID>
<CUST>MD-STLOUIS</CUST>
<DEPARTMENT>EN</DEPARTMENT>
<ATTN>J.DOE</ATTN>
<TEL>8001111111</TEL>
<EMAIL>JDOE@MD-STLOUIS.COM</EMAIL>
<DUE_DATE format="ISO-8601" >19990821</DUE_DATE>
<ITEMNO>52</ITEMNO>
   <PARTNUM dimension="28">12T20-2</PARTNUM>
   <QUANTITY>3000</QUANTITY>
<ITEMNO>53</ITEMNO>
   <PARTNUM dimension="52">12T20-2</PARTNUM>
   <QUANTITY>3000</QUANTITY>
</BID>
```

ments that appear in both the bid request and the bid have a different element-type name in each. For this reason, before sending the bid to the customer, the vendor's metadata engine will translate the element-type names CUST, ATTN, and DUE_DATE to UNIT, CONTACT, and BID_OOB, respectively.

34.3 | Legacy data flow

Legacy data flow is a concept that underlies much of the promise of XML, and therefore much of what you have been reading about in this book. It is the notion of making legacy data speedily available wherever it is needed in the enterprise, and in a form that is suitable for use at that point.
   Specifically:

- Data flows from *data generation points* to *data use points* through the enterprise network.
- Data use points determine the usage of the data. The term "usage" includes aggregation, transformation, rendition, and presentation. Therefore, the same data may be used in different ways at different use points.
- *Data semantics* – the meaning assigned to data – determines its usage. Therefore, a data use point may ascribe its own semantics to the data it receives.

- Data flow is autonomous.

There are many advantages implicit in this concept.

- First and most importantly, it provides a conceptual framework in which enterprise data is truly integrated and thereby becomes a competitive advantage.
- Second, it refutes the notion that an enterprise monoculture in terminology, acronyms, etc., is essential to its success. Data is made available to all groups, and each group interprets it in the way that is useful to its process or task. There is a kind of data ubiquitousness that may prove to be the key ingredient of success.
- Third, data use points may use data in multiple ways: to generate documents as input to their applications, for external use such as e-commerce databases, or for statistical purposes such as data mining.
- Fourth, the concept embraces a full range of data atomicity, structure, and type. For example, data atomicity may range from a single product ID to a departmental organizational chart; data structures may range from lists, tables, and tree structures to entire documents; and datatypes may range from conventional numeric data to complex non-numeric data such as company logos.

34.3.1 *Usage scenarios*

In the legacy data flow model, the traditional role of documents as collators and interpreters of data is not diminished; rather it is enhanced. Legacy data flow will simply make documents and enterprise communication more precise, and enterprise processes faster and less prone to errors or delays. The usage scenarios described below illustrate these points.

catalog generation
The enterprise product catalog generation process speeds up due to quicker data updates and less need for manual editing and error checking. The "busy-wait" periods in data exchange between enterprise departments are eliminated.

e-commerce server

The enterprise e-commerce server database can better reflect product availability and pricing changes. This is especially true when complex product configurations or multiple pricing models are involved. Human data entry errors, catalog maintenance delays, and other factors that bedevil product databases are reduced.

corporate merger

A corporate merger can be consummated more efficiently if both corporations' legacy data are organized on legacy data flow principles. Disruption in either partner's operations during the initial days of the merger can be reduced by initially providing bridges between the two data flows. Later, the best practices of each enterprise can be incorporated in the merged organization by retaining the corresponding data flows.

data event reporting

A tripwire reporting facility based on the occurrence or non-occurrence of data events may be implemented. Examples include triggers based on critical parts availability, financial flows, personnel issues, etc. More sophisticated versions may provide a data filtering mechanism based on the semantic content of data such as email.

34.3.2 *XML-based legacy data flow*

XML provides the ideal technology framework for implementing the legacy data flow concept. XML, through its tagged data and metadata structure, provides the means to "describe" the data to each use point. Two items of essential metadata are needed for legacy data to work. XML can be used to describe both. They are:

- Context metadata
- Semantic property metadata

Context is key because the same data may be interpreted differently in different contexts. A use point may therefore use or ignore data depending on context. Context includes such information as the means by which the data was generated (legacy application name, for example), the data generation point, generation date, time, etc. It would also contain the name of a larger data structure of which it is a part.

Semantic property information on the other hand is metadata that is intrinsic to the data itself; it therefore remains unchanged in different contexts. Put in the context of legacy data flow, it is the interpretation of the data according to the data generating point.

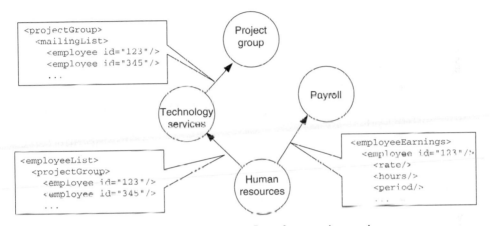

Figure 34-2 XML-based legacy data flow for employee data

Figure 34-2 depicts a simplified partial data flow of employee information between four departments in a corporation: the human resources (HR) department, the technology services department, the payroll department, and the project group. Each arc represents data flow between its end points. On each arc, the context and semantic property metadata are shown as callouts; the actual data is not illustrated.

The information channel can be implemented as a centralized Information channel. The actual flows that occur may occur at different times: possibly bi-weekly between HR and payroll, and at unscheduled times between technical Services and project group. Generally, we can expect today's processes to implement efficient data flow when it is regularly scheduled, as between HR and payroll. However, unscheduled data flows are rarely as successful.

34.3.3 *XML communication server*

One way to implement the concept of legacy data flow is to start with a preliminary list of data elements around which individual flows are then constructed. These flows will be multi-point data flows, unlike the e-commerce examples that we discussed earlier.

Moreover, each data element will have its own individual data flow tree or graph. In addition, we need to decide the mode of initiation of each flow: time-triggered or event-triggered.

To manage these flows simultaneously, we define an *XML communication server*. The XML communication server processes XML metadata just like the metadata engine, so it should not be surprising that many of the functions of the two overlap. Among these are homonymic and synonymic transformations of metadata, data formatting, aggregation, and extraction.

However, managing the individual data flows still remains the most important task handled by the XML communications server. In doing so, it must construct one or more contexts for a given data element at the generation point. Similarly, at each use point, the XML communication server must first evaluate the context, decide the course of action (accept or ignore), extract data and other related information, and then perform the metalanguage transformations necessary to insert the data in the use center's database.

34.3.4 *Data repositories*

The legacy application data repository is a source of information regarding data relationships. Many such repositories were constructed during the analysis phase of Y2K compliance projects. In particular, the data dictionaries are the starting points for building legacy data flows.

Each legacy application has its own data dictionaries, which are relatively isolated from other data dictionaries. In the legacy data flow implementation, care must be taken to ensure that these repositories are not modified in a manner that leaves them incompatible with the legacy applications they serve.

The bridge between these legacy data repositories is the XML communications server metadata repository. This repository consists of one or more metadata dictionaries spanning multiple legacy applications. Data element descriptions, semantic property descriptions, context specifications, and metadata transformation grammars are some of the objects in the metadata repository.

34.4 | Legacy data challenges

Despite the name, legacy applications are not frozen in time, but are continuously evolving. The challenge is therefore in being able to maintain compatibility between legacy data changes and the metadata descriptions of legacy data. Sometimes these changes are very subtle.

For example, the windowing technique described earlier for Y2K fixes involves no change in the structure of the application data, but only in its interpretation. A metadata repository must be able to interpret this change, perhaps at the level of individual date elements.

Another example is where apparently irrelevant data (e.g. COBOL record FILLERS) is interpreted as meaningful data by the legacy application, due to new application enhancements.

High-throughput on-line transaction-oriented legacy systems may pose another challenge. It may be difficult to design XML modules that will provide metadata transformation synchronized to the transaction rate.

Such examples are not rare scare stories, but rather common occurrences in the world of legacy applications. They are the outcome of a requirement to maintain compatibility with "old" legacy data and the systems that rely on it.

Acquiring reusable renditions

Application Discussion

- Faithful rendition
- Enriched content
- Contextual metadata

Sponsor: Liquent, http://www.liquent.com

Contributing expert: Jim Nichols

Chapter

35

One reason for XML's popularity in content management is its ability to preserve abstractions. However, there are situations in which it is important to preserve renditions, but still do all the things with them that a content system can do. Now there are XML-based technologies that allow you to acquire faithful renditions, analyze and enrich them, and manage and manipulate them at the component level. All it takes is the right metadata and the right schema!

B efore SGML and XML became popular there was little or no *content management* in the sense we've been discussing it in this book. That is, there was no ability to manage fine-grained structured abstractions at the component level and assemble and render customized documents on demand.

There were *document management systems (DMS)*, which provided repository functions for whole documents. Their watchword was *print fidelity* – being able to reproduce the exact original printed page from the stored document. There was good reason to promote a capability that many needed, particularly in regulated industries, but it was also pretty much the only thing those systems could do with the data.

But those two extremes leave something lacking: a middle ground that allows component-level access to renditions, with metadata to support document assembly and reuse. And, of course, the sometimes vital ability to reproduce the original rendition with full fidelity.

The technology exists today to address that middle ground, but two key design questions must be resolved:

- How do you harvest the right metadata?
- How do you construct a suitable document type schema?

XML plays a role in the answers to both of them. Let's look at the metadata first.

35.1 | Metadata for reusable renditions

To gather the needed metadata, we first have to find it!

In a typical enterprise, it can occur anywhere along the MOM-to-POP usage spectrum we discussed in Chapter 3, "The XML usage spectrum", on page 60.

35.1.1 *Machine-oriented messaging (MOM)*

MOM information is typically business process data, created and managed within applications. These can include legacy applications and such mainstream systems as enterprise resource planning (ERP) and customer relationship management (CRM).

The vast majority of MOM communication is from one program to another. However, a business often communicates MOM information to people – employees and partners – to support decision-making or to respond to queries. For example, a company might provide a customer with the "current stock levels", or the "contact address" of a particular employee.

MOM information, because it is created by a program, is explicitly marked and has known semantics. As a result, it is easy to harvest as both content and metadata.

35.1.2 *People-oriented publishing (POP)*

POP information could as well exist in paper form as electronic. It is typically created, received, and archived over time by employees, often without central management.

As with MOM information, a business communicates POP information to internal and external audiences to drive decision-making and in response to queries. Examples include:

- a salesperson giving a prospect a sales proposal,

- a customer receiving technical support notes for a product, and
- an employee receiving a health benefits summary during an open enrollment period.

POP information, because it is created by people, is not so rigorous in form or content as MOM information. As a result, much of its metadata is implied, rather than explicitly marked, and different harvesting techniques must be used.

35.1.3 *Content and context*

MOM and POP information both consist of content and metadata in their own right. In addition, the context in which the information is used provides further metadata, generated by the processes that operate on the information.

It is even possible for MOM applications to provide contextual metadata for POP information, as when a word processing document is circulated by email.

To make the most effective use of information assets, metadata must be harvested from both the content and the context.

35.1.3.1 Content metadata

Content metadata includes *structural properties*, which can be derived from the formatting and punctuation. These include elements like headings, paragraphs, and sentences.

Content also has *subject properties*, which must be derived by linguistic and semantic analysis of the data. The analysis can yield keywords, concepts, linguistic properties, and relationships with other content.

The analysis of subject properties also contributes to recognition of structural properties. For example, several contiguous paragraphs on the same topic could be recognized as subelements of a parent "section" element.

Content metadata is what allows information to be divided into components for reuse. It tends to be static, unless the content itself changes.

35.1.3.2   Contextual metadata

Contextual metadata is generated in the course of processing information. It includes properties generated when a document is created and when it is converted to XML. However, unlike content metadata, contextual metadata is dynamic. Each time a document is processed, more metadata is generated.

Contextual metadata can add significant value to a document.

Consider a customer receiving a compilation of technical support notes for various service requests. Each note could contain the identifying number and status of the corresponding service request, obtained from the technical support CRM system.

The customer not only receives the requested technical information, but is also likely to be satisfied that his service request is being looked after efficiently.

35.2 | A schema for reusable renditions

Of course we will use XML to store the content and its associated metadata. To meet our requirements for component-level management of enriched renditions, the document type schema will need to provide for three kinds of information:

faithful rendition
> A perfect rendition of the original content in a form that allows it to be presented on a variety of devices.

enriched content
> The original content, enriched with XML markup containing structural and subject metadata.

contextual metadata
> Metadata inherent in processes that have acted on the content (e.g., "date created" from a word processor; "customers who have received it" from email).

35.2.1 *Faithful rendition*

There are industries in which faithful rendition is crucial, typically those subject to government regulation. One is the pharmaceutical industry.

Consider a new drug application to the US Food and Drug Administration. During the review process, it is quite common for the agency to inquire about particular information contained within the application. If the sponsor and reviewer aren't viewing the information in the exact same format and layout, serious communication difficulties could arise.

This issue is considered so vital that the US regulations governing the process mandate that all paper and electronic copies of applications be identical.

To achieve the required fidelity, a system should begin by using the original software that created the document to produce a rendition that is then converted into XML. Given the astounding variety of document and data object formats in the world, this is a non-trivial task.

For example, the specs for one system, *Liquent Xtent*™, indicate support for 145 formats! The system converts them into an XML-based faithful rendition by utilizing two W3C standards: Scalable Vector Graphics (SVG) and XSL formatting objects (XSL-FO).

35.2.1.1 Scalable Vector Graphics (SVG)

We've previously discussed the difference between *raster graphics*, which are rendered arrays of points, and *vector graphics*, which describe pictures with geometric formulas.

Figure 35-1 shows how a page containing a simple drawing would be represented using a raster notation.

In contrast, SVG is a sophisticated notation that supports vector graphics, text, and even embedded raster images for photographs and the like, all in full color. And all in XML, which is a first for a notation with that kind of graphics expressive ability.

Example 35-1 shows the page in Figure 35-1 as it might be represented in an XML-based vector notation like SVG.[1]

---

1. The example uses simplified element type names and coordinates, not the actual SVG notation. However, it conveys the idea accurately.

```
00000000100000000000000000000000000000000000
00000000100000000000000000000000000000000000
00000000100000000000000000000000000000000000
00000000100000000000000000000000000000000000
00000000100000000111000000000000111111110000000
00000000100000001000100000000010000001000000
00000000100000010000010000000010000001000000
00000000100000010000010000000010000001000000
00000000100000010000010000000010000001000000
00000000100000001000100000000010000001000000
00000000100000000111000000000000111111110000000
00000000100000000000000000000000000000000000
00000000100000000000000000000000000000000000
00000000100000000000000000000000000000000000
00000000100000000000000000000000000000000000
```

Figure 35-1   Raster representation of a page

Example 35-1. XML-based vector representation of the page in Figure 35-1

```
<Page>
  <HSize>44</HSize>
  <VSize>15</VSize>
  <Line>
    <StartX>9</StartX>
    <StartY>1</StartY>
    <EndX>9</EndX>
    <EndY>15</EndY>
  </Line>
  <Circle>
    <CentreX>19</CentreX>
    <CentreY>8</CentreY>
    <Radius>4</Radius>
  </Circle>
  <Box>
    <TopLeftX>31</TopLeftX>
    <TopLeftY>5</TopLeftY>
    <BottomRightX>38</BottomRightX>
    <BottomRightY>11</BottomRightY>
  </Box>
</Page>
```

SVG is an approved W3C Recommendation with strong support and many implementations. It has sufficient expressive power to retain the fidelity of the original rendition for both print and electronic presentation.

35.2.1.2   XSL-FO

SVG is designed to represent a picture accurately and therefore works well for a single page. To handle content that may comprise multiple pages, *Liquent Xtent* employs the XSL-FO standard, which allows document level description of content pages.

A document is described using XSL-FO and each page within the document is described using SVG.

We discuss XSL-FO in more detail in Chapter 63, "XSL formatting objects (XSL FO)", on page 996.

35.2.2 *Enriched content*

The content of a rendition contains data and implies metadata as well. Deriving the metadata and making it explicit enhances the content. There are several techniques for doing this, including analysis of the formatting and the subject matter.

35.2.2.1   Formatting analysis

Formatting is analyzed by examining the same visual cues used by the reader. For example:

- Headings provide the reader with a visual cue to the start of a section in a document. We recognize these headings because they may be underlined, in bold type, in a different font size, or set apart by spacing.
- Paragraphs are recognized by indentions or gaps in the flow of text.
- Sentences are recognized through punctuation.
- Positioning allows us to recognize that a graphic is associated with a particular paragraph.

35.2.2.2   Linguistic and semantic analysis

Analysis of linguistics and semantics requires software that has more intimate knowledge of the content than the software for analyzing formatting. As there is an unbounded variety of content, systems like *Liquent Xtent* allow user-supplied components to participate in the analysis.

One objective of performing linguistic and semantic analysis on a rendition is the detection of information flow, both around objects on the page and across pages. Among other things, the analysis indicates whether objects are related.

35.2.2.3   Representing enriched content

The values of metadata properties recognized by content analysis are frequently data of the content itself. The purpose of the analysis is to make that data's role as metadata explicit by tagging it.

Often, the position of the tags and data is critical to its meaning. For example, hierarchical structure in XML is indicated by the nesting of tagged elements. Similarly, the position of a tagged index term is critical because the page it is on is part of the metadata.

These facts mean that the representation of enriched rendered content must allow for the intermixing of two kinds of markup vocabulary:

basic formatting objects
> These include paragraphs, headings, and graphics, with relationships among them and style properties such as fonts and color. *Liquent Xtent*, for example, uses XHTML for this purpose.

custom vocabularies for linguistic and semantic metadata
> The W3C Recommendation *Modularization of XHTML* allows custom vocabularies to be intermixed in XHTML text. Alternatively, the custom vocabularies can be used exclusively and XSLT stylesheets can be used to generate output for particular output devices. The faithful rendition would still be available when needed.

35.2.3 *Contextual metadata*

Contextual metadata is inherent in the processing of information. It can be harvested at all stages of processing.

To start with, the same technology that enables a system to convert scores of document and data representations to an XML faithful rendition can also gather contextual metadata. For example, *Liquent Xtent* can harvest metadata from a *Word* document that uses heading styles, or that has property values for title, subject, author, and category.

Metadata can also be obtained through interfaces to content management systems, databases, mail systems, and other processes. These can typically be added by users in the same way as analysis components.

Every use of a document presents another opportunity to harvest metadata. Consider a pharmaceutical company that uses a mail system to communicate between doctors and its medical informatics group. Each message can yield metadata on how the document has been used, along with feedback from the doctors regarding the usefulness of the content. The metadata can improve the responses to doctor inquiries.

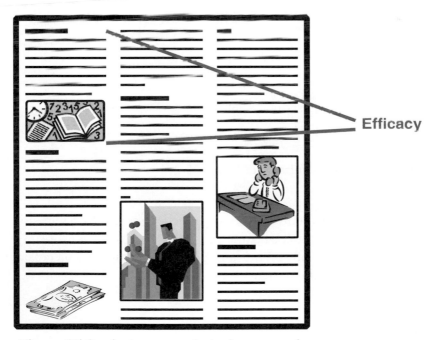

Figure 35-2 A pharmaceutical sales proposal

35.3 | A reusable rendition example

Figure 35-2 depicts a successful presentation made by a pharmaceutical company to a managed care organization. It resulted in the drug being added to the formulary and a percentage increase in the number of prescriptions written.

An XML representation of the enriched content is shown in Figure 35-3. It uses a custom vocabulary to express the structural metadata gathered by the content analysis.

```
<Proposal>
    <Drug Name>New Drug XX</Drug Name>
    <Efficacy>
        <Text>
            <Keywords>infection, congestive heart failure</Keywords>
        </Text>
        <Visuals>
        </Visuals>
    </Efficacy>
    <Customer>
        <Name>HMO One</Name>
        <SizeOfSale>2000000<SizeOfSale>
    </Customer>
    ......
</Proposal>
```

Figure 35-3   XML representation of Figure 35-2

Note the `Keywords` element, which was added as a result of semantic analysis and is part of the enriched content.

The `Customer` element, however, is an example of contextual metadata, acquired from a sales tracking system.

Schemas and Design

- Schema design and development
- Schema management
- Vocabulary development
- XML application design

Part Ten

Nature abhors a schema-less database equally as much as she abhors a vacuum. Create a data table in a spreadsheet and the program immediately searches for field names, and supplies them even if you haven't.

Although XML will let you create a document without an explicit formally-written expression of the document type schema, the benefits of having one are enormous. These chapters will provide insight into schemas, whether you write them using XML DTD declarations, or one of the new schema definition languages.

We start with a hands-on introduction to schema design, focusing on concepts rather than syntax. We then consider the issues of schema management and the enormous impact it can have on your business.

Vocabularies – sets of named element types and attributes – are the building blocks of schemas. Since the vocabulary determines the information that will be available at your portal and for use by your applications, you ultimately have to develop your own. We show you how to get started.

Finally, we examine the complete XML design process. It doesn't end with schemas, it begins with them!

Building a schema for a product catalog

Friendly Tutorial

- ▌ Schema design considerations
- ▌ Step-by-step schema design
- ▌ DTD declarations and schema notations
- ▌ Datatypes

Sponsor: TIBCO Software Inc., http://www.extensibility.com

Contributing expert: Lee Buck

36

The better your schema, the better your data! In the case of product catalogs, you could add: And the better your business! In this chapter we will walk you through the analysis and design of a schema for an online product catalog.

The online catalog is in many respects the heart of electronic commerce. With XML, it can provide a standard and platform-independent way of exchanging information between resellers, manufacturers and customers

Such exchanges can be thought of as information flows between the various organizations. We'll look at one such flow between manufacturers and the folks at a fictitious website called www.we-sell-everything.com.

We'll use a schema to define what information may exist in the flow, where it may appear and how it should be used. This schema establishes a vocabulary by which we can exchange information and a contract that ensures that the information conforms to our expectations. It must reflect the requirements of our product catalog application.

36.1 | Online catalog requirements

Online catalogs have no bounds. Electronic catalogs provide resellers and manufacturers the opportunity to personalize the customer's experience. Rather than merely publishing a conventional print based catalog on the

Internet, our catalog example will use XML to build part of the framework for a catalog application. This application will build upon existing information resources to provide enriched content interaction and access.

Because XML objects are processable both as documents and as data, the catalog can include not only blocks of descriptive text but also database information. The two will allow our site to provide the user with flexible presentation of the information as well as powerful comparison facilities. This content may be in the form of character text and audio and video files.

The components of our online catalog will enable personalized product pricing for prospects and customers. By including promotional codes and rebate information, the reseller and manufacturer gain added pricing flexibility. Additionally, the catalog will link complementary products to create dynamic solution offerings.

By creating an online catalog, results of customer buying habits can be determined quickly. Using the appropriate approach for schema design, changes to the catalog can be deployed quickly, further enhancing results.

36.2 | Design considerations

Schema design involves a number of issues.

Validation

XML DTDs provide a strong foundation for ensuring that all the necessary pieces of information are present at the right places in a document (i.e. required elements are included, inappropriate ones are not, attributes are supplied when required, etc.). DTDs can also offer some help in constraining the value of a particular attribute or data content of an element. (See 36.3, "Datatypes", on page 548.) The *XML Schema* definition language (XSDL) is a more comprehensive language that also offers these facilities.[1]

Modularity

Modular schemas are one of the best means to build a flexible and reusable schema repository. A modular approach to schema

---

1. And lots of other facilities as well. See the advanced tutorial in Chapter 60, "XML Schema (XSDL)", on page 918.

creation delivers application flexibility and component reuse. Libraries of modular schemas can facilitate e-commerce in heterogeneous environments. Taking a modular approach to schema design is an important goal for our little project. In our case it will mean pulling out the notion of an address and placing it into a budding corporate standards schema which will contain such often repeated element types.

Relationship modeling

Schemas provide several facilities to model the relationships between pieces of information. One is the structure of the document: the context in which an element appears. Another is ID/IDREF relationships. These permit all kinds of relationships to be modeled independently of the structure of the document. In our example we'll use these two facilities to model the relationships involved.

Collaboration

Collaborative design efforts help ensure that schemas reflect diverse corporate needs. Schemas will be shared between organizations to help ensure successful e-commerce applications. Resellers and manufacturers will want to collaborate on schemas to establish mutually agreeable rules for data interchange.

Elements vs. attributes

Many pieces of information which we want to model could be represented either as elements or as attributes. While each has its own strengths and limitations, the choice between them is often a matter of style. In our case we'll tend to use attributes for atomic data with a corresponding datatype and use elements for organizing concepts and for representing structures of data items.

Iterative design and schema flexibility

Schemas are living documents that must change as business requirements change. When such change occurs, two sets of compatibility issues arise: a) can existing XML documents be validated against the new schema and b) can existing processes handle documents conforming to the new schema? Careful design can maximize the potential for answering "yes" to both. For our example, we'll design the `promotion` element type to accommodate new kinds of promotions in the future.

36.3 | Datatypes

A *datatype* is a category of information, usually the kind that comes in small pieces and is used to build bigger ones. The examples in Table 36-1 will convey the idea better than any formal definition. They are a subset of those defined in the W3C Datatypes spec (Chapter 59, "Datatypes", on page 888).

Table 36-1   Common datatypes

string	decimal	IDREFS
boolean	float	date
anyURI	integer	time

It is good for a schema to be able to identify and enforce the use of datatypes because it strengthens the contract between the producer and the consumer of an XML document. In e-commerce applications such as our catalog, we need to assure the integrity of the information to the maximum extent possible at the earliest moment. We'll want to specify datatypes for the attribute values in our schema.

36.4 | The design

Our catalog is to come from one or more manufacturers. It needs to contain information about each manufacturer, the products available and any special promotions available for the products.

To build the schema we'll use *XML Authority*™. A trial version is provided on the CD-ROM; it is part of the TIBCO *TurboXML*™ IDE. To follow along, install and open the program and click "New Schema."

36.4.1 *The catalog*

We'll model a catalog as the root element of the document. It contains a repeatable sequence of elements which provide information about each of the concepts: manufacturer, product, and promotion. Our model is as shown in Figure 36-1.

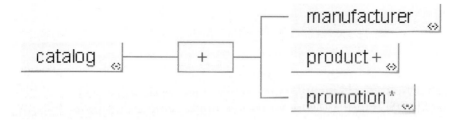

Figure 36-1   catalog **content model** (manufacturer, product+, promotion*)+

Figure 36-1 is produced by *XML Authority*. It provides a concise visualization of the structure of our schema. A brief explanation of its symbology:

- Square brackets represent a sequence of elements
- Angled brackets represent a choice between elements
- Occurrence symbols alone represent grouping of elements
- The icons at the right of an element represent what an element may contain: other elements, untyped character data, or typed data.

A catalog element will need various bits of housekeeping information like its effective date and its expiration date. More robust implementations might well contain routing information, authentication and other bells and whistles but we'll keep it simple. We'll model the dates as attributes as shown in Figure 36-2:

Figure 36-2 illustrates an attributes table in *XML Authority*. If you are following along, bring up the window by clicking "Attribute Types" in the toolbar and enter the information as shown above.

🗋 Attribute Type	Element	Data Type
● date.expires	catalog	date
● date.issued	catalog	date

Figure 36-2   `catalog` attributes

36.4.2 *Manufacturer*

A `manufacturer` element will contain name and address information, as shown in Figure 36-3. The former we'll model as an `ID` attribute type since we need it to uniquely identify a particular manufacturer (see Figure 36-4).

The address information provides a simple example of a powerful concept in schema design: modularization. It enables us to build an inventory of reusable chunks that can be referenced from multiple schemas. The address model shown is rather limited and inappropriate to our global audience. By separating it out into its own schema, we'll be able to isolate the necessary enhancements from our design efforts (as long as they are done in a compatible way).

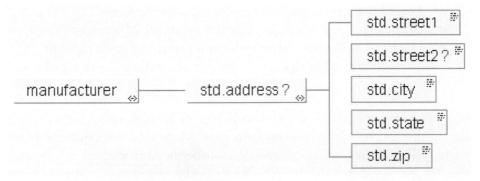

Figure 36-3   Content models of `manufacturer` (`vstd.address?`) and `std.address` (`std.street1, std.street2?, std.city, std.state, std.zip`)

name   manufacturer id

Figure 36-4   `manufacturer` **attributes**

36.4.3 *Product*

The `product` element type provides basics like name, SKU (essentially its bar-code), and SRP (standard retail price). These we'll model as attributes. Importantly, we'll model SKU as an `ID` attribute so we can refer to it later from within a promotion. We can then also use SKUs in a `complements` attribute to refer to other products that are complementary to this product (i.e. taken as a whole they comprise a complete solution). We want to be able to include a picture or other such media about the product so we'll define a `media` attribute that locates such media.

We'll also include a mixed element type for a product description that permits portions of the description to be marked as a feature or a benefit (see Figure 36-5 and Figure 36-6). This simple refinement of the description enables a much richer set of presentation possibilities on our website. More advanced designs would include a much richer set of potential markup here, providing maximum flexibility to our website designers to present the information in various ways.

Figure 36-5   Content models of `product` (`description?`) and `description` (`feature` | `benefit`)*

36.4.4 *Promotion*

Finally we have the `promotion` element type. A `promotion` element may contain information about two different types of price reduction: `bundle`, which provides for a lower price for a particular product when one or more other products are purchased at the same time, and `discount`, which pro-

◆ complements	product	idrefs
◆ media	product	entity
◆ product.name	product	text (cdata)
◆ sku	product	id
◆ srp	product	currency

Figure 36-6   `product` **attributes**

vides volume-based pricing (see Figure 36-7 and Figure 36-8). In the future, as shown in Figure 36-7, `rebate` could be added without affecting existing documents.

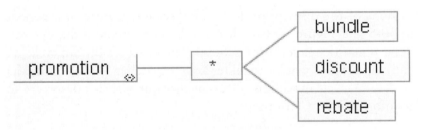

Figure 36-7   `promotion` **content model after adding** `rebate` (`bundle` | `discount` | `rebate`)*

◆ other.skus	bundle	idrefs
◆ sku	bundle	id
◆ price	bundle	currency
◆ sku	discount	id
◆ min.qty	discount	integer
◆ pct.off	discount	float

Figure 36-8   **Attributes of** `promotion` **subelements**

36.4.5 *The big picture*

We did it. Taken as a whole our schema's structure looks like Figure 36-9.

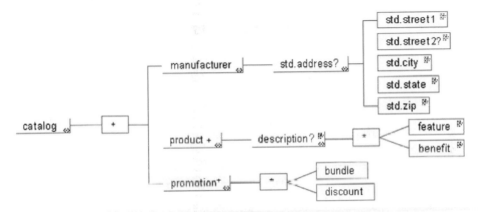

Figure 36-9   Document type structure

36.5 | Schema definition languages

We designed our schema at a conceptual level, using a tool that presented a visualization of the schema definition. Software, however, requires a character string representation of the schema definition. We show several examples in this section. (With *XML Authority*, you can export your schema definition in a variety of notations by choosing "Export" from the File menu.)

36.5.1 *DTD declarations*

In Example 36-1 we can take a look at part of the schema, expressed as DTD declarations. Notice the use of `a-dtype` fixed attributes to specify the datatype for various attributes.

A single `a-dtype` names the datatypes for all of an element type's attributes that need them. In order to link each datatype name with its attribute, the `a-dtype` value is a list of pairs, each attribute name being followed by its datatype name.[2]

Example 36-1. Schema excerpt expressed as DTD declarations

```
<!ELEMENT catalog   (manufacturer , product+ , promotion* )>
<!ATTLIST catalog   date.issued  CDATA      #IMPLIED
                    date.expires CDATA      #IMPLIED
                    a-dtype      NMTOKENS   #FIXED 'date.issued date
                                                   date.expires date'>
<!ELEMENT manufacturer   (std.address? )>
<!ATTLIST manufacturer   name     ID        #IMPLIED >
<!ELEMENT product (description? )>
<!ATTLIST product sku           ID         #REQUIRED
                  product.name  CDATA      #IMPLIED
                  srp           CDATA      #REQUIRED
                  complements   IDREFS     #IMPLIED
                  media         ENTITY     #IMPLIED
                  a-dtype       NMTOKENS   #FIXED 'srp currency'>
<!ELEMENT promotion   (bundle | discount )*>
<!ELEMENT bundle   EMPTY>
<!ATTLIST bundle   price         CDATA      #REQUIRED
                   complements   IDREFS     #REQUIRED
                   sku           ID         #REQUIRED
                   a-dtype       NMTOKENS   #FIXED 'price currency'>
<!ELEMENT discount EMPTY>
<!ATTLIST discount min.qty       CDATA      '1'
                   pct.off       CDATA      #REQUIRED
                   sku           ID         #REQUIRED
                   a-dtype       NMTOKENS   #FIXED 'min.qty integer
                                                   pct.off float'>
```

36.5.2 *XML Schema definition language (XSDL)*

Example 36-2 shows the XSDL version of most of the element types defined in Example 36-1. The XSDL definition is an XML document. Note that the datatype is specified individually for each attribute definition, using the type attribute.

---

2. a-dtype is defined in the W3C Note at
   http://www.w3.org/TR/dt4dtd and is explained in 59.6.3, "XML
   DTDs", on page 916. The CD-ROM contains open source software that
   lets programmers support a-dtype with both the DOM and SAX interfaces.

Example 36-2. Schema excerpt expressed in XSDL

```
<xsd:element name="catalog">
<xsd:complexType>
 <xsd:sequence>
  <xsd:element ref="manufacturer"/>
  <xsd:element ref="product" minOccurs="1" maxOccurs="unbounded"/>
  <xsd:element ref="promotion" minOccurs="0" maxOccurs="unbounded"/>
 </xsd:sequence>
 <xsd:attribute name="date.issued" type="xsd:date"/>
 <xsd:attribute name="date.expires" type="xsd:date"/>
</xsd:complexType>
</xsd:element>
<xsd:element name="manufacturer">
<xsd:complexType>
 <xsd:sequence>
  <xsd:element ref="std.address" minOccurs="0" maxOccurs="1"/>
 </xsd:sequence>
 <xsd:attribute name="name" type="xsd:ID"/>
</xsd:complexType>
</xsd:element>
<xsd:element name="product">
<xsd:complexType>
 <xsd:sequence>
  <xsd:element ref="description" minOccurs="0" maxOccurs="1"/>
 </xsd:sequence>
 <xsd:attribute name="sku" type="xsd:ID" use="required"/>
 <xsd:attribute name="product.name" type="xsd:string"/>
 <xsd:attribute name="srp" type="currency" use="required"/>
 <xsd:attribute name="complements" type="xsd:IDREFS"/>
 <xsd:attribute name="media" type="xsd:ENTITY"/>
</xsd:complexType>
</xsd:element>
<xsd:element name="promotion">
<xsd:complexType>
 <xsd:choice minOccurs="0" maxOccurs="unbounded">
  <xsd:element ref="bundle"/>
  <xsd:element ref="discount"/>
 </xsd:choice>
</xsd:complexType>
</xsd:element>
```

36.5.3 *Microsoft XML-Data*

The manufacturer element type, expressed in the Microsoft XML-Data schema definition language, appears in Example 36-3. As with XSDL, the schema definition is an XML document. The datatype is specified individually for each attribute type definition, using the dt:type attribute.

Example 36-3. manufacturer expressed in XML-Data

```
<ElementType name="manufacturer" content="eltOnly" order="seq">
  <element type = "s:std.address" minOccurs="0" maxOccurs="1"/>
  <AttributeType name = "name" dt:type = "ID"/>
  <attribute type = "name"/>
</ElementType>
```

36.6 | A sample document

A sample document that conforms to the schema looks like Example 36-4. (In *XML Authority*, you can get a head start on such a sample document by choosing Export->Example XML Document from the File menu. It will create a template for you to populate.)

36.7 | Conclusion

Our catalog schema provides the foundation for building an e-commerce website. By formulating and expressing our information flows using XML schemas we are assured that we can connect with our business partners no matter what type of technical infrastructure they may have. We can maxi-

Example 36-4. Sample `catalog` document instance

```
<catalog date.issued = "2001-05-31" date.expires = "2001-06-30">
<manufacturer name = "Stuff-o-rama">
    <std.address>
        <std.street1>127 Walking Way</std.street1>
        <std.city>Chapel Hill</std.city>
        <std.state>NC</std.state>
        <std.zip>27514</std.zip>
    </std.address>
</manufacturer>

<product sku = "12-3783-23" product.name = "foozle" srp = "29.99">
<description>
The foozle is the finest in plastic oven-ware.
Its <feature>patented melt-away containment
</feature>means that <benefit>you'll never have
to wash another dish.</benefit>
</description>
</product>

<product sku = "12-2412-23" product.name = "singey" srp = "19.99">
<description>
The singey aluminum oven mitts are ideal for
accessories for any kitchen. Available in three
sizes with convenient <feature>teflon
coating</feature> to <benefit>ensure a steady
grip.</benefit>
</description>
</product>

<promotion>
    <bundle sku="12-2412-23" price="14.99" other.skus="12-3783-23"/>
    <discount sku = "12-2412-23" min.qty = "10" pct.off = "10" />
    <discount sku = "12-2412-23" min.qty = "20" pct.off = "15" />
    <discount sku = "12-2412-23" min.qty = "50" pct.off = "20" />
</promotion>
</catalog>
```

mize the business impact of the information and respond quickly to new opportunities as they emerge.

> *Tip*   You can get started with schema development using the free trial of XML Authority on the CD-ROM that accompanies this book.

Schema management

- Major Bank
- Centralized schema repository
- Schema development standards
- Cooperative development and reuse

Contributing expert: Priscilla Walmsley

37

Data is precious, and the companies with a lot of it, know it. For them, data format design is solely for the ordained, who are skilled and devoted champions of efficiency through standardization and reuse. But now, thanks to XML, anyone with a text editor can create data formats and the cats are out of the bag. Here's how one company herded them all in the same direction.

The flexibility and extensibility of XML make it a powerful tool for information exchange. But this flexibility can result in chaos if it isn't carefully managed. The Data Management group at Major Bank[1] took a close look at the way XML document types were defined in their organization and did not like what they saw...

37.1 | The situation

Banking is a highly competitive industry where providing customers with accurate, up-to-date information is crucial. Major Bank is involved in a number of XML projects, including online banking, instant credit approval, consolidation of customer statements, and an online concierge service for premier customers.

The document types for these projects, which are highly complex, are mostly developed internally. However, some come from industry standards (e.g. OFX/IFX), business partners, customers, and specific technologies

---

1. A fictional name for a real(ly) major bank!

(e.g. IBM's *MQSeries*). Most projects are currently using DTDs, although some are experimenting with schema definitions.

Data Management at Major Bank is responsible for overall IT standards and architecture. Their main objective is to protect and manage the information assets of the company, and to reduce the costs and risks associated with developing and maintaining information structures.

The Data Management team decided to take a look at the current projects involving XML to determine what types of standards and services would be useful in this area. What they found was a mixed bag of independent XML efforts that were in various stages of development. They had already begun to build legacy XML systems!

37.1.1 *Inconsistent, incompatible efforts*

Six different business units were independently defining XML document types. As a result, many element types were defined redundantly, and in some cases incompatibly. For example, there were four different definitions for the element type address.

This redundancy was a problem for several reasons:

- It will be unnecessarily difficult for these applications to exchange data in the future.
- Extra effort was expended to design the same components twice.
- The groups that developed them did not have the benefit of one another's expertise.
- Redundant or overlapping definitions cause confusion and increase the maintenance effort and learning curve associated with the applications.

37.1.2 *Lack of understanding of existing schemas*

The individual projects had all created DTDs that were stored as plain text files in a variety of places, including various file systems, Web servers, and source code management systems. In many cases, the DTDs were stored redundantly in multiple locations and no definitive version was identified.

Several projects had modularized their DTDs, which is good design, but it was difficult to tell how the pieces related to one another. If a developer modified the contents of one file, he had only a vague understanding of how that impacted the other DTD files in the set.

The documentation for these DTDs was equally elusive. It existed in a variety of formats, including *Word* documents, HTML, PDF, and comments distributed throughout the DTD itself. Some projects had no documentation at all, while others had documentation that was too general to shed light on the individual declarations in the DTD.

37.1.3 Dramatic variations in vocabulary and style

The only consistency in the document types defined by the individual project teams was that they all used more or less correct DTD syntax. The individual DTDs were designed very differently. Some were highly modularized, while others had hundreds of declarations in the same DTD file. Some made heavy use of attributes, while others used none at all.

Most importantly, the vocabulary used in the various DTDs was not consistent. One group's definition of Customer was the same as another group's Applicant. Abbreviations for the same term varied by DTD. Some used user-friendly names, while others used COBOL-like names such as PROD-ORD-NUM.

There were stylistic differences, too. Capitalization varied from uppercase to lowercase to "camel case", even within the same DTD. The use of namespaces was unpredictable at best.

37.1.4 Versions, versions everywhere

Although most of the company's XML projects were in their initial phases, they already had several versions of DTDs in use. The number of versions was expected to increase dramatically as they went live with more projects and added more business partners.

In many cases, these versions would need to be managed simultaneously on an ongoing basis, in order to support different sets of customers. For example, in one project an individual personalized relationship was set up with each customer, which necessitated customized (and not necessarily mutually compatible) extensions for each of them.

In addition, the projects anticipated ongoing changes to all schemas, whether they were developed internally, designed by an industry standards group, or provided by a business partner. The rapid growth of the scope of e-commerce and normal progression in business processes made this instability inevitable.

37.2 | Schema management as a solution

After assessing the situation, the Data Management team determined that they needed a centralized repository to store and manage their XML schemas and DTDs (Figure 37-1).

Figure 37-1   Schema repository

Data Management identified several benefit areas that they expected from this solution.

37.2.1 Schema categorization and documentation

The immediate primary objective was to encourage reuse of schema components among project teams. In order to encourage new projects to use existing DTDs, these DTDs would have to be well-documented and highly accessible to interested parties.

The team first deployed the repository as a tool for user-friendly viewing of existing DTDs, especially very large ones. The tool included the ability to search for DTDs by subject area and keywords. The existing documentation was also incorporated into the schema repository.

37.2.2 Schema relationships

One of the most significant benefits of a centralized schema repository is the ability to see how schemas relate to one another. The Data Management team felt that it was essential to cross-reference element types among multiple schemas, a function provided automatically by the repository. This ability allowed a user to immediately assess the impact of changing an element type on schemas throughout the organization.

Data Management also needed a facility for documenting synonym relationships among element types with different names. Many schemas used by the organization did not conform to the standard vocabulary, especially the industry standard schemas and legacy schemas. Keeping track of the relationships among synonymous element types would further the ability to assess the impact of a change.

The synonym relationships also provided the foundation for more complex transformation relationships among schemas and element types. One project generated XML documents from DB2 and VSAM legacy sources, combined them, and transformed the result into a different XML document that conformed to a schema defined by a credit bureau.

In this case, the schema repository served as a place to define the relationships among these schemas, including the transformation information required to convert documents from one to another. The XSLT for the transformations could then be generated automatically from that information.

37.2.3 *Version control*

Because of the growing web of versions, the Data Management team determined that a centralized approach to schema management would have to include support for versioning. They wanted not only to store multiple versions of a schema, but also to understand exactly what the differences were between them, and whether backward compatibility was maintained.

In many cases, several different versions of a schema would be used in production at the same time by different business partners. These multiple versions of schemas needed to be managed simultaneously.

37.2.4 *Schema standardization*

Another objective of centralized schema management was to encourage consistent style in the many DTDs and schemas that were developed internally. People throughout an organization can more quickly understand DTDs and their conforming XML documents when all schema definitions use the same element type names, with the same capitalization and hyphenation. This consistency in turn reduces maintenance time and costs, allowing the organization to adapt to change more quickly.

It was also expected that standardizing schema creation would help to encourage good schema design practices. Schema designers were likely to mimic the examples of well-designed schemas found in the repository. Additionally, centralized management would give Data Management an opportunity to review the schemas that were submitted to ensure that they were designed well.

37.3 | The plan of attack

After familiarizing themselves with the existing projects and the types of DTDs and schemas that were likely to be created, the Data Management team was ready to define the services and procedures necessary to manage the organization's XML environment.

37.3.1 *Create standards and guidelines*

The Data Management team had no desire to become a roadblock to fast-paced, mission-critical projects. They simply wanted to provide guidance and assistance to those projects. Accordingly, they set up a procedure to perform a design review each time a new schema was submitted to the repository.

A set of design criteria were incorporated into the repository against which schema definitions could optionally be evaluated. Violations are provided in a report. Let's look at the criteria established by Major Bank.

37.3.1.1 Documentation

Is the schema definition properly documented? Could a user who is not familiar with this DTD understand it by reading the documentation?

37.3.1.2 Modularity

Is the schema definition designed as a set of modular, reusable components?

37.3.1.3 Reuse

Does the schema definition reuse existing, approved components wherever possible?

37.3.1.4 Style

Is the style of the schema definition consistent with organizational standards?

- Capitalization: Are element-type names mixed case, starting with a capital letter?

- Special characters: Hyphens are permitted in names; underscores are not.
- Have namespaces been omitted?
- Do any names exceed 32 characters in length?

37.3.1.5   Extensibility

Does the schema definition allow for future extensions? For example, is there a data item defined as an attribute that should be an element type because it may be broken down further in the future?

37.3.1.6   Accuracy

Does the schema definition accurately describe the business rule? The schema designer may not be a DTD expert and may misuse, for example, choice or sequence separators.

37.3.1.7   Wider applicability

There is a temptation to create schemas that are useful only for a specific application purpose. In some cases this may be appropriate. However, there are other times when it is better to create a schema that has broader applicability.

For example, a business unit that handles only domestic accounts might fail to define a `Country` element type as part of an address. They should consider defining it as an optional element for the purposes of consistency and future usability.

37.3.2   *Define a corporate e-commerce vocabulary*

Major Bank had already developed an approved glossary of terms designed to encourage consistent vocabulary in production systems. The glossary, which consisted of data element names, abbreviations, and definitions, was referenced during the creation of databases, program code, and other information structures.

For example, the glossary dictated that all data structures should use the term "customer", abbreviated as cust, instead of client or account_holder.

The Data Management group determined that this same glossary should also apply to the creation of XML schemas and DTDs, ensuring consistent use of terms. As a result, they extended the repository product to allow links to their online glossary.

37.3.3 *Create reusable building blocks*

There is no one "super-schema" that can satisfy the requirements of every group in an organization. Different business units often have conflicting definitions of even the most basic terms, like account, transaction, and customer. Trying to force them to model their data the same way is costly and results either in over-engineered models that try to capture everything, or overly simplistic models that cover only the lowest common denominator.

Therefore, instead of trying to design a universal model for their e-commerce data, the Data Management team decided to think smaller. They determined that the most reusable components were the most atomic, so they set out to build small units that could easily be popped into new applications.

Element types like Address, and ContactInfo were among the first developed. For the most part, these element types were defined using existing corporate entity-relationship models, and in some cases legacy systems. They used a program to convert the models into markup declarations and load them into the repository.

Schema components in the repository are tracked according to their life cycle stage. The glossary-derived element type definitions were identified as being at the "approved" stage, which allowed them to be reused in new projects. Project teams were not forced to use approved element types, but were encouraged to do so and notified when their DTDs missed an opportunity.

37.3.4 *Populate the schema repository*

Data Management next set out to populate the repository fully. They imported all of the DTDs in use in the company into the repository in order to evaluate them against the established design criteria. That enabled them to identify areas where the existing DTDs did not conform to the new company standards. Documentation for the DTDs was imported as well.

Several subject area categories were defined, and each of the existing DTDs was placed into one or more of those categories. This allowed users who were interested in finding and reusing schema components to search for them by subject area. The documentation could also be used as the basis for searching.

37.3.5 *Organize for future growth*

The Data Management team realizes that the use of XML in Major Bank will explode in the next several years. Therefore, they set out to organize roles and responsibilities to support this future growth.

The roles include a schema administrator who maintains the contents of the schema repository, a trainer who provides general XML courses, and a subject matter expert in schema design. The team also developed detailed procedures for the use of the schema repository in a complex, multi-version environment.

37.4 | Conclusion

Data Management's strategy was to become a service provider. They had neither the authority nor the desire to force project teams to conform to their standards. The fast-paced environment in which systems are developed today would not allow that.

Instead, the group established itself as a resource for the design, reuse, and understanding of Major Bank's schemas. In doing so, they created an XML environment that is less costly to maintain and expand, better integrated into the organization's business processes, and easier to tailor to individual customer needs.

Building your e-commerce vocabulary

Tool Discussion

- Creating a schema
- Capturing business semantics
- Reuse for e-commerce

Contributing expert: Priscilla Walmsley

Chapter 38

> Your computers may walk the walk, but can they
> talk the talk? In today's e-commerce, just as in human
> discourse, vocabulary is vital. Your computer and
> those of your business partners might speak the same
> language – XML, of course – but do they attach the
> same meaning to the words? Let this chapter be your
> guide to straight talk!

he people in your company have a vocabulary that they use
when talking about your business. Words like *part*, *adjust-
ment*, and *transaction* have a specific meaning when used in
the context of your organization, and they're not just meaningful to people.

38.1 | Why do you need an e-commerce vocabulary?

Your specialized company vocabulary might have developed initially as
purely human discourse, but information systems have since influenced it
and made it more structured and precise. While developing those systems,
users, programmers, and data analysts have painstakingly documented the
terms and data elements used in your business. They have described what
the words mean, how they relate to one another, what type of data they represent, and how to determine that data's validity.

Now e-commerce challenges us to share data with external business partners, customers, and suppliers. That means all parties must be using the
same words to ensure that they understand each other. In XML terms, they
must agree on schemas that define those words: the corporate e-commerce
vocabulary.

38.2 | Where do schemas come from?

Sorry to say, the stork doesn't bring them. You either have to build them or
borrow them.

38.2.1 *Building a new schema*

In some cases, your organization will have the luxury of defining the schemas that are to be used for data interchange with your trading partners.
This may be the case if you are a large organization with many small trading
partners.

We call this a luxury because there are lots of ways to model data. It is
certainly convenient if you have the opportunity to use a vocabulary and
data structure that closely match your own.

Consider two possible variations in something as elemental as telephone
contact information, for example.

1. One way to model the phone number would be to allow for
   two specific phone numbers: day and evening. Many systems
   are currently designed this way.
2. Other systems may be designed to allow an unlimited number
   of phone numbers, with a description for each (e.g. "home",
   "mobile", "office", "pager", etc.).

To complicate things further, a different vocabulary might be used in
each of these models. One may use the term "business phone" to represent
what the other system calls "office number". Neither of these approaches is
necessarily better, just different.

Being the creator of the schema reduces the amount of work required to
convert your existing data structures to XML documents. For example, if

you used the second model in your database and you had to use someone else's schema that was based on the first model, you would need to search through your data for each "home" phone number and convert it to "evening". Although this task may seem trivial taken alone, hundreds of these minor conversions require time to analyze and process.

Another benefit of owning the vocabulary is that the people in your organization will understand it intuitively and find it easier to assess the impact of a change. Also, if you eventually open up your schema to competing companies, they will have the extra task of converting their vocabulary to match yours.

38.2.2   Borrowing an existing schema

In many cases, you will not be creating the schemas you will use for interchange with other parties. Instead, you will be using schemas defined by an industry standards group, trading partner, or vendor. In this case, it may seem that capturing your own corporate vocabulary is less important, since a vocabulary is already provided for you. This is a fallacy.

It is essential to understand the interface between your own systems and the data you share with your trading partners. You won't be revising your internal systems to conform to the interchange schemas. Rather, you will be converting data back and forth between your internal systems and the external ones, and all the schemas will be subject to change over time.

Developing your internal vocabulary for e-commerce allows you to split the problem into two independent parts:

1. Capturing your existing data and metadata in its original format and translating it to XML using a vocabulary you understand; and
2. Translating the semantic meanings from one XML schema to another.

38.3 | Capturing existing business semantics

You may recall that we said earlier that, while developing your systems,

... users, programmers, and data analysts have painstakingly documented the terms and data elements used in your business. They have described what the words mean, how they relate to one another, what type of data they represent, and how to determine that data's validity.

That's the good news!

The bad news is that your corporate vocabulary is probably not neatly documented in a single place, but rather embedded in legacy systems on various platforms. These legacy systems are often cryptic, but they contain the key to understanding the data that will be exchanged.

A vast resource of information about your business processes exists embedded in your legacy systems and models. The reason for building an e-commerce vocabulary is to expose this system information, or metadata, and thereby allow it to be used easily in e-commerce applications.

Fortunately, there's more good news: Business semantics gathering tools can scan existing systems and models and unify them in a common, tree-structured XML-based model. Let's see how that is done.

38.3.1 *Relational databases*

A large percentage of the data that is to be used in e-commerce applications currently resides in relational databases. These databases were designed by database administrators and developers who understood the business logic behind the data.

The catalogs of relational databases precisely describe the data they contain. From an ODBC data source, a semantics gathering too should be able to extract relational database information, including table layouts, table and column descriptions, datatypes, and primary and foreign keys.

38.3.2 *Electronic data interchange (EDI)*

The EDI standard dictionaries provide a semantically rich model for e-commerce. If your organization is using EDI, chances are many of your existing processes use the EDI vocabulary, or at least understand it.

Much of the semantics of the EDI standards can be leveraged for use in XML-based e-commerce systems. For example, EDI defines thousands of atomic data elements in detail, including lengthy lists of valid values for each one. There is no need to throw this information away and start from scratch.

Example 38-1 shows how XML can represent EDI semantics.

Example 38-1. Excerpt from a schema definition of an ANSI X12 EDI data element

```
<simpleType name="element-482">
<annotation>
  <documentation>Payment Action Code</documentation>
</annotation>
<restriction base="string">
  <maxLength value="2" />
  <enumeration value="AJ">
    <annotation>
      <documentation>Adjustment</documentation>
    </annotation>
  </enumeration>
  <enumeration value="ER">
    <annotation>
      <documentation>Evaluated Receipts Settlement</documentation>
    </annotation>
  </enumeration>
  <enumeration value="FL">
    <annotation><documentation>Final</documentation></annotation>
  </enumeration>
  <enumeration value="NS">
    <annotation>
      <documentation>Not Specified</documentation>
    </annotation>
  </enumeration>
  <enumeration value="PA">
    <annotation>
      <documentation>Payment in Advance</documentation>
    </annotation>
  </enumeration>
  <enumeration value="PO">
    <annotation>
      <documentation>Payment on Account</documentation>
    </annotation>
  </enumeration>
  <enumeration value="PP">
    <annotation>
      <documentation>Partial Payment</documentation>
    </annotation>
  </enumeration>
</restriction>
</simpleType>
```

38.3.3 *Program data structures*

Large mainframe files contain most of the production data that is not stored in relational databases. Programmers have written complex *copybooks* to represent this data, including names and datatypes of the elements in these files, and valid values in some cases. A gathering tool should be able to parse a copybook and match it to a corresponding XML tree structure.

38.3.4 *Logical models*

Your company may have logical models of your business systems and processes. These models have additional descriptive information to supplement your corporate e-commerce vocabulary.

For example, a database administrator may have created an entity-relationship model of a database for an accounting system. The model contains detailed information about each column in the database, including use cases, examples, and valid values. A business semantics gathering tool should incorporate such models into your e-commerce vocabulary.

38.3.5 *Repositories*

Some organizations have already put a lot of effort into capturing and managing their corporate metadata. These organizations have built metadata repositories, which centrally store system information such as database layouts, copybook structures, and logical models. The tool should leverage these efforts by extracting metadata from commercially available repository products.

38.3.6 *Customized sources*

Many organizations have metadata stored in proprietary or less-common formats. For example, some systems may be documented in customized HTML files. A business semantics gathering tool should be extensible to handle these situations; for example, by means of scripts or plug-in modules that understand unsupported data formats.

38.4 | Reuse for e-commerce

After capturing the existing semantic business definitions, the next step is to make them useful for e-commerce systems.

38.4.1 *Editing and refining*

Because descriptive data is often incomplete, or is merged from many sources, some manual refinement might be required. It is helpful if your semantics gathering tool allows editing of the descriptive information in the new XML data definitions.

38.4.2 *Schema generation*

After the descriptive information has been refined, users can generate DTDs and schema definitions that incorporate the new vocabulary. These DTDs might represent only fragments of complete document types.

For example, a schema generated from a relational table may contain customer header information only. This is desirable, since schemas are more likely to be used and reused if they are modular. An XML document could contain data from many different subject areas (e.g. customer information, sales data, and product information), and several XML documents might use the same customer information.

38.4.3 *Managing the vocabulary*

Capturing your existing vocabulary and preparing it for e-commerce is an important initiative. However, the bulk of the effort is wasted if that vocabulary languishes in text files somewhere and is never reused.

It is important to provide access to the corporate e-commerce vocabulary so that it can be understood and reused freely. There are schema repositories that allow you to store and manage the definitions centrally.

XML design

Tool Discussion

- Integrated Development Environment (IDE)

- DTD and schema design

- Stylesheet design

- User interface design

- Software on CD-ROM

Sponsor: Altova, http://www.xmlspy.com

Contributing expert: Alexander Falk

Chapter

39

One important benefit of XML for application developers is that it permits a clean separation of design from programming. Most aspects of XML design can be represented in XML documents: DTDs, schema definitions, XML templates, stylesheets – even some user interfaces. In this chapter we'll look at these documents and the tools for creating them.

ML documents are the key to XML applications – not just as data that applications process, but as the specifications that control the execution. These documents possess all the benefits of XML, a notable one being that they can be created and revised with common text editing tools.

But since XML data lends itself so well to sophisticated content processing, it is logical to ask whether content systems can be used for XML specifications as well.

39.1 | Integrated Development Environment (IDE)

Program developers have long employed a specialized form of content system called an *Integrated Development Environment (IDE)*. Such systems provide a framework for managing the source code associated with a programmer's part of a project and controlling execution of the tools he needs. These may include a source code editor, a compiler, and an interactive debugger with which he can interact with the running program. Programming IDEs often have an open architecture that allows the use of tools other than the built-in ones.

IDEs are now available for XML designers as well. As they offer interesting and often powerful alternatives to text editors, we'll use one to illustrate this chapter. The product is the *XML Spy Suite* from Altova, which incorporates an IDE and some additional tools.

As an example, we will design an application for publishing datasheets for a family of aircraft.

39.2 | DTD and schema design

We've been looking at schema design in detail in this part of the book, so here we'll just touch on it briefly in the context of the overall application design process.

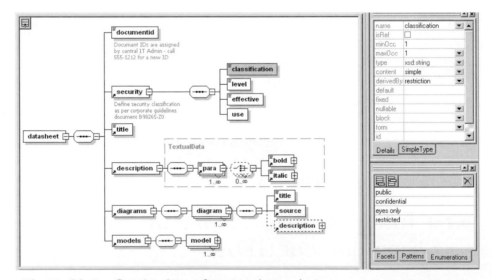

Figure 39-1   Graphical interface to schema design

The first step is to create a DTD or schema definition that will accommodate all the information we need to include in our datasheet. The designer must identify all of the data elements needed and define content models and attributes for them.

In this case, we also want some automatic consistency checking functions without having to build them into application code. For example, we want to assure that the data content value of the MaxPassengers element must be in the range of 200 to 600. We therefore decide to use the *XML Schema definition language* (XSDL), which offers this facility.

Figure 39-1 shows a visual interface for schema design. To define the content model, the user can manipulate the graphical representation directly using drag and drop utilities, as well as by modifying element type properties using the property windows on the right. This hides much of the complexity of XSDL, and enables the designer to focus on the semantic aspects of the design.

A schema editor typically offers both graphical and textual views, and supports several schema languages and conversions among them. A schema editor could also support the generation of content model documentation in several formats (e.g. HTML, *Microsoft Word*) and include graphics, source text, annotations, and cross-references.

Figure 39-2   XSLT stylesheet generator

39.3 | Stylesheet design

We next need to create XSLT stylesheets for each environment in which the datasheets will be published. We'll do the first one for a desktop Web browser, using HTML as the target rendition language. For a printed book we might have wanted XSL-FO, or WML for a wireless device.

Figure 39-2 shows a visual XSLT design tool. The content model tree for datasheet is on the left and a rendered template appears in the design pane on the right. This display enables users to drag and drop element types from the tree view directly into the design pane. Individual element types or groups of them can be selected in either pane and styling can be applied directly to the selected items.

The design pane constantly reflects the visual characteristics of the stylesheet. Text and graphical design elements can be entered into it directly, thereby adding *boilerplate* to the stylesheet; that is, rendered material that is not bound to a specific XML document instance.

Figure 39-3   Stylesheet editor for developers

Figure 39-3 is an excerpt from a stylesheet that might have been generated from Figure 39-2. For a complex stylesheet, operating with this interface is more in the realm of programming than design. However, it may be necessary in order to accomplish results that can't be expressed graphically. An IDE can make the task easier through auto-completion and intelligent editing facilities that provide information about available XSL instructions, as well as HTML elements, attributes, and entities.

39.4 | Test case editing

To test our stylesheet we'll need to create some actual aircraft datasheets. We could, as always for XML, use an ordinary text editor or word processor in plain text mode.

But as XSLT stylesheets and XSDL schema definitions are XML documents, an IDE that offers textual editing tools for those document types will normally handle arbitrary types. That means designers can use the IDE editor to create test cases.

XML Spy, for example, has that facility, but it also offers another view that may be of interest to designers. This "enhanced grid" view is shown in Figure 39-4. It can display any sequence of repeating elements as a table, with attributes and sub-elements shown as columns. Notice the modification elements at the bottom of the main pane.

39.5 | User interface design

The tech writers and engineers who will create datasheets in a production environment will typically prefer to see the documents in rendered form, rather than deal directly with the XML markup. One possible visual editing interface for datasheets is shown in Figure 39-5. It was generated from the previously designed schema and stylesheet.

In addition to rendering the content as it is entered, the software validates the document in real time and lists currently valid element types in the upper right pane. It also validates datatype constraints in the schema. If a user were to mistakenly enter 3000 instead of 300 for the number of passengers, an error would be flagged.

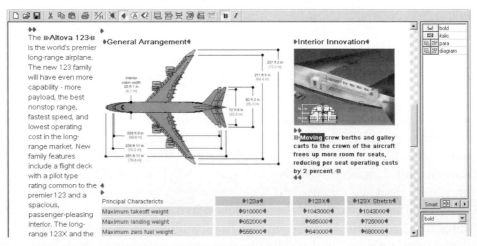

Figure 39-4   Enhanced grid view

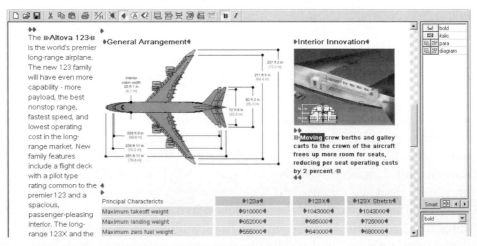

Figure 39-5   Stylesheet-driven user interface

Other choices for interface design include whether and how to display tags, whether to display the list of allowable element types, appropriate toolbar buttons and menu commands, etc.

39.6 | Storage and management

As with any content processing effort, XML application design requires a means of storing and managing project documents. An IDE may offer some project-based document organization, but it normally relies on external repositories for storage, access control, versioning, and other management functions.

Figure 39-6 Project view with external repository access

Figure 39-6 shows a hierarchical organization of project documents on the left and the details of the selected document on the right. The pop-up window is the interface to an external repository that controls access to the documents.

Depending on the IDE, such repositories could take many forms, including:

- Source control systems, as used in program development.
- XML content and database management systems.
- Schema management systems.
- WebDAV servers.
- ODBC-compliant database systems (with conversion transforms).

39.7 | Conclusion

In this chapter we have looked at XML design for an aircraft datasheet application. Much of the design was recorded as XML documents – schema definitions, stylesheets, test cases, etc. – which makes the design process, in effect, an XML content processing application.

Software development in general has been treated as a content processing application for many years. Developers have employed products called "Integrated Development Environments (IDE)" as a specialized form of content processing system. Now these systems are available for XML design as well. We used one to show how specialized XML-aware editing and design tools can enhance XML application design.

 Tip   You can get hands-on experience with XML design using the trial version of XML Spy that is available on the CD-ROM.

Voice

- VoiceXML
- Voice in a mobile environment
- Adding telephony to websites

Part Eleven

One of the prized souvenirs of markup language pioneers is a coffee mug that states "SGML spoken here". The joke, of course, is that SGML, like modern Latin, is strictly a written language.

Linda Goldfarb used to embroider that statement onto bibs for SGML community newborns. The joke there was that any sounds uttered by the bib wearer were as likely to be SGML as any other language.

The SGML community's latest newborn – we refer now to XML still can't speak for itself. But increasingly it is becoming the means of controlling what is spoken. XML-based languages like VoiceXML, coupled with advances in speech recognition and synthesis, are making the Web a spoken medium. In this part you'll learn how to voice-enable your website, and how XML can be a vehicle for voice control – or voice control for a vehicle!

VoiceXML in a mobile environment

Case Study

▌ Introduction to the VoiceXML language

▌ Architecture of a VoiceXML application

▌ A moving case study

Sponsor: IBM Corporation, www.alphaWorks.IBM.com

Contributing experts: Chuck Lam, Ying Lee, Lucas Ryan and Daniel Jue

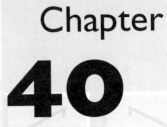

40

Keyboards and mice are hardly a natural way to communicate, as anyone with carpal tunnel syndrome can tell you! What people are really good at is talking, and computers finally have the hardware that lets them understand and talk back. Now XML is making it easier to program that hardware, driving new applications and giving a whole new meaning to the term "mobile environment".

endors would like us to become dependent on ubiquitous computing and information services. They want us to manage emails, check stock quotes, and do other tasks at any time, anywhere.

But early adopters are finding that miniature screens, micro keyboards, and stylus scribbles are not the ideal interface. They are impediments to widespread utilization of ubiquitous services.

Fortunately, improvements in speech recognition and automated text-to-speech technologies are finally making voice interfaces feasible. The challenge now is making them easy to develop.

In this area, as in so many others, XML is coming to the rescue, here in the form of *Voice Extensible Markup Language (VoiceXML)*. VoiceXML is an XML-based markup language for developing voice applications. It was defined by the *VoiceXML Forum* (`http://www.voicexml.org`), an industry consortium of over 300 companies.

40.1 | Why VoiceXML?

VoiceXML is attractive to developers for many reasons. Some of the major ones are:

- It abstracts away the complexity of speech processing from application developers. The application developer does not need to know anything about the signal processing techniques to make speech work.
- It is based on the client-server architecture of the Internet, and its component architecture is similar to many existing Web technologies.
- A VoiceXML application can share the back-end infrastructure of a graphical Web application, particularly if the back-end data layer is based on XML.
- VoiceXML allows portable applications that can scale from small-footprint speech processing systems like IBM's *Embedded ViaVoice* to full-blown speech servers, such as IBM's *Websphere Voice Server*.
- Numerous VoiceXML outsourcers (*voice portals*) will host the speech processing system and telephony equipment for application developers.

Today the most popular voice applications are interactive voice services (IVR) using the telephone. These include voice dialing, information retrieval such as voice-mail management, and transactions such as stock trading.

These are popular initial applications because:

- their limited vocabulary is well suited for highly accurate speech recognition, and
- the expensive hardware (speech recognizer, text-to-speech generator, etc.) can be centralized and amortized among many users.

40.2 | Components of a VoiceXML application

Figure 40-1 illustrates a typical VoiceXML application architecture. Its main components are:

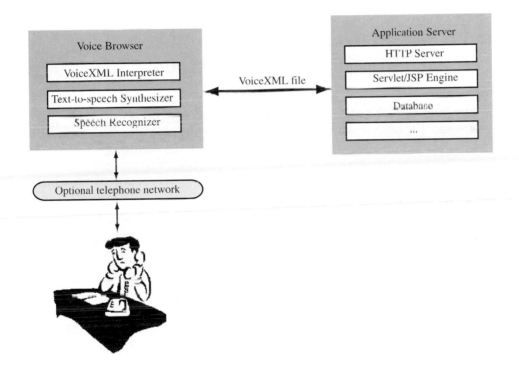

Figure 40-1 A typical VoiceXML application architecture

application server
> It hosts the application logic and serves the appropriate VoiceXML files.

VoiceXML file
> Like an HTML file, a VoiceXML file specifies what to present and the allowable inputs from the user.

Voice browser

It is analogous to an HTML browser. It renders the speech and converts the user's voice input into a machine-understandable form. The browser and end user might require a telephone network to communicate.

Let's look at each of these components in more detail.

40.2.1 *VoiceXML file*

A VoiceXML file is an XML document conforming to the VoiceXML DTD. A partial example is shown in Example 40-1.

The top-level element types, such as `form`, are called *dialogs*. They are composed of `field` elements, which specify audible prompts and the `grammar` of user inputs that can validly respond to the prompts.[1]

40.2.2 *Application server*

The back-end database and application logic are exactly the same as for a graphical Web application. They can be developed using familiar technologies such as a Java servlet/JSP engine, a Web server using the HTTP or HTTPS protocol, and a conventional DBMS.

The presentation layer, however, now renders the output as a VoiceXML file instead of HTML. If the application content is already in XML, the change to the presentation layer may be as simple as specifying a different XSLT stylesheet.

---

1. The notation for grammars is not defined by the VoiceXML spec, which considers them comparable to graphic formats; vendors define their own. The content of the `grammar` element in this example is character data. The strings that look like `option` tags are not actually XML.

40.2.3 *Voice browser*

The Voice browser does the heavy-duty work of speech processing and interpretation of VoiceXML files. It thereby frees application developers from the complexity of speech recognition and text-to-speech processing.

The user interacts with the browser in much the same way as with an HTML browser, except now the user "views" the content verbally instead of visually. Some voice browsers even support the navigation concepts of HTML browsers, such as bookmarks, "go back", and "go forward".

There are even full-duplex voice browsers that allow a user to *barge in*. That is, the user can issue a command or a response before the browser has finished speaking. In older half-duplex systems, the user must wait for the prompts to complete before speaking. The barge-in feature allows experienced users of an application to navigate rapidly, while still allowing novices to be guided by prompts.

40.3 | A VoiceXML case study

We've previously discussed the vital role XML plays in automotive documentation. You could, if you were as inclined to bad puns as we are, call it a "driving force", a technology that accelerates in the parsing lane, etc.

But VoiceXML is leading us to even greater transports of inspired wordplay, and to some inspired technology as well. We'll[2] now look at an application that adds a new component to the concept of a mobile environment – self-propulsion!

40.3.1 *The IBM alphaWorks TechMobile*

The automobile is a natural environment for voice technology. A driver should keep eyes on the road and hands on the wheel, so exclusive dependency on a graphical user interface isn't feasible.

To demonstrate how its technologies can work in this setting, IBM alphaWorks has created the *TechMobile*, shown in Figure 40-2.

---

2. Please admire our restraint: we might have said "wheel"!

Figure 40-2   The *TechMobile*

40.3.2 *Features*

The voice controller inside the *TechMobile* utilizes IBM's *ViaVoice* for speech recognition and text-to-speech processing. It supports the following functions:

- Check email.
- Control the car's MP3 player.
- Lock and unlock the car doors.
- Flash the headlights.
- Control the air conditioning system, including fans.
- Raise and lower the windows.

And just for fun, one can activate a voice-controlled number-guessing game by saying "I'm bored."

The same functions are also accessible through an onboard touch-sensitive screen that acts as an HTML browser interface. Because of modular architecture and VoiceXML's hiding of the underlying speech processing, much of the application logic is shared by the HTML interface and the VoiceXML interface.

40.3.3 *Architecture overview*

The architecture of voice applications for a car differs from that of voice applications for phones in several aspects. One is that a phone is a "thin" client, whereas a car is a "thick" client. That is, phones are more constrained in terms of physical size, power consumption, and price, which in turn affects the available computational power, memory size, etc.

Because of these constraints, the voice browser in a telephony application typically acts as a proxy and resides separately from the phone client itself. In a car environment, however, the voice browser can be installed internally.

Moreover, as most functions of the application server are for controlling the car itself, it makes sense to design the system so that all components are inside the car. Doing so limits the use of wide area wireless networks (which can be unreliable) to functions like email that inherently require them.

VoiceXML makes such a distributed architecture possible without painful trade-offs. The voice browser and all application logic for controlling the car, including the server, are inside the car; in effect, they form an intranet.

External application services, such as email, are hosted remotely from the car. VoiceXML has a linking feature that enables both internal and external services to be presented to the user as a seamless whole.

40.3.4 *How the system works*

Example 40-1 is an edited skeleton of the actual VoiceXML text used in the *TechMobile*. It is activated when entering the car.

The first form element, named "Introduction", greets the driver with the words:

> Welcome to IBM alphaWorks *TechMobile*. You can control different functions by voice command.

The goto element then directs the browser to the next form, called "ChooseFunction", which begins by defining a grammar of valid user inputs.

The grammar also indicates whether any inputs are considered synonymous by the application. For example, the inputs "mail" and "email" both

Example 40-1. A VoiceXML application

```
<?xml version="1.0"?>
<vxml version="1.0">
<form id="Introduction">
  <block>
    <audio>Welcome to I.B.M alphaWorks TechMobile.</audio>
    <pause>200</pause>
    <audio>
      You can control different functions by voice command.
    </audio>
    <pause>200</pause>
    <goto next="#ChooseFunction"/>
  </block>
</form>
<form id="ChooseFunction">
  <field name="function">
    <grammar><![CDATA[
      [
        [mail email]                         {<option "EMAIL">}
        [music mp3]                          {<option "MUSIC">}
        [door doors]                         {<option "DOORS">}
        [headlights headlight light lights] {<option "HEADLIGHTS">}
      ]
    ]]></grammar>
    <prompt>
      <audio>
        Please choose a function. Doors, MP3, headlights, or email.
      </audio>
      <pause>2000</pause>
    </prompt>
    <filled>
      <result name="DOORS">
        <audio>You selected doors.</audio>
        <goto next="#ControlDoor"/>
      </result>
      <result name="EMAIL">
        <audio>You selected email.</audio>
        <goto next="http://email.server.net/servlet/CheckEmail"/>
      </result>
      ...
```

select the same option, "EMAIL". Similarly, both "music" and "mp3" select the "MUSIC" option.

The "ChooseFunction" form next prompts the user to:

Please choose a function: doors, MP3, headlights, or email.

As the voice browser supports the barge-in feature, the user can respond with a selection before hearing the complete prompt.

The `filled` element contains a `result` for each selectable function. The `result` confirms the user's choice audibly (`audio`) and directs the browser to `goto` the associated `form`.

For internal functions, the `form` can be in the same VoiceXML file, as is the case for "ControlDoor". For external services, like "EMAIL", the location of the `form` is specified by a URI.

40.3.5 *Conclusion*

Cars and computers have been talking back to us for a long time. Now they are starting to listen to, and understand, us as well. Although the hardware and software for low-level voice control are complex, VoiceXML can hide that complexity from the application developer.

As a result, voice-based interfaces are becoming more prevalent. And, as the *TechMobile* demonstrates, even if they can't yet drive towards a brilliant future by themselves, they can at least make sure the doors are safely locked for the journey!

 Tip   IBM alphaWorks has provided a suite of free software for you on the CD-ROM.

Adding telephony to your website

Case Study

- **▌** Human/machine dialog
- **▌** Interactive voice systems
- **▌** Telephony application development
- **▌** Building a customer notification system

Sponsor: Voxeo Corporation, http://www.voxeo.com

Contributing expert: Lee Anne Phillips

Chapter 41

Can we talk? Well, if one of us is human and the
other a computer, probably not. At least not in any
meaningful way. But recent advances in voice
recognition and synthesis, telephony switches, and
XML-based languages are leading us toward true
dialog – and a new definition of what it means to have
XML call out to you!

Personalized dialog – directed at ourselves alone – is the most
engaging form of verbal communication. Voice-enabled computers, however, typically just parrot monologs. Now new
technology, based on XML, is letting computers take the first steps toward true dialog. The dialog is conducted by telephone, and one of the
parties can be your website.

41.1 | The need for human/machine dialog

There is a growing dependency on self-service in most of our day-to-day
business transactions. From supermarkets to gas stations, from parking
meters to banking at the automated teller machine, the only interaction
with human beings most of us have while shopping is with the clerk at the
checkout stand.

In fact, in many stores it's difficult even to find a human being not
actively involved in taking money from customers. This is commerce pared

down to its bare essentials, with every resource being dedicated to supplying goods for a price, and as little as possible spent on ancillary activities.

But we often need advice or information along with our purchase, or want a service instead of goods. The new self-service paradigm often precludes any such interaction without waiting in a long queue.

And if that queue is for telephone support, it is punctuated at best by cheery messages describing the approximate wait time, and at worst by inane insistence on offering unwanted automated service instead.

But phone calls don't have to be this one-sided.

41.2 | Interactive voice systems

While we're still some years away from talking freely to our computers with the expectation of a coherent reply, the conversation has become far less one-sided. Advances in automated speech recognition and speech synthesis make it at least possible to give a simple order, with a reasonable expectation of a simple action or report being generated in response.

We're seeing this happen in several areas, including:

interactive voice response (IVR)
> Auto-attendant, telesales, telephone banking, call center integration, self-help menus and fax-back services, teleconferencing, and automatic callback.

Web by telephone
> Calendars and contacts, FAQs and support content, weather, travel directions, stock quotes, personalized news, directories, and listings.

personal communications
> Follow-me/find-me, Internet call waiting, intelligent call forwarding, email by phone, reply by phone, voicemail replacement, and unified messaging.

instant notification

Travel information, consumer and business auctions, stock trades and price changes, important email, network equipment failure, meetings and appointments, and instant messaging.

41.3 | Telephony application development

One of the inhibitors to better computer telephony has been the cost and difficulty of implementation.

Until recently, the total number of qualified telephony application developers in the world numbered in the thousands. Developing an application and tying it to corporate data was an arduous and expensive process, typically involving:

- Proprietary hardware with dedicated telephone interface cards.
- Proprietary APIs requiring knowledge of telephony.
- Programming without visual program design tools.
- Platforms that did not include interfaces to provisioning or billing services.
- Direct interaction with multiple regional telephone companies and knowledge of local rules.

The situation today is changing for the better:

- Open XML-based standards, such as VoiceXML, are being developed for voice and telephony, hiding much of the technical complexity from developers.
- Web telephony service providers, such as Voxeo Corporation, lease bandwidth and ports, eliminating the need to purchase proprietary hardware or deal with telephone companies.
- Visual design tools are available for telephony application development, such as Voxeo's *Designer*, shown in Figure 41-1.

Let's see how a telephony application can be developed for your website using these new facilities.

Figure 41-1   Telephony application design tool

41.4 | Case study: customer notification system

We'll construct a simple client-notification application for an imaginary company, the Underland Stagecoach Company. The application's sole function will be to notify a passenger when a planned trip has been canceled. Callers leave a telephone number and, if the trip is canceled, the system calls to deliver the unfortunate news.[1]

---

1. The complete source code for a demonstration form of this application is available on the accompanying CD-ROM.

41.4.1 *Background and strategy*

Underland is an industry leader in terms of automation and online bookings and now wants to extend that leadership into new areas. The company's existing website offers a typical online reservation and trip planning interface. It works well for travelers with access to a computer.

The telephone notification system was planned to be the first step in a process integrating the entire customer relationship management system with a full-fledged XML-based ERP system. All parts of all company databases would then be accessible by means of industry-standard query formats.

Since the existing database was working effectively, the initial stages of the project did not address the data infrastructure. Nor did it touch the design of the existing corporate website, shown schematically in Figure 41-2.

Figure 41-2 Website with traditional visual interface

Instead, an additional interface was added to provide telephone access to the same information, as depicted in Figure 41-3.

41.4.2 *Designing for telephonic interaction*

The website's existing HTML page for client notification has a total of forty navigation choices, including ten choices that duplicate a client-side image map as text, to accommodate visually disabled clients.

Telephone interfaces cannot support such rich navigation options without extremely careful design; it's usually better to simplify. In this case, the

Figure 41-3   Website in Figure 41-2 extended for telephony

telephonic equivalent was pared down to a single choice: to request the notification service.

Navigating the entire site from one phone number was determined to be too confusing for practical use. Instead, a group of toll-free numbers was reserved for the most common interactions, allowing very shallow menu trees to be used in all parts of the site. This solution was reasonable because telephone numbers are inexpensive.

People don't remember what they heard and said very well, so telephone interfaces can't carry much context with them. A visual site can display an entire page of data that the user can glance at to refresh his memory; a voice browser can only read that data aloud.

As people can stand just so much reminding, confirmation and reminder phrases were made:

- short and to the point, to avoid boring listeners; and
- interruptible, so a user could skip what he didn't want to hear.

41.4.3   *How the application works*

Let's look at some key steps in the application to see how they work.

41.4.3.1   Database access

Callers are tentatively identified by the *Caller ID* passed in from the phone network. A database lookup is performed on the incoming phone number to load an initial caller information set.

As the database access was already part of the website, acquiring the needed information for the voice interface was just a matter of selecting it.

41.4.3.2   Verifying the notification number

The opening dialog brands the service and asks whether the *Caller ID* phone number received is the correct number for notification. If so, the user is thanked and notification proceeds. If not, the user is prompted for the notification number, that number is verified, and only then does the notification proceed.[2]

A future enhancement will allow Underland's system to deal with several alternative numbers at which the user might be found ("follow-me/find-me").

41.4.3.3   Developing a spoken grammar

People talk in ways characteristic of their neighborhoods and cultural heritage. Trying to enforce a stilted vocabulary frustrates users, so they attempt to bypass the system in order to talk to a "real person" who can understand them.

As the cost drivers for this project depend on minimizing such bypass attempts, the user interaction has to be natural and flexible. Extensive grammars must be provided covering the most common ways in which people can say the responses sought by the system. Fortunately, most of these grammars are pre-written.

Example 41-1 shows a grammar for a simple yes or no response, as used in this application.

Note the large number of variations available for these two words. Even more are possible, like:

- "right-o" and "not on your life"
- military "affirmative" and "negative", or
- utterances that a computer has trouble understanding, like the difference between "uh, uh" and "uh huh".

---

2. In the demonstration code on the CD-ROM, a random name is selected from the database and the challenge and verification are skipped.

Example 41-1. Yes/no grammar for a VoiceXML application

```
LIB_YES_NO [
  [ yes
    yeah
    yup
    sure
    okay
    correct
    right
    ( ?( ?yes that's ) [ right correct ] )
    ( ?yes it is )
    ( you got it )
    ( yes i do )
    ( yes i would )
    ( yes it is correct )
  ] {return("yes")}
  [ no
    nope
    incorrect
    wrong
    ( no way )
    ( no it isn't )
    ( ?no [ it's that's ] not [ correct right ] )
    ( ?no it isn't )
    ( ?no it is not )
    ( ?no it's not )
    ( no i don't )
    ( no i do not )
    ( no i wouldn't )
  ] {return("no")}
```

More like these could easily be added, but doing so isn't usually necessary as long as the original set of variations is sufficiently broad. Users will typically learn and use an appropriate vocabulary within the limits of their natural speech, since we do that in everyday life when talking to a child, a young adult, a peer, or a person in authority.

41.4.3.4   Handling keyed input

For some parts of a dialog, it is natural for the user to employ the telephone keypad. Grammars can be defined for keyed input in much the same way as for spoken input. These are called *DTMF grammars*, after the name of the signalling standard used in touch-tone phones.

Example 41-2 shows a portion of the application that uses a DTMF grammar.

Example 41-2. Keypad input and recognition

```
<form id="GetNewPhone">
  <field name="newnumber">
    <grammar src="dtmf_phonenumber.gram#MAINMENU"/>
    <prompt>
      <audio src="audio/enter_phone.wav"/>
    </prompt>
    <!-- If silence then tell user that we didn't  -->
    <!-- hear any input. Reprompt the user.        -->
    <noinput>
      <audio src="audio/no_hear_pressed.wav"/>
      <reprompt/>
    </noinput>
    <!-- If the user's key input isn't matched by the grammar -->
    <!-- we need to tell the user we didn't understand,       -->
    <!-- then reprompt the user to enter the number again.    -->
    <nomatch>
      <audio src="audio/figure_out_pressed.wav"/>
      <reprompt/>
    </nomatch>
    <!-- Give the user a little help. -->
    <help>
      <audio src="audio/please_enter_number.wav"/>
      <reprompt/>
    </help>
    <filled>
      <assign name="selectedphone" expr="newnumber"/>
      <goto next="#ConfirmPhone"/>
    </filled>
  </field>
</form>
```

The `field` listens for a keyed phone number and prompts the user if none is entered, or if it doesn't match the grammar. Once the system recognizes a valid phone number, it proceeds (in the `filled` element) to direct the browser to a `form` that will confirm the number.

41.4.3.5   Delivering the goods

The last step in the application is to make a telephone call. As VoiceXML has no direct call-handling capabilities, the Underland used the CallXML language developed by Voxeo.

Example 41-3 shows the CallXML code that makes the outbound call.

Example 41-3. Initiate call, detect answer, announce

```
<callxml>
<block label="UserCallBack">
  <!-- Wait before calling user back. -->
  <wait value="$outbound_wait"/>
  <!-- Make outbound call to user. -->
  <call value="$numtocall" callerID="$callerid"
        maxtime="30s"/>
  <!-- Wait until the call is answered. -->
  <onanswer>
    <!-- Greet the user. -->
    <playAudio format="audio/wav"
               value="audio/cxml_hello_passenger.wav"/>
    <!-- Synthesize the user's name. -->
    <text>$randomName.</text>
    <!-- Give user the bad news and say goodbye. -->
    <playAudio format="audio/wav" value="audio/cxml_bad_news.wav"/>
    <playAudio format="audio/wav" value="audio/cxml_goodbye.wav"/>
    <!-- Done delivering bad news, so hang up. -->
    <hangup/>
  </onanswer>
</block>
...
</callxml>
```

Note the `onanswer` element. The user is greeted with a recording (`playAudio`), but his name, which was obtained from the database access, is rendered as text-to-speech (`text`).

As the number of human names is impossibly large, it was necessary to use machine synthesis rather than access a recorded vocabulary of names. In other places, where there was a smaller number of possible announcement candidates, a more natural sound was achieved by recording them all.

41.4.4 *Deploying the application*

Based on projections made by polling users on its website, Underland foresaw an ROI great enough to justify the system. However, this conservative approach ignored the possibility of luring computer-challenged customers into the expanded system by promoting the new service through conventional media.

Initial provisioning and deployment of the application took about five minutes, using the facilities of one of the online telephony service providers (in this case, the Voxeo community site).

Going into production required two additional days, as Underland and the service provider had to sign a service level agreement. The agreement guaranteed the bandwidth that would be available and the number of calls that would be handled simultaneously.

Semantic Web

▌ Extended linking

▌ Topic maps tutorial

▌ RDF and its applications

▌ Application integration with topic maps

Part Twelve

The W3C vision of the Semantic Web is one where data is defined and linked so that machines can do more than display it to people; they can share it among themselves to automate tasks and integrate applications. In other words, the very things we've been discussing in this book.

This part focuses on the weak "link" in the vision!

Hyperlink anchors today use physical addresses (URIs). Although the links themselves represent topical (semantic) associations, there is no hint of the *reason* why things might be linked. And although search engines operate in topical space, they are totally undisciplined and routinely return thousands of irrelevant pages.

XML can be used today to cure these problems. Extended linking supports meaningful relationships. RDF metadata allows rich descriptions of Web resources. And topic maps can chart the Web's information space so you can use topical querying and addressing and never get lost.

In fact, we'll see that topic maps can do more than navigate the Semantic Web, they can help you build it by integrating your applications!

Extended linking

Application Discussion

∎ Extended linking defined

∎ XLink applications

∎ XPointers

∎ Strong link typing

Contributing experts: Steven R. Newcomb and Victoria T. Newcomb of Coolheads Consulting, http://www.coolheads.com

42

> Extended linking and strong link typing will let the Web traverse to locations where it has never been. Those concepts are explained simply and clearly in this chapter.

Future generations of Web browsers and editors will reduce the effort required to keep our personal affairs organized and our corporate memories up to the minute. The productivity of many kinds of work will be enhanced, and in many ways. It's all going to happen basically because of two simple enhancements to the Web paradigm.

The W3C's XML Linking Language ("XLink," "extended linking") 1.0 Recommendation proposes to give all of us the ability to annotate documents, and to share those annotations with others, even when we cannot alter the documents we are annotating. In other words, we won't have to change a document in order to supply it with our own annotations – annotations that a browser can make appear as though they were written right into the annotated document.

42.1 | The shop notes application

As an example, consider a technician's set of online maintenance manuals. These are electronic books that the technician is not (and should not be) authorized to change. With HTML hyperlinks, the technician cannot write a note in a manual that can take future readers of that manual, including himself, to his annotations. Nor can the technician's annotations be displayed in their proper context – the parts of the manual that they are about.

42.1.1   *What is extended linking?*

By using *extended linking*, when the technician makes an annotation, he does so purely by editing his own document; no change is made to the read-only manual document that he is annotating.

The big difference between "extended" linking and HTML linking is this. With an HTML (or "simple") link, traversal can only begin at the place where the link is; traversal cannot begin at the other end. With an "extended" link, however, you can click on any of the link's anchors, and traverse to any other anchor, regardless of where the link happens to be.

Tip   Extended linking allows the starting anchor of a link to be different from the link itself. Instead of HTML's "A" tagged element that is linked to one other element, you can have (say) an "L" tag that links two or more other elements to one another.

A simple link (top of Figure 42-1) is always embedded ("inline") in (for example) the InstallLog text from which it provides traversal; the link cannot be traversed by starting at the target anchor (for example, the Installation procedure document).

An extended link (bottom of Figure 42-1) can appear in a separate document, and provide traversal between the corresponding parts of two other documents: for example, the technician's shop notes document ("TechLog") and the read-only installation manual. Because the location of this particular link is not the same as any of its anchors, it is said to be "out-of-line" (not embedded).

In our example, an annotation takes the form of just such an extended link element.

Figure 42-1   Simple vs. extended linking.

42.1.2 *Displaying extended links*

One way to realize the benefits of extended links is to display an icon at each anchor that indicates something about the other anchor. (The mechanism that supports this is discussed in greater detail under "Strong link typing", below.)

For example, as shown in Figure 42-2, a reader of the installation manual on the right will know that, if he clicks on the exclamation point displayed near Task 2, he will see a shop note about that task. If he clicks on the pound sign, he will be shown the serial number of a part that was installed according to the procedure, recorded in an "InstallLog" document.

Similarly, a reader of the annotation in the shop notes document ("TechLog") will know that clicking on the "I" icon will bring him to the installation instruction that the annotation discusses.

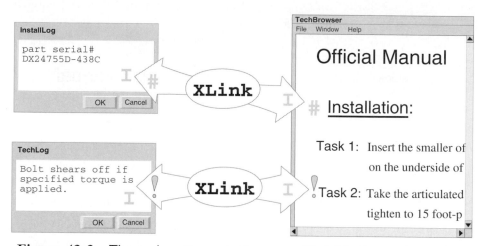

Figure 42-2   The exclamation point icon near Task 2 indicates that a shop note is available.

42.1.3 *Notes survive to new versions of manuals*

The technician's annotations – his "shop notes" – accumulate over time, and they represent a valuable asset that must be maintained. If the technician were to write shop notes inside each manual, when a new version of a manual is received it would be a chore to copy annotations from the old manual to the new manual.

With extended linking, however, the annotations are not in the old version; they are in a separate document. Therefore, the shop notes don't disappear when an annotated manual is replaced by a newer version.

That is because each link is equipped with "pointers" – pieces of information that can tell a browser where (for example) clickable icons should be rendered that indicate the availability of an annotation. Each such "XPointer" (as it is called) can point at anything in any XML document.

In our technician's shop, when a manual is replaced by a new version, the XPointers keep on working, even with the new manual, so the new manual is instantly and automatically equipped with the old manual's annotations.

In most cases, the XPointers don't have to be changed, because they continue to point at the right things, even in the new manual. If, because of differences between the old and new versions of the manual, some XPointers in the shop notes don't still point at the right things (or perhaps have nothing to point at any more), certain techniques can be used to detect each such situation. By dealing with these problem spots, the maintainers of the shop notes can minimize their efforts.

Moreover, XPointers and extended links enhance the potential for achieving high levels of quality and consistency, even when there are voluminous shop notes that annotate many manuals.

42.1.4 *Vendors can use the notes*

Some shop notes may also have value to the vendors of the manuals they annotate; they may beneficially influence subsequent versions of the manual. An editor of the manual can load (i.e., make his browser aware of) all the shop notes of many repair shops; this has the effect of populating the manual with icons representing the annotations of all the shops. The most common trouble spots in the manual will be made obvious by the crowds of annotation icons that they appear to have accumulated (Figure 42-3).

The fact that the shop notes take the form of interchangeable XML documents that use standardized extended links makes the task of sharing internal shop notes with manual vendors as easy as sending them any other kind of file. There is no need to extract them from some other resource, or to format them in such a way that they can be understood by their recipients. They are ready to work just as they are, in the tradition of SGML, HyTime, HTML, and now XML.

42.2 | Other applications of extended linking

The above "shop notes" example is just a sample of the kinds of enhancements that extended linking will bring to our interactions with information resources. Some of the broader implications are a bit more startling.

Figure 42-3   Task 18 evidently prompted three kinds of annotations in four different shop logs.

42.2.1 *Public resource communities of interest*

For example, many web sites today contain HTML links to public resources. One is the U.S. Government's online service for translating any U.S. postal code into its corresponding Congressional district and the name of its current incumbent Representative:

```
http://www.house.gov/zip/ZIP2Rep.html
```

However, if those HTML links were to become XLink extended links, an XLink-enabled browser could render this U.S. government Web page in such a way as to add to it a catalog of the activists and lobbying organizations who refer readers of their websites to this particular U.S. government resource. The "marketplace of ideas" represented by the aggregate of such organizations is thus revealed in a new and interesting way.

42.2.2 *Guidance documents*

Another startling possibility is the association of browser-controlling metadata with any and all Web resources.

In this scenario, a document of annotations (or a set of such documents) can be a user's companion during excursions on the Web. These annotations might make suggestions to users as to where to find more recent material, or they might even take control of the browser's link traversal ability in order to protect children from disturbing material.

While the latter XLink-enabled possibility may sound inimical to the freedom of speech, in fact it enhances liberty. It provides a new public medium for free speech: documents that censor the Web and/or otherwise provide guidance to Web travelers in the form of annotations that appear only in their designated contexts.

Of course, no adult is required to use any such guidance document, just as no one is required to read any particular book, but it's easy to predict that many will pay for the privilege of using many kinds of such "guidance documents".

More importantly, everyone will have the tools to write such guidance documents, so the technical ability to provide guidance (and, yes, even to provide censorship services) will be widely distributed, rather than being dangerously concentrated in a few generalized rating services. The creation and maintenance of guidance documents may well become a thriving cottage industry. Anyone can be a critic.

In the case of electronic commerce, it's easy to imagine that vendors will attempt to provide guidance documents designed to annotate the online sales catalogs of their competitors. In response, some providers of online sales catalogs will take steps to render the pointers in these kinds of guidance documents invalid and unmaintainable.

Regardless of all this, the overall impact on electronic commerce will certainly be positive; increasing the meaningful interconnectedness of the Web will help more people find exactly what they're looking for.

And it may turn out to be a mistake, in many cases, for catalog owners to attempt to render the pointers used to annotate their catalogs invalid, because similar pointers could be used, for example, by impartial consumer testing organizations to attach "best buy" recommendations to certain products. The guidance documents of consumer testing organizations will probably be quite popular, and well worth the cost of using them.

42.2.3 *Computer-augmented memory*

Extended linking has the potential to make radical improvements in our ability to keep track of what we are doing. Someday, we can expect to automatically annotate each piece of information we work with in such a way that, in effect, it refers future readers to the work we did with respect to it.

In other words, practically everything we do can be usefully seen as an annotation of one or more other pieces of work. If everything we do is, in some sense, an annotation of one or more other things, everything we do can all be found far more easily, starting from any piece of work anywhere in the "chain" (or, more likely, "tree" or "graph") of relevant information.

This is because extended linking allows all links to be bidirectional. (Or, rather, "n-directional", to account for extended links with more than two ends.) All of the connections among our affairs can then be tracked more or less automatically, so that each of us can enjoy a radical reduction in filing, cross-indexing, and other organizational chores, and with vastly increased ability to find what we're looking for quickly and easily.

Obviously, this same idea is even more significant in the realm of corporate memory. Even with today's behemoth enterprise integration technologies, it's still too hard to figure out what has happened, who is doing what, how various plans and projects are going to integrate, and where the relevant paperwork can be found.

Going a step further, there is an International Standard (ISO/IEC 13250) that seeks to exploit extended linking in such a way as to create living, easily explored and maintained "topic maps" of sets of information resources (see Chapter 43, "Topic maps: Knowledge navigation aids", on page 628). This goal sounds almost insanely ambitious, but extended linking, in combination with strong link typing (see below), should make it practical and achievable.

The topic maps paradigm elegantly solves consistency and usability problems faced by people who must collaborate in developing indexes and glossaries, or who must merge multiple indexes into master indexes. When applied to the Web, topic maps are analogous to the Global Positioning System provided by earth-orbiting satellites, allowing Web users to determine their current locations in a multidimensional "topic space".

42.2.4 *Intellectual property management*

The advent of extended linking also offers interesting new possibilities for the management and exploitation of intellectual property.

For example, metadata regarding the licensing policies of owners of Web resources could be associated with those resources by means of extended links. Such metadata could be changed when the resources are sold or licensed, without requiring any changes to the assets themselves.

This method greatly reduces the likelihood of inadvertent damage to the assets, and greatly increases the ease with which ownership and/or management policies can change. There is already an official, internationally-ratified ISO standard for using extended linking for exactly this purpose.

Such activity policies, and the means by which they are associated with online assets, could well become a source of private law that will strongly influence the development of intelligent agents.

42.3 | Strong link typing

With the XLink extended link facility, there is no limit to the number of links that can be traversed from a single point in a single document. Many different documents can contain links to the very same anchor, with the result that, theoretically, at least, an unlimited number of traversals are possible, starting from a single point. In addition, there are no limits on the kinds of annotations that can be made, nor on the purposes to which such annotations may be put.

Therefore, it makes sense to provide some easy way to sort the annotations (i.e., the links) into categories. For example, some kinds of annotations will be made in order to provide "metadata" about the document, and these will often take effect in some way other than by rendering an icon on the display screen. Some kinds of annotations are interesting only for specialized purposes.

42.3.1 *Hiding the installation log*

Going back to our earlier example, the technician can create an annotation that indicates the serial number of a new part that he installed in accordance with a particular maintenance procedure. The fact that such an annotation is available would be of interest only to someone who was auditing the installation of parts; it probably wouldn't appear even to the technician, despite the fact that it was he who created the annotation.

The technician's installation log annotation can be hidden from most people because it is "strongly typed": it has been clearly and unambiguously labeled as to its intended meaning and purpose, so all browsers can see what kind of link it is. In effect, the link says, "I am a Part-Installation-Log-Entry". People who aren't interested in part installation records can arrange for their browsers to hide them.

42.3.2 *Why do we need strong link typing?*

People may still choose to be made aware of other kinds of annotations made by our technician. For example, other technicians may wish to read our technician's accounts of any special situations that he has experienced when attempting to follow a particular instruction, or about successful and unsuccessful experiments with substitute parts.

The notion of "strong link typing" is virtually absent from HTML links. Basically, in HTML, the browser software knows where the user can go, but not why the author of the document being browsed thought the user might like to go there. The human reader can usually divine something from the context about the material that will be shown if the "anchor" hyperlink is traversed, but the browser itself is basically unable to help the user decide whether to click or not to click, so it can't hide any available traversals.

To be able to hide the availability of unwanted kinds of links can save a lot of time and effort. So the W3C XLink Recommendation also provides for the addition of strong typing features, not only to extended links, but also to the "simple" links that closely resemble the familiar HTML "anchor" (<a>) element. Thus, browsers can start supporting strong link typing promptly, even before they can handle extended linking.

42.3.3 *Anchor role identification*

The notion of strong link typing includes the notion of "anchor role" designation.

For example, the simple link at the top of Figure 42-1 characterizes its target anchor as an installation instruction; in the diagram, this is indicated by the "I" icon in the arrowhead. Similarly, the extended link at the bottom of Figure 42-1 characterizes one of its anchors as a shop note (the exclamation point) and the other anchor as an installation instruction (another "I" arrowhead).

Thus, a link can do more than just identify itself by saying, for example, "I am a Part Installation Log Entry". It can also specify which of its anchors fulfill which roles in the relationship it expresses.

For example, our Part Installation Log Entry link can say, in effect, "I signify that part [pointer to entry in parts catalog or inventory record] was installed in [pointer to information that identifies the unit being maintained] in accordance with maintenance directive [XPointer to instruction in manual]".

In other words, the log entry link is a three-ended link whose anchor roles might be named "replacement-part" (indicated with a "#" icon), "maintained-unit" ("@" icon), and "maintenance-directive" ("I" icon) (Figure 42-4).

The fact that an anchor plays some specific role in a relationship often determines whether the relationship is interesting or even relevant in a given application context.

42.4 | Conclusion

It is easy to see that the impact of extended linking will be significant, and that technical workers and electronic commerce will be early beneficiaries. Extended linking will enhance the helpfulness and usefulness of the Web

Figure 42-4   Link with two traversal possibilities at each anchor, distinguishable because of anchor role identification.

environment. The burden of many kinds of paperwork will be very sub-stantially mitigated.

On the horizon, there appears to be serious potential for significant improvements in the availability of all kinds of knowledge, due to the possi-bility of creating and interchanging topic maps. Intellectual property man-agement, and the Web-based utilization of intellectual property, will become easier and more orderly.

All of these benefits, and probably many more, emanate from two very simple enhancements of the Web paradigm in the XLink and XPointers Recommendations of the World Wide Web Consortium:

- Allowing the starting anchor of a link to be different from the link itself; and

■ Strong link typing, in which links plainly exhibit the kind of relationship they represent, and the roles their anchors play in that relationship.

Tip   For more on XLink, see Chapter 65, "XML Linking Language (XLink)", on page 1018. XPointer is covered in Chapter 64, "XML Pointer Language (XPointer)", on page 1004. The text of the XLink and XPointer specs are on the CD-ROM.

Topic maps: Knowledge navigation aids

Friendly Tutorial

▌ Topic maps in a nutshell

▌ Indexes, glossaries, and thesauri

▌ Topic map applications

▌ Tools for topic maps

Sponsor: XCare.net, `http://www.ontopia.net`

Contributing experts: Hans Holger Rath and Steve Pepper, of the ISO topic map standards group (ISO/IEC JTC1/SC34/WG3)

43

Here's another reason we need the Semantic Web. True story: Charles was searching an online shopping site for a CD by the doo-wop greats, the Flamingos. Because of his interest, he was also offered a pink neon bird sculpture. That site needs topic maps! This chapter explains why, and might lead you to think that yours does too.

ver want to fire your Web search engine for bringing you thousands of useless pages? Or to navigate from one Web page to another on the same subject when there is no link between them? Then you want topic maps.

When you ask your Web browser to search for "Mozart", that composer is the "topic" of your search and you hope to find Web pages that are in some way devoted to it. The browser might actually find such pages, but they will probably be lost among the thousands of pages in which "Mozart" is simply a word that occurs in passing and in no way the main topic of the page.

Similarly, when you look up "Mozart" in the index of a book, you hope to find the pages whose topic is Mozart.

So topics are a familiar concept, one that we work with all the time. What then are topic maps and why do we need them?

Well, suppose you want to find out about operas composed by German composers that were influenced by Mozart. There is no way to formulate such a query in a Web search engine. You can try to use a set of relevant keywords such as "opera + Germany + composer + Mozart", but you are guaranteed to get an enormous number of useless hits. You are also guaranteed to miss some of the most interesting pages. More importantly, even if the search were extremely accurate, you would still have to wade through all the resulting documents simply to find the names of the works you are interested in.

How much easier if you could simply query your index for all *operas* "written by" *composers* associated with *Germany* ("born in" or "lived in") and with *Mozart* ("influenced by")!

The key difference between the two approaches is that the former simply uses a full text index built from the raw content of a set of information resources. The latter, however, utilizes an index that encapsulates the structure of the underlying knowledge.

The latter solution is actually an example of a *topic map*; that is, a structured network of hyperlinks above an information pool. Each node in the network represents a named topic (e.g. Germany, Mozart, Wagner). The links connecting the nodes express the associations between the nodes (e.g. written by, lived in, influenced by).

From this it should be clear that indexes are actually very simple forms of topic maps. So, too, are glossaries and thesauri. This chapter will explain the basic concepts of topic maps, how they relate to the kinds of navigational aids we are already familiar with, what additional benefits they provide, and how to create and use them. We'll also look at some applications and consider requirements for topic map tools.

43.1 | Topic maps in a nutshell

A topic map models a domain of knowledge in terms of:

- the topics of that domain,
- their interrelationships (or "associations"), and
- occurrences of relevant information resources. [1]

We'll explain those concepts in this section, along with a few more:

- topic types,
- association types,

---

1. The map can be interchanged as an XML or SGML document conforming to the International Standard ISO/IEC 13250, which also standardizes the conceptual model.

- occurrence roles,
- identity,
- facets, and
- scope

43.1.1 *Topic and topic type*

In the context of an encyclopedia, a *topic* might represent subjects such as "Germany", "Bavaria", "Munich", the king "Ludwig II", or the opera "Lohengrin" by the composer "Richard Wagner": anything that might have an entry (or indeed a mention) in the encyclopedia.

The subject represented by a topic can be any "thing" whatsoever – a person, an entity, a concept, really *anything*, regardless of whether it exists or has any other specific characteristics, about which anything whatsoever may be asserted by any means whatsoever. Exactly what one chooses to regard as topics in any particular application will vary according to the needs of the application, the nature of the information, and the uses to which the topic map will be put.

A topic can have a number of characteristics. First of all, it can have a *name* – or more than one. The standard provides an element form for *topic name* which consists of at least one *base name*, and optional *display* and *sort* names.

A topic also has a *topic type* – or perhaps multiple topic types. Thus, Germany would be a topic of type "country", Bavaria a topic of type "state", Munich and Würzburg topics of type "city", Ludwig II a topic of type "king", etc. In other words, topic types express typical *class-instance* relationships or the *is a* relation (see Figure 43-1).

Figure 43-1   Topic names and types (represented by different symbols)

Topic types are themselves defined as topics. In order to use them for typing, you have to explicitly declare "country", "state", "city", etc. as topics in your topic map, and this then allows you to say more about them using the topic map model itself.

43.1.2 *Topic occurrence and occurrence role*

A topic can have one or more *occurrences*. An occurrence of a topic is a link to an information resource (or more than one) that is deemed to be somehow relevant to the subject that the topic represents. It could be an article about the topic in an encyclopedia, a picture or video depicting the topic, a simple mention of the topic in the context of something else, a commentary on the topic, or any of a host of other forms in which an information resource might have some relevance to a given subject.

Such resources are generally outside the topic map document itself, and they are "pointed at" using whatever addressing mechanisms the system supports, typically XPointer or HyTime.

Occurrences may be of any number of different types (we gave the examples of "article", "illustration", "mention" and "commentary" above). Such distinctions are supported in the standard by the concept of the *occurrence role* (see Figure 43-2). As with topic types, each occurrence role is formally considered to be a topic, although the actual occurrences are not.

43.1.3 *Indexes and glossaries*

As described so far, topics and occurrences provide a model for explicitly stating which subjects a pool of information pertains to and how. That is basically what an index also does.

Figure 43-2   Occurrences of topics in an information pool and their various occurrence roles (represented by different line types).

In Example 43-1, the index terms are topics and the page numbers are their occurrences.

Example 43-1. An index is a simple form of topic map.

Germany 17, 77
Mozart 72
Wagner 49
Würzburg 22

But topic maps offer more. Through the concept of *occurrence roles*, they generalize and extend the conventions used to distinguish different kinds of references from one another.

In Example 43-2 the use of different typefaces indicates different *roles* played by the occurrences on pages 17 and 77 (perhaps a *main description* and a *mention*).

Example 43-2. An index with occurrence roles

Germany **17**, 77

Some books contain more than one index (index of names, index of places, etc.). *Topic types* provide the same facility, but extend it in several directions to enable the creation of multiple, dynamic, user-controlled indexes organized as taxonomic hierarchies.

Glossaries, too, can be implemented using just the bare bones of the topic map standard that has been described so far. Like an index, a glossary is also a set of topics and their occurrences, ordered by topic name. Here, though, the occurrence role is "definition".

Example 43-3. A glossary is a topic map.

Federal Republic of Germany: see *Germany*.

...

Germany: Federal republic in the northern part of central Europe, population (1998) approx. 82 million.

...

Würzburg: City in Bavaria, Germany on the river Main, 90 km south-east of Frankfurt. 128.000 inhabitants (1998).

Note that "Federal Republic of Germany" does not have a definition. It is just another topic name for the topic that also has the name "Germany", and in this map there can be only one definition per topic.

The definitions in Example 43-3 are instances of just one kind of occurrence – those that play the role of "definition". With a topic map it is easy to create and maintain much more complex glossaries than this; for example, ones that use multiple kinds of definitions (perhaps suited to different kinds of users).

43.1.4 *Topic association and association type*

Topic maps don't stop here, however. They go far beyond just providing a mechanism for creating more robust and powerful indexes and glossaries. The key to their true potential lies in their ability to model *relationships* between topics, and for this the topic map standard provides a construct called the *topic association*.

A topic association is (formally) a link element that asserts a relationship between two or more topics. Examples might be as follows:

- Munich *is in* Bavaria.
- Bavaria *is in* Germany.
- Wagner was *born in* Leipzig.
- Lohengrin was *composed by* Wagner.
- Wagner was *influenced by* Mozart.

Just as topics can be grouped according to type (country, state, city, etc.) and occurrences according to role (definition, article, illustration, commentary, etc.), so too can associations between topics be grouped according to their type. The *association types* of the five relationships in the list above are "is in", "born in", "composed by" and "influenced by" (see Figure 43-3). As with most other things, the various association types are themselves regarded as topics [2]

43.1.4.1   Association role

Each topic that participates in an association has a corresponding *association role* which states the role played by that topic in the association. In the case of the relationship "Wagner was born in Leipzig" those roles might be "person" and "birthplace"; for "Lohengrin was written by Wagner" they might be "opera" and "composer".

Like topic types, individual association roles must be declared as topics in order to be used.

43.1.4.2   Association topology

In the topic map model, associations do not have a direction; that is, they are not one-way (or "unilateral"). The "born in" relationship between Wagner and Leipzig implies what might be called a "fostered" relationship between the city and the composer ("Leipzig fostered Wagner"), and the "composed by" relationship between Lohengrin and Wagner is also a "composed" relationship between the composer and his opera ("Wagner composed Lohengrin").

Sometimes associations are *symmetrical*, in the sense that the nature of the relationship is the same whichever way you look at it. For example, the

---

2. That is to say, the *value* of an association type (e.g. "is in") is a topic, not the "association type" construct itself.

corollary of "Wagner was a friend of Ludwig II" would be that "Ludwig II was a friend of Wagner". Sometimes the association roles in such symmetrical relationships are the same (as in this case: "friend" and "friend"), sometimes they are different (as in the case of the "husband" and "wife" roles in a "married to" relationship).

Other association types, such as those that express superclass/subclass and some part/whole relationships, are *transitive*: If we say that Munich is in Bavaria, and that Bavaria is in Germany, we have implicitly asserted that Munich is in Germany and any topic map search engine should be able to draw the necessary conclusions without the need for making the assertion explicitly. Much of the real power of topic maps results from using transitive relations between topics, types, and roles for querying the map.

Figure 43-3   Associations of various types between topics (represented by different line types)

43.1.5 *Thesauri and semantic networks*

Typed topic associations extend the power of topic maps to the modeling of thesauri and other networks of information and knowledge.

A *thesaurus* is a network of interrelated terms (along with their definitions, examples, or whatever) within a particular domain. There exist various standards for thesauri that predefine relationship types, such as "broader term", "narrower term", "used for", and "related term", all of which correspond directly to association types in a topic map. Other thesaurus constructs, such as "source", "definition", and "scope note" would be modeled as occurrence roles in a topic map.

One advantage of applying the topic map model to thesauri is that it becomes possible to create hierarchies of association types that extend the thesaurus schema without deviating from accepted standards (for example, by subclassing "used for" as "synonymous for", "abbreviation for", and "acronym for"). Further advantages would be gained from using the facilities for scoping, filtering and merging described in the next three sections.

"Semantic networks", "associative networks" and "knowledge" (or "conceptual") "maps" are terms used within the fields of semantics and artificial intelligence to describe various models for representing knowledge structures within a computer. Many of these already correspond closely to the topic/association model. Adding the topic/occurrence axis provides a means for "bridging the gap" between these fields and the field of information management, thereby establishing a basis for true knowledge management.

43.1.6 *Scope*

When I refer to "Paris", you know immediately that I am talking about the capital city of France. Or do you? How do you know that I'm not talking about the town of the same name in Texas or the hero of Troy? Presumably because you are assuming a *scope* set by some form of context, whether it be a particular subject area under discussion or a generally accepted default.

The concept of scope is important for avoiding ambiguities like this and for increasing the precision with which assertions can be made. In topic maps, any assignment of a characteristic to a topic, be it a name, an occurrence or a role in an association, is considered to be valid within certain limits, which may or may not be specified explicitly. The limit of validity of such an assignment is called its *scope*; scope is defined in terms of *themes*, and themes are modeled as topics.

So, in topic maps where the scope is defined by the themes "France", "USA", and "Greek mythology", the name "Paris" could be used unambiguously. Similarly the association expressing the assertion that "Leipzig *is in* East Germany" could be qualified by giving it the scope "1949-90".

43.1.7 *Subject identity*

Sometimes the same subject is represented by more than one topic. This can be the case when two topic maps are merged. In such a situation it is necessary to have some way of establishing the identity between seemingly disparate topics.

This can be done in either of two ways:

- Explicitly, by specifying the same *subject identity* for the two topics; or
- Implicitly, through the *topic naming constraint*, which states that any topics that have the same name in the same scope refer to the same subject.

The ability to merge topic maps opens up the possibility of *federating knowledge*. Topic maps can even be used to federate knowledge expressed according to different ontologies.

43.1.8 *Facets*

The final feature of the topic map standard to be considered in this introduction is the concept of the *facet*. Facets basically provide a mechanism for assigning property-value pairs to information resources. A facet is simply a property (such as "language" or "security level"); its values are called *facet values*. Facets are typically used for applying metadata which can then be used for filtering the information resources.

43.2 | Applications of topic maps

We will consider two applications. They both involve publishing, but topic maps have broad applicability in other areas as well.

43.2.1 *Reference work publishing*

In the age of digital information all commercial publishers face major new challenges, but perhaps none more so than publishers of reference works, especially encyclopedias and dictionaries. Not only has the advent of the World Wide Web finally forced all such publishers to think seriously about moving into electronic publishing; it has also turned out to be perhaps their biggest and most threatening competitor.

The reason for this, of course, is that the raw material from which reference works are fashioned consists for the most part of "hard facts" that cannot be owned. The knowledge that Wagner was born in Leipzig or that the population of Germany is about 82 million cannot be copyrighted. Almost every piece of information to be found in any modern, commercial encyclopedia can be found somewhere on the Internet for free. So how is a reference work publisher to compete?

43.2.1.1 Adding value

Paradoxically, the answer lies in the fact that most users today do not need more information — if anything, they need less, because they are already drowning in enormous quantities of it. At the very least, they need the ability to be able to find their way to relevant information as quickly as possible and to be able to filter out the "noise" created by all the information for which they have no use. They also need to be able to trust the information they receive, to know that it is reliable and up-to-date. Thus, two of the most important "value-adds" that commercial publishers can provide are

- tools and methods for finding the required information in a timely manner; and
- the confidence that the information so found can be trusted.

Topic maps can greatly assist the discovery of relevant information. In addition, the topic paradigm turns out to provide an *organizing principle* for many kinds of information that helps ensure its timeliness and accuracy.

43.2.1.2   A typical topic map

Encyclopedia articles are – at a very abstract level – about persons, geographical objects, history, culture, and science. These are the main *topic types*. Existing classification systems list further subclasses of these topic types, such as:

- historic person (monarch [emperor, king, queen], politician, [president, chancellor], explorer), artists (writer [novelist, poet], painter, sculptor, composer, musician), scientists (mathematician, physicist, chemist, biologist, physician);
- country, state, landscape, city/town, river, mountain, island.

The *occurrence roles* point to the resources of an encyclopedia publisher. Typical data assets are articles, definitions, mentions of the topic in an article, pictures/images, audio, and video clips.

Even more interesting (because of the value added to the publication) are the *association types* that are used to structure the mass of cross-references normally found in such works. Common examples are:

- ruled over, conquered;
- painted, composed, wrote, played, discovered, invented;
- parent of, child of;
- located in, larger than;
- took place, before, after;
- discovered by, conquered by, founded by, invented by.

Some of these are simply different names for the same association type viewed from different perspectives (e.g. conquered/conquered by, parent of/child of). Others exhibit the important property of transitivity (e.g. located in, larger than).

It is a good idea to identify transitive relationships like these because the topic map engine can use this information to generate more intelligent answers to the queries of the user.

An encyclopedia that is based on and governed by a comprehensive topic map has a number of unique advantages:

- Navigation is much easier and much more consistent.
- The user interface (indeed, multiple user interfaces) can be generated automatically from the topic map.

- New information resources are easily integrated.
- Multiple viewpoints of the same subject matter can be represented.
- The map itself becomes an asset in its own right, independent of the information resources it covers.

43.2.2 *Technical documentation*

Technical documentation for a complex product could consist of thousands of pages, or megabytes of textual data. Corporate publishers have to manage and publish the documentation for different product versions and product variants. More ambitious corporate publishers add reader-related information to the publications ("skill level" is the typical example) or publish different views of the same material ("Overview", "Reference Manual", "Questions and Answers", etc.).

Versions, variants, and views require a more complex organization of the text than the sequential ordering of a printed book. XML alone cannot meet these requirements; publishers must also change the information management paradigm.

43.2.2.1   Text modules

Modularization of the text is the first step towards an appropriate solution. The existing chapter-section-subject structure of book-oriented technical documentation is split up into hundreds or thousands of separate text modules (information objects). The modules consist of "self-contained" text about a given subject (e.g. "Installation"). Hyperlinks connect the modules.

Hierarchical subject codes – assigned as metadata – allow quick access when querying the database containing the modules.

These two characteristics (self-contained text, hierarchical subject codes) indicate a class of technical documentation that is an ideal candidate for a topic map application.

43.2.2.2   A typical topic map

The identification of *topic types* can be based on the subject code classification. If this is not available, the technical design of the product or semantic markup in the documentation will give the necessary hints. In software documentation for example, the topic types might consist of "program block", "command group", "command", "macro", "parameter", "error", etc.

The *occurrence roles* would relate to existing modularized material. Data modules, functional diagrams, tables, screen shots, error messages, and syntax examples are among the possibilities.

Finally, *association types* can be derived from knowledge of the relationships between the topic types already identified: "command group A *consists of* commands X, Y, and Z", "command X *has parameters* P and Q", etc.

43.3 | Tool support for topic maps

Possibilities for tool support exist at each phase of the topic map life cycle.

43.3.1 *Topic map design*

The design of topic maps is an incremental process. The definition of the various types and roles and sub-/super-classes of them should be done under the control of a topic map design tool. Doing so will help ensure the consistency of the map.

Outside the scope of the topic map standard, but nevertheless very useful, are constraining conditions that can drive consistency checks. They make it possible to check whether transitive associations are used correctly, whether the types of topics in an association correspond to the respective association roles, etc.

Another part of the topic map design is the generation of all the topics, associations, and occurrences. In a large application these can be numbered in the thousands or even millions. The design tool has to offer an easy access to all these objects of the map.

As in a content management system, user access rights play an important role in a topic map design tool. Permission for creating, changing, and deleting parts of the map could be assigned to different user groups with different responsibilities, and the system has to take care that these rules are enforced.

43.3.2 *Creation and maintenance*

The boundary between the design and the creation of a topic map is fluid. Only the initial design will distinguish the declaration of types and roles on the one hand, and the topics, associations, and occurrences on the other. During the maintenance of the map these will be done concurrently – maybe by different user groups.

The editors (designer, author) of the topic map need a visualization tool besides the consistency checker. The visualization tool produces a rendition of the map that is similar to the one the end-users will see. The querying possibilities should also be similar.

The initial creation of the map out of an existing information pool can probably be supported by an automatic rule-based process. This process can be compared to the conversion of word processor files to XML. Both add explicit structure to apparently "flat" data.

A conversion for topic maps takes as its input information objects in which the topics and associations exist only implicitly, and produces a linked and structured knowledge base as output.

43.3.3 *Exchange of topic maps*

The publication of topic maps will be done electronically, since paper-based presentations of any but the simplest of topic maps are to all intents and purposes impossible. The topic map document architecture defined in the standard is the interface between topic map design and creation tools, and the topic map browser – the rendition and navigation tool of the end-user.

Note that this interchange standard does not address application-specific semantics such as the "association topology" properties described earlier. Work is currently underway in the ISO and the topic map community to address this requirement through a "Topic Map Constraint Language".

43.3.4 *Navigating a map*

There are two ways to navigate a topic map: by traversing the links or by directly addressing the nodes through queries.

Traversal of a large link network – possibly consisting of millions of nodes and links – requires an easy-to-use and easy-to-understand user interface. Very sophisticated colorful graphical user interfaces with nodes and edges that move in accordance with physical laws (like magnetism or gravity) might be eye-catchers.

However, a familiar interface like a Web search engine might prove to be practical. Figure 43-4, for example, shows the *Ontopia Topic Map Navigator*, which is built on top of the *Ontopia Topic Map Engine*. The left pane allows you to navigate within the topic map. By clicking occurrences, you can see appropriate resources presented in the right pane (in this case, a composer bio and an opera synopsis).[3]

Figure 43-4   The *Ontopia Topic Map Navigator*

Querying a topic map requires a query language covering the concepts of the topic map standard and desirable application-specific semantics (associations, transitivity). The user needs additional support when defining a

---

3. You can try it for yourself. There is a free copy of an Ontopia topic map browser on the CD-ROM.

query – the information available in the map can be offered to the user by the query interface, e.g. in a menu-like style.

There should also be the possibility to "build-in" the knowledge that, say, the (virtual) topic type "clarinetist" is in fact a synthesis of all topics of type "person" that are connected via a "player of" association with the topic "clarinet". This will allow the user to work in a very intuitive manner and ensure very precise query results.

43.4 | Conclusion

Topic map capabilities are starting to appear in products for content management, source code control, product data management, and groupware, among others.

Topic maps also complement the Resource Description Framework (RDF).[4] RDF makes it possible to assign metadata to information resources in the World Wide Web. Topic maps can utilize this metadata to automatically build a navigational layer – "conceptual map" – of the resource domain.

And as we have seen, topic maps have also been designed to be merged easily, and to mediate between different ontologies. All of these facts underscore the importance of topic maps to the Semantic Web.

Analysis   The ability to apply multiple topic maps to arbitrary information pools has enormous potential for the World Wide Web. Website owners and independent third parties can develop and apply topic maps to collections of websites, thereby providing an overall information context for them. Instead of relying solely on physical addresses, which have no information context, a surfer could check his location in an applicable topic map to see where he is in an information space. In other words, topic maps can act as the global positioning system (GPS) for the World Wide Web.

---

4. Discussed in Chapter 44, "RDF: Metadata description for Web resources", on page 646.

RDF: Metadata description for Web resources

- ▮ Resource Description Framework (RDF)

- ▮ Resources and resource identifiers

- ▮ RDF schemas

- ▮ Harvesting metadata

- ▮ Metadata queries

Sponsor: Profium Ltd., http://www.profium.com

Contributing experts: Dr. Janne Saarela and Dr. Martyn Horner

To paraphrase Will Rogers: "I never metadata I didn't like!" The problem is that we don't meet with enough of it. The Web floods us with information, but not enough metadata to organize that information and make it navigable. RDF is another technology that offers the promise of a Semantic Web, and powerful information routing for the enterprise as well.

he World Wide Web has made it possible to spread information further and in greater quantities than ever before. So much so that most of us are drowning in it!

44.1 | What is metadata?

Finding what you need on the Web is becoming harder and harder. Tools like search engines, which are everyone's key to the Web, must become ever more ingenious to sort out the good from the bad, the harmful, and the simply irrelevant.

The solution depends on metadata.

44.1.1 *Indexes are metadata*

Search engines traditionally deal directly with information. They find it by looking through the text of Web pages. This is like browsing in a library, going from shelf to shelf and book to book, when the fast way to the book you need is through the library index.

Making such indexes for the Web and keeping them current is the job of the Web's librarians. Modern search engines are investing more and more computing power for this purpose. An index is a form of *metadata*: "data about data" or "information about information".

In a library, the book you want – or on the Web, the content you want – is a *resource* that your work (or recreation!) requires. To find that resource, you must first know some metadata about it, and knowledge about resources is what RDF is all about.

44.1.2 *Properties are metadata*

RDF stands for *Resource Description Framework*. A description of a thing is actually a description of its characteristics, or *properties*, another form of metadata. RDF is a method of recording such descriptions.

The basic unit of RDF is the *statement*. It makes a single connection between a resource and the value of one of that resource's properties. A book, for example, can have such properties as:

- author,
- publisher,
- page count,
- publication date,
- books that it refers to,
- books that refer to it, and so on.

Each of these properties has a name – "author", "publisher", etc. – that is, in some sense, universal. The RDF statement associates a resource through a property to the resource's value of that property; that value is particular to the resource. In other words, RDF brings together the universal – property names – and the particular – property values of resources.

The property value may be a literal character string or a number. However, it might also be something else in the information landscape – perhaps a book, a Web page or a person – in which case that, too, is a resource to which connections can be made.

The association of resources with other resources constructs a "web" of metadata potentially as rich and detailed as the World Wide Web that it describes. Because information has no worth if it can't be found, the metadata adds value to its underlying information and therefore has value in its own right.

44.2 | RDF data model

RDF is normally represented in XML, but XML itself only provides semantics for generic characteristics of all structured information, such as:

- the identification of data elements of named types, but not the meaning of the types;
- hierarchical relationships among the elements; and
- the existence of named properties (attributes) of elements, but not their meaning.

RDF, like other XML applications, provides additional meaning. In this case, the *RDF data model*.

44.2.1 *Resources*

The core concept of RDF is the recognition of a resource. The simplistic way to think of a resource is as a URI, but there are subtleties lurking behind that simplification.

As we try to locate useful items in our information universe, we necessarily assume that they will stay still long enough to be located. We think of the target of our search as a physical item   a document, a person, an institution, even a piece of text or a number – and we believe that it is constant, at least until we locate it.

Of course, this is a false belief.

People change even as you try to find them: they grow older and perhaps wiser. Documents can be updated even when they have the good manners to stay in the same place. Equally, they can stay unchanged (and maintain their usefulness to you) even though they are moved around physically on a computer's disk.

The important mental step to take here is to think of your search target not as the item itself, but as a *resource*: something that contains the *relevant essence* of the item. In other words, the aspects of the item that you need to rely on for your present purposes.

So locating a person as an email address might be quite sufficient for business purposes, even though your correspondent's appearance and geographical location might have changed. If the "person" is an institution, it might even have changed its entire physical identity.

However, those kinds of change don't matter. The resource for your purpose is the relevant essence of the person; in this case, the email address.

Conceiving of resources in this way allows references to them to survive many changes over time and space.

44.2.2 *Resource identifiers*

In the real data universe of the World Wide Web, resources are identified by URIs.

A URI doesn't actually say where a resource is to be found, but gives a (supposedly reliable) procedure for locating it. Location should be possible over a practically useful stretch of time and from a reasonable range of equipment. The access procedures of the Web – DNS name servers, routers, proxies, etc. – work to guarantee that the URI will provide access to the indicated resource.

The concept of URI is therefore tightly bound to the concept of resource. However, the concept of resource, as we have seen, is less tightly bound to a physical item than one might have thought.

Now that we understand what a resource is, we can use the term more precisely. A resource, as identified by a URI, is both unique and universal. We therefore apply the term not only to items being connected by an RDF statement, but also for the property names and other fixed points in the RDF data model.

For example, we will shortly refer to some property names taken from a vocabulary called "Dublin Core". The "creator" property from this vocabulary would formally be referred to by its full resource identification: `http://purl.org/dc/elements/1.1/creator`.

44.2.3 *Triples*

An element of RDF is called a `triple`. It connects a resource – the "subject" – via a universal property name – the "predicate" – to a particular property value – the "object".

subject
> This can be any resource.

predicate
> This resource is a member of a relatively restricted set of resources.

object
> This is either another resource or a literal character string or number.

These three elements of a triple – subject, predicate and object – form a *statement*.[1] Resources can participate in multiple statements, as shown in Figure 44-1.

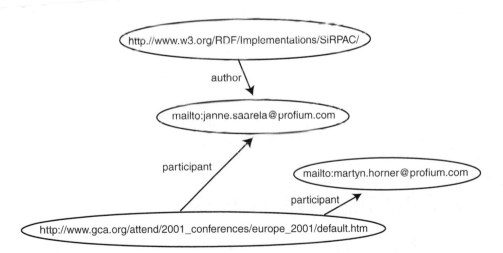

Figure 44-1 Graphical representation of three RDF statements

---

1. The term is an accurate English grammar metaphor for an RDF triple.

44.3 | RDF schemas

RDF offers the facility of constructing type systems called *RDF schemas*.

The RDF type system follows the object-oriented modeling paradigm, utilizing classes and properties. Membership in a class implies the sharing of common characteristics of the class.

Properties, however, are not bound to classes: any property can be exhibited by any type of object.

RDF schemas provide a formal means to describe the semantics of properties. The semantics are expressed in one or more natural languages. Applications can make use of this information to prompt users who are unfamiliar with a property.

In the same way that XML DTDs and schemas can be used to validate XML documents, RDF schemas can be used to validate RDF data model instances. However, just as with XML, validation is an option; applications can choose to deal only with the data.

We've discussed several metadata vocabulary initiatives in this book. Some of them have bindings to RDF schemas, for example:

Dublin Core, www.dublincore.org
> Dublin Core defines bibliographic metadata, such as "creator", "date", and "format". Bindings of its properties exist for markup languages like HTML, as well as for RDF.

PRISM, www.prismstandard.org
> PRISM defines metadata for the syndication and post-processing of media industry content. Its properties include "event", "industry", "location", "expiration time", and "has alternative".

44.4 | Putting RDF to work

RDF, like WebDAV and topic maps, is a technology widely promoted for its potential to contribute to the Semantic Web. Fortunately, as with those other technologies, we can start with a more tractable domain!

At the enterprise level, RDF can be applied with a single vocabulary, designed to suit the activity. A quality-controlled process can be put in place for creating RDF metadata models. And because there is a known target audience, firm criteria can be established for functionality and performance.

Let's take a high level look at the stages in utilizing RDF, using an RDF-based product to illustrate: Profium's *Smart Information Router (SIR)*.

44.4.1 *Harvesting metadata*

An RDF application begins by storing the input information stream, at the same time harvesting metadata from it. The metadata could occur in several forms, both implicit and explicit:

annotated

Some XML documents are annotated with metadata in the form of additional elements and attributes. This markup might have been inserted with an XML editor during editing, or applied with a suitable tool during conversion to XML.

derived

Metadata that isn't explicitly marked can be derived from the data content using tools that can be attached to the input process. These *metadata enrichment* programs use various levels of machine intelligence and heuristics to extract metadata from plain text.

intrinsic

In between the previous two there are representations, such as SOAP and NewsML, where metadata must be present as an integral part of the delivery mechanism. Unlike derived metadata, parsing is straightforward and unambiguous. And unlike annotated metadata, it has to be there or the information couldn't have been delivered in the first place!

The product can compensate for a degree of irregularity in the input stream. It also maps between vocabularies and can derive metadata from the stream itself, such as "source", "dates", "ownership", etc.

The result of this stage is a managed pool of content and a web of metadata to describe it.

44.4.2 *Querying*

Metadata, as we have seen, represents information about information. Therefore, to find answers to questions about the information, you must first ask (slightly different) questions about the information about the information.

These questions can become even more complex than that sentence!

Generally, though, it is easier to ask about metadata than about data, since the vocabulary is controlled and specific to the enterprise.

For example, you could ask regarding a financial news feed:

> Find any mention of Nokia's activities in Helsinki during the years 1995 to 2001 and compare the reports from Reuters and United Press International; I only read English.

If you had no metadata repository, but only the text in a huge collection of files, you would have to devise some pretty clever search algorithms. They would need to look for:

- the names "Nokia" and "Helsinki" (and only in context: no use looking for activities in the little Finnish town of Nokia, since Nokia has long since moved to Espoo!);
- numbers that look like the specified dates (all of them, in all formats);
- the copyrighted texts from the news agencies; and
- something to ensure that the text is in English.

Imagine what a Web search engine would do with this problem!

Profium SIR provides a browser-based graphical interface to assist in formulating queries like this one. It is shown in Figure 44-2.

Queries can be simple ("documents by author Smith") or complex, involving comparisons and correspondences and levels of sub-queries. The visual form of the query is converted into an internal form for execution, or into XML for interchange.

Figure 44-2   The *Profium* SIR query editor

44.4.3 *Routing*

The value of RDF metadata is not just in *finding* information in a large information base. It also allows us to *evaluate* that large body of information by executing queries on a much smaller sample.

That in turn provides an automatic means of determining what to do with the content – send it by email, transmit it to a PDA, publish it on paper, broadcast it via TV – and what sort of embellishments one can add – styles, annotations, branding.

Think of it as "semantic-based routing". Formatting and delivery can be controlled according to the semantic metadata.

> *Tip*   The CD-ROM includes a free RDF parser from Profium, in the form of a Java class library and a sample application.

Application integration using topic maps

Application Discussion

- Distributed objects
- Workflow topic maps
- Application integration architecture

Sponsor: XCare.net, `http://www.xcare.net`

Contributing expert: Suriya Narayanan

Chapter

45

It's midnight ... do you know where your applications are? There was a time when the answer was "wrapped in a rubber band in my desk drawer", but that time is gone forever. Today's Web applications are composed of a multitude of cooperating components. You might not even know *what* they are, let alone where they are. Unless, of course, you've got a topic map!

 ong, long ago, in a data processing center far, far away, applications were implemented as monolithic programs. Today, with the evolution of the Web and the driving forces behind it, distributed object computing has become the prevailing architecture for developing applications.

45.1 | Distributed objects

Just about any application can be modeled and developed as a collection of objects in a network, collaborating to accomplish what the application is expected to accomplish. The network where the applications run can span the globe or be limited to a single computer's internal bus.

An object has an *interface* that exposes its *methods* – operations performed on the object. Objects can invoke one another's methods while collaborating, in order to perform the application functionality.

Even a legacy application that was developed back in that ancient data processing center can participate. It can be *wrapped*, using an appropriate *object wrapper*, to provide an object-oriented interface and object-oriented access to its functionality.

45.1.1 *Navigating the object ocean*

What if we treated the operations on the distributed objects as topics in a topic map?[1] More precisely, we want to treat the methods defined in the classes as topics, and the methods on specific instances of the classes – the objects – as the corresponding topic occurrences.

Recall that associations are relationships between topics. The fact that the topic "method A" is calling the topic "method B" is an *association* between the two topics. The *association roles* that the topics – the methods – play in that association would be `caller` and `callee`.

45.1.2 *Mapping control flow*

What happens when you navigate a topic map that represents the methods of distributed objects? As the *control flow* – the logic – of the application is captured in the topic map, the application executes as those methods are called during the navigation.

This is an important notion.

Programmers have customarily included the control flow in the code. After all, this is a good part of what programming is all about and is actually fun to do! Is it even feasible, let alone desirable, to move control flow out of the code in this way?

The answer lies in the granularity of the objects and methods that we choose to model in the topic map.

At the micro, physical data structure level, encapsulating the control flow in the code is unavoidable. Although in principle even this control flow could be represented in a topic map, that map would be too large, too focused on the physical aspects, and too detailed to serve any useful purpose.

---

1. If you aren't certain of what that means, take a few moments to read the tutorial in Chapter 43, "Topic maps: Knowledge navigation aids", on page 628.

However, if the objects and methods being modeled as a topic map are at a sufficiently high level – representing abstractions of real-life business objects – then the topic map of the object interactions is immediately meaningful. Such topic maps are useful for integration because they model the workflow of the business.

45.1.3 *Workflow*

Workflow is a discipline for modeling real-life systems as a sequence of tasks, with the ability to make some branching decisions along the way.

For example the processing of a sales order in a business can be modeled as a workflow. A workflow could also describe how a patient is handled when visiting the physician's office. You can see a workflow illustrated in Figure 45-1; we'll discuss it in detail later on.

A well-designed workflow is *loosely-coupled*, meaning that the components that implement the individual tasks know nothing about one another's internals or data formats, only about their formally-defined interfaces. In contrast, traditional applications (including the components themselves) are termed *tightly-coupled* because their internal objects do have intimate knowledge of one another.

45.1.3.1 Topic maps and workflow

As we have seen, a topic map can model interactions of meaningful high-level business objects. As those interactions represent the workflow of the business, we are effectively modeling business workflow with topic maps.

Given tools to define and manage distributed object topic maps, and a runtime platform for map navigation, topic maps could become vehicles for application integration without heavy-duty programming.

45.1.3.2 Content and workflow

Business objects return business data, which has formally-defined semantics and a known format. It is the same sort of data found in relational databases and spreadsheets.

Enterprises also have large amounts of free-form creative data, such as reports, plans, procedures, and similar documents. Chapter 43, "Topic maps: Knowledge navigation aids", on page 628 explained how to navigate around such content using topic maps.

Suppose that in addition to business objects, a workflow were to include distributed objects that generated free-form content from a topic map. That content topic map would be distinct from the distributed object topic map, although as both are topic maps they could be stored and managed in the same topic map database, using the same access mechanisms.

However, the distributed object topic map could model the operations of the content-generation objects together with the operations on the application business objects. Doing so would facilitate tighter integration of free-form content with business process data.

Let's look at an architecture that could support such workflows.

45.2 | Architecture for application integration

Figure 45-1 illustrates an architecture for application integration by means of topic maps. It is based on an actual implementation of a topic-based integration platform developed by XCare.net.

The architecture provides for application business objects and content generation objects. Their behavior is controlled by topic maps of their interactions and topic maps of the content.

The primary components of the architecture are the three managers: the context manager, the semantic manager, and the service manager. These components essentially act as brokers, by connecting a client browser service request to an appropriate server component.

45.2.1 Context manager

The context manager is responsible for managing the session and maintaining its state. As the user navigates the information space described by the topic map, the context manager maintains the state across the navigations and makes session-level data available to the other components.

Figure 45-1   Application integration architecture using topic maps

45.2.2 *Semantic manager*

The semantic manager has the most to do of all the managers. Its role is to navigate the topic maps that model the interactions of the application business objects. The semantic manager also manages the topic maps database.

45.2.2.1   Topic maps

The semantic manager understands workflows that are represented as `topicmap` XML documents, like the one shown in Example 45-1.

45.2.2.2   Association evaluators

The semantic manager evaluates the associations defined in the topic maps by running *association evaluators (AEs)* that are included in the association definitions. In XCare.net's implementation, AEs are snippets of Java code that have access to the context in which they are running.

The runtime context for AEs consists of:

- the user's security principal,
- the state data managed by the context manager,
- the object instances of the classes that are defined as topics in the topic map, and
- the specific set of HTTP request parameters that the browser sent.

The semantic manager provides the runtime environment for the AEs.

45.2.3 *Service manager*

The service manager's primary responsibility is to bridge the connections among the application objects, the content generation objects, and the external systems. It is essentially a specialized directory service for locating those things.

The service manager isn't fundamental to the architecture, but it helps draw the line between those software components that are responsible for the integration and those that need to be integrated.

45.3 | A simple workflow example

Let's look at a simple example of a workflow topic map.

Suppose you decide to take your spouse out on a surprise date to dinner, followed by a show or a movie. This "system" can be modeled using the workflow in Figure 45-2.

The topic map representing this workflow model is in Example 45-1. It begins with a bit of housekeeping in which it defines the "types" of things that occur in the map, then topics for the complete workflow (SurpriseDate) and for the exit from it (GoHome).

The map then defines the HaveDinner, EnjoyTheShow and EnjoyTheMovie topics.

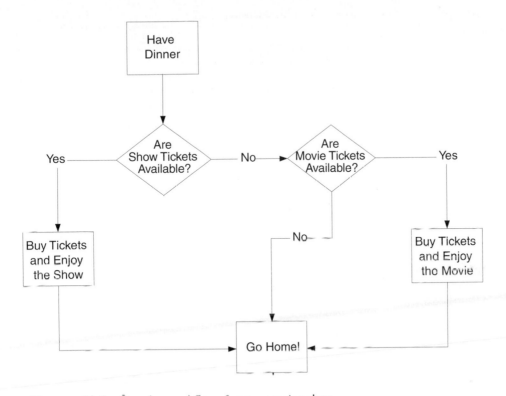

Figure 45-2 Simple workflow for a surprise date

These topics represent class-methods of objects, not their specific instances. The instances will not be determined until a runtime instantiation of the workflow is made. Associations representing paths through the workflow are defined. They associate the topics that represent the workflow steps.

Example 45-2 shows a topic map representing such a runtime instantiation. Again, housekeeping topics occur, as do the class-method topics HaveDinner, EnjoyTheShow and EnjoyTheMovie. This time, however, the latter three topics have occurrences, which are references to object-methods.

The workflow instance topic map inherits from the workflow definition topic map the associations that define the flow of control.

Example 45-1. Simple workflow definition topic map

```
<topicmap>
<!-- "Types" for categorizing topics and associations -->
<topic id="class-method"/> <!-- For topics -->
<topic id="control-flow"/> <!-- For control flow -->
<topic id="caller"/>  <!-- Calling object in association -->
<topic id="callee"/>  <!-- Called object in association -->
<topic id="AE"/>      <!-- Association evaluator -->
<!-- Topics -->
<topic id="SurpriseDate" types="class-method">
  <topname><basename>SurpriseDate</basename></topname>
</topic>
<topic id="GoHome" types="class-method">
  <topname><basename>GoHome</basename></topname>
</topic>
<topic id="HaveDinner" types="class-method">
  <topname><basename>HaveDinner</basename></topname>
</topic>
<topic id="EnjoyTheShow" types="class-method">
  <topname><basename>EnjoyTheShow</basename></topname>
</topic>
<topic id="EnjoyTheMovie" types="class-method">
  <topname><basename>EnjoyTheMovie</basename></topname>
</topic>
<!-- Associations -->
<assoc type="control-flow">
  <assocrl type="caller" href="SurpriseDate"/>
  <assocrl type="callee" href="EnjoyTheShow"/>
  <assocrl type="AE"     href="AreShowTicketsAvailable()"/>
</assoc>
<assoc type="control-flow">
  <assocrl type="caller" href="SurpriseDate"/>
  <assocrl type="callee" href="EnjoyTheMovie"/>
  <assocrl type="AE"     href="AreMovieTicketsAvailable(Cabaret)"/>
</assoc>
<assoc type="control-flow">
  <assocrl type="caller" href="SurpriseDate"/>
  <assocrl type="callee" href="GoHome"/>
  <assocrl type="AE"     href="Always()"/>
</assoc>
</topicmap>
```

45.4 | A compound workflow example

Real life workflows are more complex than the simple workflow defined above. But the complexity usually derives from the repetition of simple

Example 45-2. Simple workflow instance topic map

```
<topicmap>
<!-- "Types" for categorizing topics -->
<topic id="class-method"/> <!-- For topics -->
<!-- Topics and occurrences -->
<topic id="SurpriseDate" types="class-method">
  <topname><basename>SurpriseDate</basename></topname>
  <occurs type="object-method" href="OurDate"/>
</topic>
<topic id="HaveDinner" types="class-method">
  <topname><basename>HaveDinner</basename></topname>
  <occurs type="object-method" href="BonesSteakHouse"/>
</topic>
<topic id="EnjoyTheShow" types="class-method">
  <topname><basename>EnjoyTheShow</basename></topname>
  <occurs type="object-method" href="Ragtime"/>
</topic>
<topic id="EnjoyTheMovie" types="class-method">
  <topname><basename>EnjoyTheMovie</basename></topname>
  <occurs type="object-method" href="Cabaret"/>
</topic>
<topic id="GoHome" types="class-method">
  <topname><basename>GoHome</basename></topname>
  <occurs type="object-method" href="OurHome"/>
</topic>
</topicmap>
```

workflows in various combinations. In other words, the supposedly complex workflow is actually a compound one, consisting of a hierarchy of simple workflows with relatively straightforward logic relating them.

Topic maps lend themselves well to representing compound workflows because they are easily combined. Any of the topics in a topic map can be a topic map in its own right.

Suppose we complicate the SurpriseDate workflow in Figure 45-2. Let's say that the kids need to be taken care of before the surprise date with your spouse can begin.

The new workflow, shown in Figure 45-3, is conceptually more complex, but actually simpler than Figure 45-2 in practice, as it is built on top of the SurpriseDate workflow. Its topic map is shown in Example 45-3.

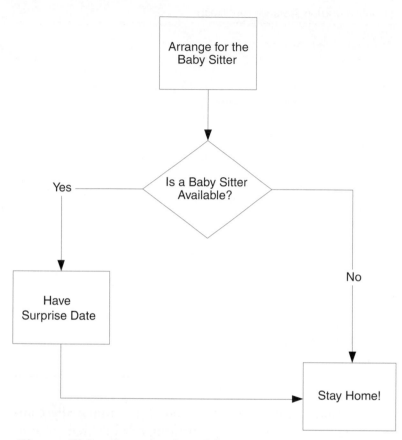

Figure 45-3   Compound workflow

45.5 | Conclusion

We have seen many examples in this book of using XML for data sharing among disparate applications. XML workflow topic maps offer an elegant technique for coordinating the execution of those applications. Industries, such as healthcare, where there is currently a serious lack of effective integration among systems, could especially benefit from topic-based integration.

Example 45-3. Compound workflow topic map

```
<topicmap>
<!-- "Types" for categorizing topics and associations -->
<topic id="class-method"/> <!-- For topics -->
<topic id="control-flow"/> <!-- For control flow -->
<topic id="caller"/>  <!-- Calling object in association -->
<topic id="callee"/>  <!-- Called object in association -->
<topic id="AE" />     <!-- Association evaluator -->
<!-- Topics -->
<topic id="KidlessDate" types="class-method">
  <topname><basename>KidlessDate</basename></topname>
</topic>
<topic id="GoHome" types="class-method">
  <topname><basename>GoHome</basename></topname>
</topic>
<topic id="ArrangeBabySitter" types="class-method">
  <topname><basename>ArrangeBabySitter</basename></topname>
</topic>
<topic id="SurpriseDate" types="class-method">
  <topname><basename>SurpriseDate</basename></topname>
</topic>
<!-- Associations -->
<assoc type="control-flow">
  <assocrl type="caller" href="KidlessDate"/>
  <assocrl type="callee" href="ArrangeBabySitter"/>
  <assocrl type="AE"     href="IsBabySitterAvailable()"/>
</assoc>
  <assocrl type="caller" href="KidlessDate"/>
  <assocrl type="callee" href="SurpriseDate"/>
  <assocrl type="AE"     href="DoesWorkflowExist()"/>
</assoc>
<assoc type="control-flow">
  <assocrl type="caller" href="KidlessDate"/>
  <assocrl type="callee" href="GoHome"/>
  <assocrl type="AE"     href="Always()"/>
</assoc>
</topicmap>
```

Web Services

- The vision and the reality
- Applications and technologies
- Deploy your own Web service!

Part Thirteen

The hype about Web services has been voluminous and relentless.

One reader of this book even asked whether we would be changing the focus from XML to Web services. Our reply was that you wouldn't notice the difference! And that's regardless of what you think Web services is. (Besides thinking that it's ungrammatical!)

Some think it is business integration on steroids: companies finding one another automatically and purchasing services without human intervention.

Some think it is universal content processing: user access to any data from any computing device at any location.

And programmers, who have to do the work, think about the reality: some improved technologies for distributed computing.

But all of these thoughts involve XML. Web services is *XML* Web services, the culmination of everything you've been reading. In this part, we'll look at both the vision and the reality.

The Web services vision

Application Discussion

- Next-generation Internet
- Web-based services using XML
- Core services
- Integrated user experience

Sponsor: Microsoft Corporation, `http://msdn.microsoft.com/xml`

Contributing experts: Microsoft staff

Chapter

46

Some say Web services is revolutionary; others that it is merely an incremental change to distributed processing. But enhancing a technology sufficiently can lead to a point at which amazing new applications are possible. If Web services really is a revolution, it may be the first in history to be led by the parties in power!

Picture an online world where constellations of PCs, servers, smart devices and Internet-based services can collaborate seamlessly. Businesses will be able to share data, integrate their processes, and join forces to offer customized, comprehensive solutions to their customers. And the information you or your business need will be available wherever you are – whatever computing device, platform or application you are using.

Today, all we *can* do is picture it.

46.1 | Can we get there from here?

In many respects, today's Internet still mirrors the old mainframe world. It's a server-centric computing model, with the browser playing the role of dumb terminal. Much of the information your business needs is locked up in centralized databases, served up a page at a time to individual users.

Worse, Web pages are simply a "picture" of the data, not the data itself, forcing many developers back to "screen scraping" to acquire information.

And integrating that underlying data with your business' existing systems – never mind those of your partners – is a costly and frustrating challenge.

Compounding this frustration is the fact that today's standalone applications and Web sites create islands of functionality and data. You have to navigate manually between Web sites, devices and applications, logging in each time and rarely being able to carry data with you. You have to keep constant track of which particular application or device or Web site gives you which level of access to which particular data. Tasks that ought to be simple – such as arranging a meeting with colleagues from partner companies and automatically updating every attendee's calendar – are a nightmare. Productivity is one of the main casualties.

Solving such problems is the key challenge for the next generation of the Internet. A revolution is needed.

46.2 | A revolution is upon us – again!

Fortunately, one is easily found.

Revolutions are a way of life in the computer industry. Only 20 years ago, the world was still in the mainframe era. Few people had access to or used computers. When they did, it was only through the company IT department. The PC, the graphical user interface, and the introduction of the Internet changed all that. They democratized computing for hundreds of millions of people and transformed the computer into a mass-market product.

Since then, standards such as HTML and HTTP have exponentially increased people's use of the Internet. These base protocols for viewing content on the Web (and the associated software for "browsing" this content) grew Web usage to what it is today – a key activity in the daily lives of business employees and consumers.

And it is HTML's sibling, XML, that is enabling the revolution that will make the next generation of the Internet possible. As we have seen throughout this book, XML enables developers to describe data being exchanged among PCs, smart devices, applications and Web sites. Because XML separates the underlying abstract data from the way that data is rendered and displayed, the data itself is "unlocked" so that it can easily be organized, programmed, edited and exchanged.

XML is a lingua franca for the Internet age. Just as the Web revolutionized the way users talk to applications, XML can transform the way applications talk to one another.

46.3 | Web services

As developers become more familiar with XML, they are moving beyond simply using it for data. With the help of XML-based technologies such as SOAP, WSDL, and UDDI,[1] they are creating a new type of software, called *Web services*, that uses XML to provide Web-based services.

The vocabulary here has some subtle distinctions:

- *Web-based services* are services of any kind delivered over the Web.
- *Web services technologies* are WSDL and two XML-based protocols: SOAP and UDDI.
- *Web services* are Web-based services implemented with Web services technologies.

Web services programs are configurable and reusable, much like component software, and they are accessible anywhere via the Internet. Programs using this model will run by coordinating multiple Web sites, drawing on information and services from each of them, and combining and delivering the result in customized form to any device.

Because Web services breaks down the distinctions between the Internet, standalone applications and types of computing devices, businesses can collaborate on integrated and customized solutions.

For example:

- A company offering an online electronic-payment service can expose it to partners, so they can deliver it as part of their own offerings regardless of the platform they are using.

---

1. SOAP is described in 2.11.3, "Protocols", on page 52; WSDL and UDDI were introduced there and are described in more detail in Chapter 47, "Web services technologies", on page 680.

- An airline can link its online reservation system to that of a car-rental partner, so travelers can book a car at the same time they book a flight.
- An online auction company can notify bidders when they are outbid or have won an auction, or could partner with other firms to offer alternative shipping, fulfillment or payment options.

46.3.1 *Basic principles*

This new Internet-based integration methodology has four basic principles.

Internet connection

The first principle is that systems connect through the Internet – a safe assumption given the high availability and low-cost connectivity it provides.

Service discovery

Second, there needs to be a simple way to find services on the Internet with which businesses can work. UDDI and WSDL fulfill that function. Traditional means are usable as well, such as word of mouth or printed directories. However, UDDI and WSDL, by formalizing the process, help to automate it.

Common data representation

Third, a common language is needed to ensure that information can be shared with others. XML is the ingredient that makes this possible. XML provides a common data representation so that your business partners and customers won't need to use a particular programming language, application, or operating system to interact with your systems.

Common communication protocol

The final principle is that there must be a common protocol for actually conducting business; for example, to call the service, book the appointment, order the part, or deliver the information. SOAP is this protocol. It enables systems to talk to one another and make requests.

These four principles embody flexible technologies that can bind disparate systems with different programming languages, thereby unifying personal computing, enterprise computing, and the Web.

46.3.2 *Expected benefits*

Web services should provide several benefits for businesses. It is hard to describe them without some hype, but that's the nature of revolutions.

- Easier integration

  Your software will more easily integrate with other pieces of software – from the desktop to the mainframe – both within your enterprise and at external sites. These integration capabilities will enable you to forge closer ties with business partners and pursue development of joint business processes.

- Faster application development

  As the impact of Web services grows, developers will deliver more and more software and services, including legacy applications, that operate within the Web services programming model. If there is existing code that can help on a project, you can find and integrate it through Web services instead of reinventing it.

- Easier personalization

  Data can be accessed from common data sources rather than collected and maintained on an application-by-application basis. You can simply request common data as needed and transform it dynamically to deliver individualized results.

46.4 | Implementing the vision

As you might expect, a vision with this much excitement – not to mention economic potential – is shared by more than one computer company. In fact, because the Web services technologies are industry-backed open specifications, virtually every major software and hardware vendor is building implementation tools.

And in principle, they should all interoperate. After all, integration is the reason for building them in the first place!

For example, Microsoft's platform for building, deploying, operating and integrating Web services is called *.NET*. One of its interesting characteristics is the incorporation of Web services developed with the platform as part of the platform. Like the familiar development concept of the class library, with its reusable code, the platform has a reusable core set of Web services.

46.4.1 *Authentication services*

The first of these core services is known as *Microsoft Passport*. Independent websites such as online magazines can use this service to verify that Web users are who they claim they are. This is known as *authentication*.

A *Passport* user can automatically log in to any site that is connected to the *Passport* Web service. Rather than ask you for a password, the site merely verifies that you are currently logged into *Passport*.

Microsoft states that, as of this writing, *Passport* provides authentication services for 160 million accounts.

46.4.2 *The integrated user experience*

One of the aims of applications built with Web services – and certainly one of the claims – is that the end user experience will be something very different from today's.

Because Web services link applications, services, and devices together in connected solutions, the claim goes, software arrives as part of an integrated and simplified experience. Users will be able to act on information any time, any place, from any smart device.

The concept is illustrated in Figure 46-1.

But integrating all of the Web services and client software a particular user needs, and presenting them anywhere on any device, requires more than just an authentication service.

CLIENTS   WEB SERVICES   SERVERS

Figure 46-1 Combining Web services to create "user experiences"

46.4.3 *Other core services*

.NET My Services™ is Microsoft's planned successor to *Passport*. The services provide more than authentication. They allow a user to keep a wide variety of personal information in a shared remote database instead of on a single device.

That means that no matter what machine you use anywhere in the world, the same information will be available. Third-party websites will be able to access the part of the information you allow them to have. For example, you could share your contact list with an online greeting card site so that you would not have to reenter it.

The initial services are shown in Example 46-1.

It will be possible to use these services through Web browsers as well as through the SOAP Web services protocol. Because they are core services,

Example 46-1. Initial set of *.NET My Services*

```
myAddress
    electronic and geographic addresses for an identity
myProfile
    name, nickname, special dates, picture
myContacts
    electronic relationships, address book
myLocation
    electronic and geographical location and rendezvous
myNotifications
    notification subscription, management and routing
myInbox
    email and voice mail, including existing mail systems
myCalendar
    time and task management
myDocuments
    document storage
myApplicationSettings
    application settings
myFavoriteWebSites
    favorite URLs and other Web identifiers
myWallet
    receipts, payment instruments, coupons, transaction records
myDevices
    device settings, capabilities
myServices
    services provided for an identity
myUsage
    usage report for above services
```

developers will be able to incorporate their functionality into the Web services they develop.

Analysis   Web services is a very far-reaching and ambitious vision, with implications for all Web users and, if the goals are achieved, for much of the economy as well. All of the major software and hardware vendors are promoting Web services, and Microsoft has made it central to its plans for the future. Reliability, security and privacy of the services will obviously be of paramount importance. Regardless, from a purely technical standpoint it is fascinating to see plans for such a wide array of services based on XML and XML-based protocols.

Web services technologies

Application Discussion

▌ Service discovery

▌ Web Services Description Language (WSDL)

▌ Universal Description, Discovery, and Integration

Chapter

47

Computer programs are brittle. It is easier for applications to talk to people than to other applications. That's why Web services specifications are less mature than pure Web specifications. Although the grand vision of Web services may take years to arrive, the same could have been (and was!) said of XML itself when the First Edition of this book was published. Just so you won't miss the leading edge, here's how the Web services technologies work.

There are three major Web services technologies: SOAP, WS-DL, and UDDI. In 2.11.3, "Protocols", on page 52 we covered SOAP in some detail and briefly introduced the others. Now we'll take a closer look at the other two. Unlike SOAP, whose object-orientation is pretty much limited to its name, WSDL and UDDI are imbued with the object-oriented model.[1]

47.1 | Web Services Description Language

If I agree to provide you with some XML documents, we will also agree on the document type. That agreement is usually recorded formally in a DTD or schema definition. The definition is like a recipe: It lists the ingredients of a dish – in this case, the data elements of the documents that I'm serving.

---

1. If you are a developer, you are probably similarly imbued. Other readers may want to review 49.5.1.1, "What is an object?", on page 718.

If I agree to provide you information through an XML-based protocol, you'll want to know the offerings I have available and how to request each one. For this you'll need a description of my service, which I can express formally using the Web Services Description Language (WSDL). The service description is like a menu from a take-out restaurant: It tells you in great detail what is available and your options for getting it.

Figure 47-1 shows the components of WSDL in the form of a stack. Ignore the details for now; just focus on the middle column.

47.1.1 *Starting at the top: service*

WSDL is a layered specification. Each layer depends upon the layer directly below it. There is a certain elegance to layered designs. When you are working with them, you can concentrate on one layer at a time. Using this technique, let's explore WSDL by working from the top down with an application example.[2]

Logically enough for a language that describes Web services, the top concept is the *service*. In our case, it is a global meteorological service offered to subscriber corporations. It might, in turn, get its information from other Web services run by national meteorological departments.

47.1.2 *Dividing up work: port*

A service could offer multiple functions, called *operations*. To balance the resources for supporting them, the service could span multiple physical computer systems. Access to particular groups of operations is provided by *ports*. Each port could exist on a different machine or multiple ports could be on the same machine. That is totally up to the Web service creator.

Each port has a name. Perhaps one port would serve the temperatures, another the humidity and a third the barometric pressure. It would all depend on what was most convenient for the person constructing the service. Let's call our ports `temperature`, `humidity` and `pressure`. They might have Web addresses such as:

---

2. A sample WSDL document from a different example is shown in 48.4, "Describing our service with WSDL", on page 700.

Figure 47-1 The WSDL stack

- http://temperature.weatherworld.com/
- http://humidity.weatherworld.com/ and
- http://pressure.weatherworld.com

We could have put two ports on the same machine if that was convenient.

Because ports are URL-specific, it makes no sense for this part of a Web service to be defined in an industry standard, as you might define an industry standard DTD or schema. The other parts of a WSDL definition are more reusable than the ports.

47.1.3   *Choosing a transport protocol: binding*

Now that we know where on the Internet to go for the ports that give access to different operations of the service, we need to know how to communicate with them. For that, each port must specify a *binding*.

Recall from 2.11.3, "Protocols", on page 52 that protocols tend to build on one another. A binding is basically a way of defining a new protocol based on an existing one. In this case, the existing protocol is the *transport protocol* that is used to transport the messages from place to place. It makes sense to build on top of an existing transport protocol because otherwise you would have to specify the exact order of the bits travelling down the wire. That would be a total waste of time!

In this case we are going to build our new meteorological protocol on top of SOAP. We could also specify a binding based on the older HTTP protocol that is used by Web browsers. However, each port may support only one binding. For the service to support both transport protocols, we would have to define separate ports, with names like `temperature_soap`, and `temperature_http`. Both ports would support the same operation; only the transport protocol would differ.

The WSDL spec describes how to use WSDL with SOAP and HTTP. Third parties could define how to use WSDL with (for example) XML-RPC or the popular mail protocol SMTP. Any existing transport protocol could be used, but somebody, somewhere would have to write a document explaining how WSDL and the protocol fit together.

The binding does more than just choose the transport protocol. It also specifies some details about how to use the transport protocol for each operation. These details depend upon which transport protocol you have chosen. For instance if you choose SOAP, you get to choose options that are available in the SOAP specification and generally tweak the layout of the SOAP messages that are sent across the network.

47.1.4 *Getting abstract: port type*

Each binding is associated not only with a transport protocol but also with a *port type*, which is a set of operations provided by the service. All the operations of a service are grouped into one or more port types. In our example, we've created three port types with one operation each, temperature, humidity and pressure.

This is the layer at which we start to lift off from the very concrete into the land of the abstract. The bindings and ports were concrete in that they defined how the information would be laid out in terms of SOAP messages (or HTTP messages) and where on the Internet the messages would physically go.

Port types are abstract. They do not say what exactly should go on the wire nor where that information should go. Rather they define in the abstract what sort of things can be said. That means, for example, that an industry group could define a single port type for handling temperatures and then specify a variety of bindings for it.

Doing so would allow some Web services to handle temperatures using SOAP (the most popular Web services protocol), some to use XML-RPC (the older protocol), and some to use HTTP (the protocol for the existing Web). Service providers could compete based on which concrete bindings they provide for the same abstract port types.

47.1.5 *Defining behavior: operation*

Each port type has a name and a set of *operations*. Any Web service that claims to support the port type must have concrete bindings for each of the operations. Just as a DTD or schema requires many XML documents to have the same element structure, all ports of the same type must support the same operations.

Operations are defined in terms of input, output, and faults.

Imagine a real-world service for delivering pizza. To place an order, you must give the pizzeria a list of toppings, an address and a credit card number. In WSDL terms these are the *input* to the process.

Hopefully you will eventually get a pizza. This is called the *output*. If something goes wrong, you can expect a phone call along the lines of "we could not find your house" or "we could not process your credit card." These error messages are called *faults*.

47.1.6 *The information unit: message*

In our meteorological example, the output certainly is not a pizza and a fault is not a phone call. Web services deal in information represented as XML. The unit of information sent back and forth between programs is an XML *message*. Operations define their input, output and faults in terms of messages.

The operation `query_temperature` would have as its input a geographical location. Users are probably interested in the temperature where they live! We would therefore define a message type for asking about the temperature at a particular point on the globe. It might also allow the user to specify whether the result should be in celsius or fahrenheit. The output would be another XML message, containing the temperature represented as an integer.

We might send fault messages for requesting an unsupported location (e.g. Antarctica) and for requesting an unsupported temperature unit (e.g. Kelvin).

Let us say we called our output message type `temperature_report`. The interesting thing about this element type is that it could be useful in a totally different operation, wherein a remote weather station reports the temperature to our server. For that operation, it would be an input message rather than an output.

In other words, the remote station would contact us and send a `temperature_report` message as input. Later, an end-user could request the neighborhood temperature and we would send another `temperature_report` message, this time as output.

47.1.7 *Composing messages: part and type*

Each message has one or more components, called *parts*. Every part is an element, either one whose content is a datatype defined in the *XML Schema* specification, or one that conforms to a defined complex element type.

For instance the input to our `query_temperature` operation would need a latitude and longitude. Each of these could be a part with data content conforming to the *XML Schema* integer datatype.

Alternatively, we could define a single complex `position` element type with subelements or attributes for the latitude and longitude. We would then refer to that one element type in our message part definition.

It is possible to define new element types by embedding their definitions right in the Web service description, or else by referring to external schema definitions. You can define types that are very simple, such as credit card number, or very complex, such as purchase order.

Creating definitions in WSDL is easiest with the *XML Schema* definition language (XSDL), but other schema languages can be used as well.

47.1.8 *Summary of WSDL*

Here is a summary of the WSDL hierarchy shown in Figure 47-1, working from the top down. Now the details we encouraged you to skip the first time should be meaningful.

service
> A Web service performs operations. These are grouped into one or more sets, called "port types." Each port type is accessed from one or more ports.

ports
> A port establishes a binding between a port type and a Web address for accessing the port type's operations. There could be several ports of the same type, each bound to a different transport protocol. The addresses of a service's ports could point to the same or different machines.

bindings
> Bindings are the links between the physical implementation of a Web service and the abstract interface. Each binding specifies how a particular transport protocol is used for the operations of a given port type.

port types
> The operations provided by a Web service are grouped into one or more port types. Port types define the abstract interface to a Web service.

operations

An operation could consume a particular input and/or produce a particular output. If errors occur, it could also produce faults. Inputs, outputs, and faults are types of messages.

messages

Messages are XML documents. They are made up of parts.

parts

A part is an element of a specific type.

types

Part types can be complex element types (with subelements and/or attributes) or simple datatypes. They are typically defined in XSDL.

The layers obviously go from most complex ("a complete Web service") to simplest ("a single element"). They also go from concrete implementation ("send these bits, to this URL, on this machine, using this transport") to abstract interface ("the types of things we are talking about are temperatures and air pressures").

Most importantly, the layers go from most specific to most reusable. Compare the definition "Sal's Pizza on the corner of Main Street and First Avenue" with the generic term "pizzeria". The first is very specific because it includes a concrete location. Web services also have one or more concrete locations because they are provided by the ports.

It is the lower layers that are reusable and might be defined by an industry consortium rather than a specific company. There is not necessarily anything company-specific about bindings, operations, messages or element types. In many circumstances it would make sense to share these and have multiple competing implementations.

But it would never make sense to share ports themselves. It is no more possible to "compete" by sharing a port than it would be to open two pizzerias at the same address!

47.2 | UDDI

Now we know how to check the temperature or order a pizza. But from whom? What if you wanted to find a weather information service or pizzeria? You might know in the abstract what sort of service (bindings, operations, etc.) you want, but you wouldn't necessarily know how to find all of the relevant service providers.

47.2.1 *Finding a service provider*

Universal Description, Discovery, and Integration (UDDI) is a project to create the Web services world's equivalent of a phone book. When you want to find a service in your town, you pick up the **Universal** yellow pages business **Description** listings and scan through them to **Discover** one that meets your requirements. Then you might **Integrate** the listing with your wallet through the "scissors" protocol!

UDDI is based on SOAP and WSDL. Service providers will use it to let Web services consumers know that their services exist, just as yellow pages help off-line consumers to know that businesses exist.

UDDI is different from existing business directories because of its integration with Web services. For instance, the UDDI business registry is actually a Web service itself, so programmers can contact it and ask it questions through SOAP. UDDI and SOAP are also integrated in a more important way. The UDDI registry can report what Web services are available from a particular business.

In theory a computer could connect to a UDDI registry, use SOAP to search it for a Web service implementing a "real-time currency conversion" operation, connect to that service and do the conversion without human intervention.

The information available through UDDI is typically described as falling into one of three categories, based on the telephone book metaphor:

white pages
>   These describe an organization's name, address and contact information.

yellow pages
> Yellow pages categorize businesses by industrial category and geographical location.

green pages
> The so-called green pages are technical descriptions of how to interact with each organization's services.

47.2.2 *UDDI data structures*

A UDDI *registry* is a database of *business entities, business services, binding templates* and *tModels*. These are known as the four UDDI *data structures*.

47.2.2.1   Business entities

Business entities are records of corporations or departments. They contain names, contacts, descriptions and other identifying information.

A business entity is uniquely identified by a `businessKey`, which is a long random-looking string of numbers and letters known as a *Universally Unique ID (UUID)*.

47.2.2.2   Business services

Business services are records of the services provided by a business entity. These can be true Web services. However, they can just as easily be traditional offline services, such as phone lines, or non-automated services, such as email.

Each service has a UUID called a `serviceKey`. It also has other identifying information, such as a name and a description. Most importantly, each service refers to one or more `bindingTemplates`.

47.2.2.3   Binding templates

Binding templates specify how to contact the company and consume the service. The most important subelement of the binding template is the access point, which tells how to communicate with the service.

Valid types of access point are:

- `mailto` for email,
- `http` for Web browsers or SOAP,
- `https` for secure HTTP,
- `ftp` for File Transfer Protocol,
- `fax` for fax machine, and
- `phone` for telephone.

47.2.2.4   tModels

tModels[3] are typically used as assertions that a service meets a certain specification. As UDDI is designed to be extremely general, the structure of tModels will vary widely.

tModels can be used to refer to almost any kind of service description. The description can be as technically precise as a WSDL definition or as informal as a prose document.

For Web services, of course, the formal tModels are the useful ones. Other businesses, however, simply cannot be described in that way. What is the input and the output of a dentist? Is biting his finger a fault?

47.2.3   *Will it work?*

UDDI is still very immature and in some cases it is also controversial. There is some question about who should run this "big registry in the sky." Would the operator be some sort of regulated utility just another service provider?

Some wonder whether there is even a good reason to think that service discovery will be any different in the Web services world. Perhaps businesses will continue to find one another through advertisements in magazines, introductions through social networks, and other traditional means. Business does require a certain level of trust after all!

---

3. The word tModel does not really stand for anything.

47.3 | Implementation

It is important to keep in mind that no matter how related they may seem, Web services technologies and Web-based delivery of services are two different things. This is particularly confusing right now because the industry is moving on both fronts at once, which causes people to think that they are the same thing.

Obviously there are already services on the Web that are not based on the new Web services technologies. *HotMail* and *Google* are two examples.

Many people will also use Web services technologies in ways that have nothing to do with providing services to Web browsers. You could easily use SOAP inside your company, for example, or to communicate only with your existing partners through pre-existing leased lines.

Similarly, Web services technologies have nothing technically to do with subscription-based software services, although some of those services are being built *using* Web services technologies.

47.4 | Conclusion

Although the specifications are under active development, much of the promise of Web services remains a dream of the future, not a here-and-now reality. Retain a degree of skepticism.

On the other hand, you can understand why this prospect has so excited the executives of every major software company.

Computers already talk to each other, with and without human supervision. The complexity of this communication will only increase in the future. Just as XML helps you manage the complexities of data representation, the new XML-based Web services technologies will help you with the complexities of computer communication.[4]

---

4. And remember, Web services is a proven concept. Churches in L.A. have been holding them for years.

Deploying a Web service

Application Discussion

- From legacy application to Web service

- Describing a service with WSDL

- Registering a service with UDDI

- Software on CD-ROM

Sponsor: IBM Corporation,
http://www.ibm.com/developerworks/webservices

Contributing expert: Doug Tidwell

Chapter

48

We've seen the grand vision for Web services and looked at the technology that could make that vision a reality. In this chapter we'll get down to the details and see just how easily you can deploy a Web service — even if it's the first program you ever wrote!

Web services as a grand vision of dynamically interoperating software uniting business partners who've never met isn't quite here yet. However, the need for independent programs to cooperate has been around for quite a while. As software, Web services is just the latest means of accomplishing that task.

We'll show you how you can deploy a Web service with technology that's available today.

48.1 | Who does what to whom?

In the Web services world, there are three basic operations, commonly known as *publish*, *find*, and *bind*.

publishing
The process a Web service uses to advertise itself.

find
The operation by which an application finds a Web service.

bind
> The act of attaching to the Web service and using its methods.

These operations involve three parties: *service providers*, *service requestors*, and *service brokers*.

service provider
> An application that publishes and provides a service over a network.

service requestors
> Applications that hope to find a particular service and bind to it.

service broker
> A business that brings service providers and requestors together by operating a registry of services.

To publish a Web service, the provider adds a description of that service to the registry. To find a Web service, the requestor describes a service and the broker returns information about the Web services that match the request. Once the requestor has selected a particular service, the requestor contacts the provider and e-business ensues.

48.2 | A dull but familiar example

Let's look at a sample program. We'll take an underwhelming piece of code and deploy it as a Web service. The point of this example is to demonstrate that virtually any program can be a Web service, which means even the legacy applications that keep your business running.

Example 48-1 shows our sample application. [1]

---

1. The code in Example 48-1 is a slightly modified version of the "Hello, World" application made famous by Brian Kernighan and Dennis Ritchie, everyone's first program. This version is placed in the public domain with the proviso that it may not be used to develop weapons of mass destruction. No animals were harmed during the development, debugging, deploying, or deploring of this application.

Example 48-1. Source code for a less-than-exciting Web service

```
public class HelloWorld
{
  String message = "Hello, World!";

  public String getMessage()
  {
    return message;
  }

  public void setMessage(String m)
  {
    message = m;
  }
}
```

The application provides two methods, getMessage and setMessage. The getMessage method simply returns the current message, whatever it might be, while setMessage allows an application to change the message.

Note that nowhere in the code is there even a hint of modern technologies such as SOAP, XML, or networking. Despite this lack of sophistication, we can still deploy this program as a Web service.

48.3 | Making our code a Web service

Deployment of our example is done with the Apache SOAP toolkit, available at xml.apache.org. To deploy the service, we simply give it a name, define the Java class that implements the service, the names of the methods, and other details as needed. All this is done through a Web form on the SOAP administration console, depicted in Figure 48-1.

We give our Web service an ID, define the methods that it supports (for various reasons, we might not want to support all of a class's public methods in our Web service), and a few other details.

How does a client application invoke this Web service after we've deployed it? Example 48-2 shows a fragment of the Java code needed to invoke our service.[2]

---

2. For simplicity's sake, Example 48-2 omits some of the details, such as defining the encoding used for our data, and setting up a vector of parameters for our method.

Figure 48-1   Apache SOAP toolkit administration console

Example 48-2. Client application for our Web service

```
URL url = new URL("http://localhost:8080/soap/servlet/rpcrouter");
String urn = "urn:Services:HelloWorld";
Call call = new Call();
call.setTargetObjectURI("urn:Services:HelloWorld");
call.setMethodName("getMessage");
. . .
Response response = call.invoke(url, "");
```

This code also uses the Apache SOAP toolkit, which defines the `Call` and `Response` objects that are used to invoke the service. The application creates the `Call` object, fills in the data for the method call (the method name, the parameters, etc.), then calls the `Call.invoke` method.

Example 48-3 is a SOAP message that requests invocation of the `getMessage` method.

Note the line beginning `<hw1:getMessage`. That element tells the SOAP router how to map the information in the XML message document to a particular Java class. The name of the invoked method is the XML element type name, `getMessage`.

Example 48-3. Request for the getMessage method

```
<?xml version='1.0' encoding='UTF-8'?>
<SOAP-ENV:Envelope
xmlns:SOAP-ENV="http://schemas.xmlsoap.org/soap/envelope/"
xmlns:xsi="http://www.w3.org/1999/XMLSchema-instance"
xmlns:xsd="http://www.w3.org/1999/XMLSchema">
<SOAP-ENV:Body>
<hw1:getMessage xmlns:hw1="urn:Services:HelloWorld"
SOAP-ENV:encodingStyle="http://schemas.xmlsoap.org/soap/encoding/">
</hw1:getMessage>
</SOAP-ENV:Body>
</SOAP-ENV:Envelope>
```

Example 48-4 is the XML document that carries the response. It is in the return subelement of the getMessageResponse element.

Example 48-4. Response to the request in Example 48-3

```
<?xml version='1.0' encoding='UTF-8'?>
<SOAP-ENV:Envelope
xmlns:SOAP-ENV="http://schemas.xmlsoap.org/soap/envelope/"
xmlns:xsi="http://www.w3.org/1999/XMLSchema-instance"
xmlns:xsd="http://www.w3.org/1999/XMLSchema">
<SOAP-ENV:Body>
<hw1:getMessageResponse xmlns:hw1="urn:Services:HelloWorld"
SOAP-ENV:encodingStyle="http://schemas.xmlsoap.org/soap/encoding/">
<return xsi:type="xsd:string">Hello, World!</return>
</hw1:getMessageResponse>
</SOAP-ENV:Body>
</SOAP-ENV:Envelope>
```

As we have seen, the entire remote method call is done using XML. An XML document describes the method to be invoked and carries the parameters for that method. The SOAP router returns an XML document containing the results of the method call. Notice also that the results of the method call are described with an *XML Schema* data type: string in this example.

Web services has enabled us to deploy a completely unremarkable piece of code as a Web service. Any application that can access the SOAP router can invoke the methods of our Web service. That means that legacy applications can become Web services with little or no modification.

Be aware that SOAP is designed to be completely neutral with regard to operating system, programming language, and object model. SOAP defines the interfaces we'll use, but we don't have to worry about the platform that's running the Web service, or the language used to write it. We're simply building an XML document and sending it to a particular URL, then receiving another XML document in response. XML's role as the universal representation for structured data makes this possible.

Notice, however, that all of the important information here (such as the URL of the SOAP router, the ID of the service, and the name of the method) is fixed. Our client application can use our Web service remotely, but it can't use any other Web service. With a way to find that information at runtime, we could set the values of those strings and invoke any method of any SOAP service on any server. That's where WSDL comes in.

48.4 | Describing our service with WSDL

If Web services are to be discovered at runtime, we need a standard way of describing them. A service provider who publishes information about a Web service must do so using a standard XML vocabulary. Service requestors searching for it had better describe their needs with the very same vocabulary. WSDL is designed to be that vocabulary.

Example 48-5 shows the WSDL document that describes our *Hello World* service.

Everything a client would need to invoke the methods of our Web service is there. You can see most of the elements that we discussed in 47.1, "Web Services Description Language", on page 681. The interface elements are shown first (`message` and `portType`), then their implementation (`binding` and `service`).

We won't go into all of the details, but note the following:

`urn:Services:HelloWorld`
> This is the ID of the service. It occurs several times in the document.

`name` **attribute of** `operation`
> The values of these attributes (there are two occurrences) are the names of the methods.

Example 48-5. Our Web service described in WSDL

```
<definitions name="HelloWorldDefinitions"
  targetNamespace="http://www.HelloWorld.com/wrapperedService"
  xmlns="http://schemas.xmlsoap.org/wsdl/"
  xmlns:tns="http://www.HelloWorld.com/wrapperedService"
  xmlns:soap="http://schemas.xmlsoap.org/wsdl/soap/"
  xmlns:xsd="http://www.w3.org/1999/XMLSchema">
<message name="InsetMessageRequest">
  <part name="meth1_inType1" type="xsd:string"/></message>
<message name="IngetMessageRequest"/>
<message name="OutgetMessageResponse">
  <part name="meth2_outType" type="xsd:string"/></message>
<portType name="HelloWorldPortType">
  <operation name="setMessage">
    <input message="tns:InsetMessageRequest"/></operation>
  <operation name="getMessage">
    <input message="tns:IngetMessageRequest"/>
    <output message="tns:OutgetMessageResponse"/></operation>
</portType>
<binding name="HelloWorldBinding" type="tns:HelloWorldPortType">
  <soap:binding style="rpc"
    transport="http://schemas.xmlsoap.org/soap/http"/>
  <operation name="setMessage">
    <soap:operation soapAction="urn:Services:HelloWorld"/>
    <input><soap:body
      encodingStyle="http://schemas.xmlsoap.org/soap/encoding/"
      namespace="urn:Services:HelloWorld" use="encoded"/>
    </input>
  </operation>
  <operation name="getMessage">
    <soap:operation soapAction="urn:Services:HelloWorld"/>
    <input><soap:body
      encodingStyle="http://schemas.xmlsoap.org/soap/encoding/"
      namespace="urn:Services:HelloWorld" use="encoded"/>
    </input>
    <output><soap:body
      encodingStyle="http://schemas.xmlsoap.org/soap/encoding/"
      namespace="urn:Services:HelloWorld" use="encoded"/>
    </output>
  </operation>
</binding>
<service name="HelloWorld">
  <documentation>Class HelloWorld as service</documentation>
  <port binding="tns:HelloWorldBinding" name="HelloWorldPort">
    <soap:address
      location="http://localhost:8080/soap/servlet/rpcrouter"/>
  </port>
</service>
</definitions>
```

`part` **subelements of** `message`
>   Attributes of these elements specify the number and type of each argument passed to or returned from the methods.

`location` **attribute of** `address`
>   This element is in the SOAP namespace. The attribute value is the URL of a SOAP router, which serves as the Web address for our service.

An XML application can parse the information here, connect to the SOAP router, and supply the needed details such as method names, arguments, etc.

One nice feature of WSDL is that tools are currently available to generate most of it for us. Example 48-5 was generated by IBM's *XML and Web Services Development Environment*.[3] The tool can, among other things, examine a JavaBean and generate a WSDL document from it. It can also generate bean skeletons from a WSDL. This allows you to benefit from Java's strong, static type checking and simplify your Web services calling code.[4]

A standard way to describe Web services is all well and good, but we also have to put the descriptions where service providers and service requestors can find them. That's what UDDI is designed to do.

48.5 | Using a UDDI registry

The UDDI spec defines how registries of Web services should work. There are four kinds of information defined in a UDDI registry, with a separate XML element type for each:

`businessEntity`
>   Information about businesses

---

3. The tool can be found on the CD-ROM accompanying this book.
4. Of course, generating WSDL in this way doesn't provide the flexibility of late binding and loose coupling that we've been describing, but it does get you started quickly. It's like converting a rendered document to XML by putting tags around the style codes; you lose the power of an abstraction that can be reused in a variety of ways

businessService
> Information about services

bindingTemplate
> Information about individual templates or methods

tModel
> Information about the specifications or standards implemented by
> a given service (which we'll discuss in a minute).

All of the data structures and APIs in the UDDI specification are representable in XML.

Example 48-6 shows a businessEntity element that describes our company.

Example 48-6. The XML representation of a UDDI BusinessEntity object

```
<businessEntity businessKey="">
  <name>DougCo Manufacturing</name>
  <description xml:lang="en">
    Sample business created to exercise a UDDI registry
  </description>
  <contacts>
    <contact>
      <personName>Doug Tidwell</personName>
      <phone useType="voice">1-919-555-5583</phone>
      <phone useType="fax">1-919-555-2389</phone>
      <email>dtidwell@us.ibm.com</email>
      <address>
        <addressLine>1234 Main Street</addressLine>
        <addressLine>Anytown, TX  73958</addressLine>
      </address>
    </contact>
  </contacts>
</businessEntity>
```

We could use this document to define a new BusinessEntity object in the registry. The businessKey attribute is empty; that tells the registry to assign a unique identifier to our object.

When a service requestor finds a business that implements the *Hello World* service, it receives the service provider's businessKey. It might then use the businessKey to request service details by sending the XML document in Example 48-7 to the registry.

Example 48-7. Request for *Hello World* service details

```
<find_service generic='1.0' xmlns='urn:uddi-org:api'
    businessKey='00038F2D-EC27-95A6-BA21-2399DEA396E7'>
    <name>Hello World service</name>
</find_service>
```

In response to the query in Example 48-7, the registry would return an XML document with a serviceList element that describes the services in more detail. We can then use the information from that element for further queries, drilling down through the information in the registry until we find the exact service we are looking for. Example 48-8 shows what a bindingTemplate for a specific service might look like.

Example 48-8. Binding template for a *Hello World* service

```
<bindingTemplate bindingKey="28BC2890-28CC-380C-3131-8FFCA08A7309"
                 serviceKey="821B38A9-38AC-8103-8CA2-03829A38CC28">
  <description xml:lang="en">
    Hello World interface, provides get and set support
  </description>
  <accessPoint URLType="http">
    http://localhost:8080/uddi/servlet/uddi/
  </accessPoint>
  <tModelInstanceDetails>
    <tModelInstanceInfo
        tModelKey="uuid:83C9AFB0-DD83-280A-381C-FF829A9380CB">
      <description xml:lang="en">
        Hello World interface
      </description>
    </tModelInstanceInfo>
  </tModelInstanceDetails>
</bindingTemplate>
```

The information in Example 48-8 tells us the access point for the service. However, it doesn't contain detailed information about the APIs that the service provides. That's where the TModel concept comes in.

The set of potential Web services is so vast and varied that UDDI doesn't attempt to provide a vocabulary for describing them all. Instead, The TModel element type was created as a way to reference other specifications. This TModel could reference the WSDL description in Example 48-5, for example.

In other words, if there is an externally-defined specification for the *Hello World* service, we can use UDDI queries to find the unique identifier for the *reference* to that spec. We can then use that identifier (the `tModelKey`) to find all service providers that support that same specification. When we find one, we can use the SOAP messages we discussed earlier to invoke the methods defined in the spec.

48.6 | What's next?

The technologies we've reviewed so far are an important step on the way to dynamic applications that are built from a variety of services discovered at runtime. There are a number of things yet to come, however, such as:

service provider ratings
> You might find twenty providers that implement the *Hello World* service; how have other users rated those twenty providers?

micropayments
> Although no one is likely to pay for a *Hello World* service, there are lots of other services that might charge for the service they provide. If a stock quote service charges one cent for each quotation, for example, their cost per transaction will be less than one cent – squarely in the micropayment range.

contract terms
> If our application decides to use a given Web service, there may be times when we need legally binding agreements for our use of the service. What happens if the service provides incorrect information? What happens if the service is unavailable? How much will each invocation of the service cost? It would be extremely useful if these terms could be negotiated automatically by agents.

48.7 | Conclusion

Although the sample program we've used in this chapter doesn't do anything useful, it does demonstrate how to use Web services software to deploy even unsophisticated code over a network. The enabling technology behind all of this is XML.

Analysis   Whether publishing or searching for a service, describing the service's methods and parameters, or interacting with the service itself, everything in Web services involves an XML document. As Web services grows in importance, XML will become the backbone of the Web of the future.

Infrastructure

- Programming technology
- XML file compression
- XML in low-level system functions

Part Fourteen

So far in this book, any mention of "infrastructure" was in the context of XML being a vital part of the infrastructure provided by information distribution and electronic business applications.

In the following chapters, however, we dig down a lot further and see the role that XML plays in the infrastructure that supports those very applications.

We've seen throughout the book how products support XML for content management and data integration, and in this part we'll see how programming technology supports many of those products.

We'll also look at how file compression – increasingly important in these days of growing network loads and low-speed wireless access – can be enhanced by taking advantage of the predictability of XML documents.

Finally, we'll get a glimpse into a future where XML is ubiquitous, even finding its way into low-level system functions and specialized hardware.

XML processing

Tool Discussion

▮ XML processing stack

▮ Object-oriented programming

▮ Data mapping and binding

▮ The stack in action

Sponsor: Hewlett-Packard Company, http://www.hp.bluestone.com

Contributing expert: Richard Friedman

Chapter

49

A *stack* is an effective model for discussing items that are built upon one another, where the upper layers are dependent on those below. We've seen several stacks already, showing relationships among protocols and among components of business integration systems. In this chapter we'll see why programmers choosing XML development tools like products that stack up well!

Recall our discussion of protocols in 2.11.3, "Protocols", on page 52? We pointed out that protocols build on one another, a relationship that is normally modeled as a multi-layered stack. And remember the stack in Figure 16-2? It is a "high-level" view, meaning that each layer of the stack could be broken down into multiple components.

The stack metaphor is extremely popular among developers, for reasons that we'll discuss shortly. But remember that a stack is just a model, a convenient way of discussing something. A high-level stack might be fine for teaching the concepts of a subject[1] but it could lack the precision needed at the more detailed level required for implementing a product.

49.1 | The XML processing stack

A more detailed stack for XML processing is shown in Figure 49-1. It has four layers: transport, parsing, document handling, and data binding. We

---

1. At least we hope so!

can use this stack in several ways. When describing software behavior, the stack indicates that each layer incorporates functions from the layer below it. In terms of data flow, it indicates that data enters at the bottom layer and flows up to the top.

Data mapping and binding — objects, relational tables, legacy applications

Document handling — BPM, extended validation, data transformation, CBR

Parsing — parser, validator, data structure constructor

Transport — HTTP/S, SMTP, FTP, JMS, file, ...

Figure 49-1   The XML processing stack

transport

The bottom layer is the point at which data enters the stack. Despite the term "transport", the entry could be through various methods, including local disks as well as network access.

parsing

In this layer the unparsed XML text string is converted into a form that can be used by the rest of the stack's functions. Markup is separated from the data, which is stored in a data structure that is accessible to subsequent processing.

document handling

Processing in this layer includes such functions as validation and routing. More generally, it includes all of the post-parsing services that are built into generic XML-processing tools. We have a dedicated layer for parsing because it is such an important and near-universal service, while the services in this layer can be skipped for many applications.

data binding

Third-layer operations often involve integration with databases and legacy systems. In these cases, the fourth layer of the stack controls the means by which the XML data is used to update these systems.

The stack architecture has a significant benefit for XML processing. It clearly defines where data passes from one layer to the next, which allows common interfaces to be developed. Because of those interfaces, for example, a variety of parsers can be substituted interchangeably in the parsing layer of a well-designed system.

But bear in mind that not every application requires every layer of the stack, and some programs span multiple layers.

Let's look more closely at each layer of the stack.

49.2 | Transport

In Figure 49-1 the bottom layer of the stack is labeled "transport", which implies some movement of data, typically over a network. Realistically, this layer should perhaps be labeled "data sources", as an XML document could come from many different places.

For example, it could exist as a file on a local disk, as part of an electronic mail message, or as a file on a Web or FTP server, in addition to being transmitted over a network. But as we just saw, regardless of how a document arrives at the point of processing, there is a consistent interface for entering the parsing layer. The stack architecture hides the physical characteristics of the transport layer and provides a normalized view of it.

Even with normalization, network-specific issues can emerge. That is because an XML message will sometimes need to pass through proxy servers and firewalls before reaching its intended destination. Therefore, it is wise to be careful about external dependencies, such as remote schema definitions, external subsets of document type definitions, stylesheets, and external entities in general.

49.3 | Parsing

The parsing layer ensures that a document meets the requirements for being a well-formed XML document. This means it needs to meet the specifications defined in the W3C XML 1.0 Recommendation. However, other things happen in this layer as well.

49.3.1 *Schema validation*

The parsing layer is the point for *validating* the XML document; that is, testing whether the document conforms to the constraints imposed on documents of its type. These constraints are in addition to those that a parser tests to determine whether the document is a well-formed XML document.

Initially, document type definitions (DTDs) were the only method of defining these constraints, which primarily affect the structure, element types, and attributes of a document. Because DTDs are a fundamental part of the XML recommendation, validation against a DTD is performed by the XML parser itself. Parsers that can validate are called – with astounding clarity for high tech nomenclature – *validating parsers*.

Other methods of element and datatype validation have been introduced, using XSDL, TREX, *Schematron*, or other schema definition languages to express the constraints. These offer simple data validation as well, which formerly had to be performed by the operations layer of the stack.

49.3.2 *Data structure construction*

The parsing layer is also the place where a document is transformed from a string of Unicode characters into a conveniently accessible data structure.

The parser reads an XML document and produces a stream of *parser events*. These events describe the markup and data in the order found in the document. The stream typically conforms to the Simple API for XML (SAX). For many applications, the stream is the data structure that is passed to the next layer.

For others, the event stream is used to construct a tree structure that corresponds to the conceptual hierarchical document represented by the nested start- and end-tags of the XML document character string. In principal, two kinds of tree structure can be built:

- A generic tree structure whose nodes are XML constructs of the conceptual document, such as elements and attributes. It typically conforms to the W3C Document Object Model (DOM), which provides an interface for accessing and manipulating the tree.
- An application-specific tree structure whose nodes are application-defined constructs, such as `Buyer`, `Shipper`, and `LineItem` in a purchase order application.

Application trees are not actually built in this layer; we'll look at them later in layer four. The data structure produced in the parsing layer is always generic, either an event stream or a tree.

49.4 | Document handling

There are many operations that support development of XML applications. We'll look at some key ones:

- extended validation
- data transformation
- Content-based routing (CBR)
- Business process management (BPM)
- method invocation

As all of them operate on the data structure returned by the parsing layer, they can be intermixed and sequenced as needed.

49.4.1 *Extended validation*

Extended validation is constraint checking that cannot be handled by the schema languages you have available. It must be done by your application code.

Validators for newer schema languages can perform such constraint checking as determining whether a content data string matches a pattern, or whether a numeric attribute value is within a certain range. These constraints, however, are imposed on individual element types or attributes.

In contrast, extended validation can enforce dependencies and other relationships. An element type might be optional in the schema definition because it is required only when another element type or particular attribute value is present.

For example, `AdministrativeContact` might be an optional element type in a particular document type. However, if a `ShipTo` element exhibits a value for the `Notify` attribute, the `AdministrativeContact` element is then required.

HP Bluestone finds that, when processing business documents, constraints like these account for over 40% of processing beyond schema-level validation. The W3C XPath recommendation provides a standard notation for addressing parts of an XML document. XPath makes it possible to express complex constraints clearly, among its many other uses.

49.4.2 *Data transformation*

Like extended validation, transformation is another heavily used operation. The transformations are typically controlled by XSLT stylesheets, as we have seen in previous chapters. XSLT relies on XPath as the notation for indicating which parts of a document are affected by particular transformation actions.

In a typical application, it is common for the XML data to be transformed many times. As long as the results of intermediate transformations are in the same form of data structure as the sources, no difficulty is presented.

49.4.3 *Content-based routing*

Content-based routing (CBR) is an operation that routes message documents to different destinations according to the message content. To make this possible, two things are required:

- The CBR engine must be able to interpret the notation of the messages.
- The user must be able to specify what things the CBR engine should look for and which destinations to use if they are found.

Traditional CBR relies on the occurrence of particular character strings in the message content. A routing rule, for example, might look for occurrences of "priority" followed by any number of spaces, followed by "rush", followed by any characters, followed by "purchase order". It could cause such messages to be routed to a purchasing process running on a high-performance server.

XML-based CBR, however, can go much further. Because the messages can be parsed and data structures built, the rich addressing capabilities of XPath are available for expressing routing rules. For example, the rule `//PurchaseOrder[@priority="rush"]` selects all messages containing purchase orders with "rush" as the value of their `priority` attribute, without regard to the precise character strings occurring in the text.

Note that CBR has a characteristic not found in the other layer three operations we have discussed so far. Once it routes the data to another program, that program takes over responsibility for it and may start at the transport layer again. The same is true of business process management, which we discuss next.

49.4.4 *Business process management*

Business process management (BPM) manages the flow of data through a series of complex automated processes. It is used by XML applications to initiate further processing of an XML document. For example, a supply chain application might use BPM to route a purchase order document through various purchasing processes.

In some systems, an XML document is also used to represent the business process itself. This form of implementation is increasing as Web services cause businesses to rely on sharing business processes as part of doing business electronically.

49.5 | Data mapping and binding

This layer of the stack contains facilities for converting XML documents to data structures. We've placed it at the top because, from a data flow standpoint, conversion is frequently the last step in the generic processing of the document, prior to application-specific processing or storage. However, these facilities could be invoked by components of other layers. For example, because they are bidirectional, the transport layer might use them to convert from a legacy application format to XML.

This form of data conversion is often called *data binding*. Regardless of the name, the conversion depends on the process of *mapping*; that is, defining the correspondence between components of the XML document and components of the data structure.

We'll consider three conversion targets: objects, relational tables, and the data stores maintained by legacy applications.

49.5.1   *Objects*

Many approaches to programming have been popular since computers were invented. The current overwhelming favorite is called *object-oriented programming*.

49.5.1.1   What is an object?

The object-oriented view of data is that data is *encapsulated* in *objects*, along with programs, called *methods*, that operate on the data. Encapsulation means the data is hidden, so a program, for example, that wants to read and update the data can't do so directly. Instead, it *invokes* one or more of the object's methods to do the job. The means of invoking the exposed methods, and the format of the data they receive and return, are part of the *interface* to the object.

The things you can do with an object, then, depend completely on the methods that the creator of the object *exposes* (i.e. makes available) through the interface. Methods aren't limited to reading and updating, but could involve complex operations on the data.

The standardized Document Object Model that is created by the parsing layer, as its name suggests, consists of objects. It is a *generic XML object* because its data structure and methods reflect XML constructs like elements, attributes, and data. The interface to a DOM is defined by the W3C DOM recommendation. Implementations are widely available.

49.5.1.2 Application objects

Generic XML objects are not the only data structure that could be created by the parsing layer. It could also create an event stream that could be used to create application-specific data structures. These too could be objects, *application objects*, with methods created for the particular application rather than generic DOM methods. Programs can use these methods to operate on the data structure in terms of application constructs, rather than XML constructs.

For example, the DOM exposes methods that allow reading and updating of elements, but knows nothing about the meaning of the element types. In contrast, an application-specific data structure could be encapsulated as a "purchase order" object, with exposed methods to calculate shipping and taxes.

Java™ programmers have developed a specification that should simplify XML data binding to application objects. The *Java Architecture for XML Binding (JAXB)* provides for automatic generation of application-specific mappings by compiling the DTD or schema definition.

49.5.2 *Relational tables*

There are two classic approaches to mapping XML documents to the table structures supported by a *Relational Database Management System (RDBMS)*. They are illustrated in Figure 49-2.

There are three main components of the diagram:

element structure
> The element structure of a document is shown in the upper left corner.

right database
> The mapping that produces the relational tables to the right of the element structure creates a separate table for each level of the hierarchy. Each table has a key column that relates it to its parent row. Although this approach minimizes duplication of data, performance degrades as the hierarchy increases in depth.

Figure 49-2   Relational table mappings

bottom database

    The mapping that produces the table below the element structure takes a different approach. It sacrifices storage space for improved performance by duplicating entries. The table becomes both wider and deeper as the hierarchy increases in depth.

49.5.3 *Legacy applications*

An enterprise's *legacy applications* are systems built with technologies other than those used for new projects. They usually represent a significant challenge for data mapping, not because of the technologies involved per se, but because the legacy system's data structures, schemas, and APIs are often poorly documented and not fully understood. The problem is compounded when several different legacy applications share data and each uses a different field name for the same data item.

    The notorious Y2K problem actually proved a boon for legacy data mapping because organizations were forced to create coherent data dictionaries in order to locate fields in which dates were stored.

49.6 | The stack in action

Now that we've seen the entire XML processing stack, we can look at how it operates. We'll first describe a product implementation of the stack, then an application scenario executed by the product.

49.6.1 *Product implementation*

HP Bluestone's *Total-e-Server (TES)* is a certified J2EE application environment that supports development of server-based applications. Figure 49-3 illustrates the components of *TES* that perform the functions of each of the stack's layers. We'll discuss each layer briefly:

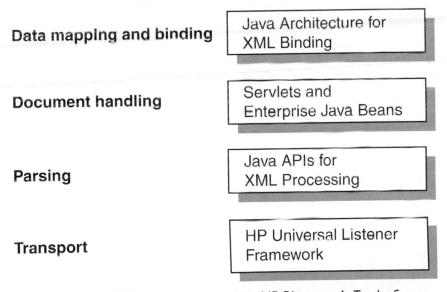

Data mapping and binding — Java Architecture for XML Binding

Document handling — Servlets and Enterprise Java Beans

Parsing — Java APIs for XML Processing

Transport — HP Universal Listener Framework

Figure 49-3   XML processing stack in HP Bluestone's *Total-e-Server*

Data mapping and binding
> This layer is implemented by the Java Architecture for XML Binding, which provides for automatic generation of application-specific mappings by compiling the DTD or schema definition.

Document handling

Total-e-Server has an extensible framework for implementing XML document handlers. These handlers offer services for content-based routing, extended validation, and the other operations we've discussed.

Parsing

The product offers a parsing interface that is compliant with the Java APIs for XML Processing (JAXP). It allows multiple Java XML parsers to be used and additional facilities for management.

Transport

The HP Bluestone *Universal Listener Framework™ (ULF)* offers the ability to watch for incoming XML from a number of input sources, such as e-mail, FTP, file systems, etc. When an XML document is received it is immediately moved to the parsing layer of the stack.

49.6.2 *Application scenario*

In this uncompelling but illustrative scenario, a PurchaseOrder XML document is received from a trading partner over the Internet and processed:

1. An instance of the ULF component is configured to listen for HTTP POST requests.
2. Upon receipt of a document, parsing is attempted using an XML parser. If the document is well-formed XML, the parse will continue and generate a W3C DOM representation of the document. Otherwise, it will fail and a failure notice will be returned to the trading partner.
3. The DOM structure is passed to an XML document handler that is configured as a content-based router. This component identifies the document type and passes the document to the appropriate handler for that type. In this case, the document will be passed to the PurchaseOrder document handler.[2]

---

2. Alternatively, the document type could have been identified by additional information provided on the POST, thereby avoiding the need for CBR.

4. The `PurchaseOrder` document handler performs some complex validation and transforms the DOM structure into the required Java class structure. If the transformation is successful, an acknowledgment is transmitted to the trading partner. If not, a non-acknowledgment is sent.

Java technology for XML development

■ Tools for tool-building

■ Java APIs for XML

■ Middleware development services

■ Software on CD-ROM

Sponsor: Sun Microsystems, http://java.sun.com/xml

Contributing experts: Sun Microsystems staff

Chapter

50

When the definitive history of gastronomical influences on technological development is written, it may well record that Sun Microsystems had more to do with satisfying the coffee cravings of programmers than Starbucks. Certainly, if you sniff around the software that supports XML applications, you're bound to smell the Java!

S everal of the products that we've used to illustrate the chapters of this book have something in common: They are written in the *Java*™ programming language. If they support EDI or other forms of business integration, they may also use the *Java 2 Platform, Enterprise Edition* (J2EE).

But we don't say much about these common characteristics in those chapters. For one thing, we'd be repeating ourselves a lot if we did.[1] But more importantly, we'd be getting off-topic.

The chapters in which those products appear occur in application-oriented parts of the book. For that reason, we focus on *what* the products do with XML, rather than *how* they accomplish it. In contrast, the purpose of this chapter is to provide – in a single place – a look at some of the *Java* technology that influences a product's ability to process XML.

Some might argue that the main influence is metaphysical: there is a profound *rightness* about using XML and *Java* together in that both were designed for the Web, both are internationalized (because they support Unicode), and both are designed for portability.

---

1. We repeat ourselves a lot as it is, but we generally restrict the repetition to emphasizing important XML concepts.

More than portability! They are designed to *let information be free*, to liberate it from the bonds of operating systems, to let it travel unhindered throughout the network that is the computer...

Right.

Metaphysics notwithstanding, in this chapter we'll focus strictly on technical capabilities. We'll look at implementations of the SAX and DOM interfaces and other Java APIs for XML, plus services for developing XML middleware.

Note   In 2.11, "Programming interfaces and models", on page 50, we covered some basic concepts that are necessary for this chapter: parsing, APIs, DOM, and SAX.

50.1 | Java APIs for XML Processing (JAXP)

SAX and DOM are the most popular APIs for XML parsing. However, using them in a program typically requires knowledge of the specific implementation of the parser.

Java APIs for XML Processing (JAXP) is a specification that provides *plugability* for SAX and DOM parsers created by different vendors.[2] That is, it removes the need for detailed implementation knowledge and thereby minimizes the changes that must be made to an application program when its developer chooses a different vendor's parser.

50.1.1   *What parsers do*

An XML parser must ensure that the XML document is *well-formed*, which means (in a nutshell) that the tags are properly constructed, every start-tag has an associated end-tag, and the elements they identify are always nested properly, one within the other.

---

2. JAXP also provides plugability for XSLT processors.

Proper nesting means that the title element, for example, is always fully inside or fully outside the chapter element, not overlapping. The title element can't start outside the chapter, and then finish inside it.

When validating, a parser goes even further and verifies that the XML document lives up to the restrictions and specifications declared in the document's DTD or schema definition.

All XML parsers must be able to check for well-formedness. Those that can also validate against a DTD are known as (surprise!) *validating parsers*. Either kind can be used with the SAX and DOM APIs.

50.1.2   *The SAX API*

You can think of this interface as "serial access" for XML.

Recall from 2.11, "Programming interfaces and models", on page 50 that SAX is "event-driven". The parser reads through an XML document once, from start to finish. At each parsing event, such as recognizing the start or end of an element, it notifies the application. It also provides the information associated with the event, such as the element-type name, attributes and their values, or content data characters.

The SAX API is fast and it uses little memory, which recommends it for server applications and simple programs that only read data or make only small changes to it.

The basic outline of the SAX parser is shown in Figure 50-1. First the SAXParserFactory generates an instance of the parser. The XML text is shown coming into the parser from the left. As the parser runs, it invokes the appropriate operations (called "methods"), which are organized into the four groups (called "interfaces") shown on the right.

What those methods actually do is determined by the application programmer, who might not even implement all of them. A typical application provides at least the ContentHandler methods. A robust one will implement the ErrorHandler interface as well.

Here is a summary of the major SAX functions, grouped by the interfaces in which they are defined:

SAX ParserFactory

The SAX ParserFactory class defines the newInstance() method, which lets the user determine which parser to use at runtime. For example, the user might choose to use a parser from a different

Figure 50-1   SAX API

vendor, or choose a validating parser rather than a nonvalidating parser.

SAX Parser

The parser reads the XML text and recognizes parsing events, as described above.

ContentHandler

The information about the events the parser recognizes is sent to the ContentHandler for processing. This is where the application developer puts the code that processes the data.

ErrorHandler

When the parser encounters an error, it tells the ErrorHandler. Sometimes the application can ignore the error and continue. Sometimes the error makes it impossible for the parser to continue, in which case the application would issue an error message.

DTDHandler

The DTDHandler tells when a DTD is being parsed. Another interface, DeclHandler, can then be used to process DTD events.

EntityResolver

This interface provides methods that are invoked when the parser must access text that is outside the document entity.

50.1.3 *The DOM API*

You can think of this interface as "random access" for XML, because you can access any part of the data at any time.

The Document Object Model is a collection of objects in your program. You can manipulate the object model in any way that makes sense. You can modify data, remove it, or insert new data. When your application is through making changes, it can then write the structure out as an XML document. Interactive applications can use the DOM API to maintain the parsed document while displaying a rendition for users to read and edit.

While the SAX API is fast, it is only good for reading data. You can't use it to write XML, or to modify an XML document that has been parsed. The DOM API fills those needs.

On the other hand, the DOM can't be used to read XML. SAX can, though, so SAX and DOM can work together hand in hand. Similarly, DOM can't write data out, but XSLT can be used with DOM for this purpose.

Figure 50-2 shows how the JAXP reference implementation utilizes the SAX and DOM APIs to construct a Document Object Model.

The `DocumentBuilder` class is just an elaborate SAX `ContentHandler`. As event information arrives from the parser, the DocumentBuilder uses it to construct a DOM representation of the parsed document.

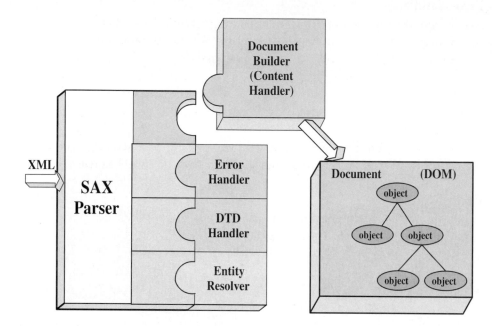

Figure 50-2   DOM construction

   The DOM API provides a relatively familiar tree structure of objects. It also provides a framework to help generate an XML document from the object tree.

   On the other hand, constructing the DOM requires reading the entire XML document and holding the object tree in memory, so it is much more CPU and memory intensive. For that reason, the SAX API may be preferable for server-side applications and data filters that do not require an in-memory representation of the entire document at once.

50.1.4 *Related APIs*

There are two other APIs that are useful in conjunction with XML parsing but are not part of the JAXP specification: JDOM and JAXB. JDOM is an acronym with no official meaning (although "Java DOM" comes readily to mind). JAXB stands for "Java Architecture for XML Binding".

   To understand what they do, recall that two kinds of tree structure can be constructed from an XML document, either:

- a generic tree structure whose nodes are XML constructs of the conceptual document, such as elements and attributes; or
- an application-specific tree structure whose nodes are application-defined constructs, such as `Buyer`, `Shipper`, and `LineItem` in a purchase order application.

The W3C DOM is a generic structure. JDOM is as well, but it is optimized for Java programming.

In contrast, JAXB provides for automatic generation of mappings to support application-specific structures. It does so by compiling the DTD or schema definition.

50.2 | XML middleware services

The *Java 2 Platform, Enterprise Edition* is a set of middleware services for developing enterprise applications. XML is supported in J2EE as a standardized data representation for information interchange.

J2EE includes such technologies as:

- *Enterprise JavaBeans™* (EJB) technology, for server-centric component-based programming
- *Java Servlets*, for extending web server functionality
- *JavaServer Pages™* (JSP), for dynamically generating Web content, including XML documents
- *Java API for XML Messaging* (JAXM), for asynchronous SOAP-based XML document messaging.
- *Java Database Connectivity* (JDBC™), for accessing databases and other tabular data sources

Figure 50-3 illustrates how J2EE facilities are used to construct a business-to-business e-commerce application. There are two businesses, each with its own secure intranet of database servers, application servers, client systems, etc.

In both businesses, applications on the intranet communicate across an internal firewall to the company's Web server, using JSP and/or Servlets. The communication protocol is HTTP(S) and the data is represented in XML.

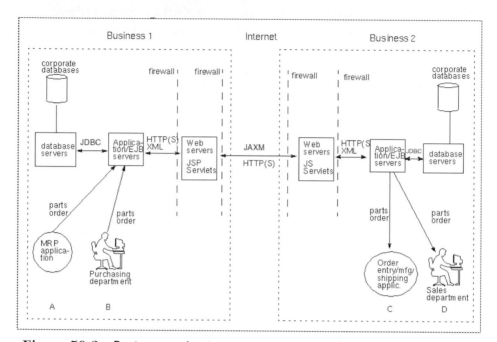

Figure 50-3   Business-to-business e-commerce application

An external firewall protects the Web server from the Internet. Other businesses can communicate with the Web server only by using HTTP(S) to cross the external firewall. JAXM can be used over HTTP(S) to package the messages.

50.2.1   *Business 1*

Business 1 is an end-product manufacturer. It runs a Materials Resource Planning (MRP) application on its intranet that calculates when to order parts, and in what quantities. It also has a purchasing department that places special orders interactively.

50.2.1.1   Automated parts ordering

Area A of Figure 50-3 illustrates the automated ordering process.

The MRP application generates order data, which is converted to a "parts order" document represented in XML using techniques like those described in Part 3, "E-commerce", on page 164 of this book. The parts order is transmitted to an EJB server, then to the Web server, and eventually across the Internet to a parts supplier, such as Business 2.

50.2.1.2   Interactive parts ordering

The interactive purchasing process is shown in area B of Figure 50-3.

Purchasing personnel interact with a browser-based application, similar to those described in Part 2, "Three-tier applications", on page 120 of this book. JSP pages are used to collect the purchasing data and generate "parts order" XML documents that are sent to the parts supplier over the Internet.

50.2.2   *Business 2*

Business 2 is an OEM parts manufacturer. It runs an order-entry, manufacturing, and shipping application on its intranet that automatically books and processes e-commerce orders. However, its application server is programmed to route non-routine orders, such as very large orders and rush orders, to the sales department for interactive processing.

50.2.2.1   Automated sales processing

Area C of Figure 50-3 depicts the automated sales processing. It is essentially the inverse of Business 1's automated order processing and uses similar techniques.

The parts order document is parsed and its data is incorporated in a sales order in the form accepted by the order entry application. That application enters the order into the manufacturing system. It also generates and sends a confirmation of the order to Business 1, including pricing and shipping dates.

50.2.2.2   Interactive sales processing

Interactive sales processing is shown in area D of Figure 50-3.

The parts order XML document is rendered on the client under the control of an XSLT stylesheet. Sales personnel review and approve the order and enter it into the system.

Tip   Sun has provided some free Java software for you on the CD-ROM.

Compression techniques for XML

Application Discussion

- Generic compression
- XML-aware compression
- Schema-specific compression

Sponsor: Intelligent Compression Technologies, Inc.,
http://www.ictcompress.com

Contributing expert: Bill Sebastian

Chapter

51

XML has had a great impact on messaging, and an even greater one on the length of the messages! Short XML messages can be more tag than data, even as much as double or triple. Fortunately, diet plans are available for your overweight documents. We'll show you how they work in this chapter.

onsider the stock market quotation in Example 51-1 on page 740. It is 582 bytes in length, but only 281 bytes of that is data. In other words, using XML has more than doubled the size of this message, with a corresponding increase in storage and transmission costs. Worse yet, because increased transmission time means decreased response time, customer satisfaction is reduced.

The cure for this problem is called *data compression*.[1] There are various techniques and a range of possible results. Let's see how our example can be reduced to 407 bytes, or even to an amazing 29 bytes – a 95 percent reduction!

---

1. In this phrase, "data" refers to the full text of the document, not just the data characters. In fact, it is the markup that is usually compressed the most.

51.1 | Data compression techniques

Data compression is the encoding[2] of text so that the same information can be stored in a smaller number of bytes. The text can therefore be transmitted faster and stored in less space. After the compressed ("coded") file has been received or retrieved, it is decoded to restore the original text.

Figure 51-1 shows how an encoder and decoder can be placed on either side of the transmission network. For example, the encoder could be embedded in a server and the decoder could be invoked by a Web browser or embedded in a client applet.

Figure 51-1   Using compression to accelerate file transmission

There are several approaches to compression that can be taken for XML documents:

generic compression
> The many implementations of the ubiquitous "zip" format are examples of *universal coders*, so-called because they neither know nor care whether they are processing a shopping list or a photograph of Mars. Zip coding reduced Example 51-1 by 30 percent. Although zip's flexibility makes it useful for many applications, its performance can be improved on substantially by programs that know more about the text to be compressed.

XML-aware compression
> Data compression systems work by preparing models that predict text. More knowledge of a file improves the models and provides better predictions. Better predictions in turn result in greater compression. Knowing the rules of XML can provide such an

---

2. Data compression is an important technology with its own accepted terminology. In this chapter we use "code" and its derivatives in the data compression sense, not in the XML sense of "character encoding".

improvement, although knowing the particular document type can provide even more.

schema-specific compression

This approach employs maximum knowledge of the file. It reduced our example from 582 bytes to 29. Let's take a closer look at the technology involved.

51.2 | Schema-specific compression

These compression systems are available from vendors like Intelligent Compression Technologies, Inc. Its *XML-Xpress* utilizes two types of knowledge that are available for most XML applications:

- Knowledge of the document type properties, such as structure, obtained from the schema definition or DTD.
- Statistical knowledge of the text that the document type knowledge makes it possible to obtain.

51.2.1 *Document type knowledge*

XML provides a general method for marking up data. Any file that follows the general markup rules is a well-formed XML document. However, XML applications impose additional constraints that are defined by a DTD or schema definition. These constraints usually include specifying the elements that will occur in a document and the order they are likely to appear.

For example, a schema definition or DTD for Example 51-1 might tell a compression system that the first element was going to be a QReply whose content would begin with an ID sub-element.

Structural knowledge allows the XML markup to be encoded (i.e., compressed) efficiently. For example, if an element type requires two subelements (A, B), the decoder can reconstruct the tags even if the element type names are missing from the encoded file. As it knows exactly where the start- and end-tags of the two elements will be located, it can determine from the DTD what strings to write at those places.

Example 51-1. Reply to stock quote request

```
<QReply>
  <ID>0</ID>
  <SYM>QCOM</SYM>
  <EX>O</EX>
  <LAST>+61.75</LAST>
  <VOL>+13490800</VOL>
  <BID>+61.84</BID>
  <ASK>+61.85</ASK>
  <BIDVOL>+25</BIDVOL>
  <ASKVOL>+5</ASKVOL>
  <BIDTIC>U</BIDTIC>
  <CUR>USD</CUR>
  <EXID>NMS</EXID>
  <HI>+61.85</HI>
  <LO>+55.75</LO>
  <NETCHG>+4.39</NETCHG>
  <OPEN>+56.72</OPEN>
  <PERCHG>+7.65</PERCHG>
  <PQ></PQ>
  <UPC71></UPC71>
  <NEWHI>n/a</NEWHI>
  <NEWLO>n/a</NEWLO>
  <CURYLD>+0.00</CURYLD>
  <DIV>+0.00</DIV>
  <DIVPDT>30 DEC 1999</DIVPDT>
  <EPS>+0.09</EPS>
  <EXDIVDT>31 DEC 1999</EXDIVDT>
  <PE>+644.49</PE>
  <YRHI>+120.0000</YRHI>
  <YRLO>+42.7500</YRLO>
  <TIME>20:01</TIME>
  <DATE>01 MAY 2001</DATE>
</QReply>
```

Similarly, for an element type whose content requires one of two subelements (A|B) with no attributes, we only need to store a binary decision in the encoded file as to which of the two was present.

The sample file in Example 51-1 lends itself exceptionally well to this kind of treatment, as it consists of a mandatory sequence of elements with no attributes. Removing the tags can reduce the encoded size from 582 bytes back nearly to the original (pre-XML) 281 bytes. The next problem is how to get the 281 bytes of uncompressed data down to just 29 bytes of encoded data.

51.2.2 *Data knowledge*

Once we've used a schema to identify each element of an XML document, we can look at a representative sampling of documents to develop models of the content of those elements.

51.2.2.1 Statistical analysis

For example, statistical analysis of sample stock quotes as shown in Example 51-1 might reveal that most companies on the NYSE price their stocks in "USD", or that share prices over 200.00 only occur in the dreams of the shareholders.

In addition to analyzing individual elements, we can also look at relationships among them and, for example, discover that the asking price usually is greater than the bid price. With this type of information we can create compression models that reduce the number of bytes needed to encode the data.

51.2.2.2 An example: the ASK element

To see how statistical analysis works, let's look at the operations used to process the ASK element. Its data content is the string +61.85.

The compression system recognizes the datatype as a fixed decimal with a 2-digit fraction. It converts the character text to the binary value "6185". From this, it subtracts the previously encoded BID value of "6184", which exploits the relationship between these items that was observed when analyzing the sample files. Subtraction produces the remainder "1", which occurs about 25% of the time for this pair of elements in the sample documents.

Now we can encode the remainder, using what compression scientists call an *entropy coder*. The encoding of a value that occurs 25% of the time will use about two bits. As the original data +61.85 used up 48 bits (six bytes), these two bits represent a compression ratio of 24:1. So on this particular entry, we did much better than the 10:1 average needed to reduce the original 281 bytes of data to 29 bytes.

These examples illustrate the algorithms that allow schema-specific XML compression to obtain compression gains 15 times greater than zip on this test set.

51.2.3 *Schema model file (SMF)*

Real-time communication applications require extremely fast encoding. In these cases, reading and interpreting a complicated schema definition or analyzing sample documents in real time is obviously impractical. Instead, that information is captured once, in advance, in a *schema model file (SMF)*.

An SMF is generated by an automated offline routine that reads a schema definition or DTD and creates parsing models that allow the real-time encoders to operate at the highest speed.

An SMF can also include encoding models developed by statistical analysis, as we just described. Such models are especially helpful for achieving maximum compression performance with smaller files.

Each SMF supports a specific schema. To compress an XML file, the real-time encoder needs to have access to the SMF that supports the schema to which the file conforms, as shown in Figure 51-2.

Figure 51-2 Using a schema model file

The same SMF is provided to both the encoder and the decoder. Those programs can support any number of schemas, as long as they have the appropriate SMFs.

51.2.4 *Database query responses*

For some XML applications, the text that needs to be compressed consists of responses to queries for information contained in a large database. While the database as a whole may conform to a schema, the query responses may consist of arbitrary elements arranged in an order that does not follow the schema definition.

For this reason the SMF incorporates access to the Document Object Model (DOM) of the database, which enables access to arbitrary elements. As long as those elements conform to their type definitions, schema-specific compression is possible.

51.3 | Choosing a compression technique

Schema-specific XML compression provides the ultimate in compression performance. It also has drawbacks, including more complicated maintenance and higher cost. For some applications, the performance benefits will justify the drawbacks. For others, application developers may want to explore some of the alternatives.

51.3.1 *No compression*

The easiest solution is to send the text in its original form. This is feasible when storage sizes and transmission times are not significant concerns. It may be the only option if the application does not allow the installation of decoders on the client side.

51.3.2 *Generic compression*

The next easiest solution is to use a universal coder, like zip. Such coders usually work by building a table of strings that are repeated frequently in the document. The occurrences of the strings are then replaced with short pointers to the appropriate table entry.

Zip can be quite effective on XML documents, in some cases achieving compression ratios as high as 10:1. The first step in evaluating compression options for an application is usually to try zip and see if it provides an adequate solution. It is a relatively fast coder as well and free implementations are available.

Other universal coders may provide better compression than zip, but may be slower or cost money. One example is *Universal-Xpress* from Intelligent Compression Technologies, Inc.

51.3.3 *XML-aware compression*

Generic compression systems have been developed for XML documents. Some, like *XmlZip*, from Vitria XmlSolutions, are wrappers around the standard zip algorithm, allowing it to be used more easily and effectively in XML applications. Others, such as *XMill*, from Dan Suciu and Hartmut Liefke, utilize XML's tags to isolate data into homogeneous blocks and improve on compression of both tags and data.

These coders, both of which are available on the CD-ROM, are easier to set up and maintain than schema-specific coders because there is no need to deal with individual schemas or DTDs.

51.3.4 *Homespun schema-specific remedies*

Developers who know little about compression might look at their XML files, see all the repeated tags, and then cleverly write routines that replace the tags with codes referenced in a schema-specific table. Except for very small files, this approach is rarely an improvement over zip.

51.3.5 *Schema-specific compression*

This approach has the potential to perform extremely well, as we have seen. However, the very schema knowledge that makes superior performance possible necessarily introduces some costs.

schema changes

Schema model files must be changed or added when a schema is changed or newly supported. However, if an SMF isn't available, the coding automatically falls back to a generic algorithm.

file footprint

> SMF files use space proportional to the number of schemas supported and their complexity, typically from 20KB to 600KB. The size of the compression engine itself is static, usually around 200KB.

installation

> Installation may require statistical analysis or other custom work in order to achieve the best possible compression results.

These costs tend to scale with the benefits, and should easily be justified for the right kind of documents. For short tags interspersed in lots of data, there is little improvement over generic compression. But for documents with many small elements and no attributes, such as those created by tagging the items of a financial database, the technology offers the highest possible compression performance.

51.4 | Conclusion

Although XML makes the use and interchange of data easier and more flexible, it can substantially increase the number of bytes that must be transmitted and stored. Several compression techniques can reduce that number, resulting in faster transfer times and more economical use of storage resources. The highest compression is achievable by techniques that employ knowledge of XML, especially knowledge of specific schemas and a sampling of their conforming documents.

> *Tip* Try schema-specific compression for yourself with the demonstration on the CD-ROM that accompanies this book.

New directions for XML applications

Application Discussion

- Performance analysis
- XML does television
- Load balancing and routing

Sponsor: Intel Corporation, http://www.intel.com/eBusiness

Contributing experts: Walter Shands, Murali Rajappa, John Abjanic, and Randy E Hall

> XML is going where no markup language has gone before. Thanks to a company that really knows about bits and bytes, XML is now in low-level, performance-oriented applications. You can even find it on television — or at least in the computer that provisions your television!

In the 30-year history of markup languages, we have seen several major trends in application emphasis:

- The first wave, using GML and SGML, was large-scale industrial publishing on paper.
- The second wave, using HTML, was (and is) online information presentation.
- The third wave, using XML, is electronic business and application integration.

And now XML is starting to make inroads in performance-oriented areas that were never before open to an "inefficient" text-based interchange representation. Let's see how Intel Corporation is leading XML into the 21st century.

52.1 | Performance analysis

For a long time a debate raged – and in some quarters is still raging – about the wisdom of using XML for messaging in distributed systems. Despite the many obvious benefits of platform neutrality, human readability, self-description, standardized support, and the rapid deployment and inexpensive maintenance that goes with such characteristics, there is always the last resort of the nay-sayers – resources. After all, the anti-XML argument goes, with an overhead of 300% in a message like `<price>10.00</price>`, XML is clearly an unacceptable drain on performance.

So there is a delicious irony in the fact that one of Intel's envelope-stretching XML applications is ... (fanfare) ... performance analysis!

52.1.1 Remote data collection

The company's *VTune* performance analyzer helps developers identify program hot spots and provides advice on how to remedy them. To do that, it needs to collect and present data from distributed machines running on *Microsoft Windows* or *Linux* operating systems. Windows supports remote data collection via Distributed Component Object Model (DCOM), but DCOM is not available on the Linux operating system

52.1.2 A clean solution ... with SOAP!

The solution lay in the use of XML requests formatted according to the Simple Object Access Protocol (SOAP). The SOAP specification defines rules for representing both messaging data and remote method invocation requests within a document.

Each request consists of a mandatory header, optional application-specific data conforming to the HTTP Extension Framework, and an envelope. Schema definitions provide support for multiple namespaces and ensure that datatype fidelity is maintained across process and server boundaries.

The remote data collection process in *VTune* works as shown in Figure 52-1:

Figure 52-1 Remote data collection in *VTune*

Example 52-1. SOAP request

```
POST  ... HTTP/1.1
Host: ###.###.###.###
Content-Type: text/xml
Content-Length: ###
SOAPMethodName. urn:SamplingCollector:IVTCollector#DoStart
<Envelope>
  <Body>
    <m:DoStart xmlns:m='urn:SamplingCollector:IVTCollector'>
    </m:DoStart>
  </Body>
</Envelope>
```

1. The *VTune* client, which runs on the *Microsoft Windows* platform, makes a Component Object Model (COM) call to a remote collection proxy object.
2. The remote collection proxy collector opens a socket connection to the *Linux* machine.

3. The remote collection proxy collector formats a SOAP request containing a collector name, interface name, method name to execute, and parameter data (Example 52-1).

4. The remote collection proxy collector sends the request to the *Linux* machine.

5. A stub collector on the *Linux* machine either invokes an executable or makes a method call to a sample collector implemented in a C programming language driver.

6. The stub collector collects data and constructs a SOAP response (Example 52-2).

7. The stub collector sends the XML response back to the *VTune* client application.

Example 52-2. SOAP response

```
200 OK
Content-Type: text/xml
Content-Length: ###
<Envelope>
  <Body>
    <m:DoStartResponse
      xmlns:m='urn:SamplingCollector:IVTCollector'>
      <result>OK</result>
    </m:DoStart>
  </Body>
</Envelope>
```

The current SOAP specification is focused on requests and responses over HTTP. XML, however, can be layered on top of other protocols – including SMTP and WAP – making remote data collection possible from cellular phones and other hand-held devices. The SOAP capabilities in the *VTune* performance analyzer support remote data collection on non-*Windows* machines in a way that could permit adding protocols in the future.

52.2 | Coming soon to a television near you ...

XML-TV?

Not exactly, but XML provides such a clean and predictable way to exchange data between disparate systems that it's a natural for an application where no errors can be tolerated. For this reason XML is being deployed in the distribution of digital television (DTV) programming, for consumers to view via DTV-enabled PCs, digital TV sets, and set-top boxes.

Such programming, for example, enables viewers to check an electronic program guide, send electronic greeting cards, take interactive quizzes, watch movie trailers, check sports statistics, and more – all on demand.

52.2.1 *Distribution system design*

In one set-top box system, the content served includes regular television channels, interactive programming in which the user becomes an active participant, and Web-based media.

Service providers are organized in a hub configuration, wherein a primary network operations center (PNOC) supports multiple franchised network operations centers (FNOCs) located in different cities. The PNOC broadcasts content that is cached locally and redistributed by the FNOCs. This approach conserves PNOC/FNOC bandwidth and reduces content delivery latency when serving Web pages.

Subscriber data for specific services resides at both the PNOC and FNOC sites, with the PNOC owning the master record. To ensure that customers receive the services they request, the PNOC subscription center's information must be replicated to the FNOC.

Because the PNOC and FNOC most likely have different subscriber database implementations, the data must be exchanged in a format that disparate systems can easily understand. In the current implementation, the PNOC's master subscriber database is implemented using Oracle database products running on Microsoft *Windows NT* servers. At the FNOC, *Linux* servers host databases for local data storage of customer subscription data.

52.2.2 *Adding a subscriber*

A document type definition is used to describe the subscriber data to be exchanged. In this case, the DTD acts as a contract between the PNOC and the FNOC so the data elements from the customer document, shown in Example 52-3, are correctly mapped to database columns in tables.

Example 52-3. New account request

```
<Action RefNo="999999999999" Actiontype="Add Record">
  <IP_Address>192.168.2.7</IP_Address>
  <MAC_Address>00:D0.B7:1C:B7:5D</MAC_Address>
  <FNOC_ID>FNOC1</FNOC_ID>
  <Hostname>fnoc1.cn.now.com</Hostname>
  <LoginId>carmen</LoginId>
  <Password>password</Password>
  <ActiveService><Service>modem</Service></ActiveService>
</Action>
```

The process for adding a new subscriber is illustrated in Figure 52-2. It is described as follows:

Figure 52-2   Adding a subscriber

1. The FNOC sends a new account request to the PNOC.
2. Subscriber information is inserted into the PNOC customer database.
3. The PNOC customer database generates an XML document containing subscriber information.
4. The system transmits the XML subscriber record document via satellite to the FNOC.
5. The FNOC receives the data and inserts it into its local database.
6. The FNOC configures the subscriber's set-top box for the requested services.

Subscriber updates and deletions are handled in a similar fashion.

As this example makes clear, XML can be used to represent data exchanged between components of a multi-vendor and multi-platform system. With XML, best-of-breed products can be packaged in new and innovative ways to provide services that otherwise would require porting all pieces to a common operating system.

52.3 | Performance enhancement

Remember the raging debate about the wisdom of using XML in distributed systems because it is supposedly such a drain on performance?

Well, here is another delicious irony: Intel is using XML in specialized networking hardware to ... (fanfare) ... enhance performance!

52.3.1 *Load balancing and routing*

One way to guarantee that network transactions are processed in a reliable and expedient manner is to build an infrastructure of high-end servers that can support unpredictable traffic loads. In industries where demand is volatile or difficult to predict, this option could prove to be expensive and could limit the ability to respond to the rapid pace of change.

A more economical and flexible alternative is to offload certain capabilities from the main application processing servers onto specialized devices. A single such "accelerator" or "director" can serve multiple application servers and improve their performance by several means.

The devices operate in domains that system designers call *load balancing* and *routing*. Let's look at what they do.

52.3.1.1   Offload routine tasks

An accelerator can perform such routine tasks as decoding an encrypted message before forwarding it to an application server for fulfillment. It can also encrypt the reply before sending it to the client.

52.3.1.2   Route requests for best response time

On busy websites, several application servers perform the same task. A network device can enhance client response times by routing each request to the server that can fulfill it most quickly. The device typically needs to know (or calculate) the speed of each server and the number of messages enqueued on it.

52.3.1.3   Route requests based on message content

This technique is used for websites that perform multiple services and use different application servers for each. It requires a device that acts like a bank receptionist who decides whether to send you to the loan officer or the new account representative. The device looks at the incoming message to make the routing decision.

For example, URI references can be analyzed to distinguish content requested by clients performing online transactions, from content typically requested by casual surfers. In this way, users performing online transactions can be given higher priority access to server resources (and better response times) than other users.

The choice of server for fulfillment of a request is determined by a table that associates pattern-matching expressions with server names. Possible expression types might include:

- Filetype expressions, such as `*.asp` or `*/order.htm`

- Path expressions, such as `/home/*` or `/home/images/*` or `/home/images/a*`
- Unique file expressions, such as `/index.html`
- Wildcard expressions, such as `*`
- Negations of the other expression types, such as `!*.gif` or `!*/index.html`

52.3.2 *XML content matching*

The phenomenal growth in the use of XML for e-commerce and other applications suggests that a richer source of information might be available for routing: the data and metadata in XML messages.

As an example of a device that indeed uses that richer source, let's look at the Intel *NetStructure 7280 XML Director*. It incorporates a rules-based XML engine that can identify and classify incoming XML requests based on data within the XML object.

Once classified, the device can then transparently prioritize and direct the "most important" XML transactions, according to predefined business rules. Those could be transactions from key trading partners, those with a high dollar value, or perhaps those that are considered time-sensitive.

52.3.2.1 How the rules-based engine works

How can the *XML Director* route XML transactions to application servers based on business parameters such as "all orders over $50,000 *and* from the Western region"?

Rules, in the form of expressions using a subset of the XPath abbreviated syntax, are associated with specific servers. If a message satisfies a rule, it is routed to the associated server.

One application of the rules engine is to identify the XML framework, if any, used by a message, such as *BizTalk* or *RosettaNet* (see 5.2, "Commerce frameworks", on page 97). The message can then be directed to the appropriate back-end server for processing.

52.3.2.2   An XML-based routing scenario

For example, Figure 52-3 illustrates an implementation that uses three groups of servers:

- Set 1 for high-value transactions of the *RosettaNet* framework.
- Set 2 for high-value transactions of the *BizTalk* framework.
- Set 3 for medium and low-value transactions of both *RosettaNet* and *BizTalk* frameworks, plus regular HTTP traffic that may at times contain XML messages.

Figure 52-3   *NetStructure 7280 XML Director* configuration

All three server sets can handle any transaction; the dedication to specific frameworks is strictly to increase performance for the high-value transactions.

The *XML Director* can be configured so that if the traffic volume becomes too great for Set 1, either of the other sets can temporarily be enlisted.

52.3.3 *Other XML Director capabilities*

As Figure 52-3 shows, the *XML Director* is installed inline between the router and the XML servers. No changes to the existing XML implementation are needed.

The product enables businesses to offload Secure Sockets Layer (SSL) encryption and decryption processing from the server, offering up to 150 times faster processing for secure transactions. The decryption is a prerequisite for inspecting the data packets for their XML tags; it reduces server workloads as a by-product. The device can handle up to 1200 new SSL connections per second.

The *XML Director* can also use URI reference analysis, port number, and virtual IP address as routing criteria.

The device is capable of detecting failing or overloaded XML servers and resubmitting the requests to another server for processing. High availability is supported via a serial cable connection to a backup *XML Director*; if the primary device goes offline, the backup will automatically pick up the load.

Analysis   The dominant use of XML today is for e-business, squarely at the MOM end of the application spectrum. Most of the original thinking about XML, however, has appeared to be at the POP end, where ideas like extended linking and topic maps promise to revolutionize our whole approach to information. So it may have come as a surprise to see that originality is occurring in the mundane, message moving arena as well. Intel's XML applications defy conventional notions of the "appropriate" places to use markup technology.

XML Core
Tutorials

- Basic XML markup
- Document type definitions
- Entities
- Advanced features
- How to read the W3C XML Recommendation
- Full spec on CD-ROM

Part Fifteen

This part continues the XML tutorial that we began in Part One. If you haven't read Part One in its entirety, please go back and do so, as we introduced some critically important ideas there.

In this part, you'll learn every useful detail of the Extensible Markup Language. At the end you'll be able to read the markup of both DTDs and document instances.

The part is intended to be read in order, with one exception. As you read the first four chapters you'll notice that here and there we've included excerpts from the W3C XML 1.0 specification. The tutorials are written so that *you can skip the spec excerpts*. They are not required for continuity; they are there so that the hard-core techies among you can get down with the deepest details.

But they need a little tutorial of their own to be read, which is why we have Chapter 57, "Reading the XML specification". Dig into that when – and if – you decide to read the spec excerpts, or to tackle the full spec itself, which is on the CD-ROM.

XML basics

Friendly Tutorial

- Syntactic details
- The prolog and the document instance
- XML declaration
- Elements and attributes

Chapter

53

X ML's central concepts are quite simple, and this chapter outlines the most important of them. Essentially, it gives you what you need to know to actually create XML documents. In subsequent chapters you will learn how to combine them, share text between them, format them, and validate their structure.

Before looking at actual XML markup (don't worry, we'll get there soon!) we should consider some *syntactic* constructs that will recur throughout our discussion of XML documents. By *syntax* we mean the combination of characters that make up an XML document. This is analogous to the distinction between sounds of words and the things that they mean. Essentially, we are talking about where you can put angle brackets, quote marks, ampersands, and other characters and where you cannot! Later we will talk about what they mean when you put them together.

After that, we will discusses the components that make up an XML document instance[1]. We will look at the distinction between the prolog (information XML processors need to know about your document) and the instance (the representation of the actual document itself).

---

1. Roughly, what the XML spec calls the "root element".

53.1 | Syntactic details

XML documents are composed of characters from the *Unicode* character set. Any such sequence of characters is called a *string*. The characters in this book can be thought of as one long (but interesting) string of text. Each chapter is also a string. So is each word. XML documents are similarly made up of strings within strings.

Natural languages such as English have a particular *syntax*. The syntax allows you to combine words into grammatical sentences. XML also has syntax. It describes how you combine strings into well-formed XML documents. We will describe the basics of XML's syntax in this section.

53.1.1 *Grammars*

Natural language syntax is described with a *grammar*. XML's syntax is also. Some readers will want to dig in and learn the complete, intricate details of XML's syntax. We will provide grammar rules for them as we go along. These come right out of the XML specification. If you want to learn how to read them, you should skip ahead to Chapter 57, "Reading the XML specification", on page 862. After you have read it, you can come back and understand the rules as we present them. We advise most readers to read the chapters without worrying about the grammar rules, and then only use them when you need to answer a particular question about XML syntax.

You can recognize grammar rules taken from the specification by their form. They will look like Spec Excerpt 53-1.

Spec Excerpt (XML) 53-1. An example of a grammar rule

```
xhb ::= 'a' 'good' 'read'
```

We will not specifically introduce these rules, because we do not want to interrupt the flow of the text. They will just pop up in the appropriate place to describe the syntax of something.

53.1.2 *Case-sensitivity*

XML is *case-sensitive*. That means that if the XML specification says to insert the word "ELEMENT", it means that you should insert "ELEMENT" and not "element" or "Element" or "ElEmEnT".

For many people, particularly English speaking people, case-insensitive matching is easier than remembering the case of particular constructs. For instance, if a document type has an element type named img English speakers will often forget and insert IMG. They confuse the two because they are not accustomed to considering case to be significant. This is also why some people new to the Internet tend to TYPE IN ALL UPPER CASE. Most vocabularies of SGML, including HTML, are designed to be case-insensitive. Designers of these vocabularies argue that this eliminates case as a source of errors.

Others argue that the whole concept of case-insensitivity is a throwback to keypunches and other early text-entry devices. They also point out that case-sensitivity is a very complicated concept in an international character set like Unicode for a variety of reasons.

For instance, the rules for case conversion of certain accented characters are different in Quebec from what they are in France. There are also some languages for which the concept of upper-case and lower-case does not exist at all. There is no simple, universal rule for case-insensitive matching. In the end, internationalization won out in XML's design.

So mind your "p's" and "q's" and "P's" and "Q's". Our authoritative laboratory testing by people in white coats indicates that exactly 74.5% of all XML errors are related to case-sensitivity mistakes. Of course XML is also spelling-sensitive and typo-sensitive, so watch out for these and other by-products of human fallibility.

Note that although XML is case-sensitive it is not case-prejudiced. Anywhere that you have the freedom to create your own names or text, you can choose to use upper- or lower-case text, as you prefer. So although you must type XML's keywords exactly as they are described, your own strings can mix and match upper- and lower-case characters however you like.

For instance, when you create your own document types you will be able to choose element type names. A particular name could be all upper-case (SECTION), all lower-case (section) or mixed-case (SeCtION). But because XML is case-sensitive, all references to a particular element type would have to use the same case. It is good practice to create a simple convention such as all lower-case or all upper-case so that you do not have to depend on your memory. Unfortunately there is not a single dominant convention in the XML world. One popular convention is all lower-case with dashes. Another one uses upper-case for the start OfEveryWord. A variation of that uses upper-case for only the secondAndSubsequentWords.

53.1.3 *Markup and data*

The constructs such as tags, entity references, and declarations are called *markup*. These are the parts of your document that are supposed to be understood by the XML processor. The parts that are between the markup constitute the *character data*. The XML processor does not concern itself with character data. Whereas it rips markup apart and analyzes it, the processor merely passes the character data on to the application.

Recall that the processor is the part of the program dedicated to separating the document into its constituent parts. The application is the "rest" of the program. In a word processor, the application is the part that lets you edit the document; in a spreadsheet it is the part that lets you crunch the numbers.

We haven't explained all of the parts of markup yet, but they are easy to recognize. All of them start with less-than (<) or ampersand (&) characters. Everything else is character data.

Spec Excerpt (XML) 53-2. Markup

Markup takes the form of start-tags, end-tags, empty-element tags, entity references, character references, comments, CDATA section delimiters, document type declarations, and processing instructions.

Spec Excerpt (XML) 53-3. Grammar for character data

```
[14] CharData ::= [^<&]* - ([^<&]* ']]>' [^<&]*)
```

Spec Excerpt (XML) 53-4. Grammar for character range

```
[2] Char ::= #x9 | #xA | #xD | [#x20-#xD7FF]
                  | [#xE000-#xFFFD] | [#x10000-#x10FFFF]
```

53.1.4 *White space*

There is a set of characters called *white space* characters that XML processors treat differently in XML markup. They are the "invisible" characters: space (Unicode/ASCII 32), tab (Unicode/ASCII 9), carriage return (Unicode/ASCII 13) and line feed (Unicode/ASCII 10). These correspond roughly to the spacebar, tab, and Enter keys on your keyboard.

When the XML specification says that white space is allowed at a particular point, you may put as many of these characters as you want in any combination. Just as you might put two lines between paragraphs in a word processor to make a printed document readable, you may put two carriage returns in certain places in an XML document to make your source file more readable and maintainable. When the document is processed, those characters will be ignored.

In other places, white space will be significant. For instance you would not want the processor to strip out the spaces between the words in your document! Thatwouldmakeithardtoread. So white space outside of markup is always preserved in XML and white space within markup may be preserved, ignored, and sometimes combined in weird, and wonderful ways. We will describe the combination rules as we go along.

Spec Excerpt (XML) 53-5. White space

[white space] consists of one or more space (#x20) characters, carriage returns, line feeds, or tabs.

Spec Excerpt (XML) 53-6. Grammar for white space

```
[3]  S  ::= (#x20 | #x9 | #xD | #xA)+
```

53.1.5 *Names and name tokens*

When you use XML you will often have to give things names. You will name logical structures with element type names, reusable data with entity names, particular elements with IDs, and so forth. XML names have certain common features. They are not nearly as flexible as character data.

Letters or underscores can be used anywhere in a name. There are thousands of characters that XML considers a "letter" because it includes characters from every language including ideographic ones like Japanese Kanji. Characters that can be used anywhere in a name are known in XML terms as *name start* characters. They are called this because they may be used at the start of names as well as in later positions.

This implies that there must be characters that can go in a name but cannot be the first character. You may include digits, hyphens and full-stop (.) characters in a name, but you may not start the name with one of them. These are known as *name characters*. Other characters, like various symbols and white space, cannot be part of a name at all.

You cannot make names that begin with the string "xml" or some case-insensitive variant like "XML" or "XmL".

There is another related syntactic construct called a *name token*. Name tokens are just like names except that they *may* start with digits, hyphens, full-stop characters, and the string XML. In other words, name tokens do not treat the start of the token as being special.

Spec Excerpt (XML) 53-7. Name tokens

An Nmtoken (name token) is any mixture of name characters.

It follows from these rules that every valid name is also a valid name token, but Example 53-1 shows some name tokens that are not valid names.

Example 53-1. Name tokens

```
.1.a.name.token.but.not.a.name
2-a-name-token.but-not.a-name
XML-valid-name-token
```

Like almost everything else in XML, names and name tokens are matched case-sensitively. Names and name tokens may not contain white space, punctuation or other "funny" characters other than those listed above. The remaining "ordinary" characters (including letters from non-Latin alphabets) are called *name characters* because they may occur anywhere in a name.

Spec Excerpt (XML) 53-8. Names

A Name [begins] with a letter or one of a few punctuation characters, and [continues] with letters, digits, hyphens, underscores, colons, or full stops, together known as name characters. Names beginning with the string "xml", [matched case-insensitively] are reserved for standardization in this or future versions of this specification.

Spec Excerpt (XML) 53-9. Grammar for names and name tokens

```
[4]  NameChar ::= Letter | Digit | '.' | '-' | '_' | ':' |
                   CombiningChar | Extender
[5]  Name ::= (Letter | '_' | ':') (NameChar)*
[6]  Names ::= Name (S Name)*
[7]  Nmtoken ::= (NameChar)+
[8]  Nmtokens ::= Nmtoken (S Nmtoken)*
```

53.1.6 *Literal strings*

The data (text other than markup) can contain almost any characters. Obviously, in the main text of your document you need to be able to use punctuation and white space characters! But sometimes you also need these characters *within* markup. For instance, an element might represent a hyperlink and need to contain a URL. The URL would have to go in markup, where characters other than the name characters are not usually allowed.

Literal strings allow users to use funny (non-name) characters within markup, but only in contexts in which it makes sense to specify values that might require those characters. For instance, to specify the URL in the hyperlink, we would need the slash character. Example 53-2 is an example of such an element.

Example 53-2. Literal string in attribute value

```
<REFERENCE URL="http://www.documents.com/document.xml">...
</REFERENCE>
```

The string that defines the URL is the literal string. This one starts and ends with double quote characters. Literal strings are always surrounded by either single or double quotes. The quotes are not part of the string.

Spec Excerpt (XML) 53-10. Literal data

Literal data is any quoted string not containing the quotation mark used as a delimiter for that string. Literals are used for specifying the content of internal entities, the values of attributes, and external identifiers.

You may use either single (') or double (") quotes to mark (*delimit*) the beginning and end of these strings in your XML document. Whichever type of quote the string starts with, it must end with. The other type may be used within the literal and has no special meaning there. Typically you will use double quotes when you want to put an actual single-quote character in the literal and single quotes when you want to embed an actual double quote. When you do not need to embed either, you can take your pick. For example, see Example 53-3.

Example 53-3. Quotes within quotes

```
"This is a double quoted literal."
'This is a single quoted literal.'
"'tis another double quoted literal."
'"And this is single quoted" said the self-referential example.'
```

The ability to have quotes within quotes is quite useful when dealing with human speech or programming language text as in Example 53-4.

Example 53-4. Quoted language

```
"To be or not to be"
'"To be or not to be", quoth Hamlet.'
"'BE!', said Jean-Louis Gassee."
'$B = "TRUE";'
```

Note that there *are* ways of including a double quote character inside of a double-quoted literal. This is important because a single literal might (rarely) need both types of quotes. We'll talk about the most important of these mechanisms in 53.7.1, "Predefined entities", on page 781.

53.2 | Prolog vs. instance

Most document representations start with a header that contains information about the actual document and how to interpret its representation. This is followed by the representation of the real document.

For instance, HTML has a HEAD element that can contain the TITLE and META elements. After the HEAD element comes the BODY. This is where the representation of the actual document resides. Similarly, email messages have "header lines" that describe who the message came from, to whom it is addressed, how it is encoded, and other things.

An XML document is similarly broken up into two main parts: a *prolog* and a *document instance*. The prolog provides information about the interpretation of the document instance, such as the version of XML and the document type to which it conforms. The document instance follows the prolog. It contains the actual document data organized as a hierarchy of elements.

Spec Excerpt (XML) 53-11. Grammar for entire document

```
[1] document ::= prolog element Misc*
```

53.3 | The logical structure

The actual content of an XML document goes in the document instance. It is called this because if it has a document type definition, it is an instance of a class of documents defined by the DTD. Just as a particular person is an instance of the class of "people", a particular memo is an instance of the class of "memo documents". The formal definition of "memo document" is in the memo DTD.

Here is an example of a small XML document.

Example 53-5. Small XML document

```
<?xml version="1.0"?>
<!DOCTYPE memo SYSTEM "memo.dtd">
<memo>
<from>
   <name>Paul Prescod</name>
   <email>papresco@prescod.com</email>
</from>
<to>
   <name>Charles Goldfarb</name>
   <email>charles@sgmlsource.com</email>
</to>
<subject>Another Memo Example</subject>
<body>
<paragraph>Charles, I wanted to suggest that we
<emphasis>not</emphasis> use the typical memo example in
our book. Memos tend to be used anywhere a small, simple
document type is needed, but they are just
<emphasis>so</emphasis> boring!
</paragraph>
</body>
</memo>
```

Because a computer cannot understand the data of the document, it looks primarily at the *tags*, the markup between the less-than and greater-than symbols. The tags delimit the beginning and end of various elements. The computer thinks of the elements as a sort of tree. It is the XML processor's (aka parser's) job to separate the markup from the character data and hand both to the application.

Figure 53-1 shows a graphical view of the logical structure of the document. The memo element is called either the *document element* or the *root element*.

The document element (memo) represents the document as a whole. Every other element represents a component of the document. The from and to elements are meant to indicate the source and target of the memo. The name elements represent people's names. Continuing in this way, the logical structure of the document is apparent from the element-type names.

Experts refer to an element's real-world meaning as its *semantics*. In a particular vocabulary, the semantics of a P element might be "paragraph" and in another it might mean "pence".

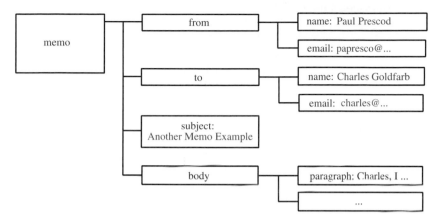

Figure 53-1   The memo XML document viewed as a tree

If you find yourself reading or writing markup and asking: "But what does that *mean?*" or "What does that look like?" then you are asking about semantics.

Computers do not yet know anything about semantics. They do not know an HTTP protocol from a supermodel. Vocabulary designers must describe semantics to authors some other way. For instance, they could send email, write a book or make a major motion picture (well, maybe some day).

What the computer does care about is how an element is supposed to look when it is formatted, or how it is to behave if it is interactive, or what to do with the data once it is extracted. These are specified in *stylesheets* and computer programs. There is a project to help computers to understand semantics. This is called the Semantic Web project and is a long-term goal of the World Wide Web Consortium.

53.4 | Elements

XML elements break down into two categories. Most have content, which is to say they contain characters, elements or both, and some do not. Those that do not are called *empty elements*. Elements within other elements are called *subelements*.

Example 53-6 is an example of an element with content.

Example 53-6. Simple element

```
<title>This is the title</title>
```

Most elements have *content*. Elements with content begin with a start-tag and finish with an end-tag. The "stuff" between the two is the element's content. In Example 53-6, "This is the title" is the content.

XML start-tags consist of the less-than (<) symbol ("left angle bracket"), the name of the element's type, (sometimes termed a *generic identifier* or *GI*), and a greater-than (>) symbol ("right angle bracket"). Start-tags can also include attributes. We will look at those later in the chapter. The start-tag in Example 53-6 is `<title>` and its element type name is "title".

Spec Excerpt (XML) 53-12. Grammar for start-tags

```
[40] STag ::= '<' Name (S Attribute)* S? '>'
```

XML end-tags consist of the string "</", the same generic identifier (or *GI*) as in the start-tag, and a greater-than (>) symbol. The end-tag in Example 53-6 is `</title>`.

You must always repeat the generic identifier in the end-tag. This helps you to keep track of which end-tags line up with which start-tags. If you ever forget one or the other, the processor will know immediately, and will alert you that the document is not well-formed. The downside of this redundancy is that it requires more typing. Some people like belts and some prefer suspenders. The XML Working Group likes belts *and* suspenders.

Spec Excerpt (XML) 53-13. Grammar for end-tags

```
[42] ETag ::= '</' Name S? '>'
```

Note that less-than symbols in content are always interpreted as beginning a tag. If the characters following them would not constitute a valid tag, then the document is not well-formed.

Caution   Many people use the word "tag" imprecisely. Sometimes they mean "element-type name", sometimes "element type" and sometimes they actually mean "tag". This leads to confusion. In XML, tags always start with less-than symbols and end with greater-than symbols. Nothing else is a tag. Tags are not defined in DTDs; element types are defined in DTDs.

It is possible for an element to have no content at all. Such an element is called an *empty element*. One way to denote an empty element is to merely leave out the content. But as a shortcut, empty elements may also have a different syntax. Because there is no content to delimit, they may consist of a single empty-element tag. That looks like this: `<MyEmptyElementTag/>`.

The slash at the end indicates that this is an empty-element tag, so there is no content or end-tag coming up. The slash is meant to be reminiscent of the slash in the end-tag of an element with both tags. This is just a shortcut syntax. XML processors do not treat empty-element tags differently from elements that merely have no content between the start- and end-tag.

Spec Excerpt (XML) 53-14. Grammar for empty-element tags

```
[44] EmptyElemTag ::= '<' Name (S Attribute)* S? '/>'
```

Usually empty elements have *attributes*. Occasionally an empty element without attributes will be used to flag a particular location in a document. Example 53-7 is an example of an empty element with an attribute.

Example 53-7. Empty element with attribute

```
<EMPTY-ELEMENT ATTR="ATTVAL"/>
```

Remember what the slash at the end means! You will see it often and it is easy to miss when there are attributes like this. The slash indicates that this is an empty element so that the processor need not look for a matching end-tag.

In summary, elements are either empty or have content. Elements with content are represented by a start-tag, the content, and an end-tag. Empty elements can either have a start-tag and end-tag with nothing in between, or a single empty-element tag. An element's type is always identified by the generic identifiers in its tags.

The reason we distinguish element types from generic identifiers is because the term "generic identifier" refers to the syntax of the XML document – the characters that represent the actual document. The term "element type" refers to a property of a component of the actual document.[2]

Spec Excerpt (XML) 53-15. Grammar for elements

```
[39] element ::= EmptyElemTag | STag content ETag
[43] content ::= (element | CharData | Reference |
                  CDSect | PI | Comment)*
```

53.5 | Attributes

In addition to content, elements may have *attributes*. Attributes are a way of attaching characteristics or properties to elements of a document. Attributes have *names*, just as real-world properties do. They also have *values*. For instance, two possible attributes of people are their "shoe size" and "IQ" (the attributes' names), and two possible values are "12" and "12" (respectively).

In a DTD, each attribute is defined for a specific element type and is allowed to exhibit a certain type of value. Multiple element types could provide attributes with the same name and it is sometimes convenient to think of them as the "same attribute" even though they technically are not.

Attributes have semantics also. They always *mean* something. For example, an attribute named `height` might be provided for `person` elements (allowed occurrence), exhibit values that are numbers (allowed values), and represent the person's height in centimeters (semantics).

---

2. The grammar in Spec Excerpt 53-15 is from the first edition of the XML Recommendation. It is clearer than the the second edition version, which was revised to deal with an obscure interaction with another production.

Here is how attributes of person elements might look:

Example 53-8. Elements with attributes

```
<person height="165cm">Dale Wick</person>
<person height="165cm" weight="165lb">Bill Bunn</person>
```

As you can see, the attribute name does not go in quotes, but the attribute value does.

Spec Excerpt (XML) 53-16. Grammar for Attributes

```
[41] Attribute ::= Name Eq AttValue
[25] Eq ::= S? '=' S?
```

Like other literals (see 53.1.6, "Literal strings", on page 767 for a refresher), attribute values can be surrounded by either single (') or double (") quotes. When you use one type of quote, the other can be used within that attribute value. As we discussed earlier, this makes it convenient to create attribute values that have the quote characters within them. This is shown in Example 53-9.

Example 53-9. Attribute values can have quotes in them

```
<PERSON HEIGHT='80"'> ... </PERSON>
<PERSON QUOTE="'To be or not to be'">...</PERSON>
```

A DTD constrains an attribute's allowed occurrence and values. One possibility is to require an attribute to be specified for all elements. For example, a military document might require section elements to have a security attribute with the value unclassified, classified, or secret. Example 53-10 demonstrates.

Example 53-10. Security attribute declaration

```
<!ATTLIST SECTION
          SECURITY (unclassified | classified | secret) #REQUIRED >
```

The attribute would need to be specified for each `section` element as shown in Example 53-11.

Example 53-11. Security attribute specification

```
<SECTION SECURITY="unclassified">...</SECTION>
```

It would be a validity error to create a `section` element without a `security` attribute.

Usually empty elements have attributes. Sometimes an element with sub-elements can be modeled just as well with an empty element and attributes. Example 53-12 shows two ways of modeling a `person` element in an email message.

Example 53-12. Alternative `person` element

```
<FROM><NAME>Paul Prescod</NAME>
      <EMAIL>"papresco@prescod.net"</EMAIL>
</FROM>
vs.
<FROM NAME="Paul Prescod" EMAIL="papresco@prescod.net"/>
```

Yet another way to do it would be to let the person's name be data content as shown in Example 53-13.

Example 53-13. Another alternative `person` element

```
<FROM><PERSON EMAIL="papresco@prescod.net">Paul Prescod
      </PERSON>
</FROM>
```

As you can see, there can be many different ways to represent the same construct. There is no one right way to do so. In the case of `person`, the last version shown is the most typical because the character data of a document generally represents what you would expect to see in a "print-out".

But that is not a hard and fast rule (after all, renditions vary widely). Because there are so many ways to represent the same thing, it is advisable to use a DTD. The constraints in a DTD can maintain consistency across a range of documents, or even within a single large document. There may be many ways to represent a particular concept, but once you choose one, let the DTD help you stick to it.

Spec Excerpt (XML) 53-17. Grammar for attribute values

```
[10] AttValue ::= '"' ([^<&"] | Reference)* '"'
                 | "'" ([^<&'] | Reference)* "'"
```

53.6 | The prolog

XML documents may start with a prolog that describes the XML version ("1.0", for now), document type, and other characteristics of the document.

The prolog is made up of an *XML declaration* and a *document type declaration*, both optional. Though an author may include either, neither, or both, it is best to try to maximize the amount of prolog information provided. This will make later processing more reliable.

The XML declaration must precede the document type declaration if both are provided. Also, comments, processing instructions, and white space can be mixed in among the two declarations. The prolog ends when the first start-tag begins.

Example 53-14 is a sample prolog as a warm-up.

Example 53-14. A simple prolog

```
<?xml version="1.0"?>
<!DOCTYPE book SYSTEM "http://www.oasis-open.org/.../docbookx.dtd">
```

This DTD says that the document conforms to XML version 1.0 and declares adherence to a particular document type, book.

Spec Excerpt (XML) 53-18. Grammar for prologs

```
[22] prolog ::= XMLDecl? Misc* (doctypedecl Misc*)?
[27] Misc ::= Comment | PI | S
```

53.6.1 *XML declaration*

The XML declaration is fairly simple. It has several parts and they fit together one after another.

A minimal XML declaration looks like this:

Example 53-15. Minimal XML declaration

```
<?xml version="1.0"?>
```

Example 53-16 is a more expansive one, using all of its parts.

Example 53-16. More expansive XML declaration

```
<?xml version="1.0" encoding="UTF-8" standalone="yes"?>
```

There is one important thing to note in the last example. It looks like a start-tag with three attributes, but it is *not*. The different parts of the XML declaration just happen to look like attributes. Well, not quite "just happen": it could have had a completely different syntax, but that would have been harder to memorize. So the parts were chosen to look like attributes to reduce the complexity of the language. One important difference between XML declaration parts and attributes is that the parts are strictly ordered whereas attributes can be specified in any order.

Spec Excerpt (XML) 53-19. Grammar for XML declarations

```
[23] XMLDecl ::= '<?xml' VersionInfo EncodingDecl? SDDecl? S? '?>'
```

53.6.1.1 Version info

The *version info* part of the XML declaration declares the version of XML that is in use. It is required in all XML declarations. At the time of writing, the only valid version string is "1.0". But if you always use the version string, you can be confident that future XML processors will not think that your document was meant to conform to XML version 2.0 or 3.0 when and if those languages become available. Since they do not exist yet, you cannot know if your documents will be compatible with them.

In fact, the only reason that the XML declaration is optional is so that some HTML and SGML documents can be used as XML documents without confusing the software that they usually work with. You can imagine that an older browser would not react nicely to an HTML document with an XML declaration. But this "backwards compatibility" consideration is only temporary. Future versions of XML may require the XML declaration.

The XML version information is part of a general trend towards information representations that are *self-identifying*. This means that you can look at an XML document and (if it has the declaration) know immediately both that it is XML and what version of XML it uses. As more and more document representations become self-identifying, we will be able to stop relying on error-prone identification schemes like file extensions.

Spec Excerpt (XML) 53-20. Version information

```
[24] VersionInfo ::= S 'version' Eq
                     ("'" VersionNum "'" | '"' VersionNum '"')
[25] Eq ::= S? '=' S?
[26] VersionNum ::= ([a-zA-Z0-9_.:] | '-')+
```

53.6.1.2 Encoding declaration

An XML declaration may also include an *encoding declaration*. It describes what character encoding is used. This is another aspect of being self-identifying. If your documents are encoded in the traditional 7-bit-ASCII used on most operating systems and with most text editors, then you do not need to worry about the encoding-declaration. 7-bit-ASCII is a subset of a Unicode encoding called *UTF-8* which XML processors can automatically detect and use. If you use 7-bit ASCII and need to encode a character outside of 7-bit-ASCII, such as the trademark sign or a non-English character, you can do so most easily by using a numeric character reference, as described in 56.2, "Character references", on page 849.

It normally not a problem to type non-ASCII characters directly into an XML document, using a Unicode-aware text editor, as these editors generally create UTF-8 documents directly. You need only use the encoding declaration if you are using some national or regional encoding like Russia's KOI8-R, Western Europe's ISO-8859-1 or Japan's Shift-JIS. If you want to use one of these encodings you should put the encoding name in the encoding declaration as shown in Example 53-17.

Spec Excerpt (XML) 53-21. Grammar for encoding declarations

```
[80]EncodingDecl ::= S 'encoding'
                 Eq ('"' EncName '"' | "'" EncName "'" )
[81]EncName ::= [A-Za-z] ([A-Za-z0-9._] |'-')*
```

Example 53-17. Encoding declaration

```
<?xml version="1.0" encoding="KOI8-R"?>
```

53.6.1.3   Standalone document declaration

An XML declaration can include a *standalone document declaration*. It declares what components of the document type definition are necessary for complete processing of the document. This rarely used, arguably useless declaration is described in 56.5, "Standalone document declaration", on page 857.

53.6.2   *Document type declaration*

After the XML declaration (if present) and before the first element, there may be a *document type declaration* which declares the document type that is in use in the document. A "book" document type, for example, might be made up of chapters, while a letter document type could be made up of element types such as ADDRESS, SALUTATION, SIGNATURE, and so forth.

The document type declaration is at the heart of the concept of *structural validity*, which makes applications based on XML robust and reliable. It includes the markup declarations that express the *document type definition (DTD)*.

The DTD is a formalization of the intuitive idea of a document type. The DTD lists the element types available and can put constraints on the occurrence and content of elements and other details of the document structure. This makes an information system more robust by forcing the documents that are part of it to be consistent.

Since XML was first standardized, alternatives to DTDs have been developed. You have probably heard of the various schema languages. The official W3C schema language is discussed in Chapter 60, "XML Schema (XSDL)", on page 918.

53.7 | Markup miscellany

This section contains information on some more useful markup constructs. They are not as important or as widely used as elements, attributes and the XML declaration, but they are still vital parts of a markup expert's toolbox.

53.7.1 *Predefined entities*

Sometimes when you are creating an XML document, you want to protect certain characters from markup interpretation. Imagine, for example, that you are writing a user's guide to HTML. You would need a way to include an example of markup. Your first attempt might be to create an `example` element and do something like this Example 53-18.

Example 53-18. An invalid approach to HTML examples in XML

```
<p>HTML documents must start with a DOCTYPE, etc. etc. This
is an example of a small HTML document:
<sample>

  <!DOCTYPE HTML PUBLIC "-//W3C//DTD HTML 3.2 Final//EN">
  <HTML>
  A document's title
  <H1>A document's title</H1>
  </HTML>

</sample>
```

This will not work, however, because the angle brackets that are supposed to represent HTML markup will be interpreted as if they belonged to the XML document you are creating, not the mythical HTML document in the example. Your XML processor will complain that it is not appropriate to have an HTML DOCTYPE declaration in the middle of an XML document! There are two solutions to this problem: predefined entities and CDATA sections.

Predefined entities are XML markup that authors use to represent characters that would otherwise be interpreted as having a special meaning, such as a start-tag or an entity reference. There are five *predefined* ("built-in") entities in XML. These were included precisely to deal with this problem. They are listed in Table 53-1.

Table 53-1   Predefined entities

Entity reference	Character
&amp;	&
&lt;	<
&gt;	>
&apos;	'
&quot;	"

Why these specific five characters? See Spec Excerpt 53-22 and Spec Excerpt 53-23 for the answer.

Spec Excerpt (XML) 53-22. Predefined entities

The ampersand character (&) and the left angle bracket (<) may appear in their literal form only when used as markup delimiters, or within a comment, a processing instruction, or a CDATA section. [...] If they are needed elsewhere, they must be escaped using either numeric character references or the strings "&" and "<" respectively.

Spec Excerpt (XML) 53-23. Attribute values

To allow attribute values to contain both single and double quotes, the apostrophe or single-quote character (') may be represented as "'", and the double-quote character (") as """.

An entity for the right angle bracket is provided primarily for symmetry. It is also sometimes useful to avoid putting a special string called *CDEnd* (discussed in 53.7.2, "CDATA sections", on page 783) into your document. But you do not have to use this entity in most cases.

We can use references to the predefined entities to insert these characters, instead of typing them directly. Then they will not be interpreted as markup. Example 53-19 demonstrates this.

Example 53-19. Writing about HTML in XML

```
<p>HTML documents must start with a DOCTYPE, etc. etc. This
is an example of a small HTML document:
<sample>
    &lt;!DOCTYPE HTML PUBLIC " //W3C//DTD HTML 3.2 Final//EN">
    &lt;HTML>
    &lt;HEAD>
    &lt;TITLE>A document's title
    &lt;/TITLE>
    &lt;/HEAD>
    &lt;/HTML>
</sample>
```

When your XML processor parses the document, it will replace the entity references with actual characters. It will not interpret the characters it inserts as markup, but as "plain old data characters" (character data).

53.7.2 *CDATA sections*

While predefined entities are convenient, human beings are not as good at decoding them as computers are. Your readers will get the translated version, so they will be fine. But as the author, you may spend hours staring at character entity references while you are editing your XML document in a text editor (if you choose not to use a graphical XML editor). You may also spend hours replacing special characters with character entity references. This can get annoying.[3]

Another construct, called a *CDATA section*, allows you to ask the processor not to interpret a chunk of text as containing markup: "Hands off! This

---

3. This is especially nasty when you are writing an XML book, where examples tend to contain many angle brackets.

isn't meant to be interpreted." CDATA stands for "character data". You can mark a section as being character data using this special syntax as shown in Example 53-20.

Example 53-20. CDATA section

```
<![CDATA[ content  ]]>
```

Example 53-21 and Example 53-22 are other examples.

Example 53-21. Writing about HTML in a CDATA section

```
<![CDATA[
<HTML>
This is an example from HTML for Dumbbells!
<p>It may be a pain to write a book about HTML in HTML,
but it is easy in XML!
</HTML>
]]>
```

Example 53-22. Java code in a CDATA section

```
<![CDATA[
if( foo.getContentLength() < 0  && input = foo.getInputStream() )
    open = true;
]]>
```

As you can see, it does not usually matter what you put in CDATA sections because their content is not scanned for markup. There is one obvious exception (and one not-so-obvious corollary). The string that ends the CDATA section,]]> (known as *CDEnd*), cannot be used inside the section. Use Example 53-23 as a cautionary tale.

Example 53-23. Illegal CDATA usage

```
<![CDATA[
 Javascript code: if( a[c[5]]> 7 ) then...
]]>
```

The first occurrence of CDEnd (]]>) in the middle of the Javascript expression will terminate the section. You simply cannot use a CDATA section for content that includes CDEnd. You must end the section and insert the character as in Example 53-24.

Example 53-24. Legal CDATA usage

```
<![CDATA[
 Javascript code: if( a[c[5]]]]>><![CDATA[ 7 ) then...
]]>
```

This is quite painful and can cause a problem for embedding programming languages. But even in those languages, CDEnd is probably a fairly rare character string, so you should just keep an eye out for it.

The non-obvious corollary is:

 Caution   CDEnd (]]>) should only be used to close CDATA sections. It must not occur anywhere else in an XML document.

This is an absolute requirement, not just a recommendation. Because of it you can easily check that you have closed CDATA sections correctly by comparing the number of CDEnd strings to the number of sections. If you do not close a CDATA section correctly, some of your document's markup may be interpreted as character data. Since (]]>) is not something that typical documents contain, this restriction is rarely a problem.

With all of these warnings, CDATA sections may sound tricky to use, but they really aren't. This book, for example, has several hundred. Mistakes involving CDATA sections are usually quite blatant, because either markup will show up in your rendered document, or data characters will be interpreted as markup and probably trigger an error message.

Predefined entities and CDATA sections only relate to the interpretation of the markup, not to the properties of the real document that the markup represents.

Spec Excerpt (XML) 53-24. Grammar for CDATA sections

```
[18] CDSect ::= CDStart CData CDEnd
[19] CDStart ::= '<![CDATA['
[20] CData ::= (Char* - (Char* ']]>' Char*))
[21] CDEnd ::= ']]>'
```

53.7.3 *Comments*

Sometimes it is useful to embed information about a document or its markup in a manner that will be ignored by computer processes and renditions of the document. For example, you might insert a note to yourself to clean up the wording of a section, a note to a co-author explaining the reason for a particular section of the document, or a note in a DTD describing the semantics of a particular element. This information can be hidden from the application in a *comment*. Comments should never be displayed in a browser, indexed in a search engine, or otherwise processed as part of the data of the actual document.

Example 53-25. A comment

```
<!-- This section is really good! Let's not change it. -->
```

Comments consist of the characters "<!--" followed by almost anything and ended by "-->". The "almost anything" in the middle cannot contain the characters "--". This is a little bit inconvenient, because people often use those two characters as a sort of dash, to separate thoughts. This is another point to be careful of, lest you get bitten.

Comments can go just about anywhere in the instance or the prolog. However, they cannot go within declarations, tags, or other comments. Example 53-26 is a document using some comments in several correct places.

Markup is not recognized in comments. You can put less-than and ampersand symbols in them, but they will not be recognized as the start of elements or entity references.

Example 53-26. Comments all over the place

```
<?xml version="1.0"?>
<!-- There is no other version yet! -->
<!-- Now on to the doctype -->
<!DOCTYPE SAMPLE [
  <!-- This is a comment in the
  doctype declaration internal subset! -->
  <!ELEMENT SAMPLE (#PCDATA)>
  <!-- This is a very simple DTD. -->
]> <!-- Here comes the "root" or "document" element. -->
<SAMPLE>This is some character data.
<!-- That was some character data. -->
</SAMPLE>
<!-- That's all folks -->
```

Comments are a good place to describe the semantics of element types and attributes. So you might use a comment to tell other DTD maintainers and authors that an element type with a cryptic name like p is actually intended to model paragraphs and not (for example) British currency. Comments are not just about being helpful to other people. After all, even expert document type designers have a limited and imperfect memory. Some day even you will wonder exactly what it was you meant by a particular element-type name. The DTD comments will help. The job that you are saving might be your own!

Spec Excerpt (XML) 53-25. Grammar for comments

```
[15]    Comment ::= '<!--'((Char - '-')|('-'(Char - '-')))*'-->'
```

53.8 | Summary

An XML document is composed of a prolog and a document instance. The prolog is optional, and provides information about how the document is structured both physically (where its parts are) and logically (how its elements fit together). Elements and attributes describe the logical structure. As we will see, *entities* describe the physical structure. To use a rough analogy, the entities are like a robot's body parts, the elements are his thoughts, and stylesheets and software provide his behavior.

Creating a document type definition

Friendly Tutorial

- Document type declaration

- Element type declarations

- Attribute list declarations

788

Chapter

54

reating your own document type definition or schema definition is like creating your own markup language. If you have
ever chafed at the limitations of a language with a fixed set of
element types, such as HTML or TEI, then you will embrace the opportunity to create your own language.[1] DTDs are XML's built-in mark-
up-language definition language.

Another way of expressing your ideas formally is by creating a schema
definition using XSDL, which we discuss in Chapter 60, "XML Schema
(XSDL)", on page 918, or one of the other new schema languages. Schema
definitions allow even more power (and complexity!) than DTDs, so they
are also important to learn.

We feel that it is important for serious XML users to understand both.
Because schema definitions employ DTD concepts, learning one will help
you learn the other. Indeed, *XML Schema* datatypes, covered in Chapter 59,
"Datatypes", on page 888, can even be used in conjunction with DTDs.

We should note again that it is possible to keep a document type definition completely in your head rather than writing the declarations for a
DTD or schema. Sometimes DTD designers do that while they are testing

---

1. With its own set of limitations!

out ideas. Usually, though, you actually commit your ideas to declarations so that a validating processor can help you to keep your documents consistent.

Note also that, for the present, we are maintaining the distinction, discussed in 6.3, "Document type, DTD, and markup declarations", on page 110, between a document type, the XML markup rules for it (DTD), and the markup declarations that declare the DTD. Those *DTD declarations* are connected to the big kahuna of markup declarations – the *document type declaration*.

54.1 | Document type declaration

A document type declaration for a particular document might say "This document is a concert poster." The document type definition for the document would say "A concert poster must have the following features." As an analogy: in the world of art, you can *declare* yourself a practitioner of a particular movement, or you can *define* the movement by writing its manifesto.

The XML spec uses the abbreviation DTD to refer to document type definitions because we speak of them much more often than document type declarations. The DTD defines the allowed element types, attributes and entities and can express some constraints on their combination.

A document that conforms to its DTD is said to be *valid*. Just as an English sentence can be ungrammatical, a document can fail to conform to its DTD and thus be *invalid*. That does not necessarily mean, however, that it ceases to be an XML document. The word valid does not have its usual meaning here. An artist can fail to uphold the principles of an artistic movement without ceasing to be an artist, and an XML document can violate its DTD and yet remain a well-formed XML document.

As the document type declaration is optional, a well-formed XML document can choose not to declare conformance to any DTD at all. It cannot then be a valid document, because it cannot be checked for conformance to a DTD. It is not invalid, because it does not violate the constraints of a DTD.

XML has no good word for these merely well-formed documents. Some people call them "well-formed", but that is insufficiently precise. If the document were not well-formed, it would not be XML (by definition). Saying that a document is well-formed does not tell us anything about its conformance to a DTD at all.

For this reason, we prefer the terms used by the ISO for full-SGML: *type-valid*, meaning "valid with respect to a document type", and *non-type-valid*, the converse.

Example 54-1 is an XML document containing a document type declaration and document type definition for mailing labels, followed by an instance of the document type: a single label.

Example 54-1. XML document with document type declaration

```
<!DOCTYPE label[
    <!ELEMENT label (name, street, city, state, country, code)>
    <!ELEMENT name (#PCDATA)>
    <!ELEMENT street (#PCDATA)>
    <!ELEMENT city (#PCDATA)>
    <!ELEMENT state (#PCDATA)>
    <!ELEMENT country (#PCDATA)>
    <!ELEMENT code (#PCDATA)>
]><label>
<name>Rock N. Robyn</name>
<street>Jay Bird Street</street>
<city>Baltimore</city>
<state>MD</state>
<country>USA</country>
<code>43214</code>
</label>
```

The document type declaration starts on the first line and ends with "]>". The DTD declarations are the lines starting with "<!ELEMENT" Those are *element type declarations*. You can also declare attributes, entities and notations for a DTD. The element type declarations that contain #PCDATA (parsed character data) allow textual data content.

Recall from 2.4, "Entities: The physical structure", on page 36 that an XML document can be broken up into separate objects for storage, called "entities".[2] The document type declaration occurs in the first (or only) entity to be parsed, called the "document entity".

In Example 54-1, all of the DTD declarations that define the label DTD reside within the document entity. However, the DTD could have been partially or completely defined somewhere else. In that case, the document

---

2. Loosely, an entity is like a file.

type declaration would contain a reference to another entity containing those declarations.

A document type declaration with only external DTD declarations looks like Example 54-2.

Example 54-2. Document type declaration with external DTD declarations

```
<?xml version="1.0"?>
<!DOCTYPE label SYSTEM "http://www.sgmlsource.com/dtds/label.dtd">
<label>
...
</label>
```

They keyword SYSTEM is described more completely in 55.9.1, "System identifiers", on page 842. For now, we will just say that it tells the processor to fetch some resource containing the external information. In this case, the external information is made up of the declarations that define the label DTD. They should be exactly the ones we had in the original label document. The big difference is that now they can be reused in hundreds, thousands, or even millions of label documents. Our simple DTD could be the basis for the largest junk mailing in history!

All document type declarations start with the string "<!DOCTYPE". Next they have the name of an element type that is defined in the DTD. The root element in the instance (described in 53.4, "Elements", on page 771) must be of the type declared in the document type declaration. If any of the DTD declarations are stored externally, the third part of the document type declaration must be either "SYSTEM" or "PUBLIC". We will cover "PUBLIC" later. If it is "SYSTEM", the final part must be a "URI" pointing to the external declarations. A URI is, for all practical purposes, a URL. URIs are discussed in 64.2, "Uniform Resource Identifiers", on page 1006.

Spec Excerpt (XML) 54-1. DOCTYPE declaration

```
[28] doctypedecl ::= '<!DOCTYPE' S Name (S ExternalID)? S? ('['
                     (markupdecl | PEReference | S)* ']' S?)? '>'
[75] ExternalID  ::= 'SYSTEM' S SystemLiteral
                     | 'PUBLIC' S PubidLiteral S SystemLiteral

[29] markupdecl ::= elementdecl | AttlistDecl | EntityDecl
                     | NotationDecl | PI | Comment
```

54.2 | Internal and external subset

In Example 54-1, the DTD declarations were completely *internal*. They were inside of the document type declaration. In Example 54-2, they were completely external. In many cases, there will be a mix of the two. This section will review these options and show how most XML document type declarations combine an internal part, called the *internal subset* and an external part, called the *external subset*.

From now on, as we'll almost always be writing about DTD declarations, we'll refer to them as "the DTD". We'll resort to the finer distinctions only when necessary for clarity.

We will start with an example of a DTD in Example 54-3.

Example 54-3. Garage sale announcement DTD.

```
<!ELEMENT GARAGESALE (DATE, TIME, PLACE, NOTES)>
<!ELEMENT DATE (#PCDATA)>
<!ELEMENT TIME (#PCDATA)>
<!ELEMENT PLACE (#PCDATA)>
<!ELEMENT NOTES (#PCDATA)>
```

These markup declarations would make up an ultra-simple DTD for garage sale announcements.[3] As you may have deduced, it declares five element types. We will get to the syntax of the declarations soon. First we will look at how they would be used. These could reside in a separate file called `garage.dtd` (for instance) and then every document that wanted to conform to them would declare its conformance using a document type declaration. This is shown in Example 54-4.

Instead of a complete URL, we have just referred to the DTD's file name. Actually, this is still a URL. It is a *relative URL*. That means that in a standard Web server setup, the XML document entity and its DTD entity reside in the same directory. You could also refer to a full URL as we do in Example 54-5.

The relative URL is more convenient while you are testing because you do not need to have a full server installed. You can just put the two entities

---

3. A garage sale is where North Americans spend their hard-earned money on other people's junk, which they will eventually sell at their own garage sales.

Example 54-4. Conforming garage sale document.

```
<!DOCTYPE GARAGESALE SYSTEM "garage.dtd">
<GARAGESALE>
<DATE>February 29, 1998</DATE>
<TIME>7:30 AM</TIME>
<PLACE>249 Cedarbrae</PLACE>
<NOTES>Lots of high-quality junk for sale!</NOTES>
</GARAGESALE>
```

Example 54-5. Specifying a full URL

```
<!DOCTYPE GARAGESALE SYSTEM
           "http://www.tradestuff.com/stuff.dtd">
<GARAGESALE>
...
</GARAGESALE>
```

in the same directory on your hard drive. But your DTD and your instance can get even more cozy than sharing a directory. You can hoist your DTD into the same entity as the instance as in Example 54-6.

Example 54-6. Bringing a DTD into the same entity as the instance

```
<!DOCTYPE GARAGESALE
[
<!ELEMENT GARAGESALE (DATE, TIME, PLACE, NOTES)>
<!ELEMENT DATE (#PCDATA)>
<!ELEMENT TIME (#PCDATA)>
<!ELEMENT PLACE (#PCDATA)>
<!ELEMENT NOTES (#PCDATA)>
]>
<GARAGESALE>
...
</GARAGESALE>
```

The section between the square brackets is called the *internal subset* of the document type declaration. For testing, this is very convenient! You can edit the instance and the DTD without moving between entities. Since entities usually correspond to files, this means that instead of moving between two files, you need only edit one.

Although this is convenient, it is not great for reuse. The DTD is not available anywhere but in this file. Other documents cannot conform to this DTD without copying the declarations into their internal subset.

Often you will combine both approaches. Some of the DTD declarations can go in an external entity where it can be reused, and some of it can go in the same entity as the instance. Often graphic entities (see 55.6, "Unparsed entities", on page 833) would be declared in the internal subset because they are specific to a document. On the other hand, element type declarations would usually be in the *external subset*, the external part of the document type declaration. Example 54-7 demonstrates.

Example 54-7. Reference to an external subset

```
<!DOCTYPE GARAGESALE SYSTEM "garage.dtd"[
<!ENTITY LOGO SYSTEM "logo.gif">
]><GARAGESALE> ... </GARAGESALE>
```

The declarations in the internal subset are processed before those in the external subset. This gives document authors the opportunity to override[4] some kinds of declarations in the shared portion of the DTD.

Note that the content of both the internal subset and the external subset makes up the DTD. garage.dtd may have a .dtd extension but that is just a convention we chose to emphasize that the file contains DTD declarations. It is *not* necessarily the full set of them. The full set of DTD declarations is the combination of the declarations in the internal and external subsets.

Caution   Many people believe that the file containing the external subset is "the DTD". Until it is referenced from a document type declaration and combined with an internal subset (even an empty one) it is just a file that happens to have markup declarations in it. It is good practice, however, when an external subset is used, to restrict the internal subset to declarations that apply only to the individual document, such as entity declarations for graphics.

It is often very convenient to point to a particular file and refer to it as "the DTD" for a given document type. As long as the concepts are straight

---

4. Actually, preempt.

in your mind, it does seem a trifle simpler than saying "the file that contains the markup declarations that I intend to reference as the external subset of the document type declaration for all documents of this type".

54.3 | Element type declarations

Elements are the foundation of XML markup. Every element in a valid XML document must conform to an element type declared in the DTD. Documents with elements that do not conform could be well-formed, but not valid. Example 54-8 is an example of an element type declaration.

Example 54-8. Element type declaration.

```
<!ELEMENT memo (to, from, body )>
```

Element type declarations must start with the string "<!ELEMENT", followed by the name (or *generic identifier* of the element type being declared. Finally they must have a *content specification*. The content specification above states that elements of this type must contain a to element followed by a from element followed in turn by a body element.

Spec Excerpt (XML) 54-2. Element type declaration

```
<!ELEMENT' S Name S contentspec S? '>'
```

Element type names are XML *names*. That means there are certain restrictions on the characters allowed in them. These are described in 53.1.5, "Names and name tokens", on page 765. Each element type declaration must use a different name because a particular element type cannot be declared more than once.

Caution   Unique element type declaration. Unlike attributes and entities, element types can be declared only once.

54.4 | Element type content specification

Every element type has certain allowed content. For instance a document type definition might allow a chapter to have a title in its content, but would probably not allow a footnote to have a chapter in its content (though XML itself would not prohibit that!).

There are four kinds of content specification. These are described in Table 54-1.

Table 54-1   Content specification types

Content specification type	Allowed content
EMPTY content	May not have content. They are typically used for their attributes.
ANY content	May have any content at all.
Mixed content	May have character data or a mix of character data and subelements specified in mixed content specification.
Element content	May have only subelements specified in element content specification

54.4.1 *Empty content*

Sometimes we want an element type that can never have any content. We would give it a content specification of EMPTY. For instance an image element type like HTML's img would include a graphic from somewhere else. It would do this through an attribute and would not need any subelements or character data content. A cross-reference element type might not need content because the text for the reference might be generated from the target. A reference to an element type with the title "More about XML" might become "See *More about XML* on page 14".

You can declare an element type to have empty content by using the EMPTY keyword as the content specification. See Example 54-9.

Example 54-9. Empty element type

```
<!ELEMENT MY-EMPTY-ELEMENT EMPTY>
```

54.4.2 *ANY content*

Occasionally, you want an element type to be able to hold any element or character data. You can do this if you give it a content spec of ANY as in Example 54-10.

Example 54-10. Element type with ANY content

```
<!ELEMENT LOOSEY-GOOSEY ANY>
```

This is rarely done. Typically we introduce element type declarations to express the structure of our document types. An element type that has an ANY content specification is completely unstructured. It can contain any combination of character data and subelements. Still, ANY content element types are occasionally useful, especially while a DTD is being developed. If you are developing a DTD for existing documents, then you could declare each element type to have ANY content to get the document to validate. Then you could try to figure out more precise content specifications for each element type, one at a time.

54.4.3 *Mixed content*

Element types with *mixed content* are allowed to hold either character data alone or character data with child elements interspersed. A paragraph is a good example of a typical mixed content element. It might have character data with some mixed in emphasis and quotation subelements. The simplest mixed content specifications allow data only and start with a left parenthesis character ("("), followed by the string #PCDATA and a final close parenthesis (")"). Example 54-11 demonstrates.

Example 54-11. Data-only mixed content

```
<!ELEMENT emph (#PCDATA)>
<!ELEMENT foreign-language ( #PCDATA ) >
```

You may put white space between the parenthesis and the string #PCDATA if you like. The declarations above create element types that cannot contain subelements. Subelements that are detected will be reported as validity errors.

In other words, these elements do not really have "mixed" content in the usual sense. Like the word "valid", XML has a particular meaning for the word that is not very intuitive. Any content specification that contains #PCDATA is called mixed, whether subelements are allowed or not.

We can easily extend the DTD to allow a mix of elements and character data. This is shown in Example 54-12.

Example 54-12. Allow a mix of character data and elements

```
<!ELEMENT paragraph (#PCDATA|emph)*>
<!ELEMENT abstract (#PCDATA|emph|quot)*>
<!ELEMENT title ( #PCDATA | foreign-language | emph )* >
```

Note the trailing asterisk. It is required in content specifications that allow a mix of character data and elements. The reason it is there will be made clear when we study content models. Note also that we can put white space before and after the vertical bar ("|") characters.

These declarations create element types that allow a mix of character data and subelements. The element types listed after the vertical bars ("|"), are the allowed subelements. Example 54-13 would be a valid title if we combine the declarations in Example 54-12 with those in Example 54-11.

Example 54-13. Sample data

```
<title>this is a <foreign-language>tres gros</foreign-language>
       title for an <emph>XML</emph> book</title>
```

The title has character data ("This is a"), a foreign-language subelement, some more character data ("title for an"), an emph subelement and some final character data "book". We could have reordered the emph and foreign-language elements and the character data however we wanted.

We could also have introduced as many (or as few) `emph` and `foreign-language` elements as we needed.

54.5 | Content models

The final kind of content specification is a "children" specification. This type of specification says that elements of the type can contain only child elements in its content. You declare an element type as having *element content* by specifying a content model that has only element type names, instead of a mixed content specification or one of the keywords described above.

A content model is a pattern that you set up to declare what subelement types are allowed and in what order they are allowed. A simple model for a `memo` might say that it must contain a `from` followed by a `to` followed by a `subject` followed by a `paragraph`. A more complex model for a `question-and-answer` might require `question` and `answer` elements to alternate.

A model for a `chapter` might require a single `title` element, one or two `author` elements and one or more `paragraphs`. When a document is validated, the processor would check that the element's content matches the model.

A simple content model could have a single subelement type as in Example 54-14.

Example 54-14. A single subelement

```
<!ELEMENT WARNING (PARAGRAPH)>
```

This says that a WARNING must have a single PARAGRAPH within it. As with mixed content specifications, you may place white space before or after the parentheses. We could also say that a WARNING must have a TITLE and then a PARAGRAPH within it as in Example 54-15.

Example 54-15. Two subelements

```
<!ELEMENT WARNING (TITLE, PARAGRAPH)>
```

The comma (",") between the "TITLE" and "PARAGRAPH" GIs indicates that the "TITLE" must precede the "PARAGRAPH" in the "WARNING" element. This is called a *sequence*. Sequences can be as long as you like (Example 54-16).

Example 54-16. Longer sequence

```
<!ELEMENT MEMO (FROM, TO, SUBJECT, BODY)>
```

You may put white space before or after the comma (",") between two parts of the sequence.

Sometimes you want to have a *choice* rather than a sequence. For instance Example 54-17 shows a declaration for an element type that allows a FIGURE to contain either a GRAPHIC element (inserting an external graphic) or a CODE element (inserting some computer code).

Example 54-17. Allowing choice

```
<!ELEMENT FIGURE (GRAPHIC|CODE)>
```

The vertical bar character ("|") indicates that the author can choose between the element types. We say that this is a *choice* group. You can put white space before or after the vertical bar. You may have as many choices as you want:

Example 54-18. Multiple Choices

```
<!ELEMENT FIGURE (CODE|TABLE | FLOW-CHART| SCREEN-SHOT)>
```

You may also combine choices and sequences using parenthesis. When you wrap parenthesis around a choice or sequence, it becomes a *content particle*. Individual GIs are also content particles. You can use any content particle where ever you would use a GI in a content model:

Example 54-19. Content particles

```
<!ELEMENT FIGURE (CAPTION, (CODE|TABLE|FLOW-CHART|SCREEN-SHOT) )>
<!ELEMENT CREATED ((AUTHOR | CO-AUTHORS), DATE )>
```

The content model for FIGURE is thus made up of a sequence of two content particles. The first content particle is a single element type name. The second is a choice of several element type names. You can break down the content model for CREATED in the same way.

You can make some fairly complex models this way. But when you write a DTD for a book, you do not know in advance how many chapters the book will have, nor how many paragraphs each chapter will contain. You need a way of saying that the part of the content specification that allows captions is *repeatable* – that you can match it many times.

Sometimes you will also want to make an element optional. For instance, some figures may not have captions. You may want to say that part of the specification for figures is optional.

XML allows you to specify that a content particle is optional or repeatable using an *occurrence indicator*. Table 54-2 shows the three occurrence indicators.

Table 54-2   Occurrence indicators

Indicator	Content particle is...
?	Optional (0 or 1 time).
*	Optional and repeatable (0 or more times)
+	Required and repeatable (1 or more times)

Occurrence indicators directly follow a GI, sequence or choice. The occurrence indicator cannot be preceded by white space.

Example 54-20 illustrates how we can make captions optional on figures:

Example 54-20. Captions are optional.

```
<!ELEMENT FIGURE (CAPTION?, (CODE|TABLE|FLOW-CHART|SCREEN-SHOT))>
```

We can allow footnotes to have multiple paragraphs:

Example 54-21. Footnotes have multiple paragraphs

```
<!ELEMENT FOOTNOTE (P+)>
```

Because we used the "+" indicator, footnotes must have at least one paragraph. We could also have expressed this in another way:

Example 54-22. Multiple paragraphs: the sequel

```
<!ELEMENT FOOTNOTE (P, P*)>
```

This would require a leading paragraph and then 0 or more paragraphs following. That would achieve the same effect as requiring 1 or more paragraphs. The "+" operator is just a little more convenient than repeating the preceding content particle.

We can combine occurrence indicators with sequences or choices:

Example 54-23. Occurrence indicators and sequences

```
<!ELEMENT QUESTION-AND-ANSWER (INTRODUCTION,
                               (QUESTION, ANSWER)+,
                               COPYRIGHT?)>
```

It is also possible to make all of the element types in a content model optional:

Example 54-24. Optional content

```
<!ELEMENT IMAGE (CAPTION?)>
```

This allows the IMAGE element to be empty sometimes and not other times. The question mark indicates that CAPTION is optional. Most likely these IMAGE elements would link to an external graphic through an attribute. The author would only provide content if he wanted to provide a caption.

In the document instance, empty IMAGE elements look identical to how they would look if IMAGE had been declared to be always empty. There is no way to tell from the document instance whether they were declared as empty or are merely empty in a particular case.

54.5.1 *Mixed content models*

We have already talked about mixed content but we should look at it a little more in light of our new understanding of content models. They say that a little knowledge can be a dangerous thing. It's true! Now that you know about content models, you can interpret the syntax for mixed content a little bit better.

Example 54-25. Mixed content again

```
<!ELEMENT abstract (#PCDATA|emph|quot)*>
```

Take a look at Example 54-25 We can see now that this model is similar to element-only content models. What it really says is that you can have a mix of as many parsed characters and elements (emph and quot, in this example) as you like.

First you could select to add some data characters (choosing the #PCDATA branch of the choice group) and then the asterisk would allow you to select from the group again. You could select a quot and then select again and so forth. In this manner you would build up a list of character data, emph elements and quot elements.

Here is where this knowledge becomes a little dangerous. You might think that you could use #PCDATA however and wherever you want in a content model. That is not true. You must use it in the exact pattern we have shown you. The #PCDATA must be the first token in the group. The group must always be a choice, never a sequence. The other components must be element type names, never parenthesized groups. The symbol at the end must always be an asterisk ("*"). It can never be a plus ("+"). You can only omit the asterisk if the mixed content model allows character data but no elements, as in Example 54-26.

It is somewhat confusing to call the model in Example 54-26 "mixed" because it only allows character data. Nevertheless, that is the correct terminology. If it helps, you can remember that it is always possible to mix char-

Example 54-26. Mixed content with no elements

```
<!ELEMENT abstract (#PCDATA)>
```

acter data with character references, entity references, processing instructions and other kinds of markup. Really, the only markup that is prohibited in an element like that is subelement markup.

54.6 | Attributes

Attributes allow an author to attach extra information to the elements in a document. For instance a code element for computer code might have a lang attribute declaring the language that the code is in. On the other hand, you could also use a lang subelement for the same purpose. It is the DTD designer's responsibility to choose a way and embody that in the DTD. Attributes have strengths and weaknesses that differentiate them from subelements so you can usually make the decision without too much difficulty.

The largest difference between elements and attributes is that attributes cannot contain elements and there is no such thing as a "sub-attribute". Attributes are always either text strings with no explicit structure (at least as far as XML is concerned) or simple lists of strings. That means that a chapter should not be an attribute of a book element, because there would be no place to put the titles and paragraphs of the chapter. You will typically use attributes for small, simple, unstructured "extra" information.

Another important difference between elements and attributes is that each of an element's attributes may be specified only once, and they may be specified in any order. This is often convenient because memorizing the order of things can be difficult. Elements, on the other hand, must occur in the order specified and may occur as many times as the DTD allows. Thus you must use elements for things that must be repeated, or must follow a certain pattern or order that you want the XML parser to enforce.

These technical concerns are often enough to make the decision for you. But if everything else is equal, there are some usability considerations that can help. One rule of thumb that some people use (with neither perfect success nor constant abject failure) is that elements usually represent data that is the natural content that should appear in every print-out or other rendition, Most formatting systems print out elements by default and do not print out attributes unless you specifically ask for them. Attributes represent data that is of secondary importance and is often information about the information (*"metadata"*).

Also, attribute names usually represent properties of objects, but element-type names usually represent parts of objects. So given a `person` element, subelements might represent parts of the body and attributes might represent properties like weight, height, and accumulated karma points.

We would advise you not to spend too much of your life trying to figure out exactly what qualifies as a part and what qualifies as a property. Experience shows that the question "what is a property?" ranks with "what is the good life?" and "what is art?". The technical concerns are usually a good indicator of the philosophical category in any event.

54.6.1 *Attribute-list declarations*

Attributes are declared for specific element types. You declare attributes for a particular element type using an *attribute-list declaration*. You will often see an attribute-list declaration right beside an element type declaration:

Example 54-27. My first ATTLIST

```
<!ELEMENT PERSON (#PCDATA)>
<!ATTLIST PERSON EMAIL CDATA #REQUIRED>
```

Attribute declarations start with the string "<!ATTLIST". Immediately after the white space comes an element type's generic identifier. After that comes the attribute's *name*, its *type* and its *default*. In the example above, the attribute is named `EMAIL` and is valid on `PERSON` elements. Its value must be *character data* and it is required — there is no default and the author must supply a value for the attribute on every `PERSON` element.

Spec Excerpt (XML) 54-3. Attribute-list declarations

```
[52]   AttlistDecl ::=  '<!ATTLIST' S Name AttDef* S? '>'
[53]   AttDef ::=  S Name S AttType S DefaultDecl
```

You can declare many attributes in a single attribute-list declaration.[5]

Example 54-28. Declaring multiple attributes

```
<!ATTLIST PERSON EMAIL CDATA #REQUIRED
                 PHONE CDATA #REQUIRED
                 FAX CDATA #REQUIRED>
```

You can also have multiple attribute-list declarations for a single element type:

Example 54-29. Multiple declarations for one element type

```
<!ATTLIST PERSON HONORIFIC CDATA #REQUIRED>
<!ATTLIST PERSON POSITION CDATA #REQUIRED
                 ORGANIZATION CDATA #REQUIRED>
```

This is equivalent to putting the declarations altogether into a single attribute-list declaration.

It is even possible to have multiple declarations for the same attribute of the same element type. When this occurs, the first declaration of the attribute is binding and the rest are ignored. This is analogous to the situation with entity declarations.

Note that two different element types can have attributes with the same name without there being a conflict. Despite the fact that these attributes have the same name, they are in fact different attributes. For instance a SHIRT element could have an attribute SIZE that exhibits values SMALL, MEDIUM and LARGE and a PANTS element in the same DTD could have an attribute also named SIZE that is a measurement in inches:

Example 54-30. Two size attributes

```
      <!-- These are -->
<!ATTLIST SHIRT SIZE (SMALL|MEDIUM|LARGE) #REQUIRED>

      <!-- two different attributes -->
<!ATTLIST PANTS SIZE NMTOKEN #REQUIRED>
```

---

5. That's why it is called a list!

It is not good practice to allow attributes with the same name to have different semantics or allowed values in the same document. That can be quite confusing for authors.

54.6.2 *Attribute defaults*

Attributes can have *default values*. If the author does not specify an attribute value then the processor supplies the default value if it exists. A DTD designer can also choose not to supply a default.

54.6.2.1   Default values

Specifying a default is simple. You merely include the default after the type or list of allowed values in the attribute list declaration:

Example 54-31. Default values

```
<!ATTLIST SHIRT SIZE (SMALL|MEDIUM|LARGE) MEDIUM>
<!ATTLIST SHOES SIZE NMTOKEN "13">
```

Any value that meets the constraints of the attribute list declaration is legal as a default value. You could not, however, use "***" as a default value for an attribute with declared type NMTOKEN any more than you could do so in a start-tag in the document instance.

54.6.2.2   Impliable attributes

Sometimes you want to allow the user to omit a value for a particular attribute without forcing a particular default. For instance you could have an element SHIRT which has a SIZE attribute with a declared type of NMTOKEN. But some shirts are "one size fits all". They do not have a size. You want the author to be able to leave this value out and you want the processing system to *imply* that the shirt is "one size fits all". You can do this with an *impliable* attribute:

Example 54-32. Impliable attribute

```
<!ATTLIST SHIRT SIZE NMTOKEN #IMPLIED>
```

The string "#IMPLIED" gives any processing program the right to insert whatever value it feels is appropriate. This may seem like a lot of freedom to give a programmer, but typically implied attributes are simply ignored. In the case of our SHIRT, there is no need to worry about "one size fits all" shirts because anybody can wear them. Authors should only depend upon the implied value when they do not care or where there is a well-defined convention of what the lack of a value "really" means. This is again a case of semantics and would be communicated to the author through some other document, DTD comment or other communication mechanism.

It is easy for an author to not specify a value for an attribute that is not required: just do not mention the attribute. Note that specifying an attribute value that is an empty string is *not* the same as not specifying an attribute value:

Example 54-33. Empty versus non-existent

```
<SHIRT>          <!-- This conforms to the declaration above   -->
<SHIRT SIZE=""> <!-- This does *not* conform to the declaration. -->
```

54.6.2.3   Required attributes

The opposite situation to providing a default is where a document type designer wants to force the author to choose a value. If a value for an attribute is important and cannot reliably be defaulted, the designer can require authors to specify it with a *required* attribute default:

Example 54-34. Required attribute

```
<!ATTLIST IMAGE URL CDATA #REQUIRED>
```

In this case, the DTD designer has made the URL attribute required on all IMAGE elements. This makes sense because without a URL to locate the image file, the image element is useless.

54.6.2.4   Fixed attributes

It may be surprising, but there are even times when it is useful to supply an attribute value that cannot be overridden at all. This is rare, but worth knowing about. Imagine, for instance, that an Internet directory provider decides to write a robot[6] that will build a table of contents for websites automatically. It does so by extracting the first-, second-, and third-level section titles of every document indexed by the directory.

The difficulty is that different DTDs will have different element-type names for titles. HTML-like DTDs use H1 for the first level, H2 for the second, etc. Other DTDs might use HEAD1, HEAD2, and HEAD3, or CHAPTER, SECTION, and SUBSECTION.

Even if the robot knows about these DTDs, what about all of the others? There are potentially as many DTDs in existence as there are XML documents! It is not feasible to write a robot that can understand every document type.

The vendor needs to achieve some form of standardization. But it cannot force everyone to conform to the same DTD: that is exactly what XML is supposed to avoid! Instead, it can ask all document creators to label the elements that perform the *role of* section titles. They could do this with an attribute, such as TITLE-LEVEL. The robot can then use the content of those elements to generate its index.

Each DTD designer thinks through the list of element types to add the attribute to. They specify what their element types mean in terms of the indexing system understood by the robot. They don't want authors changing the value on an element by element basis. They can prevent this with *fixed* attributes:

Example 54-35. Fixed attributes

```
<!ATTLIST CHAPTER    TITLE-LEVEL CDATA #FIXED "FIRST">
<!ATTLIST SECTION    TITLE-LEVEL CDATA #FIXED "SECOND">
<!ATTLIST SUBSECTION TITLE-LEVEL CDATA #FIXED "THIRD">
```

6. A *robot* is an automatic Web information gatherer.

Now all of the appropriate elements are marked with the attribute. No matter what else is in the DTD, the robot can find what it is looking for.

54.6.3 *Attribute types*

An important feature of attributes is that attributes have *types* that can enforce certain *lexical* and *semantic* constraints. *Lexical* constraints are constraints like "this attribute must contain only numerals". Semantic constraints are along the lines of "this attribute must contain the name of a declared entity". These constraints tend to be very useful in making robust DTDs and document processing systems.

However, it is vital to remember that *the value of an attribute is not necessarily the exact character string that you enter between the quotation marks.* That string first goes through a process called *attribute-value normalization* on its way to becoming the attribute value. Since attribute types apply to the *normalized value*, we had better digress for a moment to master normalization.

54.6.3.1 Attribute value normalization

XML processors normalize attribute values to make authors' lives simpler. If it were not for normalization, you would have to be very careful where you put white space in an attribute value. For instance if you broke an attribute value across a line:

Example 54-36. Normalization

```
<GRAPHIC ALTERNATE TEXT="This is a picture of a penguin
    doing the ritual mating dance">
```

You might do this merely because the text is too long for a single line in a text editor.

This sort of thing is normalized by the XML processor. The rules for this are a little intricate, but most times they will just do what you want them to. Let's look at them.

All XML attribute values are entered as quoted strings. They start and end with either single-quotes ("'") or double-quotes ("""). If you want to embed a single-quote character into an attribute value delimited by single quotes or a double-quote character into an attribute value delimited by double quotes, then you must use an entity reference as described in 53.7.1, "Predefined entities", on page 781.

The first thing the XML parser does to prepare for normalization is to strip off the surrounding quotes.

Then, character references are replaced by the characters that they reference. As we discussed earlier, character references allow you to easily insert "funny" characters.

Next, general entity references are replaced. This is important to note. While it is true that entity references are not allowed in markup, unnormalized attribute values are *text* – a mixture of markup and data. After normalization, only the data remains.[7].

If the expansion for an entity reference has another entity reference within it, that is expanded also, and so on and so forth. This would be rare in an entity used in an attribute value. After all, attribute values are usually very short and simple. An entity reference in an attribute value cannot be to an external entity.

Newline characters in attribute values are replaced by spaces. *If* the attribute is known to be one of the tokenized types[8] (see below), then the parser must further remove leading and trailing spaces. So `"    token    "` becomes `"token"`. It also collapses multiple spaces between tokens into a single space, so that `"space    between"` would become `"space between"`.

Caution   The distinction between unnormalized attribute value text and normalized attribute value data trips up even the experts. Remember, when reading about attribute types, that they apply to the normalized data, not the unnormalized text.

---

7. Philosophically, attribute values are metadata, but it is an article of faith in the XML world that metadata is data.
8. If, in other words, attribute-list declarations were provided and the processor is either a validating processor or a non-validating processor that decides to read them.

54.6.3.2   CDATA and name token attributes

The simplest type of attribute is a *CDATA* attribute. The CDATA stands for "character data". The declaration for such an attribute looks like this:

Example 54-37. CDATA Attributes

```
<!DOCTYPE ARTICLE[
<!ELEMENT ARTICLE>
<!ATTLIST ARTICLE DATE CDATA #REQUIRED>
...
]>
<ARTICLE DATE="January 15, 1999">
...
</ARTICLE>
```

Character data attribute values can be any string of characters. Basically anything else is legal in this type of attribute value.

Name token (NMTOKEN) attributes are somewhat like CDATA attributes. The biggest difference is that they are restricted in the characters that name tokens allow. Name tokens were described in 53.1.5, "Names and name tokens", on page 765. To refresh your memory, they are strings made up of letters, numbers and a select group of special characters: period ("."), dash ("-"), underscore (" ") and colon (".").

Example 54-38. Name token attribute type

```
<!DOCTYPE PARTS-LIST[
...
<!ATTLIST PART DATE NMTOKEN #REQUIRED>
...
]>
<PARTS-LIST>
...
<PART DATE="1998-05-04">...</PART>
...
</PARTS-LIST>
]>
```

An empty string is not a valid name token, whereas it would be a valid CDATA attribute value.

Name tokens can be used to allow an attribute to contain numbers that need special characters. They allow the dash, which can be used as a minus sign, the period, which can be a decimal point, and numbers. These are useful for fractional and negative numbers. You can also use alphabetic characters to specify units.

Name tokens can also be used for naming things. This is similar to how you might use variable names in a programming language. For instance, if you used XML to describe the structure of a database, you might use name tokens to name and refer to fields and tables. The restrictions on the name token attribute type would prevent most of the characters that would be illegal in field and table names (spaces, most forms of punctuation, etc.). If there is a reason that all fields or record names must be unique, then you would instead use the *ID* attribute type discussed in 54.6.3.4, "ID and IDREF attributes", on page 815.

If it is appropriate to have more than one name token, then you can use the NMTOKENS attribute type which stands for "name tokens". For instance Example 54-39 shows how you might declare a DTD representing a database.

Example 54-39. Name tokens attribute type

```
<!DOCTYPE DATABASE [
...
<!ELEMENT TABLE EMPTY>
<!ATTLIST TABLE NAME NMTOKEN #REQUIRED
                FIELDS NMTOKENS #REQUIRED>
...
]>
<DATABASE>
...
<TABLE NAME="SECURITY" FIELDS="USERID PASSWORD DEPARTMENT">
...
</DATABASE>
```

One other difference between CDATA attributes and NMTOKEN attributes is in their *normalization*. This was discussed in 54.6.3.1, "Attribute value normalization", on page 811.

54.6.3.3   Enumerated and notation attributes

Sometimes as a DTD designer you want to create an attribute that can only exhibit one of a short list of values: "small/medium/large", "fast/slow"; "north/south/east/west". *Enumerated attribute types* allow this. In a sense, they provide a choice or menu of options.

The syntax is reminiscent of choice lists in element type declarations:

Example 54-40. Choice lists

```
<!ATTLIST OPTIONS CHOICE (OPTION1|OPTION2|OPTION3) #REQUIRED>
```

You may provide as many choices as you like. Each choice is an XML *name token* and must meet the syntactic requirements of name tokens described in 53.1.5, "Names and name tokens", on page 765.

There is another related attribute type called a *notation* attribute. This attribute allows the author to declare that the element's content conforms to a declared notation. Here is an example involving several ways of representing dates:

Example 54-41. Different date representations

```
<!ATTLIST DATE TYPE NOTATION (EUDATE|USDATE|ISODATE) #REQUIRED>
```

In a valid document, each notation allowed must also be declared with a notation declaration.

54.6.3.4   ID and IDREF attributes

Sometimes it is important to be able to give a name to a particular occurrence of an element type. For instance, to make a simple hypertext link or cross-reference from one element to another, you can name a particular section or figure. Later, you can refer to it by its name. The target element is labeled with an *ID* attribute. The other element refers to it with an *IDREF* attribute. This is shown in Example 54-42.

The stylesheet would instruct browsers and formatters to replace the cross-reference element with the name of the section. This would probably be italicized and hyperlinked or labeled with a page number if appropriate.

Example 54-42. ID and IDREF used for cross-referencing

```
<!DOCTYPE BOOK [
...
<!ELEMENT SECTION (TITLE, P*)>
<!ATTLIST SECTION MY-ID ID #IMPLIED>
<!ELEMENT CROSS-REFERENCE EMPTY>
<!ATTLIST CROSS-REFERENCE TARGET IDREF #REQUIRED>
...
]>
<BOOK>
...
<SECTION MY-ID="Why.XML.Rocks"><TITLE>Features of XML</TITLE>
...
</SECTION>


...
If you want to recall why XML is so great, please see
the section titled <CROSS-REFERENCE TARGET="Why.XML.Rocks"/>.
...
</BOOK>
```

Note that we made the section's MY-ID optional. Some sections will not need to be the target of a cross-reference, hypertext link or other reference and will not need to be uniquely identified. The TARGET attribute on CROSS-REFERENCE is required. It does not make sense to have a cross-reference that does not actually refer to another element.

IDs are XML names, with all of the constraints described in 53.1.5, "Names and name tokens", on page 765. Every element can have at most one ID, and thus only one attribute per element type be an ID attribute. All IDs specified in an XML document must be unique. A document with two ID attributes whose values are the same is invalid. Thus "chapter" would not be a good name for an ID, because it would make sense to use it in many places. "introduction.chapter" would be a logical ID because it would uniquely identify a particular chapter.

IDREF attributes must refer to an element in the document. You may have as many IDREFs referring to a single element as you need. It is also possible to declare an attribute that can potentially exhibit more than one IDREF by declaring it to be of type IDREFS:

Example 54-43. IDREFS attribute

```
<!ATTLIST RELATED-CHAPTERS TARGETS IDREFS #REQUIRED>
```

Now the TARGETS attribute may have one or more IDREFs as its value. There is no way to use XML to require that an attribute take two or more, or three or more, (etc.) IDREFs. You will recall that we could do that sort of thing using content models in element type declarations. There is no such thing as a content model for attributes. You could model this same situation by declaring RELATED-CHAPTERS to have content of one or more or two or more (etc.) CHAPTER-REF elements that each have a single IDREF attribute (named TARGET in Example 54-44).

Example 54-44. IDREF attributes

```
<!DOCTYPE BOOK[
...
<!ELEMENT RELATED-CHAPTERS (CHAPTER-REF+)>
<!ELEMENT CHAPTER-REF EMPTY>
<!ATTLIST CHAPTER-REF TARGET IDREF #REQUIRED>
...
]>
<BOOK>
...
<RELATED-CHAPTERS>
<CHAPTER-REF TARGET="introduction.to.xml"/>
<CHAPTER-REF TARGET="xml.rocks"/>
</RELATED-CHAPTERS>
...
</BOOK>
```

As you can see, element type declarations have the benefit of having content models, which can define complex structures, and attributes have the benefit of attribute types, which can enforce lexical and semantic constraints. You can combine these strengths to make intricate structures when this is appropriate.

54.6.3.5 ENTITY attributes

External unparsed entities are XML's way of referring to objects (files, CGI script output, etc.) on the Web that should not be parsed according to XML's rules. Anything from HTML documents to pictures to word processor files fall into this category. It is possible to refer to unparsed entities using an attribute with declared type *ENTITY*. This is typically done either to hyperlink to, reference or include an external object. This is shown in Example 54-45.

Example 54-45. Entity attribute type

```
<!DOCTYPE BOOK[
<!ATTLIST BOOK-REF TARGET ENTITY #REQUIRED>
...
<!ENTITY another-book SYSTEM
        "http://www.buyOurBooks.com/TheOtherBook.html" NDATA HTML>
...
]><BOOK>
...
<BOOK-REF TARGET="another-book">
...
</BOOK>
```

You can also declare an attribute to be of type *ENTITIES*, in which case its value may be the name of more than one entity. It is up to the application or stylesheet to determine whether a reference to the entity should be treated as a hot link, embed link or some other kind of link. The processor merely informs the application of the existence and notation of the entity. You can find information on unparsed entities and notations in Chapter 55, "Entities: Breaking up is easy to do", on page 822 and 54.7, "Notation Declarations", on page 819.

54.6.3.6   Summary of attribute types

There are two *enumerated* attribute types: *enumeration* attributes and NOTATION attributes.

Seven attribute types are known as *tokenized* types because each value represents either a single token (ID, IDREF, ENTITY, NMTOKEN) or a list of tokens (IDREFS, ENTITIES, and NMTOKENS).

The final type is the CDATA string type which is the least constrained and can hold any combination of XML characters as long as "special characters" (the quote characters and ampersand) are properly entered. Table 54-3 summarizes.

Table 54-3   Summary of attribute types

Type	Lexical constraint	Semantic constraint
CDATA	None	None
Enumeration	Name Token	Must be in the declared list.
NOTATION	Name	Must be in the declared list and a declared notation name.
ID	Name	Must be unique in document.
IDREF	Name	Must be some element's ID.
IDREFS	Names	Must each be some element's ID.
ENTITY	Name	Must be an unparsed entity's name.
ENTITIES	Names	Must each be unparsed entity's name.
NMTOKEN	Name Token	None
NMTOKENS	Name Tokens	None

54.7 | Notation Declarations

Notations are referred to in various parts of an XML document, for describing the data content notation of different things. A data content notation is the definition of how the bits and bytes of class of object should be interpreted. According to this definition, XML is a data content notation, because it defines how the bits and bytes of XML documents should be interpreted. Your favorite word processor also has a data content notation. The notation declaration gives an internal name to an existing notation so that it can be referred to in attribute list declarations, unparsed entity declarations, and processing instructions.

The most obvious place that an XML document would want to describe the notation of a data object is in a reference to some other resource on the web. It could be an embedded graphic, an MPEG movie that is the target of a hyperlink, or anything else. The XML facility for linking to these data resources is the entity declaration, and as we discussed earlier, they are referred to as *unparsed entities*. Part of the declaration of an unparsed entity is the name of a declared notation that provides some form of pointer to the external definition of the notation. The external definition could be a public or system identifier for documentation on the notation, some formal specification or a helper application that can handle objects represented in the notation.

Example 54-46. Notations for unparsed entities

```
<!NOTATION HTML SYSTEM "http://www.w3.org/Markup">
<!NOTATION GIF SYSTEM "gifmagic.exe">
```

Another place that notations arise are in the notation attribute type. You use this attribute type when you want to express the notation for the data content of an XML element. For instance, if you had a date element that used ISO or EU date formats, you could declare notations for each format:

Example 54-47. Notations for data content

```
<!NOTATION ISODATE SYSTEM "http://www.iso.ch/date_specification">
<!NOTATION EUDATE SYSTEM "http://www.eu.eu/date_specification">
<!ELEMENT TODAY (#PCDATA)>
<!ATTLIST TODAY DATE-FORMAT NOTATION (ISODATE|EUDATE) #REQUIRED>
```

Now the DATE-FORMAT attribute would be restricted to those two values, and would thus signal to the application that the content of the TODAY element conforms to one or the other.

 Note   You can specify datatypes more precisely for data content and attribute values by using the facilities described in Chapter 59, "Datatypes", on page 888.

Finally, notations can be used to give XML names to the targets for processing instructions. This is not strictly required by XML, but it is a good practice because it provides a sort of documentation for the PI and could even be used by an application to invoke the target.

This seems like a good way to close this chapter. DTDs are about improving the permanence, longevity, and wide reuse of your data, and the predictability and reliability of its processing. If you use them wisely, they will save you time and money.

Tip   Learning the syntax of markup declarations so that you can write DTDs is important, but learning how to choose the right element types and attributes for a job is a subtle process that requires a book of its own. We suggest David Megginson's Structuring XML Documents, also in this series (ISBN 0-13-642299-3).

Entities:
Breaking up is
easy to do

Tad Tougher Tutorial

■ Parameter and general

■ Internal and external

■ Parsed and unparsed

Chapter

55

ML allows flexible organization of document text. The XML constructs that provide this flexibility are called *entities*. They allow a document to be broken up into multiple storage objects and are important tools for reusing and maintaining text. Entities are used in many publishing-oriented applications of XML but are much less common in machine to machine applications.

55.1 | Overview

In simple cases, an entity is like an abbreviation in that it is used as a short form for some text. We call the "abbreviation" the *entity name* and the long form the *entity content*. That content could be as short as a character or as long as a chapter. For instance, in an XML document, the entity dtd could have the phrase "document type definition" as its content. Using a reference to that entity is like using the word DTD as an abbreviation for that phrase – the parser replaces the reference with the content.

You create the entity with an *entity declaration*. Example 55-1 is an entity declaration for an abbreviation.

Example 55-1. Entity used as an abbreviation

```
<!ENTITY dtd "document type definition">
```

Entities can be much more than just abbreviations. There are several different kinds of entities with different uses. We will first introduce the different variants in this overview and then come back and describe them more precisely in the rest of the chapter. We approach the topic in this way because we cannot discuss the various types of entity entirely linearly. Our first pass will acquaint you with the major types and the second one will tie them together and provide the information you need to actually use them.

Another way to think of an entity is as a box with a label. The label is the entity's name. The content of the box is some sort of text or data. The entity declaration creates the box and sticks on a label with the name. Sometimes the box holds XML text that is going to be *parsed* (interpreted according to the rules of the XML notation), and sometimes it holds data, which should not be.

If the content of an entity is XML text that the processor should parse, the XML spec calls it a *parsed entity*. The name is badly chosen because it is, in fact, unparsed; it will be parsed only if and when it is actually used.

If the content of an entity is data that is not to be parsed, the XML spec calls it an *unparsed entity*. This name isn't so great either because, as we just pointed out, an XML text entity is also unparsed.

We'll try to minimize the confusion and to avoid saying things like "a parsed entity will be parsed by the XML parser". But we sure wish they had named them "text entity" and "data entity".

The abbreviation in Example 55-1 is a parsed entity. Parsed entities, being XML text, can also contain markup. Example 55-2 is a declaration for a parsed entity with some markup in it.

Example 55-2. Parsed entity with markup

```
<!ENTITY dtd "<term>document type definition</term>">
```

The processor can also fetch content from somewhere on the Web and put that into the box. This is an *external* entity. For instance, it could fetch a chapter of a book and put it into an entity. This would allow you to reuse the chapter between books. Another benefit is that you could edit the chapter separately with a sufficiently intelligent editor. This would be very useful if you were working on a team project and wanted different people to work on different parts of a document at once. Example 55-3 demonstrates.

Example 55-3. External entity declaration

```
<!ENTITY intro-chapter SYSTEM "http://www.megacorp.com/intro.xml">
```

Entities also allow you to edit very large documents without running out of memory. Depending on your software and needs, either each volume or even each article in an encyclopedia could be an entity.

An author or DTD designer refers to an entity through an *entity reference*. The XML processor replaces the reference by the content, as if it were an abbreviation and the content was the expanded phrase. This process is called *inclusion*. After the operation we say either that the entity reference has been *replaced* by the entity content or that the entity content has been *included*. Which you would use depends on whether you are talking from the point of view of the entity reference or the entity content. The content of parsed entities is called their *replacement text*.

Example 55-4 is an example of a parsed entity declaration and its associated reference.

Example 55-4. Entity Declaration

```
<!DOCTYPE MAGAZINE[
...
<!ENTITY title "Hacker Life">

]>
<MAGAZINE>
<TITLE>&title;</TITLE>
...
<P>Welcome to the introductory issue of &title;. &title; is
geared to today's modern hacker.</P>
...
</MAGAZINE>
```

Anywhere in the document instance that the entity reference "&title;" appears, it is *replaced* by the text "Hacker Life". It is just as valid to say that "Hacker Life" is *included* at each point where the reference occurs. The ampersand character starts all general entity references and the semicolon ends them. The text between is an entity name.

Spec Excerpt (XML) 55-1. General entity reference

```
[68]   EntityRef ::=   '&' Name ';'
```

We have looked at entities that can be used in the creation of XML documents. Others can only be used to create XML DTDs. The ones we have been using all along are called *general* entities. They are called general entities because they can generally be used anywhere in a document. The ones that we use to create DTDs are called *parameter* entities.

We would use parameter entities for most of the same reasons that we use general entities. We want document type definitions to share declarations for element types, attributes and notations, just as we want documents to share chapters and abbreviations. For instance many DTDs in an organization might share the same definition for a paragraph element type named *para*. The declaration for that element type could be bundled up with other common DTD components and used in document type definitions for memos, letters and reports. Each DTD would include the element type declaration by means of a parameter entity reference.

Unparsed entities are for holding data such as images or molecular models in some data object notation. The application does not expect the processor to parse that information because it is not XML text.

Although it is an oversimplification, it may be helpful in your mind to remember that unparsed entities are often used for pictures and parsed entities are usually used for character text. You would include a picture through an unparsed entity, since picture representations do not (usually!) conform to the XML specification. Of course there are many kinds of non-XML data other than graphics, but if you can at least remember that unparsed entities are used for graphics then you will remember the rest also. Example 55-5 demonstrates.

Example 55-5. Unparsed entity declaration

```
<!ENTITY picture SYSTEM "http://www.home.org/mycat.gif" NDATA GIF>
```

We use unparsed entities through an entity attribute. A processor does not expand an entity attribute, but it tells the application that the use occurred. The application can then do something with it. For instance, if the application is a Web browser, and the entity contains a graphic, it could display the graphic. Entity attributes are covered in 54.6.3.5, "ENTITY attributes", on page 817.

55.2 | Entity details

> *Caution*   Like other names in XML, entity names are case-sensitive: &charles; refers to a different entity from &Charles;.

It is good that XML entity names are case-sensitive because they are often used to name letters. Case is a convenient way of distinguishing the upper-case version of a letter from the lower-case one. "Sigma" would represent the upper-case version of the Greek letter, and "sigma" would be the lower-case version of it. It would be possible to use some other convention to differentiate the upper- and lower-case versions, such as prefixes. That would give us "uc-Sigma" and "lc-Sigma".

Entities may be declared more than once (Example 55-6), but only the first declaration is *binding*. All subsequent ones are ignored as if they did not exist.

Example 55-6. Contradicting entity declarations

```
<!ENTITY abc "abcdefghijklmnopqrst"> <!-- This is binding. -->
<!ENTITY abc "ABCDEFGHIJKLMNOPQRST"> <!-- This is ignored. -->
<!ENTITY abc "AbCdEfGhIjKlMnOpQrSt"> <!-- So is this.       -->
```

Declarations in the internal DTD subset are processed before those in the external subset, as described in Chapter 54, "Creating a document type definition", on page 788. In practice, document authors can override parameter entities in the external subset of the DTD by declaring entities of the same name in the internal subset.

Entities are not difficult to use, but there are several variations and details that you should be aware of. We have already covered the major varieties, but only informally.

There is one special entity, called the *document entity* which is not declared, does not have a name and cannot be referenced. The document entity is the entity in which the processor started the current parse. Imagine you download a Web document called `catalog.xml`. Before a browser can display it, it must start to parse it, which makes it the document entity. It may include other entities, but because parsing started with `catalog.xml`, those others are not the document entity. They are just ordinary external entities.

If you click on a link and go to another XML Web page, then the processor must parse that page before it can display it. That page is the document entity for the new parse. In other words, even the simplest XML document has at least one entity: the document entity. The processor starts parsing the document in the document entity and it also must finish there.[1]

The document entity is also the entity in which the XML declaration and document type declaration can occur.

You may think it is strange for us to call this an entity when it is not declared as such, but if we were talking about files, it would probably not surprise you. It is common in many computer languages to have files that include other files. Even word processors allow this. We will often use the word entity to refer to a concept analogous to what you would think of as a file, although entities are more flexible. Entities are just "bundles of information". They could reside in databases, zip files, or be created on the fly by a computer program.

55.3 | Classifications of entities

There are many interesting things that you can do with entities. Here are some examples:

- You could store every chapter of a book in a separate file and link them together as entities.

---

1. To put it mystically: it is the alpha and the omega of entities.

- You could "factor out" often-reused text, such as a product name, into an entity so that it is consistently spelled and displayed throughout the document.
- You could update the product name entity to reflect a new version. The change would be instantly visible anywhere the entity was used.
- You could create an entity that would represent "legal boilerplate" text (such as a software license) and reuse that entity in many different documents.
- You could integrate pictures and multimedia objects into your document.
- You could develop "document type definition components" that could be used in many document type definitions. These would allow you to reuse the declarations for common element types (such as paragraph and emphasis) across several document types.

Because XML entities can do so many things, there are several different varieties of them. But XML entities do not break down into six or eight different types with simple names. Rather, you could think of each entity as having three properties that define its type. This is analogous to the way that a person could be tall or short and at the same time male or female and blonde or brunette.

Similarly, entities can be *internal* or *external*, *parsed* or *unparsed* and *general* or *parameter*. There is no single word for a short, male, brunette, and there is similarly no single word for an internal, parsed, parameter entity.

Caution   Some combinations of entity types are impossible. Obviously an entity cannot be both internal and external, just as a person could not be both blonde and brunette. It turns out that due to restrictions on unparsed entities, there are five combinations that are valid and three that are not.

Most of the rest of this chapter will describe the five types of entities in greater depth. We will use one convention that might be confusing without this note. In a section on, for instance, internal parsed general entities, we may describe a constraint or feature of all general entities. When we do so, we will use the word "general entity" instead of "internal general entity". This convention will allow us to avoid repeating text that is common among entity types. We will refer back to that text from other sections when it becomes relevant.

55.4 | Internal general entities

Internal parsed general entities are the simplest type of entity. They are essentially abbreviations defined completely in the document type declaration section of the XML document.

All internal general entities are parsed entities. This means that the XML processor parses them like any other XML text. Hence we will leave out the redundant word "parsed" and refer to them simply as internal general entities.

The content for an internal general entity is specified by a string literal after the entity's name. The string literal may contain markup, including references to other entities. An example is in Example 55-7.

Example 55-7. Internal general entity

```
<?xml version="1.0"?>
<!DOCTYPE SAMPLE SYSTEM "sample.dtd"[
    <!ENTITY xml "Extensible Markup Language">
]>
<SAMPLE>
    &xml;
</SAMPLE>
```

Internal general entities can be referenced anywhere in the content of an element or attribute value, including an attribute default value (in the DTD). They can also be referenced in the content of another general entity. Because they are general entities, they cannot be used to hold markup declarations for expansion in the DTD. They can only hold element or attribute content. Because of this, Example 55-8 is not well-formed. The only contexts in which general entities can occur in a DTD are entity replacement values and attribute default values.

The grammar rules for internal general entities are described in Spec Excerpt 55-2.

Example 55-8. Illegal: General entity cannot contain markup declarations

```
<?xml version="1.0"?>
<!DOCTYPE SAMPLE[
    <!ENTITY xml "Extensible Markup Language">
    &xml;
]>
```

Spec Excerpt (XML) 55-2. Internal general entities

```
[70]   EntityDecl ::=  GEDecl | PEDecl
[71]   GEDecl ::=  '<!ENTITY' S Name S EntityDef S? '>'
[73]   EntityDef ::=  EntityValue | (ExternalID NDataDecl?)
[9]    EntityValue ::=  '"' ([^%&"] | PEReference | Reference)* '"'
                       | "'" ([^%&'] | PEReference | Reference)* "'"
```

55.5 | External parsed general entities

Every XML entity is either internal or external. The content of internal entities occurs right in the entity declarations. External entities get their content from somewhere else in the system. It might be another file on the hard disk, a Web page or an object in a database. Wherever it is, it is located through an *external identifier*. Usually this is just the word SYSTEM followed by a URI (see 64.2, "Uniform Resource Identifiers", on page 1006).

In this section, we are interested specifically in external parsed general entities. Example 55-9 is an example of such an entity.

Example 55-9. External parsed general entity

```
<!ENTITY ent SYSTEM "http://www.house.gov/Constitution.xml">
```

It is the keyword SYSTEM that tells the processor that the next thing in the declaration is a URI. The processor gets the entity's content from that URI. The combination of SYSTEM and the URI is called an external identifier because it identifies an external resource to the processor. There is another kind of external identifier called a PUBLIC identifier. It is denoted by the keyword PUBLIC. External identifiers are described in 55.9, "External identifiers", on page 841.

External parsed general entities can be referenced in the same places that internal general entities can be — the document instance and the replacement text of other general entities — except not in the value of an attribute.

55.5.1 *External parsed entity support is optional*

XML processors are allowed, but not required, to validate an XML document when they parse it. The XML specification allows a processor that is not validating a document to completely ignore declarations of external parsed entities (both parameter and general). There is no way to control this behavior with the standalone document declaration or any other XML markup.

The reason for this is improved Web surfing performance. The XML working group thought that it was important for processors to be able to download the minimum amount of data required to do their job and no more. For instance, a browser could display unresolved external parsed entities as hypertext links that the user could click on to receive. Because the entity would only be downloaded on demand, the original page might display faster.

Unfortunately this is very inconvenient for authors, because it means that external parsed entities are essentially unreliable in systems that you do not completely control (e.g. the Internet vs. an intranet).

Caution   *External parsed entity processing is optional!*
    XML processors can ignore external parsed entities. If you use them to store parts of your documents, those parts will only show up at the browser vendor's option.

In practice this probably means that you should not put documents that use external entities on the Web until a pattern for browser behavior emerges. In the meantime, tools like James Clark's *sgmlnorm* can read an XML document that uses external entities and expand all of the entities for you.[2] We hope that future versions of the XML specification will make external entity inclusion mandatory.

55.6 | Unparsed entities

Every XML entity is either an *unparsed* entity or a *parsed* entity. Unparsed entities are external entities that the XML processor does not have to parse. For example a graphic, sound, movie or other multimedia object would be included through an unparsed entity. You can imagine the number of error messages you would get if an XML processor tried to interpret a graphic as if it were made up of XML text!

It is occasionally useful to refer to an XML document through an unparsed entity, as if it were in some unparsable representation. You might embed a complete letter document in a magazine document in this way. Rather than extending the magazine DTD to include letter elements, you would refer to it as an unparsed entity. Conceptually, it would be handled in the same way a picture of the letter would be handled. If you refer to it as an unparsed entity, the processor that handles the magazine does not care that the letter is actually XML.

All unparsed entities are external entities because there is no way to express non-XML information in XML entities. They are also all general entities because it is forbidden (and senseless) to embed data in XML DTDs. Hence, the term "unparsed entity" implies the terms "general" and "external".

Syntactically, declarations of unparsed entities are differentiated from those of other external entities by the keyword NDATA followed by a *notation* name.

Spec Excerpt (XML) 55-3. Non-XML data declaration

```
NDataDecl ::=   S 'NDATA' S Name
```

The name at the end is the name of a declared notation. Notation declarations are described in 54.7, "Notation Declarations", on page 819. The

---

2. *sgmlnorm* is on the CD-ROM.

processor passes this to the application as a hint about how the application should approach the entity.

If the application knows how to deal with that sort of entity (for instance if it is a common graphics notation) then it could do so directly. A browser might embed a rendition of the entity. It might also make a hyperlink to the entity. If it needs to download or install some other handler such as a Java program or Active-X control, then it could do so. If it needs to ask the user what to do it could do that also. The XML specification does not say what it must do. XML only expects processors to tell applications what the declared notation is and the applications must figure out the rest.

In the rare case that the entity is an XML document, the application might decide to process it, create a rendition of it, and then embed it. Alternatively, it might decide to make a hyperlink to it.

55.7 | Internal and external parameter entities

XML entities are classified according to whether they can be used in the DTD or in the document instance. Entities that can only be used in the DTD are called *parameter* entities. For instance, you might want to wrap up a few declarations for mathematical formulae element types and reuse the declarations from DTD to DTD.

The other entities can be used more generally (throughout the entire document instance), and are called *general* entities. Authors can use general entities as abbreviations, for sharing data among documents, including pictures, and many similar tasks.

There is an important reason why the two types are differentiated. When authors create documents, they want to be able to choose entity names without worrying about accidently choosing a name that was already used by the DTD designer. If there were no distinction between entities specific to the DTD and general to the document instance, according to XML's rules, the first declaration would win. That means that either the author would accidently take the place of ("clobber") a declaration that was meant to be used in the DTD, and thus trigger a cryptic error message, or the DTD designer's entity would clobber the entity that was meant to go in the document instance, and a seemingly random string of DTD-text would appear in the middle of the document! XML prevents this by having two different types of entities with distinct syntaxes for declaration and use.

Parameter entities are distinguished from general entity declarations by a single percent symbol in their declaration, and by a different syntax in their use. Example 55-10 is an example of a parameter entity declaration and use.

Example 55-10. Parameter entity

```
<!DOCTYPE SAMPLE[
    <!-- parameter entity declaration -->
<!ENTITY % sample-entity "<!ELEMENT SAMPLE (#PCDATA)>">
    <!-- parameter entity use -->
%sample-entity;
]>
<SAMPLE>
</SAMPLE>
```

This entity is declared with a syntax similar to that of general entities, but it has a percent sign between the string <!ENTITY and the entity's name. This is what differentiates parameter entity declarations from general entity declarations. If you want a general entity you just leave the percent character out.

The entity contains a complete element type declaration. It is referenced on the line after it is declared. Parameter entity references start with the percent-sign and end with the semicolon. The parser replaces the entity reference with the entity's content. In Example 55-10, the processor replaces the reference with the element type declaration "<!ELEMENT SAMPLE (#PCDATA)>". It then parses and interprets the element type declaration as if it had occurred there originally. The element type is declared and so the example is valid.

Spec Excerpt (XML) 55-4. Parameter Entity Declaration

```
[72]  PEDecl ::=  '<!ENTITY' S '%' S Name S PEDef S? '>'
[74]  PEDef ::=   EntityValue | ExternalID
[75]  ExternalID ::=  'SYSTEM' S SystemLiteral
             | 'PUBLIC' S PubidLiteral S SystemLiteral
[69]  PEReference ::=  '%' Name ';'
```

Parameter entities can be external, just as general entities can be. But they can never be unparsed. Parameter entities exist to provide building blocks for reusing markup declarations and making DTDs more flexible. It would not make sense to tell the XML processor not to process one! An example of an external parameter entity is in Example 55-11.

Example 55-11. External parameter entity

```
<!DOCTYPE SAMPLE[
    <!-- parameter entity declaration -->
<!ENTITY % sample-entity SYSTEM "pictures.ent">
    <!-- parameter entity use -->
%sample-entity;
]>
<SAMPLE>
</SAMPLE>
```

Parameter entities cannot be referenced in the document instance. In fact, the percent character is not special in the document instance, so if you try to reference a parameter entity in the instance, you will just get the entity reference text in your data, like "%this;".

Entities can only be referenced after they have been declared. General entities may appear to be referenced before they are declared but that is a mere trick of the light.

Example 55-12. General entity usage

```
<!ENTITY user "This entity uses &usee;.">
<!ENTITY usee "<em>another entity</em>">
```

Example 55-12 is legal because the entity replacement for &usee; does not take place until the point where the user entity is *referenced*.

With one exception (described below), general entities can only be expanded in the document instance. So the fact that user refers to usee is recorded, but the replacement is not immediately done. Later, in the document instance, the author will refer to the user entity using the general entity reference, &user;. At that point, the inclusion of its replacement text will trigger the expansion of the &usee; entity reference and the inclusion of its replacement text.

The exception is general entity references in default attribute values. These must be expanded immediately – in the DTD so that they can be checked for validity. These general entities must have been declared before they are used. Whether this exception is important or not depends on how much you use general entities in default attribute values.

Note that the text of a general entity can contain references to other general entities that are declared after it, while the text of a parameter entity cannot reference later-declared parameter entities. That is because parameter entity references are resolved when an entity declaration containing them is *parsed* (i.e., at declaration time). In contrast, general entity references are not resolved until the entity whose declaration contains them is *referenced*, which usually occurs in the document instance, after all DTD declarations have been processed. Referencing can also occur in a default value of an attribute declaration, after all relevant general entity declarations have been processed.

55.8 | Markup may not span entity boundaries

Parsed entities may contain markup as well as character data, but elements and other markup must not span entity boundaries. This means that a particular element may not start in one entity and end in another. If you think of entities as boxes, then an element cannot be half in one box and half in another. Example 55-13 is an example of illegal entity use:

Example 55-13. Elements spanning entity boundaries.

```
<!DOCTYPE SAMPLE [
    <!ENTITY start "<title>This is a">
    <!ENTITY finish "title</title>">
]>

&start;&finish;
```

This document is not well-formed. When the entity references are replaced with their text, they create a title element. This element spans the entities.

Other markup cannot span entities either. Declarations, comments, processing instructions and entity references must all finish in the entity in which they started. This applies to the document entity as much as any other. Markup strings and elements may not start in the document entity and finish in an included entity. This is a subtle but important rule. Documents which fail to conform are not well-formed.

In Example 55-14, entities are used in ways that are illegal. They are all illegal because they start markup without finishing it or finish it without starting it.

Example 55-14. Illegal entities

```
<!DOCTYPE TEST[
    <!ENTITY illegal1 "This will soon be <em>illegal">
    <!ENTITY illegal2 "This will too <em>">
    <!ENTITY illegal3 "This will also </em>">
    <!ENTITY illegal4 "And so will <!-- this">
    <!ENTITY illegal5 "And this &too;">
    <!-- note that none of these are illegal yet. -->
...
]><TEST>
<!-- These references are all illegal -->
&illegal1; <!-- Start-tag in entity with no end-tag there. -->
&illegal2; <!-- Start of tag in entity -->
&illegal3; <!-- End-tag in entity with no start-tag there. -->
&illegal4; <!-- Comment start but no end in entity. -->
&illegal5; <!-- Entity reference starts in entity. -->
</TEST>
```

The entities in Example 55-15 can be used legally or illegally. They do not necessarily represent the start or end of elements or markup, because they do not contain the strings that are used to start a tag ("<"), comment ("<!--"), general entity reference ("&") or other markup. Entity content is interpreted as markup if the replacement text would be interpreted as markup in the same context. In other words, the processor expands the entity and then looks for markup. If the markup it finds spans entity boundaries, then it is illegal.

In this case, it is not the declared entities themselves that are causing the problem, but the fact that elements, entities and markup started in the document entity must end there, just as in any other entity. The context of an entity reference is very important. That is what decides whether it is legal or illegal.

This is true even of entities that hold *complete* tags, elements, comments, processing instructions, character references, or entity references. References to those entities are legal anywhere their replacement text would be

Example 55-15. Sometimes legal entities

```
<?xml version="1.0"?>
<!DOCTYPE TEST[
<!ELEMENT TEST (#PCDATA)>
<!ENTITY maybelegal1 "em>"> <!-- May not be part of tag -->
<!ENTITY maybelegal2 "-->"> <!-- May not be comment delimiter -->
<!ENTITY maybelegal3 "ph>"> <!-- May not be part of tag -->
]>
<TEST>
&maybelegal1; <!-- Legal: Interpreted as character data -->
&maybelegal2; <!-- Legal: Interpreted as character data -->
&maybelegal3; <!-- Legal: Interpreted as character data -->

<&maybelegal1; <!-- Illegal: Markup (tag) spans entities -->
<!-- &maybelegal2; Ignored: entity ref ignored in comment -->
<em&maybelegal3;    <!-- Illegal: Markup (tag) spans entities -->
</TEST>
```

legal. The same applies to *validity* (conformance to a document type definition). Example 55-16 is well-formed, but not valid, because the fully expanded document would not be valid. Validity is covered in Chapter 54, "Creating a document type definition", on page 788.

Example 55-16. Well-formed but not valid

```
<?xml version="1.0"?>
<!DOCTYPE TEST[
  <!ELEMENT EVENT (TIME, DESCRIPTION)>
  <!ELEMENT TIME (#PCDATA)>
  <!ELEMENT DESCRIPTION (#PCDATA)>
  <!ENTITY accident "<ERROR>Error</ERROR>">
]>
<EVENT>&accident;</EVENT>
```

The document in the example is well-formed. Both the EVENT and ERROR elements start and end in the same entity. It meets all of the other rules required for it to be well-formed. But it is not valid, because accident's replacement text consists of an ERROR element which is not valid where the entity is referenced. (in the EVENT element).

Conceptually, validation occurs after all entities have been parsed.

Spec Excerpt (XML) 55-5. General entity definition

```
[70]   EntityDecl ::=  GEDecl | PEDecl
[71]   GEDecl ::=  '<!ENTITY' S Name S EntityDef S? '>'
[73]   EntityDef ::=  EntityValue | (ExternalID NDataDecl?)
[72]   PEDecl ::=  '<!ENTITY' S '%' S Name S PEDef S? '>'
[74]   PEDef ::=  EntityValue | ExternalID
```

55.8.1 *Legal parameter entity reference*

Neither general entities nor parameter entities may span markup boundaries, but parameter entities have other restrictions on them. There are precise places that parameter entity references are allowed. Within the internal subset, the rules are simple: parameter entities can only be expanded in places where full markup declarations are allowed. For them to be legal in these contexts they must always contain one or more markup declarations.

Example 55-17. Multiple markup declarations in one parameter entity

```
<!ENTITY % several-declarations
                "<!ELEMENT FOO (#PCDATA)>
                <!ELEMENT BAR (#PCDATA)>
                <!ELEMENT BAZ (#PCDATA)>">
%several-declarations;
```

Because of the way XML handles white space, the replacement text for the entity declaration in Example 55-17 is parsed as it would if the entity declaration had occurred on a single line. In this case we have defined the literal entity value over several lines to make the DTD more readable. When we refer to the parameter entity "several-declarations", the three element types are declared.

The rules for parameter entities in the external subset are much more complex. This is because parameter entities in the external subset are not restricted to complete markup declarations. They can also be parts of a markup declaration. XML restricts parameter entities in the internal subset to full declarations because the internal subset is supposed to be very easy to process quickly by browsers and other processors. The external subset allows more complex, powerful parameter entity references. For instance, in the external subset, Example 55-18 would be a legal series of declarations.

Example 55-18. Entities in the external subset

```
<!ENTITY % ent-name "the-entity">
<!ENTITY % ent-value "This is the entity">
<!ENTITY %ent-name; "%ent-value;">
```

Both the name and the replacement text of the final entity declaration are specified through parameter entity references. Their replacement texts become the entity's name and replacement text.

The tricky part is that there are only particular places that you can use parameter entity references in markup declarations. You might wonder, for instance, if you could replace the string "<!ENTITY" with a parameter entity reference. You might guess that this is impossible because XML does not allow a markup declaration to start in one entity and end in another. You would guess correctly. It would be harder to guess whether you could use an entity reference to fill in the string "ENTITY" which follows the "<!" It turns out that this is illegal as well.

To be safe, we would advise you to stick to using parameter entities only to hold full markup declarations and portions of another entity's replacement text until you are familiar with the text of the XML specification itself. The specification relies on knowledge of grammatical tokens to constrain the places that parameter entity replacement is allowed in the external subset. Those token boundaries are only described in the complete grammar.

55.9 | External identifiers

External identifiers refer to information outside the entity in which they occur. There are two types. System identifiers use URIs to refer to an object based on its location. Public identifiers use a publicly declared name to refer to information.

Spec Excerpt (XML) 55-6. External identifier

```
[75]   ExternalID ::=   'SYSTEM' S SystemLiteral
                      | 'PUBLIC' S PubidLiteral S SystemLiteral
```

55.9.1 *System identifiers*

The *SystemLiteral* that follows the keyword SYSTEM is just a URI. Example 55-19 is another example of that.

Example 55-19. System identifier

```
<!ENTITY ent SYSTEM "http://www.entities.com/ent.xml">
```

You can also use relative URIs to refer to entities on the same machine as the referring entity. A relative URI is one that does not contain a complete machine name and path. The machine name and part of the path are implied from the context. Example 55-20 demonstrates.

Example 55-20. Local external general entity

```
<!ENTITY local SYSTEM "local.xml">
```

If this were declared in a document at the URI http://www.baz.org/, then the processor would fetch the replacement text from http://www.baz.org/local.xml.

These URIs are relative to the location of the referring entity (such as an external parameter entity or the external subset of the DTD) and not necessarily to the document entity. If your document entity is on one machine, and it includes some markup declarations from another machine, relative URIs in the included declarations are interpreted as being on the second machine.

For example, your document might be at http://www.myhome.com. It might include a DTD component with a set of pictures of playing cards from http://www.poker.com/cards.dtd. If that DTD component had a

URI, `4Heartss.gif`, it would be interpreted relative to the poker site, not yours.

55.9.2 *Public identifiers*

It is also possible to refer to a DTD component or any entity by a name, in addition to a URI. This name is called a "public identifier". If a few entities become widely used in XML circles then it would be inefficient for every-one to fetch the entities from the same servers. Instead, their software should come with those entities already installed (or else it should know the most efficient site from which to download them, perhaps from a corporate intranet). To enable these smarter lookup mechanisms, you would refer to those DTDs by public identifiers, as shown in Example 55-21.

Example 55-21. Referencing a DTD by public identifier

```
<!DOCTYPE MEMO PUBLIC "-//SGMLSOURCE//DTD MEMO//EN"
               "http://www.sgmlsource.com/dtds/memo.dtd">
<MEMO> </MEMO>
```

The public identifier is a unique name for the entity. It should be unique world-wide. Usually they contain corporate or personal names to make them more likely to be unique. If the software knows how to translate the public identifier into a URI, it will do so. If not, it will use the system iden-tifier.

Right now, the translation from public identifier to URI is typically either hard-wired into a processor or controlled through files called "entity catalogs". Entity catalogs list public identifiers and describe their URIs, in the same way that phone books allow you to look up a name and find a number. Documentation for XML software should mention the format of the catalogs it supports, if any.

In the future there may be intranet- and Internet-wide systems that will look up a public identifier and download the DTD from the site that is closest to you. The Web's designers have been promising this feature for years and XML is ready when they deliver. In the meantime, the system identifier following the public identifier will be used.

55.10 | Conclusion

As you can see, XML separates issues of logical structure from those of the physical storage of the document. This means that document type designers do not have to foresee every possible reasonable way of breaking up a document when they design the document type. This is good, because that sort of decision is best made by those who know their system resource limits, bandwidth limits, editor preferences, and so forth. The document type designer, in contrast, takes responsibility for deciding on a good structure for the document.

Advanced features of XML

Friendly Tutorial

- Conditional sections
- Character references
- Processing instructions
- Standalone declaration

The features in this chapter are advanced in the sense that only advanced users will get around to reading them. They do not require advanced degrees in computer science or rocket science to understand. They are just a little esoteric. Most XML users will get by without ever needing to use them.

56.1 | Conditional sections

Conditional sections can only occur in the external subset of the document type declaration, and in external entities referenced from the internal subset. The internal subset proper is supposed to be quick and easy to process. In contrast, the external subset is supposed to retain some of the full-SGML mechanisms that make complicated DTDs easier to maintain. One of these mechanisms is the conditional section, which allows you to turn on and off a series of markup declarations.

Like the internal and external subsets, conditional sections may contain one or more complete declarations, comments, processing instructions, or nested conditional sections, with optional white space between them.

A conditional section is turned on and off with a keyword. If the keyword is INCLUDE, then the section is processed just as if the conditional section markers did not exist. If the keyword is IGNORE, then the contents are ignored by the processor as if the declarations themselves did not exist, as in Example 56-1.

Example 56-1. Conditional sections

```
<![INCLUDE[
 <!ELEMENT magazine (title, article+, comments* )>
 ]]>
<![IGNORE[
 <!ELEMENT magazine (title, body)>
 ]]>
```

This is a useful way of turning on and off parts of a DTD during development.

The real power in the feature derives from parameter entity references. These are described in 55.7, "Internal and external parameter entities", on page 834.

If the keyword of the conditional section is a parameter entity reference, the processor replaces the parameter entity by its content before the processor decides whether to include or ignore the conditional section. That means that by changing the parameter entity in the internal subset, you can turn on and off a conditional marked section. In that way, two different documents could reference the same set of external markup declarations, but get slightly (or largely) different DTDs. For instance, we can modify the example above:

Example 56-2. Conditional sections and parameter entities

```
<![%editor[
 <!ELEMENT magazine (title, article+, comments* )>
 ]]>
<![%author[
 <!ELEMENT magazine (title, body)>
 ]]>
```

Now editors will have a slightly different DTD from authors. When the parameter entities are set one way, the declaration without comments is chosen:

Example 56-3. Internal subset of a document type declaration

```
<!DOCTYPE MAGAZINE SYSTEM "magazine.dtd"[
   <!ENTITY % editor "IGNORE">
   <!ENTITY % author "INCLUDE">
]>
```

Authors do not have to worry about comments elements that they are not supposed to use anyway. When the document moves from the author to the editor, the parameter entity values can be swapped, and the expanded version of the DTD becomes available. Parameter entities can also be used to manage DTDs that go through versions chronologically, as an organization's needs change.

Conditional sections are also sometimes used to make "strict" and "loose" versions of DTDs. The loose DTD can be used for compatibility with old documents, or documents that are somehow out of your control, and the strict DTD can be used to try to encourage a more precise structure for future documents.

56.2 | Character references

It is not usually convenient to type in characters that are not available on the keyboard. With many text editors, it is not even possible to do so. XML allows you to insert such a character with a *character reference*. If, for instance, you wanted to insert a character from the "International Phonetic Alphabet", you could spend a long time looking for a combination of keyboard, operating system and text editor that would make that straightforward. Rather than buying special hardware or software, XML allows you to refer to the character by its *Unicode number*.

Here is an example:

Example 56-4. Decimal character reference

```
<P>Here is a reference to Unicode character 161: &#161;.</P>
```

Unicode is a character set. The character numbered 161 in Unicode happens to be the inverted exclamation mark. Alternatively, you could use the *hex* (hexadecimal) value of the character number to reference it:

Example 56-5. Hex character reference

```
<P>Here is a different reference to Unicode character 161: &#xA1;.
```

Hex is a numbering system often used by computer programmers that translates naturally into the binary codes that computers use. The *Unicode Standard book* uses hex, so those that have that book will probably prefer this type of character reference over the other (whether they are programmers or not).

Here are the specifics on character references from the XML spec:

Spec Excerpt (XML) 56-1. Character reference

```
CharRef ::=   '&#' [0-9]+ ';'
    | '&#x' [0-9a-fA-F]+ ';'
```

Spec Excerpt (XML) 56-2. Interpreting character references

If the character reference begins with "&#x", the digits and letters up to the terminating ; provide a hexadecimal representation of the character's code point in ISO/IEC 10646. If it begins just with "&#", the digits up to the terminating ; provide a decimal representation of the character's code point.

ISO/IEC 10646 is the Borg of character set standards. It seemingly includes every character from every other character set and leaves room for characters not yet created. Unicode is an independently developed industry-standard character set that is identifiable as a subset of ISO/IEC 10646. For XML purposes, there's no real need to distinguish them.

Note that character references are not entity references, though they look similar to them. Entities have names and values, but character references only have character numbers. In an XML document, all entities except the predefined ones must be declared. But a character reference does not require a declaration; it is just a really verbose way to type a character (but often the only way).

Because Unicode numbers are hard to remember, it is often useful to declare entities that stand in for them:

Example 56-6. Entity declaration for a Unicode character

```
<!ENTITY inverted-exclamation "&#161;">
```

Most likely this is how most XML users will refer to obscure characters. There will probably be popular character entity sets that can be included in a DTD through parameter entity references. This technique will free users from learning obscure character numbers and probably even from learning how to use character references.

56.3 | Processing instructions

XML comments are for those occasions where you need to say something to another human being without reference to the DTD, and without changing the way the document looks to readers or applications. Processing instructions are for those occasions where you need to say something to *a computer program* without reference to the DTD and without changing the way that the document is processed by other computer programs. This is only supposed to happen rarely.

Many people argued that the occasions would be so rare that XML should not have processing instructions at all. But as one of us said in *The SGML Handbook*: "In a perfect world, they would not be needed, but, as you may have noticed, the world is not perfect." It turns out that processing instruction use has changed over the years and is not as frowned upon as it was in the early days of SGML.

Processing instructions are intended to reintroduce software-specific markup. You might wonder why you would want to do that. Imagine that you are creating a complex document, and, like a good user of a generalized markup language, you are concentrating on the structure rather than the formatting. Close to the deadline you print the document using the propri-etary formatting system that has been foisted on you by your boss. There are many of these systems, some of which are of fantastic quality and others which are not.

Your document looks reasonable, but you need a way to make the first letter of each paragraph large. However, reading the software's manual, you realize that the formatter does not have a feature that allows you to modify the style for the first letter of a word. The XML Purist in you might want to go out and buy a complete formatting system but the Pragmatist in you knows that that is impossible.

Thinking back to the bad-old days of "What You See is All You Get" word processors, you recall that all you really needed to do is to insert a code in the beginning of each paragraph to change the font for the first letter. This is not good "XML Style" because XML Purists do not insert formatting codes and they especially do not insert codes specific to a particular piece of software – that is not in the "spirit" of generalized markup. Still, in this case, with a deadline looming and stubborn software balking, a processing instruction may be your best bet. If the formatter has a "change font" command it may be accessible through a processing instruction:

Example 56-7. Processing instruction

```
<CHAPTER>The Bald and the Dutiful
<P><?DUMB-FORMATTER.FONT="16PT"?>N<?DUMB-FORMATTER.END-FONT?>ick
took Judy in his arms</P>
```

If you find yourself using many processing instructions to specify formatting you should try to figure out what is wrong with your system. Is your document's markup not rich enough? Is your formatting language not powerful enough? Are you not taking advantage of the tools and markup you have available to you? The danger in using processing instructions is that you can come to rely on them instead of more reusable structural markup. Then when you want to reuse your information in another context, the markup will not be robust enough to allow it.

Processing instructions start with a fixed string "<?". That is followed by a name and, after that, any characters except for the string that ends the PI, "?>".

Here are the relevant rules from the XML specification:

Spec Excerpt (XML) 56-3. Processing Instruction

```
[16]   PI ::=   '<?' PITarget (S (Char* - (Char* '?>' Char*)))? '?>'
[17]   PITarget ::=   Name - (('X' | 'x') ('M' | 'm') ('L' | 'l'))
```

This name at the beginning of the PI is called the *PI target*. This name should be standardized in the documentation for the tool or specification. After the PI target comes white space and then some totally proprietary command. This command is not processed in the traditional sense at all. Characters that would usually indicate markup are totally ignored. The command is passed directly to the application and it does what it wants to with it. The command ends when the processor hits the string "?>". There is absolutely no standard for the "stuff" in the middle. Markup is not recognized there. PIs could use attribute syntax for convenience, but they could also choose not to.

It is possible that more than one application could understand the same instructions. They might come from the same vendor or one vendor might agree to accept another vendor's commands. For instance in the early days of the Web, the popular NCSA (National Center for Supercomputing Activities) Web Server introduced special commands into HTML documents in the form of special HTML comments. Because the NCSA server was dominant in those days, many servers now support those commands.

Under XML we would most likely use processing instructions for the same task. The virtue of XML processing instructions in this case is that they are explicitly instructions to a computer program. In our opinion, one of the central tenets of generalized markup is that it is important to be *explicit* about what is going on in a document. Reusing markup constructs for something other than what they were intended for is not explicit.

For instance, since comments are meant to be instructions to users, an ambitious Web Server administrator might decide to write a small script that would strip them out to save download time and protect internal comments from being read by others. But if instructions to software (like the NCSA server commands) were hidden in comments, they would be stripped out as well. It would be better to use the supplied processing instruction facility, which was designed for the purpose.

Better still (from a purist's point of view) would be a robust XML-smart mechanism for accomplishing the task. For instance, one thing that the NCSA servers do is include the text of one HTML file into another. XML's entity mechanism (see Chapter 55, "Entities: Breaking up is easy to do", on page 822) can handle this, so you do not need processing instructions in that case.

If you want to insert the date into a document, then you could connect the external entity to a CGI[1] that returns the date. If you want to insert information from a database then you could have software that generates XML entities with the requested information.

Sometimes, though, the processing instruction solution may be the most expedient. This is especially the case if your application vendor has set it up that way. If your document is heavily dependent on a database or other program, then it is not very "application independent" in any case. If a document is inherently dependent on an application then you may decide that strictly adhering to generalized markup philosophy is just too much work. In the end you must choose between expediency and purity. Most people mix both.

Processing instructions are appropriate when you are specifying information about a document that is unrelated to the actual structure of the document. Consider, for instance, the problem of specifying which stylesheets go with which XML documents on a web site. Given enough money and time you could erect a database that kept track of them. If you already had your XML documents in a text database then this would probably be the most efficient mechanism. If you did not have a text database set up, then you could merely keep the information in a flat text file. But you would have to keep that external information up-to-date and write a program to retrieve it in order to do formatting. It would probably be easier to simply stick the information somewhere in the file where it is easy to find (such as at the beginning).

You could add a STYLESHEET element or attribute to each document, but that could cause three problems. First, it would violate the XML Purist principle that elements should represent document components and not formatting or other processing information. Second, if you are using DTDs with your documents then you must add the element or attribute to each DTD that you will be using. This would be a hassle.

The third reason to use processing instructions instead of elements is the most concrete: you may not be able to change those DTDs. After all, DTDs are often industry (or international!) standards. You cannot just go monkeying around with them even if you want to. Instead, you could put a processing instruction at the start of each document. Processing instructions are not associated with particular DTDs and they do not have to be declared. You just use them.

---

1. CGI is the "Common Gateway Interface", a specification for making Web pages that are generated by the server when the user requests them, rather than in advance.

As we described in 62.9, "Referencing XSLT stylesheets", on page 993), XML provides a processing instruction for associating stylesheets:

Example 56-8. Stylesheet PI

```
<?xml-stylesheet
          href="http://www.sgmlsource.com/memo.xsl"
          type="text/xsl"?>
```

Note that the stylesheet processing instruction does not really add anything to the content or structure of the document. It says something about how to *process* the document. It says: "This document has an associated stylesheet and it is available at such and such a location." It is not always obvious what is abstract information and what is merely processing information. If your instruction must be embedded in documents of many types, or with DTDs that you cannot change, then processing instructions are typically your best bet.

The XML *encodingPI* is an example of another processing instruction. It says what character encoding the file uses. Again this information could be stored externally, such as in a database, a text file or somewhere else, but XML's designers decided (after weeks of heated discussion) that it would be most convenient to place it in the XML document itself rather than require it to be stored (and transmitted across the Internet) externally.

If you go back to 53.6.1, "XML declaration", on page 778 you will also notice that the XML declaration has the same prefix ("<?") and suffix ("?>") as processing instructions do. Formally speaking, the XML declaration is a special form of processing instruction. From an SGML processor's point of view, it is a processing instruction that controls the behavior of a particular class of software: XML processing software. Software that treats XML as just another kind of SGML will ignore it, as they do other types of processing instructions.

To summarize: PIs (processing instructions) were invented primarily for formatting hacks but based on our experience with SGML we know that they are more widely useful. There are already predefined processing instructions in the XML specification for some kinds of processing. Processing instructions will probably be used for other things in the future. Everything that can be accomplished with PIs would be accomplished by other means in a perfect world of pure generalized markup, but in the real world they are often convenient.

56.4 | Special attributes and newlines

There are two attribute names that the XML specification treats as special whenever it encounters them. If a document is to be valid then it must have declarations for these attributes but if it is well-formed but not valid then it may just use them undeclared, as it would any other attribute.

The attribute `xml:lang` is a convention for stating the language of the content of an element. This is language not in some esoteric computer sense but in the normal, human languages sense. The attribute's value is typically a language code like "`en`" for English and "`fr`" for French.

It is also common to follow the language code with a dash and a country code to indicate a more precise dialect. The country codes are the same ones used in Internet domain names: "uk", "us", "ca" etc. If you do serious internationalization work you should check the XML specification for the full details.

The attribute `xml:space` is a hint to an application about how it should handle whitespace in an element. For instance, an XML editor might use the attribute to know whether it is appropriate to collapse several spaces into a single one or to convert newline characters into spaces. The two valid values are `default` and `preserve`. Default means that an application should do whatever it usually does with whitespace – collapse, delete, preserve or anything. Preserve means that the application should not change the whitespace in any way.

Both of these attributes are *inherited*. That means that an attribute applies to the element and all descendants unless some descendant has a conflicting value for it. In that case the descendant's attribute value would be in effect for that element and *its* descendants, but the ancestral value would again be in effect after that element ends.

Regardless of the value of these attributes, XML processors must always convert end-of-line markers to a single Unix-style newline character. It does not matter what platform (e.g. Windows, Macintosh, Unix) the document is processed on nor what platform it was created on. The various end-of-line conventions are all converted automatically to the Unix convention before the application sees the data. This means that software programs can behave in exactly the same way on all platforms and documents.

56.5 | Standalone document declaration

We should start by saying that the standalone document declaration is only designed for a small class of problems, and these are not problems that most XML users will run into. We do not advise its use. Nevertheless, it is part of XML and we feel that you should understand it so that you can understand why it is seldom useful.

A DTD is typically broken into two parts, an external part that contains declarations that are typically shared among many documents, and an internal part that occurs within the document and contains declarations that only that document uses (see Chapter 54, "Creating a document type definition", on page 788). The external part includes all external parameter entities, including both the external subset of the document type declaration and any external entities referenced from the internal subset.

The DTD describes the structure of the document, but it can also control the interpretation of some of the markup and declare the existence of some other entities (such as graphics or other XML documents) that are required for proper processing. For instance, a graphic might only be used in a particular document, so the declaration that includes it (an *entity declaration*) would usually go in the internal subset rather than the external one.

Processors that validate a document need the entire DTD to do so. A document is not valid unless it conforms to both the internal and external parts of its DTD. But sometimes a system passes a document from program to program and it does not need to be validated at each stage. For instance, two participants in an electronic data interchange system might agree that the sender will validate the document once, instead of having both participants validate it.

Even though the receiving processor may not be interested in full validation, it may need to know if it understands the document in exactly the same way that the sender did. Some features of the DTD may influence this slightly. Documents with defaulted attributes would be interpreted differently if the attribute declarations are read rather than ignored. Entity declarations would allow the expansion of entity references. Attribute values can only be normalized according to their type when the attribute declarations are read. Some white space in content would also be removed if the DTD would not allow it to be interpreted as text.

If a process can reliably skip a part of the DTD dedicated exclusively to validation, then it would have less data to download and process and could let the application do its work (browsing, searching, etc.) more quickly. But it would be important for some "mission critical" applications to know if they are getting a slightly different understanding of the document than they would if they processed the entire DTD.

The *standalone document declaration* allows you to specify whether a processor needs to fetch the external part of the DTD in order to process the document "exactly right." The Standalone document declaration may take the values (case sensitive) of yes and no.

A value of yes says that the document is *standalone* and thus does not depend on the external part of the DTD for correct interpretation. A value of *no* means that it either depends on the external DTD part or it might, so the application should not trust that it can get the correct information without it. You could always use no as the value for this attribute, but in some cases applications will then download more data than they need to do their jobs. This translates into slower processing, more network usage and so forth.

Example 56-9. A standalone document declaration that forces processing of the internal subset.

```
<?xml version="1.0" standalone="no"?>
<!DOCTYPE MEMO SYSTEM "http://www.sgmlsource.com/memo.dtd" [
<!ENTITY % pics SYSTEM "http://www.sgmlsource.com/pics.ent">
 %pics;
]>
<MEMO></MEMO>
```

Example 56-9 will tell the application that unless the processor fetched the pictures, the application might get a different understanding of the document than it would if it processed the whole document. For instance, the MEMO element might have defaulted attributes.

But if the value is *yes*, the receiving application may choose not to get the external part of the DTD. This implies that it will never know what was in it. Still, it needs to be able to trust the accuracy of the declaration. What if the security level for a document is set in an attribute and the default level is top-secret? It would be very bad if a careless author could obscure that with a misleading standalone document declaration. In the scenario we outlined, the sender has already validated the document. So the sender has enough information to check that the information is correct. The XML specification requires a validating processor to do this (see Spec Excerpt 56-4).

Spec Excerpt (XML) 56-4. Standalone document declaration

The standalone document declaration must have the value "no" if any external markup declarations contain declarations of:

- attributes with default values, if elements to which these attributes apply appear in the document without specifications of values for these attributes, or
- entities (other than amp, lt, gt, apos, quot), if references to those entities appear in the document, or
- attributes with values subject to normalization, where the attribute appears in the document with a value which will change as a result of normalization, or
- element types with element content, if white space occurs directly within any instance of those types.

The last one is very likely to happen. Often people use white space between tags to make the source XML document readable, but that can slightly change the interpretation of the document. Validating processors will tell applications that there are some contexts where character data is not legal, so the white space occurring in those places must be merely formatting white space (see 54.5, "Content models", on page 800). If an application that does not want to validate a document is to get exactly the same information out of the document, it must know whether there are any elements where white space should be interpreted just as source formatting. We say that this sort of white space is *insignificant*.

The standalone document declaration warns the application that this is the case so that mission critical applications may download the DTD just to get the right information out of the document, even when they are not interested in validating it.

The standalone document declaration is fairly obscure and it is doubtful if it will get much use outside of a few mission critical applications. Even there, however, it is safest to just get the external data and do a complete validation before trusting a document. You might find that it had been corrupted in transit.

56.6 | Is that all there is?

We've pretty much covered all the details of XML, certainly all that are likely to see extensive use. There are some things we didn't touch on, such as restrictions that must be observed if you are using older SGML tools to process XML. As the generalized markup industry is retooling rapidly for XML, such restrictions will be short-lived and, we felt, did not warrant complicating our XML tutorial.

In any case, you are now well-prepared – or will be after reading Chapter 57, "Reading the XML specification", on page 862 – to tackle the XML spec yourself. You'll find it in the XML SPECtacular section of the CD-ROM that accompanies this book.

Tip   We can also recommend Bob DuCharme's *XML: The Annotated Specification*, which is published in this series (ISBN 0-13-082676-6). It is extensively annotated and has over 170 new usage examples.

Reading the XML specification

Tad Tougher Tutorial

- Grammars
- Rules
- Symbols

Chapter

57

The XML specification is a little tricky to read, but with some work you can get through it by reading and understanding the glossary and applying the concepts described so far in this book. One thing you'll need to know is how to interpret the *production rules* that make up XML's *grammar*. This chapter teaches how to read those rules.

When discussing a particular string, like a tag or declaration, we often want to discuss the parts of that string individually. We call each part of the string a *token*. Tokens can always be separated by white space as described above. Sometimes the white space between the tokens is required. For instance we can represent the months of the year as tokens:

Example 57-1. Tokens

JANUARY FEBRUARY MARCH APRIL MAY JUNE

White space between tokens is *normalized* (combined) so that no matter how much white space you type, the processor treats it as if the tokens were separated by a single space. Thus the example above is equivalent to the following:

Example 57-2. Tokens after normalization

JANUARY FEBRUARY MARCH APRIL MAY JUNE

Whenever we discuss strings made up of tokens, you will know that you can use as much white space between tokens as you need and the XML processor will normalize it for you.

57.1 | A look at XML's grammar

There are two basic techniques that we could use to discuss XML's syntax precisely. The first is to describe syntactic constructs in long paragraphs of excruciatingly dull prose. The better approach is to develop a simple system for describing syntax. In computer language circles, such systems are called *grammars*. Grammars are more precise and compact. Although they are no less boring (as you may recall from primary school), you can skip them easily until you need to know some specific detail of XML's syntax.

As a bonus, once you know how to read a grammar, you can read the one in the XML specification and thus work your way up to the status of "language lawyer".[1] As XML advances, an ability to read the specification will help you to keep on top of its progress.

The danger in this approach is that you might confuse the grammar with XML markup itself. The grammar is just a definitional tool. It is not used in XML applications. You don't type it in when you create an XML document. You use it to figure out what you *can* type in. Before "the new curriculum", students were taught grammar in primary school. They would be taught parts of speech and how they could combine them. XML's grammar is the same. It will tell you what the parts of an XML document are, and how you can combine them.

Grammars are made up of production *rules* and *symbols*. Rules are simple: they say what is allowed in a particular place in an XML document.

---

1. You too can nitpick about tiny language details and thus prove your superiority over those who merely use XML rather than obsess over it.

Rules have a symbol on the left side, the string "::=" in the middle and a list of symbols on the right side:

Example 57-3. A Rule

```
people ::= 'Melissa' 'Tiffany' 'Joshua' 'Johan'
```

If this rule were part of the grammar for XML (which it is not!) it would say that in a particular place in an XML document you could type the names listed in the order listed.

The symbols on the right (the names, in the last example) define the set of allowed values for the construct described by the rule ("people"). An allowed value is said to *match*. Rules are like definitions in a dictionary. The left side says what is being defined and the right side says what its definition is. Just as words in a dictionary, are defined in terms of other words, symbols are defined in terms of other symbols. Rules in the XML grammar are preceded by a number. You can look the rule up by number. If an XML document does not follow all of the XML production rules, it is not *well-formed*.

57.2 | Constant strings

The most basic type of symbol we will deal with is a *constant string*. These are denoted by a series of characters in between single quote characters. Constant strings are matched case-sensitively (as we discussed earlier). Here are some examples:

Example 57-4. Matching constant strings

```
AlphabetStart ::= 'ABC'
Example1 ::= '<!DOCTYPE'
```

This would match (respectively) the strings

Example 57-5. Matches

```
ABC
<!DOCTYPE
```

When we are discussing a constant string that is an English word or abbreviation, we will refer to it as a *keyword*. In computer languages, a keyword is a word that is interpreted specially by the computer. So your mother's maiden name is not (likely) a keyword, but a word like #REQUIRED is.

Symbols in XML's grammar are separated by spaces, which means that you must match the first, and then the second, and so on in order.

Example 57-6. Representing sequence

```
AlphabetStartAndEnd ::= 'ABC' 'XYZ'
NumbersAndLetters ::= '123' 'QPZ'
```

These would match:

Example 57-7. Sequence matches

```
ABCXYZ
123QPZ
```

Note that a space character in the grammar does not equate to white space in the XML document. Wherever white space can occur we will use the symbol "S". That means that wherever the grammar specifies "S", you may put in as much white space as you need to make your XML source file maintainable.

Example 57-8. Whitespace

```
SpacedOutAlphabet ::= 'ABC' S 'XYZ'
```

matches:

Example 57-9. Matching whitespace

```
ABC XYZ
ABC        XYZ
ABC                    XYZ
```

This is the first example we have used where a single rule matches multiple strings. This is usually the case. Just as in English grammar there are many possible verbs and nouns, there are many possible strings that match the rule `SpacedOutAlphabet`, depending on how much white space you choose to make your XML source file maintainable.

Obviously XML would not be very useful if you could only insert predefined text and white space. After all, XML users usually like to choose the topic and content of their documents! So they need to have the option of inserting their own content: a *user defined string*. The simplest type of user defined string is *character data*. This is simply the text that isn't markup. You can put almost any character in character data. The exceptions are characters that would be confused with markup, such as less-than and ampersand symbols.

57.3 | Names

The XML specification uses the symbol "Name" to represent names. For example:

Example 57-10. Names

```
PersonNamedSmith :: = Name S 'Smith'
```

When we combine the name, the white space and the constant string, the rule matches strings like these:

Example 57-11. Matching names

```
Christina Smith
Allan      Smith
Michael     Smith
Black        Smith
Bla_ck         Smith
_Black          Smith
```

57.4 | Occurrence indicators

Sometimes a string is *optional*. We will indicate this by putting a question mark after the symbol that represents it in a rule:

Example 57-12. Optional strings

```
Description ::= 'Tall' S? 'dark'? S? 'handsome'? S? 'person'
Tall person
Tallperson
Tall handsomeperson
Tall dark person
Talldarkhandsomeperson
```

Notice that optionality does not affect the order of the tokens. For example, dark can never go before tall. We can also allow a part of a rule to be matched multiple times. If we want to allow a part to be matched one or more times, we can use the plus symbol and make it *repeatable*.

Example 57-13. Repeatable parts

```
VeryTall ::= 'A' S ('very' S)+ 'tall' S 'person.'
A very tall person.
A very very tall person.
A very very very tall person.
```

An asterisk is similar, but it allows a string to be matched zero or more times. In other words it is both repeatable and optional.

Example 57-14. Both repeatable and optional

```
VerySmall ::= 'A' S ('very' S)* 'small' S 'person.'
A small person.
A very small person.
A very very small person.
A very very very small person.
```

Symbols can be grouped with parentheses so that you could, for instance, make a whole series of symbols optional at once. This is different from making them each optional separately because you must either supply strings for all of them or none:

Example 57-15. Grouping with parentheses

```
Description2 ::= 'A' S ('tall' S 'dark' S 'handsome' S)? 'man.'
```

This rule matches these two strings (and no others):

Example 57-16. Matching groups

```
A tall dark handsome man.
A man.
```

We will sometimes have a choice of symbols to use. This is indicated by separating the alternatives by a vertical bar:

Example 57-17. Optional parts

```
Description3 ::= 'A' S ('short'|'tall') S
                ('fair'|'tan'|'dark') S ('man'|'woman') '.'
A tall dark man.
A short fair woman.
A short tan man.
A tall dark woman.
```

Note that we broke a single long rule over two lines rather than having it run off of the end of the page. This does not in any way affect the meaning of the rule. Line breaks are just treated like space characters between the symbols.

We can combine all of these types of symbols. This allows us to make more complex rules.

Example 57-18. Combining types of symbols

```
Book ::= (('Fascinating'|'Intriguing') S ('XML'|'SGML') S 'Book')
              | ('Yet another HTML' S 'Book')
Fascinating XML Book
Yet another HTML Book
Intriguing SGML Book
```

So in this case, you should treat the first large parenthesized expression (saying good things about SGML and XML books) as one option, and the second (saying not as good things about HTML books) as another. Inside the first set, you can choose different adjectives and book types, but the ordering is fixed and there must be white space between each part.

57.5 | Combining rules

Finally, rules can refer to other rules. Where one rule refers to another, you just make a valid value for each part and then put the parts together like building blocks.

Example 57-19. Combining rules

```
FunnyDate ::= Month S Day ',' Year
Month ::= 'Jan'|'Feb'|'Mar'|'Apr'|'May'|'Jun'
                |'Jul'|'Aug'|'Sep'|'Oct'|'Nov'|'Dec'
Day ::= ('1'|'2'|'3')?
                ('1'|'2'|'3'|'4'|'5'|'6'|'7'|'8'|'9'|'0')
Year ::= '1998'|'1999'|'2000'|'2001'|'2002'
```

This would match strings such as:

Example 57-20. Matching strings

```
Jan 21,1998
May 35,2000
Sep 2,2002
```

As you can see, this is not quite a strict specification for dates, but it gets the overall form or *syntax* of them right.

57.6 | Conclusion

We've explained the bulk of what is needed to understand XML's production rules. There are a few more details that you can find in section 6 of the XML spec itself. It is included in the XML SPECtacular on the CD-ROM.

Schema
Tutorials

- Namespaces
- Datatypes
- XML Schema definition language (XSDL)
- Full specs on CD-ROM

Part Sixteen

This part covers three approved recommendations from the World Wide Web Consortium. You'll need a pretty firm grasp of the material in Part 15, "XML Core Tutorials" before you tackle any of these.

And like that part, it is necessary to read these chapters in order as they build on one another.

Namespaces are seeing a lot of use. They have some value for documents that use DTDs, as well as for schema definitions. You need to know something about them before reading the other chapters in this part, but you don't need to cover everything.

Datatypes is a prerequisite for the XML Schema definition language (XSDL), but here too only the basics are needed.

Namespaces

Friendly Tutorial

- Unique names
- URI-based namespaces
- Namespaces and DTDs

Chapter

58

he *Namespaces in XML* specification is an extension to XML that answers the burning question: Are we talking about the same subject?

Using namespaces it is possible to create elements with the generic identifier para in two different documents, with two different document types (or no explicitly-declared document types at all) and write software and queries that recognize that both represent a paragraph. This might not seem like much of a feat, but consider that in a third document an element with that element-type name might represent a paramedic (consider an employment record from the television show "ER"), a paranormal encounter (in a document from the FBI's "X-Files") or a paralegal (court records).

Even a fully spelled-out word can be ambiguous. A list can be a list of items or the angle of list (tilt) of a seagoing vessel. Besides, if two different people invented two different document types, they might use the words "list" and "para" to mean the same basic thing but their underlying model of paragraphs and lists might be different. One might expect elements of type "list" to be ordered. The other might want to allow lists to have a header.

Everyone in the world is allowed to invent document types, so we need to be clear about the origin of our element types. If you have a document database containing both ship records and technical manuals, a database-wide query needs to be able to figure out which `list` is which – even if the documents do not have DTDs.

Despite the general agreement on the need for this sort of *disambiguation*, we should mention that the XML namespaces concept is not universally embraced as the best solution. In fact XML namespaces are downright controversial. After reading this chapter you can make up your own mind.

Nevertheless, namespaces are already in widespread use. Many World Wide Web Consortium specifications already build upon the namespace mechanism and will do so in the future. Primary among these are the *XML Schema* definition language (XSDL), Extensible Stylesheet Language (XSL), and the Simple Object Access Protocol (SOAP). Namespaces look like they are here to stay.

58.1 | Problem statement

Namespaces are easiest to understand if we work in the realm of well-formed documents without DTDs. We will address the relationship to DTDs later on.

You may be familiar with email programs that can recognize and visually highlight URLs and email addresses. This works nicely in the program, but when the email is saved to disk or forwarded to a less intelligent email program, that highlighting is lost. It might be better if the program could actually introduce markup representing the highlighting. That way other applications could get the benefit of the email program's analysis and recognition. We could use `web` and `email` element types to capture this information.

Our system would work fine for a while, but the time would come when people would want to send XML documents (remember, well-formed but DTD-less XML documents) through email. We might want to allow our system to continue to work on these documents. The problem is that it is a bad idea for us to presume that any element with an element type name of `web` or `email` was meant to refer to our element types.

Perhaps an XML document will come through the email with a `web` element that is meant to represent spider webs or knowledge webs. Perhaps the `web` elements really do represent URLs, but they use an attribute to hold the address instead of content. Then we have the same meaning but a different internal structure.

What we need to do is clearly separate our names from other people's names. We need to have different so-called *namespaces*. We do this in the real world all of the time.

What would you do if you needed to refer to a particular John Smith without confusing him with any other John Smith. You qualify the name: "John Smith from London." That sets up a namespace that separates Londoners from everyone else.

If that isn't sufficient then you further qualify the namespace: "John Smith from East London". That makes a namespace that separates Easterners from everyone else. You could narrow it down even more: "John Smith from Adelaide Street in East London." The trick is qualifying names in order to separate them from other names. The separate groups of names are known as "namespaces."

58.2 | The namespaces solution

Given that what we want to do is qualify names, the most obvious idea is to have a prefix that does the qualification. `myEmailProgram:web` or `myEmailProgram:email`. This seems to work at first, but eventually two people will make program names that clash. In fact, there will be a strong tendency to use three-letter acronyms. There are only so many of these acronyms!

In the real world people constantly choose names that other people also choose. Even city names can clash: consider how many there are named "Springfield"! If people are allowed to choose names without any central authority then they will eventually choose names that clash.

The World Wide Web Consortium could set up a registry of these acronyms and names. But that would require a great deal of effort both in setting up the registry and in registering individual namespaces.

A better mechanism would be to use a registry that already exists. One such registry is the domain name registry. We could use prefixes like: `mycompany.com:email`. We would call "mycompany.com" the *namespace* and "email" a particular name in that namespace.

This solution is getting much closer but it still is not as democratic as we would like. One problem is that domain names cost $70.00 USD (or did when the *Namespaces in XML* specification was formalized) and applying for them was a difficult, slow process. What if an ordinary America Online (AOL) user wants to develop a namespace? Does he have to register a domain name?

Every AOL user has a little bit of space to put files and assign a URL such as `http://www.aol.com/EmailAppGuy`. If we could use that as the basis for a namespace identifier, then we would open up the namespace-creating process to a larger number of people.

This idea also works for organizations other than Internet Service Providers. Consider a big company like General Electric. Various parts of the company may develop XML namespaces. The company probably already has a mechanism for delegating Web URIs (typically "http:" URLs). It makes sense to reuse that mechanism for XML namespaces.

There is a more future-thinking reason why URIs are better than domain names. As part of the Semantic Web project, it will be possible to associate metadata with things that are addressed by URIs. If namespaces are associated with URIs, it will be possible to associate metadata with them.

Example 58-1 shows what URL-based namespace prefixes might look like.

Example 58-1. Mythical (illegal!) URL-based namespace prefix

```
<http://www.aol.com/EmailAppGuy:email>email@machine.com
</http://www.aol.com/EmailAppGuy:email>
```

There are two problems with these prefixes. First, they are not legal XML names because of all of the funny characters such as slashes and dots. Second, they are plug-ugly and incredibly verbose. We need a way to set up a local abbreviation. The *Namespaces in XML* specification defines the mechanism for setting up such abbreviations.

58.2.1 *Namespace prefixes*

The *Namespaces in XML* specification defines a rule that attributes that start with the prefix `xmlns:` should be interpreted as prefix-defining attributes. The name immediately following the prefix is a local abbreviation for the namespace.

The attribute value is a URI. You can use any URI (typically a URL) that you would normally have control over. Throughout the element exhibiting that attribute, the prefix stands for the namespace identifier. Example 58-2 demonstrates.

Example 58-2. Using XML namespaces

```
<eag:email xmlns:eag="http://www.aol.com/EmailAppGuy">
  email@machine.com
</eag:email>
```

The actual prefix you use is not relevant. It is just a stand-in for the URI. So, for example, when creating an XSL stylesheet you do not need to use the xsl: prefix for names defined in the XSL spec. Doing otherwise might be confusing, but it is totally legal.

Note that the details of the URI are not relevant either. It does not matter whether there is a document at that location or whether the client machine is Internet-connected. There is no need to connect to the Internet to check the contents of the document at that address.

The data (or lack of data) at the other end of the URI is absolutely irrelevant to the namespaces design. Its only goal is to have a long, globally unique string to use in comparisons.

That's an important point! Namespaces work with broken URIs because namespaces only disambiguate names, they don't define names. The URIs therefore don't have to address the definitions of the names in the namespace (although they may).

The only requirement is that you really do control the URI that you use. It is your responsibility to guarantee that nobody else (your spouse?) will accidently but legitimately use the same URI and mean something different by it. It is also good practice to put a date (at least a year) in your URIs. Then, if you lose control of the URI or domain over the course of time, you can still be sure that nobody will use it as a namespace.

58.2.2 *Scoping*

The prefix scheme is still pretty verbose, but it is some improvement. It looks better when you realize that namespace declarations are *scoped* by their declaring elements. That means that they apply to the element, its children, and the children's children and so forth unless some child has a declaration that specifically overrides the first declaration. Example 58-3 shows a document that uses a namespace associated with the myns prefix many times despite declaring it only once.

Example 58-3. Overriding namespace scopes

```
<myns:a xmlns:myns="http://www.someurl.com/2002">
    <myns:b>
    </myns:b>
    <myns:c>
        <myns:d>
        </myns:d>
    </myns:c>
</myns:a>
```

Therefore you could declare namespaces in the document (root) element and have them apply throughout the entire document! Example 58-4 demonstrates.[1]

Example 58-4. XML namespace scope

```
<html:html
    xmlns:eag="http://www.aol.com/EmailAppGuy"
    xmlns:html="http://www.w3.org/TR/WD-HTML40"
    xmlns:math="http://www.w3.org/TR/REC-MathML/">
 <html:title>George Soros Personal Wealth Page</html:title>
 <html:h2>Counting My Cash</html:h2>
 <html:p>As you know, my cash rivals the gross national
product of some small countries. Consider the following
equation:
 <math:reln>
  <math:eq/>
  <math:ci>wealth</math:ci>
  <math:ci>gnp</math:ci>
 </math:reln>
 If you have any ideas of how I could spend
 this money. Please contact
 <eag:email>georges@aol.con</eag:email>.
</html:p>

</html:html>
```

---

1. Note that .con is the new high-level domain for Internet scams.

Although it is seldom necessary, it is also possible to redefine namespaces that were previously declared in an "outer scope". The inner declaration is effective on the declaring element, its attributes and all of its sub-elements (unless it is overridden also). Example 58-5 demonstrates four different myns:p elements with no relationship to each other (from the point of view of the XML namespaces specification). Each contains an myns:q element which is in the namespace of whichever myns:p contains it.

Example 58-5. Overriding namespace scopes

```
<myns:p xmlns:myns="http://www.someurl.com/2000">
  <myns:q>First namespace.</myns:q>
  <myns:p xmlns:myns="http://www.anotherurl.com/2001">
    <myns:q>Second namespace.</myns:q>
    <myns:p xmlns:myns="http://www.someotherurl.com/2002">
      <myns:q>Third namespace.</myns:q>
    </myns:p>
  </myns:p>
  <myns:p xmlns:myns="http://www.yetanother.com/2003">
    <myns:q>Fourth namespace.</myns:q>
  </myns:p>
<myns:p>
```

Although this is possible, it is much simpler to use unique prefixes for different namespaces and to declare namespaces on the root element. The ability to override namespaces is most useful in a minority of data-transfer applications. Declaring namespaces once at the top reduces the namespace clutter thoughout the document.

58.2.3 Default namespace

We can minimize the impact even more by removing some of the prefixes. There is a special namespace called the *default namespace*. This namespace is defined without a prefix, so element-type names in the scope of the definition that have no prefix are considered to be in this namespace.[2] If you expect to use many elements from a particular namespace, you can make it the default namespace for the appropriate scope. In fact, you can even have

---

2. You can think of the default namespace as having a null prefix, if that helps any.

a document in which the namespaces correspond cleanly to the elements and there are no prefixes at all, as Example 58-6 demonstrates.

Example 58-6. Two default namespaces: HTML and MathML

```
<html
    xmlns="http://www.w3.org/TR/WD-HTML40">
  <title>George Soros Personal Wealth Page</title>
  <h2>Counting My Cash</h2>
  <p>As you know, my cash rivals the gross national
product of some small countries. Consider the following
equation:
  <reln xmlns="http://www.w3.org/TR/REC-MathML/">
    <eq/>
    <ci>wealth</ci>
    <ci>gnp</ci>
  </reln>
  If you have any ideas of how I could spend
this money.</p>
</html>
```

Note that the default namespace is HTML both before and after the `reln` element. Within the `reln` element the default namespace is MathML. As you can see, we can eliminate many of the prefixes but still keep the relationship between the element-type names and the namespaces.

We can also establish a scope in which names without prefixes have no namespace, by using an empty URI. In Example 58-7, `notes` and `to-do` are not in the MathML namespace.

Example 58-7. A scope for local names

```
  <reln xmlns="http://www.w3.org/TR/REC-MathML/">
    <eq/>
    <ci>wealth</ci>
    <ci>gnp</ci>
    <notes xmlns="">
      <todo>check the math</todo>
    </notes>
  </reln>
```

58.2.4 *Attribute names*

Attribute names can also come from a namespace, which is indicated in the usual way by prefixing them with a namespace prefix. For instance, the current working draft of XLink uses the namespace mechanism to allow XLink attributes to appear on elements that themselves come from some other namespace. Example 58-8 shows such attributes.

Example 58-8. Attributes in XLink namespace

```
<myLink xmlns:xlink="http://www.w3.org/XML/XLink/0.9"
   xlink:type="simple">
...
</myLink>
```

It does not matter what the namespace of the element type is. The XLink attributes are in the XLink namespace even when they are exhibited by an element type that is not in the XLink namespace.

In fact, even attributes without prefixes are not in the same namespace that their element type is in. Nor are they in the default namespace. Attributes without prefixes are in no namespace at all.[3]

From a processing standpoint, the lack of a namespace doesn't matter. The attribute name can still be specified in a stylesheet pattern or utilized by the template for the element type's template rule.

In other words, an `html:img` element could have an `href` attribute and that attribute could be processed properly even though it is not formally part of the `html` namespace. Any application that knows how to handle `html:img` will know what to do with an `href` attribute.[4]

From a data modeling standpoint, unprefixed attributes are normal. They are defined by the semantics of their specific element types. In con-

---

3. From the syntactic standpoint of the *Namespaces* spec, that is. All names have to be in *some* namespace or they couldn't function as names. An unprefixed attribute is in a (non-syntactic) namespace that is *defined* by its element type, which, as we said, is not the same as the namespace that its element type itself is *in*. The `href` attribute of `html:img`, for example, is in the (non-syntactic) `html:img` namespace, while its element type, `img`, is in the (syntactic) `html` namespace.

4. That's because, as we saw in the last footnote, `href` is in the `html:img` namespace.

trast, prefixed attributes have semantics that apply to the class of all element types. XLink is a good example because, in principle, any element can be linked.

58.3 | Namespaces and DTDs

You read about DTDs and type-validation in Chapter 54, "Creating a document type definition", on page 788 and might have wondered why that chapter had no mention of namespaces. That's because namespaces were invented after DTDs.[5] Therefore, type-validation does not behave as you would expect it to behave had it been designed with namespaces in mind.

In fact, the base XML language has no inherent knowledge of namespaces. There is no special part of an element-type name or attribute name called the prefix. The name is all one string that, when name spaces are used, just happens to have a colon in it. The colon could just as easily be an underscore, dot or happy face character from the XML point of view. It is not a special character.

You might think, from learning about namespaces, that it would be possible to have two different `list` element types in the same DTD. However, you can only do that if you give them different prefixes. But in DTDs, prefixes must be *hard-wired onto the names*. They are not namespace prefixes and you cannot depend on the default namespace: a DTD is permitted only one element type declaration for the element type `list`.

Declaring `my:list` and `your:list` would be fine. These are seen as no more the same than `my_list` and `your_list` or `my.list` and `your.list`. But once you define the element types this way, you cannot default them or change the prefix. A validating parser would not recognize `list` as a synonym for `my:list`. These are no more related than `list` and `my_list` or `foo` and `bar`.

Therefore, when you create a DTD that uses namespaces, you must declare every `prefix:name` combination individually, exactly as you would if the : were just another name character (which it is!).

Example 58-9 illustrates declarations for two different `email` element types. The prefixes disambiguate them, but not in the same way that name-

---

5. About 30 years after, but who's counting.

space prefixes would. As far as an XML validator is concerned, these are two nine-letter element-type names that differ in their first three letters.

Example 58-9. Disambiguating two `email` element types

```
<!ELEMENT eag:email ...>
<!ATTLIST eag:email
    xmlns:eag CDATA #FIXED "http://www.aol.com/EmailAppGuy">
<!ELEMENT cmp:email ...>
<!ATTLIST cmp:email
    xmlns:cmp CDATA #FIXED "http://www.compuserve.com/email">
```

Note that the `xmlns` attributes are fixed. That is because the prefixes are hard-wired to the names; they can't be changed in a valid document instance regardless of what the *Namespaces* spec says. If authors try to act otherwise, the document will become invalid.

Defining each namespace attribute with a fixed value protects against such mistakes. The parser will issue an error message if an author tries to specify a different namespace value in the document instance.

Fixing namespace attributes enforces markup practices that make a document both type-valid and namespace compatible. It is the sensible thing to do.[6]

A DTD can also simulate scoping and default namespaces, as shown in Example 58-10.

Example 58-10. Scoping and default namespaces in a DTD

```
<!ELEMENT music ...>
<!ATTLIST music
    xmlns CDATA #FIXED "http://www.ihc.org/smdl">
<!ELEMENT math ...>
<!ATTLIST math
    xmlns CDATA #FIXED "http://www.w3.org/TR/REC-MathML/">
```

However, remember that the declared names in a valid document are the *only* names. Example 58-10 works only when the subelement types of `music` and `math` have different names from one another.

---

6. In fact, it makes so much sense that it probably should have been a requirement of the *Namespaces* spec. The XML implementation in *Internet Explorer 5* enforces it as though it were.

One final example to drive home the point: In Example 58-11, the first namespace prefix has no effect. The two element-type names are different in a valid document, even though they are the same according to the *Namespaces* spec.

Example 58-11. `rap:music` isn't `music`

```
<!ELEMENT music ...>
<!ATTLIST music
    xmlns CDATA #FIXED "http://www.rude-noises.go">
<!ELEMENT rap:music ...>
<!ATTLIST rap:music
    xmlns:rap CDATA #FIXED "http://www.rude-noises.go">
```

Remember: The rule is that colons and namespace declarations are not relevant or special to a DTD validator. Always define fixed values for your namespace attributes and your documents should be able to get the best of both worlds.

58.4 | Are namespaces a good thing?

We said in the introduction to this chapter that namespaces are controversial. We've seen how namespace prefixes cause clutter and how redefining them causes confusion. Why then were they considered so vital that they were rushed to Recommendation status almost as soon as XML was approved?

And why does the spec allow all that flexibility in their use?

As the application parts of this book show, the predominant use for XML on the Web is data integration. In those applications, a middle-tier server may aggregate XML fragments from many sources into a single well-formed (but not valid) document and send it to a client for processing.

Because only computers ever see those documents, prefix clutter doesn't matter. It adds to the overhead somewhat, but it could also aid in debugging.

And reusing prefixes for different namespaces doesn't matter in those applications either, since the software can base its processing strategy on the full URI, rather than the short nickname. Namespace-aware applications and specifications such as XPath and XML Schema work on the full namespace name, not the short prefix.

Furthermore, there are cases where namespace prefixes cause less clutter than alternative approaches might have. In XSL specifications, for example, the prefixes disambiguate the markup that controls the XSL processing from the markup of the generated text in the templates.

But more than that, namespaces provide a mechanism for universal vocabularies of element type names that can be used in all document types. Namespaces provide a way to define element types so that their names are unique throughout the world. As long as everyone adheres to the namespaces convention there can be no confusion about whether element types with identical names belong to one vocabulary or another.

Datatypes

- Datatype requirements
- Built-in datatypes
- User-derived datatypes
- Using datatypes in DTDs

Chapter

59

erhaps the most widely used aspect of the W3C *XML Schema* project is the datatype work. It was made a separate Part 2 of the *XML Schema* spec, with the intention "that it be usable outside of the context of *XML Schema* for a wide range of other XML-related activities".

In this chapter, we describe the basic concepts of XML datatypes and show how they can be used both in the *XML Schema* definition language (XSDL – Part 1 of the spec) and in "other XML-related activities" such as XML DTDs and WSDL Web service descriptions.

59.1 | Understanding the problem

The DTD fragment in Example 59-1 shows the declaration for an attribute whose value is intended to be a year.

Example 59-1. Attribute declaration in a DTD

```
<!ATTLIST poem pubyear NMTOKEN #IMPLIED>
<!-- Publication year should be four-digits -->
```

Although the pubyear value is supposed to represent a year, XML's set of attribute types cannot say that directly. We've chosen the closest datatype built into XML but it is not very close. All of the pubyear values in the start-tags shown in Example 59-2 would be valid.

Example 59-2. Legal pubyear NMTOKEN values

```
<poem pubyear="1922">
<poem pubyear="0">
<poem pubyear="99999999999999999999999">
<poem pubyear="-3">
<poem pubyear="3.14159265">
<poem pubyear="Hello_World">
<poem pubyear=":">
<poem pubyear="----">
```

Wouldn't it be nice if the declaration for a pubyear attribute (or even for a pubyear element type) could specify that its value (or content) must be a four-digit number between 1000 and 2100?

This would make it easier to write robust applications that use that data. If your application must check whether this poem is in the public domain yet, it might add 75 to that pubyear value and compare the result with the current year to see if the poem is more than 75 years old.

You can only do this calculation reliably if you know that the value is an integer. You could do this by writing error-checking code, but one major goal of all schemas (including DTDs) is to reduce the need for custom error-checking code.

Programmers want to plug in an off-the-shelf, validating XML processor and have it check the mundane details of datatype conformance. When they get a weekly salary value out of a document they don't want to write code to make sure that it's a usable number before they subtract it from another number.

Most importantly, end users want to be able to do the checks with off-the-shelf processors also. By design, XML allows processing without validation – it doesn't even require schemas or DTDs! Some XML software may avoid validation for performance reasons, assuming the document was validated when it was created.

Datatypes answer important questions about the description and validation of element data content and attribute values.

With datatypes you could express things like "a date element should contain data that conforms to the syntax YYYY-MM-DD" or "an email address attribute value must be of the form xxxxxx@yyyyy.zzz".

59.2 | Datatype requirements

A system to support datatypes must meet three requirements:

- There must be a way to validate that the data really conforms to the restrictions of the datatype. There should be no February 30 in a date, every email address needs an @ symbol and so forth.
- There must be a way for an application to convert data from XML into programming language datatypes. For instance an attribute value might be the string "123" but the internal representation in a programming language would be a series of bits in an optimized format. Dates could be represented not as strings but as objects with properties representing years, months, days etc. In some systems, dates are represented in terms of the number of seconds that have passed since some event.
- There must be a way to define new datatypes. Just as XML allows you to define new element types, you would want to be able to define datatypes that are specific to your project. A geographer might define a latitude/longitude notation. A mathematician might define a notation for matrices.

XML Schema Datatypes is the standard that addresses these issues.

59.3 | Built-in datatypes

The *XML Schema Datatypes* spec defines two categories of datatype: primitive and derived. All primitive datatypes are defined in the spec and are therefore among the *built-in datatypes*. You may not create your own.

A derived datatype is defined in terms of one or more existing datatypes. It might be a specialized or extended version of another datatype. You may make your own derived datatypes. The spec also includes several among its built-in datatypes, which are therefore supported by every implementation.

Figure 59-1 illustrates the built-in datatypes, showing the derivations.

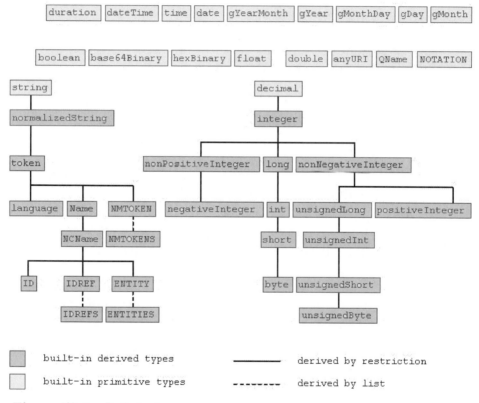

Figure 59-1   Built-in datatypes

59.3.1 *Primitive datatypes*

The *primitive datatypes* are the building blocks of all others. Most are also useful just by themselves.

59.3.1.1 Common programming datatypes

The first five we will cover include common datatypes in most programming languages and database management systems.

string

> Equivalent to CDATA in a DTD – an arbitrarily long sequence of characters. You might use this for a `title` element's datatype.

boolean

> True and false values. The data may be any one of the following strings: `false` or `0` for false values or `true` or `1` for true values. You might use this for a datatype that represented whether a checkbox in a graphical user interface should be turned on by default (true) or turned off by default (false).

decimal

> Arbitrary precision decimal numbers. These can represent anything numerical: height, weight, financial amounts, etc. Decimal numbers may have a fractional part that follows a period as in `5.3`. Decimal numbers may be preceded by a plus (+) or minus (–) sign to represent whether they are negative or positive.

float

> Single precision 32-bit floating point numbers. This is a form of number that is very efficient for numerical computation on 32-bit computers. Floats may have a fractional part and may also be preceded by a plus or minus sign. Compared to decimals, floats are less precise. They are an approximation. Sometimes the number you put into the computer will not be exactly the number you get out later![1]

double

> Double precision 64-bit floating point numbers. These numbers are more precise than single-precision floats but are still approximations.[2]

---

1. If you do use them, they may have exponents (preceded by "e" or "E", as in "2.5E5") and may take the values "NaN", "INF" and "-INF".
2. And the same footnote applies!

59.3.1.2   XML datatypes

anyURI

This extremely important primitive datatype is used for URIs (typically URLs). These may include so-called *fragment identifiers* after a pound sign. For instance if the URI refers to an XML document the fragment identifier may be an XPointer.[3]

QName

This primitive datatype is based on the XML namespaces specification. It stands for a namespace-qualified name. In other words, a QName is a name that may have a colon in it. If it does, the text before the colon should be a namespace prefix for a namespace that has been declared. If it does not, the names should be interpreted as belonging to the default namespace. See Chapter 58, "Namespaces", on page 874 for more information on namespaces.

NOTATION

This datatype corresponds to the XML NOTATION attribute type.

59.3.1.3   Binary datatypes

There are two datatypes for representing binary data. The first is called hexBinary because it uses the *hex* notation, popular among practitioners of the occult and programmers of the UNIX operating system. There are sixteen hex digits.[4] The digits 0 through 9 represent the same thing they do in ordinary decimal numbers. The letter a represents 10, b represents 11 and so forth through f representing 15. Hex is popular not only because of its mystical powers but also because a few simple calculations can turn two hex digits into a value between 0 and 255, which is exactly the amount that can be held in a single byte.

The other datatype is called base64Binary because it represents base64-encoded data. Base64 is not as simple to translate into bytes without

---

3. See Chapter 64, "XML Pointer Language (XPointer)", on page 1004 for more information on XPointers.
4. In fact, hex is short for hexadecimal, which is the base-16 numbering system.

a computer but uses less space than hex. Hex doubles the size of the data. Base64 increases it by only a third, approximately.

59.3.1.4 Durations

The remaining primitive datatypes are all related to time: durations in this section and absolute dates and times in the next.

The `duration` datatype is based on the ISO 8601 date format standard. It represents a length of time, such as an hour or 3.56 seconds. Durations can be represented with a precision of seconds or fractions of a second. They can also span thousands of years.

A duration always starts with P; for example, P2Y. The 2Y that follows the P means two years (the gestation period for some elephants!).

Instead of measuring in years, you could measure in months: P3M would be three months (the amount of time it takes to get a new phone line installed in some cities).

You can also measure in years and months: P1Y3M means one year and three months (the shelf-life of a boy band). You can also count in days (with or without years or months): P3D (length of the Battle of Gettysburg).

But wait...that's not all. Durations can get as fine grained as a fraction of a second. If you want to deal in time units shorter than a day you use the designator T after you've listed all of the day/month/year parts (or directly after the P if you are interested only in hour/minute/second units).

For instance P1YT1M represents one year and one minute (which is the amount of time that a VCR with a P1Y warranty is likely to survive). As you can see, M represents both month and minute, which is why you must include the T designator that separates the date part from the time part. If you have an hour, a minute or a second part you must have the T.

In addition to minutes you may use H for hour and S for second. S is the only part of the duration that may have a fractional part. PT3M43.13S represents three minutes and 43.13 seconds (the world record for running a mile).

The different parts of the date and time must always come in the same order: P, years, months, days, T, hours, minutes, seconds. Remember that the P is always required and the T is required if there are hours/minutes/seconds. Everything else is optional.

59.3.1.5   Dates and times

The `date` datatype represents a specific calendar date in the form `YYYY-MM-DD`. For instance the date of the Beatles' debut on Ed Sullivan would be `1964-02-09` – February 9th, 1964.

Negative dates are also allowed, to represent BCE (BC) dates. For instance `-0133-06-01` represents the approximate date of a Roman slave revolt lead by a man called Aristonicus – June 1, 133 BCE.

The `time` datatype represents a time that recurs every day. Times have the form `hh:mm:ss`. The seconds may have a fractional part. So `14:12:34.843` represents 2:12 and 34.843 seconds in the afternoon. It is *not* legal to leave the seconds out, even if they are not relevant: `14:12:00`.

To indicate that the time is expressed in *coordinated universal time (UTC)*, also known as Greenwich mean time (GMT), add a `z` to the end of the time: `14:20:00Z`.

It is also possible (and a good idea!) to specify a time zone for a time, as an offset from GMT. Do this by appending a `-` or `+` sign and a number of hours and minutes in the form `hh:mm`, such as `08:15:00-08:00` (8:15 Pacific time) or `11:20:00+03:30` (11:20 Tehran time). The time zone is optional but if you leave it out then it will be impossible to compare times across time zones.

As you might guess, it is possible to combine a date and time into a `dateTime`. A `dateTime` has a `T` between the date and time parts: `1929-10-29T11:00:00-05:00`.

59.3.1.6   Recurring dates and times

The `gDay`, `gMonth` and `gMonthDay` datatypes represent a day that recurs every month (e.g. the first or fifteenth day of each month), a month that recurs every year (let's say July – or any other month!) and a particular date that recurs every year (such as Valentine's day). The `g` in their names indicates that they are based on the Gregorian calendar.

The `gDay` datatype is in the form `---DD`. There are three leading dashes, so the 8th of every month would be `---08`.

The `gMonth` datatype, `--MM`, is similar. However, there are only two leading dashes, so every June would be `--06`.

The gMonthDay datatype is in the form --MM-DD. For instance, Caesar's "Ides of March" (March 15th) would be --03-15 and a gMonth of --02 represents the month of February of every year.

These datatypes represent durations from the very first instant of the date to the very last. To improve precision, any of them may be followed by a time zone indicator.

The gYear and gYearMonth represent particular years or months in history or in the future. The year is a four-digit number and a gYearMonth is a four-digit number followed by a two-digit number: 2002-06. Either may be preceded by a negative sign (-) to represent BCE dates. They may also be followed by a time zone indicator.

59.3.2 *Derived datatypes*

The *derived datatypes* are based on the primitive ones. The *XML Schema Datatypes* spec defines some derived datatypes and provides facilities for users to define their own.

The ones defined in the spec are listed below. They fall into several categories.

59.3.2.1 Restricted numeric datatypes

These are numeric datatypes more specific (*restricted*) than the primitive datatypes.

59.3.2.1.1 *Integers*

integer
> Decimal number (no matter how large or small) with no fractional part.

positiveInteger
> Integer greater than zero

negativeInteger
> Integer less than zero.

nonPositiveInteger
> Integer less than or equal to zero.

nonNegativeInteger
> Integer greater than or equal to zero.

59.3.2.1.2 *Computer word lengths*

This group allows data to be restricted to values that specific computers can handle efficiently. Most modern computers handle everything from 8-bits to 32-bits well. A 64-bit computer handles long and unsignedLong most efficiently and other values less so.

byte
> 8-bit signed number (between -128 and 127)

unsignedByte
> 8-bit non-negative number (between 0 and 255)

short
> 16-bit number (between -32768 and 32767)

unsignedShort
> 16-bit non-negative number (between 0 and 65535)

int
> 32-bit number (between -2147483648 and 2147483647)

unsignedInt
> 32-bit non-negative number (between 0 and 4294967295)

long
> 64-bit number (between -9223372036854775808 and 9223372036854775807)

unsignedLong
> 64-bit non-negative number (between 0 and 18446744073709551615) (whew!)

59.3.2.2 Derived XML datatypes

Several derived datatypes are based on XML attribute types and other constructs.

59.3.2.2.3 *XML attribute types*

Some derived datatypes emulate XML attribute types. They are easy to recognize because they are the only built-in datatypes with upper-case names.

ID
>   An identifier unique to a single element in a document.

IDREF
>   A reference to a unique ID in the document.

IDREFS
>   A whitespace-separated list of IDREF values.

ENTITY
>   The name of an unparsed entity in the document.

ENTITIES
>   A whitespace-separated list of ENTITY values.

NMTOKEN
>   A string with certain character constraints (53.1.5, "Names and name tokens", on page 765) placed upon it.

NMTOKENS
>   A whitespace-separated list of NMTOKEN values.

Note that some of these datatypes are single tokens and others are lists. The ones that are lists are created by *deriving by list* rather than *deriving by restriction*. We will show you how to do these yourself later on.

59.3.2.2.4 *Other XML constructs*

There are other datatypes for XML constructs.

Name

While XML has a "name" construct, (described in 53.1.5, "Names and name tokens", on page 765), the corresponding SGML NAME attribute datatype was a casualty of the minimalist XML design approach. NMTOKEN had been the closest, but now *XML Schema* has restored the datatype as Name (note the capitalization!).

language

The built-in, derived datatype called language accepts the same values as the xml:lang attribute discussed in 56.4, "Special attributes and newlines", on page 856.

NCName

Earlier we discussed the primitive datatype QName that is based on a concept from the XML namespaces specification. A QName is a name that may have a namespace prefix (and therefore a colon). There is a derived datatype that is the opposite of a QName called NCName. This stands for no-colon name which means (drum roll please...) a name with no colons in it. You can use this when you want to avoid namespace behavior in a datatype.

normalizedString

This datatype is for strings in which whitespace characters such as carriage return and tab characters should be replaced by spaces. If you use this datatype or derive from it, the schema processor will handle this normalization for you.

token

This datatype is for strings that collapse groups of adjacent whitespace into a single space and strip leading and trailing spaces. Many of the datatypes we have already discussed are derived from the token datatype in order to inherit its whitespace handling features. These are: language, Name, NMTOKEN and NCName, ID, IDREF and ENTITY.

59.4 | Defining user-derived datatypes

The XML Schema definition language (XSDL) provides a facility for defining user-derived datatypes, using the simpleType definition element.

The element must contain a child element for the desired form of derivation: list, union, or restriction.

derivation by list
> Derivation by list is quite straightforward. You merely take an existing datatype (like gYear) and create a new datatype that accepts a list of them (we could call it gYears).

derivation by union
> This sort of derivation merges two or more datatypes into one that supports values of either sort. For instance a datatype representing months might allow either gMonth integers or string names by deriving by union from Name and gMonth.

derivation by restriction
> This form of derivation narrows down the values allowed by an existing datatype. For instance you could take the datatype gYear and restrict it to years in a particular century.

The child element might optionally be preceded by an annotation element, as shown in Example 59-3.

> *Note*   Annotation elements can hold more than documentation, and XSDL elements in general have other properties that support self-documentation and application processing of schema definitions. As these facilities are not germane to deriving datatypes for general use, they are discussed in 60.3.2, "Schema components", on page 924.

59.4.1 *Derivation by list*

You derive by list when you want to allow occurrences of the datatype in the document to contain multiple values rather than just one. For instance to

Example 59-3. A `simpleType` definition

```
<xsd:simpleType name="mynewType">
    <xsd:annotation>
        <xsd:documentation>Important new type</xsd:documentation>
    </xsd:annotation>
    <xsd:restriction base="someOtherType">
        ...
    </xsd:restriction>
</xsd:simpleType>
```

allow multiple dates you could derive a `dates` datatype[5] from the primitive `date` datatype as in Example 59-4.

Caution   Items in lists are always separated by whitespace. If a datatype allows embedded whitespace (such as `string`), deriving a list from it may produce unexpected results.

Example 59-4. Deriving a list from a named datatype

```
<xsd:simpleType name="dates">
  <xsd:annotation>
    <xsd:documentation>Multiple dates</xsd:documentation>
  </xsd:annotation>
  <xsd:list itemType="xsd:date"/>
</xsd:simpleType>
```

In Example 59-4, the list was derived from an existing named datatype. It is also possible to derive a list from a newly-defined anonymous datatype. Rather than putting an `itemType` attribute on the `list`, you would merely put a `simpleType` element in the `list` element content.

The embedded `simpleType` will be used just as if you had defined it elsewhere, given it a name and referred to it with the `itemType` attribute. Example 59-5 demonstrates.

---

5. XSDL would call this a simple type, rather than a datatype, but in this chapter it is clearer to call it a datatype.

Example 59-5. Deriving a list from an anonymous datatype

```
<xsd:simpleType name="pubDates">
  <xsd:list>
    <xsd:simpleType>
       ... derivation of pubDate ...
    </xsd:simpleType>
  </xsd:list>
</xsd:simpleType>
```

59.4.2 Derivation by union

Derivation by union is a way of combining existing datatypes into one datatype. For instance you might want to allow dates to be specified according to any one of:

- the built-in Gregorian date datatype,
- a notation based on the ancient Aztec calendar, or
- the Hebrew calendar.

If we define our datatypes so that they are syntactically distinct then we can easily create a union of them. One way to easily distinguish Aztec and Hebrew dates is to start them with the letters A and H, respectively, because we know that built-in dates start with a number. Example 59-6 demonstrates such a union datatype.

Example 59-6. Union datatype

```
<xsd:simpleType name="AnyKindaDate">
  <!-- we could put an annotation here -->
  <xsd:union memberTypes="myns:AztecDate myns:HebrewDate xsd:date">
     <!-- we could put another annotation here -->
  </xsd:union>
</xsd:simpleType>
```

If we carelessly defined our notations so that some Aztec dates could also be recognized as Hebrew or Gregorian dates, then the Aztec interpretation would win over the other ones because it is listed first in the memberTypes attribute.

Instead of – or in addition to – a memberTypes attribute, you could also put simpleType elements within the union to define anonymous in-line datatypes, just as we did for lists. Unlike lists, however, which are derived from a single datatype, we can define as many anonymous datatypes as we like. Each of them contributes to the union just as if it had been defined externally and referenced.

If we wanted to, we could define a union of two different kinds of lists. Perhaps we would allow a list of Hebrew dates or a list of Aztec dates. Conversely, we could define a list of a union datatype. For instance, a list derived from `AnyKindaDate` would be a list of a union.

Many complex combinations of different kinds of derivation are possible.

59.4.3 *Deriving datatypes by restriction*

Another way to derive a datatype is by restriction. In this case, you add constraints to an existing datatype, either built-in or user-derived.

By definition, a datatype derived by restriction is more constraining than its base datatype. Any value that conforms to the new derived datatype would also have to conform to the original base datatype.

Restrictions are created with the `restriction` element. You may have a single `restriction` as a child of the `simpleType` element. You can refer to a named base datatype with the `base` attribute, or define an anonymous base datatype by including a simple type in the content.

There is a fixed list of ways that you can constrain a given datatype. These are called *constraining facets*. There are twelve of them, each represented by a specific element type. They occur as sub-elements of the `restriction` element. The allowable ones depend on the base datatype.

They have several points in common:

- They all allow a single optional `annotation` sub-element and no other.
- Each has a required `value` attribute that specifies the constraining value. The exact meaning and allowable values of the attribute depend on the specific facet and the base datatype.
- They work together.

The last item requires some explanation.

If you define a datatype with a minimum value and then refine it by restriction to make a new datatype with a maximum value, the new datatype has *both* the minimum value constraint from the base datatype *and* the maximum value constraint from the derived datatype. If you defined yet a third datatype by restriction based on the new datatype, it would add still other restrictions.

This principle applies even when the same facet is applied at two different levels. So you could define a datatype that represents the set of numbers greater than 10,000 by setting a minimum value constraint. In a datatype derived from that you could set another minimum value constraint raising the minimum value to 20,000.

Values must now be both greater than 10,000 and greater than 20,000, which is the same as saying just that they must be greater than 20,000. In one sense both restrictions apply, but really the more constraining derived datatype overrides the base datatype.[6]

59.5 | Constraining facets

This section describes the twelve `facet` elements that are used when deriving by restriction. They fall into six categories: range, length, decimal digit, enumeration, white space, and pattern.

59.5.1 *Range restrictions*

The simplest kind of restriction available for numeric and date datatypes is a range restriction. For instance we might want to define a user-derived datatype called "publication year" as a year that must fall between 1000 and 2100. Example 59-7 defines a `pubYear` datatype with these characteristics.

The `minInclusive` element sets the minimum value allowed for the new `pubYear` datatype and the `maxInclusive` element sets the maximum value allowed.

Alternatively, we could use the `maxExclusive` and `minExclusive` elements. They also set upper and lower bounds, but the bounds exclude the

---

6. There is a way to prevent such overrides, but as it is rarely needed, we don't cover it here.

Example 59-7. Defining a restricted range integer datatype

```
<xsd:simpleType name="pubYear">
  <xsd:annotation>
    <xsd:documentation>A publication year</xsd:documentation>
  </xsd:annotation>
  <xsd:restriction base="xsd:gYear">
      <xsd:minInclusive value="1000"/>
      <xsd:maxInclusive value="2100"/>
  </xsd:restriction>
</xsd:simpleType>
```

named value. In other words, a `maxExclusive` value of 2100 allows 2099 but not 2100.

59.5.2 *Length restrictions*

There are three length constraining facets: `minLength` and `maxLength`, which work together or separately to set lower and upper bounds on a value's length, and a facet called simply `length` which requires a specific fixed length.

Length means slightly different things depending on the datatype that it is restricting.

list

If the datatype is a list (e.g. `IDREFS`) then the length facets constrain the number of items in the list.

string

If the datatype derives from string (directly or through multiple levels of derivation) then the length facets constrain the number of characters in the string.

binary

Applied to a binary datatype, length facets constrain the number of bytes of decoded binary data.

59.5.3 *Decimal digit restrictions*

There are two facets that only apply to decimal numbers and types derived from them. These are `totalDigits` and `fractionDigits`.

The first constrains the maximum number of digits in the decimal representation of the number and the second constrains the maximum number of digits in the fractional part (after the .). For instance it would make sense when dealing with dollars to constrain the `fractionDigits` to two.

59.5.4 *Enumeration restrictions*

You can also define a datatype as a list of allowable values by using several enumeration elements. In Example 59-8, we define a `dayOfWeek` datatype.

Example 59-8. Defining an enumerated datatype

```
<xsd:simpleType name="workday">
  <xsd:restriction base="xsd:string">
    <xsd:enumeration value="Sunday"/>
    <xsd:enumeration value="Monday"/>
    <xsd:enumeration value="Tuesday"/>
    <xsd:enumeration value="Wednesday">
      <xsd:annotation>
        <xsd:documentation>Halfway there!</xsd:documentation>
      </xsd:annotation>
    </xsd:enumeration>
    <xsd:enumeration value="Thursday"/>
    <xsd:enumeration value="Friday">
      <xsd:annotation>
        <xsd:documentation>Almost done!</xsd:documentation>
      </xsd:annotation>
    </xsd:enumeration>
    <xsd:enumeration value="Saturday"/>
  </xsd:restriction>
</xsd:simpleType>
```

Note that an enumeration element, like all facet-constraining elements, may have an annotation sub-element.

Enumeration elements work together to restrict the value to one of the enumeration values. Enumeration elements are so strict that they supersede any of the base datatype's constraints. Where other constraints say things like "the value must be higher than X or look like Y", enumerations say: "the value must be one of these values and not anything else".

The enumeration values must be legal values of the base datatype. Therefore, if an enumeration datatype derives from another enumeration datatype, the derived datatype may only have values that the base datatype has.

59.5.5 *The* whiteSpace *facet*

The whiteSpace facet is a little bit different from the others. Rather than constraining the value of a datatype, it constrains the processing. The facet can have one of three values:

preserve
    The datatype processor will leave the whitespace alone.

replace
    Whitespace of any kind is changed into space characters.

collapse
    Sequences of whitespace are collapsed to a single space and leading and trailing whitespace is discarded.

The built-in datatypes all use the value collapse, except for string and types derived from it. Those types include normalizedString, which in turn is a base type for token. As we discussed in 59.3.2.2.2, "Other XML constructs", on page 899, all of the datatypes that represent names of things (language, Name, NMTOKEN, etc.) derive from tokens.

59.5.6 *The pattern facet*

The most sophisticated and powerful facet is the pattern facet. Patterns have a value attribute that is a *regular expression*.

Variants of regular expression syntax are used in several aspects of XML. DTDs use one to describe content models.[7] The XML specification itself is written in terms of a grammar built of regular expressions.[8]

The regular expressions that constrain datatypes are based on those used in various programming languages. They have especially close ties to the Perl programming language which integrates regular expressions into its core syntax.

Note   *The full regular expression language is quite complicated because of deep support for Unicode. There are also shortcuts to reduce the size of regular expressions. We do not cover all of these. Instead we concentrate on the 80% of regular expression features that are used most of the time.*

Example 59-9 illustrates some interesting patterns. We'll explain what goes into them in the following sections.

Example 59-9. Pattern examples

```
<xsd:simpleType name="even-number">
    <xsd:restriction base="xsd:decimal">
        <xsd:pattern value="\d*[02468]"/>
    </xsd:restriction>
</xsd:simpleType>

<xsd:simpleType name="old-fashioned-domain-name">
    <xsd:restriction base="xsd:string">
        <xsd:pattern value="\w+\.(com|net|org|gov)"/>
    </xsd:restriction>
</xsd:simpleType>

<xsd:simpleType name="phone-number">
    <xsd:restriction base="xsd:string">
        <xsd:pattern value="(\d{3}-)?\d{3}-\d{4}"/>
    </xsd:restriction>
</xsd:simpleType>
```

---

7. See 54.5, "Content models", on page 800.
8. They are called "productions" and are discussed in Chapter 57, "Reading the XML specification", on page 862.

59.5.6.1   Constructing regular expressions

The simplest regular expression is just a character. a is a regular expression that matches the character "a". There is only one string in the world that matches this string.

If we put other letters beside the "a" then the regular expression will match them in order. abcd matches "a" and then "b" and then "c" and then "d". Once again there is only one string that matches that expression.

59.5.6.1.5   *Quantifiers*

A slightly more sophisticated regular expression will match one or more occurrences of the last letter "d": abcd+. Just as in DTD content models, the plus symbol means "one or more of this thing". "This thing" is whatever comes just before the plus symbol – typically a character. Just as in content models, there are also ? and * symbols available. They stand for "zero or one of the thing" and "zero or more of the thing". We call these quantifiers.

There is another quantifier that is not available in DTD content models. It uses curly braces ({}) with one or two numbers between them. The quantifier {3} means that there should be three occurrences of the thing.

So ba{3}d matches "baaad". It is also possible to express a range: ba{3,7}d matches "baaad", "baaaad", "baaaaad", "baaaaaad" and "baaaaaaad". The lower bound can go as low as zero, in which case the item is optional (just as if you had used a question mark).

The upper bound can be omitted like this: ba{3,}d. That means that there is no upper bound. That expression is equivalent to baaaa*d which is itself equivalent to baaa+d. All three expressions match three or more occurrences of the middle letter "a".

We can put these ideas together. For instance ab{2,5}c+d{4} matches one "a" followed by two to five "b"s followed by one or more "c"s followed by exactly 4 "d"s. Example 59-10 demonstrates.

Example 59-10. Quantifiers in a regular expression

```
<xsd:simpleType name="reg-exp-example">
   <xsd:restriction base="xsd:string">
      <xsd:pattern value="ab{2,5}c+d{4}"/>
   </xsd:restriction>
</xsd:simpleType>
```

59.5.6.1.6 *Alternatives and grouping*

Regular expressions use the | symbol to represent alternatives just as DTD content models do.

Consider the regular expression yes+|no+. It matches "yes", "yess", "yesss", "no", "noo", "nooo" and so forth.

However, there is a big difference between content models and regular expressions. The primitive tokens in content models are elements. So in that context yes is judged as one "yes" element. In the world of regular expressions we are dealing with individual characters, so yes is three characters and yes+ repeats only the last character, not the rest.

If we do want to repeat the whole word yes, we can use parentheses (just as in content models). The regular expression (yes)+|(no)+ matches the strings "yes", "yesyes", "yesyesyes", "no", "nono", "nonono".

We can even use parentheses to group the whole expression: (yes|no)+. This expression allows us to match multiple occurrences of "yes" and "no". For example: "yes", "no", "yesyes", "yesno", "noyes", "nono", "yesyesyes", "yesnoyes" and so forth.

59.5.6.1.7 *Special characters*

There are ways to refer to function characters:

- \n represents the newline (or line-feed) character.
- \r represents the return character.
- \t represents the tab character.

So a\nb represents the letter "a" followed by a newline followed by "b".

There are also ways to refer to the characters that would normally be interpreted as symbols. For instance the + character might be necessary in a regular expression involving mathematics.

- Convert a symbol into an ordinary character by preceding it with the symbol \. So \? is translated into the ordinary character (not special symbol) ?.
- Convert a backslash symbol to a character like this: \\. Convert two of them like this: \\\\.
- The symbol characters you need to handle in this way are:

  \ | . - ^ ? * + { } ( ) [ ]

59.5.6.2   Character classes

It is often useful to be able to refer to lists of characters without explicitly listing all of the characters. For instance it would be annoying to need to enter (1|2|3|4|5|6|7|8|9|0) whenever you want to allow a digit.

Plus there are many Unicode characters that are considered digits that are not in this set. Examples include TIBETAN DIGIT ZERO, GUJARATI DIGIT TWO and DINGBAT NEGATIVE CIRCLED DIGIT NINE. It would not be internationally correct to ignore those!

These sets of reusable characters are known as *character classes*. They are represented by a backslash character followed by a letter.[9]

59.5.6.2.8   *Built-in character classes*

This particular character class, digits, is represented by \d. So \d+ means one or more digits, while \d+a\d{2,5} means one or more digits, and then the letter "a", and then two to five more digits. The opposite of this character class is indicated by an upper-case \D, meaning anything that is not a digit.

Another major character class is indicated simply by a period (.). It matches any character except a newline or linefeed character. So d.g matches "dig" and "dog" but also "d~g" and "d%g". The middle character could even be Kanji or Cherokee (both components of Unicode!).

The character class \s represents any whitespace character (space, tab, newline, carriage return). \S is its opposite. It represents any non-whitespace character.

\i represents the set of "initial name" characters – basically letters, the underscore and the colon.[10] \I is its opposite: anything that is not an initial name character. \c represents the set of all name characters. \C is its opposite.[11]

---

9. Note that the backslash does two different jobs. It turns symbol (punctuation) characters into ordinary characters and ordinary letters into character classes.

10. The class was renamed from the proper XML terminology of *name start characters* so that \n could have its common regular expression meaning of "newline".

11. See 53.1.5, "Names and name tokens", on page 765 for a refresher on both of these character classes.

\w represents what you might call "word" characters: basically letters, digits, and some symbols (e.g. currency, math). That is to say, characters that are not punctuation, separators or the like. \w+ will roughly match a word; \W represents the opposite – the characters that are not considered word characters.

59.5.6.2.9 *Constructing a character class*

You can also create character classes in your regular expressions (though you cannot give them fancy backslash-prefixed names!). The syntax to do this is called a *character class expression* and it uses square brackets ([]).

For instance to represent the first four characters in the alphabet you would say [abcd]. This simple example could just as easily be represented as (a|b|c|d) but the character class notation allows a couple of tricks that are difficult to emulate with the | symbol.

When you construct a character class expression you can specify ranges. For instance [a-z] represents the characters from "a" through "z" in Unicode (which are the same as in the English alphabet). You can even put multiple ranges together: [a-zA-Z0-9].

Inside square brackets, the characters *, +, (,), {, } and ? are just characters. They have no special meaning. Backslash (\) remains special because we use that to refer to the built-in character classes (\d for digits and so forth). Here is a character class that matches all of them and also matches Unicode digit and word characters: [*+(){}\d\w].

It is also possible to construct a "negative" character class which includes all of the characters that you do not list. You do this by starting your character class expression with a caret (^) symbol. So to match every character except "a" and "z", you would use the regular expression: [^az]. If you wanted to match everything except the characters *from* "a" *to* "z", you could do that like this: [^a-z].

59.6 | Using datatypes

Although *XML Schema* datatypes were originally designed for use with XSDL, they can also be used with DTDs and in other contexts. In fact several schema languages, such as RELAX NG, have chosen to use them. As the next section demonstrates, datatypes do not have to be used in schemas at all!

59.6.1 *Instance documents*

It is typical for a schema processor to infer the datatype of an element based on the element-type name and matching declarations in some schema. It is possible, however, for an element to explicitly declare its datatype using an attribute named `type` in the namespace:

```
http://www.w3.org/2001/XMLSchema-instance
```

This namespace is conventionally given the prefix `xsi` so the attribute value typically has the qualified name `xsi:type`. Of course you may declare any prefix you like.

59.6.1.1 Built-in datatypes

This in-line datatype information is useful when your goal is not schema validation, but rather just informing applications about the data. The application can use this information to create appropriate object types in a programming language. Example 59-11 shows how datatype usage can be declared in a document instance that conforms to an XSDL schema definition.

Example 59-11. Instance syntax for built-in datatypes

```
<doc xmlns:xsi="http://www.w3.org/2001/XMLSchema-instance"
     xmlns:xsd="http://www.w3.org/2001/XMLSchema">
  <mynum xsi:type="xsd:decimal">409</mynum>
  <mystr xsi:type="xsd:string">You're so fine!</mystr>
</doc>
```

For other document instances, where the full XSDL namespace isn't needed, the second namespace declaration would be:

```
xmlns:xsd="http://www.w3.org/2001/XMLSchema-datatypes
```

59.6.1.2 User-defined datatypes

There are two ways to package the simple type definitions for your derived datatypes:

- As simple type definitions within the full XSDL schema definition you are using for your documents; or
- As a set of simple type definitions to be used in conjunction with a DTD or schema definition written in another schema language. The definitions would be contained in an `xsd:schema` element and would be defined in a target namespace.[12]

If your schema defines datatypes in the namespace `http://www.myns.org/2000/datatypes` then you can refer to those datatypes using the syntax shown in Example 59-12.

Example 59-12. Instance syntax for user-defined datatypes

```
<doc xmlns:xsi="http://www.w3.org/2001/XMLSchema-instance"
     xmlns:dt="http://www.myns.org/2000/datatypes">
  <mynum xsi:type="dt:myType">3^?</mynum>
  <mystr xsi:type="dt:myOtherType">codeName</mystr>
</doc>
```

59.6.2 Web Services Description Language (WSDL)

The Web Services Description Language allows you to merge XSDL complex types and simple datatypes into your service descriptions. For instance you could say that the first element in a message must always be a `pubYear`. Example 59-13 demonstrates how you can embed a schema element with a datatype definition within a service description.

The example first initializes three namespaces, one that we will define ourselves (the one relating to publishing), one for *XML Schema* (so we have access to *XML Schema* datatypes) and one for WSDL itself. In the WSDL `types` element we embed a `schema` element containing the definition of the `pubYear` datatype. Then we use this datatype as a part of the WSDL message.

---

12. See 60.3.1, "Namespaces", on page 923.

Example 59-13. Web service description

```
<!-- namespace declarations -->
<ws:definitions
  xmlns:pub="http://www.publisher.com"
  xmlns:xsd="http://www.w3.org/2001/XMLSchema"
  xmlns:ws="http://schemas.xmlsoap.org/wsdl/">
  <ws:types>
    <!-- embedded datatype definition -->
    <xsd:schema targetNamespace="http://www.publisher.com">
      <xsd:simpleType name="pubYear">
        ... definition here ....
      </xsd:simpleType>
    </xsd:schema>
  </ws:types>

  <!-- message based on datatype-->
  <ws:message name="publisherReport">
    <ws:part name="year" type="pub:pubYear"/>
    <ws:part name="title" type="xsd:string"/>
  </ws:message>
  ...
</ws:definitions>
```

59.6.3 *XML DTDs*

Since *XML Schema* datatypes were designed after DTDs[13], there is no built-in provision in DTD declarations for declaring the use of these datatypes. Instead, users and software developers have adopted a convention for making the association.

It is called *Datatypes for DTDs (DT4DTD)* and is defined in the W3C Note at `http://www.w3.org/TR/dt4dtd`. DT4DTD is supported in the Java Architecture for XML Binding (JAXB).

Tip   DT4DTD is also supported by open source software, which is available on the CD-ROM, and by the XML Authority schema editor described in Chapter 36, "Building a schema for a product catalog", on page 544, a trial version of which is also available on the CD-ROM.

13.About 30 years after, but who's counting.

The convention uses two reserved attribute names, which are declared with fixed values:

e-dtype

> The datatype of the element's data content. The attribute is only needed when the data content is other than `string`.

a-dtype

> The datatypes of all the attributes that have them. The attribute value is a list of pairs, each consisting of an attribute name followed by its datatype. The `a-dtype` attribute is only needed when using a datatype that can't be declared with an XML attribute type (that is, a datatype other than `string`, NMTOKEN, ID, etc.).

If a datatype is not a built in datatype, you can optionally declare a notation of the same name to reference its definition. An implementation can use that information to invoke the software program that checks and/or processes the data.

In Example 59-14, the `a-dtype` attribute declares the datatypes for the pubyear and linecount attributes. The datatype of linecount is built-in, but the datatype of pubyear is user-derived so there is a NOTATION declaration that references its definition.

Example 59-14. Declaring datatypes for attributes

```
<!NOTATION pubYear          SYSTEM "datatypeDefs.xml#pubYear">
<!ATTLIST   poem
            a-dtype   CDATA #FIXED "pubyear    pubYear
                                    linecount  nonNegativeInteger"

            pubyear   CDATA #IMPLIED
            linecount CDATA #IMPLIED >
```

59.7 | Conclusion

XML Schema Datatypes provides a useful library of built-in datatypes and a powerful facility for deriving your own from them. These datatypes can be used in XSDL schema definitions, in DTDs, and in non-XSDL schema languages.

XML Schema (XSDL)

Tad Tougher Tutorial

- *XML Schema* definition language

- Syntax and declarations

- Simple and complex types

- Locally-scoped elements

- Schema inclusion

A n XML DTD is a specific case of a more general concept called a schema definition. The dictionary defines *schema* as a "general conception of what is common to all members of a class." A schema definition takes that "conception" and turns it into something concrete that can be used directly by a computer.

There are many types of schema in use in the computer industry, chiefly for databases. DTDs are different in that the class for which they declare "what is common to all members" is a class of XML documents.

The popularity of XML has brought DTDs to entirely new constituencies. The database experts and programmers who are taking to XML in droves are examining it from the standpoint of their own areas of expertise and familiar paradigms.

All of these creative folks have ideas about what could be done differently. The World Wide Web Consortium has incorporated these ideas into a design for an enhanced schema definition facility called the *XML Schema definition language (XSDL)*.

The name of the language is often shortened to "XML Schema", but we reserve that phrase for the name of the W3C spec. We call the language XSDL so you'll know when we are referring to the "schema definition language" as opposed to:

- a particular "schema definition",
- a conceptual "schema", or
- the *XML Schema* specification.

The words "XML schema", unfortunately, could refer to any of those four things.

Caution   The XML Schema spec is several times longer than the XML specification itself. It is also quite intricate and formal. This chapter will informally teach a subset that is sufficiently functional for most projects and yet simple enough that we can teach it all in one chapter.

60.1 | A simple sample schema

Let's start our explanation of XSDL by introducing a sample DTD and an equivalent schema definition and comparing the two.

60.1.1 *Sample DTD*

The sample DTD in Example 60-1 demonstrates some of the most important features of DTD declarations. Example 60-2 shows a document that conforms to that DTD.

Example 60-1. Poem DTD

```
<!ELEMENT  poem   (title, picture, verse+)>
<!ATTLIST  poem
    publisher CDATA      #IMPLIED
    pubyear   NMTOKEN    #IMPLIED
    xmlns     CDATA      #FIXED "http://www.poetry.net/poetns"
>
<!ELEMENT  title     (#PCDATA)>
<!ELEMENT  verse     (#PCDATA)>
<!ELEMENT  picture   EMPTY>
<!ATTLIST  picture   href      CDATA #REQUIRED
                     a-dtype   CDATA #FIXED "href anyURI">
```

The DTD defines a `poem` element type that consists of a `title` element followed by a `picture` and one or more `verse` elements. The poem element type has two optional attributes: `publisher` and `pubyear`. The namespace is fixed in the DTD for reasons discussed in Chapter 58, "Namespaces", on page 874.

The `picture` element type's required `href` attribute is declared as a CDATA attribute. We use the "Datatypes for DTDs" convention (59.6.3, "XML DTDs", on page 916) to require that the attribute always have a URL value.

Example 60-2. Poem document

```
<!DOCTYPE poem SYSTEM "poem.dtd">
<poem xmlns="http://www.poetry.net/poetns"
    publisher="Boni and Liveright" pubyear="1922">
<title>The Waste Land</title>
<picture href="pic1.gif"/>
<verse>April is the cruellest month, breeding</verse>
<verse>Lilacs out of the dead land</verse>
</poem>
```

60.1.2 *Equivalent schema definition*

Example 60-3 is an XSDL definition for the poem document type. There are several notable differences between this example and Example 60-1.

- Perhaps the most obvious is that instead of using the syntax of DTD declarations, a schema definition is represented as an XML document.
- There is a dependency on namespaces, which are heavily utilized.[1] The `schema` element declares the prefix `xsd` for names defined in XML Schema and `poem` for names that are defined within this schema definition.
- There is a built-in syntax that can be used to declare datatypes: the `type` attribute. Actually, it is used for more than datatypes; it is arguably the most important concept in XSDL, as we'll soon see.

---

1. Namespaces are discussed in Chapter 58, "Namespaces", on page 874.

Example 60-3. Poem schema definition in XSDL

```
<?xml version="1.0"?>
<xsd:schema xmlns:xsd="http://www.w3.org/2001/XMLSchema"
        xmlns:poem="http://www.poetry.net/poetns"
    targetNamespace="http://www.poetry.net/poetns">
  <xsd:element name="poem">
    <xsd:complexType>
      <xsd:sequence>
        <xsd:element ref="poem:title"/>
        <xsd:element ref="poem:picture"/>
        <xsd:element ref="poem:verse" maxOccurs="unbounded"/>
      </xsd:sequence>
      <xsd:attribute name="publisher" type="xsd:string"/>
      <xsd:attribute name="pubyear" type="xsd:NMTOKEN"/>
    </xsd:complexType>
  </xsd:element>
  <xsd:element name="title" type="xsd:string"/>
  <xsd:element name="verse" type="xsd:string"/>
  <xsd:element name="picture">
    <xsd:complexType>
      <xsd:attribute name="href" use="required" type="xsd:anyURI"/>
    </xsd:complexType>
  </xsd:element>
</xsd:schema>
```

60.2 | Elements and types

Notice the four `element` elements[2] in Example 60-3: `poem`, `title`, `verse` and `picture`. They perform roughly the same task as the element-type and attribute-list declarations in a DTD, but they do it differently.

In a DTD, an element-type declaration and related attribute-list declaration declare the properties of a class of elements:

1. the element-type name;
2. the data structure of the content; and
3. attributes provided for the class, including attribute types and default values.

In XSDL, a `complexType` element can define *and name* a data structure and attributes *independently of declaring an element type*. There is also a

---

2. Yes, `element` elements.

`simpleType` element, but it can define and name only the simplest data structures: various forms of character strings, such as datatypes.

The unqualified word *type* in XSDL is reserved for just these two types: complex types and simple types.[3]

An `element` element, then, declares the element-type name and data structure type of a class of elements. The type could be defined within the content of the `element` element, as in the case of `poem` in Example 60-3, in which case the type itself is not named.

Alternatively, if the type was defined and named elsewhere, the declaration could use a `type` attribute, as shown for the `title` element. As the `xsd` prefix in the attribute value suggests, the `string` type is not actually defined within this schema. XSDL automatically provides named simple type definitions for all of the built-in datatypes. Those names are in the *XML Schema* namespace.

The two methods of declaring data structure types for elements are equivalent, and are equally applicable to complex and simple types. That includes user-derived datatypes, which, as we saw in 59.4, "Defining user-derived datatypes", on page 901, are actually simple types.

60.3 | Structure of a schema definition

A schema is defined by one or more *schema documents*. Their root element is a `schema` element. Its attributes can define applicable namespaces, and its content components include elements like those we have been discussing, plus annotation elements.

60.3.1 *Namespaces*

The `schema` element must have a declaration for the XML schema namespace, `http://www.w3.org/2001/XMLSchema`. It could either assign a prefix (`xsd` and `xs` are two popular ones) or it could make *XML Schema* the default namespace. The prefix (if any) is used both for schema component elements and in references to built-in datatypes.

---

3. In fact the XSDL spec barely mentions any other types (element, attribute, data, etc.), perhaps to avoid confusion with the unqualified use of "type".

To validate documents that use namespaces, you can specify a `targetNamespace` for the schema, as shown in Example 60-3. Components that are children of the `schema` element are called *global schema components*. They declare and define items in the schema's target namespace.

The example also declares the `poem` prefix for the schema's target namespace. It is used within the schema definition to refer to the elements, attributes and types declared (or defined) by global schema components.

The instance document in Example 60-2 utilizes the same namespace, `http://www.poetry.net/poetns`. However, as it is declared as the default namespace, no prefix is declared or used.

Note that the value of the `name` attribute of a component, such as a type definition or element declaration, does not have a namespace prefix. A component name always belongs to the target namespace. It is only when the declared or defined objects are referenced that the prefix may be used.

Within a namespace different kinds of components can normally have the same name. The exception is simple and complex types, as there are many places where they are treated interchangeably. Elements, however, are not types, so an element declaration component may use the same name as a complex or simple type. There is no more relationship between them than between a guy named Bob at your office and the guy named Bob on your favorite television show (unless you work in Hollywood!).

60.3.2 *Schema components*

The XSDL elements we have been discussing, such as `element` and `simpleType`, occur in the content of a `schema` element and are collectively known as *schema components*. Those, like `element`, that correspond to DTD declarations, are also called (surprise!) *declaration components*.

As XSDL schemas are themselves defined in XML documents, it was possible to provide techniques to make them self-documenting and capable of being processed by applications other than schema processors. These include unique identifiers, extension attributes, and annotation elements.

60.3.2.1 Unique identifiers

All schema components are defined with an optional `id` attribute. You can therefore assign unique identifiers to make the components easier to refer to using XPointers, XLinks and other hyperlinking techniques. Each value assigned to an `id` attribute must be different from any other assigned anywhere in the schema document.

60.3.2.2 Extension attributes

Schema components may be extended with arbitrary attributes in any namespace *other* than the *XML Schema* namespace. For instance you could add attributes from the XLink namespace or from the RDF namespace.

If you had software that helped you to visualize the schema, extension attributes could be used to store the graphical coordinates of the various elements. If you used software that converted XML schemas to a relational database schema, you might use the extension attributes to guide that process.

60.3.2.3 The `annotation` element

Any XSDL component may have an `annotation` element as its first sub-element. The `schema` element, however, goes above and beyond the call of duty! It may have as many `annotation` sub-elements as you like. It is good practice to have at least one annotation at the beginning as an introduction to the document type.

An `annotation` element may have zero or more `documentation` and `appinfo` children elements.

The `documentation` element is used to add user-readable information to the schema. Any elements are permitted; they needn't be defined in the schema. The benefit of using annotation elements rather than XML comments is that it is much easier to use rich markup such as XHTML or Docbook. Application software can extract this documentation and use it for online help or other purposes.

An `appinfo` element adds some information specific to a particular application. These are extension elements; they work like the extension attributes we discussed earlier. You may use them for the same sorts of tasks, but the elements can have an internal structure while attributes can only contain data characters. Your extension elements should be in a namespace that will enable your applications to recognize them.

60.3.3 *Complex types*

Example 60-4 shows the definition of an `address` type. It also shows two element declarations that utilize it.

Example 60-4. Elements built on an `address` type

```
<xsd:complexType name="address">
  <xsd:sequence>
    <xsd:element ref="myns:line1"/>
    <xsd:element ref="myns:line2"/>
    <xsd:element ref="myns:city"/>
    <xsd:element ref="myns:state"/>
    <xsd:element ref="myns:zip"/>
  </xsd:sequence>
  <xsd:attribute name="id" type="xsd:ID"/>
</xsd:complexType>
<xsd:element name="billingAddress" type="myns:address"/>
<xsd:element name="shippingAddress" type="myns:address"/>
```

In XSDL, types are defined independently of elements and may be associated with more than one element-type name. In the example, the `address` type is used by both `billingAddress` and `shippingAddress`.

This example shows some of the power of complex types: we can create structural definitions as reusable units that make element declaration and maintenance easier. Types are similar to the virtual or abstract classes used in object-oriented programming.

Types do not themselves define elements that will be used directly. Example 60-4 would not permit an `address` element in a valid document. Instead the type is a set of reusable constraints that can be used as a building block in element declarations and other type definitions.

XSDL does not require you to give every type a name. If you only intend to use a type once, you could put the definition for it right in an element declaration, as in Example 60-5.

Example 60-5 was created from Example 60-4 by wrapping the `complexType` in an `element` and moving the name attribute. You could do the same with a `simpleType`. Note that the element declaration has no `type` attribute. You need to choose whether to refer to a named type or embed an unnamed type definition.

Example 60-5. Inline type definition

```
<xsd:element name="address">
  <xsd:complexType>
   <xsd:sequence>
     <xsd:element ref="myns:line1"/>
     <xsd:element ref="myns:line2"/>
     <xsd:element ref="myns:city"/>
     <xsd:element ref="myns:state"/>
     <xsd:element ref="myns:zip"/>
   </xsd:sequence>
   <xsd:attribute name="id" type="xsd:ID"/>
  </xsd:complexType>
</xsd:element>
```

To create a type that allows character data in addition to whatever is specified in its content model, you may add a `mixed="true"` attribute value to the `complexType` element.

To declare the element-type empty, we could have left out the `sequence` element.

60.3.4 *Content models*

Just as in DTDs, content models allow us to describe what content is allowed within an element. Many of the concepts are very similar to DTDs. Just as DTDs allow you to express sequences and choice, so too does XSDL. Nevertheless, XSDL has a few more tricks up its sleeves.

60.3.4.1 Sequences

Sequences are equivalent to content models of the form `A,B,C` in DTDs. This one would indicate that there must be an `A` element followed by a `B` element followed by a `C` element. The XSDL equivalent is shown in Example 60-6.

An `element` element might declare things directly, or else indirectly by referencing an existing `element` declaration. The declarations in the example do the latter, as indicated by the use of `ref` attributes instead of `name` attributes. Note that an element reference must be prefixed if it lives in a namespace (which it will if declared in a schema with a `targetNamespace`).

Example 60-6. sequence element

```
<xsd:sequence>
   <xsd:element ref="myns:A"/>
   <xsd:element ref="myns:B"/>
   <xsd:element ref="myns:C"/>
</xsd:sequence>
```

60.3.4.2   Choices

DTDs also have a | operator that represents a choice rather than a sequence. A|B|C means A or B or C. Example 60-7 shows the XSDL equivalent.

Example 60-7. choice element

```
<xsd:choice>
   <xsd:element ref="myns:A"/>
   <xsd:element ref="myns:B"/>
   <xsd:element ref="myns:C"/>
</xsd:choice>
```

60.3.4.3   Nested model groups

For more complex content models, model groups can be nested. For example, we can duplicate the DTD content model (title,picture,verse+, (footnotes|bibliography)) with a choice element within a sequence element, as shown in Example 60-8.

Example 60-8. Sequence with nested choice

```
<xsd:sequence>
  <xsd:element ref="poem:title"/>
  <xsd:element ref="poem:picture"/>
  <xsd:element ref="poem:verse" maxOccurs="unbounded"/>
  <xsd:choice>
    <xsd:element ref="poem:footnotes"/>
    <xsd:element ref="poem:bibliography"/>
  </xsd:choice>
</xsd:sequence>
```

The declaration for `verse` states that it may have multiple occurrences through its `maxOccurs` attribute. There is a corresponding `minOccurs` that defaults to "1" – meaning at least one is required by default.

Inside of sequences and choices it is also possible to use `any` and `group` elements. `any` is like a DTD's `ANY`. It means that any content is allowed. It has various bells and whistles to allow you to narrow down what you mean by "any". Most document types do not require this feature so we will not go into any detail.

The `group` element allows you to refer to a named "model group definition". You can use these model group definitions to reuse parts of content models by referencing them.

60.3.4.4 `all` elements

There is an *and connector* (&) in SGML that is not included in XML DTDs because it is difficult to implement. It appears in XSDL in a simplified form. The `all` element specifies that all of the contained elements must be present, but their order is irrelevant. So you could enter "A B C", "A C B", "B A C" and all of the other combinations of the three. Example 60-9 demonstrates.

Example 60-9. `all` element

```
<xsd:complexType name="testAll">
  <xsd:all>
    <xsd:element ref="myns:A"/>
    <xsd:element ref="myns:B"/>
    <xsd:element ref="myns:C"/>
  </xsd:all>
</xsd:complexType>
```

`all` must only be used at the top level of a complex type definition. `all` is also unique in that it may only contain `element` elements, not sequences, choices, groups etc.

60.3.5 *Attributes*

The poem and picture element declarations in Example 60-3 both contain attribute declarations equivalent to those in our original DTD. Example 60-10 shows the declarations for the poem element's optional publisher and pubyear attributes.

Example 60-10. Attribute declarations

```
<xsd:attribute name="publisher" type="xsd:string"/>
<xsd:attribute name="pubyear" type="xsd:NMTOKEN"/>
```

They are optional because there is no use attribute in their definitions. You can also make them required with use="required".

Example 60-11 shows two attribute declarations. One uses a built-in datatype and the other a user-defined simple type.

Example 60-11. Built-in and user-defined types

```
<xsd:attribute name="href" use="required" type="xsd:anyURI"/>
<xsd:attribute name="pubdate" type="myns:pubyear"/>
```

Attribute declarations can also occur within a named attributeGroup element, which allows them to be reused in complex type definitions and in other attribute groups.

attribute elements have a default attribute that allows you to specify a default value for optional attributes. To supply a default value that cannot be overridden (just as you might use #FIXED in a DTD), supply it using the fixed attribute rather than the default attribute.

60.4 | Declaring schema conformance

How does an XML document tell a processor that it conforms to a particular XSDL schema definition? Usually it doesn't!

In theory, you can determine which schema definition to use from the root element type, file type, or other cues. In practice, the namespace is typically used.

There is a convention specified in the *XML Schema* specification to allow the document author to give a more explicit hint to the receiver. Example 60-12 demonstrates.

Example 60-12. Referring to a schema definition

```
<myns:mydoc
    xmlns:myns="http://www.myns.com/myns"
    xmlns:xsi="http://www.w3.org/2001/XMLSchema-instance"
    xsi:schemaLocation="http://www.myns.com/myns
                        http://www.mysite.com/myxsdl.xsd">

</myns:mydoc>
```

Note the declaration of the xsi namespace prefix. It identifies a namespace that is specifically for putting *XML Schema* information into instance documents. There is a global attribute in this namespace called schemaLocation that allows a document to point to an appropriate schema definition.

The attribute value is defined as a list of paired URIs. The first one in each pair is a namespace URI. The second one is the URI for a schema document. As the schema processor works its way through the instance document, it can find the applicable schema for an element or attribute by looking up its namespace.

The sender of a document may also provide the receiver with a schema through an API, command line, or graphical interface. Eventually, a trusted repository may supply the schema or DTD, as we describe in Chapter 67, "Repositories and vocabularies", on page 1070.

Although there is nothing wrong with using these hints just to check whether a document is valid, often you want to check whether it validates against some particular schema. In that case you don't want your software to use hints, you want it to use the schema you've provided.

The manner in which you tell the software what schema to use for a particular namespace will depend on the software. One convention is merely to configure the software with a list of schemas. The software can read the schemas and collect the list of target namespaces from the targetNamespace attributes. Then, when it sees a particular namespace in a document it can use the appropriate schema to validate it. Because *you* provide the list of schemas in the beginning, you know exactly what schemas are being used to validate no matter what is in the document.

60.5 | Schema inclusion

DTDs can share text by means of external parameter entities. For example, the common parameter entity declared and referenced in Example 60-13 tells an XML processor to treat the DTD as if the two lines of Example 60-14 had been inserted at the fourth line.

Example 60-13. DTD with an external parameter entity reference

```
<!ELEMENT  book     (title,chapter+)>
<!ELEMENT  chapter (title,par+)>
<!ENTITY % common   SYSTEM "common.dtd">
%common;
```

Example 60-14. common.dtd file referenced in Example 60-13

```
<!ELEMENT title (#PCDATA)>
<!ELEMENT par    (#PCDATA)>
```

The *schema inclusion* facility works similarly. It allows a schema definition to treat another schema definition's contents as part of its own. Example 60-15 uses the include element to incorporate declarations from the schema in Example 60-16. The declarations are thenceforth treated as part of the book.xsd schema.

In addition to inclusion, XSDL also has support for importing and redefinition of other schemas. Importing is for combining schemas that describe different namespaces. A redefinition allows you to include another schema and override bits and pieces of the included schema. For instance you could redefine the type of an element or attribute that you are including.

60.6 | Additional capabilities

So far we have pretty much just taken concepts from DTD declarations and represented them as XML elements conforming to the schema document type. Schemas get more interesting when they allow us to do things that are difficult or impossible in DTDs.

Example 60-15. book.xsd schema definition including declarations from common.xsd

```
<xsd:schema xmlns:xsd="http://www.w3.org/2001/XMLSchema"
        xmlns:myns="http://www.myns.net/myns"
   targetNamespace="http://www.myns.net/myns">
  <xsd:include schemaLocation="common.xsd"/>
  <xsd:element name="book">
    <xsd:complexType>
      <xsd:sequence>
        <xsd:element ref="myns:title"/>
        <xsd:element ref="myns:chapter" maxOccurs="unbounded"/>
      </xsd:sequence>
    </xsd:complexType>
  </xsd:element>
  <xsd:element name="chapter">
    <xsd:complexType>
      <xsd:sequence>
        <xsd:element ref="myns:title"/>
        <xsd:element ref="myns:par" maxOccurs="unbounded"/>
      </xsd:sequence>
    </xsd:complexType>
  </xsd:element>
</xsd:schema>
```

Example 60-16. *common.xsd* schema definition

```
<xsd:schema xmlns:xsd="http://www.w3.org/2001/XMLSchema"
        xmlns:myns="http://www.myns.net/myns"
   targetNamespace="http://www.myns.net/myns">
  <xsd:element name="title" type="xsd:string"/>
  <xsd:element name="par" type="xsd:string"/>
</xsd:schema>
```

We'll now describe those additional functions briefly. We'll try to provide just enough detail to allow you to decide whether to investigate them further.[4]

---

4. For further information the spec is on the CD-ROM, but as we noted earlier, it's not a casual read!

60.6.1 *Locally-scoped elements*

Element-type names in a DTD are global; any element type can be referenced in any other element type's content model. So if you define `title` you can use it in chapters, sections and anywhere else you see fit.

Once you have defined your DTD, authors can use the `title` element in each of the contexts that you have specified. In each of those contexts the element type is exactly the same: it has the same name, attributes and allowed content.

XSDL has a facility that allows you to say that titles in one context should have a different attribute set and content model from titles in another – even if they are in the same namespace! In effect, you can declare two element types with the same name. The name is *bound* to a different element-type definition in each context.

You can do this by declaring an element type within the declaration for another element type. Example 60-17 shows two different title element types declared within the same schema. They each use a different user-derived datatype.

Example 60-17. Two locally-scoped `title` declarations

```
<xsd:element name="book"><xsd:complexType>
  <xsd:sequence>
    <xsd:element name="title"><xsd:complexType>
      <xsd:attribute name="booktitle" use="required"
                     type="xsd:string"/>
      <xsd:attribute name="ISBN" use="required"
                     type="myns:ISBNFormat"/>
    </xsd:complexType></xsd:element>
    <xsd:element ref="myns:chapter"/>
  </xsd:sequence>
</xsd:complexType></xsd:element>

<xsd:element name="employee"><xsd:complexType>
  <xsd:sequence>
    <xsd:element name="empId"/>
    <xsd:element name="title"><xsd:complexType>
      <xsd:sequence>
        <xsd:element ref="myns:jobtitle"/>
        <xsd:element ref="myns:company"/>
      </xsd:sequence>
    </xsd:complexType></xsd:element>
  </xsd:sequence>
</xsd:complexType></xsd:element>
```

In documents conforming to this schema, a `title` element within a `book` element must conform to the `title` element declared within the `book` element declaration, complete with the required `ISBN` and `booktitle` attribute values.

A `title` element within an `employee` element, however, must conform to the `title` element declared inside the example's `employee` element declaration.

60.6.2 *Type derivation*

Type derivation is the creation of a new type as a variation of an existing one (or a combination of several existing ones). This is much like the way object-oriented classes inherit from other classes. The derived type will have a content model that is an extension of the base type's.

We discussed derivation of simple types in 59.4, "Defining user-derived datatypes", on page 901. In Example 60-18 we see the derivation of a complex type, `internationalAddress`. It adds a new child element, called `countryCode`, to the `address` type we defined in Example 60-4.

Example 60-18. One type extends another

```
<xsd:complexType name="internationalAddr">
  <xsd:complexContent>
    <xsd:extension base="myns:address">
      <xsd:sequence>
          <xsd:element ref="myns:countryCode"/>
      </xsd:sequence>
    </xsd:extension>
  </xsd:complexContent>
</xsd:complexType>
```

With this definition, an `internationalAddr` is just like an `address`, but after specifying the details of the `address` you must also specify a `countryCode`.

You can also derive a type by *restriction*. That means that you add constraints, such as making an attribute or subelement required when it was previously optional. This is very similar to the equivalent concept for datatypes.

60.6.3 *Identity constraints*

There could be several elements in a document that logically represent a set. For example, records of the employees in a company might be represented as elements in an XML document.

Each element in a set must have a unique name or *key* that distinguishes it from all other elements in the set. For example, the employee records key could be an `empid` attribute or sub-element.

These *identity constraints* can get even more complicated: we might wish to declare that there must be no two customers with the same first name, last name, and address.

XSDL has sophisticated features for defining unique keys and the means of referencing them. It uses XPath for the purpose. For instance you could define the list of customers with one XPath expression and use a second to describe how each member of the set is unique.[5]

60.7 | Conclusion

XSDL is a sophisticated new tool in the toolbox of schema developers. It has the virtue of supporting modern ideas of inheritance, namespaces and schema lookup. At the same time it is somewhat controversial because it is so large and complex. The subset described in this chapter should be both useful and manageable.[6]

---

5. The discussion in 62.6.2, "Keys", on page 986 gives an idea of the problem and the approach to solving it.
6. For the whole story, we recommend Priscilla Walmsley's *Definitive XML Schema*, published in this series.

Transform & Navigation Tutorials

- XML Path Language (XPath)
- XSL Transformations (XSLT)
- XSL formatting objects (XSL-FO)
- XML Pointer Language (XPointer)
- XML Linking Language (XLink)

Part Seventeen

This part covers transform and navigation specifications from the World Wide Web Consortium. Again, you'll need a pretty firm grasp of the material in Part 15, "XML Core Tutorials" before you tackle any of these. You'll also need to know something about namespaces, from Part 16, "Schema Tutorials"

But unlike those parts, it isn't necessary to read every one of these chapters in order unless you are trying to sop up all the good technical stuff that you can. Here's a roadmap in case you are only interested in specific subjects.

XPath is a prerequisite for both stylesheets and XPointers, but again you don't need to master all the details before moving on.

XSLT is a prerequisite for XSL-FO. XSL-FO and XPointer aren't prerequisites for anything else, although understanding XPointer will add to your appreciation of the power of XLink. XLink isn't a prerequisite either.

XML Path Language (XPath)

Tad Tougher Tutorial

- XPath applications
- XPath data model
- Location expressions

Contributing expert: G. Ken Holman of Crane Softwrights Ltd.,
http://www.CraneSoftwrights.com, **author of** *Practical Transformation Using XSLT and XPath*

A ll XML processing depends upon the idea of *addressing*. In order to do something with data you must be able to locate it. To start with, you need to be able to actually find the XML document on the Web. Once you have it, you need to be able to find the information that you need within the document.

The Web has a uniform solution for the first part. The XML document is called a *resource* and *Uniform Resource Identifiers* are the Web's way of addressing resources. The most popular form of Uniform Resource Identifier is the ubiquitous Uniform Resource Locator (URL).

The standard way to locate information *within* an XML document is through a language known as the *XML Path Language* or *XPath*. XPath can be used to refer to textual data, elements, attributes and other information in an XML document.

XPath is a sophisticated, complex language. We will cover its most commonly used features, most of which are available using an abbreviated form of its syntax.

61.1 | XPath applications

Over the next few years, XPath is likely to become a basic building block of XML systems. Let's look at just a few possible applications of XPath.

61.1.1 *User scenarios*

Consider the process of stylesheet creation. A paragraph of text in one chapter may refer to another chapter through a cross-reference. During style application it makes sense to fetch the title of the referenced chapter and its chapter number. The stylesheet could then insert those pieces of information into the text of the cross-reference. For example, the marked-up phrase "`Please see <crossref refid="introduction.chapter">`" might be rendered as "Please see 'Chapter 1, Introduction'." XPath can be used within XSLT to find the appropriate chapter, find its title and locate the text of the title.

Now consider an e-commerce application. It might receive a purchase order from another system. In order to do accounting it would need to know the prices of the purchased items. In XPath notation it would locate "`/po/item/price`", meaning all of the prices in all of the items in the current purchase order document.

Finally, imagine an ordinary Web surfer of the near future. He might be reading his favorite recipes Web page. Unbeknownst to him, the page is written in XML (this is the near future, after all!). As he scrolls through, he finds a recipe that he would really love to share with his brother-in-law. He clicks the right mouse button at the beginning of the recipe. One of the choices in the popup menu might be: "email this address."

The menu item would instruct the browser to email a string of characters, termed a *URI reference* to a particular email address. The URI reference would uniquely identify not just the Web page but also the particular `recipe` element. The first part of the string would be an ordinary URI, pointing to the Web page. The last part would be an *XPointer*. XPointers are a customization of XPath for use in URI references.

As you can see, XPath is going to be a valuable tool in all sorts of XML processing.

61.1.2 *Specifications built on XPath*

XPath was developed when the groups responsible for XSLT and XPointer realized that they had to provide many of the same functions and could develop a shared solution.

These two World Wide Web Consortium specifications depend upon XPath today. XPointer uses XPath to build Web addresses (URI references) that reference parts of XML documents. URI references can address individual points and elements, as in our recipe example. They can also address lists of elements, attributes or characters.

The XSL Transformations language (XSLT) uses XPath for transformation and style application. As in our cross-reference example, XPath can be used to retrieve information from somewhere else in the document. XPath can also be used to declare that certain XSLT style rules apply to particular elements in the input document.

The *XML Schema* definition language (XSDL) also uses XPaths. It uses them to express so-called identity constraints. Using identity constraints you could require that every `employee` or `customer` element has a unique `person-id` sub-element. An XPath would be used to select the `employee` and `customer` elements and another XPath would select the contained `person-id` subelements. There is even a schema language that uses XPath to express *all* constraints. It is called *Schematron*.

XPath's syntax was carefully chosen. XPath is used by XPointer in URI references and by both XPointer and XSLT in attribute values of XML documents. XPath needed to easily fit into attribute values, browser URL fields and other places where XML's element within element syntax would be too verbose. Accordingly, XPath's syntax is very concise and does not depend on an XML parser.

XPath is designed to be extensible. W3C specifications and other XPath applications can create extensions specific to the application's problem domain. XPointer and XSLT already extend XPath.

61.1.2.1 An XLink example

Example 61-1 shows an XLink with an `xlink:href` attribute. The attribute value contains a URI reference. The reference contains an XPointer (starting with the string `xpointer`). The characters within the parentheses are an XPath expression.

Example 61-1. XLink use of XPath

```
<A xlink:type="simple"
   xlink:href="info.xml#xpointer(id('smith')/info[@type='public'])">
   Mr. John Smith
</A>
```

To summarize, Example 61-1 contains an XLink which contains a URI reference which contains an XPointer which in turn contains an XPath expression. Don't worry. We will take you through each part gently!

61.1.2.2   An XSLT example

An example of the XSLT use of the same XPath expression is the `select` attribute of Example 61-2.

Example 61-2. XSLT selecting based on XPath

```
<xsl:apply-templates select="id('smith')/info[@type='public']"/>
```

This `select` attribute finds the element identified `smith` and identifies the `info` subelements with the attribute `type` having the value "`public`". It then processes each of those `info` elements with an XSLT *template rule*. The applicable rule is found by matching each element against an XSLT pattern in the template's match attribute. Example 61-3 demonstrates.

Example 61-3. XSLT use of XPath

```
<xsl:template match="info[@type='public']">
   ...
</xsl:template>
```

61.2 | The XPath data model

It is only possible to construct an address – any address – given a model. For instance the US postal system is composed of a model of states containing cities containing streets with house numbers. To some degree the model falls naturally out of the geography of the country but it is mostly artificial.

State and city boundaries are not exactly visible from an airplane. We give new houses street numbers so that they can be addressed within the postal system's model.

Relational databases also have a model that revolves around tables, records, columns, foreign keys and so forth. This "relational model" is the basis for the SQL query language. Just as SQL depends on the relational model, XPath depends on a formal model for the logical structure and data in an XML document.

61.2.1 *Sources of the model*

You may wonder if XML really needs a formal model. It seems so simple: elements within elements, attributes of elements and so forth. It *is* simple but there are details that need to be standardized in order for addresses to behave in a reliable fashion. The tricky part is that there are many ways of representing what might seem to be the "same" information. We can repre sent a less than symbol in at least four ways:

- a predefined entity reference: <
- a CDATA section: <![CDATA[<]]>
- a decimal Unicode character reference: <
- a hex Unicode character reference: <

We could also reference a text entity that embeds a CDATA section and a text entity that embeds another text entity that embeds a character reference, etc. In a query you would not want to explicitly search for the less-than symbol in all of these variations. It would be easier to have a processor that could magically *normalize* them to a single model. Every XPath-based query engine needs to get exactly the same data model from any particular XML document.

The XML equivalent of the relational model is termed, depending on the context, either a *grove*, an *information set* or a *data model*. The *grove* concept comes from ISO and is thus important when you are working with International Standards like HyTime, Topic Maps and DSSSL.

The XML Information Set is another model of the important information in an XML document. W3C specifications are built on top of the Information Set. Whereas the grove is generalized and can include both XML and non-XML data notations, the information set is specific to XML.

XPath is a W3C specification and is only for addressing into XML documents, so its data model is derived from the W3C XML Information Set.[1]

The XPath specification does not use the Information Set directly. The Information Set takes a more liberal view of what is "important" than XPath does. Therefore XPath has a concept of a *data model*: an Information Set with some XPath-irrelevant parts filtered out.

For instance the Information Set says that it may be important to keep track of what entity each element resides within. The XPath developers chose not to care about that information and it is not, therefore, part of the XPath data model.

61.2.2 *Tree addressing*

The XPath data model views a document as a tree of nodes, or *node tree*. Most nodes correspond to document components, such as elements and attributes.

It is very common to think of XML documents as being either families (elements have child elements, parent elements and so forth) or trees (roots, branches and leaves). This is natural: trees and families are both hierarchical in nature, just as XML documents are. XPath uses both metaphors but tends to lean more heavily on the familial one.[2]

XPath uses genealogical taxonomy to describe the hierarchical makeup of an XML document, referring to children, descendants, parents and ancestors. The parent is the element that contains the element under discussion. The list of ancestors includes the parent, the parent's parent and so forth. A list of descendants includes children, children's children and so forth.

Insofar as there is no culture-independent way to talk about the first ancestor, XPath calls it the "root". The root is not an element. It is a logical construct that holds the document element and any comments and processing instructions that precede and follow it.[3]

---

1. Perhaps one day a grove-based XPath might be invented. It might allow querying arbitrary information types based on topic metadata.
2. Politicians take note: in this case, family values win out over environmentalism!
3. In the full Information Set, the root is called the document information item and it also contains information about the document's DTD.

Trees in computer science are very rarely (if ever) illustrated as a natural tree is drawn, with the root at the bottom and the branches and leaves growing upward. Far more typically, trees are depicted with the root at the top just as family trees are. This is probably due to the nature of our writing systems and the way we have learned to read.[4] Accordingly, this chapter refers to stepping "down" the tree towards the leaf-like ends and "up" the tree towards the root as the tree is depicted in Figure 61-1. One day we will genetically engineer trees to grow this way and nature will be in harmony with technology.

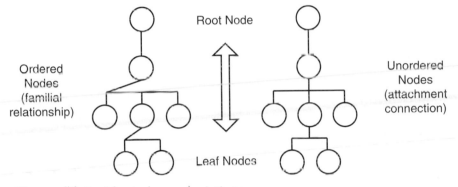

Figure 61-1 Vertical tree depictions

61.2.3 *Node tree construction*

A *node tree* is built by an XPath processor after parsing an XML document like that in Example 61-4.

Example 61-4. Sample document

```
<?xml version="1.0"?>
<!--start-->
<part-list><part-name nbr="A12">bolt</part-name>
<part-name nbr="B45">washer</part-name><warning type="ignore"/>
<!--end of list--><?cursor blinking?>
</part-list>
<!--end of file-->
```

4. To do: rotate all tree diagrams for Japanese edition of The XML Handbook.

In constructing the node tree, the boundaries and contents of "important" constructs are preserved, while other constructs are discarded. For example, entity references to both internal and external entities are expanded and character references are resolved. The boundaries of CDATA sections are discarded. Characters within the section are treated as character data.

The node tree constructed from the document in Example 61-4 is shown in Figure 61-2. In the following sections, we describe the components of node trees and how they are used in addressing. You may want to refer back to this diagram from time to time as we do so.

61.2.4 *Node types*

The XPath data model describes seven types of nodes used to construct the node tree representing any XML document. We are interested primarily in the root, element, attribute and text node types, but will briefly discuss the others.

For each node type, XPath defines a way to compute a *string-value* (labeled "value" in Figure 61-2). Some node types also have a "name".

61.2.4.1   Root node

The top of the hierarchy that represents the XML document is the root node.

It is important to remember that in the XPath data model the root of the tree representing an XML document is *not the document (or root) element of the document*. A root *node* is different from a root *element*. The root node *contains* the root element.

The nodes that are children of the root node represent the document element and the comments and processing instructions found before and after the document element.

61.2.4.2   Element nodes

Every element in an XML document is represented in the node tree as an element node. Each element has a parent node. Usually an element's parent

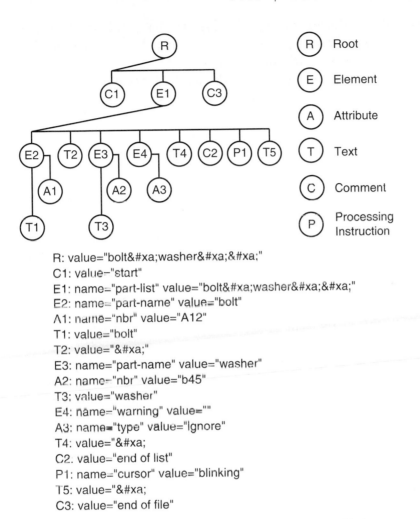

R: value="bolt
washer

"
C1: value="start"
E1: name="part-list" value="bolt
washer

"
E2: name="part-name" value="bolt"
A1: name="nbr" value="A12"
T1: value="bolt"
T2: value="
"
E3: name="part-name" value="washer"
A2: name="nbr" value="b45"
T3: value="washer"
E4: name="warning" value=""
A3: name="type" value="Ignore"
T4: value="

C2: value="end of list"
P1: name="cursor" value="blinking"
T5: value="

C3: value="end of file"

Figure 61-2   Node tree for document in Example 61-4

is another element but the document element has as its parent the root node.

Element nodes can have as their children other element nodes, text nodes, comment nodes and processing instruction nodes.

An element node also exhibits properties, such as its name, its attributes and information about its active namespaces.

Element nodes in documents with DTDs may have unique identifiers. These allow us to address element nodes by name. IDs are described in 54.6.3.4, "ID and IDREF attributes", on page 815.

The string-value of an element node is the concatenation of the string-values of all text node descendants of the element node in the document order. You can think of it as all of the data with none of the markup, organized into one long character string.

61.2.4.3   Text nodes

The XML Recommendation describes character data as all text that is not markup. In other words it is the textual data content of the document and it does not include data in attribute values, processing instructions and comments.

Caution   *The word "text" means something different in XPath from its meaning in the XML Recommendation (and the rest of this book!). We'll try to minimize the confusion by always saying "text node", even when the context is clear, reserving "text" as a noun for its normal meaning.*

XPath does not care how a character was originally represented. The string "<>" in an XML document is simply "<>" from the data model's point of view. The same goes for "&60;&62;" and "<![CDATA[<>]]>". The characters represented by any of these will be grouped with the data characters that precede and follow them and called a "text node." The individual characters of the text node are not considered its children: they are just part of its value. Text nodes do not have any children.

Remember that whitespace is significant. A text node might contain nothing else. In Figure 61-2, for example, nodes T2, T4, and T5 contain line feed characters, represented by hexadecimal character references.

61.2.4.4 Attribute nodes

If an element has attributes then these are represented as attribute nodes. These nodes are not considered children of the element node. They are more like friends that live in the guest house.

An attribute node exhibits name, string-value, and namespace URI properties. Defaulted attributes are reported as having the default values. The data model does not record whether they were explicitly specified or merely defaulted. No node is created for an unspecified attribute that had an #IMPLIED default value declared. Attribute nodes are also not created for attributes used as namespace declarations.

Note that an XML processor is not required to read an external DTD unless it is validating the document. This means that detection of ID attributes and default attribute values is not mandatory.

61.2.4.5 Other node types

Namespace nodes keep track of the set of namespace prefix/URI pairs that are in effect at a particular point in a document. Like attribute nodes, namespace nodes are attached to element nodes and are not in any particular order.

Each comment and processing instruction in the XML document is instantiated as a comment or processing instruction node in the node tree. The string-value property accesses the content of these constructs, as you can see in Figure 61-2.

61.3 | Location paths

An instance of the XPath language is called an *expression*. XPath expressions can involve a variety of operations on different kinds of operands. In this chapter we will focus on two operand types: function calls and location paths.

A *location path* is the most important kind of expression in the XPath notation. Its syntax is similar to the familiar path expressions used in URLs and in Unix and Windows systems to locate directories and files.[5]

61.3.1 *Basic concepts*

A location path has a starting point, which XPath calls its *context node*. In a file system path, it might be a computer, a disk drive, or a directory. In an XPath location path it could be, for example, the document element node or some other element node.

The purpose of the location path is to select nodes from the document by locating the desired nodes relative to the initial context node.

Arguably, the simplest location path is "/". This selects the root node (not the document element node).

61.3.1.1 Stepping down the hierarchy

We can extend this location path to select the document element node instead of the root node. "/mydoc" will select a document element node named "mydoc". The name of an element node is the element-type name of the element it represents.

> *Note*   From now on, as long as we are discussing node trees, we'll often just say "element" instead of "element node".

We have taken a step "down" the tree. We can take another step: "/mydoc/section". This will select every section element that is a child of the mydoc element.

Each slash-separated (/) path component is a *step*.

Any amount of whitespace can be present between the parts of a location path. Steps can be written across a number of lines or spaced apart to be more legible to a reader.

---

5. There is an illustrated tutorial on path expressions in 29.2, "XML Path Language (XPath)", on page 448.

61.3.1.2   Predicates

So far we have seen how to build single and multi-level location paths based on element-type names. However, the type name is not the only thing that is interesting about an element. For example, we might want to filter out elements that have (or do not have) particular attributes with particular values. Or we may be interested in the first or seventh element, or just the even-numbered ones.

We can express these constraints with qualifiers called *predicates*. Any step can be qualified. The location path in Example 61-5, for example, selects the seventh paragraph from each section with a security attribute whose string-value is "public".

Example 61-5. Selecting the seventh para from each public section

```
/mydoc/section[@security="public"]/para[7]
```

61.3.1.3   Selection

Note that we use the word *select* carefully. We could say that the expression *returns* certain nodes but that might put a picture in your head of nodes being ripped out of the tree and handed to you: "Here are your nodes!"

Rather, what you get back is a set of locations – pointers to the nodes. Imagine the result of a location path as a set of arrows pointing into the node tree, saying: "Your nodes are here!"

61.3.1.4   Context

The context node keeps changing as we step down the path. As each step is evaluated, the result is a set of nodes – in XPath talk, a *node-set*. The node-set could have one or more nodes, or it could be empty.

The next step is then evaluated for each member of that node-set. That is, each member is used as the context node for one of the evaluations of the next step. The node-sets selected by each of those evaluations are combined (except for any duplicates) to produce the result node-set.

Consider what happens in Example 61-5.

1. The XPath processor first evaluates the "/". The root node becomes the initial context node.
2. Next it looks for every child of the context node with the name "mydoc". There will be only one member of that node-set because XML allows only a single root element. It becomes the context node for the next step, which is evaluated only once.
3. Next the processor looks for all of the section children in the context of the mydoc element that have the appropriate attribute value and returns their node-set. The next step will be evaluated once for each selected section node, which is the context node for that evaluation.
4. We're almost done. The processor looks for the seventh para several times, once for each section in the node-set. It puts the selected para nodes together into the final node-set and returns a set of pointers to them: "Your nodes are here!".

The initial context does not always have to be the root node of the document. It depends on the environment or application. Whatever application (e.g. database or browser) or specification (e.g. XSLT or XPointer) is using XPath must specify the starting context.

In XSLT there is always a concept of the *current node*. That node is the context node for location paths that appear in XSLT transforms. In XPointer, the starting context is always the root node of the particular document, selected by its URI. In some sort of document database, we might be allowed to do a query across thousands of documents. The root node of each document would become the context node in turn. XPath itself does not have a concept of working with multiple documents but it can be used in a system that does.

In addition to the current node, an application could specify some other details of the context: it could supply some values for variables and functions that can be used in the XPath expression. It could also include namespace information that can be used to interpret prefixed names in a location path.

61.3.1.5 Axes

But wait. That's not all! Up to now we've always stepped down the tree, to a child element. But we can also step *up* the tree instead of down and step many levels instead of one.

We can step in directions that are neither up nor down but more like sideways. For example we can step from elements to attributes and from attributes to elements.

We can also step from an element directly to a child of a child of a child (a descendant).

These different ways of stepping are called *axes*.

For example, the *descendant axis* (abbreviated `//`) can potentially step down all the levels of the tree. The location path "`/mydoc//footnote`" would select all footnotes in the current document, no matter how many levels deep they occur.

The *parent axis* uses an abbreviated syntax (`..`) that is similar to that for going up a directory in a file system. For instance we could select all of the elements *containing* a footnote like this: "`/mydoc//footnote/..`".

The *attribute axis* (abbreviated "`@`") steps into the attribute nodes of an element.

The *namespace axis* is used for namespace information associated with an element node.

There are a number of less commonly used axes as well. You can find out more about them in the XPath specification.

61.3.1.6 Node tests

The attribute and namespace axes each have only one type of node, which is (necessarily!) its principal node type.

The other axes, however, have element as the principal node type but have comment, processing instruction, and text node types as well. We'll refer to such an axis as a *content axis* and its nodes as *content nodes*.

A step normally selects nodes of the principal type. In the case of content axes, a node test can be used to select another type. For example, the node test `text()` selects text nodes.

61.3.2 *Anatomy of a step*

We've now seen enough of the basics to take a formal look at the parts of a location step. There are three:

- An axis, which specifies the tree relationship between the context node and the nodes selected by the location step. Our examples so far have used the child axis.
- A node test, which specifies the node type of the nodes selected by the location step. The default type is element, unless the axis is one that can't have element nodes.
- Zero or more predicates, which use arbitrary expressions to further refine the set of nodes selected by the location step. The expressions are full-blown XPath expressions and can include function calls and location paths. In Example 61-5 the first predicate is a location path and the second uses an abbreviation for the `position()` function.

In this tutorial, we've only been using abbreviated forms of the XPath syntax, in which common constructs can often be omitted or expressed more concisely. Example 61-6 shows the unabbreviated form of Example 61-5. Note the addition of explicit axis names (`child` and `attribute`) and the `position()` function call.

Example 61-6. Unabbreviated form of Example 61-5

```
/child::mydoc/child::section[attribute::security="public"]
             /child::para[position()=7]
```

In the remainder of the chapter, we'll take a closer look at each of the three parts: node tests, axes, and predicates.

61.3.2.1 Node tests

Some node tests are useful in all axes; others only in content axes.
    Node tests for all axes are:

`*`

> any node of the principal type; i.e., element, attribute, or namespace.[6]

`node()`

> any node of any type

Node tests solely for content axes are:

`text()`

> any text node

`comment()`

> any comment node

`processing-instruction()`

> any processing-instruction node, regardless of its target name

`processing-instruction(target-name)`

> any processing-instruction node with the specified target name

Here are some examples of node tests used in a *content* axis:

`processing-instruction(cursor)`

> all nodes created from a processing instruction with the target name "cursor"

`part-nbr`

> all nodes created from an element with the element-type name `part-nbr`

`text()`

> all text nodes (contrast below)

`text`

> all nodes created from an element with the element type name `text`

---

6. The asterisk *cannot* be used as a prefix (`"*ara"`) or suffix (`"ara*"`) as it is in some regular-expression languages.

`*`

all nodes created from elements, irrespective of the element-type name

`node()`

all nodes created from elements (irrespective of the element-type name), contiguous character data, comments or processing instructions (irrespective of the target name)

61.3.2.2   Axes

The most important axes are described here.

61.3.2.2.1   *Child*

The default axis is the child axis. That means that if you ask for "`/section/para`" you are looking for a `para` in a `section`. If you ask merely for "`para`" you are looking for the `para` element children of the context node, whatever it is.

61.3.2.2.2   *Attribute*

When using the symbol "`@`" before either an XML name or the node test "`*`", one is referring to the attribute axis of the context node.

The attribute nodes are attached to an element node but the nodes are not ordered. There is no "first" or "third" attribute of an element.

Attribute nodes have a string-value that is the attribute value, and a name that is the attribute name.

Some examples of abbreviated references to attribute nodes attached to the context node are:

`@type`

an attribute node whose name is "`type`"

`@*`

all attributes of the context node, irrespective of the attribute name

61.3.2.2.3 *Descendant*

We can use the double-slash "//" abbreviation in a location path to refer to the descendant axis.[7] This axis includes not only children of the context node, but also all other nodes that are descendants of the context node.

This is a very powerful feature. We could combine this with the wildcard node test, for example, to select all elements in a document, other than the document element, no matter how deep they are: "/doc//*".

Some examples:

`/mydoc//part-nbr`

> all element nodes with the element-type name `part-nbr` that are descendants of the `mydoc` document element; that is, all of the `part-nbr` elements in the document

`/mydoc//@type`

> all attribute nodes named `type` attached to any descendant element of the `mydoc` document element; i.e., all of the `type` attributes in the document

`/mydoc//*`

> all elements that are descendants of the `mydoc` document element; i.e., every element in the document except the `mydoc` element itself

`/mydoc//comment()`

> all comment nodes that are descendants of the `mydoc` document element

`/mydoc//text()`

> all of the text nodes that are descendants of the `mydoc` document element; i.e., all of the character data in the document!

---

7. You may read in the XPath spec that the axis referred to by the abbreviation is actually the descendant-or-self axis. However, that is merely a technical device to enable the abbreviation to have the desired effect of referencing all descendants. The formal expansion of the abbreviation introduces another step, which would otherwise have caused children of the context node to be excluded. We refer to "//" as standing for the descendant axis because that's the way it acts.

We do not have to start descendant expressions with the document element. If we want to start somewhere farther into the document we can use "//" in any step anywhere in the location path.

We could also begin with "//". A location path that starts with "//" is interpreted as starting at the root and searching all descendants of it, including the document element.

61.3.2.2.4 Self

The self axis is unique in that it has only one node: the context node. This axis can solve an important problem.[8]

For instance in an XSLT transformation we might want to search for all descendants of the current node. If we begin with "//" the address will start at the root. We need a way to refer specifically to the current node.

A convenient way to do this is with an abbreviation: a period (.) stands for the context node.[9]

So ".//footnote" would locate all footnote descendants of the context node.

61.3.2.2.5 Parent

The parent axis (..) of a content node selects its parent, as the axis name suggests. For a namespace or attribute node, however, it selects the node's attached element.

You could therefore search an entire document for a particular attribute and then find out what element it is attached to: "//@confidential/..". You could go on to find out about the element's parent (and the parent's parent, etc.): "//@confidential/../..".

61.3.2.2.6 Ancestor

There is also a way of searching for an ancestor by name, but it does not have an abbreviated syntax. For example, "ancestor::section" would look for the ancestor(s) of the context node that are named "section".

---

8. In fact, we suspect it was invented for that purpose only. It is another ingenious hack, like the one in the previous footnote, for enabling convenient abbreviations to be mapped onto a coherent normalized form.

9. This "dot-convention" also comes from the file system metaphor. Unix and Windows use "." to mean the current directory.

This location path locates the titles of sections that contain images: "`//image/ancestor::section/title`".

61.3.3 *Our story so far*

Here are some examples of location paths using features we have covered so far:

`item`

> `item` element nodes that are children of the context node

`item/para`

> `para` element nodes that are children of `item` element nodes that are children of the context node; in other words, those `para` grandchildren of the context node whose parent is an `item`

`//para`

> `para` element nodes that are descendants of the root node; in other words, all the `para` element nodes in the entire document

`//item/para`

> `para` element nodes that are children of all `item` element nodes in the entire document

`//ordered-list//para`

> `para` element nodes that are descendants of all `ordered-list` element nodes in the entire document

`ordered-list//para/@security`

> `security` attribute nodes attached to all `para` element nodes that are descendants of all `ordered-list` element nodes that are children of the context node

`*/@*`

> attribute nodes attached to all element nodes that are children of the context node

```
../@*
```
attribute nodes attached to the parent or attached node of the context node

```
.//para
```
`para` element nodes that are descendants of the context node

```
.//comment()
```
comment nodes that are descendants of the context node

Tip   The XPath specification includes numerous other examples of location paths. You can find it on the CD-ROM.

61.3.4 *Predicates*

It is often important to filter nodes out of a node-set. We might filter out nodes that lack a particular attribute or subelement. We might filter out all but the first node. This sort of filtering is done in XPath through *predicates*. A predicate is an expression that is applied to each node. If it evaluates as false, the tested node is filtered out.

We'll discuss some common types of predicate expressions, then look at some examples.

61.3.4.1   Expression types

61.3.4.1.7 *Node-sets*

A location path expression can be used as a predicate. It evaluates to `true` if it selects any nodes at all. It is false if it does not select any nodes. So Example 61-7 would select all paragraphs that have a footnote child.

Example 61-7. Using a location path as a predicate
```
//para[footnote]
```

Recall that the evaluation of a step in the path results in a node-set, each member of which is a context node for an evaluation of the next step.[10]

One by one, each member of the result node-set, which in this case is every paragraph in the document, would get a chance to be the context node. It would either be selected or filtered out, depending on whether it contained any footnotes. Every paragraph would get its bright shining moment in the sun when it could be ".".[11]

A number of predicates can be chained together. Only nodes that pass all of the filters are passed on to the next step in the location path. For example, "//para[footnote][@important]" selects all paragraphs with important attributes and footnote children.

Like other location paths, those in predicates can have multiple steps with their own predicates. Consider the complex one in Example 61-8. It looks for sections with author child elements with qualifications child elements that have both professional and affordable attributes.

Example 61-8. A complex location path predicate

```
section[author/qualifications[@professional][@affordable]]
```

61.3.4.1.8 String-values

Not all predicates are location path expressions. Sometimes you do not want to test for the existence of some node. You might instead want to test whether an attribute has some particular value. That is different from testing whether the attribute exists or not.

Testing an attribute's value is simple: "@type='ordered'" tests whether the context node has a type attribute with value "ordered".

In XPath, every node type has a string-value. The value of an element node that is the context node, for example, is the concatenation of the string-values from the expression: ".//text()". In other words, it is all of the character data content anywhere within the element and its descendants.

---

10. In other words, Example 61-7 is really an abbreviation for "//para[./footnote]".

11. Unfortunately, the moment is brief and the price of failure is exclusion from the selection set.

So we can test the data content of a section's `title` child element with "`section[title='Doo-wop']`" and both of the sections in Example 61-9 would match.

Example 61-9. Matching sections

```
<section><title>Doo-wop</title>
...
</section>

<section><title>Doo-<emph>wop</emph></title>
...
</section>
```

61.3.4.1.9 *Context position*

There is more to the context in which an expression is evaluated than just the context node. Among the other things is the node's *context position*, which is returned by a function call: `position()=number`.

In practice, an abbreviation, consisting of the number alone, is invariably used. A number expression is evaluated as `true` if the number is the same as the context position.

Context position can be a tricky concept to grasp because it is, well, context sensitive. However, it is easy to understand for the most common types of steps.

In a step down the child axis (`a/b`) the context position is the position of the child node in the parent node. So "`doc/section[5]`" is the fifth section in a `doc`. In a step down the descendant axis (`a//b[5]`) it still refers to the position of the child node in its *parent node*, not its numerical order in the list of matching nodes.

XPath also has a function called "`last()`". We can use it to generate the number for the last node in a context: "`a//b[last()]`". We can also combine that with some simple arithmetic to get the next-to-last node: "`a//b[last()-1]`".

61.3.4.2 Predicate examples

Here are some examples, using the predicate types that we've discussed:

`item[3]`
> third `item` element child of the context node

`item[@type]/para`
> `para` element children of `item` elements that exhibit a `type` attribute and are children of the context node

`//list[@type='ordered']/item[1]/para[1]`
> first `para` element child of the first `item` element child of any `list` element that exhibits a `type` attribute with the string-value "ordered"

`//ordered-list[item[@type]/para[2]]//para`
> `para` elements descended from any `ordered-list` element that has an `item` child that exhibits a `type` attribute and has at least two `para` element children (whew!)

This last example is illustrated in Figure 61-3.

The XPath spec includes numerous other examples of using predicates. XPath is a powerful expression language, including operators and functions that operate on node-sets, numbers, strings, and booleans.

61.4 | ID function

The most common high-level expression in XPath is the location path, which we have explored in some detail. And, as we have seen, a location path can also be used at lower levels – as a predicate expression, for example.

Another form of expression that returns a node-set is a function call to the `id(string)` function. The main use of the function is to select the element node whose ID is the same as the string. For example, "`id('final')`". selects the element node whose unique identifier is "final".

An ID function and a location path can be used in the same expression. One way is to create the union of the two, as in Example 61-10. The result node-set is the element whose ID is "final", plus all `para` elements descended from `ordered-list` elements.

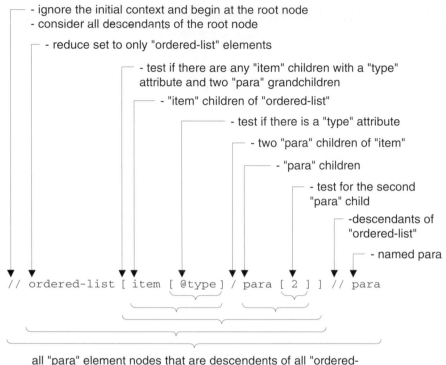

- ignore the initial context and begin at the root node
- consider all descendants of the root node
- reduce set to only "ordered-list" elements
- test if there are any "item" children with a "type" attribute and two "para" grandchildren
- "item" children of "ordered-list"
- test if there is a "type" attribute
- two "para" children of "item"
- "para" children
- test for the second "para" child
- descendants of "ordered-list"
- named para

```
// ordered-list [ item [ @type] / para [ 2 ] ] // para
```

all "para" element nodes that are descendents of all "ordered-list" element nodes of the entire document node tree that have at least two "para" element node children of an "item" child that has a "type" attribute specified or defaulted

Figure 61-3 Evaluating multiple steps

Example 61-10. Union expression

```
id('final') | /ordered-list//para
```

Another way to combine the two is to use the ID function as the initial context node of a location path, to create a path expression like that in Example 61-11. It locates the `title` child of the element whose ID is "A12345".

Example 61-11. Path expression

```
id('A12345')/title
```

Instead of a literal string, the argument could be a node whose string-value would be used, as in "`id(@IDREF)`". This expression locates the element referenced by the IDREF attribute of the context node.

61.5 | XPath's future

At this writing, the W3C is developing a new version of XPath and an XPath-based query language.

61.5.1 XPath 2.0

This version of XPath will have built-in handling for all *XML Schema* datatypes.

It will be especially useful to have built-in support for date and time calculations and ordering. Those sorts of operations are extremely difficult in XPath as it exists.

XPath 2.0 is also slated to have functions for doing mathematical set operations (union, intersection, difference etc.) on node lists and datatype sequences.

61.5.2 XML Query Language (XQuery)

There is also a new query language being developed that builds upon XPaths. *XQuery* will be a new context for using XPaths – a full query language for XML. Advocates distinguish it from XPath alone by pointing out that *XQuery* can return more than just selections of nodes from the input document: it can actually return XML fragments synthesized from information in XML documents. Example 61-12 shows a hypothetical example using a proposed syntax for *XQuery*.

Example 61-12. XQuery example

```
<emp empid = {@id}>
   {./name}
   {./job}
</emp>
```

This example generates a new `emp` element with an `empid` attribute from an `id` attribute and `name` and `job` sub-elements of the input document. XQuery's syntax is very much in flux so this example is only intended to get across the idea.

As we will see later, it is also possible to do these sorts of things using XSLT. XQuery uses a query approach ("find me some information, fit it into this pattern and return it") to the problem, while XSLT uses a transformational approach ("please transform this input document into a new vocabulary").

Although the approaches are different, there are tasks that can be accomplished either way. As time goes by it will become clearer when one approach is more appropriate than the other.

61.6 | Conclusion

XPath is an extremely powerful language and is destined to be as important in the XML world as SQL is in the relational world. Although XPath has depths that we could not address even in a "tad tougher" tutorial, we have covered all of the most common features.

With all these features one can very powerfully address the nodes of the XML data model. XPath is already in use in both XPointer and XSLT. Microsoft has added XPath support to its DOM through a function called "`selectNodes`". Future versions of the DOM will likely have XPath support as a standard feature. In short, XPath seems on track to become a central part of many XML systems.

XSL Transformations (XSLT)

Friendly Tutorial

- Template rules
- Patterns
- Templates
- Referencing stylesheets

Chapter

62

he *Extensible Stylesheet Language Transformations (XSLT)* is a spin-off of the *Extensible Stylesheet Language (XSL)*, which applies formatting to XML documents in a standard way.[1]

We've have seen XSLT used at a high level in the application chapters, now we'll look at the details of how it works. But be aware that the full details on XSLT could fill a book[2] and we don't cover them all here. The objective of this chapter is to provide a basic understanding for the way that XSLT stylesheets cause XML documents to be processed.

XSLT's processing model is very similar to that of many XML processing tools. Unlike general purpose programming languages, XML-aware tools can take care of some of the tedious parts of processing so that you can concentrate on your application needs. If you understand XSLT then you will be able to use other languages and systems much more effectively.

---

1. We discuss XSL in Chapter 63, "XSL formatting objects (XSL-FO)", on page 996.
2. The one we recommend is *Definitive XSLT and XPath* by Ken Holman, published in this series.

62.1 | Transformation vs. rendition

XSL is designed to apply style to an XML document by using XSLT to *transform* it into a rendition, represented by XSL formatting objects (XSL-FO). The XSL processor may then display the rendered document on a screen, print it, or convert it to some other rendition representation, such as PDF, PostScript, Microsoft's RTF, or even voice synthesis!

But "style" in the world of generalized markup encompasses every kind of processing. The transformation could be very powerful and complex, as XSLT can reorder, duplicate, suppress, sort, and add elements. There are many applications besides formatting where such transformations would be useful.

Consider an electronic commerce application where many companies must communicate. Each of their internal systems may use similar but different document types. To communicate they need to translate their various document types into a common one. An XSLT transformation provides a sophisticated but simple way to do so.

To summarize: name notwithstanding, XSLT is more than just a style language. While it can transform documents into XSL-FO renditions, it can also transform them into other XML abstractions, and into other rendered representations as well.

62.2 | XSLT stylesheets

Most XSLT looks more or less like ordinary XML. Simple XSLT stylesheets are merely a specialized form of XML markup designed for specifying the transformation of other XML documents. You can think of XSLT as just another document type.

The XSLT language defines element types and attributes, constrains them to occurring in particular places, and describes what they should look like. However, because of its heavy use of XML namespaces it is not possible in general to use a validating parser to ensure that an XSL document conforms to the XSL specification.

A stylesheet that transforms a document into another XML document might have a root element that looks like Example 62-1.

The root element is `xsl:stylesheet`. It must have a namespace declaration for XSLT. It makes sense to use the same declaration and `xsl:` prefix

Example 62-1. XSLT stylesheet using XML output elements

```
<xsl:stylesheet xmlns:xsl="http://www.w3.org/1999/XSL/Transform"
                version="1.0">
<xsl:output method="xml"/>
    <!-- template rules go here -->
</xsl:stylesheet>
```

every time. You can also specify the output method to be used by the processor, choosing between XML, HTML and plain text.

The `xsl:stylesheet` element is usually filled with template rules. The template rules describe how to transform elements in the source document. Of course almost every element type could be processed differently from every other element type so there are many rules in an XSLT stylesheet. Particular elements could even be processed differently if they share a type but have different attributes or occur in a different context.

62.3 | Using HTML with XSLT

Many XSLT implementations allow transformations from XML into HTML. This is good for serving to today's mainstream browsers (4.x and up) and the legacy (2.x, 3.x) browsers that most websites must still support.

It also takes advantage of many Web designers' knowledge of HTML. If you format a document using element types from HTML instead of from the formatting object vocabulary, the page will look to a browser as if it had been created in HTML directly. You can think of this process as a conversion from XML markup to HTML markup. Internet Explorer 5.0 can actually do this conversion right in the browser.

Because basic HTML is widely understood, we will use HTML element types in most of our examples. We will restrict our usage to only a few HTML types, namely:

- h1 and h2 element types for top-level and second-level headings,
- p element type for paragraphs
- body element type to contain the document's content; and the
- em element type to emphasize a series of characters.

A stylesheet that generates HTML elements might have a root element that looks like Example 62-2.

Example 62-2. XSLT stylesheet using HTML elements

```
<xsl:stylesheet xmlns:xsl="http://www.w3.org/1999/XSL/Transform"
                version="1.0">
<xsl:output method="html"/>
    <!-- template rules go here -->
</xsl:stylesheet>
```

There is a subtlety in how this transformation works. An XSLT stylesheet typically converts XML to XML. It is true that an XML document can look very much like an HTML document if it uses HTML element types, as we saw in our discussion of XHTML in 4.1.3, "Extensible HTML (XHTML)", on page 77.

However, XHTML is not quite what older browsers understand as HTML. Real HTML, for example, uses a different syntax for empty elements.

Fortunately, most XSLT processors can generate real HTML. The `xsl:output` instruction in Example 62-2 invokes this feature.

62.4 | Rules, patterns and templates

In the application sections of this book, we looked at many products that mapped parts of a source document into a result document. They did so to convert from a word processor file to XML, to create stylesheets, to convert from XML to a legacy data format, etc. Often, they used a graphical interface to allow the user to define the transformation and generated XSLT or some earlier or variant version of it, or proprietary equivalent.

In XSLT, the mapping construct is called a *template rule*. During XSLT processing every element, character, comment and processing instruction in an XML document is processed by some template rule. Some of them will be handled by template rules that the stylesheet writer created. Others are handled by *built-in* template rules that are hard-coded into every XSLT processor.

Template rules consist of two parts, the *pattern* and the *template*. Be careful with the terminology: a template is not a template rule. The pattern describes which source nodes (elements, textual data strings, comments or processing instructions) should be processed by the rule. The template describes the XML structure to generate when nodes are found that match the pattern.

In an XSLT stylesheet, a template rule is represented by an `xsl:template` element.[3] The pattern is the value of the `xsl:template` element's `match` attribute, and the template proper is the element's content.

Template rules are simple. You do not have to think about the order in which things will be processed, where data is stored or other housekeeping tasks that programming languages usually require you to look after. You just declare what you want the result to look like and the XSLT processor figures out how to make that happen. Because everything is done through declarations we say that XSL is a *declarative* language. One important benefit of declarative languages is that they are easy to *optimize*. Implementors can use various tricks and shortcuts in order to make them execute quickly.

62.5 | Creating a stylesheet

XSLT's processing model revolves around the idea of *patterns*. Patterns are XPath expressions designed to test nodes. Patterns allow the XSLT processor to choose which elements to apply which style rules to. XSLT's pattern language is basically XPath with a few extensions and restrictions. Patterns are used in the `match` attribute of template rules to specify which elements the rule applies to.

XPath expressions are also used in XSLT template rules to select other elements (and other nodes) so that the stylesheet can process them also.

62.5.1 *Document-level template rule*

Consider a document with a `book` element type which can contain `title`, `section` and `appendix` element types. `section` and `appendix` elements can contain `title`, `para` and `list` subelements. Titles contain `#PCDATA` and no subelements. Paragraphs and list items contain `emph` and `#PCDATA`. Example

---

3. It would have been clearer had they called it an `xsl:template-rule` element, but they didn't.

62-3 is a DTD that represents these constraints and Example 62-4 is an example document.

Example 62-3. DTD for book example

```
<!ELEMENT book (title, (section|appendix)+)>
<!ELEMENT section (title, (para|list)+)>
<!ELEMENT appendix (title, (para|list)+)>
<!ELEMENT title (#PCDATA)>
<!ELEMENT para (#PCDATA|emph)*>
<!ELEMENT emph (#PCDATA)>
<!ELEMENT list (item)+>
<!ELEMENT item (#PCDATA|emph)*>
```

Example 62-4. Book document instance

```
<book>
    <title>Chicken Soup for the Chicken's Soul</title>
    <section>
        <title>Introduction</title>
        <para>I've always wanted to write
            this book.</para>
    </section>
</book>
```

First the XSLT processor would examine the root element of the document. The XSLT processor would look for a rule that applied to books (a rule with a *match pattern* that matched a book). This sort of match pattern is very simple. Example 62-5 demonstrates.

Example 62-5. Simple match pattern

```
<xsl:template match="book">
  <!-- describe how books should be transformed -->
</xsl:template>
```

We can choose any basic structure for the generated book. Example 62-6 shows a reasonable one.

The template in this template rule generates a body to hold the content of the document. The tags for the body element are usually omitted in HTML but we will want to add some attributes to the element later. The body is called a *literal result element*.

Example 62-6. Generated book structure

```
<xsl:template match="book">
  <body>
    <h1><!-- handle title --></h1>
    <!-- handle sections -->
    <hr/> <!-- HTML horizontal rule -->
    <h2>Appendices</h2>
    <!-- handle appendices -->
    <hr/>
    <p>Copyright 2000, the establishment.</p>
  </body>
</xsl:template>
```

62.5.2 *Literal result elements*

The XSLT processor knows to treat body as a *literal result element* that is copied into the output because it is not an XSLT instruction (formally, it is not in the XSLT namespace). Elements in templates that are not part of the XSLT namespace are treated literally and copied into the output. You can see why these are called templates! They describe the form of the result document both by ordering content and by generating literal result elements. If the XSLT processor supports legacy HTML output, and the HTML output method is being used to serialize the result, then it will know to use legacy HTML conventions.

The h1, h2 and hr elements are also literal result elements that will create HTML headings and horizontal rules. The stylesheet is represented in XML so the specification for the horizontal rule can use XML empty-element syntax. Finally the document has a literal result element and literal text representing the copyright. XSLT stylesheets can introduce this sort of *boilerplate* text.

62.5.3 *Extracting data*

The template also has comments describing things we still have to handle: the document's title, its sections and the appendices.

We can get the data content from the title element with the xsl:value-of instruction. It has a select attribute which is a pattern. If this pattern names a simple element type then it will match a subelement of the *current* element.

In this case the current element is the `book` element. That is the element matched by the `match` attribute. Example 62-7 shows what that would look like.

Example 62-7. Extracting data from a subelement

```
<h1><xsl:value-of select="title"/></h1>
```

62.5.4 *The* `apply-templates` *instruction*

The next step is to handle sections and appendices. We could do it in one of two ways. We could either create a new template rule for handling sections or we could handle sections directly in the `book` template rule.

The benefit of creating a new rule is that it can be used over and over again. Before we create the new rule we should ensure it will get invoked at the right point. We will use a new instruction, `xsl:apply-templates`. Example 62-8 shows this instruction.

Example 62-8. The `xsl:apply-templates` instruction

```
<xsl:apply-templates select="section"/>
```

The `xsl:apply-templates` instruction does two important things.

1. It finds all nodes that match the `select` attribute pattern.
2. It processes each of these in turn. It does so by finding and applying the template rule that matches each node.

This important principle is at the heart of XSLT's processing model.

In this case, the *select* pattern in the `xsl:apply-templates` element selects all of the book's subelements of type `section`. The `xsl:apply-templates` instruction always searches out the rule that is appropriate for each of the selected nodes. In this case the `xsl:apply-templates` instruction will search out a rule that applies to sections. The expanded template is in Example 62-9.

Example 62-9. Handling section elements

```
<xsl:template match="book">
  <body>
    <h1><xsl:value-of select="title"/></h1>
    <xsl:apply-templates select="section"/>
    <hr/>
    <h2>Appendices</h2>
    <xsl:apply-templates select="appendix"/>
    <p>Copyright 2000, the establishment</p>
  </body>
</xsl:template>
```

62.5.5 *Handling optional elements*

Our sample document does not have appendices but the stylesheet should support anything that the DTD allows. Documents created in the future may have appendices.

Our stylesheet generates the title element followed by section elements (in the order that they occurred in the document) followed by appendix elements (also in *document order*).

If our DTD allowed more than one title subelement in a book element then this stylesheet would generate them all. There is no way for a stylesheet to require that the document have a single title. These sorts of constraints are specified in the DTD.

Our DTD does permit documents to have no appendices. Our title and horizontal rule separating the appendices from the sections would look fairly silly in that case. XSLT provides an instruction called xsl:if that handles this situation. We can wrap it around the relevant parts as shown in Example 62-10.

Example 62-10. Using xsl:if

```
  <xsl:if test="appendix">
    <hr/>
    <h2>Appendices</h2>
    <xsl:apply-templates select="appendix"/>
  </xsl:if>
```

The xsl:if instruction goes within a template. We could drop it into our book template as a replacement for our current appendix handling.

The instruction also contains another template within it. The contained template is only instantiated (generated) if there is some element that matches the pattern `appendix` exhibited by the `test` attribute.

As with the `select` attribute, the context is the current node. If there is no node that matches the pattern in the `test` attribute then the entire contained template will be skipped.

There is another instruction called `xsl:choose` that allows for multiple alternatives, including a default template for when none of the other alternatives match.

62.5.6 *Reordering the output*

If the DTD had allowed titles, sections and appendices to be mixed together our stylesheet would reorder them so that the title preceded the sections and the sections preceded the appendices.

This ability to reorder is very important. It allows us to use one structure in our abstract representation and another in our rendition. The internal structure is optimized for editing, validating and processing convenience. The external structure is optimized for viewing and navigation.

Reordering is easy when you know exactly the order in which you want elements of various types to be processed. In the case of the body, for example: titles before sections before appendices. But within a section or appendix, reordering is somewhat trickier because we don't know the complete output order.

That is, we need to process titles before any of the paragraphs or lists, but we cannot disturb the relative order of the paragraphs and lists themselves. Those have to be generated in the document order.

We can solve this fairly easily. In DTD syntax the vertical bar (|) character means "or". It means the same in XPath pattern syntax. So we can make a rule like the one in Example 62-11.

Example 62-11. The section rule

```
<xsl:template match="section">
    <h2><xsl:value-of select="title"/></h2>
    <xsl:apply-templates select="para|list"/>
</xsl:template>
```

This rule forces titles (in our DTD there can be only one) to be handled first and paragraphs and lists to be processed in the order that they are found. The rule that we already defined for paragraphs will automatically be selected when paragraphs appear.

62.5.7 *Sharing a template rule*

Next we can handle appendices. If we wrote out the rule for appendices we would find it to be identical to sections. We could just copy the rule but XSLT has a more elegant way. We can amend our rule for appendices to say that the rule applies to sections *or* appendices. Example 62-12 demonstrates.

Example 62-12. Handling sections and appendices

```
<xsl:template match="section|appendix">
    <h2><xsl:value-of select="title"/></h2>
    <xsl:apply-templates select="para|list"/>
</xsl:template>
```

62.5.8 *Data content*

Next we can handle paragraphs. We want them each to generate a single HTML element. We also want them to generate their content to populate that element in the order that the content occurs, not in some pre-defined template order.

We need to process all of the paragraph's *subnodes*. That means that we cannot just handle emph subelements. We must also handle ordinary character data. Example 62-13 demonstrates this.

Example 62-13. Paragraph rule

```
<xsl:template match="para">
    <p><xsl:apply-templates select="node()"/>
    </p>
</xsl:template>
```

As you can see, the rule for paragraphs is very simple. The `xsl:apply-templates` instruction handles all of the bookkeeping parts for us. The `select` attribute matches all nodes: element nodes, text nodes, etc. If it encounters a text node it copies it to the result; that is a *default* rule built into XSLT. If it encounters a subelement, it processes it using the appropriate rule.

XSLT handles much of the complexity for us but we should still be clear: transformations will not always be this easy. These rules are so simple because our DTD is very much like HTML. The more alike the source and result DTDs are the simpler the transformation will be. It is especially helpful to have a very loose or flexible result DTD. HTML is perfect in this regard.

62.5.9 *Handling inline elements*

`emph` follows the same basic organization as paragraph. Mixed content (character-containing) elements often use this organization. The HTML element-type name is `em` (Example 62-14). Note that in this case we will use an abbreviated syntax for the `xsl:apply-templates` element: Because the `select` attribute defaults to `node()`, we can leave it out.

Example 62-14. Handling emphasis

```
<xsl:template match="emph">
    <em><xsl:apply-templates/></em>
</xsl:template>
```

List items also have mixed content, so we should look at the rules for lists and list items next. They are in Example 62-15.

Example 62-15. List and item rules

```
<xsl:template match="list">
    <ol>
        <xsl:apply-templates/>
    </ol>
</xsl:template>
<xsl:template match="item">
    <li><xsl:apply-templates/></li>
</xsl:template>
```

The rules in Example 62-14 and Example 62-15 work together. When a `list` is detected the literal result element is processed and an `ol` element is generated. It will contain a single `li` element for each `item`. Each `li` will in turn contain text nodes (handled by the default rule) and `emph` (handled by the `emph` rule).

62.5.10 *Final touches*

We now have a complete stylesheet but it is rather basic. We might as well add a background color to beautify it a bit. HTML allows this through the `bgcolor` attribute of the `body` element. We will not go into the details of the HTML color scheme but suffice to say that Example 62-16 gives our document a nice light purple background.

Example 62-16. Adding a background color

```
<xsl:template match="book">
  <body bgcolor="#FFDDFF">
    <title><xsl:value-of select="title"/></title>
    <h1><xsl:value-of select="title"/></h1>
    <xsl:apply-templates select="section"/>
    <xsl:if test="appendix">
      <hr/>
      <h2>Appendices</h2>
      <xsl:apply-templates select="appendix"/>
    </xsl:if>
    <p>Copyright 2000, the establishment</p>
  </body>
</xsl:template>
```

There is also one more detail we must take care of. We said earlier that the more flexible a document type is the easier it is to transform to. Even though HTML is pretty flexible it does have one unbreakable rule. Every document must have a `title` element. We've handled the `title` element from the source as a heading but HTML has different concepts of heading and title. The title shows up in the window's title bar, in the bookmark list and in search engine result lists. We need the document's title to appear as both the HTML title and as a heading element. Luckily XSLT allows us to duplicate data.

With these additions our stylesheet is complete! It is shown in Example 62-17.

Example 62-17. Complete stylesheet

```
<?xml version="1.0"?>
<xsl:stylesheet xmlns:xsl="http://www.w3.org/1999/XSL/Transform"
                version="1.0">
<xsl:output method="html"/>

<xsl:template match="book">
  <body bgcolor="#FFDDFF">
    <title><xsl:value-of select="title"/></title>
    <h1><xsl:value-of select="title"/></h1>
    <xsl:apply-templates select="section"/>
    <hr/>
    <xsl:if test="appendix">
      <hr/>
      <h2>Appendices</h2>
      <xsl:apply-templates select="appendix"/>
    </xsl:if>
    <p>Copyright 2000, the establishment</p>
  </body>
</xsl:template>

<xsl:template match="para">
    <p><xsl:apply-templates/></p>
</xsl:template>

<xsl:template match="section|appendix">
    <xsl:apply-templates select="title"/>
    <xsl:apply-templates select="para|list"/>
</xsl:template>

<xsl:template match="emph">
    <em><xsl:apply-templates/></em>
</xsl:template>

<xsl:template match="list">
    <ol>
        <xsl:apply-templates/>
    </ol>
</xsl:template>

<xsl:template match="item">
    <li><xsl:apply-templates/></li>
</xsl:template>
</xsl:stylesheet>
```

As you can see, simple XSLT transformations can be quite simple – evidence of XSLT's good design. The important thing for you to recognize is that the basic XSLT processing model is based on template rules, patterns and templates. Flow of control between rules is handled by special instructions. In fact this processing model is ubiquitous in XML processing.

62.6 | Top-level instructions

XSLT also allows you to do more complex things. It supports all of XPath, sophisticated selections, stylesheet reuse and many other advanced features. We will introduce a few of these in this section, but remind you that the preview book on the CD goes into much more detail.

Top-level instructions are those that go directly in the `xsl:transform` or `xsl:stylesheet` elements. They do not apply to any particular template but rather declare behaviors, variables and other things that affect the entire stylesheet. Except for `xsl:import` instructions, the order of top-level statements is not important. As the XSLT specification says: "Users are free to order the elements as they prefer, and stylesheet creation tools need not provide control over the order in which the elements occur."

62.6.1 Stylesheet combination

The `xsl:include` instruction includes another stylesheet. Stylesheets may not include themselves directly or indirectly. The instructions in an included stylesheet are treated exactly as if they had been typed directly in the including stylesheet. They are not second-class in any sense. Example 62-18 demonstrates the inclusion of other stylesheets through both absolute and relative URL references.

Example 62-18. Including another stylesheet

```
<xsl:include href="http://.../currency.xsl"/>
<xsl:include href="bonds.xsl"/>
```

Importing is a little bit different from *including*. Just as in the real world, things that are imported get taxed! In the XSLT context that means that they are second class. Imported rules only take effect when no rule in the main stylesheet matches. Also, import statements earlier in the document take precedence over later ones.

Import instructions *must* go at the top of a stylesheet, before other instructions in the `xsl:stylesheet` or `xsl:template` element. A stylesheet must not directly or indirectly import itself. Example 62-19 demonstrates the importation of other stylesheets through both absolute and relative URL references.

Example 62-19. Importing another stylesheet

```
<xsl:import href="http://.../stocks.xsl"/>
<xsl:import href="credit-cards.xsl"/>
```

62.6.2 *Keys*

Keys allow you to look up elements based on names, but they let you decide what attributes or subelements serve as the names. XML has a built-in element naming construct – the ID attribute – but it has several not appropriate for all naming tasks.

Consider this case: every employee in your company has a unique employee ID. Therefore it makes sense to use the `employeeID` attribute as a unique identifier for `employee` elements. You can do that by declaring its attribute type to be `ID`.

Perhaps your company also has elements for machines, with attributes for machine names. You might think it a good idea to declare `machineName` to have the attribute type `ID` as well.

But don't!

The software that generates user IDs and machine names probably has nothing to do with XML. It may be an ancient mainframe program or a brand new directory server. Either way, it has no reason to ensure that a person's `employeeID` never clashes with a machine's `machineName`.

If such a clash ever happens, XML will complain that an `employeeID` attribute has the same value as a `machineName` attribute. The problem is that XML has a single, document-wide namespace for values of ID attribute types. It has no idea that you are trying to name real-world objects, not just XML elements.

Caution The name of an individual element – its unique ID – is not the name that occurs first in the element's start-tag. That name is the element-type name, which is shared by all elements of that type. It is not the element name, as there is no construct called that in XML. Unfortunately, even people who should know better are guilty of using this, er, misnomer!

There are ways to avoid this difficulty. The most common technique is just to not use XML's ID feature for the conflicting attributes. Instead, declare the attribute's type to be NMTOKEN (or some other type) in the DTD or schema.

Another approach is to use *keys*. Keys allow a stylesheet author to tell XSLT that the employeeID attribute can serve as a unique identifier of an employee element. The word "key" is used in the database sense: it is a unique value that can be used to identify individual objects.

In this sense, "person name" is a key in a phone book. Actually that is not strictly true – two people can have the same name. That is why most phone books also publish addresses. The name and the address can be used together to form a key. XSLT keys allow this also. Two or more attributes, subelements, or other values can be combined using XPath string combination functions. Then they can be used together as a key.

You can also index a single element by multiple keys. For instance, employee elements could be indexed in one context by employee IDs and in another context by social-security numbers, depending on what you are trying to accomplish. We will not go into detail but we will give an example to give you a feeling for the flavor of declaring XSLT attributes. Example 62-20 shows a sample document.

In the sample document, employees are uniquely identified both by employee IDs and social security numbers. We will not presume that their names are unique because in large companies they are typically not.

Names are only useful if they are referenced somewhere. Elsewhere in the input document there is a description of departments. Departments are composed of references to employees by the employee ID (Example 62-21).

Example 62-20. Sample input for the stylesheet

```
<employees>
<employee employeeID="e98302">
  <social-security>000-00-0000</social-security>
  <name>Anthony Sobers</name>
</employee>
<employee employeeID="e02322">
  <social-security>111-11-1111</social-security>
  <name>Mossy Rock</name>
</employee>
</employees>
```

Example 62-21. Referring to employee elements

```
<department>
  <person empid="e98302" />
  <person empid="e02322" />
</department>
```

Keys are not declared in the XML file nor in the DTD or schema. They are declared in the XSLT stylesheet. Example 62-22 demonstrates.

Example 62-22. Declaring keys

```
<xsl:stylesheet ...>
...

    <xsl:key name="employees-by-id"
             match="employee"
             use="@employeeID"/>
    <xsl:key name="employees-by-ss"
             match="employee"
             use="social-security"/>
...
</xsl:stylesheet>
```

Every key has a name. There must only be one key with a particular name. Each key has a `match` attribute. It defines what nodes (typically elements) are addressed by the key. The `use` attribute says what value to use as the key value. In one case we are using an attribute of the element named `employeeID`. In the other case we are using the content of a subelement named `social-security`.

When we refer to the key we will use the key function. We supply the key name and a value. The XSLT processor computes a value for each node matched by the match attribute based on the use attribute. One and only one node should have the value we are looking for. That node will be returned. Example 62-23 demonstrates key use in a portion of an XSLT stylesheet.

Example 62-23. Using keys

```
<xsl:value-of select='key("employees-by-id","e98302")/name'/>
<xsl:value-of select='key("employees-by-ss","000-00-0000")/name'/>
```

It would be quite rare to use specific employee IDs or numbers in a stylesheet (unless the employee is very important!). More likely you would use a rule that processes person elements within department elements, based on empid attributes, as in Example 62-24.

Example 62-24. Using keys without explicit numbers

```
<xsl:template match="person">
Name: <xsl:value-of
        select='key("employees-by-id",@empid)/name'/>
Social: <xsl:value-of
        select='key("employees-by-id",@empid)/social-security'/>
</xsl:template>
```

62.6.3 *Whitespace handling*

In machine-to-machine applications, whitespace nodes are usually irrelevant. Even in POP-oriented applications, some whitespace is not important for processing. A new line between two section elements is just intended to make the source XML easier to read. It is not intended to affect what is seen by the ultimate readers of the rendered document.

As we saw in Figure 61-2, whitespace nodes are ordinary text nodes that happen to have only whitespace (tab, space, newline) characters in them. Nodes T2, T4, and T5 in that figure are examples.

XSLT has a feature that allows you to strip out these whitespace-only nodes based on what element they are contained within. The xsl:strip-space instruction strips space from elements of specified types in the source document. Example 62-25 shows how you would strip space from address and date elements.

Example 62-25. Stripping space

```
<xsl:strip-space elements="address date"/>
```

In some vocabularies, all element types are space-stripping. You can accomplish this by using an asterisk in the xsl:strip-space instruction. (Example 62-26)

Example 62-26. Strip space from all elements

```
<xsl:strip-space elements="*"/>
```

If a vocabulary has only a few non-whitespace stripping elements (*whitespace-preserving elements*), you can selectively override the blanket stripping statement with the xsl:preserve-space instruction. By default, whitespace is preserved.

62.6.4   *Output descriptions*

The xsl:output instruction sets various options that control what the stylesheet should generate as output. The main attribute in the instruction is the method attribute, which typically takes a value like "xml", "html" or "text".

"xml" is appropriate for (surprise!) generating XML; it is the default. "html" uses html conventions for empty-elements, processing instructions and similar constructs. The "text" output is useful when you want to generate plain text without the XSLT processor representing delimiter characters like less-than signs (<) as <, and so forth.

Other attributes can control whether the output is indented for "pretty printing", what character encoding to use, whether to add an XML declaration and/or document type declaration and other (even more obscure) output options. Most XSLT stylesheets will not need to change these options.

But if you find that the output of your stylesheet is not quite what you would expect, then xsl:output may have the answer for you.

62.6.5 *Numeric formats*

The `xsl:decimal-format` instruction allows you to describe how decimal numbers will be printed by your stylesheet. For instance, you can use this to change the character that is used to separate the decimals from the integral part of the number. Using this feature you could set that option to period for North Americans and comma for Europeans.

Other options allow you to change the "grouping-separator" between the billions, millions and thousands and to choose characters or strings to represent "infinity", "minus", "percent", "per-mille" (per thousand), "the zero digit" and "Not a number". The latter is used for error handling.

62.6.6 *Attribute sets*

`xsl:attribute-set` allows you to define a reusable set of attributes. If you have several different types of images that must share certain attributes then it is more efficient to define those in an attribute set than to repeat them all in each template rule. Example 62-27 demonstrates the basic idea.

Example 62-27 Reusable set of attribute values

```
<xsl:attribute-set name="big-image">
    <xsl:attribute name="width">500px</xsl:attribute>
    <xsl:attribute name="height">500px</xsl:attribute>
</xsl:attribute-set>
<xsl:attribute-set name="small-image">
    <xsl:attribute name="width">100px</xsl:attribute>
    <xsl:attribute name="height">100px</xsl:attribute>
</xsl:attribute-set>

... in a template ...
<img xsl:use-attribute-sets="big-image">
```

62.6.7 *Namespace alias*

Just as `xsl:output` helps you to solve the problem of how to treat a less-than sign as an ordinary data character, `xsl:namespace-alias` helps you to treat a namespace prefixed literal result element as just a literal result element, even if the namespace happens to be XSLT! This sounds strange but it could happen if you were writing an XSLT stylesheet that generates an XSLT stylesheet. Needless to say, this is not a common situation so we will not dwell on it further.

62.7 | Variables and parameters

XSLT variables and parameters are closely related. A variable is a value that a stylesheet creator stores away for use in some other part of the stylesheet. A top-level variable is one defined outside of any template. The value is automatically available for use in any template. For instance a variable could hold the company name. The value that the variable holds could even be extracted from the input XML document. Example 62-28 demonstrates.

Example 62-28. Defining a variable

```
<xsl:variable name="company-name" select="/doc/creator/company"/>
```

Variables can be referred to in XPath instructions by preceding the variable name with a dollar-sign ($). Example 62-29 demonstrates.

Example 62-29. Referencing a variable

```
<xsl:value-of select="$company-name"/>
```

A parameter is just like a variable except that the value can be overridden. How it would be overridden depends on your XSLT implementation. Command-line XSLT transformation engines typically use command-line options. Graphical environments might use options in a graphical user interface. In other words, parameters are user options that change the stylesheet's behavior. They are declared and referenced just as variables are. Example 62-30 demonstrates.

Example 62-30. Defining a parameter

```
<xsl:param name="company-name" select="/doc/creator/company"/>
```

The `select` attribute of a parameter is used as a *default value*. If the user chooses not to supply a parameter (or forgets), the default value is used.

It is also possible to have templates and parameters within templates. In that case, they are only available within that template. Parameters for a particular template are passed not from the user, but from other templates. For instance a template for a chapter might use a parameter to pass the chapter number to a template for a section. That way the section number could be derived from the chapter number easily (e.g. Section 5.4).

62.8 | Extending XSLT

XSLT permits customized extensions (the "X" in "XSLT"), supported by an XSLT processor.

The XSLT language has a mechanism that allows you to call into a component written in any programming language. You could refer to a *Java* class file, Python program, Perl script or an ActiveX control. You could even embed a small script from a scripting language such as *Javascript* or *Python*. The function can be defined right in your stylesheet!

62.9 | Referencing XSLT stylesheets

There is a W3C Recommendation that specifies how XML documents should refer to their stylesheets. Here is the relevant text:

Spec Excerpt (xml-ss) 62-1. The `xml-stylesheet` processing instruction

The `xml-stylesheet` processing instruction is allowed anywhere in the prolog of an XML document. The processing instruction can have pseudo-attributes `href` (required), `type` (required), `title` (optional), `media` (optional), `charset` (optional).

These are called *pseudo-attributes* instead of attributes. Although they use attribute syntax, they do not describe properties of an element. In real XML terms, only elements can have attributes. The only real syntactic difference between pseudo-attributes and attributes is that you must use pseudo-attributes in the order they are defined. You can use attributes in any order.

The most important pseudo-attributes for this processing instruction are `href`, which supplies a URI for the stylesheet, and `type`, which says that the stylesheet is in XSLT and not DSSSL, CSS, or some other stylesheet language.

You can also supply a `title` that the browser might use when offering a list of stylesheet choices. The `media` option allows you to specify what medium the stylesheet is for. You could, for example, have different stylesheets for print (with footnotes and page breaks), online (with clickable links), television (large text and easy scroll controls) and telephone (read aloud using inflection to render emphasis).

Example 62-31 is a sample stylesheet processing instruction (PI).

Example 62-31. Stylesheet PI

```
<?xml-stylesheet href="http://www.xmlbooks.com/memo.xsl"
                 type="text/xsl"?>
```

You can also provide multiple PIs to allow for choice by media, title or stylesheet language. Example 62-32 demonstrates this.

Example 62-32. Alternative stylesheets

```
<?xml-stylesheet rel=alternate
                 href="mystyle1.xsl"
                 title="Fancy"
                 type="text/xsl"?>
<?xml-stylesheet
                 rel=alternate
                 href="mystyle2.css"
                 title="Simple"
                 type="text/css"?>
<?xml-stylesheet
                 rel=alternate
                 href="mystyle2.aur"
                 title="Aural"
                 type="text/aural"?>
```

XSL formatting objects (XSL-FO)

- Extensible Stylesheet Language (XSL)

- Rendition on steroids!

- Introductory example

Chapter 63

T he *Extensible Stylesheet Language (XSL)* project was originally undertaken by the World Wide Web Consortium to develop
a recommendation for applying formatting to XML documents
in a standard way. Over time a part of XSL called the *XSL Transformations (XSLT)* evolved into an independently useful language for transforming one XML document to another. It is now a separately published
approved recommendation. We discuss it in Chapter 62, "XSL Transformations (XSLT)", on page 970.[1]

The remainder of the original XSL is also an approved recommendation.
It defines the semantics of formatting, in the form of a processing model
and catalog of *XSL formatting objects (XSL-FO)*, represented as XML elements. XSL supports both online and print publishing.

Under the covers, XSL borrows from two other specifications: *DSSSL*
and *CSS*.

---

1. XSLT in turn gave birth to XPath, which is discussed in Chapter 61, "XML
   Path Language (XPath)", on page 940.

DSSSL

Document Style Semantics and Specification Language is a very powerful International Standard from the ISO. DSSSL provides the transformational template application paradigm that XSLT uses.

CSS

The *Cascading Stylesheet Language*, is a popular World Wide Web Consortium specification. CSS provides much of XSL's formatting model.

63.1 | Rendition on steroids!

As we saw in Chapter 62, "XSL Transformations (XSLT)", on page 970, style is applied to XML documents by using XSLT to transform them into XSL formatting object documents. The XML *source* documents are usually marked up according to their abstract structure, with no markup (in theory at least) that is tailored for style application or any other particular kind of processing.

XSL and XSLT, therefore, form the "missing link" between the abstract data that is intended for computer processing and the formatted rendition required for comfortable reading. In technical terms, the document is transformed from an abstraction to a rendition.

Simple stylesheet languages such as CSS help documents to put on a little make-up. XSL and XSLT allow them to get a complete make-over.

XSLT can, among other things:

- move end-notes to the end of a document;
- duplicate the title of a chapter so that it appears not only in the chapter, but also in the page running head and in the table of contents;
- suppress a corporation's internal annotations and metadata;
- sort the names in a phone directory; and
- add boilerplate text such as a copyright or corporate logo.

In fact, XSLT does not so much apply a makeover as perform complete Cher-style plastic surgery!

An XSL implementation must support both the XSLT transformation to XSL-FO, plus the rendition of XSL-FO into PDF or some other page description or device stream. That could be done all at once by a single program, or in two steps:

1. XSLT transformation to an intermediate XSL-FO document.
2. Rendition of the XSL-FO document.

Note   This division of labor, not to mention the division of the XSL Recommendation itself, raises the burning question: Is a stylesheet XSL or XSLT? All stylesheets are XSLT. Those that use XSL formatting objects could also be called XSL stylesheets. However, in order to keep the process clear, in this book we use "XSLT" to characterize all stylesheets and "XSL" only for formatting objects.

63.2 | A simple stylesheet example

A stylesheet that uses the XSL formatting objects might have a root element that looks like Example 63-1.

Example 63-1. XSLT stylesheet using XSL formatting objects

```
<xsl:stylesheet xmlns:xsl="http://www.w3.org/1999/XSL/Transform"
                xmlns:fo="http://www.w3.org/1999/XSL/Format"
                version="1.0">
<xsl:output method="xml"/>
    <!-- template rules go here -->
</xsl:stylesheet>
```

Note that the output is XML. The only indication that we are using XSL-FO is the declaration of the `fo` namespace.

Let's start simply, with a style that says "Paragraphs should use a 12pt font" and "Titles should be 20 point and boldfaced." Example 63-2 adds two template rules to apply font styles to titles and paragraphs.

The rules say that whenever the XSLT processor encounters a PARA or TITLE element in an XML document, it should create a `fo:block` element.

Example 63-2. Example 62-1 with two rules added

```
<?xml version="1.0"?>
<xsl:stylesheet xmlns:xsl="http://www.w3.org/1999/XSL/Transform"
                xmlns:fo="http://www.w3.org/1999/XSL/Format"
                version="1.0">
<xsl:output method="xml"/>

    <xsl:template match="PARA">
        <fo:block font-size="12pt">
            <xsl:apply-templates/>
        </fo:block>
    </xsl:template>

    <xsl:template match="TITLE">
        <fo:block font-size="20pt" font-weight="bold">
            <xsl:apply-templates/>
        </fo:block>
    </xsl:template>

</xsl:stylesheet>
```

Because the result uses the formatting object vocabulary, an XSL processor should proceed to render the document. A renderer could also be a separate software component or program, such as a word processor or Web browser.

The renderer (word processor, browser etc.) generates a block (fo:block) of text on the screen which is separated from the text above and below it. This makes sense. Visually a paragraph is just a text block set off from other text.

The fo:block element has an attribute called font-size. This attribute is also defined by the XSL specification and will be properly interpreted by the XSL processor in the rendition stage.

Similarly, this stylesheet will look for title elements and make them bold and 20pt.

Let's take a closer look at those formatting objects.

63.3 | Formatting objects

Imagine taking an XML "manuscript" and typing it into a word processor. You would have to use the constructs provided by the word processor, such as paragraphs, bulleted lists, hypertext links and so on. In XSL terms, those constructs are the formatting objects.

XSL stylesheets will typically contain block, display graphic, display rule (for horizontal rules), table formatting objects and so forth. A table formatting object might itself contain blocks. The blocks would contain characters, and also "sequence" formatting objects that would apply formatting like italics and bold to sequences of characters.

Conceptually, these objects form a tree. The page (or Web page) is the root. Paragraphs, tables, sequences and other "container" objects are the branches, and characters, graphics and other indivisible objects are the leaves. This tree of formatting objects is called the "formatting object tree." XML documents also describe a tree so it is logical that the formatting tree should also be an XML document.

Every formatting object has *properties*. The exact set of properties that a formatting object exhibits depends on its *class*. For example, blocks may specify the space before and after the block, clickable links may specify their destinations, characters may specify their font sizes, and pictures may specify their heights and widths.

The fo:root is the root element and contains everything else. It is illustrated in Figure 63-1.

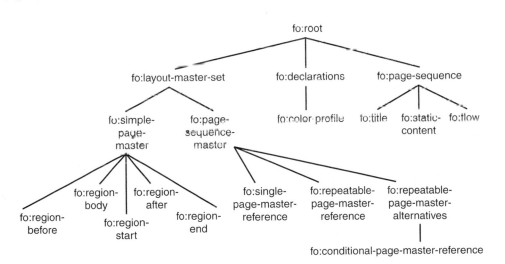

Figure 63-1   Formatting objects for pagination

Within the root you can have one or more `fo:page-sequence` elements. Each represents a series of pages – either print pages or Web pages. The main content of the document goes into `fo:flow` elements.

There are several different types of "block-level" objects that are allowed within a `fo:flow`. A few of these are listed next as a representative subset.

`fo:block`

> The `fo:block` element type holds a block of text. It can be used for paragraphs, titles, block quotations and so forth. Blocks have a huge number of properties for changing the background color, background image, font size, padding (space around block), orphans (handling of page breaks) and so forth.

`fo:external-graphic`

> The `fo:external-graphic` element type allows you to create a graphic that is formatted inline (between characters). You could use that for icons. The image is specified through a URI.

`fo:leader`

> The `fo:leader` element type creates a horizontal or vertical line. It has properties for changing the color, length, width and style (solid, dotted, dashed).

`fo:table`

> The `fo:table` element type is used for tables. It has a *table model* similar to (but not identical to) that used by HTML.

`fo:list-block`

> The `fo:list-block` element type represents a list. It can contain a sequence of `fo:list-item` elements, representing the list items, which are pairs of `fo:list-item-label`, `fo:list-item-body` elements. The label/item pairs could be used for a dictionary; the words would be the labels and the definitions would be the items. The labels could also be used for bullets or numbers in unordered and ordered lists.

`fo:basic-link`

> The `fo:basic-link` element type allows you to create hypertext clickable links to a destination specified by a URI or to another

element in the formatting object tree. This element type allows XLinks to be rendered.

`fo:page-number`

The `fo:page-number` element type generates a page number for printed documents.

> *Note* There are something over fifty formatting object types, so a complete discussion would take another book!

63.4 | Conclusion

XSL is at one time a work in progress and also a runaway success. Industry support for its spin-off, XSLT, is clear, but support for the XSL formatting capability that motivated the creation of XSLT is just beginning to take shape.

The XSL formatting object vocabulary is much more sophisticated, but also more complicated, than the HTML vocabulary that is so popular as a transformation target today. Even so, tools are already beginning to embrace the new spec.[2]

_____

2. In fact, several titles in this book series are produced using XSL.

XML Pointer Language (XPointer)

Friendly Tutorial

- Uniform Resource Identifiers (URI)

- URI references

- ID references with XPointers

Pointer is an extension and customization of XPath. XPointer allows XPath expressions to be used as parts of URIs (including URLs). Using the XPointer extension it is possible to make references deep into an XML document. That means that you can link to an element, or even a span of elements, based on things like position, element type and ID – all of the usual XPath features.

64.1 | XPointers: The reason why

There are many times when it is necessary to refer not just to another document but to a particular part of that document. We can use a simple URI to refer to another document. Once we have a document it is possible to refer to a particular node or set of nodes using XPath. The XPointer specification allows the URI and the XPath to be combined into a *URI reference*. This combination of document and node addressing is very powerful.

An XPointer-containing URI reference can be used almost anywhere that an ordinary URI can be used. Not only can you put them in hypertext links – you can also put them on the sides of buses and in previews for movies!

You could type the URI reference into a compliant Web browser and have the browser jump directly to a particular place in the document. In some situations either the browser or the server could use an XPointer to actually restrict your view to a particular section of the document. Although the major browsers do not support XPointer yet, there are many niche browsers that do.

Inter-document addressing is vital for linking. Using XPointer it is possible to link a single element in an XML document to a single character in another. The full power of XPath is available in XPointer. So it is also possible to link a set of nodes (e.g. element nodes) in one document to one or more nodes (e.g. attribute nodes) in another document.

Although XPointers are useful for linking, it is also important to remember that they can be used outside of XLink. You might see an XPointer in a URI reference in the newspaper or in an email; it would represent the address of some XML nodes, but there would be no XLink.

In fact URIs are so common today that you can even use them to represent hypertext links in MS Word or PDF documents. In the future it will be possible to use URI references with XPointers in these contexts. That will mean that it will be possible to link from deep in a Word document or PDF file to the middle of an XML document.

Let's take a closer look at URIs before we start tacking XPointers onto them.

64.2 | Uniform Resource Identifiers

The basic form of address on the Web is a *URI*, which stands for *Uniform Resource Identifier*. It comes in two flavors:

URL

Today's most common form of URI is the ubiquitous *URL* or *Uniform Resource Locator*.

URN

A newer form of URI, *Uniform Resource Name (URN)*, isn't location-dependent and perhaps will reduce the number of broken links. However, it has yet to catch on because it requires more sophisticated software support.

URLs are uniform, in that they have the same basic syntax no matter what specific type of resource (e.g. Web page, newsgroup) is being addressed or what mechanism is described to fetch it. They describe the locations of Web resources much as a physical address describes a person's location. URLs are hierarchical, just as most physical addresses are. A surface mail address is resolved by sending a letter to a particular country, and from there to a local processing station, and from there to an individual. URLs are similar.

The first part of a URL is the *protocol*. It describes the mechanism that the Web browser or other client should use to get the resource. Think of it as the difference between Federal Express, UPS, and the other courier services. The most common such protocol is `http` which is essentially the "official" protocol of the World Wide Web. The `ftp` file transfer protocol is also widely used, chiefly for large downloads such as new browser versions.

After the protocol, there is a *hostname* and then a *datapath*. The datapath is broken into chunks separated by slash (/) characters, as you have no doubt seen in hundreds of URLs. Technically, a URL ends at that point. Since URLs are just the most common form of URI, it is also safe to say that the URI ends here.

64.3 | URI references

There is another term that is confusingly similar to URI: *URI reference*. A URI reference is the combination of a URI (which could be a URL) and an optional *fragment identifier*. For instance you may have seen links into HTML documents that look like Example 64-1.

Example 64-1. Reference into HTML

```
http://www.megabank.com/banking#about
```

In the example, `#about` is a fragment identifier. It refers to a particular HTML element. XPointers are the form of fragment identifier appropriate for XML documents. They are much more flexible than HTML fragment identifiers. Essentially, XPointers are an extension to URIs (i.e., a fragment identifier syntax) to allow you to point not just *to* an XML document, but into the content of one.

For instance, on today's Web, if you wanted to quote a particular paragraph out of another document, you would go to that document and cut and paste the text into yours. If, in the future, the text on the Web changes, yours does not. If that is what you want, that is fine. But an XPointer and XLink-smart application might allow you to construct a "living document" that quotes and refers to the very latest version of the paragraph. Although these sorts of applications do exist within particular organizations, general purpose Web browsers are not yet this sophisticated.

64.4 | ID references with XPointers

The simplest form of XPointer allows you to refer to a particular element named with an ID. This is also the most robust form of XPointer, because it does not at all depend on the location of the referenced text within its document. Consider the XML document in Example 64-2.

Example 64-2. Example document

```
<?xml version="1.0"?>
<!DOCTYPE HEATWAVES SYSTEM "heatwaves.dtd">
<HEATWAVES>
<WAVE ID="summer_92_info">
    <DURATION><FROM>July 22</FROM><TO>August 2</TO></DURATION>
    <TEMPERATURE>101 Degrees</TEMPERATURE>
</WAVE>
<WAVE ID="summer_94_info">
    <DURATION><FROM>July 12</FROM><TO>July 18</TO></DURATION>
    <TEMPERATURE>100 Degrees</TEMPERATURE>
</WAVE>
<WAVE ID="summer_96_info">
    <DURATION><FROM>June 15</FROM><TO>July 18</TO></DURATION>
    <TEMPERATURE>103 Degrees</TEMPERATURE>
</WAVE>
</HEATWAVES>
```

If this document resides at `http://www.hotdays.com/heatwave.xml`, then we could refer to the second WAVE element with the URI in Example 64-3.

Example 64-3. URI with XPointer

```
http://www.hotdays.com/heatwave.xml#xpointer( id("summer_94_info") )
```

The XPointer is the last little bit of the URI, after the pound-sign (#). The text "xpointer" starts the XPointer. Inside the outer parentheses we have an XPath. Typically the XPath will be just like those defined in Chapter 61, "XML Path Language (XPath)", on page 940, but sometimes they will use extensions that are defined in the XPointer specification.

We are not restricted to XPath's id function. IDs are the most robust way to refer to elements but we can also refer to elements that do not have IDs. This is especially important if we do not control the document that we are referencing. Any XPath can be used.

If you use a namespace prefix in an XPointer, it must be declared using a special form of namespace declaration. Example 64-4 demonstrates an XPointer reference to Example 64-5. Note that the prefixes used (pfx and blah) are different. The prefixes are just local short-forms for the long namespace URI which is the same (`http://example.com/foo`).

Example 64-4. Short and long form namespace references

```
abc.xml#xmlns(pfx=http://example.com/foo) xpointer(//pfx:local)
```

Example 64-5. XML Instance

```
<blah:local xmlns:blah="http://example.com/foo"/>
```

64.5 | XPointer abbreviations

The usual syntax for XPointer is called the *full syntax*. There are also two abbreviations that save some typing for common XPointer uses.

The first shortcut is for referring to elements by their IDs. You can do this by using the ID as the whole XPointer. You can replace the keyword "xpointer" and everything else. This abbreviation is called a *bare name*. Example 64-6 demonstrates equivalent XPointers.

Example 64-6. Equivalent XPointers

```
http://www.hotdays.com/heatwave.xml#xpointer( id("summer_96_info") )
http://www.hotdays.com/heatwave.xml#summer_96_info
```

You can use IDs more concisely with this abbreviation. IDs are an excellent way to refer to an element because they are impervious to minor changes such as re-ordering or adding elements to a document.

The other abbreviation is called a *child sequence*. With a child sequence you can refer to a child or descendant element of some particular element based on its position. For instance to refer to the first child of the summer_96_info element we would add a slash after the bare name and follow that by an integer. Example 64-7 demonstrates.

Example 64-7. Child sequence

```
http://www.hotdays.com/heatwave.xml#summer_96_info/1
```

This example refers to the first subelement of the WAVE element called summer_96_info. In our sample document, this is a DURATION element. We can also refer to a subelement of a subelement (or subelement of a subelement ... you get the picture) by adding slash-separated numbers to the end. Example 64-8 addresses all of the elements within the element with ID summer_96_info and its children.

Example 64-8. Deeper child sequences

```
http://www.hotdays.com/heatwave.xml#summer_96_info/1
http://www.hotdays.com/heatwave.xml#summer_96_info/1/1
http://www.hotdays.com/heatwave.xml#summer_96_info/1/2
http://www.hotdays.com/heatwave.xml#summer_96_info/2
```

These XPointers refer (respectively) to DURATION, FROM, TO and TEMPERATURE elements.

Rather than referring to an element by ID, you can refer to it by its position relative to the start of the document by starting the abbreviated XPointer with "/1". The "/1" refers to the root (or document) element. The next number (if any) refers to one of its children. The number after that (if any) refers to a child of that child and so on. Example 64-9 refers again to the elements that are within the element with ID summer_96_info.

Example 64-9. Rooted child sequences

```
http://www.hotdays.com/heatwave.xml#/1/3/1
http://www.hotdays.com/heatwave.xml#/1/3/1/1
http://www.hotdays.com/heatwave.xml#/1/3/1/2
http://www.hotdays.com/heatwave.xml#/1/3/2
```

The "/1" refers to the root (document) element HEATWAVES. The "/3" in each XPointer refers to the third child element of HEATWAVES, the WAVE with ID summer_96_info. The trailing numbers are as before.

It is important to understand that these abbreviations are used only in XPointers, and only instead of the traditional XPath syntax. You cannot mix them with ordinary XPaths.

64.6 | Extensions to XPath

XPointer extends the XPath model to support two new concepts: *points* and *ranges*. Since a range is defined as the area between two points, we'll examine the point concept first.

XPath normally returns nodes, which represent actual pieces of a document. If you think of a row of boxes on a piece of graph paper, nodes are the boxes and points occur at the vertical blue lines that separate the boxes.

XPointer takes things even further, though. In addition to allowing points before and after a node, it also allows points between the characters of a text node.

Ranges represent an area that a user might select in a document. Just like a user interface selection, it starts at one point (between two characters of a text node or between two elements or other nodes) and goes to another point.

64.6.1 *Ranges*

Ranges can be addressed with a variety of functions introduced by XPointer's extensions to XPath.

64.6.1.1   range-to

The `range-to` function takes two XPaths and addresses a range from the point preceding the first XPath to a point following the second. For instance, if you had an element with ID "summer_92_info" and wanted to create a range that contained that element, an element named "summer_96_info", and everything in between, you could do so with the XPointer in Example 64-10.

Example 64-10. range-to

```
xpointer(id("summer_92_info")/range-to(id("summer_96_info")))
```

The XPointer takes the node addressed before the slash and generates a range to the node addressed after the slash.

64.6.1.2   string-range

The `string-range` function searches for a string in the text nodes representing the data content of an element or a set of elements, or in the values of any other node set.

The simplest form of this function takes an XPath as its first parameter and a string as its second parameter. It finds occurrences of the string in the values of the nodes and returns them as a list of ranges.

The XPath to address all title elements in a document is "//title". If we wanted to find all occurrences of the string "Extensible Markup Language" in the titles, we would do it through the XPointer in Example 64-11.

Example 64-11. string-range

```
something.xml#xpointer(
  string-range( //title, "Extensible Markup Language" ))
```

You can also refer to a particular item in the list by appending an ordinary XPath predicate (Example 64-12).

Example 64-12. 11th occurrence

```
something.xml#xpointer(
    string-range( //title, "Extensible Markup Language" )[11])
```

Sometimes you want to address only a portion of long string. Perhaps you want to select the word "Markup" but only in the context of "Extensible Markup Language". To do this you would count into the string and find that the "M" in "Markup" is the twelfth character in the complete string.

In Example 64-13, we use "12" as the third argument to string-range. The final argument says how much of the string to select beyond the "M". The word "Markup" has six letters so we use "6" as the fourth parameter.

Example 64-13. range-slice

```
something.xml#xpointer(
    string-range( //title, "Extensible Markup Language", 12, 6 ))
```

These last two parameters are optional. If you do not specify them then you select the entire string. If you leave out the last parameter then you select to the end of the requested string.

64.6.1.3   range-inside and range

The range-inside function addresses a range that starts just inside the beginning of an element or other node or a set of nodes (including sets of elements) and goes to just inside the end.

For instance range-inside(/book/title) will select a range that includes everything inside of the title but does not include the title itself. If you visualize this in terms of the XML document string, it selects the content of the title element but not the title start- and end-tags.

A related function selects the content and the tags together. It is simply called range. This function is used to select an entire node or to address a set of ranges for a set of nodes. For instance range(//title) would select the ranges of each `title` element. If you visualize this in terms of the XML document string, it selects the ranges for the content and the tags of the elements.

Note the difference between `range(//title)` and `//title`. In the range case, the result is a list of ranges. In the straightforward XPath case, the result is a list of nodes.

64.6.2   *Point functions*

XPointer can also select points without addressing a range. This capability could be used, for example, to position a cursor between characters or elements in a document.

The `start-point` function selects the point just before an element or range. For instance to create a point just before the string "XML" in a title you could use an expression like that in Example 64-14.

Example 64-14. start-point

```
foo.xml#xpointer(start-point(string-range(//title, "XML")[1]))
```

This would select the point just before the first occurrence of the string "XML" in any `title` in the document. If we change the function from `start-point` to `end-point` then we would select the point just after the "L" in "XML".

If you pass a node (typically an element) or list of nodes to the `start-point` function then it will select the first point within the node or in each of the nodes. Similarly, the `end-point` function will select the last point in the node or each of the nodes. If you want to select the point just before or after a node (not inside it) then you can combine one of these functions with the `range` function. For instance `start-point(range(//P[1]))` will select the point just before the first `P` element.

64.6.3   *Other extension functions*

XPointer adds some other functions to XPath which are unrelated to the new concepts of point and range.

The first new function is called here. It returns the node that contains the actual XPointer text, if the XPointer is in an XML document. This might be useful to find some other information that might be useful in computing the XPointer. For instance, an attribute of the same element in the XPointer source XML document might contain a string that should be matched in the target XML document.

The second new function is called origin. This function is useful only when XPointers are used with XLink. Outside of the hyperlinking context, origin is not meaningful and not legal.

origin returns the element that was used to start traversal in an XLink. In the case of out-of-line (extended) links, this is not necessarily the element that contains the XPointer.

64.6.4 *Multiple XPointer parts*

It is possible to string together several full (not abbreviated) XPointer parts to allow the system to attempt multiple addressing strategies. All you need to do is concatenate multiple strings starting with "xpointer(" and ending in ")". Each of these is called an *XPointer part*. You may separate them with whitespace if you wish.

For instance, you could start with an ID-based XPointer because they are the most robust. This strategy might fail if the ID was deleted or renamed or if the processor did not support ID processing. Then you could try a string-search strategy. This would work unless the document had been edited to delete or change the target string. You could fall back from there to a positional strategy.

Example 64-15 demonstrates (on multiple lines for clarity).

Example 64-15. Multiple XPointers in one URI

```
foo.xml#xpointer(id('summer_96_info'))
       xpointer(string-range('103 Degrees')/../..)
       xpointer( /HEATWAVES/WAVE[3] )
```

With each strategy you are less and less sure that you have addressed the thing that you wanted to address, but it may be better to take that risk than to just give up as soon as the document changes. In a Web surfing situation, users may well tolerate the occasional mistake in exchange for fewer broken links overall.

64.7 | The role of XPointers

You could say that an XPointer is mostly just a shell for an XPath, but the shell is very important. The XPointer is the glue between the URI that precedes the pound-sign and the XPath in the parentheses.

An important thing to note is that an XPointer does not *do* anything. It refers to something. Whether the object is included, hyperlinked, or downloaded depends completely on the context of the reference.

It is just like referring to a person by name. The act of referring to him doesn't really accomplish anything. You have to refer to someone before you can tell somebody to do something to him (hopefully something nice), but the reference is not the action.

For instance, you could use the XPointer in an XLink to create a hyperlink to something, or in a browser address window to download and display a particular element. It is also up to the software to decide whether the referenced element is returned alone, or in the context of its document.

For instance, if you use an XPointer in a browser window, it would probably present the whole document and highlight the referenced element. But if you use it in an inclusion link to include a paragraph, it would probably take that paragraph out of its context and present it alone in the new context. The specific behavior depends on your link processor and stylesheet.

64.8 | Conclusion

XPointer is an extension and customization of XPath. XPointer allows XPath expressions to be used as parts of URIs (including URLs). Using the XPointer extension it is possible to make references deep into an XML document. This will allow new forms of commentary, annotation and information reuse.

XML Linking Language (XLink)

Friendly Tutorial

- Linking and addressing

- Simple links

- Extended links

H ypertext links are the backbone of the World Wide Web. Documents were shuffled around the Internet long before today's Web existed, but it was the ease of moving from page to page with hypertext links that made the Web into the mass market phenomenon it is today.

However, despite their centrality, Web links have many weaknesses. The linking system that we use today is essentially unchanged from the earliest version of the Web. Unfortunately, market inertia has prevented anything more powerful from coming along ... until now.

The XML-family hyperlinking specification is called XLink. It allows links that go far beyond those provided by HTML. XLinks can have multiple end points, be traversed in multiple directions, and be stored in databases and groups independently of the documents they refer to.

Caution   XLink is still not quite there yet. Although there are partial implementations in several products, they are not mainstream. That means that we can only talk about how it might be implemented, not how it is implemented in mainstream browsers.

65.1 | Basic concepts

The most important (and sometimes subtle) distinction in any discussion of hyperlinking is that of *linking* versus *addressing*. Linking is simply declaring a relationship between two (or more) things. If we say "George Washington and Booker T. Washington share a last name" then we have linked those two people in some way.

Addressing, on the other hand, is about describing how to find the two things being linked. There are many kinds of addresses, such as mail addresses, email addresses and URLs. When you create a link in XLink, you declare a relationship between two objects referred to by their addresses (URI References). We refer to these objects as *resources*. We discuss the addresses more in 64.2, "Uniform Resource Identifiers", on page 1006.

When you follow a link one way or another, we say that you have *traversed* the link. We call the process of doing so *traversal*.

The action that starts the traversal is called its *actuation*. The ringmaster lights the fuse that *actuates* the human cannonball's *traversal* across the circus arena to a vital net resource.[1]

If you have created Web pages before, you are probably familiar with HTML's simple A element. Whether or not you are familiar with HTML, that link is a good starting point for understanding hyperlinking in general.

The A stands for *anchor*. Anchor is the hyperlinking community's term for what the XLink spec calls a *participating resource*. An HTML link has two ends, termed the *source* and *destination*. When you click on the source

---

1. A 404 error would mean that more than the link was broken!

end, (designated with an A element and href attribute), the Web browser transports you to the other end. Example 65-1 shows how this works.

Example 65-1. An HTML (not XLink) link

```
<a href="http://www.mysite.com">Go to my site!</a>
```

In this case, the a element itself describes a link, and its href attribute points to one of the resources (the destination). As we know, links connect resources, so there must be at least one more resource involved. The other resource, the source, is actually the content of the a element itself! The XLink spec calls this a *local resource*. As we will see, XLink *simple* links also use the content of the linking element as one of the resources.

There is another pervasive type of link in HTML documents. Consider the HTML markup to embed an image (Example 65-2).

Example 65-2. HTML (not XLink) image-embedding link

```
<IMG SRC="http://www.hotpics.com/jalapeno.gif">
```

That may not seem like a link but it is.[2] It declares a relationship between the containing document and the embedded image: "that picture goes in this document." HTML element types that use href attributes to address Java applets and plug-in objects are also forms of link.

Note that the destination of a link does not necessarily know that it is a destination. If you want to link to the Disney home page, you do not need to inform Disney. If a particular document has fifty a elements with href attributes, then you know that it has fifty links out. But the Web provides no way to know how many links into it there are.

In the more general *extended* link case, we will link two things such that *neither* end will "know" that the two are being linked. The link exists in some third location. This is intuitive if you go back to the definition of linking as defining a relationship. In a real-world sense, I can "link" Jenny Jones and Oprah Winfrey just by speaking of them in the same sentence. Unless they are interested in careers as XML experts, they will probably

---

2. What it *isn't* is a *navigational* link. You don't click on it to go somewhere else. Instead, its traversal is actuated automatically, as we'll see later in this chapter.

never know. XLink provides a standardized way to express this relationship in markup.

We might even want to link something that is not explicitly labeled. For instance, we might want to link the third paragraph of the fourth sub-point of the second section of a legal document to the transcript of a relevant court case.

This is analogous to the real world situation where you can either send something to a labeled location ("Please take this to the White House.") or you can give directions to the destination. In hyperlinking terms, we would consider either one of these to be an "address." Obviously there must be some way of locating a resource from a link, but it could be either an address, a label or a combination of the two: "The building is 5 blocks down the street from the White House."

65.2 | Simple links

Although XLink allows more flexible links than does HTML, it also offers simple links that are not much more complicated than HTML's links are. This sort of link is referred to as a *simple link*. A simple link has two ends, a source and a destination, just like an HTML link. One end represents a resource (usually the source) and it refers to the other end through a URI as in Example 65-3.

Example 65-3. XLink simple link

```
. . . for more information, consult
<citation xlink:type="simple"
          xlink:href="http://www.uw.ca/paper.xml">
Biemans(1997)
</citation>
```

The biggest difference between this link and the HTML link is that this element is not designated a link by its element-type name. It is not called a or any special element-type name specified in the XML or XLink specification. You can call your linking elements whatever you want to. This is an important feature, because it allows you to have many different types of linking elements in a document, perhaps with different declarations, attributes and behaviors. Just as XML allows you to use any element-type name for paragraphs or figures, XLink allows you flexibility in your linking element-type names.

The link is actually designated an XLink link by its `xlink:type` attribute. The `xlink:type` attribute describes what kind of link is being described. In this case, it is a *simple* link. The `xlink:` prefix indicates that this attribute's allowed values and semantics are defined by the XLink specification.

Formally speaking, the attribute lives in the `xlink:` namespace. Namespaces are discussed in Chapter 58, "Namespaces", on page 874. This namespace should be declared in your document: probably in the document (i.e., root) element as shown in Example 65-4.

Example 65-4. Namespace declaration in root element

```
<yourdoc xmlns:xlink="http://www.w3.org/1999/xlink">
. . .
</yourdoc>
```

For documents that will be DTD-validated, it is best to declare the `xmlns:xlink` attribute in the DTD as a fixed attribute of the root element type, as shown in Example 65-5.

Example 65-5. Namespace declaration in DTD

```
<!ATTLIST yourdoc xmlns:xlink CDATA
                  #FIXED "http://www.w3.org/1999/xlink">
```

Note   All of the examples in this chapter assume that the linking element is in the scope of a namespace declaration that sets up the `xlink:` namespace prefix.

65.2.1 *Link roles*

In HTML, link resources are either sources or destinations. The linking element is always the source. The resource referred to is always the destination.

In XML, this rigid distinction is not hard-wired. An application can make either or both resources into sources or destinations.

Consider, for instance, if a Web browser made it possible to create notes about someone else's Web site and "stick" them on to it like Post-It notes. These *annotations* might be represented as XLink *extended* links as in Example 65-6.

Example 65-6. XLink annotations

```
<annotation xlink:type="extended"
      xlink:href="http://www.mynewspaper.com">
As usual, your editorial is filled with the kind of claptrap and
willywag that gives me the heebie-jeebies!
</annotation>
```

In this case, we actually want the application to make some form of clickable "hotspot" at the *other* end, on the newspaper's Web page. Of course we don't want them to have control of the actual linking element, or else they might just choose not to show our link. So we want the link to exist in one spot and create a "hotspot" at another. This is the opposite of traditional HTML links.

In order to reverse linking roles, we must somehow tell the application that we want it to do so. One way would be to use an element-type name that the application is hard-coded to understand as having that semantic. For instance an "annotation server" might only deal with `annotation` elements, or perhaps a few different variants, and would thus know exactly how to handle it.

Another way would be to use some form of stylesheet. But you would still need to have something special in the document that would differentiate annotations from other links (perhaps the annotation element-type name). The stylesheet would provide an extra level of translation to allow your private element-type names to be interpreted as annotations by software.

Yet another way to solve this problem would be to provide an attribute that describes the role of the link in the document and hypertext system. Any of these are valid approaches, and the XLink specification provides a special `xlink:role` attribute to handle the last case. Example 65-7 is an example of that attribute in action.

Example 65-7. Role attribute

```
<hlink xlink:role="http://www.annotation.com"
    xlink:type="extended"
    xlink:href="http://www.mynewspaper.com">
As usual, your editorial is filled with the kind of claptrap and
willywag that gives me the heebie-jeebies!
</hlink>
```

In this case, the role designation has moved from the element-type name (now `hlink` instead of `annotation`) to the role attribute. Which is more appropriate will depend on your DTD, your software and your taste. XLink could perhaps dictate one style or the other, but real world usage is not that simple. For instance you might need to extend an industry standard DTD and thus have no control over element-type names. In another application, you might need to constrain the occurrence of certain kinds of linking elements, and thus need to use element-type names and content models.

The role is a URI reference. XLink does not specify what sort of data (if any) must be available at the URI's location. The URI is abstract, just like a namespace URI. It is just a long, verbose name for something that is meant to be globally unique. The only thing that matters is that you control the URI so that someone else will not use it to mean something else.

65.2.2 *Is this for real?*

You might well ask whether all of this annotation stuff is likely to happen. After all, there are all sorts of social, technical and financial difficulties related to being able to annotate someone else's Web page. Imagine annotation spam: "Tired of reading this boring technical Web page? Click here for HOT PICS!!!"

It turns out that early versions of the pre-Netscape Mosaic browser allowed remote annotations (using a proprietary linking scheme), and you could share your annotations with friends or co-workers, but not with everybody on the Web. There are various other experimental services and products that provide the same ability for the modern-day Web. However, each uses a distinct link description notation so that they cannot share.

We may or may not get to the point where everybody can publish annotations to the whole world, but we already have the technology to create annotations that can be shared by other people we know. Unfortunately, this technology has never been widely deployed.[3] Perhaps when XLink is finalized and third-party annotation products are able to interoperate, Web pages will become generally annotatable and even more linkable than they are today.

So what can you do without a world-wide link database? Well let's say that your organization was considering buying a very expensive software product. You and your co-workers might agree to submit your opinions of the product specifications published on the vendor's Website. You could make a bunch of external links from the vendor's text to your comments on it and submit that to your organizational link database. When your co-workers go to see the page, their browsers can fetch your links and actually display them as if they were part of the original document. When your co-workers click on them, the browser will take them to your annotations.

In fact, with a reasonably large link database, you could annotate any Web page you came upon in this manner. When others from your organization came upon the page, they would see your annotations. In one sense, you are editing the entire Web! Of course, the bigger your organization is, the more points of view you can see on each page. On the other hand, sometimes you might not want to share all of your comments with the entire company, so you might have a smaller departmental database which is separate, and only shared by your direct co-workers. And of course at the opposite end of the spectrum, there might be a database for everyone on the Web (if we can make link database software that scales appropriately and find someone to run it).

External links can be useful even without a link database. Without such a database, there is no easy way to distribute your links to other people, so you must communicate the links' existence in some other way. For instance, you could include a critique of a Web page as an attachment to an email. You could also build a document full of links that annotated one of your own Web pages with links to glossary and bibliographic information. The XLink specification terms such a collection a *link base*. Depending on which link base the reader used, he would get either the glossary links or the bibliographic links or both sets of links overlapping. A link base is not a full database; it is an XML document that must be parsed before it can be used.

If it makes sense to "project" a link from your home computer onto an existing website, then surely it makes just as much sense to link two existing

---

3. One product that has recently taken another run at the problem is called Third Voice™.

websites. For instance, we could make a link that is targeted towards members of the SGML newsgroup that links the World Wide Web consortium's XML Web page to a related page we know about on the Web. This link would still have two ends, but both could be sources and destinations at the same time. If so, we would term that link *bidirectional*, because you could *traverse* it from either end. Because the link would exist on your Web site, but link two other pages, we would call it a *third-party* link. And if it makes sense to link two pages, then why not three, or four, or five? Extended links allow this.

65.2.3 *Link behaviors*

XML authors usually go out of their way to avoid putting information about formatting and other types of document behavior into XML documents. We've already been through all of the benefits of keeping your information "pure". As we have said, if you just mark up your documents according to their abstractions, you can apply formatting and other behavior through stylesheets.[4]

Even though it is usually best to put behavioral information in a stylesheet, XLink provides a more direct mechanism. There are some link behaviors that are so common – almost universal – that the XML working group decided that it should provide some attributes so that users could easily specify them. This facility removes a level of indirection and thereby makes hyperlinking a little bit easier. Still, one should think thrice about adding rendition attributes to abstract documents. The stylesheet is usually the best place to describe behavior and other presentational issues.

The most interesting type of link behavior is traversal. When you click on a hyperlink, you are traversing it. If a link is intended to embed information from one resource in another, then the process of actually accomplishing the embedding is a traversal.

The behavioral descriptions are still abstract enough to allow a variety of specific behaviors, depending on the situation. For example, a printer might interpret them differently from a Web browser. Although a printer might

---

4. That is the theory, anyhow. At the time of writing, however, mainstream stylesheet languages did not support the recognition of XLinks or the execution of link behaviors. As we said in the introduction, XLinks are not quite there.

not seem like a machine that would care about hyperlinks, it might be useful to have one that could directly print Web pages and their annotations, and that could access the images to print by traversing XLinks in the Web pages.

65.2.3.1   Show

As the name implies, the `xlink:show` attribute describes how the results of a link traversal should be shown. When you click on a Web link, that is a link traversal – one initiated by your click. On the other hand, if you have ever been to a site where a Web page comes up and says: "You will be forwarded to another page in just a few seconds", then that is a link traversal that is automatic. Typically on the Web, when a link is traversed (manually or automatically) it replaces the previous document in the Web browser window. XLink allows an author to request this behavior with the `replace` value of the `show` attribute:

Spec Excerpt (XLink) 65-1. Replace

An application traversing to the ending resource should load the resource in the same window, frame, pane, or other relevant presentation context in which the starting resource was loaded.

For example see Example 65-8.

Example 65-8. A `replace` link

```
<A  xlink:type="simple"
    xlink:show="replace"
    xlink:href="http://www.gop.org/">
Click here to visit the GOP</A>
```

Sometimes you will also come across a link that actually opens a new window, so that after traversal there is a window for the new page in front of the window for the old page. XLink allows this through the new value of the show attribute.

Spec Excerpt (XLink) 65-2. New

An application traversing to the ending resource should load it in a new window, frame, pane, or other relevant presentation context.

Example 65-9 shows a link where the remote resource is launched into a new window.

Example 65-9. A new link

```
<A xlink:type="simple"
    xlink:show="new"
    xlink:href="http://www.democrats.org/">
Click here to launch a new window and visit the the Dems.</A>
```

As we have seen, a link can represent *any* relationship. We discussed the relationship between a document and an embedded graphic, but did not discuss the XLink syntax for it yet. We can say that one resource should be embedded in another using the embed option of the xlink:show attribute. Example 65-10 demonstrates.

Example 65-10. An embedded link

```
<MyEmbed xlink:type="simple"
    xlink:show="embed"
    xlink:href="http://www.democrats.org/platform.gif"/>
```

An embedded link can embed any datatype, not just graphics. You could embed a movie, sound or even another XML document:

Example 65-11. An embedded XML document

```
<MyEmbed xlink:type="simple"
    xlink:show="embed"
    xlink:href="somedata.xml"/>
```

Note that this is not like embedding text using text entities. When you use text entities, the entire behavior of those entities is defined by the XML specification. The parser manages the expansion of entities according to well-defined rules. In the case of embed, the embedding rules are dictated by the application (which might delegate the decision to a stylesheet or configuration file). Valid behaviors might include textual inclusion (as with text entities), image-like embedding in a square box or something in between. The application could also decide whether the inclusion inherits font properties.

To summarize: the big difference between embed-style links and text entities is who controls the embedding. Text entities are expanded by the XML parser and the application has no control over it. Embedded links must be expanded by the application (browser, editor, B2B engine, video game, whatever).

There are two other values for xlink:show: other and none. In both cases, the author is telling the application that it is free to determine the behavior that will accompany the traversal. With other, however, the author is saying that other markup present in the link should guide that determination. none implies that no behavior is really expected.

65.2.3.2   Actuate

The actuate attribute allows the author to describe when the link traversal should occur. For instance it could be user-triggered, such as by a mouse click or a voice command. Or else it could be automatic, such as the automatic embedding of a graphic, or an automatic forward to another Web page (e.g. "This page has moved. You will be directed to the new page momentarily.")

The onRequest value indicates that the traversal should be user-triggered. When it is combined with a a show attribute of replace, it is a typical, click-here-to-go-there link, at least in a graphical browser. On a text-based browser, it might be a type-this-number-to-go-there link. On a spoken-word browser it might be a say-this-number-to-go-there link.

When it is combined with a value of new it opens a new "context" (usually a browser window) at user command and leaves the old one open. When it is combined with a value of embed, the target resource is displayed embedded in the source, replacing the linking element.[5]

The onLoad value of the actuate attribute is used to specify that traversal should be done automatically when the document is loaded. For instance, most show="embed" links would specify automatic traversal. If you combine show="new" with actuate="onLoad", then you can create a Web page that immediately opens another Web page (like a popup advertisment). Perhaps with a stylesheet or other attribute, you could make them appear side by side. The final combination is show="replace" with actuate="onLoad". You would use this to set up a "forwarding" link, such as the one we have described, and thus forward users from one page to another.

65.3 | Extended links

In this section, we will discuss more features of *extended links*. One that we have already discussed is the ability to specify them in third-party documents. Extended links also allow for more link ends, more advanced link roles, and other good stuff. We will also be able to re-describe the simple links that we have already seen in the terminology of the more general extended link system.

65.3.1 *Locator elements*

The first extension we will undertake is links with more than two link ends. Consider, for example, that you are redirecting users to several different interpretations of a text. For instance if there were two competitive schools of thought on a topic, each hotspot in the document might allow traversal to a different interpretation of the topic. Now you have three link ends, one for the source and one for each of the interpretations of it. Just as in real life, XLink allows you to make logical links among two or more concepts.

The first big difference between simple links and extended links is that we need to figure out how to specify the address of more than one destination link. We do this by putting *locator* subelements into the extended linking element. Example 65-12 demonstrates.

---

5. In hypertext terms, this is called a *transclusion*.

Example 65-12. Multi-ended link

```
<commentary xlink:type="extended">
   <locator xlink:type="locator"
            xlink:href="roberts.xml"
            xlink:role="http://commentary.com/analysis"/>
   <locator xlink:type="locator"
            xlink:href="beam.xml"
            xlink:role="http://commentary.com/rebuttal"/>
   <locator xlink:type="locator"
            xlink:href="goodwin.xml"
            xlink:role="http://commentary.com/precis"/>
<P>My fellow Americans, this speech will go down in history...</P>
</commentary>
```

In this case, the three locators each address a resource. A sufficiently sophisticated browser displaying this document might represent each with an icon or supply a popup menu that allows access to each of the resources. It could even open a small window for each interpretation when the hotspot is selected. This could be controlled by a stylesheet or a behavior attribute. As you can see, each locator can have a different role, but they could also share roles. The role just specifies a semantic for processing the resource when processing the link, not some sort of unique identifier.

Locators can also have some other associated attributes. They can have titles, specified through a `xlink:title` attribute. These provide information for human consumption. The browser does not act on them. It merely passes them on to the human in some way, such as a popup menu, or text on the status bar.

The locator's `xlink:label` attribute is used in combination with *arcs* (next section) to declare which resources can be the start of a traversable path and to which other resources the user can traverse.

65.3.2 *Arcs*

An extended link can link many resources. You may not want to allow traversal from every resource to every other resource. In other words, you may want to restrict some *traversal paths*. XLink has a feature called arcs to allow this.

An arc defines an allowed traversal path. An arc is an element that exhibits a `xlink:type` attribute with the value `arc`. Arcs go directly within the content of the extended link element itself. If you have no arcs then all paths are traversable. If you have one, then only the paths defined by that one arc are traversable, and so forth.

If you have three resources in your link then you can have between zero and six arc elements. For instance, if your links are to Peter, Paul and Mary (or to their home pages!) then you may or may not want to allow traversal from (1) Peter to Paul, (2) Peter to Mary, (3) Paul to Peter, (4) Paul to Mary, (5) Mary to Peter and (6) Mary to Paul.

Of course, resources do not have names like Peter, Paul and Mary. Well, actually they can! We can give names to resources by putting an `xlink:label` attribute on the locators. This is shown in Example 65-13.

Example 65-13. Extended links with labels

```
<extendedlink xlink:type="extended">
  <loc xlink:type="locator"
       xlink:label="Peter"
       xlink:href="..."/>
  <loc xlink:type="locator"
       xlink:label="Paul"
       xlink:href="..."/>
  <loc xlink:type="locator"
       xlink:label="Mary"
       xlink:href="..."/>
</extendedlink>
```

Now we can set up traversal paths between them. For instance if Peter and Paul have had a little fight, then they could both talk (traverse) to Mary but not to each other. Example 65-14 demonstrates.

Example 65-14. Peter and Paul traverse to Mary

```
<loc xlink:type="arc"
     xlink:from="Peter"
     xlink:to="Mary"/>
<loc xlink:type="arc"
     xlink:from="Paul"
     xlink:to="Mary"/>
```

It turns out that there is a shorter way to say the same thing. If we leave out the `xlink:from` attribute then an XLink processor is supposed to presume that all paths to the named resource are legal. See Example 65-15.

Example 65-15. Abbreviated form of Example 65-14

```
<loc xlink:type="arc"
     xlink:to="Mary"/>
```

In this case traversal from both Peter and Paul to Mary is allowed. We might also want to allow the opposite. In that case we would use an arc with a xlink:from attribute with a value of "Mary" and no xlink:to attribute. Just to round out our example, we might allow Peter to traverse to Paul but not the reverse. (Paul is a little sedentary). Example 65-16 shows what a complete extended link would look like in that case.

Example 65-16. Extended link with arcs

```
<extendedlink xlink:type="extended">
  <loc xlink:type="locator"
       xlink:label="Peter"
       xlink:href="..."/>
  <loc xlink:type="locator"
       xlink:label="Paul"
       xlink:href="..."/>
  <loc xlink:type="locator"
       xlink:label="Mary"
       xlink:href="..."/>
  <arc xlink:type="arc" xlink:from="Mary"/>
  <arc xlink:type="arc" xlink:to="Mary"/>
  <arc xlink:type="arc" xlink:from="Peter" xlink:to="Paul"/>
</extendedlink>
```

In this example, every path is traversable except Paul to Peter. You might wonder whether there is a more concise way to say this. For instance, you might expect an anti-arc element. There is no such thing. You always specify which paths are traversable. On the other hand, if you provide no arc elements at all, all paths are traversable.

Arcs may not have xlink:role attributes but they may have an equivalent attribute called xlink:arcrole. That attribute is a URL, just as xlink:role is.

65.3.3 *Simple links and extended links*

You can do anything with extended links that you can do with simple links. In fact, a simple link is a combination of a link, a locator, a resource and an arc. In fact, this is how they are defined in the XLink spec:

Spec Excerpt (XLink) 65-3. Simple links

The purpose of a simple link is to be a convenient shorthand for the equivalent extended link. A single simple linking element combines the basic functions of an extended-type element, a locator-type element, an arc-type element, and a resource-type element.

A simple link automatically defines an arc between the local resource (the linking element) and the remote resource (the target of the xlink:href attribute). You do not need to add an arc-type element inside of it and in fact you are not allowed to.

It is both useful and convenient that simple links combine these things, but it means that we must be careful to keep the ideas separate in our heads. The link describes a relationship. The locators say what resources are being related. A simple link uses the linking element itself as one resource and the target of its xlink:href attribute as the other.

65.4 | Linkbases

It is often useful to be able to process a group of hyperlinked documents all together. For instance, if one document contains some text and another contains a rebuttal of the text, the browser might want to show them "side by side". It could also allow link traversals in one window to trigger the correct portion of the rebuttal in the other.

Such processing can only work if the browser knows about both documents at the same time. Linkbases allow you to tell the browser about all of the documents that should be processed together.

A *linkbase* element is an arc that associates one XML document with another XML document that serves as a linkbase. The linkbase is used as a source of links in addition to those in the original XML document.

Linkbases are distinguished from other arcs with an `xlink:arcrole` attribute. That attribute must have the value: `http://www.w3.org/1999/xlink/properties/linkbase`

We said before that simple links automatically define an arc. So the simplest way to declare a linkbase is with a simple link, as in Example 65-17.

Example 65-17. Reference to a linkbase

```
<xlink
  xlink:type="simple"
  xlink:arcrole="http://www.w3.org/1999/xlink/properties/linkbase"
  xlink:href="http://www.xxx.com/mylinks.xml" />
```

This will instruct an XLink processor that there are additional links to be found in the `mylinks.xml` file.

65.5 | XML Base

XML documents may sometimes contain relative URLs ("foo.xml") instead of absolute ones ("http://www.something.com/foo.xml"). For brevity, many of the examples in this chapter were relative URLs. One nice thing about relative URLs is that they are concise. Another is that you can move around a package of related documents from computer to computer and keep the links the same.

On the other hand, sometimes you want to download a single document to your computer and have all relative links point to the original documents in their original (remote) location. One way to do this would be to rewrite all of the links. This is inconvenient, however. A second option is to use the `xml:base` construct.

XML Base is not part of XLink. It is a separate specification that may be used with XLink. When it is used, all relative URLs in a document are interpreted as being relative to a base URL specified in an `xml:base` attribute. Adding this one attribute is equivalent to re-writing all of the relative URLs in the document.

Example 65-18. XML Base example

```
<doc xml:base="http://www.mysite.com/base/">
    ....
    <citation xlink:type="simple"
          xlink:href="paper.xml">
    ....
</doc>
```

It is possible to declare the base on any element and have it apply to all sub-elements, but it is simplest to just declare a single base on the root element.

65.6 | Conclusion

XLink has the power to change the Web, and our lives, in unforeseeable ways. For more of the vision, see Chapter 42, "Extended linking", on page 614. For the current version of the spec, see the *XML SPECtacular* on the CD-ROM.

Resources

- Free XML software on the CD-ROMs
- XML specifications on the CD-ROMs
- Repositories and vocabularies
- Acronyms and initialisms for XML (AIX)
- Other XML-related books

Part Eighteen

On the back cover of the first edition of this book, an inspired copywriter wrote: "The accompanying CD ROM brings together an amazing set of XML resources."

As authors, we of course don't engage in such hyperbole, except on behalf of technologies that excite us. However, we feel obligated to make the purely factual observation that the CD-ROM for this edition is far superior to the first. In fact, there are two of them!

There are over 175 free XML software packages, compared to 55 in the first edition. Please note that we use the word "free" very precisely. We mean genuinely free use, XML-centric, no time limit, uncrippled software, that is usable with your own documents.

In addition, there are 34 contributors to the Sponsor Showcase, compared to 14 in that edition. Their materials include more free software, plus trial versions of major commercial products for your evaluation, and white papers, demos, and examples.

This part includes an introduction to the CD-ROM resources, a directory of over 350 XML vocabulary projects, a dictionary of acronyms and initialisms, and for those who like to read actual books, a reader's guide to other books in this series.

Free resources
on the CD-ROM

Resource Description

- Over 175 free software packages

- IBM alphaWorks XML software suite

- XML SPECtacular

Contributing experts: Lars Marius Garshol, David A. Epstein, and
Daniel Jue

Chapter

66

Do you really need 175 XML software packages?
Not likely, but our two CD-ROMs will save a lot of
download time while you decide which you do need.
Most are described in this chapter, along with the
specifications that are on the CDs.

The two CD-ROMs that supplement *The XML Handbook* contain a wide variety of resources. There is free trial software, genuine freeware with no time limit, demos, white papers, markup and code samples, product information from our sponsors, and the full text of the most important standards and specifications.

We describe most of the free software and specs in this chapter, but not all of it; you'll need to dig into the discs for the rest.

Enjoy!

66.1 | Software featured on the covers

In this section, we briefly describe the free software and trialware that our sponsors feature on the covers of the book. We specify the platforms supported and, if it is trialware, the time limit or other usage description.

66.1.1 *NeoCore XML Information Management System (XMS)*

NeoCore XMS is a transactional database that is able to infer the structure of the data in XML documents as they are posted or modified. It is schema-independent and allows developers to store and manage XML without doing any database design, table creation, or index definition.

To client applications, *NeoCore XMS* looks like a bi-directional Web server that accepts and returns XML documents and fragments via HTTP(S). Simple Java and C++ APIs wrap the HTTP messages, creating a lightweight primary interface that is easily learned and used.

The CD contains a free unlimited personal edition of *NeoCore XMS v2.0* that runs on Windows 2000. It allows two concurrent sessions and can store up to 5MB.

66.1.2 *IBM alphaWorks XML software suite*

This suite of free software contains a wide variety of programs, most of which will run on any Java platform.

The programs are described in the next section of this chapter.

66.1.3 *Adobe FrameMaker+SGML XML/SGML editor/formatter*

FrameMaker+SGML is a tool for editing and formatting long, complex publications such as books, manuals, and catalogs. It can convert documents to XML, HTML, and PDF for publishing electronically and on the Web. The product offers both a WYSIWYG formatted interface and a document-tree structured interface; both can be used simultaneously.

The tryout version on the CD-ROM has no time limit and is fully functional, except that Save As is disabled and printing is not possible. It is available for the Mac, Windows, HP-UX, and IBM AIX platforms. Also included is product information, customer case studies, tutorials, and other materials.

66.1.4 *TIBCO Extensibility TurboXML IDE with XML Authority schema editor*

XML Authority is a graphical development tool for creating and modifying XML schemas, and for converting other data structures to XML schemas. The product can support DTDs, and can export DTDs and such schema languages as XSDL, RELAX, XML-Data, XDR, DCD, SOX, and DDML.

The trial version on the CD-ROM runs on Windows 95/98/00 and Windows NT. There is a 30-day time limit from the date of installation.

66.2 | IBM alphaWorks

IBM *alphaWorks* is a team dedicated to speeding emerging IBM technology to the marketplace, from fields as diverse as management and transaction functions, networking, security, and power management.

Its website operates on a unique premise.

66.2.1 *The alphaWorks idea*

The *alphaWorks* website is a focal point for bidirectional communication with early adopters of strategic emerging technologies. At the site, users can download "alpha-code" implementations of those technologies. More importantly, they can also access and provide feedback to IBM's top researchers and developers, through the site's technology discussion forums.

alphaWorks serves as one of IBM's primary channels for the distribution of XML technology. You can find several different categories of XML technology at the site.

1. One of the main categories, which fulfills one of *alphaWorks'* primary goals, is implementations that track the important W3C Recommendations and other related XML specifications. One of the objectives in providing these implementations is to have them available in a timely manner, often the same day that Recommendations (proposed and final, and early Notes) become public.

2. In addition to these implementations of the important XML specifications, the site also serves as a distribution point for example applications that make use of these specifications.

3. *alphaWorks* also serves as a proving ground in which experimental new XML technologies are introduced and evaluated. User feedback is monitored directly by the research and development staff, and updated according to the comments supplied by users.

4. Finally, the site offers a variety of tools and components that provide a bridge between the XML and Java spaces.

66.2.2 *XML at alphaWorks*

The list of emerging XML technologies on *alphaWorks* is already quite long and growing almost daily. Rather than try to list all of them, we'll briefly describe a representative selection. They are all included on the accompanying CD-ROM.

Data Descriptors by Example

DDbE is a Java component library for inferring an XML DTD or schema from a set of well-formed XML instances. DDbE offers parameters that permit the user to control the structure of the content models and the types used for attribute declarations. The goal of DDbE is to give users a good start at creating DTDs for their own applications.

DirectDOM Developer Kit

The DirectDOM technology allows a Java developer to build rich graphical user interfaces by manipulating documents using the W3C Document Object Model (DOM) of a browser. Development kits are available for Microsoft Internet Explorer (IE) 5.5 and Netscape 6 on Windows 95, 98, ME, NT, and 2000 platforms and for Netscape 6 on Linux. These development kits require Java 1.2.2 or higher.

LotusXSL

A Java implementation of an XSLT processor that tracks the W3C specification. It is designed to be used either as a stand-alone application, as a submodule of a larger application, or within an applet or servlet. In addition to supporting the standard DOM 1.0 API, it can also be configured to generate streaming SAX output.

P3P Policy Editor

The IBM P3P Policy Editor is a visual tool, with an easy-to-use interface, for creating a Web site's privacy policy in the P3P language, which can be interpreted by Web browsers and other user agents that support the Platform for Privacy Preferences Project (P3P) specification from the W3C. P3P allows users to automate the acceptance or rejection of a Web site's requests for information, based on user preferences set in browsers or client devices. Users are assured that their privacy is protected without having to read each Web site's privacy policy.

SVG View

Scalable Vector Graphics (SVG) is a language for describing two-dimensional graphics in XML. SVGView is a Java program that uses Java 2D and the XML Parser for Java to parse, process, and display SVG files on any XML-enabled Web browser. The viewer enables Web professionals working with SVG files to preview their forms or images.

Web Services PMT

The Web Services Process Management Toolkit combines Business Process Management technology with Web Services. It allows you to compose Web Services into a business process to achieve a defined business goal. Composing Web Services allows you to choreograph and add control logic to a set of Web Services in a business process. This technology also allows you to implement a Web Service as a business process. Using a process as implementation for a Web Service allows you to compose complex Web Services with the characteristics of a process.

Xeena

A DTD-driven XML editor. Using a visual, tree-oriented editing paradigm coupled with a context-sensitive palette of elements,

Xeena provides an intuitive, self-validating, mechanism for viewing and editing XML documents.

XMI Toolkit

XMI specifies an open information interchange model that gives developers working with object technology the ability to exchange models and data over the Internet in a standardized way, thus bringing consistency and compatibility to applications created in collaborative environments. By establishing an industry standard for storing and sharing object programming information, development teams using various tools from multiple vendors can collaborate on applications. The new XMI standard allows developers to leverage the web to exchange data among tools, applications, and repositories, to create secure, distributed applications built in a team development environment.

XML Generator

This tool creates "random" test cases for XML applications by generating them from a DTD. The cases can be stored as XML files, or accessed directly through the DOM API.

XML Interface for RPG

XML Interface for RPG, C and COBOL provides access to DOM and SAX level 1 APIs in RPG, C and COBOL programs. It allows procedural applications to create new or parse existing XML documents, facilitating the use of XML as both a datastore and IO mechanism in these languages.

XML Lightweight Extractor

Given a DTD, the XML Access Server Lightweight Extractor (XLE) allows a user to annotate the DTD to associate its various components with underlying data sources, and when requested, extracts data from the data sources and assembles the data into XML documents conforming to that DTD.

XML Parser for Java (XML4J)

A configurable XML parser written in *Java*, based on the Apache Xerces XML Parser Version 1.0.3. The package contains classes for parsing, generating, manipulating, validating, and emitting XML documents. The package is designed in a modular fashion so that a variety of specially configured parsers can be constructed.

Xplorer

Xplorer allows the users to search for XML files based on the XML file name, Document type and some advanced search options like element name and value, attribute name and value, PI, etc. It also allows users to check the validity of XML files and view a valid XML file in the XML viewer. Only valid files can be viewed in the XML viewer. If you try to view an invalid XML file, an error dialog appears and errors are logged in the Log Window.

XSL Editor

This tool allows you to import, create, and save XSL style sheets and XML source documents. It supports stylesheet development with aids for generating XPath syntax from sample documents and writing select and match expressions. It runs transforms with or without tracing and breakpoints. The user interface features a collapsible tree view of the XML source document.

XSL Trace

The IBM XSL Trace application reveals the mystery of XSL transforms! XSL Trace allows a user to visually "step through" an XSL transformation script, highlighting the transformation rules as they are fired. Additionally, an XSL Trace user can view the XML source and the corresponding XML or HTML result in "real time". XSL Trace users can set and remove "break points" on the style sheet and source document as well as highlight all source nodes processed by each style rule. The XSL Trace UI features an XML "source based" collapsible "tree view" with dynamic font resizing for "Zooming" in and out to handle small and large documents.

Tip   *You can visit the alphaWorks site,* `http://www.alphaWorks.IBM.com`, *to engage IBM researchers and developers at the earliest stages of development and to download the latest software.*

66.3 | An eXtravagance of free XML software

To make this list, software has to be genuinely free, worthwhile XML software. That means:

- It must have substantial XML-oriented functionality; no graphics packages, file utilities, or other general-purpose filler.
- It must let you do useful processing of your own documents. If you are taking the trouble to install and learn it, you should get some benefit from it.
- It can't have a time limit on its use. As above: you should be the one to decide when it's no longer interesting.
- Most of all, it's got to be pretty good stuff! Some of it is proven code that rivals the best ever written for speed and stability. Other packages are promising newcomers.

You'll find fuller descriptions of everything on the CD-ROMs, along with hyperlinks to the vendor's website for the latest versions of the programs that you like. The descriptions here are just to give you the flavor and, of course, they apply only to the version on the CDs.

 Caution   This list is incomplete! The CD-ROMs have over 175 packages. Be sure to check them out for yourself.

66.3.1 *Parsers and engines*

XML parsers, parsing toolkits, HyTime engines and DSSSL engines.

66.3.1.1   Architectural forms engines

XAF

XAF is an architectural forms engine which offers a SAX 1.0 interface to the transformed document. XAF can be used with any

SAX 1.0 parser. Only a subset of architectural forms is supported and this release is at beta level.

xmlarch

xmlarch is an architectural forms engine written in Python that works with any SAX 1.0 parser and offers a SAX 1.0 interface to the processed documents. It is also possible to receive architectural document events for several architectures in one parse pass.

66.3.1.2   XLink/XPointer engines

XPath4XT

XPath4XT is an XPath implementation that can evaluate XPath expressions against a DOM tree. XPath4XT uses XT and comes with a special version of XT which has to be used. XPath4XT uses JAXP to parse XML documets, and so requires a parser with support for JAXP.

XML::XPath

XML::XPath is a Perl implementation of XPath. It can parse XPath expressions and resolve them against a document tree built by the XPath module from SAX events or the XML::Parser.

66.3.1.3   XSL engines

FOP

FOP is a Java application that takes an XML document conforming to the formatting half of the XSL 19990421 Working Draft and produces PDF output. This way it can be used with any SAX 1.0 parser to produce PDF from XML + XSL. FOP can be invoked from the command line and read from a file, or it can be given a DOM document or a SAX DocumentHandler at run-time.

Passive TeX

Passive TeX is a TeX implementation of the XSL March 2000 WD and MathML which reads XML documents containing XSL formatting objects and MathML elements and uses LaTeX to produce formatted output. This can be used to produce well-formatted PDF, DVI or PostScript, and even supports bookmarks in the PDF output.

REXP

REXP is an XSL:fo to PDF file converter, based on the source of FOP 0.9.2. It supports a bit more of XSL than FOP does. A tiny bit of support for SVG is also there, and there will probably be more in the future.

66.3.1.4   XSLT engines

SAXON

SAXON is a Java framework for processing XML documents optimized for XML to XML/SGML/HTML conversions. Essentially, it is an XSLT implementation (1.0 recommendation) which can also be used as a Java development framework. The XSLT implementation is fast, fully conformant and provides many useful extensions. Through its API Java and XSLT code can be combined.

XT

XT is an XSLT engine that implements the final XSLT recommendation, as well as the XPath recommendation. It is officially of beta quality, but experience has shown it to be very fast, stable and conformant. It does not support the full recommendation, but does have some useful extensions. It can be used with any SAX 1.0 parser and also as a servlet.

Xalan-Java

Xalan-Java is an XSLT processor written in Java. It implements the entire final XSLT recommendation, and can produce both SAX and DOM output, with support for Java and JavaScript extensions. Xalan-Java uses Xerces-Java for XML parsing. Xalan has a JAXP API. Xalan can also compile XSLT stylesheets to Java bytecode.

Xalan-C++

Xalan-C++ is a C++ implementation of an XSLT processor, following the final XSLT recommendation. The XML parser used is Xerces.

Sablotron

The Sablotron is an XSLT processor written in C++ (as open source). The goal is to make the processor fast, compact and portable. The Sablotron has both a command-line and an API interface. Not all features of XSLT are currently implemented. The Sablotron uses expat for XML parsing.

66.3.1.5 DSSSL engines

Jade

Jade is James Clark's excellent DSSSL engine, which is really a general SGML tool for conversion from SGML to other SGML DTDs or to output formats like RTF and TeX. Jade can process XML documents and can also output XML. Jade uses SP to parse the SGML/XML input.

66.3.1.6 SGML/XML parsers

SP

SP is an SGML/XML parser, and is fast, complete, highly conformant and very stable. SP has been the parser of choice for most of the SGML community for many years and has been embedded in lots of other applications. SP supports architectural forms as well as SGML Open catalogs.

SPIN_py

SPIN is a C module that can be compiled into the Python interpreter to provide an interface to the SP SGML parser.

SPIN_tcl

SPIN is a C module that can be compiled into the tcl interpreter to provide an interface to the SP SGML parser.

66.3.1.7   XML parsers

expat

expat is a non-validating parser written in C, and is the parser previously known as XMLTok. It is used in Mozilla 5.0 and in parser modules for several different scripting languages. It is very fast and highly conformant.

TclXML

This is a validating XML parser written entirely in tcl. The parser offers both event-based and tree-based interfaces, and with Tcl 8.1 it supports Unicode.

XP

XP is written to be fully-conforming and as fast as possible, with an emphasis is on server-side production use. There is no validation, only well-formedness checking. Even though 0.5 is a beta release it is stable, conformant and fast. A SAX 1.0 driver is included. XP supports several Unicode encodings.

xmlproc

xmlproc is a validating parser written in Python. It implements nearly all of the XML Recommendation, including XML namespaces. (The home page lists the deviations.) xmlproc provides access to DTD information and also offers a DTD parsing module. xmlproc supports SGML Open catalogs and XML Catalogs. xmlproc can report errors in Norwegian and English and can be extended to support other languages as well.

Windows Foundation Classes

WFC is a collection of C++ classes for Windows programming. Included are a non-validating XML parser as well as other tools for working with XML documents. The parser has been tested on Unix too.

TclExpat

TclExpat is the expat C XML parser wrapped as a Tcl module. Version 1.1 uses the final 1.0 version of expat, which supports XML namespaces.

Expat Module for Ruby

This module wraps the expat parser for access from within the Ruby interpreter. (Ruby is an object-oriented scripting language with similarities to Perl.) It also has a DOM 1.0 implementation and XPointer support.

XML Parser Component for Delphi

This is a validating XML parser written in Delphi that parses XML documents into a DOM element tree that can then be modified and traversed. The component also allows programs to build DOM trees and write them out as an XML document. The parser supports both 8-bit and 16-bit encodings.

libxml

libxml is a validating XML parser written in C (also known as gnome-xml). It has an event-based (SAX-like) interface and can also build an in-memory DOM-like tree of the parsed document. There is also a nearly full XPath implementation, and libxml supports namespaces. An HTML parser is also included.

fxp

fxp is a validating XML parser written in Standard ML, a functional programming language in the ML family. fxp has a programming interface, and comes with some example command-line applications. It has only been tested with the Standard ML of New Jersey compiler under Unix, but might well work elsewhere as well. fxp supports XCatalog and Unicode.

Microsoft XML Parser

The Microsoft XML Parser is a COM component that can be accessed from any COM-aware application in any programming language. The parser is validating and supports the DOM 1.0, XML namespaces, a subset of the XSLT (final recommendation), a subset of XPath, and XML schemas (XDR ones, that is). The parser requires Microsoft Internet Explorer 4.01 with SP1.

HaXml

HaXml is a collection of libraries for using XML in Haskell. This includes a non-validating XML parser, an HTML parser, a library for transforming XML documents (and generating HTML) and special modules for building Haskell data structures from XML documents and dumping them back out as XML. HaXml supports Unicode if the Haskell compiler does.

PXP

PXP is a complete validating XML parser written in Objective Caml, a functional programming language in the ML family with OO features. PXP has some advanced features for building customized XML document trees and also provides access to DTD information. It supports Unicode and can read documents in many different encodings.

Xerces Java

Xerces Java is a validating XML parser with support for the DOM level 1 and 2, SAX 1.0 and 2.0, and the XML Schemas final recommendation. Xerces can be invoked through the JAXP API.

Xerces C++

Xerces C++ is a validating XML parser written in a portable subset of C++. It supports XML Namespaces, the DOM level 1 and SAX 1.0. Preliminary support for DOM level 2 and SAX 2.0 is also available.

Xerces Perl

Xerces Perl is the validating Xerces C++ parser wrapped as a Perl module. It supports the DOM level 1.

xml.expat

xml.expat is a Common Lisp wrapper for expat, allowing it to be used from Franz' Allegro Common Lisp compiler. The package basically exposes the raw expat API, and then adds some convenience macros and functions on top of that.

xmlparse

xmlparse is a validating XML parser written in C++ with full Unicode support. The parser has been tested on the OASIS conformance test suite and should be highly conformant (only 3 errors). It uses a SAX-like API and passes text to the application in UTF-8 encoding.

TinyXML

TinyXML is a non-validating parser written in Java which has been made as small as possible. It supports an event-based callback interface similar to SAX (with this the parser is only 16k), but also has a very simple tree interface.

UncommonXML

UncommonXML is more or less a Common Lisp port of the XP XML parser. It does not validate, but reads the DTD. It is currently at the alpha level.

66.3.1.8 DOM implementations

TclDOM

TclDOM is a 100% Tcl implementation of the DOM 1.0. The aim is to create a standard Tcl version of the DOM to be used with any DOM implementation/parser.

InDelv Smalltalk DOM

The InDelv Smalltalk DOM is a DOM 1.0 implementation written in Smalltalk, and comes with a non-validating Smalltalk XML parser with a SAX-like interface.

XDOM

XDOM is an open source XML parser with a DOM level 1 and level 2 (core and traversal) implementation written in Delphi. The implementation implements some convenience extensions and also deviates from the specification in a couple of places.

66.3.1.9 XML middleware

SAX

SAX 1.0 is now obsolete, and has been replaced by SAX 2.0.

DOMParser

The DOM Parser is a SAX 1.0-compliant parser that turns a DOM Document into a SAX event stream, instead of parsing an XML document.

XML::Writer

XML::Writer is a Perl module which makes it easier to generate correct XML output from Perl. It has intelligent support for XML namespaces and will automatically generate prefixes (although this can be controlled, if desired).

CGI::XMLForm

CGI::XMLForm is a Perl module that extends CGI.pm to create custom XML from HTML form input and can also create HTML form values based on XQL-like queries of XML data. CGI::XMLForm uses XML::Parser.

Python XML package

The Python XML package is a package of various Python XML tools that has been put together by the Python XML Special Interest Group, a group of volunteers led by Andrew M. Kuchling, for the convenience of Python XML developers.

PyXPath

PyXPath is a Python implementation of the 9.Jul.99 XPath working draft. It can parse and evaluate XPath expressions, but currently cannot do matching. It requires PyDOM.

GPS

GPS is a general implementation of the grove data model (from the HyTime ISO-standard). It implements both groves and property sets, in two different implementations. One is an in-memory structure, the other uses the ZODB object database for persistence.

Pyxie

Pyxie is a powerful XML processing library written in Python which can be used to develop XML processing software which is event-driven, tree-based or event-driven with tree access. Pyxie requires the Python XML package.

SAX2

SAX is a simple event-based API for XML parsers. It is not an official standard, since it was developed by the participants of the xml-dev mailing list instead of a standards body. However, SAX is very much a de facto standard, since it is supported by most XML parsers and is used by lots of applications

xmlBlaster

xmlBlaster is a pure Java publish/subscribe MOM server (message-oriented middleware) which exchanges XML-encoded messages between publishers and subscribers. Communication with the server is based on CORBA (using JacORB), and subscribers can use XPath expressions to filter the messages they wish to receive.

Protege

Protege is a very advanced knowledge-based framework for developing domain-specific systems. It has been developed and used by the medical informatics community for years and has lately been extended with support for RDF. So Protege does much much more, but can also be used for generating editors for specific RDF applications. It understands both RDF and RDF schemas.

JDOM

JDOM is an API for representing the XML document tree structure similar to the DOM, but much simpler and designed specifically for Java using the collections API. JDOM structures can be built from XML files, DOM trees and SAX events and can be converted to the same.

66.3.1.10   RDF parsers

ICS-FORTH Validating RDF Parser

The ICS-FORTH VRP can parse RDF documents and validate them against an RDF Schema. It is intended to be embedded in other software as a library.

RDF Filter

RDF Filter is an event-based RDF parser built on top of SAX 2.0. It fires callback methods for RDF input events and is suitable for use with large RDF documents, since it does not build the full in-memory structure.

66.3.2 *Editing and composition*

Tools for interactive creation, modification and composition of XML documents.

66.3.2.1   XML editors

Amaya

Amaya is the W3C testbed browser, and is an HTML and XHTML browser (and editing tool) with CSS support. It supports the MathML 2.0 XML DTD and can edit and display presentational MathML graphically; Amaya can also display some SVG. There is support for simple XLinks. Amaya can read HTML documents written in XML, and save HTML documents as XHTML.

Emile

Emile is an XML editor that reads the DTD to provide short-cuts for the user during editing. Emile can export documents as HTML.

PECEL

PECEL is an XML data entry tool geared towards data applications more than document applications. It is tree-based, and uses a DTD to guide the user during document creation. PECEL also has a template function for creating document templates. PECEL uses XML4J for parsing.

Merlot

Merlot is an open source XML editor for data-oriented applications rather than document-oriented applications. It has a plugin API that allows the editing of some elements to be customized for specific DTDs.

66.3.3 *Control information development*

Tools for creating, modifying and documenting DTDs, XSL style sheets etc.

66.3.3.1 XSL editors

xslide

xslide is a major Emacs mode for editing XSL style sheets that has both syntax coloring, automatic completion and convenience functions to run XSL engines. xslide was tested in Emacs 20.3.1.

66.3.3.2 XSL checkers

XSL Lint

XSL Lint is a Perl script that checks XSLT style sheets for mistakes. It is at the alpha level.

66.3.3.3 DTD parsers

DTDParse

DTDParse is a Perl module that can parse a DTD into an in-memory structure. This structure can then be used in various kinds of programs that need DTD information. It comes with several scripts that can produce DTD documentation using this module.

DTDParser

DTDParser is a Java module for parsing XML DTDs separately from any XML document. The parser can parse from any kind of stream and builds an object structure representing the DTD. This structure can then be accessed to extract information about the DTD and also be modified.

66.3.4 *Conversion*

Tools for scripted creation and modification of XML documents.

66.3.4.1   General S-converters

X-Tract

X-Tract is an interpreter for XML Script, an XML transformation language with XML syntax. XML Script can be seen as a non-standard version of XSLT, with different syntax and based more on a traditional imperative programming model, rather than the functional model of XSLT. It uses the Xerces parser.

MetaMorphosis

MetaMorphosis is a tree-based XML transformation tool that can be used to convert between SGML/XML applications, to publishing formats etc. MetaMorphosis has an architecture where several parsers and output generators are available (and more can be written in Visual Basic or C++ and plugged in).

66.3.4.2   General N-converters

Majix

Majix is an RTF-to-XML converter written entirely in Java. It can handle RTF styles and also lets you customize it to fit your own XML DTDs.

Tidy

Tidy is a tool that can read your XML and HTML markup and detect and to some extent also fix errors in it. This can be used to clean up bad HTML and XML and also to convert from poor HTML to XML. Tidy can also pretty-print your markup, and has special features for dealing with the HTML produced by MS Word '97 and 2000. It is to some extent also aware of ASP, JSP and PHP directives and will ignore these.

DB2XML

DB2XML is a tool for generating XML from database queries. It is a GUI-driven application written in Java, but can also be used as a servlet and as a command-line application. The XML generated is configurable, and metadata (types etc) can optionally be included, dates can be customized and currency representation can be localized. The generated XML can be processed with an XSLT stylesheet, using the embedded LotusXSL XSLT engine.

Java HTML Tidy

Java HTML Tidy is a reimplementation of Tidy in Java. JTidy, as it is also known, can parse non-conforming HTML documents into a DOM tree and convert them to valid HTML.

66.3.5 *Electronic delivery*

Tools for electronic delivery and display of XML documents.

66.3.5.1 XML browsers

Mozilla

This is version 5 of Netscape Navigator, which can display XML documents with CSS style. It also has some support for MathML. Please note that this is a beta release.

InDelv XML Client

The InDelv XML Client is an XML browser written in Java that uses XSLT stylesheets to display the documents. It can also be used to edit documents. The client also supports XPath and XPointer.

66.3.5.2   Web publishing

Cocoon
> Cocoon is a Java servlet framework that can be used to publish XML on the web as HTML. It tries to establish a three-layer framework for this, with the three layers being content (ie: XML source documents), style (ie: XSL style sheets) and a so-called logicsheet.

66.3.6   *Document Storage and Management*

Tools for supporting document management, such as document databases and search engines.

66.3.6.1   XML document database systems

XML-DBMS
> XML-DBMS is a Java library that can be used to move data from XML to a relational database and also back again. Through the use of a mapping document the structure of the original document is preserved.

66.3.6.2   XML search engines

XML::QL
> XML::QL is a Perl implementation of the proposed XML-QL XML query language (note: this is not XQL), built directly on top of XML::Parser.

Xtract

> Xtract is a document search tool for with a query language loosely based on XQL. Xtract can handle both HTML and XML documents, but is currently at beta level.

XSet

> XSet is an XML search engine oriented towards performance. It keeps its working set in memory (using paging to support large documents) and can be accessed through RMI. The query language is very simple.

66.4 | The XML SPECtacular

The CD includes a collection of the relevant standards and specifications that you can browse, search, and print. There is a brief description of each.

For each document, we've included a link to a website where you can learn more about the underlying project and obtain the latest version of the spec. Where copyright and production considerations allowed, we've also included a browseable copy on the CD-ROM.

In this listing, we've only included brief summaries of specs for which the full text exists on the CD.

66.4.1 *W3C base standards*

The following standards are either approved W3C Recommendations or are in development.

XML: Extensible Markup Language

> Here it is: the XML standard itself. For a standard it is mercifully short and readable, and clearly written. This is definitely recommended reading! Note that this is the second edition of the specification, where numerous errors and ambiguities have been fixed.

Namespaces in XML

This standard enables XML element-type names to be globally unique. This can be used in many ways, such as to mix elements from different vocabularies in a single document, as RDF and XSLT do.

DOM1: Document Object Model - level 1

The DOM is an important XML standard that is often used to implement many of the others. It describes a standardized API for accessing, manipulating and building XML and HTML document structures in memory, and is often the basis for implementations of XSL, XPointer, XQL and many other standards. It is also intended to be used by browsers and editors.

DOM2: Document Object Model - level 2

The DOM is an important XML standard that is often used to implement many of the others. It describes a standardized API for accessing, manipulating and building XML and HTML document structures in memory, and is often the basis for implementations of XSLT, XPointer, XQL and many other standards. It is also intended to be used in browsers and editors.

RDF: Resource Description Framework - Model and Syntax Specification

RDF promises to become an important part of the infrastructure of the Web in the future. It provides a framework for describing resources on the Web and as such holds great promise of providing new means of navigation on the Web and better guidance for Web robots.

XPath: XML Path Language

XPath provides an expression language that can be used to search XML documents, to filter them, to address into them and to compute values from them. It is an extremely versatile and useful standard, and it provides the foundation for both XSLT and XPointer.

XLink: XML Linking Language

XLink is a crucial part of the XML standards family as it describes hyperlinking in XML documents and takes major steps beyond the hyperlinking provided by HTML.

XPointer: XML Pointer Language

XPointer is a companion standard to XLink that describes mechanisms for addressing a particular part of a document with a hyperlink. It is based on XPath, so it may be a good idea to look at the XPath specification before diving into XPointer.

XML Fragment Interchange

This standard describes how to exchange fragments of XML documents while retaining interesting parts of the context of the fragment, such as the DTD reference, ancestor information for the fragment, etc.

XML Information Set

This standard is much more important than it may seem at first glance. The XML recommendation itself only describes a syntax for representing the data in XML documents, but an actual data model for XML documents is not provided there. And, when you think about it, the only reason we have the syntax is to enable us to exchange documents and then recreate the data described by the document inside our systems and programs. And this is what the XML Information Set provides: a formal data model for XML documents.

XML Schema Part 1: Structures

This is perhaps one of the most important standards in the set of XML-related standards. XML already has DTDs, which can be used to define what particular types of XML documents can and cannot contain. Schemas go beyond the features offered by DTDs in order to offer functionality required in the many new areas where XML is currently being used.

XML Schema Part 2: Datatypes

This specification provides the features used to define the datatypes of element content and attribute values. This can be used to declare that an element contains dates or URLs, and similarly for attributes. Although datatypes are part of the work on schemas, they can also be used in DTDs. (There is open source software on the CD-ROM that supports such use.)

XSL: Extensible Stylesheet Language

This is another important standard which provides a means of rendering XML documents in a way that is optimized for end-users of the information. This can be as visually formatted documents or as aurally formatted documents destined for text-to-speech synthesis.

XSLT: XSL Transformations

XSLT is an XML-based language for describing transformations on XML documents. This can be used to convert between XML document types, to HTML or to XSL flow objects as described in the XSL standard.

Associating stylesheets with XML documents

This very simple standard describes how to reference a style sheet from an XML document in a stylesheet-language- and application-independent way. A useful reference.

CSS2: Cascading Style Sheets - level 2

CSS is the style sheet standard that is implemented in browsers today and can be used right now. It is simple, but effective and elegant. Software that can support CSS-based display of XML is already here and more should be just round the corner.

66.4.2 *W3C XML applications*

These application standards are either approved W3C Recommendations or are in development.

SMIL: Synchronized Multimedia Integration Language

SMIL is an XML application that can be used to integrate a set of multimedia objects into a coherent presentation complete with hyperlinks and synchronization. SMIL can be integrated with XHTML and SVG.

MathML: Mathematical Markup Language

MathML is the long-awaited solution to a problem many scientists and teachers have struggled with: how to publish mathematical formulae on the web. It also provides a solution for exchanging formulae between programs.

XHTML: The Extensible HyperText Markup Language

XHTML is a reformulation of HTML 4.0 in XML syntax, and is intended to be the basis for further work on HTML. This work is likely to consist of both a modularization of XHTML as well as extensions to it.

SVG: Scalable Vector Graphics

SVG is an XML application that can be used to describe two-dimensional vector graphics, text and raster images. This allows for styling images with style sheets, and hyperlinking into (and out of) images.

66.4.3 *Other specifications*

These standards are developed by industry consortia, collaborations of several vendors, or informal user groups.

SAX 2.0: Simple API for XML

SAX is a general event-based API for XML parsers. Using SAX enables application programmers to write applications and utilities that are parser-independent. SAX is not presently being standardized by an official standards body. It is a de facto standard developed by the participants on the xml-dev mailing list.

XMLNews

XMLNews is a set of specifications for exchanging news items, and allows optional richness of markup. There are two specifications: XMLNews-Story which is a document type for news stories, and XMLNews-Meta which is a document type for news story metadata records.

XSA: XML Software Autoupdate

XSA is an XML-based system for automatically discovering new releases of software products. Software developers publish an XSA document which describes all their software products, and list maintainers and other interested parties poll these documents to discover new releases and address changes.

Repositories and vocabularies

Resource Description

■ Schemas, DTDs and other specifications

■ Vertical and cross-industry

■ Repositories

■ Industry vocabularies

Contributing expert: Lilia Prescod

> There are so many XML projects in the world that it can be hard to find the ones that apply to you. Here's a guide.

T he growth in XML activity has been so frantic that it seems as though there is now a vocabulary, or several, for every industry and application. We've prepared this chapter to help you find the ones that might apply to your situation. It lists over 350 vocabularies that were available when we wrote this book.

The list is not totally comprehensive. Even if it were, there are new vocabularies being created every day, so you'll want to know how to find them yourself. A good place to start is with one of the websites that accumulates XML vocabularies.

67.1 | Registries and repositories

There is so much happening in the XML world that it can be hard to find the work that has already been done. In particular, it can be tricky to find out if there is a DTD, schema or standard that applies to the problem you are trying to solve. It would be helpful if there were an official place to find all XML-related schemas and specifications.

A list of these DTDs, schemas, and other specifications is known as a *registry*. The good news is that registries exist. The bad news is that there are several of them and none of them has complete coverage yet. Still, searching three or four websites for an applicable specification is better than searching the entire Web!

Over time, the backers of these registries would like them to become Internet backbone technologies like the Domain Name Service or the IP number allocators. This eventuality will require the sites to move beyond a role as simple yellow pages and into a more sophisticated role of schema server and integrator: not just registry but also *repository*.

The path from here to there is not entirely clear. But it is clear that there is a lot at stake. The owner of the Internet's "XML Schema Server" will have a lot of influence on uses of XML.

67.1.1 *xml.org*

xml.org, `http://www.xml.org`, is a project of the Organization for the Advancement of Structured Information Standards (OASIS). Its site incorporates a content management system, which allows the site to serve as both a registry (search engine) and a repository (storage site) for DTDs, schemas and other standards documents. Groups and individuals who create such documents can store them at the xml.org site.

xml.org is considered a resource for "XML specifications, schemas and vocabularies". At this point, the repository does not require any particular schema language or adherence to a particular framework. It is framework and technology neutral. This is good in that it maximizes contributor freedom and opportunity to innovate. The downside is that all of these specifications may not work together nicely because there are no published guidelines for making them work together.

OASIS wants xml.org to become more than a standalone repository. It should also become an index to a variety of other, technically compatible repositories. In other words, it should one day be able to delegate queries to affiliated repositories run by other companies.

67.1.2 *uddi.org*

uddi.org, `www.uddi.org`, is a registry of Web services that uses the UDDI protocol that we described in 47.2, "Universal Description, Discovery, and Integration", on page 689

A UDDI registry is organized into three different kinds of information records:

white pages
> They contain general contact information about organizations.

yellow pages
> These list organizations by business category or location.

green pages
> These include the technical aspects of conducting business, including Web service descriptions and schemas.

uddi.org has a much more formal structure than xml.org and is designed to help potential business partners find each other. xml.org, in contrast, is organized around schemas appropriate to particular industries.

UDDI is still in its infancy but there are big goals for the project, which at this writing had over 200 "community members", including all of the major platform vendors. It is already possible to experiment with the service, either interactively through a Web browser or from a programming language through SOAP.

67.1.3 *BizTalk repository*

The BizTalk repository, `http://www.biztalk.org`, is for schemas that are compatible with the BizTalk framework. Although the repository is run primarily by Microsoft there is also an "advisory board" made up of outsiders.

BizTalk schemas need to pass a verification test. This is a double-edged sword. In theory, these tests can impose some level of quality control and interoperability requirements. This could help independently created schemas to work together. These tests will inevitably reject some schemas or specifications that are useful despite the fact that they do not adhere to the BizTalk framework specifications.

If you are looking for schemas for use within the BizTalk framework, then the BizTalk repository should be the first place you go. Otherwise, you should probably use one of the other repositories with a more general collection of schemas.

67.1.4   *Other registries*

xml.org and uddi.org dream of being the backbone of the Web's XML infrastructure, but some sites are interested primarily in being registries for schemas hosted elsewhere. These sites are older than the ones we've just discussed, and in some domains they are more complete.

The first such site was Robin Cover's, `www.oasis-open.org/cover`. Robin has cataloged markup-related information since the earliest SGML days, before there was even a Web as we know it. His Web pages have come to be known as the "Cover pages" (get it)?

Robin's pages are more than a schema registry and also less. They are more than a schema registry because they track software, Web pages, printed books and everything else pertaining to XML and SGML. The Cover pages are one-stop shopping for consumers of XML news and information. On the other hand, the pages do not actually store the schemas in question and cannot serve them to client software on demand.

Our Australian friend, James Tauber, runs another schema index with the imaginative name "schema.net", `http://www.schema.net`. Well, okay, the name itself is rather obvious; the imagination was in grabbing the domain name before anyone saw the importance of schemas!

67.2 | Public vocabularies

We use the catch-all term *vocabulary* to refer to all sorts of element-type and attribute specifications. Some are DTDs, some use one of the new schema definition languages, and some use informal English prose.

Some vocabularies define complete, self-contained document types, both POP-like and for messages. Some define only parts of the document because their designers expect them be augmented by other vocabularies that define the other parts.

In the following list, we've grouped the vocabularies into 77 categories, which are in turn grouped into eight super-categories. For each project, there is a URL. For your convenience, the list is also available on a page on the CD-ROM so you can let your browser link directly to the project sites. That list also includes a brief description of each vocabulary.

67.2.1 *Business Systems*

Application integration

Open Applications Group Interface Specification (OAGIS)
`http://www.openapplications.org`

Calendaring

iCalendar
`http://www.imc.org/rfc2445`
vCard and vCalendar
`http://www.imc.org/pdi/`

Catalog

Open Catalog Format (OCF)
`http://www.martsoft.com/docs/ocf/ocf.htm`
Open Catalog Protocol (OCP)
`http://www.martsoft.com/ocp/`
Product Data Markup Language (PDML)
`http://www.pdml.org/pdmlintro.html`
eCatalog XML (eCX)
`http://www.ecx-xml.org/`

Commerce

BizTalk Framework 2.0
`http://www.microsoft.com/biztalk/techinfo/framwork20.asp`
Business Process Modeling Language (BPML)
`http://www.bpmi.org/faq.esp`
Business Rules Markup Language (BRML)

`http://www.research.ibm.com/rules/commonrules-overview.html`

CommerceXML (cXML)

`http://www.cxml.org/home/`

Common Business Library (xCBL)

`http://www.xcbl.org/`

Electronic Business XML Initiative (ebXML)

`http://www.ebxml.org/geninfo.htm#what`

Electronic Commerce Modeling Language (ECML)

`http://www.ecml.org/`

Global Uniform Interoperable Data Exchange (GUIDE)

`http://www.bizcodes.org/GUIDE/`

Guideline XML

`http://www.edifecs.com/b2b_resources_guideline.jsp`

Implementation Guide Markup Language (IgML)

`http://www.foresightcorp.com/igmldev/`

Internet Open Trading Protocol (OTP)(Trade)

`http://www.ietf.org/html.charters/trade-charter.html`

Marine Trading Markup Language (MTML)

`http://www.mtml.org/`

Network Trade Model (NTM)

`http://www.risk.sungard.com/ntm/`

Open Buying on the Internet (OBI)

`http://www.openbuy.org/`

RosettaNet

`http://www.rosettanet.org`

Small and Medium Sized Business XML (SMBXML)

`http://www.smbxml.org/`

Trading Partner Agreement Markup Language (tpaML)

`http://www-106.ibm.com/developerworks/library/tpaml.html`

Transaction Authority Markup Language (XAML)

`http://www.xaml.org/`

Universal Commerce Language and Protocol (UCLP)

`http://www.w3.org/TR/NOTE-uclp/`

Visa XML Invoice Specification

`http://www-s2.visa.com/ut/dnld/spec.ghtml`

eCo Framework

`http://www.commerce.net/projects/currentprojects/eco/`

eXchangeable Routing Language (XRL)

`http://tmitwww.tm.tue.nl/staff/wvdaalst/Workflow/xrl/`

Customer information

Customer Profile Exchange Network (CPExchange)
http://www.cpexchange.org/
GlobalAddress
http://www.and.com/standards/repository.html
Unified Customer Reporting (UCR)
http://www.haifa.il.ibm.com/projects/software/ucr/index.html
eXtensible Customer Information Language (xCIL)
http://members.ozemail.com.au/~sakthi/dtd/dtd.html
eXtensible Name and Address Language (xNAL)
http://members.ozemail.com.au/~sakthi/dtd/dtd.html

Data mining

Predictive Model Markup Language (PMML)
http://www.dmg.org/public/techreports/pmml-1 0.html

Electronic data interchange (edi)

ACORD EDI (AL3)
http://www.acord.org/
ANSI ASC X12/XML
http://www.x12.org/
Formal Language for Business Communication (FLBC)
http://www-personal.umich.edu/~samoore/research/flbc/index.htm
l
TranXML
http://www.transentric.com/products/commerce/tranxml.asp
XEDI
http://www.xedi.org/about.html
XML/EDI (Electronic Data Interchange)
http://www.xmledi-group.org/

Finance

Bank Internet Payment System (BIPS)
http://www.fstc.org/projects/bips/
Common Markup for micropayment per-fee-links

`http://www.w3.org/TR/Micropayment-Markup/`

Extensible Business Reporting Language (XBRL)

`http://www.xfrml.org/`

FinXML

`http://www.finxml.org/`

Financial Information Exchange Markup Language (FIXML)

`http://www.fixprotocol.org/cgi-bin/rbox/Welcome.cgi`

Financial Information eXchange (FIX)

`http://www.fixprotocol.org/cgi-bin/rbox/Welcome.cgi`

FpML (Financial products Markup Language)

`http://fpml.org/`

Interactive Financial eXchange (IFX)

`http://www.ifxforum.org/`

Investment Research Markup Language (IRML)

`http://www.irml.org/html/approach.asp`

Market Data Definition Language (MDDL)

`http://www.fisd.net/mddl/default.html`

Mortgage Industry Standards Maintenance Organization (MISMO)

`http://www.mismo.org/mismo/Mismo_faq.cfm#1`

Open Financial Exchange (OFX)

`http://www.ofx.net/ofx/default.asp`

Research Information Exchange Markup Language

`http://www.rixml.org/faqs.html#gen`

Straight Through Processing Markup Language (STPML)

`http://www.stpml.org/`

XMLPay

`http://www.verisign.com/developer/xml/xmlpay.html`

data link for intermediaries Markup Language (daliML)

`http://www.dali1441.com/dali/dalihome.nsf/daliML?openframeset`

swiftML

`http://www.swift.com/index.cfm?item_id=2642`

Human resources

HR-XML

`http://www.hr-xml.org/channels/home.htm`

Human Resources Markup Language (hrml)

`http://www.hrml.com/`

Human Resources XML (HR-XML)

http://www.hr-xml.org/channels/home.htm
Job Survey (JobSur) Markup Language (JSML)
http://www.codap.com/job_survey_jobsur.htm
XMLRsum Library
http://xmlresume.sourceforge.net/

Industrial automation

Machinery Information Management Open Systems Alliance (MIMOSA)
http://www.mimosa.org/
Virtual Instruments Markup Language (VIML)
http://nacimiento.com/VIML/

Product information

Electronic Component Information eXchange (ECIX) QuickData Protocol
Specification
http://www.si2.org/ecix/ecix_home.htm
Product Definition eXchange (PDX)
http://www.pdxstandard.org/
StepML
http://www.stepml.org/index.html

Security

XML Key Management Specification (XKMS)
http://www.w3.org/TR/xkms/
AuthXML Standard for Web Security
http://www.authxml.org/
Intrusion Detection Exchange Format (idwg)
http://www.ietf.org/html.charters/idwg-charter.html
Intrusion Detection Message Exchange Format(IDMEF)
http://www.ietf.org/internet-drafts/draft-ietf-idwg-xmlsmi-01.
txt
Security Assertion Markup Language (SAML)
http://www.oasis-open.org/committees/security/docs/draft-sstc-
saml-spec-00.PDF
Security Services Markup Language (S2ML)
http://www.s2ml.org/

Signed Document Markup Language (SDML)

`http://www.w3.org/TR/1998/NOTE-SDML-19980619/#SECTION00200`

XML Access Control (XACL)

`http://www.trl.ibm.com/projects/xml/xacl/index.htm`

XML Encoding of SPKI(Simple Public Key Infrastructure) Certificates

`http://www.alternic.org/drafts/drafts-p-q/draft-paajarvi-xml-s`
`pki-cert-00.html`

XML Key Information Service Specification (X-KISS)

`http://www.w3.org/2001/07/xkms-ws/cfp.html`

XML Key Registration Service Specification (X-KRSS)

`http://www.w3.org/2001/07/xkms-ws/cfp.html`

XML-Signature

`http://www.w3.org/Signature/`

eXtensible Access Control Markup Language (XACML)

`http://www.xacml.org/committees/xacml/index.shtml`

eXtensible Access Control Markup Language (XACML)

`http://www.xacml.org/committees/xacml/index.shtml`

Systems administration

ALURe (Aggregation and Logging of User Requests) XML Specification

`http://www.alurexml.org/`

DMTF Common Information Model (CIM)

`http://www.dmtf.org/standards/standard_cim.php`

DirXML

`http://www.novell.com/products/nds/dirxml/quicklook.html`

Directory Services Markup Language (DSML)

`http://www.dsml.org/about.html`

Extensible Log Format (XLF)

`http://www.docuverse.com/xlf/index.html`

Log File Format

`http://communicator.sourceforge.net/logstandard/log-standard-v`
`14.html#Introduction`

Log Markup Language (LOGML)

`http://www.cs.rpi.edu/~puninj/LOGML/`

Workflow

Simple Workflow Access Protocol (SWAP)

```
http://www.ics.uci.edu/~ietfswap/
```
Workflow Management Coalition (WfMC)
```
http://www.wfmc.org/
```

67.2.2 *Content management and distribution*

Content management protocols

DAV Searching & Locating (DASL)
```
http://www.webdav.org/dasl/protocol/draft-dasl-protocol-00.htm
l
```
HTTP Distribution and Replication Protocol (DRP)
```
http://www.w3.org/TR/NOTE-drp-19970825.html
```
WebDAV
```
http://www.webdav.org/
```

Content organization

Portable Site Information (PSI)
```
http://www.xml.com/pub/2000/03/22/psi/index.html
```
XEditor
```
http://www.openhealth.org/editor/
```
XML Catalog
```
http://www.ccil.org/~cowan/XML/XCatalog.html
```

Metadata

BiblioML
```
http://www.culture.fr/BiblioML/
```
Common Warehouse Metadata (CWM)
```
http://www.cwmforum.org/
```
Dublin Core
```
http://dublincore.org/
```
Encoded Archival Description (EAD)
```
http://cidc.library.cornell.edu/xml/
```
Image Metadata Aggregation for Enhanced Searching (IMAGES)
```
http://www.diglib.org/pubs/news02_01/umnpv.htm
```
Jigsaw XML Format (JigXML)

`http://www.w3.org/Jigsaw/Doc/Programmer/JigXML.html`

MAchine Readable Cataloging (MARC)

`http://lcweb.loc.gov/marc/marc.html`

MPEG-7 Description Definition Language

`http://www.csd.uwo.ca/gradstudents/students/tong/mpeg-7.html#E`
`13E5`

Manuscript Access through Standards for Electronic Records (MASTER)

`http://www.cta.dmu.ac.uk/projects/master/`

Meta Content Framework Using XML (MCF)

`http://www.w3.org/TR/NOTE-MCF-XML.html`

Open Archives Metadata Set (OAMS)

`http://www.openarchives.org/sfc/sfc_oams.htm`

Platform for Internet Content Selection (PICS)

`http://www.w3.org/PICS/`

Publishing Requirements for Industry Standard Metadata (PRISM)

`http://www.prismstandard.org/index.asp`

Resource Description Framework (RDF)

`http://www.w3.org/RDF/`

Resource Directory Description Language (RDDL)

`http://www.openhealth.org/RDDL/#intro`

Structured Graph Format (SGF)

`http://www7.scu.edu.au/programme/fullpapers/416/416.html`

Topic Maps (ISO/IEC 13250)

`http://www.topicmaps.org/`

Web Modeling Language (WebML)

`http://www9.org/w9cdrom/177/177.html`

XMLMARC

`http://xmlmarc.stanford.edu/`

XMLTV

`http://www.doc.ic.ac.uk/~epa98/work/apps/xmltv/`

bibteXML

`http://carol.wins.uva.nl/~zegerh/bibteXML/`

Mobile delivery

Open eBook

`http://www.openebook.org/specification.htm`

SyncML

`http://www.syncml.org/`

Wireless Markup Language (WML)
http://www.wapforum.org/
XML DTD for Roaming Access Phone Book
http://rfc3017.x42.com/
XML Document Navigation Language (XDNL)
http://www.w3.org/TR/2000/NOTE-xdnl-20000323/#sec-intro

Rights management

Open Digital Rights Language (ODRL)
http://odrl.net/
eXtensible Media Commerce Language (XMCL)
http://www.xmcl.org/

Syndication

Channel Definition Format (CDF)
http://www.w3.org/TR/NOTE-CDFsubmit.html
Information and Content Exchange (ICE) Protocol
http://www.icestandard.org/
NITF (News Industry Text Format)
http://www.nitf.org/
NewsML
http://www.iptc.org/NMLIntro.htm
Open Content Syndication (OCS)
http://internetalchemy.org/ocs/index.html
RDF Site Summary (RSS)
http://www.oreillynet.com/topics/rss/rss
XMLNews-Meta
http://www.xmlnews.org/docs/xmlnews-meta.html
XMLNews-Story
http://www.xmlnews.org/docs/xmlnews-story.html

Technical publishing

DocBook DTD
http://www.oasis-open.org/docbook/
Electronic Book Exchange (EBX)
http://www.ebxwg.org/

Institute of Electrical and Electronics Engineers Standard (IEEESTD)
`http://standards.ieee.org/resources/spasystem/dtd/`
ONIX International DTD
`http://www.editeur.org/onix.html`
OpenOffice.org XML project
`http://xml.openoffice.org`
Printing Industry Markup Language (PrintML)
`http://printml.org/index_en.htm`
Question and Answer Markup Language (QAML)
`http://www.ascc.net/xml/en/utf-8/qaml-index.html`
RFC2629
`http://www.faqs.org/rfcs/rfc2629.html`
Text Encoding Initiative (TEI)
`http://www.tei-c.org/`
eFirst XML for Scholarly Articles
`http://www.openly.com/efirst/`

Translation

OpenTag Format
`http://www.opentag.com/`
Translation Memory Exchange (TMX)
`http://www.lisa.org/tmx/tmx.htm`

67.2.3   Content types

Forms

Extensible Forms Description Language (XFDL)
`http://www.w3.org/TR/1998/NOTE-XFDL-19980902`
XForms
`http://www.w3.org/MarkUp/Forms/`
XML Encoded Form Values
`http://www-uk.hpl.hp.com/people/sth/doc/draft-kristensen-xml-map-00.html`
XML Forms Architecture (XFA)
`http://www.xfa.com/`

Hypertext

HyTime
http://info.admin.kth.se/SGML/Anvandarforening/Arbetsgrupper/HyTime/Reports/tr1v1.html
Virtual HyperGlossary (VHG)
http://www.vhg.org.uk/home/index.html
XML Bookmark Exchange Language (XBEL)
http://www.python.org/topics/xml/xbel/
ibtwsh: Itsy Bitsy Teeny Weeny Simple Hypertext DTD
http://www.ccil.org/~cowan/XML/

Multimedia

DIG35
http://www.digitalimaging.org/
Image Markup Language (IML)
http://faculty.washington.edu/lober/iml/
MPEG-21 Multimedia Framework
http://www.cselt.it/mpeg/standards/mpeg-21/mpeg 21.htm
Multimodal Presentation Markup Language (MPML)
http://www.miv.t.u-tokyo.ac.jp/MPML/en/
Synchronized Multimedia Integration Language (SMIL)
http://www.w3.org/AudioVideo/Activity.html
XGL File Format Specification
http://www.xglspec.org/
XML Messaging Specification (XMSG)
http://www.w3.org/TR/xmsg/

Music

4ML
http://fourml.sourceforge.net/
FlowML
http://wendy.vub.ac.be/~bschiett/saol/FlowML.html
MuTaTeD2, A system for Music Information Retrieval of Encoded Music
http://www.pads.ahds.ac.uk/carolaMuTaTeD2Home.html?hyperwave=action%3dplain.action
Music Markup Language (MML)

`http://www.mmlxml.org/`
Music Tagging Type Definition (MuTaTeD!)
`http://www.pads.ahds.ac.uk/musicMutatedAbstract.html`
MusicML
`http://www.tcf.nl/3.0/musicml/`
MusicXML
`http://www.musicxml.org/default.asp`
Standard Music Description Language (SMDL)
`http://www.techno.com/smdl.htm`
eXtensible Score Language (XScore)
`http://fn2.freenet.edmonton.ab.ca/~rgrigait/xscore/`

Outlines

Outline Processor Markup Language (OPML)
`http://www.opml.org/`

Tables

CALS table
`http://www.tiac.net/users/bingham/tables/calstbhs.htm`

Vector graphics

Extensible 3D (X3D)
`http://www.vrml.org/x3d.html`
Precision Graphics Markup Language (PGML)
`http://www.w3.org/TR/1998/NOTE-PGML`
Scalable Vector Graphics (SVG)
`http://www.w3.org/Graphics/SVG/Overview.htm8#intro`
Vector Markup Language (VML)
`http://www.w3.org/TR/NOTE-VML`

Voice

JSpeech Grammar Format (JSGF)
`http://www.w3.org/TR/jsgf/`
Java Speech Markup Language Specification (JSML)
`http://java.sun.com/products/java-media/speech/forDevelopers/J`

SML/
NISO Digital Talking Books (DTB)
`http://www.loc.gov/nls/niso/dtd.htm`
Natural Language Semantics Markup Language
`http://www.w3.org/TR/2000/WD-nl-spec-20001120/`
SABLE: A Synthesis Markup Language
`http://www.bell-labs.com/project/tts/sable.html`
Speech Recognition Grammar Specification
`http://www.w3.org/TR/speech-grammar/`
Speech Synthesis Markup Language (SSML)
`http://www.cstr.ed.ac.uk/projects/ssml_details.html`
TalkML
`http://www.w3.org/Voice/TalkML/`
Voice eXtensible Markup Language (VoiceXML)
`http://www.voicexml.org/forum_1.html`

67.2.4 *Personal communication*

Email

HTML Threading: Conventions for use of HTML in email
`http://www.w3.org/TR/1998/NOTE-HTMLThreading-0105`
MessageML
`http://www.messageml.org/`

Instant messaging

Common Profile for Instant Messaging (CPIM)
`http://www.ietf.org/internet-drafts/draft-ietf-impp-cpim-01.txt`
Instant Messaging and Presence Protocol (impp)
`http://www.imppwg.org/`
Jabber XML
`http://www.jabber.org/`

67.2.5 *Science*

Astronomy and instruments

(Astronomical) Instrument Markup Language (IML/AIML)
`http://pioneer.gsfc.nasa.gov/public/aiml/`
Astronomical Dataset Markup Language (ADML)
`http://xml.gsfc.nasa.gov/`
Astronomical Markup Language (AML)
`http://monet.astro.uiuc.edu/~dguillau/these/`
Flexible Image Transport System (FITS)
`http://fits.gsfc.nasa.gov/fits_intro.html`
Spacecraft Markup Language (SML)
`http://www.interfacecontrol.com/sml/`

Biology

Anatomical Markup Language (AnatML)
`http://www.physiome.org.nz/sites/physiome/anatml/pages/`
BIOpolymer Markup Language (BIOML)
`http://www.bioml.com/BIOML/index.html`
Bioinformatic Sequence Markup Language (BSML)
`http://www.labbook.com/products/xmlbsml.asp`
CellML
`http://www.cellml.org/public/about/what_is_cellml.html`
Gene Expression Markup Language (GEML)
`http://www.geml.org/`
Genome Annotation Markup Elements (GAME)
`http://www.bioxml.org/Projects/game/`
Taxonomic Markup Language
`http://www.albany.edu/~gilmr/pubxml/`
The Systems Biology Markup Language (SBML)
`http://www.cds.caltech.edu/erato/sbml/docs/index.html`
XDELTA (DEscription Language for TAxonomy)
`http://www.bath.ac.uk/~ccslrd/delta/index.html`
XML for Multiple Sequence Alignments (MSAML)
`http://maggie.cbr.nrc.ca/~gordonp/xml/MSAML/`

Chemistry

CHEM ESTANDARDS
http://www.cidx.org/commerce/what.html
Chemical Markup Language (CML)
http://www.xml-cml.org/
Molecular Dynamics Language (MODL)
http://violet.csa.iisc.ernet.in/~modl/

General science

Extensible Scientific Interchange Language (XSIL)
http://www.cacr.caltech.edu/SDA/xsil/
eXtensible Data Format (XDF)
http://xml.gsfc.nasa.gov/XDF/XDF_home.html
nanoML
http://www.nanotitan.com/

Geography

CaveScript XML
http://www.speleonics.com.au/cavescript/
Geography Markup Language (GML)
http://www.opengis.net/gml/01 029/GML2.html
LandXML
http://www.landxml.org/over.htm
Point Of Interest eXchange Language Specification (POIX)
http://www.w3.org/TR/poix/

Math

Mathematical Markup Language (MathML)
http://www.w3.org/Math/
Open Mathematical Documents (OMDoc)
http://www.mathweb.org/omdoc/
OpenMath
http://www.openmath.org/

Meteorology

Weather Observation Definition Format (ODF)
`http://zowie.metnet.navy.mil/~spawar/JMV-TNG/XML/OMF.html`
WeatherML
`http://www.weatherml.com/home.htm`

67.2.6   *Social*

Economics

EcoKnowMICS ML
`http://www.ecoknowmics.com/prod01.htm`

Game playing

Board Game Markup Language (BGML)
`http://www.vilab.com/bgml/home.html`
Caxton Chess XML (CaXML)
`http://www.chesscity.com/RESOURCES/XML/CaxtonXML.htm#_Toc51637`
`4582`
Chess Game Markup Language (ChessGML)
`http://www.saremba.de/chessgml/index.htm`
ChessML
`http://www.schachprobleme.de/chessml/index.html`
Quest Markup Language (QML)
`http://www.outer-court.com/goodies/qml.htm`
Smart Game Format (SGF)
`http://www.red-bean.com/sgf/`

Geneology

GedML: Genealogical Data in XML
`http://users.iclway.co.uk/mhkay/gedml/`

Humor

Adult Entertainment Markup Language (XXXML)

```
http://www.sdtimes.com/news/027/story7.htm
```
ComicsML
```
http://www.jmac.org/projects/comics_ml/
```
Mind Reading Markup Language (MRML)
```
http://www.oxy.edu/~ashes/mrml.html
```

Linguistics

ATLAS (Architecture and Tools for Linguistic Analysis Systems) Interchange Format (AIF)
```
http://www.nist.gov/speech/atlas/develop/aif.html
```

Public interest

Human Markup Language (HumanML)
```
http://www.humanmarkup.org/
```
International Development Markup Language (IDML)
```
http://www.idmlinitiative.org/index2.cfm
```
Open Philanthropy eXchange (OPX)
```
http://www.opxinfo.org/
```

Religion

Liturgical Markup Language (LitML)
```
http://www.oremus.org/LitML/
```
Theological Markup Language (ThML)
```
http://www.ccel.org/ThML/
```

67.2.7 Software development

Artificial intelligence

Artificial Intelligence Markup Language (AIML)
```
http://alicebot.org/alice/aiml.html
```
DARPA Agent Markup Language (DAML)
```
http://www.daml.org/
```
Description Logic Markup Language (DLML)
```
http://co4.inrialpes.fr/xml/dlml/
```

Information Flow Framework (IFF)
`http://www.ontologos.org/IFF/IFF.html`
Knowledge Query and Manipulation Language (KQML)
`http://www.cs.umbc.edu/kqml/`
OML/CKML
`http://www.ontologos.org/`
Ontology Inference Layer (OIL)
`http://www.ontoknowledge.org/oil/`
Petri Net Markup Language (PNML)
`http://www.informatik.hu-berlin.de/top/pnml/`
Procedural Markup Language (PML)
`http://www.cc.gatech.edu/faculty/ashwin/papers/git-gvu-98-20/`
Relational-Functional Markup Language (RFML)
`http://www.relfun.org/rfml/`
XML Belief Network File Format (XBN)
`http://research.microsoft.com/dtas/bnformat/default.htm`
XML-Based Ontology Exchange Language (XOL)
`ftp://smi.stanford.edu/pub/bio-ontology/xol.doc`

Components

Bean Markup Language (BML)
`http://www.davecentral.com/7746.html`
Koala Bean Markup Language (KBML)
`http://www-sop.inria.fr/koala/kbml/kbmltech.html`
Koala Object Markup Language (KOML)
`http://www-sop.inria.fr/koala/XML/serialization/`
Open Software Description (OSD)
`http://msdn.microsoft.com/workshop/delivery/osd/overview/osd.asp`
Software Component Documentation DTD
`http://www.componentregistry.com/`

Documentation

JavaDox
`http://www.creativepro.com/story/news/2953.html`
Object-Oriented Programing Meta-Language (OOPML)
`http://www.iro.umontreal.ca/labs/gelo/xml4se/oopml/Welcome.html`

Pattern Markup Language (PML)
http://www.yy.cs.keio.ac.jp/~suzuki/project/uxf/

Graph exchange

Graph eXchange Language (GXL)
http://www.gupro.de/GXL/
eXtensible Graph Markup and Modeling Language (XGMML)
http://www.cs.rpi.edu/~puninj/XGMML/draft-xgmml.html

Internationalization

Character Mapping Markup Language (CharMapML)
http://www.unicode.org/unicode/reports/tr22/tr22-2.2.html

Middleware

Mediation of Information Using XML (MIX)
http://www.npaci.edu/DICE/MIX/
Simple Object Access Protocol (SOAP)
http://www.microsoft.com/mind/0100/soap/soap.asp
Web Distributed Data eXchange (WDDX)
http://www.openwddx.org/faq/
Web Interface Definition Language (WIDL)
http://www.w3.org/TR/NOTE-widl
WebBroker: Distributed Object Communication on the Web
http://www.w3.org/TR/1998/NOTE-webbroker/
XML-RPC (Remote Procedure Calling)
http://www.xmlrpc.com/stories/storyReader$7

Modeling

Architecture Description Markup Language (ADML)
http://www.opengroup.org/onlinepubs/009009899/index.htm
CDIF XML-Based Transfer Format
http://www.eigroup.org/cdif/intro.html
OMG Model Driven Architecture (MDA)
http://www.omg.org/mda/

Open Information Model (OIM)
`http://www.mdcinfo.com/OIM/index.html`
UML eXchange Format (UXF)
`http://www.yy.cs.keio.ac.jp/~suzuki/project/uxf/`
UML-Xchange
`http://www.cam.org/~nrivard/uml/umlxchng.html`
XML Metadata Interchange Format (XMI)
`http://www-4.ibm.com/software/ad/library/standards/xmi.html`

Protocols

Blocks Extensible Exchange Protocol (BEEP/BXXP)
`http://beepcore.org/beepcore/`
Common Name Resolution Protocol (CNRP)
`http://www.ietf.org/html.charters/cnrp-charter.html`
Media Object Server Communications Protocol (MOS)
`http://63.220.41.20/`
Roaming Operations (roamops)
`http://www.ietf.org/html.charters/roamops-charter.html`
Voluntary Interindustry Commerce Standards (VICS) Collaborative Planning, Forecasting and Replenishment (CPFR) XML Messaging Model
`http://www.cpfr.org/`
XLANG
`http://www.gotdotnet.com/team/xml_wsspecs/xlang-c/default.htm`
XML DTD for ACAP - ACAP (Application Configuration Access Protocol) data interchange format
`http://www.alternic.org/drafts/drafts-m-n/draft-melnikov-acap-xml-01.html`
XML Encoding Rules (XER)
`http://asf.gils.net/xer/concept.html`
XML Encoding for SMS (Short Message Service) Messages
`http://www.ietf.org/internet-drafts/draft-koponen-sms-xml-01.txt`
XML Inter-ORB Protocol (XIOP)
`http://xiop.sourceforge.net/index.html`
XML MIME Transformation Protocol (XMTP)
`http://www.openhealth.org/documents/xmtp.htm`
eXtensible Name Service (XNS)
`http://www.xns.org/`

Schema languages

Document Definition Markup Language (DDML)
`http://www.w3.org/TR/1999/NOTE-ddml-19990119`
RELAX
`http://www.xml.gr.jp/relax/`
RELAX NG
`http://www.oasis-open.org/committees/relax-ng/`
Schema for Object-Oriented XML 2.0 (SOX)
`http://www.w3.org/TR/NOTE-SOX/`
Schematron
`http://www.ascc.net/xml/resource/schematron/schematron.html`
W3C XML Schema
`http://www.w3.org/XML/Schema`

Theoretical computer science

Rule Markup Language (RuleML)
`http://www.dfki.uni-kl.de/ruleml/`
Turing Machine Markup Language (TMML)
`http://www.unidex.com/turing/tmml.htm`

User interface

Extensible User Interface Language (XUL)
`http://www.mozilla.org/xpfe/xptoolkit/xulintro.html`
User Interface Markup Language (UIML)
`http://www.uiml.org/intro/index.htm`
XML Binding Language (XBL)
`http://www.w3.org/TR/2001/NOTE-xbl-20010223/`

67.2.8 Vertical industry

Advertising

Banner Mark-up Language (BannerML)
`http://www.cogitum.com/BannerML/index.htm`
NAA Classified Advertising Standards Task Force and DTD

```
http://www.naa.org/technology/clsstdtf/
```
adXML
```
http://www.adxml.org/
```

Agriculture

AgXML
```
http://www.agxml.org/index.jsp
```

Application service providers

Information Technology Markup Language (ITML)
```
http://www.itml.org/
```

Architecture, engineering, and construction

Architecture, Engineering, and Construction XML Working Group
(aecXML Working Group)
```
http://www.iai-na.org/domains/aecxml/about/aecxml_about.html
```
Green Building XML (gbXML)
```
http://www.idea-server.com/gbxml.htm
```
Materials Property Data Markup Language (MatML)
```
http://www.ceramics.nist.gov/matml/matml.htm
```

Automotive

MSR MEDOC
```
http://www.msr-wg.de/
```
NaVigation Markup Language (NVML)
```
http://www.w3.org/TR/NVML
```
Standards for Technology in Automotive Retail (STAR)
```
http://www.starstandard.org/
```
XML for the Automotive Industry - SAE J2008
```
http://www.xmlxperts.com/sae.htm#over
```

Education

IMS Metadata Specification
```
http://www.imsproject.org/metadata/index.html
```

Learning Material Markup Language (LMML)
`http://daisy.fmi.uni-passau.de/projects/PaKMaS/LM2L/`
NetQuest Tutorial Markup Language (TML)
`http://www.ilrt.bris.ac.uk/netquest/about/lang/`
Schools Interoperability Framework (SIF)
`http://www.sifinfo.org/`
Universal Learning Format (ULF)
`http://www.saba.com/standards/ulf/Overview/Frames/overview.htm`

Food services

Recipe Markup Language (RecipeML)
`http://www.formatdata.com/recipeml/index.html`

Government

Election Markup Language (EML)
`http://www.oasis-open.org/committees/election/index.shtml#documents`
ParlML
`http://www.europarl.eu.int/docman/texts/TFDM(2000)0014EN(TOC)0.htm`
Triple-s Survey Interchange Standard
`http://www.triple-s.org/index.htm`
e-government interoperability framework (e-GIF)
`http://www.govtalk.gov.uk/egif/home.html`

Hardware and electronics

Component Information Dictionary Specification (CIDS)
`http://www.si2.org/ecix/cids/index.html`
Robotic Markup Language (RoboML)
`http://www.roboml.org/`
Timing Diagram Markup Language (TDML)
`http://www.si2.org/ecix/tdml1-0/index.html`
nanoML
`http://www.nanotitan.com/`

Healthcare

Clinical Data Interchange Standards (CDISC)
`http://www.cdisc.org/`
Health Level 7 (HL7)
`http://www.hl7.org/`
Template Definition Language (TDL) for Electronic Patient Records (EPR)
`http://www.schattauer.de/zs/methods/2000/1/pdf/00010050.pdf`

Hospitality

Hospitality Industry Technology Integration Standards (HITIS)
`http://www.hitis.org/`

Insurance

Acord XML Property and Casualty
`http://www.acord.org/xml_frame.htm`
Life (XMLife)
`http://www.acord.org/standards/xml/life.htm`

Legal

Digital Property Rights Language (DPRL)
`http://citeseer.nj.nec.com/context/143250/0`
Legal Electronic Data Exchange Standard (LEDES)
`http://www.ledes.org/`
Legal XML
`http://www.legalxml.org/`
Legal XML Electronic Court Filing Draft Specification
`http://www.legalxml.org/DocumentRepository/ProposedStandards/Clear/PS_10001/PS_10001_2000_07_24.htm`
XML Court Interface (XCI)
`http://www.nmcourt.fed.us/xci/xcihome.htm`
XrML (eXtensible rights Markup Language)
`http://www.xrml.org/`

Manufacturing

Batch Control Markup Language
http://www.plantautomation.com/content/homepage/
Process Specification Language (PSL)
http://www.mel.nist.gov/psl/
Steel Markup Language (SML)
http://www.e-steel.com/home.shtml

Military

Defense Logistics Format (DLF)
http://milpac.com/specs/xml-dlf.pdf
Program Executive Office (PEO) Interchange XML Initiative (PIXIT)
http://xml.gov/scripts/efforts_pixit.cfm

Petrochemical

WellLogML
http://www.posc.org/ebiz/WellLogML
WellSchematicML
http://www.posc.org/ebiz/WellSchematicML/index.shtml

Real estate

Comprehensive Real Estate Transaction Markup Language (CRTML)
http://www.aartt.org/
Data Consortium Namespace (DCN) DTD
http://www.dataconsortium.org/documents.html
Real Estate Information Standards (REIS)
http://www.dataconsortium.org/
Real Estate Listing Management System (OpenMLS)
http://www.numerata.com/
Real Estate Transaction Specification
http://www.rets-wg.org/

Resource extraction

Epicentre XML Exchange Format (PEF XML)

```
http://www.posc.org/ebiz/pefxml/ExchangeFormat.html#gen
```
Equation of State ML (eosML)
```
http://www.posc.org/ebiz/eosML/index.shtml
```
GeophysicalML
```
http://www.posc.org/ebiz/Geophysics/index.shtml
```
Log Graphics Markup Language (LogGraphicsML)
```
http://www.posc.org/ebiz/LogGraphicsML/v1.0/index.html
```
Partner Interface Processes for Energy (PIPE)
```
http://xml-pipe.org/index.htm
```
PetroXML
```
http://www.petroxml.org/
```
ProductionML
```
http://www.posc.org/ebiz/ProductionML/index.shtml
```
eXploration and Mining Markup Language (XMML)
```
http://www.ned.dem.csiro.au/XMML/
```

Retail

Retail Enterprise Data in XML (REDX)
```
http://www.nrf-arts.org/redx.htm
```

Telecommunications

Call Policy Markup Language (CPML)
```
http://www.iec.org/exhibits/coppercom_01/
```
Call Processing Language (CPL)
```
http://www.bell-labs.com/mailing-lists/iptel/draft-ietf-iptel-
cpl-00.txt
```
XML-for-Fax (XML-F)
```
http://www.vsi.com/pdf/xmlf-spec.pdf
```
eXtensible Telephony Markup Language (XTML)
```
http://www.pactolus.com/pcs-xtml.pdf
```

Acronyms and initialisms in *The XML Handbook*

Resource Description

- Organizations
- Protocols
- Standards
- Jargon

Chapter 68

> Every product, trend, and concept created by the high tech industry spawns a new vocabulary of impenetrable, redundant, and/or meaningless phrases. The industry then attempts to avoid using that vocabulary by coining a raft of equally impenetrable abbreviations. Or so it may seem to a newcomer faced with a flood of inimical acronymical initialisms (IAI). Here's our attempt to help.

 n this chapter you'll find the initialisms and acronyms used in the body of The XML Handbook.

68.1 | Where do acronyms come from?

Twisted minds!

We know because we've coined a few ourselves.[1] But here's an explanatory bit of pedantry:

abbreviation

A short way of saying something long, like "spec" instead of "specification".

initialism

An abbreviation composed of the initials of the something long, like "XML" instead of "Extensible Markup Language". (Did we mention that people don't always follow rules perfectly?)

---

1. But only four for this book: IEC, MOM, POP, and XDBMS.

acronym

An abbreviation that would be an initialism except that it is pronounced like a word, rather than as separate letters. "PRISM" is an acronym; "XML" is an initialism.[2] "ISO" is both.[3]

68.2 | Acronyms and initialisms in *The XML Handbook*

The following table includes 267 acronyms and initialisms (including a few contractions and words that look like acronyms but aren't). We think it has every one that occurs in the body of the book, which means:

- It includes even incidental ones that aren't vital to understanding the text. Fortunately, there are lots of these.
- It also includes initialisms and acronyms that don't occur directly but are used in the definition of other ones (like "ITU").
- It probably doesn't include any that might be used in the industry but aren't used in the book.[4]
- It includes some that have no connection with XML, or even with computers. But we couldn't draw a reasonable line because if you don't understand an initialism, how can you know it isn't relevant?[5]

The table includes the spelled-out definitions of the abbreviations, but there is no attempt to explain them. In other words, this isn't a glossary. We've explained all the important terms in context in the body of the book; you can find them in the index.

---

2. Albeit a forced one.
3. And also a triumph of political correctness over sanity. It deliberately doesn't match the name "International Organization for Standardization" in order to be "language neutral". As a result, almost every English speaker calls ISO the "International Standards Organization".
4. That includes those coined for last month's hot trend. They'll probably be forgotten by next month anyway.
5. So if you always wondered what "DNA" stood for, now you can find out!

Table 68-1 Acronyms and initialisms in *The XML Handbook*

AAA	American Arbitration Association
ACL	access control list
AE	association evaluator
ANI	automatic number identification
ANSI	American National Standards Institute
AOL	America Online
ANI	automatic number identification
API	application program(ming) interface
APS	CGM Application Structure
ASCII	American Standard Code for Information Interchange
ASN.1	Abstract Syntax Notation 1
ASP	Active Server Pages

ASP	application service provider
AU	Unix audio file
AVI	Audio Video Interleave
B2B	business-to-business
B2Bi	business-to-business integration
B2C	business-to-consumer
BC	before Christ
BCE	before the Common Era
BIS	business integration services
BLOB	binary large object
BMP	Basic Multilingual Plane
BMP	bitmap
BMS	Basic Mapping Support
BP	business process
BPA	business process automation
BPM	business process management
BSP	business service provider
CallXML	Call XML
CBL	common business library
CBR	content-based routing
CD-ROM	compact disc read-only memory
CDA	content delivery agent
CDS	content delivery services
CGI	Common Gateway Interface

CGM	Computer Graphics Metafile
CIA	US Central Intelligence Agency
CICS	Customer Information Control System
CLOB	character large object
CML	Chemical Markup Language
CMS	content management system
COBOL	Common Business Oriented Language
COM	Component Object Model
CORBA	Common Object Request Broker Architecture
COTS	commercially available off-the-shelf
CPA	Collaboration-Protocol Agreement
CPP	Collaboration-Protocol Profile
CPU	central processing unit
CRM	customer relationship management
CSS	Cascading Style Sheets
CSV	comma-separated values
cXML	commerce XML
DB	database
DBMS	database management system
DCE	Distributed Computing Environment
DCOM	Distributed Component Object Model
DHCP	Dynamic Host Configuration Protocol
DHTML	Dynamic HTML
DMS	document management system

DNA	deoxyribonucleic acid
DNS	Domain Name System
DOM	Document Object Model
DSML	Directory Services Markup Language
DSO	Data Source Object
DSSSL	Document Style Semantics and Specification Language
DT4DTD	Datatypes for DTDs
DTD	document type definition
DTMF	Dual Tone Multi-Frequency
DTV	digital television
EAI	enterprise application integration
eBI	e-business integration
EBI	enterprise business integration
ebXML	Electronic Business XML
EDGAR	Electronic Data Gathering, Analysis, and Retrieval
EDI	electronic data interchange
EDIFACT	EDI for Administration, Commerce and Transport
EFT	electronic funds transfer
EIP	enterprise information portal
EJB	Enterprise JavaBeans
EMR	electronic medical records
EPS	Encapsulated PostScript
ERP	enterprise resource planning
FAQ	frequently asked question

FBI	US Federal Bureau of Investigation
FIDOM	Format-Independent DOM
FIXML	Financial Information Exchange ML
FNOC	franchised network operations center
FTP	File Transfer Protocol
GIF	Graphics Interchange Format
GM	General Motors
GML	Generalized Markup Language
GMT	Greenwich mean time
GPS	global positioning system
GUI	graphical user interface
HL7	Health Level Seven
HR	human resources
HTML	HyperText Markup Language
HTTP	Hypertext Transfer Protocol
HTTPS	HTTP over SSL
HyTime	Hypermedia/Time-based Structuring Language
IBM	International Business Machines
ICE	Information Content and Exchange
ID	identifier
IDE	integrated development environment
IDREF	identifier reference
IEC	integrated e-commerce
IEC	International Electrotechnical Commission

IETF	Internet Engineering Task Force
IFX	Interactive Financial Exchange
IIOP	Internet Inter-ORB Protocol
IP	Internet Protocol
IPTC	International Press Telecommunications Council
ISO	International Organization for Standardization
ISP	Internet service provider
IT	information technology
ITU	International Telecommunications Union
ITU-T	ITU telecommunication standardisation sector
IVR	interactive voice response
J2EE	Java 2 Platform, Enterprise Edition
JAXB	Java Architecture for XML Binding
JAXM	Java API for XML Messaging
JAXP	Java APIs for XML Processing
JDBC	Java Database Connectivity
JDOM	Java Document Object Model (unofficial meaning)
JPEG	Joint Photographic Experts Group
JSP	JavaServer Pages
JTC1	ISO/IEC Joint Technical Committee 1
KB	kilobytes
LaTeX	Lamport TeX
LAN	local area network
LCD	liquid crystal display

LDAP	Lightweight Directory Access Protocol
MAPI	Messaging API
MathML	Mathematical Markup Language
MCL	master component library
ML	markup language
MOM	machine-oriented messaging
MOM	message-oriented middleware
MPEG	Motion Picture Experts Group
MP3	MPEG 3
MRP	materials resource planning
MSMQ	Microsoft Message Queuing
MSP	managed service provider
MSXML	Microsoft XML
NDS	Netware Directory Services
NewsML	News Markup Language
NIST	US National Institute for Standards and Technology
OAG	Open Applications Group
OASIS	Organization for the Advancement of Structured Information Standards
OBI	Open Buying Initiative
OCR	optical character recognition
ODBC	Open Database Connectivity
OFX	Open Financial Exchange
OMG	Object Management Group

OPEC	Organization of Petroleum Exporting Countries
ORB	Object Request Broker
OS	operating system
PBX	private branch exchange
PC	personal computer
PDA	personal digital assistant
PDF	Portable Document Format
PHP	PHP: Hypertext Preprocessor
PIC	Pictor graphic file
PICS	Platform for Internet Content Selection
PIP	Partner Interface Process
PKI	Public Key Infrastructure
PNG	Portable Network Graphics
PNOC	primary network operations center
POP	people-oriented publishing
POP	Post Office Protocol
POST	(not an acronym: an HTTP method with a case-challenged name)
PRISM	Publishing Requirements for Industry Standard Metadata
QIR	quarterly investment review
QoS	quality of service
RADIUS	Remote Authentication Dial-in User Service
RDBMS	relational DBMS
RDF	Resource Description Framework

RELAX	Regular Language Description for XML
RMI	remote method invocation
ROI	return on investment
RPC	remote procedure call
RSS	RDF Site Specification
RTF	Rich Text Format
SAX	The Simple API for XML
SC34	ISO/IEC JTC1 Subcommittee 34
SCM	screen cam recording
SCM	supply chain management
SGML	Standard Generalized Markup Language
SIC	standard industry classification
SKU	stockkeeping unit
SME	small-to-medium enterprise
SMF	schema model file
SMIL	Synchronized Multimedia Integration Language
SMTP	Simple Mail Transfer Protocol
SNA	Systems Network Architecture
SOAP	Simple Object Access Protocol
SQL	Structured Query Language
SRP	standard retail price
SSL	Secure Sockets Layer
SVG	Scalable Vector Graphics
SyncML	Synchronization Markup Language

TCP	Transmission Control Protocol
TDCC	Transportation Data Coordinating Committee
TES	Total-e-Server
TeX	Tau epsilon Xi text formatter
TIFF	Tagged Image File Format
TLA	three-letter acronym
tpaML	Trading Partner Agreement Markup Language
TREX	Tree Regular Expressions for XML
UDDI	Universal Description, Discovery, and Integration
UI	user interface
ULF	Universal Listener Framework
UML	Unified Modeling Language
UN/CEFACT	United Nations Centre for Trade Facilitation and Electronic Business
URI	Universal Resource Identifier
URL	Universal Resource Locator
URN	Universal Resource Name
US	United States of America
USD	US dollars
UTC	coordinated universal time
UTF-8	8-bit Unicode Transformation Format
UUID	Universal Unique Identifier
VAN	value-added network
VAT	value-added tax

VoiceXML	Voice XML
VoIP	voice over IP
VPN	virtual private network
W3C	World Wide Web Consortium
WAN	wide area network
WAP	Wireless Application Protocol
WAV	wave audio file
WBXML	WAP Binary XML
WebDAV	Web Distributed Authoring and Versioning
WfMC	Workflow Management Coalition
WMF	Windows Metafile
WML	Wireless Markup Language
WP	word processing
WSDL	Web Services Description Language
WWW	World Wide Web
WYSIWYG	what you see is what you get
X.25	ITU-T standard protocols for packet switched networks
X.500	ITU-T standards for electronic directory services
X12	ANSI Accredited Standards Committee X12
XAS	XML application server
xCBL	XML Common Business Library
XDK	XML developer's kit
XDBMS	native XML DBMS
XHTML	Extensible HyperText Markup Language

XLink	XML Linking Language
XML	Extensible Markup Language
XML-DEV	XML Developers discussion group
XML-RPC	XML Remote Procedure Call
XMS	XML Information Management System
XPath	XML Path Language
XPointer	XML Pointer Language
XPP	XML Professional Publisher
XQuery	XML Query Language
xsd	XML Schema document
XSDL	XML Schema definition language
XSL	XML Stylesheet Language
XSL-FO	XSL formatting objects
XSLT	XSL Transformations
XSQL	XML SQL
XTM	XML Topic Maps
XXXML	Adult Entertainment Markup Language
Y2K	Year 2000

Other books on XML

Resource Description

▌ Program development with XML

▌ DTDs and schemas

▌ XML transformations

▌ Learning the foundations of XML

E d Mosher, Ray Lorie, and I invented the first structured mark-up language in 1969, IBM's Generalized Markup Language (GML). It led to SGML, HTML, XML, and countless applica-tions and variations on the theme.

But strangely, considering that markup is for documents, for the first two decades in which the markup language concept was gaining its now univer-sal acceptance, hardly any books were published on the subject. (Amazingly, a few survivors of that period are in Amazon.com's current retail database, including a few ancient IBM product manuals. I never tried to find out what would happen if someone actually attempted to order one.)

Well, the last two years have more than made up for the first two decades. When we went to press, my website, *All the XML Books in Print*, listed more than 150 titles. I won't repeat them all here, but I will describe the ones I recommend most highly.

These are the books from the *Definitive XML Series* that I edit for Pren-tice-Hall PTR, in which *The XML Handbook* appears.

XML isn't HTML with a capital X. It requires new ways of thinking about Web content. The authors of these books have gotten the message and know how to share it with you. I recruited them personally for my book series because I know they are genuine experts. We worked together to make their books accurate and clear, which is why I am able to recommend the books from personal knowledge.

Of course, the book you are now reading is my recommendation for an introduction to XML. It focuses on what XML is and what it can do for you, but it doesn't purport to tell you how to go about doing it. For that, there are more specialized books.

69.1 | Program development with XML

Contrary to misuse in the popular press, and by some experts who ought to know better, XML isn't a programming language. It is a markup language, of course, and that means it's a data description language. You use normal programming languages, including scripting languages, to develop XML applications. These books show you how.

69.1.1 *General principles and techniques*

XML by Example: Building E-Commerce Applications
Sean McGrath / 1998
Also published in Japanese and Portuguese.
This book will teach you XML application programming from the ground up, all the while developing a full-blown e-commerce application. Programmers can learn the XML language from this book as well.

XML Processing with Python
Sean McGrath / 2000
There is a reason that Python is attracting the best programmers away from other scripting languages, and XML is part of it. This book will teach you how to program in Python, and how to use its unique capabilities for processing XML. The software you'll need is on the CD-ROM.

Definitive XML Application Development

Lars Marius Garshol / 2002

For experienced developers, this book provides thorough and systematic coverage of XML application development: DOM, SAX, XSLT, XPath, schemas, and all the important APIs and techniques. The author was a designer of SAX and creator of the SAX Python translation.

69.1.2 Specific applications

Building Web Sites with XML

Michael Floyd / 2000

XML adds a whole alphabet soup of acronyms to the Web developer's lunch box: XSLT, DOM, SAX, schemas, and more. The founder of *Web Techniques* magazine shows you how to master these technologies, while systematically constructing an XML-based website. All the code is on the CD-ROM, to help you get your own website started.

Enterprise Application Integration with XML and Java

JP Morgenthal with Bill La Forge / 2000

There are few greater information technology imperatives for the enterprise today than integrating its legacy applications. Not only is it necessary for normal operations, but it is a prerequisite for integrated e-commerce with business partners. XML is the complement to Java that makes the integration possible, and this book shows you how to take advantage of both of them.

Program Generators with XML and Java

J. Craig Cleaveland / 2001

XML isn't just for data any more. Now you can use XML to describe the programs you need, then write a Java program template to generate them automatically. This book shows you how.

69.2 | DTDs and schemas

Nature abhors a schema-less database equally as much as she abhors a vacuum. Create a data table in a spreadsheet and the program will immediately search for field names, and supply them even if you fail to. Although XML will let you create a document without an explicit formally-written schema (also known as a "document type definition", or DTD), the benefits of having one are enormous. These books make the job easy, whether you write out the DTD using XML markup declarations, or one of the new schema languages.

Structuring XML Documents

David Megginson / 1998
Also published in Japanese.
This book covers the fundamentals of good DTD design, illustrated by popular industry DTDs. It also has full coverage of architectural forms, which allow object-oriented development of XML DTDs.

Definitive XML Schema

Priscilla Walmsley / 2002
The W3C's *XML Schema* is an incredibly powerful – and complex! – document schema language, with such new capabilities as strong typing, modularity, inheritance, and identity constraints. This book was written by one of the developers of the language. It carefully guides you through the complexity so you can tap that power for your own projects.

69.3 | XML transformations

The key to processing XML is being able to address its structures and data and transform them into a new XML document. XPath and XSLT are the W3C recommendations that govern this process. These technologies affect everything from programming to database design, and for many developers they require a new way of thinking about those problems. This book will help you down the XPath and transform your development experience!

Definitive XSLT and XPath

> G. Ken Holman / 2002
>
> Nobody has taught XSLT and XPath to more people than Ken Holman, chair of OASIS's XSLT/XPath Conformance Technical Subcommittee and long-time leader in the XML community. In this book, he draws upon his popular live training materials that have been used by thousands of developers.

69.4 | Learning the foundations of XML

XML is a proper subset of SGML and the XML Recommendation is much shorter than the SGML International Standard. But the subsetting isn't the only reason for the shorter document. The XML spec is written for parser implementors and deliberately doesn't discuss applications, philosophy, style, alternatives, and other usage issues. I don't claim that you need to learn SGML in order to use XML, but I think it would help you use it better.

The SGML Handbook

> Charles F. Goldfarb / 1991 / Oxford University Press
>
> On the other hand, if you really must know every detail of SGML, here is the official ISO Standard, annotated by yours truly (who is also the Project Editor of the Standard). I've added a structured overview of the complete language that introduces every term and concept in context. This book has been in print for more than ten years and was the essential reference used by the W3C Working Group when designing XML.

 Tip   You can find Charles' up-to-date list of *All the XML Books in Print* at `http://www.xmlbooks.com`.

Index

A

Abstractions 387-388, 422-423
    architecture 383-385
    as documents 78-79
    distinct from renditions 13, 108, 118, 273, 403,
      416, 419, 427, 506, 672
    editing with XML 419-421
    preservation 416
    reusable 417
    SGML and XML 15
Acronyms 1103-1116
Active Digital Profile
    see ADPr (Active Digital Profile)
Active Server Pages
    see ASP (Active Server Pages)
Actuation
    definition 1020
Addressing
    linking vs. 1020
Adobe Systems, Inc.
    FrameMaker+SGML 420-422, 424-425
    Illustrator™ 5, 79
    Knowledge Chain™ Builder 425
    PageMaker 509
    Portable Document Format (PDF) 74
ADPr (Active Digital Profile) 244
AEs (Association Evaluators) 661-662
Aggregation 275-276, 354
Altova
    XML Spy Suite 580, 583, 586
Anchor
    definition 1020
AOL (America Online) 878
API (Application Programming Interface) 199, 425,
    603, 703-704, 720, 726
APIs (Application Processing Interfaces) 51
    definition 51
Application integration
    architecture using topic maps 660-667
    context managers 660, 662
    semantic manager 661

    semantic managers 662
    service managers 662
Application Processing Interfaces
    see APIs (Application Processing Interfaces)
Application Programming Interface
    see API (Application Programming Interface)
Application Service Provider
    see ASP (Application Service Provider)
APS (CGM Application Structures) 315
Arc
    definition 1032
ASP (Active Server Pages) 135, 138
ASP (Application Service Provider) 256
Association Evaluators
    see AEs (Association Evaluators)
Attribute sets 991
Attribute-list declaration 807
    definition 806
Attributes 79, 302, 315, 425, 543, 553, 686, 715,
    731, 772, 776, 778, 781, 805, 814, 930
    definition 416, 774
    actuate attribute 1030
    and newlines 856
    default values 808
    elements vs. 805-806
    ENTITY 817-818
    enumerated 815, 818
    fixed 810
    ID/IDREF 815-817
    impliable 808-809
    inherited 856
    lexical constraints 811
    names 76, 774-775, 883
    notation 815, 818, 820
    required 809
    semantic constraints 811
    semantics 774
    types 819
    value normalization 811, 814
    values 774-775, 811-812
Auction Demo 135-150

O

OASIS (Organization for the Advancement of Structured Information Standards) 1072
  and ebXML 97-98
oasis-open.org 1074
Object-oriented programming
  definition 718
Objects 718
  interface 718
  invoking methods 718
  methods 718
Occurence indicators 868-870
  repeatable 868
OCR (Optical Character Recognition) 499, 514
OFX (Open Financial Exchange) 5, 102
Online catalogs 545, 549-556
  requirements 545, 546
Ontopia
  Topic Map Engine 644
  Topic Map Navigator 644
Open eBook
  Forum 91
  specification 91
Open Financial Exchange
  see OFX (Open Financial Exchange)
OpenWave™ 87
Optical Character Recognition
  see OCR (Optical Character Recognition)
Oracle Corporation 751
  Oracle9i Database™ 481-482, 484, 486
  XML SQL Utility 484
Organization for the Advancement of Structured Information Standards
  see OASIS

P

Page XML
  see PXML (Page XML)
Parameter entities
  definition 834
  general entities vs. 834-835
Parameters
  definition 992
Parsed
  definition 824
Parsers 114, 726, 729, 770
  events 714

  interfaces 727
  methods 727
Parsing 50, 503
  definition 50
  and processing 32
  as understanding 10
  XML documents 68
Participating resource 1020
Partner Interface Process
  see PIP (Partner Interface Process)
Patterns
  definition 975
PDF (Portable Document Format) 74, 338, 383, 387-388, 394-395, 509, 561
People-Oriented Publishing
  see POP (People-Oriented Publishing)
Petrochemical marketplace 203-209
  bottleneck 204
  downstream flow 204
  external information flows 207
  internal information flows 207
  mergers and acquisitions 208
  significant information flows 206
  upstream flow 204
PI (Processing Instruction) 994
  target
    definition 853
PICS (Platform for Internet Content Selection) 81-82
  element types 82
PIP (Partner Interface Process) 101
Pipes
  definition 404
Pixels
  definition 311
Platform for Internet Content Selection
  see PICS (Platform for Internet Content Selection)
PNOC (Primary Network Operations Center) 751, 753
Point
  definition 1011
Point functions 1014
POP (People-Oriented Publishing) 63-64, 95, 399, 431, 441, 532-533
  definition 64
  abstractions 65
  and MOM (Machine-Oriented Messaging) 63, 65-67, 69-70

5. TRANSFER RESTRICTIONS: The enclosed SOFTWARE is licensed only to you and may not be transferred to any one else without the prior written consent of the Company. Any unauthorized transfer of the SOFTWARE shall result in the immediate termination of this Agreement.

6. TERMINATION: This license is effective until terminated. This license will terminate automatically without notice from the Company and become null and void if you fail to comply with any provisions or limitations of this license. Upon termination, you shall destroy the Documentation and all copies of the SOFTWARE. All provisions of this Agreement as to warranties, limitation of liability, remedies or damages, and our ownership rights shall survive termination.

7. MISCELLANEOUS: This Agreement shall be construed in accordance with the laws of the United States of America and the State of New York and shall benefit the Company, its affiliates, and assignees.

8. LIMITED WARRANTY AND DISCLAIMER OF WARRANTY: The Company warrants that the SOFTWARE, when properly used in accordance with the Documentation, will operate in substantial conformity with the description of the SOFTWARE set forth in the Documentation. The Company does not warrant that the SOFTWARE will meet your requirements or that the operation of the SOFTWARE will be uninterrupted or error-free. The Company warrants that the media on which the SOFTWARE is delivered shall be free from defects in materials and workmanship under normal use for a period of thirty (30) days from the date of your purchase. Your only remedy and the Company's only obligation under these limited warranties is, at the Company's option, return of the warranted item for a refund of any amounts paid by you or replacement of the item. Any replacement of SOFTWARE or media under the warranties shall not extend the original warranty period. The limited warranty set forth above shall not apply to any SOFTWARE which the Company determines in good faith has been subject to misuse, neglect, improper installation, repair, alteration, or damage by you. EXCEPT FOR THE EXPRESSED WARRANTIES SET FORTH ABOVE, THE COMPANY DISCLAIMS ALL WARRANTIES, EXPRESS OR IMPLIED, INCLUDING WITHOUT LIMITATION, THE IMPLIED WARRANTIES OF MERCHANTABILITY AND FITNESS FOR A PARTICULAR PURPOSE, EXCEPT FOR THE EXPRESS WARRANTY SET FORTH ABOVE, THE COMPANY DOES NOT WARRANT, GUARANTEE, OR MAKE ANY REPRESENTATION REGARDING THE USE OR THE RESULTS OF THE USE OF THE SOFTWARE IN TERMS OF ITS CORRECTNESS, ACCURACY, RELIABILITY, CURRENTNESS, OR OTHERWISE.